JOYCE'S   BOOK   OF   THE   DARK

Finnegans Wake

JOYCE'S BOOK

JOHN BISHOP

1986

O F   T H E   D A R K

Finnegans Wake

The University of Wisconsin Press · M A D I S O N ,   W I S C O N S I N

Published 1986

The University of Wisconsin Press
114 North Murray Street
Madison, Wisconsin 53715

The University of Wisconsin Press, Ltd.
1 Gower Street
London WC1E 6HA, England

First printing

Printed in the United States of America

For LC CIP information see the colophon

ISBN 0-299-10820-1

For my mother,
Anne Skomsky Bishop,
in memory of my father,
Walter Bishop
(1917–1983)

Contents

Maps and Figures

Abbreviations

All references to *Finnegans Wake* in the following pages are identified by page and line number—the figure 389.18–19, for instance, designating *Finnegans Wake*, page 389, lines 18 and 19. Books and chapters of *Finnegans Wake* are given in Roman numerals: III.iv refers to Book III, chapter iv. The footnotes and marginal notes in II.ii are identified by the letters R, L, and F preceding the number of the note: 299.F2 designates the second footnote on page 299.

Other works frequently cited in the text are identified parenthetically by the following abbreviations:

D   James Joyce. *Dubliners*. New York: The Viking Press, 1961.

ID   Sigmund Freud. *The Interpretation of Dreams*. Trans. and ed. James Strachey. New York: Avon Books, 1965.

JJ   Richard Ellmann. *James Joyce*. Revised ed. New York and Oxford: Oxford Univ. Press, 1982.

L   *The Letters of James Joyce*. Vol. 1 ed. by Stuart Gilbert. New York: The Viking Press, 1957. Vols 2 and 3 ed. by Richard Ellmann. New York: The Viking Press, 1966.

NS   Giambattista Vico. *The New Science of Giambattista Vico*. Trans. Thomas Goddard Bergin and Max Harold Fisch. Revised ed. Ithaca: Cornell Univ. Press, 1984. As is customary in the scholarship on Vico, references are to paragraph number, rather than to page number.

OED   *The Oxford English Dictionary*. Compact Ed. Oxford: Oxford Univ. Press, 1971.

P   James Joyce. *A Portrait of the Artist as a Young Man*. New York: Viking, 1964.

U   James Joyce. *Ulysses*. New York: Random House, 1961.

The following abbreviations are used throughout the text to identify languages and dialects:

Alb.	Albanian	Germ.	Germanic	O.E.	Old English
Am.	American	Gi.	Gipsy	O.Fr.	Old French
Anglo-Ir.	Anglo-Irish	Gr.	Greek	O.N.	Old Norse
Arm.	Armenian	Heb.	Hebrew	Per.	Persian
Ar.	Arabic	Hu.	Hungarian	Port.	Portuguese
Br.	British	I.E.	Indo-European	Pro.	Provençal
Co.	Cornish	It.	Italian	R.R.	Rhaeto-Romanic
Da.	Danish	Ki.	Kiswahili	Russ.	Russian
Du.	Dutch	L.	Latin	Sans.	Sanskrit
Eng.	English	L.L.	Late Latin	Sp.	Spanish
Fr.	French	M.E.	Middle English	Sw.G.	Swiss German
Fi.	Finnish	Med.L.	Medieval Latin	Turk.	Turkish
Gael.	Gaelic	M.L.	Modern Latin	We.	Welsh
Ger.	German	Nor.	Norse		

Other abbreviations and symbols:

arch.	archaic
C.	century
mod.	modern
pp.	past participle
pres. p.	present participle
sl.	slang
*	designates an etymologically reconstructed form
<	"is derived from," in historical linguistics
=	"is equivalent to"
†	indicates river-names (in chapter 12)

Etymologies

Because they are susceptible to varied interpretations and constructions, the etymologies discussed in the following pages have been drawn freely from a number of sources. Works consulted in the writing of this book include the following:

Benveniste, Emile. *Indo-European Language and Society.* Trans. Elizabeth Palmer. Coral Gables, Fla.: Univ. of Miami Press, 1973.

Buck, Carl Darling. *A Dictionary of Selected Synonyms in the Principal Indo-European Tongues: A Contribution to the History of Ideas.* Chicago: Univ. of Chicago Press, 1949.

Grandsaignes d'Hauterive, R. *Dictionnaire des racines des langues européennes.* Paris: Larousse, 1949.

Liddell, Henry George, and Robert Scott. *Greek-English Lexicon.* Oxford: Oxford Univ. Press, 1871.

Onions, C. T. et al. *The Oxford Dictionary of English Etymology.* Oxford: Oxford Univ. Press, 1966.

Partridge, Eric. *Origins: A Short Etymological Dictionary of the English Language.* New York: Macmillan, 1959.

Pokorny, Julius. *Indogermanisches Etymologisches Wörterbuch.* Bern, 1959.

Shipley, Joseph T. *The Origins of English Words: A Discursive Dictionary of Indo-European Roots.* Baltimore: The Johns Hopkins Univ. Press, 1984.

Skeat, William Walter. *An Etymological Dictionary of the English Language.* Oxford: Oxford Univ. Press, 1910.

Watkins, Calvert. "Indo-European and the Indo-Europeans" and "Appendix of Indo-European Roots," in *The American Heritage Dictionary of the English Language*. Ed. William Morris. Boston: Houghton Mifflin, 1969.

Webster's New World Dictionary of the American Language. College Edition. New York: World Publishing Company, 1964.

Weekley, Ernest. *The Romance of Words*. 1949; rpt New York: Dover, 1961.

Williams, Raymond. *Keywords: A Vocabulary of Culture and Society*. New York: Oxford Univ. Press, 1976.

Acknowledgments

To thank everyone who has contributed in one way or another to the writing of this book would require the invention of a character named "Here Comes almost Everybody" who had an effect on me. Out of this warm body of people, I wish to thank in particular all those who read and discussed parts of this work as they emerged out of evolving drafts: Ann Banfield, Suzanne Bick, Craig Buckwald, Mitchell Breitwieser, James Breslin, William Chace, Vincent Cheng, Jay Fliegelman, Phillip Herring, Catherine Judd, D. A. Miller, Josephine McQuail, Mary Ann O'Farrell, Brendan O Hehir, David Riggs, Shirley Samuels, and Theoharis C. Theoharis. I owe more extended and special thanks to Michael André Bernstein, Robert Polhemus, Ralph Rader, Thomas Parkinson, and John Henry Raleigh for the suggestions and encouragement they offered after reading a penultimate version of the manuscript. Thanks go also to all those students in seminars at the University of California at Berkeley who, reminding me steadily of the general perplexities felt by readers of *Finnegans Wake*, forced me to maintain a broad perspective on the book and to refine my ways of articulating an understanding of its lucid darknesses. For their patient assistance in the nightmare business of proofreading, editing, and helping to prepare a finished manuscript, thanks go to Richard Curtis, Bronwyn Freier, Richard Gringeri, Stephen Kusche, Stanley Liljefelt, Mark Winokur, and Gabrielle Welford, my superhuman typist. I am additionally indebted to the Regents of the University of California for a research fellowship that made possible the consolidation of a manuscript, and to the English departments of the University of California at Berkeley and Stanford University for their general support.

In another vein, I owe a heavy debt of gratitude to all those students of the *Wake* without whose work the writing of this book would have been impossible. My own writing draws so freely from the following standard works of Wakean reference that a blanket statement of indebtedness must here take the place of running notational acknowledgment:

James S. Atherton, *The Books at the Wake: A Study of Literary Allusions in James Joyce's "Finnegans Wake."* 1959; rpt. Carbondale: Southern Illinois Univ. Press, 1974.

Adaline Glasheen. *Third Census of "Finnegans Wake": An Index of the Characters and Their Roles.* Berkeley and Los Angeles: Univ. of California Press, 1977.

Clive Hart. *A Concordance to "Finnegans Wake".* Minneapolis: Univ. of Minnesota Press, 1963.

Clive Hart. "Index of Motifs," in *Structure and Motif in "Finnegans Wake".* Evanston, Ill.: Northwestern Univ. Press, 1962, pp. 211–47.

Matthew J. C. Hodgart and Mabel P. Worthington. *Song in the Works of James Joyce.* New York: Columbia Univ. Press, 1959.

Roland McHugh. *Annotations to "Finnegans Wake."* Baltimore: The John Hopkins Univ. Press, 1980.

Louis O. Mink. *A "Finnegans Wake" Gazetteer.* Bloomington: Indiana Univ. Press, 1979.

Brendan O Hehir. *A Gaelic Lexicon for "Finnegans Wake."* Berkeley and Los Angeles: Univ. of California Press, 1967.

Brendan O Hehir and John M. Dillon. *A Classical Lexicon for "Finnegans Wake."* Berkeley and Los Angeles: Univ. of California Press, 1977.

Anyone familiar with these books will recognize their imprint throughout this one; I have tried, wherever possible, to derive all "translations" of Wakese into English from these sources, all unavoidable deviations from those sources being my own.

Finally I wish to express my gratitude to the staff of the University of Wisconsin Press for their care in seeing this book through production; to Allen Fitchen, director of the press, for his responsiveness, encouragement, and faith in my project, and to Jack Kirshbaum, my editor, for his patience and his counsel on everything ranging from conjunction emplacement to chapter content. Warmest thanks go to Ann Banfield, Mitchell Breitwieser, Jay Fliegelman, Catherine Judd, D. A. Miller, Mary Ann O'Farrell, Dennis Weiss, and my sisters, Jeanne and Nooshie, for their support, their enmeshment in this book's darker undertext, and their willingness to listen to "things that will not stand being written about in black and white." Somewhere among them, they heard it all.

This book is dedicated to my mother, Anne Skomsky Bishop, in memory of my father, Walter (1917–1983).

JOYCE'S BOOK OF THE DARK

Finnegans Wake

An Introduction:
On Obscurity

"IN OUR OWN NIGHTTIME"

Sooner rather than later, a reader of *Finnegans Wake* would do well to justify to himself its stupefying obscurity; for as even its most seasoned readers know, "*Finnegans Wake* is wilfully obscure. It was conceived as obscurity, it was executed as obscurity, it is about obscurity."[1] And to this one might add that nothing will ever make *Finnegans Wake* not obscure. Stories of the pains Joyce took to deepen the opacity of *Work in Progress* during its composition only intensify the impression thrown off by the finished text. Jacques Mercanton recalls finding Joyce and Stuart Gilbert "going over a passage that was 'still not obscure enough'" and gleefully "inserting Samoyed words into it";[2] Padraic Colum recalls "from time to time [being] asked to suggest a word that would be more obscure than the word already there," only to have Joyce reply "five times out of six," in what amounts to an admission that his designs were darkly principled, "I can't use it."[3] The essential question one wants answered in hearing these stories and in probing the murkinesses of the text itself is whether this relentless obscuration was really arbitrary and wilful—"sheer perversity," in Louise Bogan's phrase[4]—or whether it was leading somewhere that would repay the study, time, and labor which *Finnegans Wake* demands of its reader. Joyce himself was unevenly helpful; as he put it to Frank Budgen on the less baffling matter of *Ulysses*, "If I can throw any obscurity on the subject let me know" (*L*, III, 261).

Not very expansively, he replied to the growing news that his readers simply were not following him by wondering out loud, with lamblike innocence, to William Bird: "About my new work—do you know, Bird, I confess I can't understand some of my critics, like Pound or Miss Weaver, for instance. They say it's *obscure*. They compare it, of course, with *Ulysses*. But the action of *Ulysses* was chiefly in the daytime, and the action of my new work takes place chiefly at night. It's natural things should not be so clear at night, isn't it now?" (*JJ*, 590). Typically, he defended his methods by displacing attention from his style to his subject, as he did again when replying to objections raised by Jacques Mercanton over the obscurity of a passage in *Work in Progress:* "It is night. It is dark. You can hardly see. You sense rather."[5] In Joyce's view, all obscurity came with the terrain he surveyed, and not with his treatment of it: "If there is any difficulty in reading what I write it is because of the material I use. In my case the thought is always simple."[6] He was only pointing out in all these remarks that "obscurity" is "darkness" rendered verbal (L. *obscuritas*, "darkness"), and that the night, his subject, was intractably obscure. Only a little reflection, I think, will demonstrate that the systematic darkening of every term in *Finnegans Wake* was an absolute necessity, dictated by Joyce's subject; and that *Finnegans Wake* has exactly what so cranky a critic as F. R. Leavis wished it had and of course judged it did not: "the complete subjection—subjugation—of the medium to the uncompromising, complex and delicate need that uses it."[7]

Suppose only that Joyce accomplished the least part of what he claimed when, over and over again throughout the 1920s and 1930s, he said that he "wanted to write this book about the night" (*JJ*, 695):[8] "I reconstruct the nocturnal life."[9] What would this sort of "reconstruction" have entailed? We might begin to appreciate the difficulties he would have faced by resorting to a simple experiment, an "appeal to experience" of the sort on which all modern forms of knowing—and the novel—are based. Suppose, that is, that we charged ourselves with the task of providing in chronological order a detailed account of everything that occurred to us *not* last night (such an account would be far too sketchy to be useful) but in the first half hour of last night's sleep; or better yet, suppose that we fall asleep tonight intent on preserving for liberal study in the morning a detailed memory of the first half hour of sleep. "The charges are, you will remember, the chances are, you won't" (254.23–24). What we are likely to recall of this little slice of "Real life" (260.F3)—"you were there"—is a gap of obscurity far more stupefying than anything Joyce ever wrote. The "hole affair" (535.20 [and a "hole," unlike a "whole," has no content]) will likely summon up a sustained "blank memory" (515.33)—"What a wonderful memory you have too!" (295.15–16)—which in turn should generate vast "Questions" (I.vi) and "puzzling, startling, shocking, nay, perturbing" doubts (136.21–22) about the possibility of literately filling in this blank "m'm'ry" (460.20 ["m'm'ry," obviously, is "memory" with severe holes in it]). "Now just wash and brush up your memoirias a little bit" (507.30): even were we to simplify this exercise for the benefit of members of "the Juke and Kellikek families" (33.24–25)—these were a clan of morons, prominent both in *Finnegans Wake* and in the press of Joyce's day, whom generations of inbreeding had reduced to a state of breathtaking feeblemindedness—even were we to simplify this exercise by stipulating that we recall *anything* that passed through our minds in the half hour of "real life" under scrutiny, it isn't clear that there would be a great deal to say. Indeed, many of us will have only total "recoil" of "the deleteful hour" in question (160.35, 348.8, 446.8 [not "recall"]; 118.32). A delightful Irish saying captures perfectly this kind of "recoil": "when a person singing a song has to stop because he forgets the next verse," according to the *Annotations*, "he says 'There's a hole in the ballad.'" Some such perturbing "hole in [the] tale" (323.22 [of our "real life"]) seems also to entrench itself in the head when we begin to "recoil" the "hole affair" we endured last night. It is not simple obscurity that rises to meet us; "quite as patenly there is a hole in the ballet trough which the rest fell out" (253.20–21; cf. 211.19 [that "trough," not "through," deepens the emptiness of the "hole affair"]).

Was one dreaming throughout this half hour? And how does one know? Anyone's "m'm'ry" will attest that the average morning's catch of dreams runs exceedingly thin when compared to the length of time one lay asleep "during [the] blackout" (617.14). Indeed, some people claim never to dream at all; people who do remember dreams are not likely to remember having them every night; and only the insane will claim to remember having undergone eight hours of nonstop dreaming on any night. Authorities on the subject will help us as little as our own "maimeries" (348.7 ["maimed" "memories"]): they have conducted for centuries an "embittered and apparently irreconcilable dispute as to whether the mind sleeps at night" (*ID*, 629), arguing whether we dream continuously throughout the length of sleep and simply fail to remember most of what we dream, or whether dreaming interrupts sleep only erratically.[10] Even the most respected of these authorities will not diminish our perplexities: in Freud's view, for instance,

An Introduction

"a dreamless sleep is best, the only proper one. There ought to be no mental activity in sleep."[11] If we simply assume, however, that "no mental activity" occupied the half-hour of "real life" we wished, in detail, to reconstruct, questions of an unsuspected order of obscurity would rise up to meet us. For dreams in their own ways may be obscure, and *Finnegans Wake* may also seem obscure, but both dreams and *Finnegans Wake* will only seem radiantly translucid when compared to those lengthy intervals of "real life" that occupy us in the space of sleep outside of dreams. Much of *Finnegans Wake*, of necessity, is about just this. What happens here? And how does one know? "Remember and recall, Kullykeg!" (367.11 [Kallikak]).

One of many reasons why Joyce's repeated claims about *Finnegans Wake* have seemed so improbable for so long is that people have customarily treated the book, at Joyce's invitation, as the "representation of a dream"—doing so, however, as if dreams took place only in theory, and without concretely engaging the very strange and obscure question of what a dream is. Recollectible dreams are the rare, odd landmarks of sleep, and certainly not its norm; they rise out of the murk with a stunning clarity when compared to the darker, lengthier extents of the night that everywhere fall between. As a "nonday diary" (489.35) seeking to "reconstruct the night," *Finnegans Wake* is not about a dream in any pedestrian sense of that word; treating it as a book about a "dream" is like treating *Ulysses* as a book about "human experience": both terms are far too broad to be useful. Joyce's comments on the relationship of *Finnegans Wake* to dreams and dreaming—comments that have bothered many readers—were therefore often appropriately cagey: to Edmond Jaloux he said that the book "would be written 'to suit the esthetic of the dream'," as indeed it must if it were to portray the average night in which dreams, "erigenating from next to nothing" (4.36–5.1), punctuated the dark (*JJ*, 546); and to Ole Vinding, comparably, he said "it's like a dream" (*JJ*, 696).[12] But as many as his comments as not orient us less clearly in a "dream" per se than in "one great part of every human existence" (*L*, III, 146) "about which we know almost nothing"—in the night as an obscure totality.[13] In the critical year 1927, when it became clear to Joyce that readers who had championed *Ulysses* were withdrawing their support, and when he began cultivating their encouragement by talking about abandoning *Work in Progress* to James Stephens, he replied to Harriet Shaw Weaver's objection that parts of his new work were "incorrigibly absurd" by remarking, "There is no such absurd person as could replace me except the incorrigible god of sleep and no waster quite so wasteful" (*L*, I, 252). He was implying what he said often and elsewhere more directly: "I want to describe the night itself."[14] And of the night: "Here is the unknown."[15]

"Recoil" again that "blank memory" of the "hole affair" we all went "trough," "even in our own nighttime" (7.21). If we momentarily brush aside all the evident obscurities and arbitrarily assume that a continuous stream of "thought" purled through our minds in the half hour of "real life" we wished, in detail, to reconstruct, we would face the new problem not simply of replacing a "blank memory" with a presumed content, but of finding a means by which to do so. Particularly if we think of sleep (as opposed to "dreams") as that part of the night which cannot be remembered, this would mean finding a way of "reveiling" (220.33 [note the occluding "veil"]) an interval of life inherently barred from "mummery" (535.30 ["memory"]). Since "in the night the mummery" (310.23) is masked (or "mummed"), all such attempts to "recoil" will seem "unaveiling" (503.26). Indeed, it is as if the persons we become in the "veiled world" (139.1 [of the night]) say "good-bye" to any potentially retrievable "mummeries" as soon as they "go by": "Dear gone mummeries, goby!" (535.27). As if under hypnosis (Gr. *hypnos*, "sleep"), "[we] will remain ignorant of all . . . and draw a veil" (238.15–17).

Can we nonetheless, by some determined exertion or inferential indirection, "reconstruct" a half hour of "real life" of which we have no "mummery" and which no amount of volition ("would") or obligation ("should") allows us to know? "You wouldnt should as youd remesmer. I hypnot" (360.23–24) because sleep (*hypnos*) puts us in a trance ("mesmer") that moves us into "Metamnisia" (158.10 [Gr. "metamnêsia," "beyond forgetfulness"]); and from there, we find everything "leading slip by slipper to a general amnesia" (122.5–6). What becomes obscure now is not simply the presumed content of the "blank memory" we all "recoil," but the operation of memory itself, and of "mummery's" darker underside, in forgetting. Any reconstruction of the night would of necessity have to open up bottomless inquiries into the complementary relations of memory and amnesia, and into our relations with the past. Since memory is the network of operations that gives us a sense of indivisible "sameness"—of "identity"—in time, what would become equally obscure, even questionable, is the stability of "identity." For "as I now with platoonic leave recoil" (348.8), thinking about sleep is like being badly in "Platonic love": I have no real contact with the person in question, who seems to have taken "leave," at least of my senses. Worse, since presumably "I have something inside of me talking to myself" (522.26), but I cannot "recoil" it, it must be that "I'm not meself at all" (487.18).

"You," therefore, "may identify yourself with the him in you" (496.25–26) — where that "him" would refer to a "person suppressed for the moment" (280.12–13).

Again, however, we might bypass all these obscure problems by supposing—improbably—that something awakened us after a half-hour of sleep last night, and enabled us to rise out of the murk of our own lives with dim memories and fleeting impressions that "something happened that time I was asleep" (307.F5): a dream. Although this would put us "mehrer the murk" (506.24 ["nearer the mark"]), a Beckettian cry of relief—"At last, a brain with content!"—would be far too hastily vented; for the retrieval of this dream "from the wastes a' sleep" (64.1) would actually stir up more (Ger. *mehr*) rather than less "murk" (hence "mehrer the murk"). How do we know that the dream shakily falling together in "mummery" really happened during sleep and is not, for instance, a spontaneous after-effect of wakening? Since "we only know dreams from our memory of them after we are awake" (*ID*, 76), *not* from direct experience, everything we "know" is circumstantial, reaching us after the fact.[16] What we have rashly labeled a dream, then, might more accurately be called the "murmury" of a dream (254.18). And since all such dreams occur to us—literally—when we wake up and assume the conscious capacity to "remumble" them (295.4 ["mumble"]), to articulate them to ourselves in "murmury" (254.18 ["murmurs"]), traducing them in the process, they will help only some in allowing us to know what really happened in the clearer few minutes of the dark half-hour that we wished, in detail, to reconstruct. This distinction is one that Freud made by partitioning the dream into a "manifest content" (of which the dreamer is conscious) and a "latent content" (of which the dreamer is not): "dreams only show us the sleeper in so far as he is not sleeping";[17] the examination of "dreams is the royal road to the unconscious," not the unconscious itself (*ID*, 647). Dreams in this customary sense, as Joyce pointed out to Jacques Mercanton, are not what *Finnegans Wake* is about: "'Work in Progress'? A nocturnal state, lunar. That is what I want to convey: what goes on in a dream, during a dream. Not what is left over afterward, in the memory. Afterward, nothing is left."[18]

Even were we to disregard as sophistic the evident epistemological problems surrounding dreams, new problems would make difficult our attempts to chronicle a half-hour fragment of the dark. For the question would arise of how we might arrange the dream chronologically, in history's clock-time and in linear script. Uncertainty would contaminate our knowledge of how long the dream lasted, surely, and of when exactly in the half-hour under our consideration it occurred. But even murkier questions would occlude our sense of its evolution in time: on what image did this dream begin? and what was going on immediately preceding its formation? On what last image did the dream end? and what followed that? Merely to ask these questions is to begin noting how bottomless any dream is in its obscurity, disappearing into a point that Freud called its "navel," "where it reaches down into the unknown" (*ID*, 143n., 564). Trying to ascertain what happened before the first sketchy event that one recalls of any dream—"how the deepings did it all begin" (428.5)—seems an exercise undertaken in vain, in vanity: "Fantasy! funtasy on fantasy, amnaes fintasies!" (493.18). Thinking about these nocturnal "fantasies," one finds "everything" (L. *omnes*) "leading slip by slipper to a general amnesia" (hence "amnaes"), where thinking itself blurs out into "emptiness" (L. *vanitas*) and a contentless "void" (L. *vanus*). Any book purporting to reconstruct the night—and particularly an average night stirred by dreams—would have to show us how and why and when these "mummeries" (535.27 ["masked performances"]) bled up out of the dark "from next to nothing" (4.36–5.1), and there forced themselves into articulate "murmury."

Then, too, uncertainty would infect our knowledge not simply of the extension of the dream in linear time, but also of its own internal order in time. No one remembers the experience of sleep, if at all, as a sequence of events linked chronologically in time by cause and effect from the moment his head hit the pillow to the time the alarm clock startled him into rational accountability in the morning. Instead, memory of the night, often triggered by a random gesture or thought, seems to arise by association, dim particles of the dark standing out in "m'm'ry" and evoking others, and still others, until, by a process of mnemonic linking, one has filled in the gaps and reconstructed a spotty "m[e]m[o]ry" (460.20). How does one know that this randomly drifting form of recollection does not replicate exactly the order in which dreams sequentially unfolded in the night—apparent last part first, apparent first part in the middle, "blackholes" (549.5) everywhere else—and that what occurs to one as a jumble of disarranged impressions is not just that: a jumble of disarranged impressions, perhaps concealing a secret structure of its own, but perhaps not, upon which one imposes a coherent narrative structure after the fact in order to make logical sense of it?

Even supposing that we could dredge up a content for a half hour of "our own nighttime" and could order it sequentially, there would remain the vexing questions of what, if anything, the dream meant, and whether it was worth figuring out: not everyone agrees that dreams are meaningful; and not everyone who thinks that dreams are meaningful agrees on what dreams mean. "It is night. It is dark." And it is all very obscure. Indeed, "we are circumveiloped by obscuritads" (244.15 [note again the "circumveloping" "veil"]).

Some such exercise in "nightwatch service" (576.30) as the one we have just undertaken is crucial to any reading of Joyce's "nonday diary" because it will begin—merely begin—to "reveil" the essential obscurity of the material with which *Finnegans Wake* is literately dealing: "reading [the] Evening World" (28.20) as we experience it "even in our own nighttime" is not easy. Such "night duty" (429.23) will also begin to "reveil" why darkness and obscurity are integral aspects of Joyce's "book of the dark" (251.24), and not mere mannerisms. Had Joyce made *Finnegans Wake* less obscure than it is, he would have annihilated everything about his material that is most essential, most engaging, funniest, and most profound—rather in the same way that an intrusive sweep of "floodlights" would destroy any nightscape (134.18). The obscurity of *Finnegans Wake* is its essence and its glory. In its own artful form of "chiaroscuro," the book renders the dark matters we have considered eminently "clearobscure" (247.34 [the Eng. "chiaroscuro" derives from the It. *chiar-oscuro*, "clear-dark"]).

As for that ample "blank memory" that we have left hovering uncomfortably in mind, "shllwe help . . . you t'rigolect a bit? yismik? yimissy?" (234.25–26)—even while acknowledging that any such attempt "to recollect" must be something of a "joke" opening into areas "of facetious memory"? (147.30–31 ["t'rigolect" plays on the Fr. *rigoler*, "to joke," while that "yismik" "reveils" a resistantly unlifting "yashmak," the Moslem double veil]). At the *Wake*'s encouragement, then, "let's hear what science has to say, pundit-the-next-best-king" (505.27–28), where the obscure word is "science"; and as opposed to psychoanalysis, whose status as a science has been in question since it originated, let's make this "real science," with wires and meters and things that can be measured.

"HOW WE SLEEP"

Another, less troublesome reason why *Finnegans Wake* may have seemed so improbable as a reconstruction of the night, at least to readers of the last three decades, is that many of them will have been indoctrinated into a far different sense of sleep than the one which Joyce, living in an age dominated by psychoanalysis, would have had. Anyone who has looked into the current literature on dreams will have discovered a mass of facts about "REMs" and "K-complexes" and "alpha waves" that Joyce could not possibly have known. Since this literature inevitably affects the way in which we think about sleep, it complicates the way in which we approach a book purporting to reconstruct the night; for science claims to give true representations of things, as opposed to eccentric and perverse ones. Problematically, then, though it needs to be held in perspective, the new material cannot be ignored without in some way relegating *Finnegans Wake* to the position of a quirkily dated legpull. Fortunately, any light on the dark being useful, it helps us indirectly to fill in some of those roomy "blackholes" in our "m'm'ry." Here, then, is a vastly simplified redaction of the current "facts," and some questions they raise about sleep and about the plausibility of Joyce's "book of the dark." As it says there, "sifted science will do your arts good" (440.19–20).

The almost accidental discovery of "rapid-eye movements" (or "REMs") in a sleep laboratory in the 1950s occasioned what some have considered a revolution in the study of the night.[19] When sleep-researchers curious about the causes of these odd rolling motions in the eyes of sleeping people began systematically to awaken their dormant subjects, they almost always discovered, beneath the twitching eyelids, "dreams." Sleep accompanied by rapid-eye movements (or "REM sleep") therefore began rapidly to seem an "objective" sign of dreaming and, beyond that, a universal one. People who claimed never at all in their lives to dream, when awakened from REM sleep, recounted the most vividly detailed dreams, and as volubly as neurotics; yet when questioned about these dreams in the morning, they swore that they had dreamed nothing at all. Others awakened in the middle of REM sleep, who began comparably to recount dreams but dozed off in the middle of their telling, recalled, when immediately reawakened, having been awakened earlier, but not having dreamed. Over the decades, snowballing evidence of this kind began to show that everybody alive dreams, and several times a night, but that the extreme volatility of the "maimeries" involved makes dreams hard "t'rigolect": even people who do remember their dreams by and large seem to recall only fractions. "We foregot at wiking when . . . the bleakfrost chilled our ravery": (338.30–31 ["when the breakfast killed our reverie"]).

Because rapid-eye movements seem generally to accompany dreaming, some people have come to regard them as the "somatic correlates" of "dreams." And dreaming in turn, far from being a purely psychogenetic disturbance, has begun "to take on the proportions of an almost universal biological phenomenon"[20]—"universal" because not only adult humans, but all forms of mammalian life, including newly born infants and unborn babies in the uterus, also succumb to sleep disrupted by rapid-eye movements.[21] The general picture emerging from the study of REM sleep is one of aggregating obscurity and weirdness: it shows that nightly in sleep, roughly every ninety minutes, for durations lasting anywhere from three to fifty minutes, everybody in the world drifts into "a third state of existence," a dream-riddled limbo that has also been called "paradoxical sleep"—"paradoxical" because the person who has drifted into it is at once sleeping and not sleeping. While his body lies paralytically immobilized and couldn't move if it wanted to— "He's stiff" (6.22)—the eyes and brain seem to be partially awake and conducting complex affairs in a world of hallucinated objects. Sleep researchers had begun to observe, early in the course of these studies, evidently intricate parallels between the movements and focal adjustments made by the eyes in REM sleep, and the images that the dreaming subject believed himself to be seeing (in one famous case, the researcher wakening a sleeping person whose eyes were twitching back and forth from left to right over and over again learned that the dreamer had imagined two people throwing tomatoes at each other as he watched from a distance).[22] It was as if, then, the eyes of the dormant person had involuntarily lifted toward wakening under some internal impulsion, while the rest of the body lay paralyzed in slumber. Since the eyes seem to undergo such partial wakening during REM sleep, the findings have enlivened a debate, persisting from the nineteenth century, as to whether visual dreams are presentative or representative in character: are dreams events in which we really see, but see unreal things; or are they representative, fantasies in which we merely imagine ourselves seeing things?

Investigations next began looming in on those slight twitches and jerks which most people will casually have noted disrupting the bodies of people asleep. The study of such movements, again during REM sleep, opened the possibility that they too might well bear eerie correspondences to actions hallucinatorily undergone interior to the dreamer's dream: in one exemplary case "the right hand, left hand, and a foot executed movements in the order named, and the subject, when immediately awakened thereafter, reported that he lifted a bucket with his right hand, supported it with his left, and started to walk away."[23] Inexplicably, moreover, periodic intervals of REM sleep seemed to be followed by wholesale upheavals of the body, by the need to shift position or roll over in bed.[24]

Exercising the indefatigable ingenuity and resourcefulness of Western science, neurologists have also affixed wires and meters to people's private parts, so to ascertain that all males and females at all capable of it—even infants newly born—experience penile or clitoral erections regularly during phases of REM sleep, five times a night, every ninety minutes or so, every night, *regardless* of the dream's content (the report cited gives the case of a male succumbing to dark, vexed arousal during repeated dreams of major attack by shark and snake).[25] Since anyone overcome by an event of this magnitude in wakefulness would surely acknowledge it consciously, findings like these raise the fascinating question of how a person asleep and dreaming might register a comparable but unconscious awareness, in the imagery of the dream, of the event rocking the body. Certainly, the evidence suggests what people have always vaguely known: that dreams and sexual desire are inextricably and uneasily linked. But it also highlights the strangely blurred relations between desire and the objects desire seeks out— desire, in the case cited, evidently concealed from itself and converted into its opposite in the misinterpretation-prone head. Toward what object, then, when one "hallucinate[s] like an erection in the night" (310.23), is one pointing—"pointing up to skyless heaven like the spoon out of sergeant-major's tay" (331.1–2)? And "Whor dor the pene lie" (349.1–2 [Port. *dor*, "pain"; It. *pene*, "penis"]) in dreams from which one wakens to "recoil" only horror and terror?

Anxious to prove that dreaming had clear somatic manifestations, early sleep-research tended to discover dreams only in the night's cyclically recurrent periods of REM sleep, presuming that the brain rested in the intervals between. Later research pressing into these darker parts of sleep, however, discovered that "mental life" seemed doggedly to persist there too, though in far different forms: reluctant subjects repeatedly awakened from "non-REM sleep" reported having been dimly mulling over trivial matters bearing on work, personal problems, and other items constituting an average day's residue. Unlike the vivid dreams bled up out of REM sleep, then, a kind of dim, distorted, internal discourse seemed to seep through NREM sleep.[26] But even these discoveries seem unstable: severe nightmares and episodes of sleep-walking, for instance, seem to emerge from NREM sleep; and the question always remains whether the thoughts discovered in the dark did not rush into the vacuum of the mind at the moment of the subject's awakening. Many obscurities remain.[27]

The research is interesting because it has elevated to the status of scientific truth one of many things that has struck people as being least probable about *Finnegans Wake:* "whatever the significance of dreaming, it is important to note that consciousness—in the sense of mental experience—is not completely abolished even during the deepest stages of sleep";[28] "there is no point in the sleep cycle at which consciousness suddenly appears. It seems to be there all along" (here the obscure word is "consciousness").[29] So something very dark may indeed have been going on in that "deleteful" half-hour of "real life" that we began to reconstruct and whose blank "m'm'ry" we all "recoil." The question next arises, then, of what relation this dark thought might have to language; for where there is thought, in one view, language cannot be far behind.

The problem with all of these studies—and with their bearing on *Finnegans Wake*—is that they finally reveal less about the content and the interior of the "dream," as we experience it "in our own nighttime," than about the bodies of sleeping people. No one captivated by the dark will deny the interest of the information this work yields. But the ways in which sleeping people show themselves to wakened rationalists will finally not "reveil" what in particular goes on in the "hole affair" we went "trough" last night and which *Finnegans Wake* takes as its subject. In interesting ways, too, these studies highlight the epistemological weirdness of all reconstructions of the night and so set Joyce's in foil. Since all those many animals whose sleep is accompanied by rapid-eye movements, when you wake them, have nothing very substantial to say about their "dreams," the real "correlates" of dreams—indeed, the only real evidence of their existence—seems to lie less on eyelids than in the "murmur[ies]" and strangely nonsensical tales "remumble[d]" by the people awakened: it's in language and in tales told, where it is unclear whether science or interpretive art has primacy. And this Joyce would well have known. In one way of thinking about the "revolution" that rocked the scientific world in the 1950s, people discovered not so much "rapid-eye movements," as the electroencephalograph and the value of strategic awakenings.

For "rapid-eye movements" were indistinctly there all along, too—indistinct because immeasurable. Joyce, of course, could not possibly have known about them in any quantifiable form when he wrote about "Bindmerollingeyes" (11.6–7 [the hero of *Finnegans Wake*]) and suggested that one good way of learning more about the "floored" "mistermysterion" in question would be to "Look at this twitches!" (301.18–19, 22–23 [all of them]). But details like these (and there are many) reflect how widely nineteenth- and early twentieth-century students of the dark believed that dreams and agitations of the eyes in sleep went together—as those who write about REM sleep themselves periodically acknowledge.[30] Most insights into the nature of dreams gained through "the new science" of sleep

research had already been conjecturally formulated, though not electroencephalographically clinched, in the literature on sleep written prior to their discovery and would easily have been within Joyce's reach.

When Joyce advised his readers to "hear what science has to say," moreover (505.27), he was certainly not addressing an audience that would suddenly vanish when new scientific discoveries came along, ten years after his death. Writing in an age of great scientific volatility himself, and modeling his book on one called *The New Science*, he was inviting them to ponder the contradiction-laden destiny of all "science" whose dark object was "nescience," or unconsciousness; for "science" (from the L. *scio*, "I know") can be of "nescience" (L. *nescio*, "I don't know") only with difficulty. Beyond that too, he was calling attention to the inadequacies of science itself—"pundit-the-next-best-king"—as a way of "knowing" in a world where aesthesis and play were heavily beleaguered alternatives. So "if sciencium (what's what) can mute uns nought, 'a thought, abought the great Sommboddy within the Omniboss"—note the *somme* (Fr. "sleep") infusing this obscure "somebody"—"perhaps an artsaccord (hoot's hoot) might sing ums tumtim abutt the Little Newbuddies that ring his panch" (415.15–19). With a little laugh by the way " (hoot's hoot)," the lines apprise us that *Finnegans Wake* intends to set us straight as to "what's what" and "who's who."

THE JOYCEAN "UNGUMPTIOUS" AND THEIRS

As its spelling implies, the Joycean "UNGUMPTIOUS" has a lot of "gumption" and humor in it, and is both distinct from and yet related to the "Unconscious" in more orthodox forms. As its appearance in the text also suggests, and as many Joyceans have compellingly demonstrated, there can be no question that psychoanalysis had an impact, a deep one, on *Finnegans Wake*:[31] the term appears in a phrase directing our attention to "LIPPUDENIES OF THE UNGUMPTIOUS" (308.R2 [a "libidinous unconscious"]), in a book that has the "intrepidity" to call itself "an intrepidation of our dreams" (338.29). Like all the many psychoanalytical tags drifting through *Finnegans Wake*, these terms suggest similarities and yet differences, both of which are important to weigh.

Mere mention of Freud will raise hackles on one side of the room and banners on the other; but sleep alone will elicit a version of the same bizarre politics. Merely having proposed as an exercise the reconstruction of a halfhour fragment of dark will already have raised in most minds unresolved questions on which there will be sides to take, and about which seasonably "fashionable" and unfashionable "factions" will form. A reader of Joyce would do well to try cultivating an indifference to these partisanships, by paying attention to the *Wake* itself: there we read that one must, "for a surview over all the factionables see Iris in the Evenine's World" (285.26–27). The line invites its reader to sort these matters out not by resorting to programmatic responses, but by studying what is seen, "in fact, under the closed eyes" (107.28 [hence the "iris"]), in the "Evening World" (28.20 [the night]). It also suggests that in exploring the "Evening World," the *Wake* will, among all things else, "survey the factions" that have politicized the same dark domain.

It seems to me impossible for any reader seriously interested in coming to terms with *Finnegans Wake* to ignore *The Interpretation of Dreams*, which broke the ground that Joyce would reconstruct in his own "intrepidation of dreams" and, arguably, made *Finnegans Wake* possible: it was in the cultural air that any early twentieth-century European would have breathed, and it is everywhere implicit in Joyce's "nonday diary." Its first chapter, not least, provides an excellent summary of the nineteenth-century literature on sleep and dreams, and those that follow have not been surpassed in exploring what dreams mean and how they work. No subsequent treatment of the subject fails to show its influence. The book is important to *Finnegans Wake*, however, not simply because it treats so elaborately *of Dreams*, but because it is equally about *Interpretation*, which is any reader's only business; and it is about interpretation of a kind that unyieldingly brings the simple and central question "What does it mean?" to a species of peculiarly nonsensical, obscure, and garbled literary text—"the text of the dream" (*ID*, 552), the puzzling and troubling "murmurrandoms" (358.3) that any dreamer "remumble[s] from the night before" (note the "random" element in such "murmured memoranda").[32] Particularly because the only real evidence of "dreaming" comes in the dark language of these "murmurable" "murmoirs" (294.7, 387.34 ["memorable" because "murmured" "memoirs"]), some interpretive technique *distinct* from those brought to bear on consciously constructed narratives will be essential to a reading of what Joyce called his "imitation of the dream-state";[33] and *The Interpretation of Dreams* offers not simply the most intricately developed and detailed example of such a technique, but also an account—no matter whether critical or not— of alternative interpretive techniques as well. It is, in short, an indispensable text to bring to *Finnegans Wake*.

On the other hand, it would be foolish to disregard Joyce's well-known derogations of Freud and "the new Viennese school" (*U*, 205): all of his recorded comments on psychoanalysis were dismissive.[34] They suggest, perhaps, what should be obvious: that both as a "competent" thinker and man—a "competitor" and not a follower—and especially as an artist whose work consistently explored "the inner life," Joyce was of necessity in competition with psychoanalysis, and all the more particularly because of its claims to authority. This much, at least, is implied in remarks like the chastising aside he directed to Mary Colum when he heard that she was attending a series of lectures by Pierre Janet: "You could learn as much psychology from yourself as from those fellows."[35] And why not? A great deal has been said about the heroism of Freud's self-analysis, but relatively little about Joyce's, in the writing of *Ulysses*, which he regarded as "essentially the product of [his] whole life":[36] it would be difficult to conceive of anyone spending seven years on a text that heavily autobiographical, reworking on a daily basis the personal and literary past, without emerging from the experience radically changed. One way of reading *Ulysses*, a work thematically absorbed with the issues of fathering and self-fathering, is to see it as the process whereby an arrogant little man, a young Joyce who in fact had published under the name "Stephen Dedalus," rewrote himself so entirely as to emerge from the experience not simply with the humane capabilities of a Leopold Bloom, and not simply even with the expansive good humor and affability that every reader of the biography will know, but as one of the twentieth century's great men of letters. The book, through its microscopic examination of the inner life, altered the past in every way possible.[37]

It would do Joyce insufficient credit, then, to read *Finnegans Wake* as a "creative" reworking of understandings that might be had much more straightforwardly through a reading of Freud, and not simply because Joyce clearly went about reconstructing the night in his own idiosyncratic way, but also because if most of the night is void of recollectible dreams, a work aspiring to their interpretation would be only of partial relevance.[38] Joyce thought about psychic interiors throughout his literary career and about "nightlife" daily for almost twenty years (150.33, 407.20). It was his work. As an author who distrusted authority in all its forms, he preferred to all theory nagging, living, concrete immersion in the material under his scrutiny itself ("I hate generalities" [*JJ*, 565]). If, as he said, "*Ulysses* is related to this book as the day is to the night," we should expect *Finnegans Wake* to behave with all the uncapturable richness of a *Ulysses*, exploring its dark subject thoroughly, systematically, but not systemically.[39] Finally, too, as Joyce's comparative remarks on Freud and Vico suggest, his real authority in

An Introduction

the study of the unconscious was Vico, and even here he distanced himself carefully ("I would not pay overmuch attention to these theories, beyond using them for all they are worth" [L, I, 241]).[40]

All this is only to note that Joyce's vexed relation to Freud is sufficiently complex as not to be solved by oppositional diatribe, doctrinaire advocacy, or, above all, simple disregard. "The relation of *Ulysses* and *Finnegans Wake* to [*The Interpretation of Dreams*] is tricky and subtle," as Adaline Glasheen has rightly noted, "and deserves the fullest, deepest study."[41] Ongoing reference to *The Interpretation of Dreams* and its sequelae in the following pages is intended to open relevant perspectives and to invite running comparisons between Joyce's "UNGUMPTIOUS" and the Freudian one. I would like the reader to see in these conflations a Joycean reading of Freud, and not a Freudian reading of Joyce.

"EPISTLEMADETHEMOLOGY FOR DEEP DORFY DOUBTLINGS"

Early in the course of our "unaveiling" reconstruction of a half-hour fragment of the dark, the healthily skeptical reader will have wondered how anyone could possibly know what goes on in a part of the night unyielding to "m'm'ry" and resistant in every way to any form of direct knowing. Particularly for a writer of Joyce's realist allegiances, the question would have raised larger questions about how one knows—anything. Capable as one may be in wakefulness of explicating allusions, for instance, or speaking cannily about the collapse of representational epistemologies, it would seem a genuine deficiency in any claim to knowledge not to know the content of one's own head in an wholly representative slice of "Real life" (260.F3). "Writing about the night," then, would have deepened in its purport for Joyce, and also in its obscurity, because it would have meant not simply generating a "nonday diary," but concurrently undertaking a sustained "epistlemadethemology for deep dorfy doubtlings" (374.17–18)—a phrase that yields "two thinks at a time" (583.7). *Finnegans Wake* launches on a dark "epistemology," to be sure, bending the questions "How do I know?" (507.24) and "Where did thots come from?" (597.25 ["thoughts"]) into "one great part of [our] existence" about which we must willingly entertain "deep doubts"—and "dorfy" ones, at that. But it is also, as an "epistle-made" artifact, an "epistlemadethemology" in which the status of language and letters ("epistles") will unrelentingly be "made [a] theme."

Although it is currently one trend to see *Finnegans Wake* as a work "about language"—and it surely is—Joyce himself, whenever he was asked to clarify the book, problematically said that it was "about the night." This minor discrepancy as to what the book is "about" is extremely important, as the following pages intend to show; for while a book "about language" need say nothing at all "about the night," and in fact usually will not, a book "about the night" would of necessity have to undertake an intricate and wondrously obscure inquiry into the nature of language. "My heeders will recoil with a great leisure" (160.35 [not "recall," not necessarily "pleasure"]) that big "blank memory" left suspended in their heads after last night's orgy of "leisure." Why do no words leap into the gap and fill this roomy space? *If that [one] hids foregodden has nate of glozery*" (339.24 ["has forgotten his night of glory"]), is it because one has also "forgotten his native glossary"? If the experience of sleep entails the wholesale rubbling of language, out of what dark place in the mind do those "murmurable" "murmurrandoms" that we "recoil" in the morning come from?

The fullest possible response to the question of what happens to (literate) consciousness in the night—"Something happened that time I was asleep, torn letters or was there snow?" (307.F5)—would oblige us to wonder, at least if we think it improbable that language ever suddenly vacates the head, whether letters and literacy fell into a strange new order in the dark, like "torn letters"; or if sleep merely blanketed everything over, as if under a bleaching fall of "snow" ("We feel unspeechably thoughtless over it all here . . . " [238.36]). In this latter case, the question would arise of how language could possibly capture the nothing that language, constantly about something, is not. For not the least obscure matter pertaining to our experimental reconstruction, in detail, of a half-hour of the night—presuming we could replace a profoundly "blank memory" with "somethink" (83.14)—would be the question of what kind of language could adequately fill the spaciously "hole affair." English?—with words like "memory" and "recall," which are always of something? "Languish" too, then, is what *Finnegans Wake* is necessarily about (96.11, 232.21 ["language"]), but primarily because it is "about the night." And in an already doubt-riddled "epistlemadethemology," letters—"epistles" and words—will be an ongoing "thematic" concern.

As to the question of how Joyce in particular could possibly know the interior of the night, we have the difficult evidence of *Finnegans Wake* itself to examine, but also oblique indications from the biography and the letters. All the evidence shows Joyce entering this area with extreme caution. He began to write *Work in Progress* in March 1923, in English, tentatively, unclear as to where it would lead him (*JJ*, 551); and it took him the better part of a year, by the end of which he had sketched out half the book, to show the newly evolving work to anyone but his immediate friends, and then too, only tentatively ("May I ask you, by the way, to be rather reticent about my new book?" he wrote to Valery Larbaud [*L*, III, 87–88]). Nothing indicates that Joyce knew his "experiment in interpreting 'the dark night of the soul'" (*L*, I, 258) would exhaust two decades of his life, half of his literary career, and the odd resources of some sixty languages. Only as he warmed to his material did he begin to realize the depth and extent of its obscurities, and these obviously challenged and allured him, but also frustrated him immensely: "The task I have set myself is dreadfully difficult," he wrote to Robert MacAlmon in early 1924, "but I believe it can be done" (*L*, III, 88). And to Harriet Shaw Weaver in the same year: "There are so many problems to be solved that I can face only one at a time" (*L*, III, 96); "I have been thinking and thinking how and how and how can I and can't it" (*L*, I, 220); "It is a bewildering business. . . . Complications to right of me, complications to left of me, complex on the page before me, perplex in the pen beside me, duplex in the meandering eyes of me, stuplex on the face that reads me. And from time to time I lie back and listen to the sound of my hair growing white" (*L*, I, 222). Nobody took these laments seriously; everybody thought he was dramatizing himself while really only doodling around with puns, indulgently parading the emptiest of eruditions, or inventing some kind of private mythology. Joyce: "I am rather discouraged about this as in such a vast and difficult enterprise I need encouragement. . . . but I cannot go back" (*L*, I, 249).

Frank Budgen recalls being told by August Suter that "in the early days of the composition of *Finnegans Wake*," Joyce said, "I am boring into a mountain from two sides. The question is how to meet in the middle."[42] Suter recalls the formulation differently: when he asked Joyce about his new work, Joyce replied, "imagine a mountain which I am boring into from all sides without knowing what I am going to find."[43] The comparison was to become a well-worked favorite, varying in form with the state of the work, and in these guises show Joyce thinking about the night much as anyone only can;[44] for what happens "down there" can be inferred most clearly by working out of the two well-lit shafts through which one enters and leaves it, while falling asleep and waking up—although dreams pock the dark with innumerable random obscure points of entry. As the *Wake* puts it, of a hero obscurely called "*The Bearded Mountain*" (222.12), "there are two signs to turn to, the yest and the ist, . . . feeling aslip and wauking up" (597.10–12): "the yest" here is where night fell and where "yest"erday disintegrated ("the west"), while "ist" (or "east") is where the day will break, and where the present always reappears ("is").

One of these two openings had already been amply cleared away, for two of Joyce's earlier three works of fiction had come to deadends at the threshhold beyond which *Finnegans Wake* was darkly to move. At the end of "The Dead," "faintly falling" asleep in the Gresham Hotel, Gabriel Conroy feels "his own identity . . . fading out" as a reverie of snow drifts into his mind, to change his mind and the texture of the story as well (*D*, 223–24); and at the end of *Ulysses*, Joyce sought comparably "to convey the mumbling of a woman falling asleep."[45] To note that Joyce's fiction pressed repeatedly against the dark borderland separating wakefulness from sleep is only to note one necessity that compelled him into the writing of the *Wake*—which, after all, is only an inflected synonym for "The Dead." A second necessity was the fact of *Ulysses* itself, through which, according to T. S. Eliot, Joyce "killed the nineteenth century, exposed the futility of all styles, and destroyed his own future" (*JJ*, 528). What could Joyce have done after writing *Ulysses*? A chronicle of June 17, 1904? Or a sweeping saga of three generations of family life whose culminating item would be a writer dense with sensitivity? The logical place for him to go was down, into the night. "Having written *Ulysses* about the day, I wanted to write this book about the night" (*JJ*, 695).

The intensity with which Joyce studied dreams, read about dreams, and discussed dreams with family members and friends has been broadly documented.[46] Jacques Mercanton, who is supposed to have become the official expositor of *Finnegans Wake* had Joyce lived (*JJ*, 710), makes it seem in his recollection of Joyce that the going over of dreams may have been the first order of business of every day.[47] But it clearly went further even than this: stray remarks in his letters show Joyce waking up at night, scribbling on paper in the dark, and falling back asleep: "I composed some wondrous devices for Λd during the night," he informed Harriet Shaw Weaver, "and wrote them out in the dark very carefully only to discover that I had made a mosaic on top of other notes so I am now going to have to bring my astronomical telescope into play" (*L*, I, 235). Already he was teaching her, everywhere in the letters, how to read *Finnegans Wake*: "astronomical telescopes," unlike regular ones, work only at night, and they train on matters invisible to the light of day; they do what Joyce does in "his book of the dark." No amount of generalizing or mere assertion, however, will ultimately persuade anyone of anything. The only evidence that will show just how much Joyce thought and learned about the night is *Finnegans Wake* itself, "the Strangest Dream that was ever Halfdreamt" (307.11–12).

"SLEEP, WHERE IN THE WASTE IS THE WISDOM?"

Somewhere very early in a meditation of this sort, the busily put-upon reader will doubtlessly have paused to wonder why all of this should be important enough to merit his attention and time. Since the "hole affair" "amounts to nada in pounds or pence" (521.5–6)—since it defies "sound sense" and is not very profitable either (hence the "pounds" and "pence"), he will likely want to ask of "Sleep, where in the waste is the wisdom?" (114.19–20). Though the only fully satisfactory answer to this question can be a reading of *Finnegans Wake*, we might for now entertain a few orienting considerations.

Writers who deal with the subject are fond of pointing out that we spend one-third of our lives in sleep. The unyielding fraction, as anyone who has tried unsuccessfully to conform to a regulated eight-hour sleep schedule knows, is finally arbitrary, deriving from an Aristotelean partitioning of the day into three equal thirds of which one seems "reasonably" appropriate to the night. But the fraction is not simply arbitrary; it's conservative.[48] For the forces that tow us into sleep, arguably, are always there under the surface of things, exerting an obliviating drag on our capacities to engage resourcefully and energetically in the world, blacking us out not just in those lengthy amnesias endured every night, but—an eyelid drooping here, attention lapsing there, best intentions crumbling everywhere—in the less noticeable amnesias, lapses of attentiveness, surrenders to passivity, and withdrawals from life that undermine the living of any day. Something of this nature surely overcomes Mr. Bloom, for instance, at 10 o'clock on a hot summer morning, when, theoretically well rested, he can barely bring himself to regard the world from "beneath his veiled eyelids" because the news of an unmanageable problem has left him sluggishly stupefied and stunned, in lotus-land (*U*, 74; note also his eyelids on 71, 75). "Nowtime" is just a variant of "nighttime," according to one of the *Wake*'s careful spellings (290.17) as "night" is just "nowt" (238.27). That big "blank memory" that we have all "recoil[ed]" from "our own nighttime," after all, did not simply vanish when night did; the roomily "hole affair" lingers on vexingly, now, very much a part of our present minds. If one-third of our lives is spent in sleep, then, so too one-third of us is never fully in the here-and-now. Inviting us to be conscious of the unconscious, or, in its own idiom, wakening the dead, *Finnegans Wake* wakes us up to the dark third of us that never comes to light.

At a complementary extreme, there are the forces that work against sleep. Toward the waking end of *Finnegans Wake*, its reader meets a figure who is given to venting, usually with great moral urgency, alarming statements on the order of "I'm the gogetter that'd make it pay like cash registers" (451.4–5) and *"I've a terrible errible lot todue todie todue tootorrible-day"* (381.23–24). He represents, among much else, that part of the *Wake*'s sleeping mind whose anxiety about quotidian survival—making rational sound sense and tons of pounds and pence—is alarming him up into agony. The huffy-puffy rhythm tells it all: everyone is under pressure, "to do" "to-day" what's "due today," in "terror" and "error" and "horror," without perhaps stopping to wonder why all that pressure need be there, or where in one's life it originates. Sleep is what someone in this frame of mind doesn't want to think about, hasn't the time to think about, and can't afford to indulge in because of competing demands on his time and attention ("cash registers," "the cash system," and the whole "cash-dime problem," for example [161.7, 149.17]): "Dollarmighty!" (562.33). Sleep is a sheer, unprofitable "waste of time" (151.21). Still, since "today" is only "todie" in the terms given—since one's management of the limited amount of time in a day is only representative of one's management of the limited amount of time in a life—it may well be important to think about the night and one's dreams, before "today" slips into "to die," and to determine too where those pressurizing, sleep-annihilating demands come from and whether they need be met.

Sleep unfolds in "the darkness which is the afterthought of thy nomatter" (258.32–33): to all quotidian appearances, it is absolutely trivial, a little "after-thought" "of no great matter" to much of anyone—particularly with all those "cash registers" in the background sonorously indicating what values are to be assigned to what things. Living as we do in a world where there are all kinds of pounds and pence and sounds and sense to make, we all mean business, if not literally. Who has time to think about the night in the morning when something else is always judged to be more centrally pressing? Wondering who makes these decisions as to what has value and what does not would in itself have fascinated Joyce, and also would have let him exercise a modernist inclination to detect precisely in the trivial—a single day, for example—the richest of revelations. Sleep is the underside of the stone on whose sunlit upper surface is engraved the letter and the law of the land: no one wants to look at it. It is so trivial, so marginal, so unthinkable an "afterthought of thy nomatter," in fact, that even people writing about dreams and the centrality of the marginal and *Finnegans Wake* seem quite happy to overlook it, as if there were nothing there. So Joyce, "having done the longest day in literature"—in wording he co-opted from his brother—began "conjuring up the darkest night" (*L*, III, 140), and for many good reasons: as we follow him into "our own nighttime," we find there, as intricately writ as anywhere else, "as human a little story as paper could well carry" (115.36).

Within *Finnegans Wake*, Joyce refers to his sleepy subject as "the mountainy molehill" (474.22): the phrase advises us that he knew quite well how big a "mountain" he was making out of a "molehill" by writing six hundred pages, over two decades, "about the night"; but it also serves notice that he found in the visionless and subterranean experience of sleep (a "molehill" of sorts) a vast "mountain" of material. By tunneling into this "mountain," Joyce not simply mined open the twentieth-century's analytical fascination with sleep, dreams, and the Unconscious, but developed as well a modernist eschatology (Gr. *eschatos*, "furthest, uttermost"): "modernist" because his efforts located in a trivial "afterthought of thy nomatter," in the absolutely unthinkable, precisely what is most apocalyptic and revealing about the precariously instituted order of things; an "eschatology" because it sends knowledge and thought to their limits and uttermost ends.

Even if one wanted to and had the time, sleep is what one cannot think about because it unfolds in a bottomless fissure within which thinking and all our quotidian ways of knowing disappear. At its interior, every epistemological category on which the novel, science, and empiricism are traditionally predicated—indeed, the totality of "the real"—crumbles into rich indefinition, and vanishes; and so too does "common sense." "Common sense," then, tells us that everything about *Finnegans Wake* must necessarily lie outside the pale of "common sense": no two people can ever empirically "sense" a dream in "common," and it isn't even clear that one can. Still, if we heed with Joyce "The Value of Circumstantial Evidence" (307.24 ["dreams," for example]), boring into the core of the dark from its two familiar well-lit wakened edges, much might be inferred about the heart of the night.

The best guide to *Finnegans Wake* is concentrated reflection on "our own nighttime." Joyce told Jacques Mercanton that he countered criticism of the book by saying that "it ha[d] to do with an ideal suffering caused by an ideal insomnia. A sentence in the book describes it in those terms" [120.9–14].[49] Since "ideal insomnia" differs from real insomnia by virtue of its ideality, the sentence is inviting us to be thoughtfully vigilant "in our own night-time" and complementarily thoughtful in wakefulness about "how we sleep" (248.19). Anyone wanting seriously to read *Finnegans Wake* must at some point go to "nightschool" (430.2), take a few "Night Lessons" (II.ii), do a little "nightwatch service" (576.30), exercise some "night duty" (429.23), serve on "the vigilance committee" (34.4), and, above all, "sleep on it" (445.22–23). All of the characters inside the book do these things, and so did Joyce himself: "I am at present attending night school," he wrote jokingly to his son and daughter-in-law in 1934, and then went on to close the letter with a characteristic tag: "Good night, dear children. Nightynight everybody" (*L*, III, 320–21). Only daily reference to the "hole affair" you went "trough" last night will clarify this most "clearobscure" of books.

It was Joyce's lifelong rival, Doctor Oliver St. John Gogarty, who first reacted in exasperated disbelief to *Finnegans Wake* by calling it "the most colossal leg-pull in literature since McPherson's Ossian."[50] But even its most serious readers seem tacitly to have assumed that Joyce was only kidding when he said it was "about the night." The real obstacle to our comprehension of *Finnegans Wake* since its publication, in my view, has been a reluctance on the part of readers to think seriously about the very strange, literally unthinkable, and only apparently trivial material that it richly explores. As a consequence, Joyce's own many assertions about the book—his "reconstruct[ion of] the nocturnal life" and "imitation of the dream-state"—have been dismissed out-of-hand as improbable, or else explained away either as "conceits" that Joyce found useful for his own eccentric purposes, or as impressionistic "devices" that in practice have licensed interpretive mayhem on the one extreme hand and pedantic irrelevance on the other. As one consequence, the text perhaps most widely regarded as the great monolithic obstacle to our understanding of modernism has remained inaccessibly obscure since its publication in 1939—and not simply to the interested lay reader, but to many Joyceans as well. It is time that the putative bluff was called, and shown to be no bluff at all. *Finnegans Wake* is about "the night we will remember" (432.1–2).

"But we'll wake and see" (375.8).

CHAPTER ONE

"Reading the Evening World"

Any reader can extend his own reflections on the night into a "reading [of the] Evening World" literately reconstructed in *Finnegans Wake* (28.20) simply by examining the book's opening pages. If the *Wake* indeed "reconstructs the night," this area ought theoretically to portray the irrecollectible "thought" moving through sleep in the first few minutes after the loss of conscious thought in bed; and it ought, ideally, to conform with some plausibility to our shared sense of what that experience is like.

Immediate concessions to "common sense," then, and to what critics skeptical of *Finnegans Wake* have always maintained would not be out of order: most of what one finds here is as impenetrably obscure as the "blank memory" "recoil[ed]" from the early part of last night's sleep; whole vast spaces on the page make absolute nonsense. The essentially English first paragraph, to be sure, yields dim impressions: references to places in Dublin seem to have been unhinged from their local mooring points and rendered diffuse—"Adam and Eve's" Church inverted into a more oddly evocative "Eve and Adam's," the Liffey and Dublin Bay losing their concreteness in the looser terms "riverrun" and "bay." Propped up by that undeniably opaque second paragraph, however, these few clear impressions fall outside of any context that might render them intelligible; and appeals to authority will not necessarily help here either. Other readers may have detected "the voice of God," allegories involving the Holy Name, or clever puns in the Sanskrit here, but perhaps we do not.[1] And even if we consult the available reference works and have the allusions and foreign words explicated for us, they only render what is already unintelligible a little more clearly unintelligible.

None of this matters in the least. If one operates on the premise that *Finnegans Wake* reconstructs the night, the first preconception to abandon wholesale is that it ought to read anything at all like narrative or make sense as a continuous linear whole: nobody's "nightlife" makes sense as a continuous linear narrative whole (150.33, 407.20). Just as it is impossible to recall, minute by minute, in sequential order, the "hole affair" that one went through in sleep last night, from the time one lost consciousness until the time one awoke, so, arguably, it is impossible to read *Finnegans Wake*. Instead, the book makes sense only in much the same way that "everynight life" does (17.33). Impossible as it may be to fathom as an obscure totality, even at the level of a page, particles of immanent sense will stand out from the dark foil against which they are set, in turn to suggest connections with others, and still others, until—not necessarily in linear order—out of a web of items drawn together by association, a knot of *coherent* nonsense will begin to emerge;[2] and upon this coherent nonsense, as upon the shards of a recollected dream, some interpretation will have to be practiced in order to discover an underlying sense. "Reading [the] Evening World" as it is reconstructed in *Finnegans Wake* is like reading the evening world as one knows it in fact. This is also to note that any point of entry into this "book of the dark" will inevitably be arbitrary and confusing—as Joyce himself implicitly acknowledged by pointing out that "the book really has no beginning or end. . . . It ends in the middle of a sentence and begins in the middle of the same sentence" (*L*, I, 246). One can, given these terms, start "reading [the] Evening World" in much the same way that one starts exploring any memory of the night: anywhere. For demonstrative purposes, this reading will momentarily bypass altogether the first two murky paragraphs of the book to begin in its third paragraph:

> The fall (bababadalgharaghtakamminarronnkonnbronntonnerronntuonnthunn-trovarrhounawnskawntoohoohoordenenthurnuk!) of a once wallstrait oldparr is retaled early in bed and later on life down through all christian minstrelsy. The great fall of the offwall entailed at such short notice the pftjschute of Finnegan, erse solid man, that the humptyhillhead of humself promptly sends an unquiring one well to the west in quest of his tumptytumtoes: and their upturnpikepointandplace is at the knock out in the park where oranges have been laid to rust upon the green since devlinsfirst loved livvy.
>
> (3.15–24)

The paragraph locates us "in bed"—"early"—though it does so in a manner quite "clearobscure" (247.34). For all the book's purported verbal instability, virtually every page of *Finnegans Wake* refers comparably to "bed"

(5.20, 6.26), or to "night" (7.2), or to things associated with a night in bed: to "dusk" (4.12), "eve" (5.11), peaceful rest (6.35), "slumber" (7.21), "sunset" (9.2), even snoring and pillows (7.28, 6.24). Although these sleep-orienting terms, deployed more often than not in plain English, permeate the book and give it one kind of centricity, they enter the *Wake*'s "nightmaze" so obliquely (411.8), with such eccentricity, that they become, as here, almost unnoticeable—as if they were negligible after-thoughts of no great matter (notice how unnoticeable this "bed" becomes at 18.18, "sleep" at 4.15, and "Nap" at 9.6). Arguably, the phrase "in bed" is as obscure a term as any other in the paragraph before us, precisely because it eludes attention—and in much the same way that an interval of sleep might elude attention in waking life, a part of the whole, linking the whole, too trivial to bear much more than an "afterthought of thy nomatter" when so much else seems of greater urgency (258.32–33). Who can notice this bed with that hundred-lettered word overpowering it by its proximity? "It's like a dream," in which many a "goodridhirring" (7.19 ["good red herring"]) operates to distract attention from what may be most eccentrically central. If "precisely the most trivial elements of a dream are most indispensable to its interpretation" (*ID*, 552), however, a little attention ought to be expended here too. The phrase "in bed" will serve illustratively, as an orienting point out of which all other elements on this page—and on all those pages that surround it in this circular book—might be seen to radiate by a logic of association. In this nocturnal universe where "*Totem Fulcrum Est*" (481.4 [L. *totum fulcrum est*, "all is bed"]), it yields one kind of leverage on the dark.

The paragraph's location in bed will likely seem obscure to a reader, but only because that bed is almost entirely obscure to the formerly solid ("erst solid"), once upright ("once wallstrait") Irishman ("erse . . . man") who is laid to rest in it ("laid to rust") and who, no longer either solid or upright, seems to have sustained a very serious fall ("The fall," "the great fall," "the pftjschute" [Fr. *chute*, "fall"]). Perhaps only a minute ago our rubbled hero could have identified his head and feet with as much proud precision as any wakeful rationalist, and in several languages too. Now he hasn't the vaguest awareness of their location, of their relation either to each other or to himself, or quite fully of their existence; the paragraph resolves as a muddily blurred "humptyhillhead" sends sensory inquiries outward in space in quest of the toes to which it is presumably attached, and not simply overshoots the mark by miles, but even when all sensation is "laid to rust," finds no clear object. Any head so oblivious of its personal and spatial attachment to its own "tumptytumtoes" will likely be oblivious of itself. Normally full of inquiry, in fact, our hero's inert head is now largely capable only of "un-quiry"; the negation ("un-") of "inquiry," this would be the absence of the capacity to inquire at all.

Together, these details begin to illustrate a whole negational mannerism of the *Wake*'s language, and, as put to play here, they yield the first of innumerable moments in the book that will be preoccupied with missing persons (324.18–22), missing bodies (66.28ff., 291.15), lost properties (556.26–27), headhunting (497.7), and so forth. They simply tell us that the "unquiring" humanoid "laid to rust" "in bed" here is unconscious—unconscious, in particular, of the existence and extension of his body as an object in space. Who knows, in the middle of sleep, where his head and toes are or even that they exist? We might see the paragraph murkily beginning to "represent," then, from his own internal point of view, "mun in his natural, oblious autamnesically of his very proprium" (251.4–5)—a "man," that is, "in the state of nature" (49.24–25), "obviously" "oblivious" "of his very *proprium*" (L. everything his "own") because he is "making act of oblivion" (424.18–19) and undergoing sleep's "auto-amnesic" "blackout" (617.14 [Gr. *autamnêsia*, "obliviousness of self"]). Since "point of view" would hardly be the most accurate term to apply to anyone oblivious of his head and toes, however, it might be more accurate to think of the paragraph replicating the "eyewitless foggus" (515.30) of this "unquiring one"—where an "eyewitless foggus," the negation of an "eyewitness focus" or clear point of view, would yield only an "eyeless" and "witless" gaze through "fog" into "the darkness which is the afterthought of thy nomatter" (258.32–33). Sleep happens only in unconsciousness, in "unquiry," "after thought" shuts off, and annihilating space, it locates us in a domain where there is "no matter": "I've lost the place, where was I?" (307.F4).

In turn, we might see the paragraph beginning to introduce the subject of *Finnegans Wake*, who, "if I may break the subject gently" (165.30), has "tropped head" (34.6)—"dropped head," that is, almost as fully as if "dropped dead," largely because there was "too much" of it there to begin with (It. *troppo*, Fr. *trop*). And an "unquiry" related to the one evident on the opening page will introduce us more formally to this "unquiring one" and to his peculiar mode of "thought": "Who do you no tonigh, lazy and gentleman?" (126.2). As the wording here suggests, all "unquiry" looms dopily in on a single person (a "lazy gentleman") who is sleeping ("tonight"), void of sexual identity ("lazy and gentleman"), and largely oblivious of his own proximate presence to himself in space ("to nigh"). "Who do you no" ("know") tells us that he doesn't ("know") because he is unconscious—as throughout

Finnegans Wake, which more than once spells "know" "no." Like the "un-quiry" of which we read on page three, then, this one is less a "query" than a "queery"; indeed, "It am queery!" (512.33)—where the syntactical distortion of third person ("It is a query") to first ("I am queer") implies that all such "unquiries" emanate from the mind of a very singular first person indeed, and drift back into himself.

The relation of our "unquiring" subject to the manifold objects arrayed around him in the paragraph under our attention is accordingly complex. For as he lies "in bed," his "tropped head" questing vacantly for the toes to which it is ordinarily attached, a murky landscape "turns up" in their "place" ("*upturn*pikepointand*place*"). As the commentary on *Finnegans Wake* has made too clear, this landscape seems to stretch across Dublin from the Hill of Howth (or Howth Head ["-hillhead"]), westward to Castle Knock, once the site of a "turnpike," at the western border of the Phoenix Park ("well to the west," "up*turnpike*pointandplace," "the knock out in the park"). These localities and others named in *Finnegans Wake* are represented in Map A, which depicts the greater Dublin area, the "Howth Castle and Environs" of 3.3, within which all of *Finnegans Wake* remotely takes place. But only remotely and only evidently. For anyone oblivious of the location of his own head and toes—the closest few objects in the world—is surely oblivious of the civic landmarks that lie outside of his disintegrated bedroom; and our hero (a "host," or bartender as it will turn out) is here as throughout *Finnegans Wake* "oblifious of the headth of hosth that rosed before him, from Sheeroskouro . . . like a dun darting dullemitter" (317.32–34). The wording here tells us that the sleep-sapped head of our host ("headth of hosth") lies heavily there at the back of his mind, solid as a rock, the Head of Howth ("headth of hosth"), or any of the Dolomite Alps ("dull-emitter"); but also that this inertly "tropped head" is largely "oblivious" of itself and of all such objects in the world around it as the Liffey ("obliff-"), the "headth of hosth," and Dublin ("dun darting dullemitter" suggests Lady Morgan's phrase, "Dear Dirty Dublin"). This is because sleep has rendered it an extremely "dull emitter," incapable of much thought, though nonetheless able to bleed out weak appearances in that dark ("dun"), flickering ("darting"), "sheerly obscure" form of chiaroscuro ("Sheeroskouro") known as the dream. The objects and landforms "dully emitted" within our hero's "unquiring" and "tropped head," then, have more the status of "*impassible abjects*" (340.5) than of "passible objects" proper: degraded and emotionalized forms ("abjects"), "impassible" to anyone outside of the sleeping mind within which they appear, they have no "possible" existence in a reality collectively visible, as any nominalist would agree. There is no such "thing" as a "humptyhillhead" or a "pftjschute" ("Whoevery heard of such a think?" [460.16]) because both are more in the nature of "thinks" than "things" (583.7; cf. 83.14, 242.4). Rather than lying "out there," in Cartesian space or in a Dublin objectively capturable in "facts," they aggregate "in here," internal to our "unquiring" hero, of whom they are accordingly distorted descriptions. If, then, "by a commodius vicus of recirculation" (3.2), we "rearrive" at (3.5) any number of details already examined in the paragraph under our scrutiny, we'll find them taking on a whole new range of meanings. And what initially seemed sheer "disorder" will begin to resolve not simply into a "fine artful disorder" (126.9), but into a clear and elegant "thisorder" (540.19): "it's like a dream."

That "knock out in the park," for instance, no more clearly refers to "Castle Knock" than it does to a "knock out" pure and simple. Another cipher designating the unconsciousness of the figure "laid to rust" "in bed" here, it shows him "kayoed" (85.4 ["K.O.'d"])—"knocked out"—"parked" (454.34): a "knockout" "in these parks" (505.34, 606.24) had rendered our "pacific subject," "as close as made no matter" (85.4–7), "unspeechably thoughtless over it all" (238.36). While "hillhead" seems comparably to refer to the "Hill" of Howth on Howth "Head," the suppressed and linking term "Howth" derives from the Dano-Viking word *hoved* ("head"), so that "Howth Head," literally signifying "head head," would refer back to our "knock[ed] out" hero's "large big nonobli head" (64.30 [L. *non oblitus*, "not quite obliviated"]) with stubbornly loopy determination: "Howth Head," meaning "head head," refers throughout *Finnegans Wake* as invariably to our "knock[ed] out" "dull emitter's" "tropped head" as to anything perceptible in waking life.[3] Since, "on that same head" (471.29), the dark ground that "selfstretches" (14.31 [anthropomorphically]) between the "knock[ed] out" and his "tropped head" is largely identified here as "the park"—Phoenix—we can infer that the peculiar mound of imaginary "no matter" surveyed in this paragraph, however inertly stratified it may seem, is furtively charged with the potential of imminent and flashy resurrection. "Laid to rust" here, in other words, is simply the body of a man in bed, which will rise in the morning when, phoenixlike, he wakes. It is only at that time—when he "gets the pullover on his boots" (74.12), and starts ambulating groggily around his bedroom—that "the headless shall have legs!" (471.15).

All this is only to begin noting that the apparent content of the paragraph we are examining—or of any other paragraph in *Finnegans Wake*—resembles exactly the "manifest content" of a dream in being only a "goodridhirring"

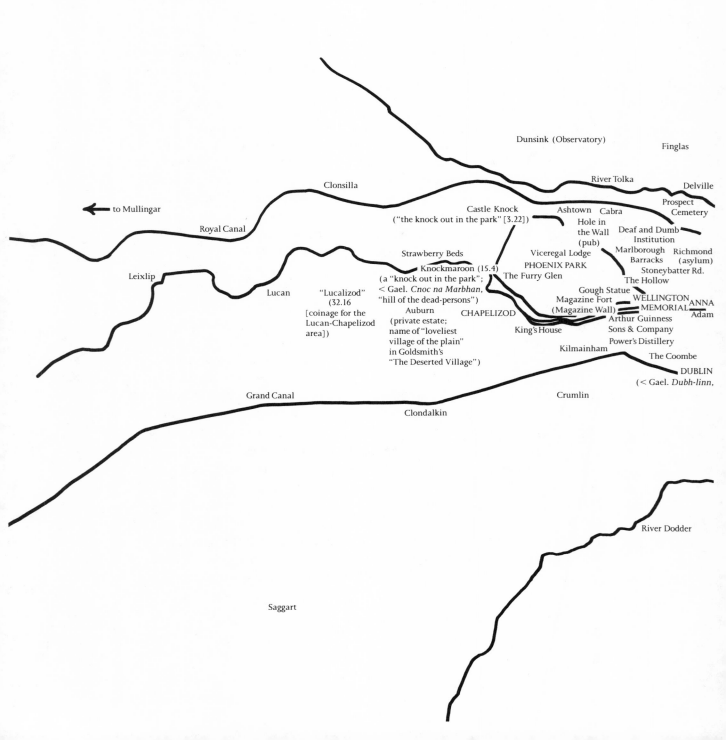

Map A
"Howth Castle and Environs" (3.3) :
Dublin by Daylight

Dunsink (Observatory)

Finglas

River Tolka

Delville

Clonsilla

Prospect
Cemetery

Castle Knock   Ashtown   Cabra
("the knock out in the park" [3.22])

to Mullingar

Royal Canal

Hole in
the Wall
(pub)

Deaf and Dumb
Institution

Strawberry Beds

Viceregal Lodge
PHOENIX PARK

Marlborough
Barracks

Richmond
(asylum)

Knockmaroon (15.4)
(a "knock out in the park";
< Gael. *Cnoc na Marbhan*,
"hill of the dead-persons")

The Furry Glen

Stoneybatter Rd.

Leixlip

Lucan

"Lucalizod"
(32.16
[coinage for the
Lucan-Chapelizod
area])

The Hollow

Gough Statue

WELLINGTON

Magazine Fort
(Magazine Wall)

MEMORIAL

ANNA
Adam

Auburn
(private estate;
name of "loveliest
village of the plain"
in Goldsmith's
"The Deserted Village")

CHAPELIZOD

King's House

Arthur Guinness
Sons & Company

Power's Distillery

Kilmainham

The Coombe

DUBLIN
(< Gael. *Dubh-linn,*

Grand Canal

Crumlin

Clondalkin

River Dodder

Saggart

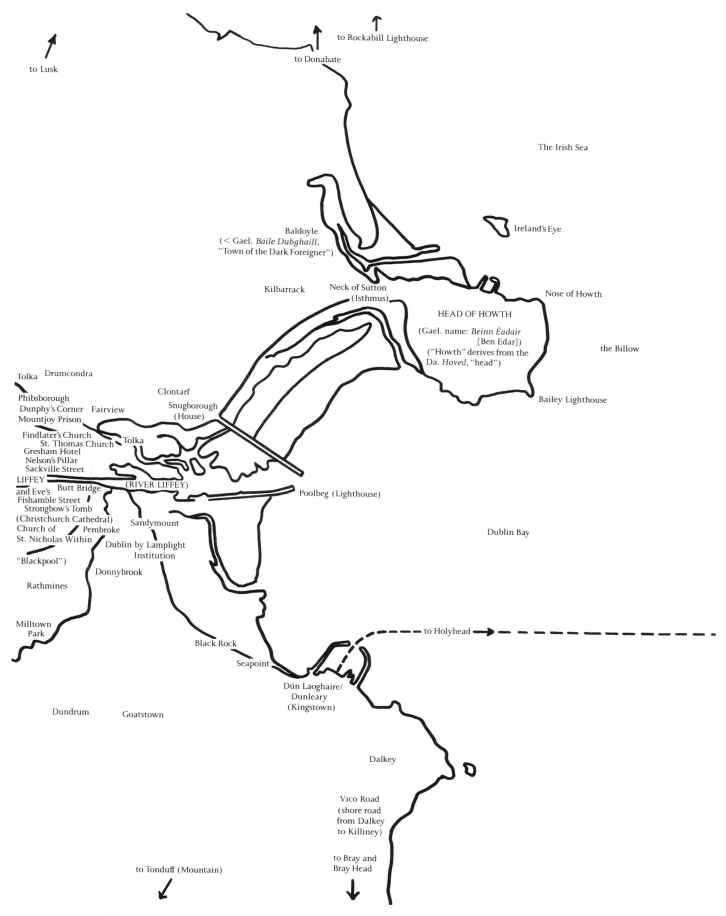

to Lusk

to Rockabill Lighthouse

to Donabate

The Irish Sea

Baldoyle
(< Gael. *Baile Dubghaill*,
"Town of the Dark Foreigner")

Ireland's Eye

Kilbarrack

Neck of Sutton
(Isthmus)

Nose of Howth

HEAD OF HOWTH

(Gael. name: *Beinn Éadair*
[Ben Edar])
("Howth" derives from the
Da. *Hoved*, "head")

the Billow

Tolka   Drumcondra

Clontarf

Bailey Lighthouse

Phibsborough
Dunphy's Corner   Fairview
Mountjoy Prison

Snugborough
(House)

Findlater's Church   Tolka
St. Thomas Church
Gresham Hotel
Nelson's Pillar
Sackville Street
LIFFEY
and Eve's   Butt Bridge   (RIVER LIFFEY)
Fishamble Street
Strongbow's Tomb
(Christchurch Cathedral)   Sandymount
Church of   Pembroke
St. Nicholas Within
"Blackpool")   Dublin by Lamplight
Institution

Poolbeg (Lighthouse)

Dublin Bay

Rathmines

Donnybrook

Milltown
Park

Black Rock

to Holyhead

Seapoint

Dún Laoghaire/
Dunleary
(Kingstown)

Dundrum   Goatstown

Dalkey

Vico Road
(shore road
from Dalkey
to Killiney)

to Tonduff (Mountain)

to Bray and
Bray Head

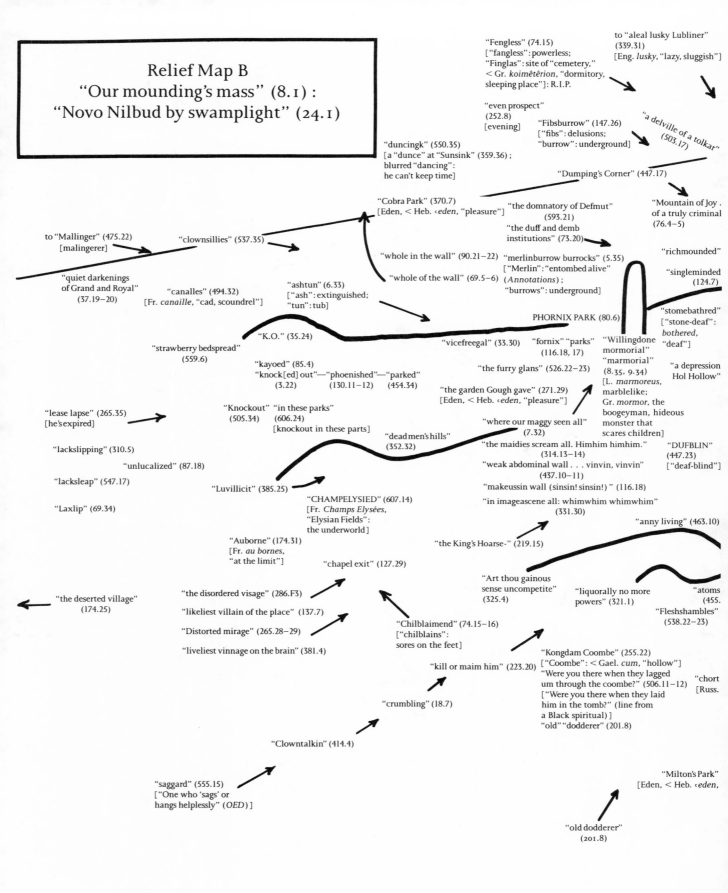

Relief Map B
"Our mounding's mass" (8.1) :
"Novo Nilbud by swamplight" (24.1)

"Fengless" (74.15)
["fangless": powerless;
"Finglas": site of "cemetery,"
< Gr. *koimêtêrion*, "dormitory,
sleeping place"]: R.I.P.

to "aleal lusky Lubliner"
(339.31)
[Eng. *lusky*, "lazy, sluggish"]

"even prospect"
(252.8)
[evening]

"Fibsburrow" (147.26)
["fibs": delusions;
"burrow": underground]

"a delville of a tolkar"
(503.17)

"duncingk" (550.35)
[a "dunce" at "Sunsink" (359.36) ;
blurred "dancing":
he can't keep time]

"Dumping's Corner" (447.17)

"Cobra Park" (370.7)
[Eden, < Heb. ‹*eden*, "pleasure"]

"the domnatory of Defmut"
(593.21)
"the duff and demb
institutions" (73.20)

"Mountain of Joy .
of a truly criminal
(76.4–5)

to "Mallinger" (475.22)
[malingerer]

"clownsillies" (537.35)

"richmounded"

"whole in the wall" (90.21–22)
"whole of the wall" (69.5–6)

"merlinburrow burrocks" (5.35)
["Merlin": "entombed alive"
(*Annotations*) ;
"burrows": underground]

"singleminded
(124.7)

"quiet darkenings
of Grand and Royal"
(37.19–20)

"canalles" (494.32)
[Fr. *canaille*, "cad, scoundrel"]

"ashtun" (6.33)
["ash": extinguished;
"tun": tub]

"stomebathred"
["stone-deaf":
bothered,
"deaf"]

PHORNIX PARK (80.6)

"strawberry bedspread"
(559.6)

"K.O." (35.24)

"vicefreegal" (33.30)

"fornix" "parks"
(116.18, 17)

"Willingdone
mormorial"
"marmorial"
(8.35, 9.34)
[L. *marmoreus,*
marblelike;
Gr. *mormor,* the
boogeyman, hideous
monster that
scares children]

"a depression
Hol Hollow"

"kayoed" (85.4)
"knock[ed] out"—"phoenished"—"parked"
(3.22)   (130.11–12)   (454.34)

"the furry glans" (526.22–23)

"the garden Gough gave" (271.29)
[Eden, < Heb. ‹*eden*, "pleasure"]

"lease lapse" (265.35)
[he's expired]

"Knockout" "in these parks"
(505.34)   (606.24)
[knockout in these parts]

"where our maggy seen all"
(7.32)

"DUFBLIN"
(447.23)
["deaf-blind"]

"lackslipping" (310.5)

"unlucalized" (87.18)

"dead men's hills"
(352.32)

"the maidies scream all. Himhim himhim."
(314.13–14)
"weak abdominal wall . . . vinvin, vinvin"
(437.10–11)

"lacksleap" (547.17)

"Laxlip" (69.34)

"Luvillicit" (385.25)

"makeussin wall (sinsin! sinsin!)" (116.18)

"in imageascene all: whimwhim whimwhim"
(331.30)

"anny living" (463.10)

"CHAMPELYSIED" (607.14)
[Fr. *Champs Elysées,*
"Elysian Fields":
the underworld]

"the King's Hoarse-" (219.15)

"Auborne" (174.31)
[Fr. *au bornes,*
"at the limit"]

"chapel exit" (127.29)

"Art thou gainous
sense uncompetite"
(325.4)

"liquorally no more
powers" (321.1)

"atoms
(455.
"Fleshshambles"
(538.22–23)

"the deserted village"
(174.25)

"the disordered visage" (286.F3)

"likeliest villain of the place" (137.7)

"Distorted mirage" (265.28–29)

"liveliest vinnage on the brain" (381.4)

"Chilblaimend" (74.15–16)
["chilblains":
sores on the feet]

"kill or maim him" (223.20)

"Kongdam Coombe" (255.22)
["Coombe": < Gael. *cum*, "hollow"]
"Were you there when they lagged
um through the coombe?" (506.11–12)
["Were you there when they laid
him in the tomb?" (line from
a Black spiritual)]
"old" "dodderer" (201.8)

"chort
[Russ.

"crumbling" (18.7)

"Clowntalkin" (414.4)

"Milton's Park"
[Eden, < Heb. ‹*eden*,

"saggard" (555.15)
["One who 'sags' or
hangs helplessly" (*OED*)]

"old dodderer"
(201.8)

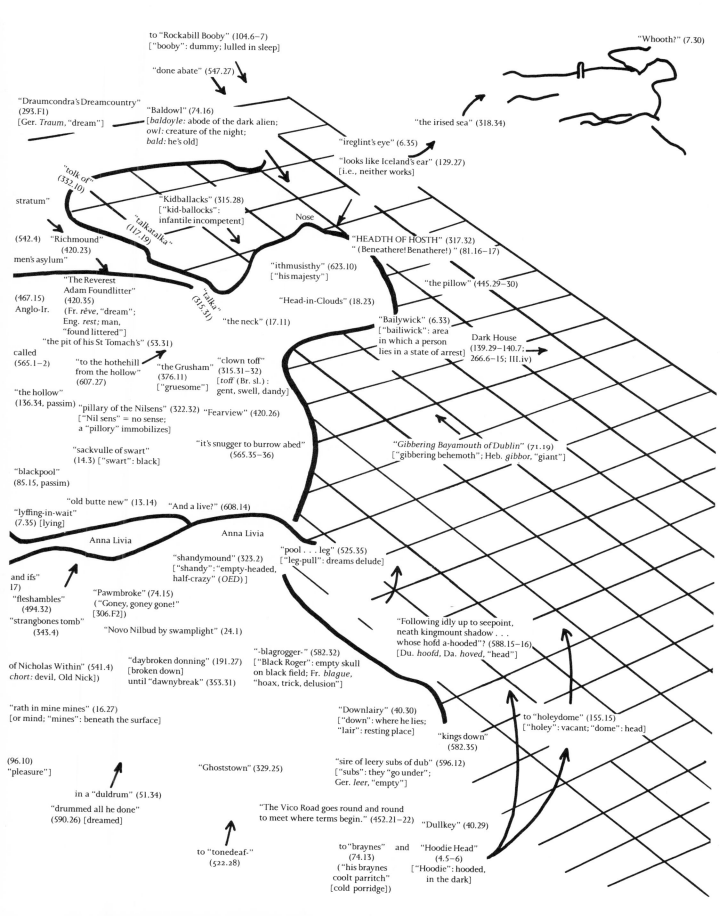

to "Rockabill Booby" (104.6–7)
["booby": dummy; lulled in sleep]

"Whooth?" (7.30)

"done abate" (547.27)

"Draumcondra's Dreamcountry"
(293.F1)
[Ger. *Traum*, "dream"]

"Baldowl" (74.16)
[*baldoyle*: abode of the dark alien;
owl: creature of the night;
bald: he's old]

"the irised sea" (318.34)

"ireglint's eye" (6.35)

"looks like Iceland's ear" (129.27)
[i.e., neither works]

"tolk of"
(332.10)

stratum"

"Kidballacks" (315.28)
["kid-ballocks":
infantile incompetent]

Nose

"talkatalka.."
(117.19)

(542.4)   "Richmound"
(420.23)

"HEADTH OF HOSTH" (317.32)
" (Beneathere! Benathere!) " (81.16–17)

men's asylum"

"The Reverest
Adam Foundlitter"
(420.35)
(Fr. *rêve*, "dream";
Eng. *rest*; man,
"found littered"]

"ithmusisthy" (623.10)
["his majesty"]

"the pillow" (445.29–30)

"talka"
(315.31)

"Head-in-Clouds" (18.23)

(467.15)
Anglo-Ir.

"the neck" (17.11)

"Bailywick" (6.33)
["bailiwick": area
in which a person
lies in a state of arrest]

Dark House
(139.29–140.7;
266.6–15; III.iv)

called
(565.1–2)

"the pit of his St Tomach's" (53.31)

"to the hothehill
from the hollow"
(607.27)

"the Grusham"
(376.11)
["gruesome"]

"clown toff"
(315.31–32)
[*toff* (Br. sl.):
gent, swell, dandy]

"the hollow"
(136.34, *passim*)

"pillary of the Nilsens" (322.32)
["Nil sens" = no sense;
a "pillory" immobilizes]

"Fearview" (420.26)

"sackvulle of swart"
(14.3) ["swart": black]

"it's snugger to burrow abed"
(565.35–36)

"*Gibbering Bayamouth of Dublin*" (71.19)
["gibbering behemoth"; Heb. *gibbor*, "giant"]

"blackpool"
(85.15, *passim*)

"old butte new" (13.14)

"And a live?" (608.14)

"lyffing-in-wait"
(7.35) [lying]

Anna Livia

Anna Livia

"pool . . . leg" (525.35)
["leg-pull": dreams delude]

"shandymound" (323.2)
["shandy": "empty-headed,
half-crazy" (*OED*)]

and ifs"
17)

"fleshambles"
(494.32)

"strangbones tomb"
(343.4)

"Pawmbroke" (74.15)
("Goney, goney gone!"
[306.F2])

"Novo Nilbud by swamplight" (24.1)

"Following idly up to seepoint,
neath kingmount shadow . . .
whose hofd a-hooded"? (588.15–16)
[Du. *hoofd*, Da. *hoved*, "head"]

of Nicholas Within" (541.4)
chort: devil, Old Nick])

"daybroken donning" (191.27)
[broken down]
until "dawnybreak" (353.31)

"-blagrogger-" (582.32)
["Black Roger": empty skull
on black field; Fr. *blague*,
"hoax, trick, delusion"]

"rath in mine mines" (16.27)
[or mind; "mines": beneath the surface]

"Downlairy" (40.30)
["down": where he lies;
"lair": resting place]

to "holeydome" (155.15)
["holey": vacant; "dome": head]

"kings down"
(582.35)

(96.10)
"pleasure"]

"Ghoststown" (329.25)

"sire of leery subs of dub" (596.12)
["subs": they "go under";
Ger. *leer*, "empty"]

in a "duldrum" (51.34)

"drummed all he done"
(590.26) [dreamed]

"The Vico Road goes round and round
to meet where terms begin." (452.21–22)

"Dullkey" (40.29)

to "tonedeaf-"
(522.28)

to "braynes"   and
(74.13)
("his braynes
coolt parritch"
[cold porridge])

"Hoodie Head"
(4.5–6)
["Hoodie": hooded,
in the dark]

(7.12), a representational smokescreen that sustains the misleading appearance of vague consonance with waking reality, while in fact indirectly representing a "latent content," and an unconscious one, which bears on "matters that fall under the ban of our infrarational senses" (19.36–20.1). The nature of this "latent content" in turn discovers itself if, at the *Wake's* repeated insistence, we "see [a] relief map" (564.10) of "Finn his park" (564.8 [not "Phoenix Park"])—where the spelling, like the entire passage in which the phrasing occurs (564.1–565.5), renders the imaginary landscape with which we are concerned explicitly anthropomorphic. One version of such a map is bodied forth in Relief Map B, which shows "Howth Castle and Environs" and other localities mentioned in *Finnegans Wake not* as they are represented by cartographic officialdom, but as they are represented throughout Joyce's "book of the dark" (the meanings of any terms on the map not immediately transparent will emerge in passing). Reference to the upper right-hand corner of this "relief map" will show that the landscape which our "knock[ed] out "dull emitter" has in mind—or, more accurately, has in his "tropped head"—latently depicts, in "Sheeroskouro," a "still" "form outlined aslumbered, even in our own nighttime" (7.20–21). Shortly to become known in *Finnegans Wake* as "our mounding's mass" (8.1), this slumbering form is that of a sleeping body.

Scattered legends about the landmass that extends between Howth Head and Castle Knock in Dublin might lead us to associate the "form outlined aslumbered" here with that of a "sleeping giant" (540.17)—perhaps even the Irish demigod "Finn MacCool" (5.10, 6.13, 139.14)—"whose head is the Hill of Howth" "and whose feet turn up among the hillocks of Phoenix Park."[4] But an association is not an identity, and the "abjects" and "thinks" our "knock[ed] out" hero has in his "tropped head" ("he was obliffious of the headth of hosth") are not really a perceived Howth or Castle Knock at all. Underlying this dormant form, then, one finds no "real giant" at all, but an altogether ordinary "man of the hooths" (619.25 [a "man of the house," and of "Howth" head]), "reclined from cape to pede" (619.27 ["cap-à-pie"]), his "heartsoul dormant mid shadowed landshape" (474.2–3). The paragraph, in short, amounts to a representation, in the condensed and displaced referential systems typical of dreams, of the sleeper's "knock[ed] out" body, which he now senses, from his own "eyewitless foggus," not as a visible object rationally knowable and mensurable in feet and inches in Cartesian *res extensa*, but, "infrarationally," as a space of inert, unthinking matter without knowable boundaries, internal to which he dwells equally at every point. More than the Dublin of any authoritative history or guidebook, this is the space within which all of *Finnegans Wake* takes place. And it, too, in its own way, will turn out to be an immense "afterthought of thy nomatter."

Sleep entails a withdrawal of all perception and consciousness from the world one "knows" by day—a world nowhere without real landscapes and everywhere cluttered with real objects (bedroom walls, bed, head). But as consciousness disintegrates in sleep, external objects vanish from perception.[5] And as objects vanish, "the sleeper turns into himself and falls back . . . into his own body," "his own body being the material substratum of the dream." "The process of falling asleep is a withdrawal" "from the object world," and "the process of dreaming is rebuilding" "a new environment formed out of the dreamer's body."[6] In yet other words, "the dreamer sinks into himself. And makes himself a whole new world; a man-made world, in the deepest sense. A whole new world, out of the body of the dreamer."[7] To say it in the idiom of the *Wake:* "And then. Be old. The next thing is. We are once amore as babes awondering in a wold made fresh" (336.15–17)—in a "world made fresh," that is, because a "world made flesh"; and a "world made flesh" because sleep, as "refleshmeant" (82.10 ["refreshment"]), puts one "back in the flesh" (67.5–6). As in dreams, all "landshapes" in *Finnegans Wake* originate in the body of the sleeper to whom they occur; and correlatively, all such "landshapes" inevitably reveal the nature of the body of the sleeper.[8]

In one form or another, the "unknown body" (96.29) of the man "tropped head" at *Finnegans Wake*—the distorted "landshape" we have begun to probe—will turn up everywhere in the book, underlying everything in it. Recurrent "cap-a-pie," "head-to-foot," "head-to-toe," and "top-to-bottom" formations, turning up all over the place, and often where one least expects them, will keep this space deviously under a reader's attention everywhere in the *Wake*.[9] Particularly in its first chapter, as a way of orienting his reader into the alien spatialities of a world made fresh, Joyce calls heavy attention to the "landshape" highlighted on the book's first page (at, for instance, 6.26–27, 6.29–35, 7.8–10, 7.13–14, 7.21–24, 10.35–36, 11.6–7, 12.19–20, 12.35–36, 14.31 ["selfstretches"], 15.25, and 17.4–5). But after the chapter moves through this succession of dreamscapes—and in the process introduces us to a kind of shorthand whereby the slumbering form that we have been examining becomes known simply as "our mounding's mass" (8.1)—any hump, lump, dump, or mountainlike form will serve to evoke the sleeper's body. The insistent appearance of this "still" "form outlined aslumbered" beneath tales apparently bearing on other places and other persons—

"impossible to remember persons in improbable to forget position places" (617.8–9)—will remind the "read[er of] the Evening World" that all of *Finnegans Wake*, because "everynight life" does (17.33), takes place in the "tropped head" of "one stable somebody" (107.31) who himself, because unconsciously "knock[ed] out," drifts through the dark with "headandheelless" obscurity (81.22–23) beneath the evident surface of things.

Momentarily, we might regard the "knock[ed] out" "dull emitter" "laid to rust" "in bed" at *Finnegans Wake* as "Headmound" (135.9 [as opposed to an alertly brainy "Edmond"]). As the name implies, he comes equipped with an amply "Vacant. Mined" (421.11)—a "vacant mind" whose "eyewitless foggus" throughout the night, and whose vast ability to "no" (not "know"), all of *Finnegans Wake* will now go on to "represent" in elaborate detail. Like all of the figmentary characters who drift through his "tropped head" in the dark, "Ah, he's very thoughtful . . . when he's not absintheminded. . . . He is, really" (464.15–18). Problematically, however, and especially for knowledgeably conscious readers, this "knock[ed] out" hero is extremely "absintheminded" throughout the length of the night—where that "absinthe," "now that I come to drink of it" (561.14 [not "think" of it]), deepens any form of quotidian "absentmindedness" conceivable to the wakeful rationalist by "alcoherently" (40.5), and as deeply as sleep, "blacking out" everything (230.10). To the likely objection that may be arising at this point—"This representation does not accord with my experience" (509.1–2)—the obvious reply is that "experience" always has a colorfully narratable content to it, whereas sleep pitches one into a "vaguum" (136.34 [a very "vague" "vacuum"]) and sends one off "touring the no placelike no timelike absolent" (609.1–2 ["absolute" "absent"]). To note further that English does not have a single word—let alone a mimetic convention—that does for the "absent" what "representation" does for the "present," is to begin seeing why *Finnegans Wake* had to be written as peculiarly as it is.[10] In portraying a man "knock[ed] out" and "tropped head," who "is not all there, and is all the more himself since he is not so" (507.3–4), Joyce is "giving unsolicited testimony on behalf of the absent . . . to those present" (173.29–31). As he put it in a letter to Harriet Shaw Weaver, joking about her account of a large dinner party, "the tangential relationships, the spiral progressions and the presence of the absent remind me of something which perhaps I wrote or ought to have written" (*L*, I, 218).

There is a happy corollary to these headier observations. As should have become evident in passing—and, if not, "see relief map" (564.10)—the man "tropped head" at *Finnegans Wake* is not very bright. Psychologically, sleep is regressive. Physiologically classified a "vegetative state," it renders our "knock[ed] out" hero something of a lush human vegetable given to pithy little thoughts on the order of "I yam as I yam" (604.23; 481.35). As a consequence of his fall (asleep), "his nut [is] cracked" (136.2), and a good half of the "turniphudded dunce" (517.7–8) becomes a severe "mental and moral defective" (177.16), if not a simple "Dimb!" "Dumb!" "dud" (6.9–10). In what Joyce called his "nocturnal comedy," then, the man "tropped head" at *Finnegans Wake* becomes, "in his own wise" (33.4 [this word merits study]), "our worldstage's practical jokepiece" and "a veritable Napoleon the Nth" (33.2–3)—"Napoleon" because he's a megalomaniac whose egocentrism moves to indefinite and extreme degrees (hence "Nth").[11] Certainly the simplest way of reading *Finnegans Wake* is to see it as one protracted and extremely funny little-moron joke, but with one important twist: the little moron turns out to be an altogether representative Western Man, and the more "know-all profoundly impressive" a Western Man in his bents and inclinations, the bigger the little moron (*L*, I, 257). For sleep takes place in a state that reveals the power of a tranquilizing ability to "no" (not "know")—and to "no" precisely those things about which Western "awethorrorty" (516.19) has consolidated the illusive belief that it can "know."[12] We might, then, think of the "the old man on his ars" (514.34) shown in Relief Map B—a beleaguered patriarch—as "Professor Ciondolone" (161.2–3 [It. *ciondolone*, "idler," "lounger"]), and, as the honorific implies, "the accomplished washout" (174.8), "in his own wise," may have a great deal to teach us; or, at least, we should give the "doped bum" *"the bumfit of the doped"* (339.26 [and "the benefit of the doubt"]).

Given the dubious relation of conscious "knowing" to the "funny and floored" figure (227.24) shown "knock[ed] out" in the relief map, some guidelines would be of use in helping us to proceed further in a "reading [of the] Evening World." For we have hardly begun to read that paragraph containing the phrase "in bed," which still stands surrounded by all kinds of murkily nonsensical terms—"Finnegan," "christian minstrelsy," that hundred-lettered thunderword, the first two paragraphs. Rather than moving linearly through a text "imitative of the dream-state," drawing on the compromised instruments of orthodox rationalism, it might better make sense to proceed much as we might in interpreting a dream. In what follows, then, "our procedure [will consist] in abandoning all those purposive ideas which normally govern our reflections," and all the more crucially because "purposive ideas," or "ideas that are *known* to us" (*ID*, 567), will teach us nothing more than what we already knew to begin with: that we "had reason as I knew and you knew and he knew all along" (158.31). No less problematically, purposive attacks on a text this obscure may cause us to straitjacket it into perhaps faultily preconceived literary expectations. Having then abandoned these preconceptions, we will "focus our attention on a single element of the dream . . . and follow out a chain of associations from [this] one element, till, for one reason or another, it seems to break off" (*ID*, 565–66). In the paragraph under our attention, for instance, this would mean isolating a single element—a syllable, word, or phrase like "in bed"—then to "Note the . . . Associations" (270.11–14), as the *Wake* cryptically puts it, that furl out of that element as it is developed, from cover to cover, throughout the book. "No connection [will be] too loose, no joke too bad, to serve as a bridge from one thought to another" in pursuing these associations, and especially no connection that arises "by assonance, verbal ambiguity . . . or by any association of the kind we allow in jokes or in play upon words" (*ID*, 568–69). Some connection of this kind has already yielded sense in thinking about the phrase "knock out"; and as that example furthermore suggests, this associative way of proceeding, far from licensing anarchy, will in the long run capture meaning in a way that no amount of calculating rationalism ("rationalization") ever could.[13] "If we then take up a second element" in the paragraph, moreover, and repeat the process with it, "it is only to be expected that the unrestricted character of our associations will be narrowed" because we will "hit upon associations that have something in common with the first chain" (*ID*, 566). As we repeat this process with a third, fourth, and fifth chain of associations, each mutually restricting and hemming each other in, their self-delimiting convergence will ultimately capture "*unknown*" or "unconscious" matters (*ID*, 567)—"matters that fall under the ban of our infrarational senses" (19.36–20.1)—with an exactitude whose purport must be its own proof.

What follows, then, is a primer, an illustration of a *process* that any reader might go through in "reading [the] Evening World." As it explores "the book of Doublends Jined" (20.15–16 ["double-ends joined"]), taking as its "allforabit" the paragraph in which our analysis began (19.2), this reading will move to "double ends" and purposes, engaging us in "two thinks at a time" (583.7). On one level, it will simply be moving through that paragraph—and others along the way—very slowly, particle by particle, ultimately to read them in some depth. But at the same time, because it will be tracing long chains of association out of such paragraphs and throughout the entire book, it will be reading *Finnegans Wake* over and over again, from cover to cover, coming to terms on each repeated reading with a distinct

JOYCE'S BOOK OF THE DARK

aspect of the whole. "Reading [the] Evening World" literately reconstructed in *Finnegans Wake* requires one to become familiar with a set of representational mannerisms peculiar to the working of the night, one of which has to do with the latent omnipresence of the sleeper's body beneath all the manifest appearances of his dream. Another of these mannerisms furls out of the word "unquiring" and, in particular, out of the syllable "un-." For "by naught" (555.5["night"]), in the "*noughttime*" (349.6), its negational power wields a spectacular force. As a way of seeing how this works, examine again the figure shown "outlined aslumbered" in Relief Map B. And "do not fail to point to yourself a depression called Holl Hollow. It is often quite guttergloomering . . . and gives wankyrious [one curious] thoughts to the head" (565.1–3).

Nothing in Particular: On English Obliterature

In a book expressly intended to prove that personality survives beyond the grave, the Spanish thinker Miguel de Unamuno proposes this interesting exercise:

> It is impossible for us, in effect, to conceive of ourselves not existing, and no effort is capable of enabling consciousness to realize absolute unconsciousness, its own annihilation. Try, reader, to imagine yourself, when you are wide awake, the condition of your soul when you are in a deep sleep; try to fill your consciousness with the representation of no-consciousness, and you will see the impossibility of it. The effort to comprehend it causes the most tormenting dizziness. We cannot conceive of ourselves as not existing.[1]

Still, he seems to overlook his own best evidence. Unimaginable as anyone conscious may find the "no-consciousness" of deep sleep, quotidian reflection suggests that billions of people actually vanish into it each day, with clockwork regularity, there in turn to conceive of nothing without much torment at all. Contemporary sleep researchers speculate that recollectible dreaming takes up roughly one and one-half hours of the average night's sleep;[2] and their tabulative ascertainments, doubtless borne out by reference to "m'm'ry," merely quantify what nineteenth-century students of dreams and Freud in essence also knew: "A dreamless sleep is best, the only proper one." What happens in these dreamless extents of the night merits our special attention now because Joyce, if he were indeed to "reconstruct the nocturnal life" in *Finnegans Wake*, would necessarily have had to account for these parts of his sleeper's dark too, in turn to provide his reader with some such "representation of no-consciousness" as Unamuno deems inconceivable. Brief examination of any page of *Finnegans Wake* will begin to reveal Joyce's success in this endeavor: the book represents nothing; or, to modulate the phrase one degree, much of it represents much the same kind of nothing that one will not remember not having experienced in sleep last night.

A writer of strong realist allegiances, as the evidence of everything he wrote before *Finnegans Wake* attests, Joyce would have beheld in the darker parts of sleep the paradoxical spectacle of an undeniably real human experience ("you were there") within which "reality," "experience," and all human knowing mutually vanished into a state that the *Wake* calls, with contradictory precision, "Real Absence" (536.5–6).[3] Because Joyce held on the authority of Vico the conviction that thought could yield access to matters "found within the modifications of our own human mind"—matters that "we cannot at all imagine and can comprehend only with great effort" (*NS*, 331, 338)—he would no more have refrained from rendering this "Real Absence" legibly particular in his "book of the dark" (251.24) than his surrogate, Shem the Penman, who "giv[es] unsolicited testimony on behalf of the absent . . . to those present" (173.29–31) in a neverseen, *Wake*-like "*édition de ténèbres*" (179.24–27 [Fr. "edition of darkness"]). Indeed, as *Finnegans Wake* neared its completion Joyce spoke of having built it "out of nothing."[4]

He was aware, of course, of problems. While he confided to Jacques Mercanton that his "whole book [was] shaky," in *Finnegans Wake* itself he described his sleeping protagonist in these more expansively concessive terms:[5]

> Thus the unfacts, did we possess them, are too imprecisely few to warrant our certitude, the evidencegivers by legpoll too untrustworthily irreperible [L. "undiscoverable, unlearnable"] where his adjugers are semmingly freak threes but his judicandees plainly minus twos. Nevertheless Madam's Toshowus waxes largely more lifeliked (entrance, one kudos; exits, free) and our notional gullery is now completely complacent, an exegious monument, aerily perennious.   (57.16–22)

If these lines simply suggest, by one reading, that the entire representational endeavor of *Finnegans Wake* is nothing but a "legpull"—a "notional gullery"—since only one untrustworthy "evidencegiver by headpoll" can witness and report on those "too imprecisely few unfacts" even potentially retrievable from "the wastes a'sleep" (64.1); they also plainly state—even as they evoke "his judicandees" (L. *his judicandis*, "the judging of these things")—that the "evidencegiver" in question is undiscoverable at this moment of the night, and that those missing "unfacts" and his absent "head" are equally "irreperible" too. While the passage acknowledges evident epistemological problems, then, it also expresses the *Wake*'s obstinate determination "nevertheless" "to show us," in a form of verisimilar portraiture that might well find place in a National Gallery ("notional gullery," "lifelike"), the "Real Absence" internal to a "completely complacent" sleeping man—here virtually indistinguishable from a brain-void waxwork dummy in turn "semmingly" pasted together of nothing ("Madame Tussaud," "waxes," "lifelike"; L. *adjugor*, "to be yoked together"; Hu. *semmi*, "nothing"). So "completely complacent" in the passage at hand is the man who lies "outlined aslumbered" from "leg" to "poll" ("legpoll") that little seems to be on his "tropped head" except for dim indications of not being there at all ("notions," "gullery"). And especially in a book about sleep entitled the *Wake*, the closing reference—to Horace's *Exegi monumentum, aere perennius* ("I have finished a monument more durable than brass")— will oblige us to begin wondering what exactly distinguishes the "Real Absence" internally endured by this figure who rests in peace, not awake, "tropped head," from the real absence internal to someone resting in eternal peace, at his wake, dropped dead.

Spectral entry into these considerations must inevitably proceed from reflection on the more easily accessible experience of dreaming, where already the *Wake*'s sleeping hero "is not all there" (507.3). And a passage in the *Wake* growing out of these lines on "our notional gullery" will yield access to the "clearobscure" character of dreams. For after moving through the reach of murky obscurity in which these lines are set (I.iii–iv), the book ultimately lifts back up toward the light of a courtroom hearing in which, by one account, "a constable gives evidence" against "Festy King, also called Pegger Festy, [who] is tried at Old Bailey for stealing coal and taking off his clothes in public."[6] This culminant legal scene bears scrutiny:

> Remarkable evidence was given, anon, by an eye, ear, nose and throat witness, whom Wesleyan chapelgoers suspected of being a plain clothes priest W.P., situate at Nullnull, Medical Square, who, upon letting down his rice and peacegreen coverdisk and having been sullenly cautioned against yawning while being grilled, smiled (he had had a onebumper at parting from Mrs Molroe in the morning) and stated to his eliciter under his morse mustaccents (gobbless!) that he slept with a bonafides and that he would be there to remember the filth of November, hatinaring, rowdy O, which, with the jiboulees of Juno and the dates of ould lanxiety, was going, please the Rainmaker, to decembs within the ephemerides of profane history, all one with

Tournay, Yetstoslay and Temorah, <u>and one thing which would</u> pigstickularly <u>strike a person of such sorely tried observational powers</u> as Sam, him and Moffat, though theirs not to reason why, the striking thing about it <u>was that he was patrified to see, hear, taste and smell, as his time of night</u>, how. . . . (86.32–87.12; emphasis mine)

Actually on trial here, as the underlining will suggest, is the evidence of the senses, their testimony baffling the sleeping man who is nowhere directly apparent in this scene but everywhere central to it because he envelopes it. While all of his Irish senses actually lie "petrified" in the motor paralysis of sleep ("he was patrified to see, hear, taste, and smell at his time of night"), they also seem contradictorily capable of bearing confused false witness, in these and subsequent lines, as they proceed to testify about subjects "unlucalised, of no address and in noncommunicables" (87.18–19), in a trial whose single "evidencegiver by headpoll" when "bluntly broached, and in the best basel to boot, as to whether he was one of those . . . for whom the audible-visible-gnosible-edible world existed" cannot exactly say that he is sure (88.4–7).[7] The formally contradictory sentence, then, intricately replicates the "real" character of perception in dreams, where vision arises "*in fact*, under the closed eyes of the inspectors [as] the traits featuring the *chiaroscuro* coalesce" (107.28–29); and where the dreamer possessed by voices, "when seized of the *facts*," actually "overhears[s] in his secondary personality as . . . [an] underreared" (38.26–28; emphasis mine). The evidence spilled up under closed lids and within dormant ears, accordingly, is as passive in form as the sentence representing it ("Remarkable evidence *was given*, *anon*, by an eye witness petrified to see" [italics mine]); and, as the highlighted adverb in turn suggests, "it ooze[s] out in Deadman's Dark Scenery Court through crossexanimation of the casehardened testis" [L. "witness"] both "anonymously" and "anon"—"immediately, without mediation" (87.33–34). The reference here to "Deadman's Dark Scenery Court" would only locate this entire trial more deeply within the body of a man who lies "casehardened" ("hardened on the surface") under the sensory closure of sleep, while internally undergoing a "cross-examination" of his own "exanimation" ("deprivation of life," or "apparent death").[8]

All of the elements in this sentence extraneous to its syntactical core— each inviting the Wakean question, "Is it a factual fact"? (529.31)—now begin to operate comparably, as negatory ciphers denoting perception "oozed out" of a body deadened to all sensory perception of the real. Those odd "Wesleyan chapelgoers," for instance—practitioners of "inner calm" who doctrinally embrace "the witness of the Spirit"—only cast further doubt on the already jeopardized evidence by branding the strange witness of whom we read an undercover Catholic.[9] Their rightful distrust of "figments in the evidential order" (96.26–27) renders this "dim seer" (96.28) indistinguishable from the *Wake*'s "patrified" hero, who sleeps undercovers and in disguise throughout the entire sentence, enjoying insuperable inner calm as he witnesses spirits and emits strange counterintelligence at the interior of "an unknown body" (96.29) void of any sensation of the real at all ("Nullnull, Medical Square"). His testimony, then, only illusively whispered "to a solicitor under Norse moustaches" and amplified by a sneeze—"(God bless!)"— actually bears on events perceived in the absence of all direct perception, as if over remotenesses of dark by means of imperceptible, because radiotelegraphed, Morse code ("morse mustaccents" plays "Morse" and the Fi. *musta* ["black"] into the English word "accents").[10] His voluble testimony also seems self-elicited ("eliciter") and quite inaudible; for the anonymous "throat-witness" sleeping throughout this entire scene, "obliffious" entirely of himself, is much more "pigstickularly" oblivious of the existence of his own shut mouth: he's "(gob-less)" [Anglo-Ir. *gob*, "mouth"], and he just lies there, "stuck like a pig." Evidence given about exact dates and times ("he would be there to remember the filth of November . . . the dates of ould lanxiety"), designates as well the absence of perceived historical time altogether—discrete "fifth" slipping into blacked-out "filth," and "the days of old anxiety" blurring away entirely into "Auld Lang Syne" (where "auld acquaintance" "be forgot" and is "never brought to mind" [389.11, 390.23, 21, II.iv]). The misheard echo of a Guy Fawkes Day chant—"Please to remember the fifth of November, gunpowder, treason and plot"—finally suggests that this entire Irish juridical nightmare, bearing obscurely on the annihilation of English reality and legality, actually threatens more the etymologically related properties of English reality and legibility.

For ultimately on trial in this strange legal scene is not simply the taxed evidence of the senses, but all the exacting rules of evidence by which the innately formless senses of sight and hearing have been disciplined over years both of personal and cultural history to bear witness on an "audible-visible-gnosible world" held intelligibly in place by those correlated institutional forces of le<u>g</u>ality, le<u>g</u>ibility, and lo<u>g</u>ic which Vico conceptually equates with intelle<u>c</u>tion and recolle<u>c</u>tion in *The New Science*, by derivation from the common root **leg-* ("tó colle<u>c</u>t, to gather") (*NS*, 240, 363). Demanding intelli<u>g</u>ent and recolle<u>c</u>tively drilled study through peeled eyes and amply opened ears, English and the reality it orders are evident to no one at birth, or in sleep. If the "person of sorely tried observational powers" represented in this scene fails adequately to register the real evidence, then (from the Latin *e-videre*, "to see clearly"), he can only fail badly to heed the laws by which that evidence is wakefully ordered. The passage therefore begins to suggest why *Finnegans Wake* had to turn obscurely "outlex" (169.3) in order accurately to reconstruct "everynight life" (17.33), where vision and evidence arise only in their own absence; but it also yields a simple corollary allowing us to distinguish dream-riffed parts of the book from its "Real Absences." For while all of sleep takes place under the closure of the senses, dreams do not quite. "Show[ing] us the dreamer in so far as he is *not* sleeping," in Freud's words, dreams submit to intelligible analysis, interpretations as variant as those surrounding any legal case, and, above all, recollection, because they lift from dormancy the trained senses of sight and hearing, inevitably articulated with elaborate memories of struggles by which the "earsighted" dreamer has learned the heard and written law (143.9–10): no recollectible dream lies far from wakened life or is void of visual or auditory image.

Yet in parts of the night reconstructed by *Finnegans Wake*, as its prostrate central figure lies "deafadumped" (590.1), his "eyballds" glazed over and "unoculated" in visionlessness (75.17, 541.27), the trained senses and all that they have been disciplined to know fall dormant as the rest of his body, whether singly or together, to leave only "the gravitational pull perceived by certain fixed residents . . . suggesting an authenticitatem of his aliquitudinis" (100.32–34 [L., "an authenticity of his somethingness"]): "Is now all seenheard then forgotten? Can it was . . ." ? (61.29–30). "Turn[ing] a deaf ear clooshed" in parts of his sleep ("clooshed" folds the English "closed" into the Gael. *cluas*, "ear"), "daff Mr Hairwigger"—"(not all hear)"—"proceed[s] . . . in the directions of the duff and demb institutions" to become incapable of any legitimate or legal hearing at all (582.7, 491.30, 536.1–2, 73.18–20). And "claud[ing] boose his eyes" (509.30)—where "claud" blurs "cloud" and "close" into the Latin *claudo* ("shut"), while the "boose" blacks brain and "both" eyes out—he turns his "seeless socks" (468.25) vacant as the gaps in empty wickets, so to lose all evidence of all evidence: "Wickedgapers, I appeal against the light. An nexistence of vividence" (366.2–3 [the orthographical modifications suggest equally the "inexistence of evidence" and the death—L. *nex*—of vivid existence]). At those darkest moments of the night in which the man "tropped head" at the *Wake* finally finds "sound eyes right but . . . could not all hear" and "light ears left yet . . . could but ill see," he simply "cease[s]. And he cease[s], tung and trit" (Da. *tung og træt*, "heavy and tired"), so to cross over the borders of "Metamnisia" (Gr. *metamnêsia*, "beyond forgetfulness") "in the waste of all peaceable worlds,"

what it was like "blindly, mutely, tastelessly, tactlessly" (92.27) not to have been there in the middle of last night's sleep, when he too drifted through "states of suspensive exanimation," enjoying a kind "of mindmouldered ease" (143.8–9, 14). Indeed, properly to identify with a central unconsciousness like "Headmound" or *His Murkesty*" (175.23), a reader has to establish less a conventionally empathetic identity than an "indentity," and "of undiscernibles" (49.36–50.1)—where the attachment of the prefix "in-" to the normally solid term "identity" directs one inward, but also negates, so to suggest that *His Murkesty* doesn't have one at all.

As the example furthermore suggests, "every dimmed letter" (424.32) comprising the "blurry wards" (425.13) of Joyce's "sordomutic" "nonday diary" (489.35)—a letter "written in smoke and blurred by mist and signed of solitude, sealed at night" (337.13–14)—is systematically darkened in order to intensify the shimmering torrent of negativity understreaking the "darkumen's" reference to no perceived reference (350.29). Given a darkly human hero ("darkumen" combines "document" and "dark human") who "is consistently blown to Adams" (313.12) in the "percepted nought" of dreamless sleep, Joyce necessarily undertakes a complementary "*abnihilisation of the etym*" (353.22), by blowing away the "black and white" of lexical English into an "outlexical" "blotch and void" (229.27) adequate to the representation of "Headmound's" "Vacant. Mined." Affixes of negation like *a-*, *ab-*, *de-*, *dis-*, *ex-*, *-less*, *im-*, *in-*, *mis-*, *non-*, and *un-*, accordingly, become as epistemologically central to *Finnegans Wake* as the personal pronouns, in turn systematically deformed, are to English; while syllabifications internal to the "blotty words" (14.14) of Joyce's "NIGHTLETTER" (308.16) are comparably bent into senses that denote the darkening or absence of sense. The English "for instance," "for inkstands" (173.34), gets blacked out and abnegated at two "unstant[s]" (143.8) in "the no placelike no timelike absolent" of the *Wake*'s "noughttime" (609.1–2), in order to capture the "Real Absence" of a hero who knows less "the existence of time in the world" than the "exsystems" (148.18) "off time" (143.5) "undeveiled" (75.5–6; cf. 403.15). Indeed, since *His Murkesty* has "tropped head" and lies "personally unpreoccupied" (558.4) at the interior of "an unknown body" (96.29) incapable of deed or act, he seems to sense through much of the night only his lack of sense and senses: "Impalpabunt, he abhears" (23.25–26 ["appears" but "ab-hears"]); "Murk, his vales are darkling" (23.23 ["Mark" only "murk"]). "Smatterafact," "*thin*" (183.7, 106.24 [rather than find a fact, "then"]), phrases in *Finnegans Wake* like "the boob's indulligence" and the "murketplots" (531.2, 368.9) would only apparently refer to "the pope's indulgence" and "the marketplace," latently referring us back inward to the "thin" and "dulled" "intelligence" lacking in a "boob" like "Headmound," who lies murkily "reduced to nothing" (499.3) "durk the thicket of slumbwhere" (580.15 ["durk" moves "dark" into the Ger. *durch*, "through," while "slumbwhere" blurs "somewhere" away in "slumber"]): "it's like a dream." So pervasive is the annihilation of reference and matter of fact in Joyce's "nonday diary," *as a marrer off act*" (345.4), that even such apparently orthodox English words as "excommunicated" (181.35) and "delightedly" (179.30) bear essentially negative meanings: in "delight time" reconstructed in this "nightynovel" (329.10, 54.21 [the "night time"]), they carry the full weight of their negatory prefixes in order to help represent an "exexive" "ex-ex-executive" (363.9, 42.8–9) who lies x'd out, "denighted" (615.15), and "Exexex! COMMUNICATED" (172.10). A reader wishing "to shed a light on" this "document," then, would do better "to shellalite on the darkumen" (350.29)—bearing in mind that "shellalite," an explosive, "obliterates": "letters be blowed!" (251.31).[13]

Now "in [this] Nichtian glossery which purveys aprioric roots for aposteriorious tongues this is nat language at any sinse of the world" (83.10–12), as the *Wake* informs its reader, calling attention to the elaborate "not language" it has devised in order to represent the *nat* (Da. "night") through which its hero suspensively drifts between the knowable past of a yesterday ("aprioric") and the potentiality of a knowable future tomorrow ("aposteriorious"). "Nat language" here means several things. "Since" the world vanished into the "*nat*" ("night"), of course, the man "tropped head" at the *Wake* has "no sinse of the world," and "this is not language in any sense of the word": "not a salutary sellable sound is since" (598.4). Since "nat language" also suggests "not language," however, the phrase indicates that the language of *Finnegans Wake* will work heavily by oppositional negation. Unlike English, that is, which conveys meaning in its ideal form by indicating the presence of corresponding ideas and things, this "not language" operates largely by indicating their "Real Absence." The "lexical" parallels into which the "outlex" (169.3) of Wakese can be translated, accordingly, indicate largely what the *Wake* is *not* about—as, for example "recoil" is *not* "recall" (quite the contrary); "Headmound" is *not* "Edmond" (quite the contrary); and "Taciturn" (17.3), whose mouth is firmly shut throughout the length of sleep, is *not* "Tacitus," who after all had a great deal to say on the subject of Germany.[14]

"Scotographically arranged" in plain "blotch and void" on "the blink pitch" (412.3, 229.27, 93.4), this "nat language" now generates as a totality a kind of portraiture opposite in every particular from that afforded by the photograph and related forms of representation: antonymically inverting the sense of "photography" (< Gr. *phôtographia*, "light-writing"), Joyce's sleep-descriptive "scotography" (< Gr. *skotos*, "darkness") makes for a kind of "darkness-writing" whose developed product, the inversion of a well-articulated positive print, is a "partly obliterated negative" that captures the "Real Absence" of an extremely "Black Prince"—"the blank prints, now extincts" (387.20)—who lies "reduced to nothing" in the "noughttime" (499.3) and so can only be captured in "black prints."[15] Where the photograph, taken through the open-eyed lens of the camera lucida (171.32), seeks to freeze the plenitude of the present in all its fleeting detail, the Wakean "scotograph," taken through "blackeye lenses" (183.17) kept as firmly "SHUT" beneath "a blind of black sailcloth" (182.32–33) as those of the eyes in sleep, seeks to capture only the absent; "exhabiting that corricatore of a harss, revealled by Oscur Camerad" (602.22–23), its "camera obscura"—dark chamber, closed lens—exposes and "exhibits" the "character" of an "obscure comrade" of ours who, because "put to bed" (It. *corricatore*, "one put to bed"), seems more to be "ex-habiting" than "in-habiting" his body, as if in a "hearse," "tropped head." "Say mangraphique may say nay por daguerre!" (339.23).[16]

Traditional forms of representation at the turn of the century, as Virginia Woolf complained, aspired perhaps too unreflectively to emulate the apparently flawless mimetic perfection of the photograph, ultimately to yield the glory of the Norman Rockwell oil and the slice-of-life narrative circulated in the *Saturday Evening Post* of Joyce's day. Compensatorily, then, the "scotographic" "blotch and void" of *Finnegans Wake* issues its reader—through "black mail," as opposed to black-and-white mail (34.33–34, 69.2, 240.12, 350.11, 457.2, 563.16, 420.17–421.14)—something of an elaborately articulated "Scatterbrains' Aftening Posht" (99.34–35), a *"Pooridiocal"* (106.11) whose each "blink pitch" "nondepicts" the "Real Absence" of sleep (Da. *aften*, "evening"), where our hero's "brains" lie "scattered" in a "posh" ("a state of slush" [*OED*]). Sentences comprising this "scotographic" "black mail," then—this "night express" (135.34) expressive of "noughttime"— might be regarded as representing all the blanks that fall in between ordinarily lexical sentences: "In the buginning is the woid, in the muddle is the sounddance and thereinofter you're in the unbewised again" (378.29–30). Manifestly a "word," "woid" points also into a "void" here, so to generate in this particular construction an obliterate negative of the creative Logos, a "muddled sentence," "wherein often," as in sleep, a reader is lucidly in the *Unbewusst* (Ger. the "Unconscious").

The observation made of a "blindfold passage" (462.35) in this "night-mail" (565.32) that "old hunks on the hill read it to perlection" (94.10)—to "perfection" in "perlection" ("a reading through" [*OED*])—does not particularly lighten the task of a conscious reader. "Old Hunks," a blind Elizabethan bear and a cipher for the *Wake*'s sleeping hero, couldn't see, and he hibernated. A good reading of the *Wake*'s "obliterated negative," then, would require a reader to work through its black and white abc's by cultivating an unrelentingly "abcedminded" (18.17) memory of the "blotch and void" "absentmindedness" experienced last night. For unlike actual photographic negatives, which are clearly visible, the "obliterated negative" of this "Scatterbrains' Aftening Posht" "render[s] all animated greatbritish and Irish objects nonviewable to human watchers" (403.23–24). Many of its "blink pitches" must therefore be construed as bearing a content as imperceptible as that of the number zero borne on unreceived radio-waves wired through "Etheria Deserta" (309.9) from "ostralian someplace" (488.20)—a world "down under" (321.32, 450.1), and a dark one (L. *ostra*, "purples")—by a "Negoist Cabler . . . who is sender of the **H**ullo **E**ve **C**enograph in prose or worse every Allso's night. . . . Noughtnoughtnought nein" (488.21–26).

Colorfully articulated nullity of this kind would equally well describe *Finnegans Wake*, itself a "**H**ullo **E**ve **C**enograph in prose and verse," which offers its reader a new kind of writing (Gr. *cainographos*, "new-writing"), expressive of the "nought" (Gr. *cenographos*, "empty-writing") imperceived by a man lying hollow in the dead of night ("Hollow Eve Cenograph"). A vague humanoid presence identifiable throughout *Finnegans Wake* primarily by the acrostic initials HCE, this "spickspookspokesman of our spectures-que silentiousness" (427.32–33 ["picturesque" "specter"]) occupies a mind structured internally much like a "cenotaph"—a tomb commemorating a body buried somewhere else—dimly stirred as if on a "Halloween" or "All Souls' Night" ("Hullo Eve," "Allso's"). Its obliterated and absent content ("Noughtnoughtnought nein"), by way of the Latin *nego* ("to say no") and the German *nein* ("no"), would yield a quadruple negative representative of the *Wake*'s ubiquitous ciphers for the "blickblackblobs" imperceived during the "blanko" "blotto" "blackout" of sleep (339.21, 64.31, 39.33, 560.2, 617.14).

While reading in the *Wake*'s "nat language" of "the **h**aardly **c**reditable **e**dventyres" of this sleeping man, then (51.14)—where the blurring of the Danish *eventyr* ("fairy tale") into the English "adventure" tells us that these "edventyres" will not be actual ones—a reader should find himself, as he sympathetically "blacks out" and "goes dead"

> Turning up and fingering over the most dantellising peaches in the lingerous longerous book of the dark. . . . I know it is difficult but when your goche I go dead. Turn now to this patch upon Smacchiavelluti! Soot allours, he's sure to spot it! (251.22–27)

The "Machiavellian" inversions of Joyce's "scotographic" "blotch and void" make *Finnegans Wake*'s the "black velvet" (242.6) of prose styles (It. *smacchia/velluti*, "cleans velvet"): its "sooty velour allures" ("Soot allours"; Fr. *zut, alors!*). Since it offers its reader not the account of a "day in the city," but of a "dayety in the sooty" (143.4–5)—where "dayety" evokes a "dumbshow" (120.7, 559.18) darker than any ever performed in Michael Gunn's Gaiety Theatre because enacted by "Makeall Gone," of "Dumnlimn" (443.16), in the "sooty" black of night—it's "blink pitches" must be scrutinized for their constant traces of the absent in the same way that "black patches," in darkness, are spotted on black velvet ("turn now to this patch upon Smacchiavelluti"; "he's sure to spot it"). "Revery warp" (211.17 [and "word"]) on the "dantellising" pages of this dark text, accordingly, makes sense in much the same way that each constituent element in a dark textile like lace does ("dantellising" suggests the French *dentelle*, "lace"): and "lace . . . Sure, what is it on the whole only holes tied together"? (434.21–22). Particled up "from next to nothing" (4.36–5.1) and set against a night-black velvet foil, *Finnegans Wake* is a comparably dark "wordspiderweb" (*L*, III, 422), an aesthetic collection of nullities held in place by a "nat language" that gives the human "noughttime" its apprehensible shape. And since all of the night, dream-stirred or not, takes place in the "Real Absence" of experience, "every dimmed letter" in Joyce's "darkumound" (386.20–21) should be examined for its reference to the absence of a man "tropped head" in the dark.

Something of how this "nat language" is put contextually to work in the linear "drema" (69.14) of *Finnegans Wake*—the entirely "nonactionable" (48.18) "drama" of a "dream" erratically experienced over the space of a night—is suggested by a return to the third chapter of the book, whose central pages have already shown "our notional gullery" lying "completely complacent" in the "vaguum" (136.34). For in this section of the *Wake*, Joyce intricately portrays HCE sinking into a part of the night "versts and versts from true civilisation, not where his dreams top their traums halt (Beneathere! Benathere!)" (81.15–16): reference to a "tram-stop" here indicates the end of the line and all "trains" of thought, just as "Beneathere!" moves us "beneath" the headland of "Ben Edar" (Howth) and therefore beneath the head altogether; the entire construction evokes a part of the "noughttime" in which "dreams stop" and the German *Traum* ("dream") halts. Chapter I.iii begins inauspiciously as a series of figures who have listened to the singing of "Osti-Fosti's" ballad in the preceding episode insubstantially vanish, together with all ordinary signs of human identity, each after the other evaporating into a succession of varied absences:

> Yet all they who heard . . . are now . . . as much no more as be they not yet now or had they then notever been. . . . Of the persins sin this . . . saga (which, thorough readable to int from and, is from tubb to buttom all falsetissues, antilibellous and nonactionable and this applies to its whole wholume) of poor Osti-Fosti . . . no one end is known. . . . *Ei fù* [It. "he was"]. His husband, poor old A'Hara . . . at the conclusion of the Crimean War [at an end in a Black Sea] . . . under the assumed name of Blanco . . . perished. . . . *Booil* [Russ. "he was"]. Poor old dear Paul Horan . . . was thrown into a Ridley's for inmates in the northern counties [an insane asylum]. . . . He was. Sordid Sam . . . at a word from Israfel the Summoner [the Islamic angel of death], passed away painlessly . . . one hallowe'en night, ebbrous [It. *ebbro*, "drunk"] and in the state of nature, propelled from Behind into the great Beyond. . . . *Han var* [Da. "he was"]. . . . her wife Langley . . . disappeared, (in which toodooing he has taken all the French leaves unveilable . . .) from the sourface of this earth . . . so entirely spoorlessly (the mother of the book with a dustwhisk tabularasing his obliteration done upon her involucrum) as to tickle the speculative to all but opine . . . that the hobo . . . had transtuled his funster's latitat to its finsterest interrimost. *Bhi she* [Gael. "he was"]. . . .   (48.6–50.17)

Then the three-page paragraph violently redacted here closes as a long conditional clause ("Again, if Father San Browne . . .") turns weirdly interrogative at its incompleted end, so to replicate formally the dissolution of sense, with sentence, in a nebulous part of the night that only question and hypothesis can begin to replicate: "and were they? *Fuitfuit* [L. 'he was he was']" (50.18–32).

That deliberately occulted phrase "he was," repeated seven times to suggest "helvetically hermetic" enclosure, structures the paragraph ("*Ei fù. Booil.* He was. *Han var. Bhi she. Fuitfuit*"). It deviously tells us that the sleeping man whose "eyewitless foggus" the paragraph replicates, himself obscured from himself, isn't quite there anymore—simply "was"—his actual disappearance determining all the figmentary ones; for all those patently ridiculous figures were "Just feathers! Nanentities" (538.7).[17] The paragraph shows HCE sinking "benighth" (480.17) all knowing of the earth ("finsterest" evokes both the toponym "Finisterre" ["earth's end"] and the German *finster* ["dark"]), as he takes a spectral "French leave" (sl. for "a sudden unnoticed departure") and "disappears spoorlessly" from dreams of worldly "habitat" into the unknown "latitat" (L. "hiding-place") of a "finsterest interrimost" which finds him dreamlessly "interred" in superlative degrees of the dark and the interior. For if dreams have their strange chronologies, dreamlessness does not, and the chapter has already generated a sequence of equations that began blurring an abnegated past and a nonexistent future into a present void of circumstance ("all they who heard . . . are now . . . as much no more as be they not yet now or had they then notever been"). As wording webbed through the middle of this dense paragraph moreover indicates, the chapter begins at the *end* of the auditory dream that was reconstructed in I.ii ("The Ballad"):

> Me drames . . . has come through! ["come true," moved to completion]. Now let the centuple celves of my egourge [the dream involved a crowd, and the 'hundred selves' now fade into a single 'cell'] . . . reamalgamerge in that indentity of undiscernibles where . . . may they cease to bidivil uns and . . . melt into peese! [melt into peace] *Han var* ["he was"].   (49.32–50.5)

Merely opening with a scotographic account of how nothingness starts seeping up into the "tropped head" of a man who has "nearvanashed himself" (61.18), I.iii now begins systematically "propogandering his nullity suit" (59.22 ["nearvanashed" recalls the literal meaning of "nirvana" in the "blowing-out" of the flame of life, while the "gander" in "propogandering" "takes flight"]). "All falsetissues" like lace, the body of this entirely "nonactionable" and "antilibellous" chapter (Gr. *antilibellos*, "against books") accordingly becomes the formal equivalent of any "empty envelope" (L. *involucrum*) absent of "all unveilable French leaves" and addressed not with letters but with the obliterate "nat language" of Wakese. The content of this "unvulope" (378.35) would be the *Wake*'s nullified hero, a "tabula rasa erased" as soon as anything enters his "Vacant. Mined" (421.11): "he has taken all the French leaves unveilable . . . the mother of the book with a dustwhisk tabularasing his obliteration done upon her involucrum" (50.8–13).

After observing that "there's nix to nothing we can do for he's never again to sea" (50.35 ["at sea," "he's never to see"]), the chapter proceeds to chronicle HCE's deepening vanishment into the "noughttime" by showing how "television kills telephony in brothers' broil" (52.18). Elsewhere in the *Wake* identified as a "nightlife instrument," the "faroscope of television" (150.32–33; < Gr. *têle*, "far off" and L. *visio*, "seeing") would suggest a form of vision radiated up "under the closed eyes" (107.28); while "telephony" would comparably suggest hearing bled up in dormant ears. Having dreamt of the singing of the ballad in I.ii, that is, HCE's hallucinatorily active eyes and ears now shut off, to leave him possessed only of "exrace eyes" (51.25–26 ["ex-human" eyes capable only of scotographic imperception]), and a mind bearing a corroding residuum of vision that generates this "touching seene" (the spelling would make this a "scene" already "seen," one washed away with all internal "see-in," into a "seeing" of this sort):

> . . . seein as ow his thoughts consisted chiefly of the cheerio, he aptly sketched . . . the touching seene. The solence of that stilling! Here one might a fin fell. Boomster rombombonant! It scenes like a landescape . . . or some seem on some dimb Arras, dumb as Mum's mutyness, this mimage of the seventyseventh kusin of kristansen is odable to os across the wineless Ere no œder nor mere eerie nor liss potent of suggestion than in the tales of the tingmount. (Prigged!)   (52.34–53.6)

That this passage intricately reworks a sentence "prigged" from Joyce's *A Portrait of the Artist as a Young Man* conveniently allows us, at Joyce's insistence, to compare the presentment of character in the earlier novel with "the representation of no-consciousness" afforded by the "blink pitches" of his scotographic "book of the dark." The relevant passage in *A Portrait* shows Stephen Dedalus looking soulfully at Dublin and meditating on the Viking "thingmote," the public assembly-place around which "the seventh city of Christendom" historically aggregated:[18]

> . . . the dim fabric of the city lay prone in the haze. Like a scene on some vague arras, old as man's weariness, the image of the seventh city of christendom was visible to him across the timeless air no more weary nor less patient of subjection than in the days of the thingmote.   (P, 167)

Dedalus may be absentminded, but far less so than the "very pure nondescript" depicted asleep in the corresponding passage from *Finnegans Wake,* who lies "still" and alone (L. *solus*) in a "situation" (Da. *stilling*) pervaded by a "silence" so deep that he could hear a pin drop ("The solence of that stilling! Here one might a fin fell"). Since the orthographical softening of "pin" into "fin" (Shelta, "man") suggests that this man himself has fallen into hushed sleep ("Finn fell"), the succeeding line evokes the reverberant felling of a "tree" (Du. *boom*): Big Pin! Even the drop of a pin, it seems, would be thunderously momentous in this part of the "nought." Moreover, what "seems" to be "scene" here ("It scenes," "some seem") is the mere "mimage" (or "mirage" of an "image") of "a landescape" that is no more clearly a dreamed "landscape" than an "escape" from "land" altogether. For this extinguished example of man's mightiness ("Mum's mutyness") now lies "mum," "dumb," in "muteness," against a "dimb" ("dim" and "dumb") background. The senses of taste and smell, evidently cultivated in great earnestness earlier in the day by the *Wake*'s hard-drinking hero, seem to have become "patrified" ("the wineless Ere," "no odor"). Anything potentially audible to him fills only an empty skull ("odable to os" [L. *os*, "bone"], Ger. *oed*, *oeder* ["empty," "more empty"], "no eer . . . " "nor liss"). Its blacked-out content therefore resembles imperceptible static washed through ether over the wireless air: "With nought a wired from the wordless either" (223.34). "There [is]," in short, "not very much windy Nous [Gr. 'mind'] blowing at the given moment through the hat of Mr Melancholy Slow" (56.28–30)—"Melancholy Slow," of course, because he just lies there, "hat" instead of "head" to evoke a heady structure void of content, and the Greek "Nous" rather than the English "mind" to suggest the "noose," at whose vacant center humans also disappear.[19]

So "patrified" are this man's five senses, "as a murder effect" (345.7), that subsequent lines invite us to wonder after the incessant manner of the *Wake* if he has merely "tropped head" or actually "dropped dead": "D.e.e.d! Edned, ended or sleeping soundlessly? Favour with your tongues!" (54.5–6 [the ceremonial Latin phrase *Favete linguis* means literally "favor with your tongues," but proverbially "listen in silence"]).[20] The lines invite us to "listen" attentively, then, but only by metamnesically "falling silent" as if in sound, soundless sleep, so to bring to mind rich "blank memory" of the "nought's" "Real Absence." Or, as Joyce himself advises in this region of his "darkumen":

> . . . all, hearing in this new reading . . . could simply imagine themselves in their bosom's inmost core, as *pro tem locums* timesported acorss the yawning (abyss), as once they were ["across" the "abyss" that opens in a body ("corse") stilled in sleep ("yawn")] . . . listening to the cockshyshooter's evensong evocation of the doomed . . . silkhouatted . . . aginsst the dusk [made insubstantial as the content of a "silhouette" or the inside of a "silk hat"] . . . while olover his exculpatory features . . . the ghost of resignation diffused a spectral appealingness. . . .   (55.33–56.17)

As the "television" bleakly radiating this dusky "landescape" under closed eyelids continues to diffuse with that "dusk," moreover, it washes out into another image of scotographic negativity (57.23–29) and finally renders "the blanche patch" representative of HCE's experience in the "nought" a blanched-out white: "winter . . . over[s] the pages of nature's book" (57.30–31) and "the shadow of the huge outlander"—the "silkhouatte" of this man somnolently slipped "out of land" and all earthly definition—vanishes sightlessly "mid pillow talk . . . through Molesworth Fields" (57.34–35) into the obscurity of another "nonactionable" and "antilibellous" legal trial, where the reader is now asked to formulate ongoing and "jostling judgements of those, as all should owe, malrecapturable days" (58.21–22):

"wowhere are those yours of Yesterdays?" (54.3). For should he live to the proverbial age of seventy, the "ordinary man with that large big nonobli head" (L. *non oblitus*, "not forgotten"), and that blanko berbecked fischial ekksprezzion" (64.30–31) will spend almost seven thousand "malrecapturable days" of his life as these in dreamless sleep—twenty years—"meet there night . . . made their nought" (67.3–4 ["mid the night, made there nought"]), "edned, ended or sleeping soundlessly." "Fischial," in these lines, would evoke both "facial" and "visual" properties of "that big nonobli head," though the term "blanko" would blank them out; while the Danish negative *eks-* ("ex-"), abnegating an English "expression" already obliterated by the Italian *sprezzato* ("broken"), would comparably x-out expression, vision, and their facial ground altogether, so to suggest on the *Wake*'s "blink pitch" how sleep can "bash in Patch's blank face beyond recognition" and render him "not a tall man, not at all man. No such parson" (63.5, 10–11).

Obliterating every term in the literate stream of consciousness whose evolving totality means Stephen Dedalus in *A Portrait*, the no less richly particularized "blotch and void" of *Finnegans Wake* yields, in this region of the book, "a poor trait of the artless" (114.32)—where "trait" might be run back etymologically to the Latin *tractus* ("a draft, a line"), and "artless" comparably construed as an etymological synonym for "inert" (from the L. *inartis* ["artless, idle"]). For the *Wake*'s "poor trait of the artless" renders in particular the scotographic "indentity" of "someone imparticular" (602.7) lying "inert," without a "trait," in the "nought." Where a work titularly conceived as *A Portrait* might well invite comparisons with pictures hung in Ireland's National Gallery, then, a "specturesque" "poortrait" like that captured by the *Wake*'s "obliterated negative" could only find room in a "notional gullery"—to whose contemplation chapter I.iii now in fact returns us as we read again of "Madam's Toshowus [lying] completely complacent, an exegious monument, aerily perennious," slipped with "bland sol" "into the nethermore" (57.26): the wording now suggests that a "blind soul" has vanished, with "the pleasant sun" (L. *sol blandus*), into a netherwordly nevermore.

Locating us beneath "an exeguous [scanty] monument"—"soon, monumentally at least . . . to be, to be his mausoleum" (56.12–14)—these lines now require brief reconsideration, by way of an "abnihilisation of the etym" like that undertaken in the etymological chart labeled figure 2.1, the top of which is all literate English, the very bottom only obliterate "nat language." For parts of sleep that lie beneath "memory" and "remembrance," according to Joyce's "adamelegy" (77.26), lie equivalently beneath "the manyoumeant"

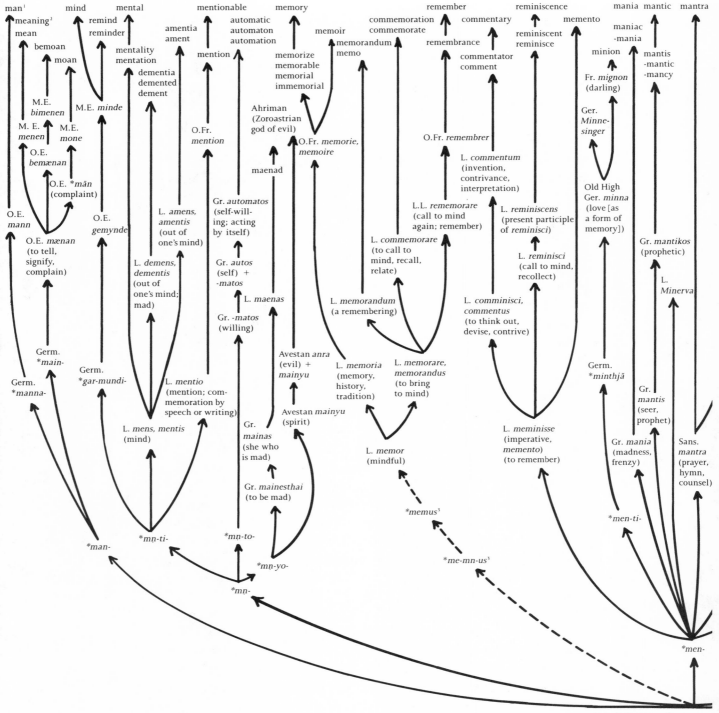

Figure 2.1. Etymological chart: *men-. "Undernearth" "the manyoumeant" (610.4, 318.31)

1. Pokorny, 700; Shipley, 248; Skeat, 350.

2. Grandsaignes d'Hauterive, 124; Shipley, 248; Skeat, 360.

3. Dotted lines indicate derivations now discredited but speculatively entertained in Joyce's day; see A. Walde and J. B. Hofmann, *Lateinisches Etymologisches Worterbuch* (Heidelberg: Carl Winter, 1940), II, p. 68.

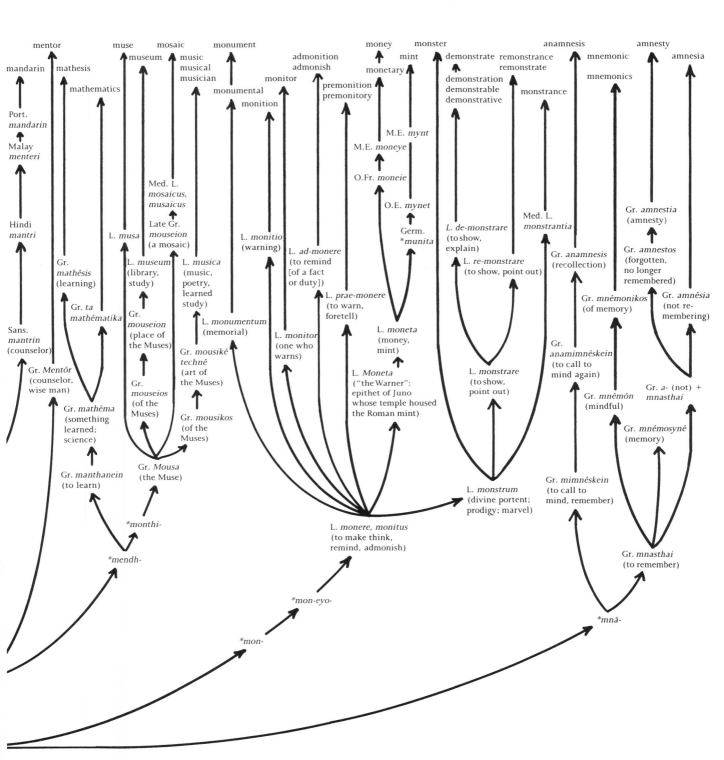

(318.31) before falling there (the term buries "man" and "meaning" under a "monument"). As the trained senses of the man "tropped head" at the *Wake* blow out and "nearvanash" in the "nought," that is—together with all the laws of which intellection and recollection are the abstract sum—so too does "memory," and the whole field of "meaning" made possible in wakefulness by the disciplined wiring of eyes and ears to legible letters and legislated "things," the latter term genetically related to the "thingmote" that Stephen Dedalus headily contemplates in *A Portrait* and that the "aerily perennious" "Headmound" certainly does not in the *Wake*'s "poor trait" (conceptually, "things" derive from the broad Teutonic term *thing* ["public assembly"] and at one time designated what a group of people such as gathered in the thingmote agreed to observe).

Since "memory" and "meaning," moreover, are only two in a long series of etymologically toppling dominoes that include "man," "mind," and "mentality," as well as "mentionability" and "commentary," parts of sleep that fall beneath "the manyoumeant"—"undernearth the memorialorum" (610.4)—lie also beyond the writing of literate "memoirs" (L. *memorialium*) and so require the obliterate reduction of the *Wake*'s sleeping subject to a "*belowes hero*" (343.17 ["below zero"])—a "whosethere outofman" (19.17)—whose life in the night becomes a vast "apersonal problem, a locative enigma" (135.25–26). And "there too a slab slobs, immermemorial" (600.26 [Ger. *immer*, "always"; "immemorial"]). For immemorial sleep finds this "very pure nondescript" with "not a knocker on his head or a nicknumber on the manyoumeant . . . wooving nihilnulls from Memoland," as "his spectrem" lies lost in "the irised sea" (318.30–34): the "memo" "woven" here would be of "nothing" (L. *nihil*), "no one" (L. *nullus*), and a "nobody" (L. *nemo*), within the closed eyes of whose "spectre" the "spectrum" has blacked out. "Reduced to nothing" in a body of matter rendered inert and drained of perception under the force of sleep, the man "tropped head" at the *Wake* so becomes, "as a murder of corpse" (254.32 ["as a matter of course"]), "the presence (of a curpse)" (224.4–5)—"*to say nothing of him* having done whatyouknow howyousaw whenyouheard whereyouwot . . . under **h**eaviest **c**orpsus **e**xemption" (362.14–17; italics mine). Not quite as dead as he will ever become, he nonetheless becomes in dreamless sleep, as dead as he will ever have occasion to know. He now lies "undernearth" "the manyoumeant" in a second sense, "laid to rust" there "under the Helpless **C**orpses **E**nactment" (423.30), and in ways that will merit further study.

As will have become evident in passing, "*A stodge Angleshman has been worked by eccentricity*" in *Finnegans Wake* (284.L1); for Joyce's "poor trait" makes of a man "tropped head" "in bed" not merely something of "a stage Englishman," but an astonishingly "stodgy" one, since he has, like "Madam's Toshowus," essentially no ideas at all. A sustained reading of *Finnegans Wake* actually does manage to draw a reader deeply into a "blank memory" of the "percepted nought" experienced in the night; and in doing so, it opens all manner of inquiry into what precisely the "Vacant. Mined" could have been about in those parts of its life when it seemed not to be there at all. By probing into these extents of emptiness, moreover, ignored by most writers on dreams, Joyce fathomlessly deepened the "mountainy molehill" of the night, finding there much more than the primitive reasoning of the dream which so compelled the attention of Vico, Freud, Lévy-Bruhl, and other students of the savage mind. In "reconstructing the nocturnal life," he was also exercising the whole twentieth-century fascination with nothingness. "My eyes are tired," he wrote to his son Giorgio three years before he completed *Finnegans Wake*. "For over half a century, they have gazed into nullity where they have found a lovely nothing" (*L*, III, 359, 361n.).

As Joyce's contemporaries were showing in countless ways over the two decades during which he sustained the writing of *Finnegans Wake*, nothingness is a formative trait and invention of the human. Nonexistent in a material reality that keeps on pouring forth stars, seasons, and generations of species with plentiful regularity, it seems not to exist outside of human minds, except when human minds themselves invested with the capability of knowing it, choose to implant it there. Since individuals tutored in all those words and abilities layered up over the Indo-European root *men-seem able to know "nothing" only in the "Real Absence" of the night, the experience of sleep becomes, at the *Wake*, the concrete reality out of which the whole category of nothingness immanently wells. Sleep's "Real Absence" is the experience of nothing, really endured, in particular.

These observations will moreover suggest how organically Joyce, one of the century's great humanists, managed to synthesize in a work essentially like *Ulysses*, but "about the night," some of the principal intellectual preoccupations of a culture already moving away from the scientific study of man into the "new scientific" study of "our whosethere outofman"; the same preoccupations that would compel twentieth-century thinkers to contemplate variously the related properties of aboriginality, prehistory, unconsciousness, and nothingness. His "knock[ed] out" "belowes hero" lies in a resonant position: a man at the dazzlingly developed height of millennia of evolved civilization—a twentieth-century Westerner—he lies "reduced to nothing" within a body "tropped head," experiencing both the extinction of his con-

Nothing in Particular

sciousness and the nothingness above which his daily life, over years of personal and ages of collective history, has been masoned and layered. His vacant passage through the "noughttime," accordingly, broadens out into endlessly stunning perspectives. While it is doubtlessly true that HCE and his wife are by day as rationally individualized citizens of the Western world as anyone

> whereat samething is rivisible by nighttim, may be involted into the zeroic couplet, palls pell inhis heventh glike noughty times ∞, find, if you are not literally cooefficient, how minney combinaisies and permutandies can be played on the international surd! (284.8–14)

As this "mythametical" discussion of surds, irrational numbers, unknowns, and zeros will suggest (286.23), the "risible, "invisible," "absurd" nothing to which "**H**ere **C**omes **E**verybody" (32.18–19) in the world is indeterminately reduced in the night bears darkly prolific powers. Since it is out of this indifferentiated state, every morning and through all the mornings in history, that all the manifold and splintered facets of the wakeful world emerge—striving individuals, nations in strife, tongues—sleep's "Real Absence" becomes, at the *Wake*, a form of "substrance" (597.7 [elemental "substance," as discovered in somebody "under a trance"]), a torrent streaming everywhere unconsciously under the evident surface of things (597.1–8ff.). Just as in real-world arithmetic, so in the nocturnal "aristmystic" of the *Wake* (293.18): if an aspect of "the logos . . . comes to nullum in the endth" in this book (298.20 ["to nothing, in the end"]), it is nonetheless and for that reason capable of modulating through an infinitely expanding series of "combinations" and "permutations" that lift it, through "nullum in the endth" (O^n), into everything—∞—"no thing making newthing wealthshowever for a silly old Sol, healthytobedder and latewiser" (253.8–9 [for a sleepily "silly old soul" waiting for "old Sol" to rise]): "Wins won is nought, twigs too is nil, tricks trees makes nix, fairs fears stoops at nothing" (361.1–3). In its richly particularlized "nat language," *Finnegans Wake* shows that the human experience of "one percepted nought" can be articulated with as much richness and zest, pathos and humor, as the plenitude of wakeful life. In ways to be made clear in passing, it finds this "nought" everywhere and always underlying and circumscribing the living of life in the Daily World. "We see nothingness," in a way distinct to Joyce, "making the world irridescent, casting a shimmer over things."[21]

Profoundly engaged by the "hole affair" it reconstructively fills in, *Finnegans Wake* manages to spin a universe, an "obliterated negative" of the one now present to literate consciousness, out of the study of sleep's "Real Absence." Much of this "huge shaping of literary anti-matter," a kind of a phenomenology of lack of mind, is difficult to read not simply because of its language, but also because its scotographic "nat language" struggles hard to convey to a rationally lettered reader, in detailed "blotch and void," experiences that lie in unconsciousness beneath "the manyoumeant."[22] Subsequent chapters, then, lead into places where, consciousness moving out of human experience and "noughttime" moving in, man is not, and "our whosethere outofman" and "belowes hero" becomes principle. The first of these infinitely expanding sites, in a work with the word *Wake* engraved on its spine and dustjacket, will inevitably be the grave, humanity's first writing, 50,000 years of it engraved on the surface of the earth before more ornate engravings and the Western alphabet proper began to flower, with spirits, around the dark locale of the tomb.

CHAPTER THREE

"Finnegan"

Momentarily, we might construe the hero of *Finnegans Wake* as "Finnegan" (3.19), though for reasons gradually to become clear, this is no more his real name than "Headmound" is. "Finnegan" is a cipher for the "perpendicular person" (60.25) shown "outlined aslumbered" in Relief Map B, and it indicates that he is quite fully *"Dead to the World"* (105.29). Our idiomatic custom of saying that people asleep are "dead to the world," however, now raises the troublesome question of how being "dead to the world," not awake, resting in peace "in bed" differs from what one foresees happening to anyone "dead to the world," at his wake, resting in peace, and also "in bed"—particularly if we dig a little more deeply into these terms.

Etymologically, the word "bed" derives from the proto-Indo-European root *bhedh-, meaning "to dig or bury" or, in nominal form, "a hollow in the ground, for sleeping" (this radical sense still survives in expressions like "vegetable bed" [18.17–19.19], "flower bed" [475.7–11], "lake bed" [76.14–32], and "bed of rock" [472.2]). While the etymology certainly sheds grim light on Indo-European man's sleeping arrangements in eras prior to the invention of "tick[s]" (26.15), "cots" (39.33), "bunk[s]" (40.19), "shakedown[s]" (40.25–26), "lodginghouses" (39.31), "bedroom suite[s]" (41.16), and "inns" (7.5), it interests us here because of the spectral resonances it inevitably generates throughout *Finnegans Wake*. If the man "tropped head" "in bed" at the *Wake* is indeed "dead to the world" and can largely only "no," how can he "know" that the "bed" in which he lies is not, "as a murder effect"

(345.7), a "bed of soil?" Or, to bend the same question back into the experience of "our own nighttime," how does anyone fully asleep and "dead to the world" know that he is not really dead to the world? And conversely, how does anyone actually dead to the world know that he is not simply asleep?

The problem is all the more perturbing because the word "bed" stands in an oddly complementary relation to the word "cemetery," which derives from the Greek *koimêtêrion* ("sleeping room," "dormitory")—in turn from the verb *koimaô* ("to put to bed")—and which customarily designates a place where people "lie in peat" (4.15 [but also "in peace"]) in much the same posture as that enjoyed by the stratified humanoid shown "tropped head" in Relief Map B, whom we might now begin to think of as "laid to rust" (3.23 [but also "rest"]), "pending a rouseruction of his bogey" (499.1 [a "resurrection of the body"]), after having been "recalled and scrapheaped by the Maker" (98.17). Since, at his *Wake*, "be there some who mourn him, concluding him dead" (489.1), it may well be that our hero has "indeeth" "tropped head" (79.17 ["in death" "indeed"]); and that "now of parts unknown" (380.23), "he went under the grass quilt on us" (380.26). For the distinction between an unconscious body (Eng. "corpse") and an unconscious "body" (L. *corpus*) is a thin one; while anyone "laid to rest" "in bed," by a slight inflection of terms, would also be "embedded."

That we drift through sleep in places primordially conceived as burial sites and are laid to rest at our wakes in places originally designating bedrooms highlights the bottomlessness of the negatively definitive term "unconscious," in turn raising questions about the indistinctly differentiated unconsciousnesses of sleep and death. What internally distinguishes eight hours of sleepily peaceful requiescence from "(*hypnos chilia eonion!*)" (78.3–4 [Gr. "sleep for thousands of ages"])? As the nineteenth-century literature on sleep alone attests, students of the dark used to stand so fascinated before the annihilative powers of the night, until modern thought channeled attention into those more accessible parts of sleep surfacing in dreams, that a representative figure like Schopenhauer could say, summarily, "there is no radical difference between sleep and death."[1] He would only have been expressing a belief so commonplace and so primal as to go back to the source of our culture, and the Greeks, for whom Death and Sleep where twin brothers, both sons of Night. According to Lessing, "the only genuine and general representation of Death" for the Greeks was "a picture of sleep;" and of sleep, of death.[2] Similarly for Joyce, any genuine "reconstruction of the nocturnal life" would have entailed a "grave word" or two

(243.30) about the interior of the coffin. "Sleep is death stirred by dreams, death is dreamless sleep."[3]

To an alert rationalist, the distinction between a person at his wake ("Rot him!" [422.9]) and a person not awake ("wake him!" [7.3]) will be all too clear: in a word, "wake not, walk not" (546.1–2). But the distinction corrodes almost entirely if one cultivates the "ideal insomnia" that *Finnegans Wake* requires and tries to enter the "eyewitless foggus" of a man "tropped head" and "dead to the world" "in bed" himself. The requisite exercise would involve sinking again into the "blank memory" preserved from last night's stint of embedment, now to observe how deeply the "hole affair" (535.20)—and a "hole" is always edged with a little loam—is "rich in death anticipated" (78.6). Sleep takes place "in your own absence" (189.31)— your own "Real Absence" (536.5–6)—where "life, it is true, will be a blank without you because avicuum's not there at all" (473.6–7). Anyone crawling into some bed "todie" (60.28, 381.23, 408.22 [not inevitably "today"]) will "recoil" how he lay there, "feeling dead" (269.F1), "very dead" (612.4), resting in peace, and "thinking himself to death" (422.9 [as opposed, for instance, to some brainy conclusion]). "Indead" (505.21, 560.18), the "hole affair" seems to force one to "dejeunerate into a skillyton be thinking himself to death" (422.8–9): "a bad attack of maggot it feels like" (410.5).

As a "thanatomimetic" state, moreover—like "playing possum" (96.33– 34)—sleep makes one an involuntary participant in eerily extended "funeral games" (332.26, 515.23, 602.22 [as opposed to "funeral earnestnesses"]). You "drop in your tracks" (26.16)—"f[a]ll stiff" (379.18 ["full stop"]). There, "tropped head," amid "the redissolusingness of mindmouldered ease" (143.14), one passes into a state of "exanimation" (143.8–9, 87.34) and then "[goes] about his business, whoever it was, saluting corpses, as a metter of corse" (37.9–10 ["as a matter of course," one "meets a corpse"]).[4] Anyone can play a few of these "funeral games" when he goes to bed "todie"—"indead," "he musts" (325.19 [because he "must"])—there to wonder how deeply the "hole affair" implicated him in "funeral fare or fun fain real" (83.22 ["real" "funeral," or one merely "feigned" in "fun"?]). Were one to ask what "did die" "doom" last night (223.12; cf. 111.2, 358.36), one good answer would be to say that "I was intending a funeral. Simply and samply" (491.2–3 [not "attending" one]); for the puristic intention of anyone "dead to the world" is in some sense easy to gauge. "On the verge of selfabyss" (40.23), "so to shape, I chanced to be stretching, in the shadow as I thought, the liferight out of myself in my . . . imaginating" (487.13–15 [I did not think, therefore I must not have been]). "Indead," "I go dead" (251.26) "every die" (283.F2 ["every day"]). And "every die" "yew yourselves" (98.36), even the "most umbrasive of yews all" (362.17 ["impressive"]) comparably lie there resting in peace in some imperceived "bed," "dead certain however of neuthing whatever" (455.21–22). All those "yews," occulting a batch of decomposed "yous" (cf. 23.36, 232.13, 469.27) would adorn the cemeterial "bed," while the *umbra* in "umbrasive" (L., "shade") would evoke a dark and chilly "underworld" (147.27) occupied by the "tropped head." "Howday you doom?" (517.31; cf. 483.18). "Strangely cult for this ceasing of the yore" (279.2–3).

The "veiled" and "blank memory" "recoil[ed]" from last night by every "tombs, deep and heavy" in the world (503.26 [every "Tom, Dick and Harry"]) opens now with problematic lucidity "to the unaveiling memory of. Peacer the grave" (503.26–27)—where the end-stopped "of" evokes a world void of objects (both of prepositions and of perception), while the "misappearance" (186.12) within the "peaceful grave" of a dubious "Peter the Great" suggests that in sleep one not only "goes dead" but also becomes, because immobily "perpetrified" (23.30 ["thoroughly petrified"]), a "Peter" of sorts (the Latinized Gr. *petrus*, in a pun that Joyce regarded as sanctioning his own, means both "Peter" and "rock").[5] One might begin simply to regard the "loamsome" (26.15) "hole affair" of sleep, then, as a species of "death he has lived through" (293.3–4)—a death of the sort that befalls Joyce's dummy-like hero. For "Charles de Simples had an infirmierity complexe before he died a natural death" (291.F8): the hint of "infirmity" lands him "in bed," where a nightly variety of "natural death" foreshadows the ultimate one.

The same kind of complementarity as that blurring together the meanings of "bed" and "cemetery" and rendering indistinct the unconsciousnesses of sleep and death links *Finnegans Wake* with the Irish-American ballad of "Finnegan's Wake." As most readers know, the ballad tells the story of a whiskey-loving hod-carrier named Tim Finnegan (4.18, 26–27) who goes to work each morning fortified by a drop of "the craythur" (4.29). "With a love of the liquor Tim was born" (4.33–34), though it proves to be his undoing:

One morning Tim felt tippling full,	(6.7–8)
His head felt heavy, his hod it did shake	(6.8–9)
He fell from the ladder and broke his skull	(6.10)
So they carried him home his corpse to wake.	
They rolled him up in a nice clean sheet,	
And laid him out upon the bed	

"Finnegan"

69

> With a gallon of whiskey at his feet
> And a barrel of porter at his head.

(6.26–27)

The mourners at Finnegan's wake—an Irish one, in which riotous gaiety co-exists with funereal grief—gradually begin arguing, and in the ensuing ructions one of them hurls a noggin of whiskey across the room. But the liquor misses its intended target and splashes instead all over the corpse of Finnegan, who revives and rises from his bed bawling out, *"Thanam o'n dhoul, do ye think I'm dead?"* (cf. 24.15 [the Gaelic phrase means "Soul of the devil" and recurs in various forms at 74.8, 258.8–9, 317.3–4, 321.29, and 499.17–18]).[6]

The bearing of the ballad on a reconstruction of the night is finally quite simple. Minimal reflection on Finnegan's fate will suggest that anybody who gets up out of bed with a mouth that big and a thirst that grand cannot really have been dead at all. In Joyce's appropriation of the ballad, "Finnegan's Wake" simply becomes a comically parabolic account of what it is like to "black out" and fall, though asleep, so to find oneself "laid out upon the bed," "dead to the world," "rehearsing somewan's funeral" (477.9)—but ultimately to undergo a thirsty "resurrection of the body" under the agency of animating "spirits" "come to mournhim" (12.14–15 ["come tomorrow"]). Sleeping, from this perspective, implicates one in effortless "rehearsing" for "the big sleep," "the long sleep," or the "long rest" of commoner idiom (25.26; *U*, 110 [the recurrent pun on "hearse" is a grim one]). But because "the remains must be removed before eaght hours shorp" at this funeral "rehearsal" (617.16,27 ["eight hours" being the length of sleep]), the "hole affair" might more accurately be called an "ephumeral" (369.33 [an "ephemeral" "funeral"]), in which the body lies "dead to the world" in merely "a protem grave" (76.21). Judging from a terse comment that Joyce himself made about "Finnegan's Wake," in a letter written after the publication of *Finnegans Wake*, this was how he read the ballad (*L*, III, 448): he noted simply that Finnegan was an exemplar of "*Scheintod*" (Ger. "apparent death," "suspended animation"). Or, as the *Wake* puts it, "Tam Fanagan's weak yat his still's going strang" (276.21–22 [he may be "still" and "dead to the world," that is, but his "spirits" sublimate as potently in the dark as any in any "still"]). No differently from anyone's experience of sleep, then, Finnegan's experience at his wake might be regarded simply as an "ephumeral" drift through "states of suspensive exanimation" (143.8–9) endured between periods of wakefulness that find him engaged in the masonry of the civilized world ("*Ho, Time Timeagen, Wake*" [415.15]). Like others who "rise afterfall" (78.7), "Finnegan" becomes one bedrock on which the *Wake* rests because being dead to the world, immemorially unconscious, is the basic state of the night, the darker ground out of which the more colorful eventfulnesses of dreams arise. This is also to begin noting that *Finnegans Wake* tells the same story that "Finnegan's Wake" does, but with a difference; for the *Wake* is about a wake as perceived not from the "point of view" of any wakeful mourners or garrulous songsters, but from the "eyewitless foggus" of the body "tropped head" "in bed."

And there are, accordingly, spooky corollaries. Insofar as the *Wake* is elaborately reconstructing the "Real Absence" that a man lying "dead to the world" at his own "ephumeral" can "no," Joyce is putting the proposition *"Suppotes a Ventriliquorst Merries a Corpse"* (105.20), where the wording in part recalls the ballad of "Finnegan's Wake" ("potes," "liquor," "merries," "corpse"), but also indicates the *Wake*'s intention of rendering, in its own spectral form of "ventriloquism," the muddy "explots" (124.29 [not exactly "exploits"]) of a corpse that is "dud" (6.10), "duddandgunne" (25.23–24), "noewhemore. Finiche!" (7.15): "you skull see" (17.18). Joyce is also saying to his reader, in concert with the dark artiste in the *Wake* who "ma[kes] his boo to the public" (423.22 [not "bow"]), "I'd love to take you for a bugaboo ride and play funfer all" (304.11–12 ["funeral"]). And, with frightening effect, he does just that, though with much "fun for all" along the way (301.13; cf. 13.15, 111.15, 120.10, 458.22 ["funeral"]). In directing our attention to the "blank memory" of the "funeral games" we all "rehearsed" last night, the *Wake* therefore obliges itself "to reconstruct for us . . . inexactly the same as a mind's eye view, how these funeral games . . . took place" (515.22–25, 33). The "hole affair" now becomes an "undertaking" in both senses of that word, with Joyce himself, like the Wakean artiste "suspected among morticians" (172.12), playing the part of the "premature gravedigger" (189.28) or "underthaner" (335.36 ["entertainer"-"undertaker"]), whose business it is to conduct for us, in a manner of "grand stylish gravedigging" (121.32), an exceedingly peculiar species of *"ante mortem"* (423.21 ["postmortem"]). As a "representation" contradictively structured around the experience of "your own absence" (189.31) in the dead of "nought" (368.36), the *Wake* offers its reader *"an admirable verbivocovisual presentment of the worldrenownced Caerholme event"* (341.18–19)—where the line seems manifestly to bear on a horse race ("the world-reknowned Carholme Event"), but only because Joyce's "nonday diary" is elaborately concerned with that variety of dark horse known as a "sleeper." Latently it indicates how fully the *Wake*, as a literary "presentment" rendering from his own "eyewitless foggus" the "Real Absence" of a man lying "dead to the world," is holding forth a sustained "presentiment" of the "world-renounced event" that will seep into the skull at the wake.

This means that *Finnegans Wake*, because sleep does, "really" takes place in some murky "bed" in a "seemetery" (17.36 [a "seeming" "cemetery," though a real *koimêtêrion*])—and in particular, "amid the semitary of Somnionia" (594.8 [L. *somnus*, "sleep"; *somnium*, "dream"]). More interestingly, "if I may break the subject gently" and again (165.30), the subject "tropped head" at this *Wake*, "becorpse" he is mindlessly "dead to the world" (509.32), is largely only "the presence (of a curpse)" (224.4–5): "He's doorknobs dead!" (378.1–2). The *Wake* in turn becomes an articulately graphic "present(i)ment"—an eerie "engravure" of sorts (13.7)—of the stilled "stream of unconsciousness" ("basin of unconsciousness"?) that has seeped in "among skullhullows and charnelcysts" (613.20–21) interior to "the presence (of a curpse)" who lies "blurried" (13.11 ["blurred," "buried"]) in some muddy "bed" in a "seemetery," "sinking" (224.25 [not "thinking"]) of "a mouldy voids" (37.9 [as opposed to a philosophical one]). Relief Map B shows "the Outrage, at Length" (602.25). And as at the wake, so at the *Wake:* one tries to "throw any lime on the sopjack" that one can (489.12).

Read from this perspective, as its title plainly indicates, the *Wake* is really about a wake, and it becomes easily one of the most amusingly scarifying "ghoststories" ever written (51.13, 359.26). It operates less by evoking colorfully decked-out "apparitions," who are always very much a part of this life, all their chatty disclaimers notwithstanding, than by calling remorseless attention to "your ghost" (24.27), to the nothing "yew" become in the dead of night, "when meet there night . . . made their nought the hour strikes" (67.3–5), and "yew" are not only "reduced to nothing" (499.3), but, "as a murder of corpse" (254.32), laid out "dead to the world" in a "seemetery." As a "NIGHTLETTER" radiotelegraphing complex "youlldied greedings" through void ether (308.16–17 ["Yuletide" because sleep, like the Incarnation, takes place "in the flesh"]), the *Wake* everywhere reminds one that "his fooneral will sneak pleace by creeps o'clock toosday" (617.20–21)—where the line, rather than giving us the time, gives us the "creeps," by suggesting how difficult internally to distinguish from "the long sleep" is the shorter sleep that every "tomb, dyke and hollow" in the book (597.6 ["Tom, Dick and Harry"]) will go through "todie" as "daylight" disintegrates into "dielate" on "this daylit dielate night of nights, by golly!" (83.27). To put all this in the assaultive idiom of the ghost story: "Boo, you're through!" (247.12). And to put it in a word that comparably encapsulates the complex tonality of gravity and levity, of "hilarity" and "tristesse" (21.12) that characterizes *Finnegans Wake* as a whole: "Boohoohoo . . . !" (379.13).

The dark "tome" now modulates into a "bog of the depths" (516.25)—a "Book of the Dead" (13.30–31, 134.36, 309.3, 580.16, 621.3)—whose graven letters begin to operate much like those on a "tomestone" (253.34), marking the spot where a man lies "dead to the world" and giving "testimony on behalf of the absent . . . to those present" (173.29–31)—though now "a testament of the rocks from all the dead unto some the living" (73.32–33). "If Standing Stones Could Speak" (306.22–23), they would say much exactly what "the menhere's always talking about" in this elaborately arabesqued "book of kills" (25.11–12, 482.33 [not "Kells"; "menhirs" are "standing stones"]): "Here line the refrains of" (44.10), "the remains of" (13.10), "the late cemented Mr T. M. Finnegan. R.I.C." (221.27 [R.I.P.]; 325.1); "may ye root to piece!" (545.36). Or, more elaborately, in three sentences that minimally fill in the "blank memory" one has of last night: "Rest in peace! But to return. What a wonderful memory you have too!" (295.15–16).

"Wurming along gradually" (84.30), it becomes evident that this "book of kills" had to be written "in the vermicular" (82.11–12 [L. *vermiculus*, "worm"])—as opposed to an identifiable "vernacular"—because its "*belowes hero*" (343.17), "the presence (of a curpse)," lives not in a perceptible "world," but in something much more like "the wormd" (354.22 ["the world" overtaken by "worm"]). Every page written "in [this] vermicular," accordingly, each already strewn over with "engraved" letters and "grave word[s]" (120.10, 243.30), becomes a kind of literate "graphplot" (284.7), holding forth a spookily articulate "present(i)ment" of the "Real Absence" interior to "a deadman" (87.33, 121.36) who lies "blurried" in a "graveplot." Systematically entangled with words like "night," "sleep," and "bed," that is, and with particles operating in the *Wake*'s "nat language," its reader will find on any of the book's "graphplots" "allsods of" terms (289.4–5) in this "vermicular"—like "loamsome," "dead," and "sods"—whose effect is everywhere to net and capture the underlying unconsciousness of a body lying "dead to the world" in a "seemetery." And "amudst" these "graphplots" (332.26), everywhere at the *Wake*, the reader will also find that in "*spectracular mephiticism there caoculates through the inconoscope . . . a still, the figure of a fellowchap in the wohly ghast*" (349.17–19), who "*among nosoever circusdances is to be apprehended*" (342.12). Since an "inconoscope" would look "in" at "icons" (or "images"), the lines suggest that no "apprehensibly" visible "spectacle" "coagulates" at the *Wake*, or at the wake, or in one's "blank memory" of the night—no "circuses," no "dances," no "circumstances," no colorfully parading members of "the fellowship in the Holy Ghost," "nor no nothing" (455.2). Instead, one maintains in the "eyewitless foggus" "recoil[ed]" from "lost life" (515.26["last night"]) the "spectacularly mephitic spectre" of a representative man ("fellowchap"), lying "still" in the dead of night, whose "explots" are vision-void and "wholly ghastly": "*caoculates*" evokes the Gaelic *caoch* ("blind"), while the English "mephitic," referring to "noxious or pestilential emanations from the earth," would summon up "the ghouly ghost" (57.6). "You had just," in short, in browsing "amudst" these "graphplots," "been cerberating a camp camp camp to Saint Sepulchre's march . . . fellowed along the rout by the stenchions of the corpse" (343.4–8). In his wakeful life, of course, the man "tropped head" at his *Wake* fairly bustles with activity ("Tramp, Tramp, Tramp") in a world defined by Church ("stations of the cross") and State ("Tramp, Tramp, Tramp the Boys are Marching" is the tune to which the patriotic song "God Save Ireland" is set). But in the "seemetery" of night, by contrast, he just lies there, a "man made static" (309.22), "camp camp camp[ing]" in one spot, so to "cerebrate" the sorrowful mysteries of "the stenchions of the corpse": "Tarara boom decay" (247.28). The peculiar tense ("you had been") puts "being" in a past that is over and done with: "Siar, I am deed" (89.28). "D.E.D." (420.30). "Dood dood dood!" (499.6).[7]

As all these many articles lifted from his "tropped head" imply, one thing is certain of the representative "fellowchap" shown stratified in Relief Map B: "he'll be the dea[th] of us" (379.20; 369.29, 460.22); and as someone at the *Wake* puts it, "I hope they threw away the mould" (146.12–13). Throughout the book, its reader will be "recurrently meeting" its hero—"Morbus O' Somebody" (88.14)—"in cycloannalism, from space to space, time after time, in various phrases of scripture as in various poses of sepulture" (254.25–28) as he drifts through the "semitary of Somnionia" in "total calm" in the "duskguise[s]" (532.27), for instance, of "Totumcalmum" (26.18["Tutankhamen"]), "the noneknown worrier" (596.10–11 ["the Unknown Warrior"]), "Morty Manning" (329.24 ["mortal man"]), "and all the deed in the woe" (11.7 ["all the dead in the world"]). Since "cycloannalism" would differ from "psychoanalysis" in exploring the profoundly unconscious state into which a person "tropped head" will move not simply "todie," but also after the "cycle" of "years" is up (L. *annus*, "year"), the term suggests that part of the *Wake*'s extended "undertaking" will be an investigation of "the morbidisation of the modern mandaboutwoman type" (151.5–6). And "that's the point of eschatology our book of kills reaches for now in soandso many counterpoint words" (482.33–34).

Life in the cemetery, judging from the vast literature on the subject, is not that empty. For instance, "skim over *Through Hell with the Papes* (mostly boys) by the divine comic Denti Alligator" (440.5–6 ["Dante Alighieri"])— where the reference to the "dental" equipment of "alligators" more or less answers the question "Death, where are thy jaws?" by referring us to the *Inferno*, the complaining members of whose men's club talkatively reveal that death has Big Ones. Although Western culture, obsessed with "spirits," has generated countless books and institutions elaborately explaining events presumed to follow the wake, in "underworld[s]" (147.27), "otherworld[s]" (385.4), "netherworld[s]" (571.35), "yonderworld[s]" (593.23), "wonderwearlds" (147.28), "mansions of the blest" (426.26), "heavens" (170.9), and puritan "Hell[s]" (63.23), it has produced very few—the *Wake* among them—troubled enough to wonder about the substantially "Real Absence" that informs the "tropped head" nightly, in "real life" (260.F3). To this telling oversight Joyce, throwing his ventriloqual voice into the dummy shown embedded in Relief Map B, sighs in exasperation, "we only wish everyone was as sure of anything in this . . . world as we are of everything in the . . . fellow that's bound to follow" (452.29–31). That we collectively "know" a great deal more about life beyond the grave than we do about life in the middle of life, in its night, no doubt attests to our culture's hysteria about the prospect of the wake; but the oddly displaced "knowledge" attests as well to a collective hysteria about what it means to have to be alive at all. Compensatorily, then, the *Wake* moves our attention into the cemetery only to pull it back into the middle of life, into the obscure "seemetery" of sleep, so to deepen the "mountainy molehill" it found there by addressing the "clearobscure" question "why is limbo where is he"? (256.23). Where do people get all their ideas of "other worlds," and what enables them to describe "the Hereweareagain Gaieties of the Afterpiece" (455.24) so elaborately?

Any number of items elicited from the "tropped head" of the man lying embedded at the *Wake* will begin opening answers to this question. For "one bed night he had the delysiums that they were all queens mobbing him. Fell stiff" (379.17–18): if these terms suggest on the one hand the dreamy "delusions" sent into the "night" by "Queen Mab" (in Br. folklore, the maker of dreams)—and "full stop"—they also evoke the "Elysium" into which someone "dead to the world" has passed by "falling stiff" and entering a "seemetery." In places like these, the *Wake* suggests—as others have elaborately argued—that some unconscious reflection on the human experience of the night seems intricately entangled in even the most complex beliefs about "eternal sleep" and the existence to which it leads—because, however short an "ephumeral" it may be, sleep brings the world to its end: "Jehosophat, what doom is here!" (255.12 ["Jehoshaphat," of Joel 3 : 12, is another site of the end of the world]).[8] In the *Wake*'s "present(i)ment" of the "Real Absence" interior to a man "tropped head," then—"no thing making newthing wealthshowever" (253.8–9)—"the death he has lived through becomes the life he is to die into" (293.3–5); and out of the mundane experience endured in the "seemetery" of "everynight life" (17.33, 36), the *Wake* discovers, in all kinds of places, projections forward through the cemetery into a presumed "nexistence" (366.2)—a "next existence," met in "inexistence," after "death" (L. *nex*). Because he is asleep, the man "tropped head" at the *Wake* is already in an "other world" (91.25)—one radically alien to and cryptically occulted from the world accessible to the light of "day's reasons" (347.24)—but an "other world" from whose experience people seem to have derived ideas of what other "other worlds" might be like.[9] Passage through a night in the "seemetery" moreover palpably embeds in human experience a sense of what it is to fall down "dead to the world" and to undergo a spectral transit through a dark "noughttime" at whose sunstruck latter end, after encountering shades and shadows and sometimes harrowing hell, one hurls back an immobilizing rock and undergoes a resurrection of the body into the sun's day, at the pearly gates of dawn, under an eastering blade of matitudinal light: "Array! Surrection!" (593.2–3 [the "insurrectionary" note is of the "Easter Rising"]).

The genuine mystery lying at the heart of all resurrection and solar myths emerges in miniature, but with undiminished strangeness, in any thinking about the "solarsystemised" process of sleep (263.24), which draws everybody in the world "seriolcosmically" (263.24–25) through periodic cycles of nonbeing and being, snuffing out and resurrecting lives like "Finnegan's" according to the design of "an archetypt" immanent in "one . . . original sun" (263.27 [an "archetype" manifest in the "sun," in turn manifesting an "architect" of "original sin"]). This "solarsystematized" arrangement builds into the architecture of the world "a sot of a swigswag, systomy dystomy, which everabody you ever anywhere at all doze. Why? Such me" (597.21–22): the "doze" here calls attention to the periodic alternation of "doing and dozing" in a world rocked under "one original sun," just as the "swigswag" of that tipsy "sot" calls attention to the alternation of "blacking out" and enlightened "sorting-out" in "everabody" given to "feeling aslip and wauking up" (597.12)—and just as the "systole" and "diastole" in "systomy dystomy" call attention to the flood and ebb of blood in the heart. Why these periods suffuse "everabody" is a fathomless question ("Search me!"), but a question nonetheless implanted in "everybody's" "body" ("Such is me"). It raises the "cyclological" question (220.30–31) of why anyone involuntarily made to "drop down dead" (323.19) in the "seemetery" of the night should wake up at all, rather than "camp camp camp[ing]" off into eternity cultivating an extremely long "blank memory." As it occurs unconsciously to the man lying "dead to the world" at the *Wake*, "I'd like myself to be continued" (452.10–11). The *Wake* in turn, now construing itself as "Tobecontinued's tale" (626.18), discovers in its to-be-continued hero's "ephumeral" disappearance in the "seemetery" of night a protoversion of other stories bearing on the "resurrection of the body" into the light of new life.[10] "The descent to the underworld is what happens to every human being when he goes to sleep. The question what is life turns out to be the question what is sleep."[11]

At the *Wake* now, as at the wake, "postmartem is the goods" (455.11–12), and "the coffin" becomes "a triumph of the illusionist's art" (66.27). And in turn, a story already "terribly difficult" to "tell" because of its emplacement in a body "laid to rust" in a "seemetery" becomes even slightly more "Tellibly Divilcult" (303.F1)—the undertones here hinting at "devil cults" because "Tobecontinued's tale" opens fantasmal perspectives on unending "nekropolitan nights" (80.1–2). Out of the "graphplots" aligned in the *Wake*'s "seemetery," accordingly, a "night of the Apophanypes" unfolds (626.4–5), a "hallowe'en night" (49.24), which affords us, as a literary "present(i)ment" of what "the presence (of a curpse)" must "sink" (628.10 [not "think"]), as it passes from one world to the next, an "epiphany" of the "Apocalypse" (hence "Apophanypes")—so to raise a great deal of hell and pull a little heaven to earth in order to bring both to light. For in this "book of the depth" (621.3), where "every hollow holds a hallow" (25.13–14), "its never dawn in the dark but the deed comes to life" (328.27–28).[12]

The *Wake* now becomes something of a "fulldress Toussaint's Wakeswalks Experdition" (455.5–6), holding out a "spictre" (299.5) of "new worlds for all!" and all "scotographically arranged" (412.2–3). While the reference to "Madame Tussaud's Waxworks Exhibition" reminds us that the man lying "dead to the world" in this "seemetery" has all the headwork of a waxwork dummy, it also suggests that he passes, while enduring a "wake"-like "perdition," into the dark of an "All Hallows' Eve" (Fr. *La Toussaint*) at whose resurrective latter end lies a "Lets All Wake Brickfaced" (359.27–28 [for "breakfast," no matter how rigorously "brick-faced"]). "So for e'er fare thee welt!," as a priest at the *Wake* puts it, "Parting's fun"! (454.1–2 [Ger. *Welt*, "world"]). "Nearvanashed" (61.18 ["Nirvana"]), the man "tropped head" at this *Wake* has passed through "the Gate of Hal" (535.5 ["hell"]) and dwells "hells where" (228.6), "in those wherebus" (239.30 ["Erebus"]) of "Veiled Horror" (156.32–33 ["Valhalla"]), "Holl Hollow" (565.2), or "Had Days" (229.13 ["Hades"]): the homey appearance of our friend "Hal" in that "gate of hell," however, tells us that his passage into an "other world" has happened not in mythic or geographic space, but interior to a body that "Had Days" when it was awake but now, "nearly vanished" in the "seemetery" of night, does not, having entered an "other world" webbed of "veiled horrors" and "hollows" and located "elsewhere" from the one open to "day's reason." Or again, having come to the end of his day on earth, our "supernoctural" hero (598.17 ["supernatural" because "nocturnal"]) finds himself translated into a "dimdom done" (594.6) blissfully void of conflict largely because he "sleeps in peace, in peace," in "peace peace perfectpeace!" (583.10, 364.20; 549.12).[13] As these examples suggest, the *Wake*'s extensive "graphplots" are "erebusqued" (38.3–4) with all the underworlds and otherworlds in the world ("erebusqued" combines "arabesqued" and "Erebus"), ultimately to make the book something of a "multilingual tombstone" (392.24–25); but these "yonderworld[s]" emerge here not because Joyce's "knock[ed] out" hero, gifted largely with the capacity to "no," "knows" Old Norse or Greek, for instance—let alone the "wherebus" of his head and toes (239.30)—but because a version of them all becomes immanent in sleep's "ephumeral," and in the nullity bubbled up in the "tropped head" passed into the "seemetery" of the night.

One way of putting into perspective what now threatens to be a survey of world eschatology, and of showing how the *Wake* might well be read as a literary "present(i)ment" of the darkly colorful nullity interior to "the presence (of a curpse)," would be to "rearrive," "by a commodius vicus of recirculation," at the opening pages of the book, once again to "take our review of the two mounds" (12.19–20 [of "humptyhillhead" and "tumptytumtoes"]). This "review of the two mounds," of course, will differ considerably from anything like *La revue des deux mondes*; for if in wakeful life the man lying "dead to the world" at his *Wake* "lives" in "*le monde*" (Fr., "the world"), at his "ephumeral" in the "seemetery," by contrast, he merely "leaves" (353.10 [not "lives"]), and in something much more like le "mound" (17.29, 18.3)—interior to which, as a glance at the "relief map" will suggest, *le monde* has disintegrated severely.[14] If the disturbingly earthy "humptyhillhead" "laid to rust" in that muddily obscure "bed" on the opening page of the *Wake* cannot find its toes or distinguish "sopjack" from "abjects," it is "becorpse" (509.32), from this perspective, it has disintegrated into a sodden parity with a terrain that muddily seeps back in, all boundaries separating it from the global totality of its native earth having melted. In a turn of "the vermicular" that puts a new slant on the name, le "mound" is all that "Headmound," "our mounding's mass," holds in his "tropped head" and can "no" (he is also given the "abusive name" "*Dirt*" more than once at his *Wake* [71.5, 72.13]). These ciphers, then, show him endearingly "being humus" (18.5), as he lies in a "seemetery," teeming with a "blank memory" the size of which only a Wakean "tomestone" could ever articulate, accoutred in "**h**is **E**ddems and **C**lay's hat" (278.F7), amid "clayed sheets" (546.1), "his clay feet, swarded in verdigrass" (7.30 ["verdigris" accumulates on humanoid figures that do not move]), participating in a *castomercies mudwake surveice*" (349.25 [not a "customary midweek service," but a "survey" of "mud" by the person "cast to mercy" at his "wake"]). Underlying everything in Joyce's "bog of the depths," one finds some such "spictre" as this, revealing "Morbus O' Somebody"—Finnegan—drifting through loam at the speed of dark in a "bed" in an obscure "seemetery." Essentially these figures evoke the unconsciousness of sleep; but because they do so, they inevitably hold forth a "present(i)ment" of the "explots" befalling "the presence (of a curpse)" when it passes through the "seemetery" and into another world—here an earthy "underworld" in which, "being humus, the same roturns" (18.5) "by a commodius vicus of recirculation" to its "hume sweet hume" (80.18; 261.5, 481.21, 606.16), where it awaits a future "resurrection of the body" and "very merry Incarnations in this land of the livvey" (308.19–20).

These nuances in the "vermicular" now oblige us to see further that the *Wake*, because sleep does, takes place "all underground" (113.32, passim), and not metaphorically. Since the perceptions withdraw from the world outside the body in sleep, to fall "back in the flesh" (67.5–6), sleep leaves one "buried" (131.15, passim), but "buried" within an animate sort of loam— "red loam" (469.3 [Heb. *Adam*])—and all the more deeply because "humus" and the "human" ("earthling") are etymologically entangled in each other (*NS*, 12). We might, then, think of the figure shown "outlined aslumbered" in the "relief map" as "Tommy Terracotta" (481.32), or more simply, as "*Terry Cotter*" (71.22) since he just lies there "being humus," brain-void and immobile as an earthenware or "terra cotta" figurine—though implicitly informed with the human.[15] Now in the night, "every morphyl man of us . . . falls back into this terrine" (80.22–23 ["tureens" are made of "terra cotta"]), "where indeeth we shall calm decline, our legacy unknown" (79.17). "Morphyl" here suggests "mortal," of course, because our hero is "dead to the world" and at a loss to know where "they drugged the buddhy" (602.26–27 [the "drugs" "knock out"; the "Buddha" in the "body" shows it "nearvanashed"]); but it also plays off the Gr. *morphê* ("shape"), out of which arises Morpheus, in Greek myth the son of Sleep and "shape-shifting" maker of dreams. If the line suggests on the one hand that in sleep "We vivvy soddy. All be dood" (264.F1 ["very sorry," "all is dead" and buried in "sod"]), it also suggests that the "terrain" in which everything is "blurried" is the dream-stirred, "vivid sod" of the living body. It is in the animate underground of this sort of red loam that the *Wake*, because sleep does, takes place.

"The sole [and 'soul'] of the settlement, below ground" (392.21), the man "tropped head" and "buried" at this *Wake* now becomes a "belowes hero" (343.17) in another sense: "a locally person of caves" (365.2), lying everywhere encrypted beneath "the manyoumeant," his life in the night takes place in an "underground heaven, or mole's paradise" (76.33, cf. 483.27)—or, more elaborately, in a "rambling undergroands" (481.15 [where the "rambling groans" in this "rumbling underground" will lead to the production of dreams]). "Dead to the world" as he may be, "**he c**ontinues highlyfictional, tumulous under **h**is **c**hthonic **e**xterior" (261.17–18)—where the signs of "tumultuous" "chthonic" activity in the "tumulus" (or "tomb") suggest that underworldly "spirits" haunt "our mounding's mass" as much as they haunt Finnegan, and as much as they haunt any "mound or barrow" (479.23–24).

"Hollow," yet "all-hallowed," the "darkumound" (386.20–21) of which the *Wake*, as literary "document," is a "present(i)ment," now becomes an "ollollowed ill" ("hill") riffed and stirred with "spirits" (7.33–34 [the "ills" keep us "in bed"]). By another turn of "the vermicular," then, we might think of le "mound" shown in Relief Map B as "Spooksbury" (442.7), or "Soulsbury" (541.29), or "Haunted Hillborough" (340.34), or, less transparently, as "Finsbury" (374.28), "Danesbury" (372.17), or "Edenberry" (66.17–18)—where the "burryripe" "burryberr[y]" in the last of these names (291.11, 376.28) would indicate that the man "tropped head" there is "all reddy berried" and "dead to the world" (421.6 ["already buried"]), but only in a vegetative state like sleep (hence the frequent spelling of "bury" as "berry" in *Finnegans Wake*).[16] As a totality, these ciphers show the man "tropped head" at the *Wake*—"sir ghostus" (532.4)—"ghosting himself" (501.32) as he lies "interred in the landscape" shown in the "relief map" (*L*, I, 254). At the same time, however, they also map out a richly extended "netherworld" (571.35) teeming with chthonic agencies that seek to erupt out of le "mound" and return into *le monde*, to wreak havoc with the world of the living and the day. Archetypal depth psychologies locate chthonic powers such as these in immaterial "depths," in the "underworld" of an Unconscious that lies not merely below ground, but "below the earth and beyond it," always and everywhere underlying the visible surface of things.[17] But in the nocturnal underworld treated at the *Wake*—an "underworld of nighties and naughties and all the other wonderwearlds" (147.28)—we should expect, as the terms imply, a great deal of this chthonic mayhem to erupt somewhere in the occulted region of our hero's "underwhere" (365.11–12 ["underwear"]), it, too, always and everywhere underlying the visible surface of the daily world (hence the "nighties" and the "underwear" evident in those "wonderwearlds"). "See relief map" (564.10 and context).[18]

One way of putting some of these new properties of the "mound" into a context, and of showing how subterranean forces stir inside it, would entail moving forward into a row of Wakean "graphplots" that show the man "dead to the world" in a "seemetery"—now construed as "Donawhu" (76.32 ["Don't know who"])—leading a "plotty existence" (76.18) in "a protem grave" (76.21) localized as usual "in the bed" (76.32). These terms suggest that though "his body still persist[s]" (76.20), it has not moved a great deal since he "tropped head" at the start of the *Wake*, having lain there statically "the whole of the while (*hypnos chilia eonion!*) lethelulled" (78.3–4), in a state "rich in death anticipated" (78.6). We read, however, of some "underground" force that seeks, while "knowing the hingeworms of the hallmirks of habitationlesness, buried burrowing in Gehinnon, to proliferate through all his Unterwealth, seam by seam, sheol om sheol, and revisit our Uppercrust Sideria of Utilitarios . . ." (78.8–11). Most of this language evokes the "eyewitless foggus" of somebody who is "dead to the world": the deceased as described in the Egyptian Book of the Dead were supposed to pass through and "know the hingemarks of the murky hallmarks" in a "habitationless" underworld in order to rise from the grave into new life;[19] and the references to the Biblical graveyard of "Gehenna" (Jer. 19:6), to "sheol" (Heb. "the grave"), and to "seams" of earth and "iron-mines" (Gr. *sidêreia*) embed us deeply in the "Underworld" (Ger. *Unterwelt*) of a "seemetery." As that furtive "burrowing" suggests, however, a dark vitality is alive in le "mound," prodding "the presence (of a curpse)" to seek the "upper crust" of earth and return to the "utilitarian" world of "siderial day." "How hominous his house, haunt it? Yesses indead it be!" (560.17–18 ["Yesses" = "Jesus!," a riser]). But because "upper crust" is also slang for "the head," we might see this "burrowing" agency striving simply to lift the "tropped head" upward out of the "seemetery" of sleep into perceptual vitality.

Purposive and urgent enough to transform a "Gehenna" into a "Gehinnon" (Ger. *geh hinnen*, "Get out of here!"), this "burrowing" progresses in a direction whose end is made clear by countless other passages that find the man lying "dead to the world" in the *Wake*'s "seemetery" "wurming along gradually" (84.30) through the "burrows" and "barrows" of "Soulsbury"; for this "burrowing" primarily moves with "burning" determination, "toborrow and toburrow and tobarrow" (455.12–13), "to burrow burning" (602.17–18 [toward "tomorrow and tomorrow" and "tomorrow morning"]): "Will it ever be next morning"? (66.10). The ciphers tell us that "deeds bounds going arise again" (55.5 ["These bones gwine to rise again!"]), "in the quicktime" (560.9 [morning]); but since we are sharing the "eyewitless foggus" of some-one embedded in a "seemetery," they also suggest that as far as "the presence (of a curpse)" can "no," "these bones" might be preparing to rise again "in the quicklime," as they murkily gather themselves together and move from "Yet stir thee, to clay, Tamor!" (255.4 [in the secret Irish tongue of *Bog* Latin, *tamor* means "earth," but the whole "vermicular" construction moves us through "yesterday, today, tomorrow"]). In the "noughttime," from this per-spective, "one world [is] burrowing on another" (275.5–6); for the "spirits" of anyone who has come to the end of his day on earth and "tropped head," disintegrating with an Old World (of yesterday and the past in all conceiv-able senses) only seek, after an annihilative gap of time in the "seemetery," "toborrow and toburrow and tobarrow" toward a resurrection of the body in a New World (of tomorrow and the future in all conceivable senses). In "To-becontinued's tale," then, as in others involving the resurrection of the body, the "spirits" are intent on returning to earth to gratify dark appetites and yearnings that arise in the "wonderwearld"—as, for instance, the appetite for "breakfarts" (453.12) or "Breakfates" (131.4).[20]

As these brief readings "in the vermicular" will suggest, the *Wake* goes about its "present(i)ment" of life in the "seemetery" so colorfully as to make a reading of "Finnegan's" "explots" at his "ephumeral" unending. Every "graphplot" in the *Wake*'s "epistola of . . . buryings" (117.28) opens onto "fresh horrors from Hades" (183.35), when not "striking up funny fu-nereels" (414.35), because a "present(i)ment" of essential unconscious-ness—"Real Absence"—was crucial to Joyce's reconstruction of the night. There are "coughings all over the sanctuary" at the *Wake* (26.26)—though the "coughing" distinctly heard in that "coffin" tells us that the man "tropped head" within it is not really "dead to the world" at all, but merely "dead to the world." As the nagging persistence of that indistinction between the twin unconsciousnesses of sleep and death suggests, these are not finally, either for Joyce or his reader, merely gamey issues, but visceral ones. By pulling one's attention into the "seemetery" of night, the *Wake* obliges its reader everywhere to discriminate between "the sleep and the ghoasts" (551.2–3)—between the "Real Absence[s]" of "sleep" and of "ghosts," as between "the sheep and the goats," and as if at "the end of the world" (hence again those "sheep and the goats"). Inevitably, it leaves its reader wondering what internally differentiates sleep and death. Inevitably, too, it leaves him meditating on what it must be to be the star of the show at a wake.

The only predictable certainty about any human life is that it will culminate in an event at which, but for one, there will be some "fun for all." Everybody knows it, and everybody has a shadowy account of what it will mean to be "propelled from Behind into the great Beyond" (49.25) as the last in a steady sequence of rude kicks delivered from the rear assails one unexpectedly on that "one finel howdiedow [when] Bouncer Naster raps on the bell with a bone" (455.13–14). Well may this "Pater Noster" resolve into a "Nasty" barroom "Bouncer" then, as he extends this "fine howdy-do" on that "fine final day" that will signal the end of the world and time ("on the bell"). The further out of consciousness one keeps one's own shady account of the wake, the more bearable life in its middle may be; yet its presence in the background, as both "The Dead" and the "Hades" episode of *Ulysses* suggest, everywhere exerts a force on the foreground and so determines the way life is lived in its middle—and all the more powerfully as death, already one of the "catastrophic cataclysms which make terror the basis of human mentality" (*U*, 697), is susceptible to profound moralization and institutionalization under the "awethorrorty" (516.19) of "Bouncer Naster." The *Wake*, like the wake, brings this "spectracular" event to the fore, to explore its power on the living.

In *The New Science*, Vico establishes an etymological equivalence between "humanity" and *humando* (L. "burying"), anthropologically reinforcing the identity by calling attention to the strangeness of that moment in prehistory in which an aspect of human consciousness flickered up out of animality as our forebears stopped leaving the corpses of their parents to rot, the prey of scavenging beasts, and instituted, in the custom of burial, "a great principle of humanity" (*NS*, 12, 337, 529). His observations suggest that consciousness of death and consciousness as a totality cannot be disentangled: one is the condition of the other. In another form, the same story is told in Genesis, concerning "*Der Fall Adams*" (70.5 [Ger. "the case of Adam"]), who underwent, through the paradoxically "fortunate fall"— "the great fall" (3.18)—an uplifting ascent into knowledge of good and evil and an immediate fall into knowledge of death. Both Vico and Genesis make an aspect of death as much a human creation as a fact of nature. "Human beings appear to be unique among the fauna inhabiting the 'biosphere' that coats the planet in being aware that they themselves and all their contemporaries are going to die, and that death has overtaken countless generations";[21] "animals are unaware of death because death is a symbolic form" (cf. *U*, 46, 101).[22] The story one has in a mind potentiated by death of what its death will entail, then, wields the power of any symbol in having the capacity to shrivel or magnify life where it is always and only known, in its middle—as Joyce, educated into a Catholicism that rendered life in its middle subservient to the demands of a moralized afterlife, would well have known (*P*, III).

"Numerous are those who, nay, there are a dozen of folks still unclaimed by the death angel in this country of ours today, humble indivisibles in this grand continuum . . . who, while there are hours and days, will fervently pray to the spirit above that they may never depart this earth of theirs" (472.28–33). Yet in the "semitary of Somnionia," "dead to the world" as Finnegan, each of these dozens is as unconscious as he will ever have occasion to know: "if he was to parish . . . before the dorming of the mawn"—before "the dawning of the morn," while "dorming" under the "moon"—"he skuld never ask to see sight or light of this world or the other world or any either world" either (91.23–25). Like Bloom during his gentle descent into "Hades," not least, the *Wake* suggests that something so natural, inevitable, and commonplace need not inevitably fill us with horror and fear, aspects of which, as states of mind and not facts of nature, are evolved out of relations with a punitive "Bouncer Naster." It goes about scattering this fear, moreover, through the exercise of great good humor and restless curiosity, so to demonstrate by the casting of light words over dark subjects, a conversion of gravity into levity, and the raising of spirits of all kinds, that the humor, pleasure, and curiosity expended during a limited "lease on mirth" (329.19 ["leases" expire, too]) is one best and ample means to a meeting of "peace on earth" and its end.

If being "dead to the world," "of corpse" (254.32), were all that "everynight life" entailed—"(Oh hell, here comes our funeral . . .)" (190.2–3)—nobody would ever go to sleep at all and everybody would die of protracted insomnia. Yet as we experience it, "in our own nighttime," sleep is pleasantly revitalizing and invigorating, culminating as it does in "Array! Surrection!" (593.2–3 [and a sundazzled "resurrection" of the body]). "Finnegan's" spooky experience, therefore, is only the bottommost layer in a book whose "every word will be bound over to carry threescore and ten toptypsical readings" (20.14–15); as it occurs to the man "tropped head" at his *Wake* at a moment in which he murkily rises out of "the living detch" to "shake off the dust and dream" (8.22, 280.35), "that's enough . . . of finicking about Finnegan and fiddling with his faddles" (531.27–29). Although there is, as these lines imply, a great deal more to *Finnegans Wake* than an extended reconstruction of "Real Absence" and the interior of the "tropped head"— not least an exploration of a night's warm dreams—"nefersenless" (415.33 [and "nevertheless"]) "this is not the end of this by no manner means" (373.35–36). For death, as the reference to the ancient Egyptian city of "Nefer-sent" implies, has a long, dark history, and the grave has historicized depths that lead downward into "the deep deep deeps of Deepereras. Buried hearts. Rest [t]here" (595.28–29).

Further study of Finnegan's "explots" in the "seemetery" therefore obliges us to "wurm along" a little more deeply "in dead men's hills" (352.31–32), by drawing illustratively on the "new science" of Egyptology and moving into "Aeships" (625.4 [or "Egypt"]). There, among "tomb people" (hence the Gael. *Aos-sidhe* in "Aeships"), somewhere "in Amongded" (418.6 ["among dead" in "Amentet," an Egyptian realm of the dead]), "we shall do a far walk (O pity) anygo khaibits" (570.28–29) as we contemplate, with "Ba's berial," the invention of the cemetery, the construction of a formalized afterlife, and the history of Western death (415.31 ["Amentet" was home of the Egyptian *khaibit*, or "shadow," and *ba*, or "soul"]). And there, too, as we "thothfully" consider "the silence of the dead, from pharoph the nextfirst down to ramescheckles the last bust thing" (415.28, 450.20–21 [with "Thoth" and "Ramses"]), we shall find sleep everywhere intimately linked by a form of dark and "secret hook-up" with "Secret Hookup" itself (360.16 [as with "Sekhet Hetep," the Egyptians' otherworldly "fields of peace"]).

"Finnegan"

CHAPTER FOUR

Inside the Coffin: Finnegans Wake *and the* Egyptian Book of the Dead

PHARAOPH TIMES

Mortuary literatures and funerary texts, as at all wakes, assume an enormous importance at Joyce's *Wake*. Sensibly, Joyce seems to find in them not only previsionary accounts of life beyond the grave, but also elaborate meditations on the experience of sleep. Since a thorough study of the use to which Joyce put myths of afterlives and other worlds in *Finnegans Wake* would in itself make a book, this chapter will undertake a reading of one particular mortuary text—the Egyptian Book of the Dead—that the *Wake* draws upon heavily in its portrayal of its hero's existence in the "semitary of Somnionia" (594.8). A treatment of the Book of the Dead, in turn, will suggest how the *Wake* bends other mythographies of postmortality into its reconstruction of the human dark.

It is impossible to overlook the vital presence of the Book of the Dead in *Finnegans Wake*, which refers to ancient Egypt in countless tags and allusions. When Joyce refers to his protagonist as a man not of "the hidden life," but of "the Hidden Life" (499.15), for instance, he is translating one of the names of the Egyptian underworld—Amenti ("the Hidden Land")—and the name of one of its prominent deities—Amen-Ra ("Ra, the Hidden One").[1] When he comments—in the phrase "To it, to it! Seekit headup!"

(454.35–36)—on the celestial aspiration that causes people to look upward toward heaven ("seek it head-up"), he is comparably alluding not only to "Sekhet Hetep" (cf. 415.34–35), but to the "Tuat," another name for the Egyptian afterworld. And when he describes the "Toussaints' wakewalks ex-perdition" as a "chamber of horrus" (455.5–6), he is alluding particularly to the mortuary locale of the "Chamber of Horus."

There are several good reasons for approaching *Finnegans Wake*, and its treatment of the wake, through a reading of the Book of the Dead. Joyce ac-tively sought to have somebody write an essay exploring the *Wake*'s af-finities with this text: as he explained in a letter to Harriet Shaw Weaver, one of the "4 long essays" in that testamentary collection which he planned to have follow *Our Exagmination* was to examine specifically the *Wake*'s re-construction of the night by reference to the Book of the Dead (*L*, I, 281; *JJ*, 613–14). Undiscouraged by his failure to recruit anyone to compile this un-written work, he became more direct and advised Frank Budgen to compose an article on *Finnegans Wake* entitled "James Joyce's Book of the Dead."[2] Budgen seems dutifully to have done this in an essay published as "Joyce's Chapters of Going Forth By Day," which, apart from its title and a casual reference, has much of value to say about the *Wake* but little to do with the Book of the Dead.[3] In the course of four decades, nonetheless, readers of the *Wake* motivated by this kind of heavy hinting have for the most part fulfilled Joyce's wishes by showing us how intricately the *Wake* alludes to the Book of the Dead.[4] Still, even the most learned of these readers have seemed uncer-tain at times of the exact portion and significance of their labors. While a consideration of "Finnegan's Wake" will have suggested the broad reasons for which Joyce would in part have modeled the *Wake*—his own book of the dead—on its Egyptian prototype, only a close examination of the Book of the Dead itself will provide more detailed answers to larger questions that any reader is likely to have about much that he meets in the *Wake*: What does the *Wake* have to do with a wake? What does either have to do with an "imitation of the dream-state"? And, above all, what does a reconstruction of the night have to do with such archaic and arcane cultural oddments as the Book of the Dead, which one finds everywhere in the *Wake*? Since Joyce clearly regarded the Book of the Dead as one of his conceptual models, some sense of its structure must precede an account of its exact role in *Finne-gans Wake*.

In its own elusive form of symbolic language the Book of the Dead af-fords us probably the oldest, most impassioned, and most fiercely sustained glimpse into events occurring at and beyond the moment of the wake that

Inside the Coffin

people of this world have ever enacted. More perhaps than any other culture, ancient Egypt has impressed upon us a paradoxical truth about the way in which our consciousness depends upon the passage into unconsciousness of past generations of men at their wakes: we know what kind of life these people enjoyed before death largely because they were so heavily preoccupied with life after death; "most of the surviving products of past generations are parts of the equipment with which they furnished the dead."[5] As the archaeological testimony of its tombs and pyramids alone suggests (62.20–21, 261.9, 553.10), dynastic Egypt was among the most necrocentric culture that this planet has known. The literature that survives from dynastic Egypt consists almost entirely of texts that were engraved into the walls of tombs, carved all over the insides and outsides of coffins, or laid beside the corpse on papyri. Even those odd documents that describe the mundane work and play of the ancient Egyptians come to us primarily out of tombs; and they tell us that even in those most convivially abandoned of times in which the wealthy hosted dances and parties, the specter of the tomb loomed large in the imaginations of the celebrants. It was a custom at Egyptian parties for someone to sing a dirge reminding all those present that the day of their own deaths was approaching; "in some cases, to drive this lesson home into the minds of the company, the host had a mummy on a sledge drawn through the dining hall."[6] As this illustration suggests, the ancient Egyptians seem to have thought about their mortality with more persistence and intensity than any other people who have lived. Indeed, as a reading of the Book of the Dead will attest, they seem to have begun preparing for their deaths as soon as they began to think.

There is, in fact, no such single work as the Book of the Dead: the title conventionally given to this odd cultural document is at best a makeshift name, adopted by scholarly convention, which comes to us by one of the most unprincipled etymological histories on record. Egyptologists adopted this title through their barterings with graverobbers, who, over the course of centuries, had come to refer to any piece of writing lifted from the desert tombs as a "deadman's book" or a "book of the dead."[7] The accuracy with which this informal title suits the content of the *Wake*, nonetheless, should by now be immediately apparent.

As Joyce scholastically pointed out to Budgen—apparently in that season in which he tried to prod Budgen into writing "James Joyce's Book of the Dead"—the title by which the Egyptians themselves knew the Book of the Dead, insofar as they knew any such odd scattering of documents as now lies before us by any single formal title at all, was the *Chapters of Com-*

ing Forth By Day, a title which throws an entirely different light on the content within.[8] The meaning latent in this "real" title, of course, suggests how Joyce would have found in the Book of the Dead's account of life in the "seemetery" a covert psychology of sleep; like the *Wake*, it turns out that the Book of the Dead can be read in either of two ways: as the stream of unconsciousness of a man dead to the world, or as the stream of unconsciousness of a man sleepily dead to the world. That Joyce was conscious of this kind of bivalent readability in his source is suggested by one of the hundred odd alternative titles for the *Wake*—and here, the Book of the Dead as well—that he lists at the beginning of chapter I.v: *"How to Pull a Good Horuscoup when Oldsire is Dead to the World"* (105.28–29). The line evokes the underlying spiritual drama on which the Book of the Dead is based: the resurrection into light of the dead god "Osiris" through the agency of his son "Horus," a resurrection which every mortal Egyptian was understood personally to reenact, with the help of the gods, after his death; but it also clearly refers to the restful sleep of the old man ("Oldsire") who lies embedded at the *Wake*, hosting premonitory, because wish-fulfilling, dreams (hence the "horoscope").[9]

As a collective cultural document, the many "Chapters of Coming Forth by Day" that make up the Book of the Dead comprise a widely varied series of "spells and incantations, hymns and litanies, magical formulae and names, [and] words of power and prayers," which together were supposed to serve the deceased man both as a guidebook to the unearthly topographies of the next world and as a catalogue of verbal talismans, reference to which would rescue him from the many dangers and hostile demons that he was expected to meet there.[10] Singly, however, none of the papyri, stone carvings, mummy bandages, amulets, "show coffins, winding sheets, . . . urns," or shards of pottery on which the words of the Book of the Dead have been found quite exactly resemble one another (77.28–29): no two of these deadman's books are identical. While Egyptologists have determined that all these sepulchral texts share many common elements—often, indeed, whole chapters inherited over a long tradition—they have also discovered that each dead man had his own eclectically personalized version of the deadman's book; while two deadmen's books might contain some of the same chapters, moreover, the chapters might be written entirely differently.

From these observations, archaeologists have inferred that every individual who could afford it consulted with his priests and scribes in the course of his lifetime and more or less ordered—as one might today order the furnishings of a living room—the writing of a guidebook that would answer his own particular needs and desires in the next world.[11] The personalized document cited here as the Book of the Dead, accordingly, deserves a title both more and less definitive. Since it is only one individualized version of thousands of books of the dead, it might more accurately be construed as *The Scribe Ani's Book of the Dead,* or, more resonantly, *Ani's Wake;* even more accurately, since it deals with events that led Ani to his resurrection into daylight after his wake, it might be entitled *Ani's Chapters of Coming Forth By Day*—or again, as *Ani Wakes.* A comparison likening a document this personal to the private furnishings of a living room, moreover, is not at all facetious: the Papyrus of Ani was painted over years, both by Ani himself and by hired scribes, on a roll of papyrus almost eighty feet long;[12] at Ani's funeral, it went into a tomb consisting of seventeen rooms, together with "vases full of wine, beer, oil, perfumes, flowers, bread, cakes, ducks, haunches of beef, and vegetables"; with the tools that Ani used to make a living in life, as well as with his bed, his pillow, his harp, his chairs and couches; with *ushabti* statuettes—magically to be evoked into life in the next world—of servants and beasts of burden;[13] and with Ani's body, which had been mummified over a period of seventy days, wrapped in linen bandages inscribed with words from the Book of the Dead, and hermetically sealed inside of two thickly veneered coffins of sycamore wood, the inner one anthropoid, each of which was written over with more words from the Book of the Dead.[14]

Less wealthy Egyptians seem to have furnished their dead with less opulent tombs—and, correspondingly, with less opulent editions of the Book of the Dead: they apparently purchased briefer, ready-made copies of books of the dead from the establishments of local scribes, who kept in stock a selection of these documents varying in length, quality, and content and who would, once the purchase was negotiated, fill the dead man's name into blank spaces in the prefabricated papyrus just before the funeral.[15] Even the poor man had his little variant of this general cultural document: wrapped in linen and laid in an open grave with his new pair of sandals and a walking stick meant to lighten his future travels, the corpse of the poor man was furnished with a few inscribed amulets and tokens intended to guard him from dangers to be met in the next life.[16]

Written roughly fourteen centuries before the birth of Christ, according to Budge's chronology, the Papyrus of Ani shares enough common elements with other books of the dead to have enabled Egyptologists to classify it as one of the many "Theban recensions"—that is, as one of several variations of the Book of the Dead which, because of their common properties, were written at a historical moment in which Thebes was a center of power in the Egyptian kingdom. And, as many students of the *Wake* have noted, "the thieves' rescension" (410.36–411.1 [or "Theban recension"]) is the one that Joyce studied when he wrote the *Wake:* indeed, his hero is "hinted at in the eschatological chapters of Humphrey's *Justesse of the Jaypees* and hunted for by Theban recensors who sniff there's something behind the *Bug of the Deaf*" (134.34–36).[17] While Atherton rightly suggests that Joyce probably consulted the Papyrus of Ani in writing *Finnegans Wake*, isolated passages in the book show that Joyce drew on another Theban recension of another deadman's book, the Papyrus of Nu: "the overseer of the house of the oversire of the seas, Nu-men, triumphant, sayeth" (493.30–31).[18] This line echoes the opening invocations in chapters of Nu's Book of the Dead, as the name "Numen" implies: "the steward of the overseer of the seal, Nu, . . . begotten of the steward of the overseer of the seal, Amen-hetep, . . . saith";[19] and it differs from comparable invocations in the Papyrus of Ani ("the scribe Ani saith"). There is, furthermore, another Theban recension of yet another deadman's book situated in Dublin, in its museum; and since Stephen Dedalus alludes knowingly to divinities of the Egyptian pantheon in *A Portrait* and *Ulysses*, it is not inconceivable that Joyce would have been aware of it.[20]

The *Wake*'s assimilation of these distinct papyri suggests not only how broadly Joyce studied this material, but also how organically he would have contoured all of it into the designs of *Finnegans Wake*. Since each copy of the Book of the Dead has as its subject a real individual, each copy of the book inherently differs from all others; yet because two distinct books of the dead, one written for a scribe, and one for a steward of the overseer of the seals, might each contain traditionally prescribed chapters identical in all matters but those of naming and phrasing, the documents are at the same time collective and universal. Any book of the dead, then, has at its center a hero like the *Wake*'s: a real individual like HCE who is also, dead to the world and "reduced to nothing" (499.3), like Here Comes Everybody.

"IN THE OTHERWORLD . . . OF TWO-TONGUE COMMON"

As one might expect from this account, the varying personal editions of each of the three main variant recensions of the Book of the Dead that we possess offer, at least in individual details, a confusing and often contradictory sense of what exactly life after death was supposed to be—which is only to note that even the most educated person, in the most stable period of Egyptian religious history, was uncertain of his exact position in a cosmos whose contours changed and shifted with Egyptian centers of powers and senses of the universe. Collectively, however, the scattered remains of that general cultural document now known as the Book of the Dead yield a broadly coherent sense of the cosmos within which the ancient Egyptian understood himself to spin out his days. It was a chilling and yet beautiful cosmography, whose architects poured their attention into the mapping of the landscape of a next and strange world. In their endeavors to peer beyond the grave, Egyptian cosmographers devised an elaborate mythology revelatory of a universe haunted by gods and demons who bore human bodies under the heads of serpents, jackals, apes, and birds, and who walked among blood-red lakes of fire and among fields of eternal peace. People lived under this cosmography and prepared themselves to die in it for almost five thousand years; it shaped the literate world almost three times longer than Christianity has, and seventeen times longer than Newtonian physics. The cryptic hieroglyphics of the dynastic Egyptians offer us, then, as legitimate an understanding of human mortality as does the scientific symbol-system that orders modern reality. And in its own way, this determined cultural probe into the phenomenon of the wake turns out to have much to do with the simple, mundane experience of sleep.[21]

Spatially, for example, the portals of entry into Amenti, the next world of the Egyptians, were located in exactly the same place as are the opening pages of *Finnegans Wake:* "well to the west" (3.21), at "the place where the sun set" at day's end, that point in space at which the sun left the world and moved, according to empirical observation, beyond it.[22] To the ancient Egyptians, in fact, the name "Amenti" denoted not only "the Hidden Land" and "the kingdom of the dead," but also "the West," and in particular those specific regions to the west of the Nile where they situated their necropoli and ritualistically buried their dead in order that they might find themselves near the gates of sunset and the other world.[23] A modern person, trained to know solar physics, will keep these many meanings clearly distinct from each other; but to the ancient Egyptian, they were all of a punlike unity: these people believed that somewhere in the west beyond their cemeteries there existed a concrete site at which the sun moved out of the world—through portals that Joyce's Book of the Dead, for instance, refers to as the "Ghoststown Gate" (329.25), the "Gate of Hal" (535.5), or simply sunset. The semantic blur implicit in the word "Amenti," finally, seems actually to have effected the architecting of Egyptian cities: since the west was the land of the dead, many ancient Egyptian cities sprang up in such a way that the living established their dwellings on the east bank of the Nile, while in the deserts on the western side of the river they built their spectral necropoli.[24]

Unlike other primitive peoples, the Egyptians did not believe that the sun moved underground when it sank below the horizon; nonetheless, since none of their explorers ever traveled far enough west into the mountains and sandseas of the Sahara actually to locate the place at which the sun caved into Amenti, the problems of its disappearance and of the advent of the night engaged their deepest attention. In modern times we express our anxieties about comparable problems of transport and disappearance by wondering of one another how we each get through the night. Less egotistical than we have learned to be, the ancient Egyptians expressed the same nyctophobic concern by wondering how the sun got through the night, disappearing as it did at sunset in one part of the world and reappearing in the morning in a chamber of the sky diametrically opposite. They solved these difficulties by evolving an elaborate metaphysics to explain the sheer physics of their world—a metaphysics that took as its two basic principles the manifest forms of two divine beings, both "hidden": Amen-Ra, the bearer of the sundisk, and Osiris Khent-Amenti (Lord of the Hidden Land of the Dead).

According to Egyptian cosmologists, the entire earth, consisting of Egypt and all known lands, was surrounded by a range of unapproachable mountains situated way beyond the peripheries of the visible world. Upon this ring of mountains rested the watery slab of the oceanic sky, across whose deeps daily Amen-Ra traveled with the sun, in a boat, as the Egyptians understood it, a boat infinitely more glorious than those which plied daily up and down the Nile, but nonetheless a comparable boat, since the fiery warmth of the solar disk had in some way to be sheltered from the quenching waters of the celestial sea.[25] Empirical reflection will suggest why the Egyptians should have imagined the outer boundaries of the real in these exact terms: Egyptian adventurers never succeeded in traveling the necessary four thousand miles to discover the sources of the Nile that Joyce makes so much of in the *Wake*; no matter how far they ventured, there always seemed to be another range of mountains in the distance, or an ocean which they could not cross; and water always came down out of the sky. Within the enclosed space of Egyptian reality formed by this ring of remotely pillaring mountains and the superincumbent slab of celestial waters, however, cosmologists understood there to be two openings: that through which the boat of the sun disappeared at night, and that through which it emerged in the morning; these were the two gates through which dead men, like Amen-Ra in his boat, entered or left the realm of the dead. Since the Egyptians spatially located the land of the dead in a region temporally equivalent to the night, Joyce was able to elicit from their accounts of supernature descriptions of the human night, so to bring the *Wake*, his modern book of the dead, into complete conceptual alignment with the Book of the Dead. Like Joyce, moreover, Egyptian cosmographers faced great difficulties in discovering what exactly happened beyond the world in the land of the dead.

Since the Egyptians had as much trouble imagining an infinitely extensive universe as we do today, they simplified the baffling conceptual problems generated in their mappings of supernature by proposing that a second, terminal range of mountains circumscribed that chain of remote mountains which already bounded the real world.[26] This understanding accomplished two things: first, it placed the hidden realm of the dead not in the inconceivable expanse of infinity, but in a finite, enclosed body of space, a dark ring of extraterrestrial supernature surrounding the known world; second, it implicitly defined a few of the basic features of the other world. Since people who lived and depended on the Nile naturally tended to conceive of any space between two ranges of mountains as a valley, it became understood that an infernal river flowed through the broad valley of Amenti. And since no one knew exactly where the Nile originated, it was understood that the river flowing through the other world was in some way a continuation of the Nile. As some Egyptian sepulchral texts explain it, a living being who wished to reach the kingdom of the dead could do so not only by dying or by traveling far enough west to reach the gate of sunset, but also by passing through the two black holes that had long been observed behind the waters of the Nile's First Cataract.[27] The supposition that the dead dwelled along the banks of a circular river in a dark, entunneled valley of this kind, finally, offered an economically simple explanation of the celestial physics that brought about the night: once the boat of Amen-Ra vanished through the portals of sunset in the southwest, it navigated its way gradually northward and then eastward through the enclosed, circular valley of Amenti— on a skewed plane with the earth, but outside the ring of peaks that bounded it—until it emerged triumphant, ten to twelve hours later, out of the gates of dawn.

Much of what happened in the Hidden Land of Amenti could now be determined empirically—by observing events that occurred on the northeast and southwest horizons of the sky at dawn and dusk, or by moving as close to the edges of the real world as possible. Since the sun often disappeared from the world and reentered it in emblazonments of scarlet, for instance, it became clear that there were regions of eternal fire in Amenti: the Egyptians were perhaps the first people to discover hell and to chart the circular architecture of the infernal world which, after three thousand years of modification, Dante would describe in his *Inferno*. Since the morning sun often seemed to have trouble pushing its way into the world out of dark accumulations of thunderclouds—indeed, since it had had to fight its way through the kingdom of night—cosmographers also assumed that in the ten or twelve hours between nightfall and sunrise, the gods accompanying Amen-Ra in his boat had to battle continuously against the forces of darkness.[28] What forms these forces took could be inferred from stories told by people who had in turn heard things from people who had traveled to the horizons of the earth—into the fiery regs and ergs of the Sahara and beyond the jungles of the Sudan, where explorers saw predatory beasts that rarely wandered into the everyday cosmos.[29]

From these varied fragments of concrete observation and hearsay of remote origin, Egyptian thinkers finally evolved a diffuse sense of the fate of Amen-Ra in the afterworld: in each of the twelve hours of the night in which it sailed or was towed through Amenti, according to many sepulchral documents, the boat of the sun passed through a continuum of twelve countries or kingdoms, all but one ruled and populated by demons and animalistic forces that mutilated and preyed on the souls of living things and that hungrily tried to overpower Ra and his company before they reached the gates of morning.[30] In that hour which corresponded to the deepest part of the night on earth, for instance, the sun entered the Kingdom of Seker, an archaic god of death, who ruled, eternally unseen, over a domain of "blackest darkness" and "bare, barren, sandy deserts, wherein lived monster serpents."[31] Since in this part of the underworld—and in this part alone—even the infernal river vanished from view, Ra and his company were forced to abandon the boat of the sunken sun and to move forward, through chinks of virtually impenetrable rock, in the body of a serpent out of whose mouth burned a weak, but illuminative fire.[32] In the next hour, in another kingdom, Ra boarded the boat of the rising sun, which his attendants towed upstream along "the secret road of Amenti," like a boat along the Nile, toward the gate of dawn.[33] As Ra circumnavigated his way around the cosmos through the other world, his name and form changed in ways concordant with the changed physical circumstances surrounding him: "I am the god Tem in rising"; "I am Khephera in the morning, Ra at mid-day, and Temu in

Inside the Coffin

the evening";[34] in the depths of the other world, he was called Afu-Ra ("the corpse of Ra").[35] The metempsychotic rhythms by which the name of Ra changed from Tem to Temu as he passed from the world of the living into the world of the dead and then back again were ones that Joyce carefully accommodated to the story of his sleeper, "Tim Finnegan," who also nightly falls dead to the world, and then reawakens, and then falls down dead again: his name "is Timb to the pearly morn and Tomb to the mourning night" (139.10–11 [in wakeful consciousness he knows that his name is "Tim," but when he's dead to the world, he becomes a form of "Tomb"]); and, "of course, he could call himself Tem, too, if he had time to? You butt he could anytom" (88.35–36). The nightmarish underworld through which the *Wake*'s "Timb" fluidly drifts between sunset and sunrise, however, is as much the world encountered in sleep as that which people have understood to be the world of the dead.

One final observation about the cosmological framework in which New Kingdom books of the dead are set will suggest how intricately Joyce modernized Egyptian tomb literature, much of it already consonant with the *Wake*. It is undoubtedly confusing to read in the Book of the Dead of the twelve divisions of the Egyptian afterworld, of the fourteen regions into which each such division was again subdivided, of the three hostile gods who guarded the doors of the palace in each subdivision, of the many predatory monsters who lurked in the darkness about each such palace, and of the rituals that the dead soul of Ra had to perform in order to pass all of these named and numbered obstacles: details like these, not really important to a modern reader, changed in every generation, with every slight shift of theocratic power, and in every personally varied copy of the deadman's book. As confusing as all this detail may be, the fundamental shape of the Egyptian otherworld remained nonetheless elegantly coherent, and simple in its beauty. Conceptually, as we have seen, the Egyptians envisioned this "hidden land" beyond the world as a ring of dark, navigable space circumgirding and encompassing reality; as a finite, enclosed body of space through which a circular river flowed, into which the light of the world disappeared at night, and within which the spirits of all things unearthly became manifest. But they also envisioned it as a human body— and, at least as we understand it, as a sleeping human body.

Whose body this was is made clear in every other phrase of every book of the dead, and in maps of the other world that Egyptologists have discovered among some tomb scriptures. It is the body of Osiris, the god who fell down dead to the world, like Tim Finnegan, and then came back to life: "My body is buried" . . . "I am he who is hidden in the great deep" . . . "the Hidden of Forms" . . . "I am in the Dweller in the Body" . . . "I am he who riseth and shineth" . . . "O Osiris, . . . wake up and be strong like unto Ra every day."[36] Unversed in modern cartography, ancient Egyptian priests and scribes therefore drew their problematic maps of "the Hidden Land" of Amenti in curious ways: at the top of the "map" reproduced in figure 4.1, for example, the other world is diagrammed as "the body of a man bent round backwards in such a way as to form a circle, and the toes touching the back of the head. This god is, the [inverted] text tells us, Osiris, and it is his body which forms the circle of the Tuat [another name for the Egyptian other world]."[37] In a map of the cosmos dating from a much earlier period of Egyptian history, an unnamed god—presumably "Osiris, Lord to the Uttermost Limit"—is depicted lying asleep, or dead, on his back, with his legs bent around over the front of his body to form a comparable circle; but here, Budge tells us, the void enclosed by the circular body, rather than the body itself, "is thought to represent the region where the dead live."[38]

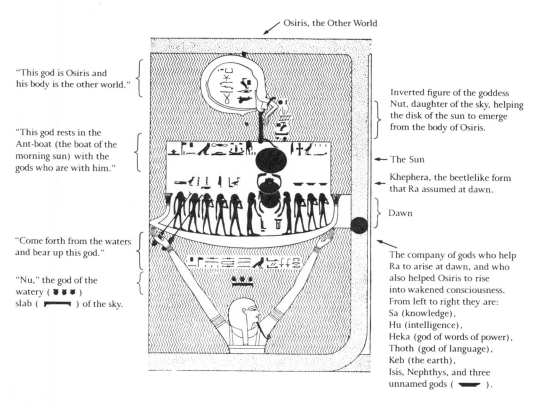

Figure 4.1. Coffin Text: Egyptian Supernature

Inside the Coffin

97

Fragments of the myth of Osiris elusively invoked in all versions of the Book of the Dead portray him as the one god in the Egyptian pantheon who came to earth and took on the mortal lineaments of humanity, reigning as a beneficent lawgiver and king of Egypt. He was, in the American idiom, permanently put to sleep by Set, not coincidentally the god of night and darkness, who confined the dead body in a casket and threw it into the sea. When Isis, the wife of Osiris, brought the corpse of her husband back to Egypt, Set thrust it below the world of light again, hacking it into fourteen pieces and separately burying the dismembered parts in hidden locations all over the earth of Egypt; from this element in the myth, Egyptians came to understand that the body of Osiris encompassed the entire material universe—"Thy body is all pervading"—rather in the way that the *Wake*'s sleeper, buried in his own body, seems to encompass the entire world in the opening pages of the *Wake*, when, dead to the world, he dreams of a landscape stretching from Phoenix Park to Howth Head without perceiving himself as the scattered central subject who contains it.[39] Despite everything that the powers of the night did to keep Osiris dead and buried, however, the superior force of the sun-god Amen-Ra woke him: moved by the entreaties of Isis, Amen-Ra sent to earth a company of gods who recollected the scattered being and returned him to life; among this company was Horus, the son of Osiris and a god of the rising sun, who now slew Set ("How to pull a good Horuscoup when Oldsire is Dead to the World"). After his resurrection, because Osiris was the only god or man ever to have died and returned to life, he became Osiris Khent-Amenti, Lord of the Underworld and the new "Prince of the night and of the thick darkness."[40] In this position, finally, he brought into the Egyptian consciousness the possibility of understanding that all mortals, after his example, might bodily enjoy life after death in another world.[41] This account of the myth of Osiris, of course, deliberately emphasizes its affinities with *Finnegans Wake*; for here, too, Joyce would have elicited from his Egyptian models a set of understandings applicable to his modern, sleeping man, who also lies in darkness on his back "pending a rouseruction of his bogey" (499.1)—his body, like Osiris's, forming the space within which another world resides.[42]

The myth of Osiris, finally, provided the ancient Egyptian with a metaphysics that perfectly complemented the celestial physics contained in the myth of Amen-Ra. When, at sunset, the boat of Ra passed from the world into the kingdom of the dead, it entered the domain and the body of Osiris, whose resurrective potencies were now put to work to repay the sun for an old favor: according to the Theban recension of books of the dead, those gods who boarded the boat of Amen-Ra in Amenti to move it toward dawn were the same gods who worked together to resurrect the scattered body of Osiris. As the solar agency of Amen-Ra helped to resurrect Osiris, so complementarily the chthonic agency of Osiris helped the sun return to dawn after it passed, at nightfall, into his body. Together, these interlinked myths suggested not only that people arose in the morning because the sun did, but also that the sun arose in the morning because some humane, creative nocturnal power was there to resurrect and wake up and see it: in understanding that the physical universe was phenomenologically rooted in a knowing human body, these ancient people would have seemed to Joyce peculiarly modern. The interdependence of these myths is suggested, moreover, in the very form and verbal texture of the scribe Ani's Book of the Dead: the Papyrus of Ani opens with a "Hymn to Ra," follows with a "Hymn to Osiris," and thereafter blurs the two figures so incessantly into a complementarity that at times it becomes impossible to say whose resurrective movement toward dawn and whose descent into nocturnal darkness is the cause and effect of whose.

Everywhere alluded to and nowhere directly told in books of the dead, the coordinated resurrection stories of Osiris and Amen-Ra establish the cultural vocabulary in which Egyptian mortuary texts are written. Apart from their religious significance, these stories rather resemble in cultural substance, and in importance to the particular work in which they occur, the coordinated resurrection stories of Tim Finnegan and Finn MacCool, to which the *Wake* everywhere alludes but nowhere directly tells: none of these four narratives make up the real plot of either of the two apparently plotless works in question, nor do they name the real protagonists; for, like the *Wake*, every version of the Book of the Dead has as its central figure a real person—the scribe Ani, the steward Nu, "the first pharaoh Humpheres Cheops Exarchas" (62.21)—who is not there, the dead man next to whose corpse the particular dead man's book was found at rest. It is his peculiarly told story, central to each of these works, that is of essential interest to us now.

APPLIED EGYPTOLOGY

One of the interesting features of New Kingdom books of the dead are the "Rubrics" included with each of their various chapters, which inform us in great detail of the ways in which those chapters were intended to be read.

Inside the Coffin

Many of these rubrics directed a reader to "know it on earth"—that is, apparently, to commit a chapter to memory before he passed into the other world;[43] other chapters were to be spoken out loud "regularly and continually millions of times,"[44] or intoned under specified ritualistic circumstances.[45] Yet other chapters were to be inscribed on the coffin or recited by relatives at the tomb.[46] Many of the chapters, however, were supposed to be recited or known after death by the dead man himself.[47] Extended sections of the Book of the Dead, consequently, put a reader into a position as difficult of access as that afforded by the *Wake:* not only does the deadman's book look forward into the life that people anticipated living after death; much of it, as the circumstances of its discovery show, was supposed to be read there. Presuming to speak directly from the point of view of the corpse, the Book of the Dead may be one of the few books on earth ideally written for an audience consisting entirely of the dead. In its utilitarian capacity as a guidebook to the other world, moreover, it had very particular information to impart to the dead man: it told him how to move from the life he had just departed to a secure place in the next world by steering his way through the annihilative duration of time that would befall him between the moment of his death and the moment of his resurrection into life after death.

Once the Egyptian dead man became translated out of the world and into the recumbent body of Osiris, he entered a region of space whose manifold terrors every book of the dead maps out in considerable detail. Fundamentally the most horrifying of these terrors seems to have been the loss of all perception and sensation in a form of "blackest night":

> The Osiris, the scribe Ani, whose word is truth, saith: —Hail, Temu [the sunken sun]! What manner of land is this unto which I have come? It hath not water, it hath not air; it is depth unfathomable, it is black as the blackest night, and men wander helplessly therein.[48]

In an "unseen" world of darkness this "thick and impenetrable,"[49] it was even more horrifying to be deprived of the capacity to move, especially if one had earlier learned that demonic predators and the agents of annihilation and decomposition prowled everywhere through the dark:

> The Osiris Ani saith: —O thou who art motionless, O thou who art motionless, O thou whose members art motionless, like unto those of Osiris. Thy members shall not be motionless, they shall not rot (or stink), they shall not crumble away, they shall not fall into decay.[50]

The dead man who traveled unprotected into this sunless world found himself powerless to accomplish even the most feeble acts of self-preservation.

Inhabiting a universe with other dead men—"those who are in inertness" and "those who are asleep in the body of Osiris"[51]—his inert body could not eat, drink, open its mouth to warn off predators, or bestir itself in the least. Unconscious and immobile, the dead man found himself utterly vulnerable:

> O I am helpless. O I am helpless. I would walk. I am helpless. I am helpless in the regions of those who plunder in Khert-Neter, I the Osiris Ani, whose word is truth. . . .[52]

Underlying the Book of the Dead, then, Joyce detected an intricately detailed reconstruction of the human night—and of vulnerable and uncomfortable sleep, in which a man awaits anxiously his resurrection from the dark. Few of us need to worry, as the originators of Egyptian myth and sepulture seem to have worried, about the vulnerable condition in which sleep—and later, burial—might leave one, especially in a torrid land where the things of the night crept at large around mud-built houses whose bedrooms could hardly have been impermeable. Yet the terrified vitality implicit in these passages allows us to know that the state of oblivious inertia being explored here is as much in the nature of sleep as of death: knowing exactly how it felt not to have been there in the night, the "spooker" of these passages (178.6 ["spooky speaker"]) seems to be projecting his memory of those unremembered parts of sleep past the moment of death into his future grave—where he meditates on his fate in cunningly elaborate ways.

From these passages, in turn, it should be evident how Joyce found the portrayal of the interior of the corpse offered in the Book of the Dead appropriately serviceable to his own portrayal of the interior of sleep. So, for example, at the end of a passage in which HCE, as "the first pharaoh Humpheres Cheops Exarchas," dreams of himself being "subjected to the horrors of the premier terror of Errorland" (62.21–25), Joyce draws on the rhetoric of English translations of the Book of the Dead to describe the oblivious imperception into which his sleeper momentarily sinks: "We seem to us (the real Us!) to be reading our Amenti in the sixth sealed chapter of the going forth by black" (62.26–27).[53] That Joyce has in mind as a "premier terror" of the dark "errorland" of sleep the loss of consciousness is suggested by the name that he repeatedly uses throughout the *Wake* to refer to the Egyptian afterworld. "Amenti" was not the name by which the ancient Egyptians themselves most commonly referred to the underworld of "the Tuat" or "Khert-Neter." Many New Kingdom books of the dead, in fact, use "Amentet," "Ament," "Amenti," and "Amenta," if at all, to name obscure subsections of the realm more widely called the Tuat. Since the *Wake*, however, is "basically English" (116.26), Joyce seems to have preferred the more obscure of these often interchangeable terms because of the less obscure English overtones it bore: "the premier terror" of the "errorland" of sleep, the terror that caused "Cheops" to drive 100,000 laborers over the twenty years it took to build his pyramid, is that of "amentia" in its fullest sense, of loss of mind and conscious life.[54]

Considering the demonic strife to which the boat of Amen-Ra was subjected on every night that it passed in Amenti, the Egyptians judged it extremely dangerous to be transported to the dark, Hidden Land if, upon one's arrival there, one found oneself inert and amental. Innumerable serpents, monsters, and demons roamed in this darkness—their means of subsistence revealed in their names: "devourer of the dead," "eater of shadows," "bone crusher," "he of the white teeth," "eater of blood," "the great god who carrieth away souls, who eateth hearts, who feedeth upon offal, who dwelleth in the darkness," and so forth.[55] A cheerless fate therefore befell the ordinary man who passed into Amenti—the poor man, that is, who was not supplied with a guidebook sufficiently informed to spare him from all possible dangers. Like every other mortal—like HCE in the opening pages of the *Wake*—he found himself immobile and unconscious when he first arrived in the dark entunnelment of the other world with his walkingstick, his windingsheet, and the meager ration of food that his impoverished relatives put into his grave. And he remained senseless, vulnerable to predators, until that single hour of the night in which the boat of the sun sailed through the region of Amenti in which he lay, bringing with its passage daylight and fresh air into the infernal gloom. This is the sort of relieved understanding that filters dimly into the "tropped head" of the *Wake*'s sleeper in the last chapter of the book when at dawn, after having lain motionless in the dark underworld of his body for the length of a night, "going forth by black," he begins to perceive, like a corpse stranded in Amenti, the light of the sun boating into his awareness:

> The eversower of the seeds of light to the cowld owld sowls that are in the domnatory of Defmut after the night of the carrying of the world of Nuahs and the night of making Mehs to cuddle up in a coddlepot, Pu Nuseht, lord of risings in the yonderworld of Ntamplin, tohp triumphant, speaketh.   (593.20–24) [56]

When HCE rises from his inertness in this underworld, he will reawaken to a whole, new day of life in a familiar city. As the ancient Egyptian understood it, however, the dead man who was lifted from immobility when the boat of Ra entered his part of Amenti wakened to his senses for only a lone dusky hour, and in that time, he had to look after his own survival in an utterly strange world. His course of action, as he had learned it on earth, was then clear: during this hour, he stumbled aimlessly forward, handicapped by the need both to fend off monsters, thirst, and hunger and to replenish his dwindling provisions, all the while trying to locate in the twilight of the new world that hidden region in the kingdom of Osiris in which he might enjoy the security of immortal life. But as soon as the boat of the sun left the region of Amenti in which he wandered, light and air vanished, and the dead man sank back into an inertness from which he would not reawaken again—if at all—until the boat of the sun reappeared. On every day that he managed to survive in the afterworld, in other words, the average Egyptian endured an almost unbroken night of vulnerable sleep. A person in these circumstances was all but doomed to be taken by a beast, if not in his sleep, then in his single hour of wakefulness; without the protection of "words of power" from a book of the dead, the duration of his life in the life after death was only a matter of days.[57]

Here, then, the Egyptians developed a strangely sophisticated concept—that of "the second death"—the like of which few other accounts of human mortality, primitive or modern, have evolved. Once we begin to consider human anxieties about the chances of survival in the other world—anxieties expressed in each of the passages from the Papyrus of Ani already quoted—life after death turns out not to offer a release from the threat of death at all. The Egyptians were hardly refusing to come to terms with the prospect of human finitude by evolving an eschatology in which a person was understood to be twice mortal, for after a deceased man perished again in the other world, he did not advance reincarnate into yet another other world, but was annihilated forever. This was the fate of the Egyptian masses, who passed from life into the sleepy realm of Amenti, and from Amenti into nothingness.[58] The concept of the second death, then, opened up dark depths in a mythography that might otherwise have failed to distinguish the "Real Absence" of sleep from that met at the end of human time. The understanding that a person could die twice, once on earth and once in the other world, made it possible for Egyptian thinkers to acknowledge that in the end the ordinary mortal passed from the world into a nothingness unfathomably deeper than that endured in the night; and they prayed, accordingly, in their strange mortuary documents, not to be among the multitudinous numbers of "those who are to be annihilated."[59] Curiously, then, the primitive incantations of the Book of the Dead turn out to be far less superstitious than many modern accounts of death. The conception of the

Inside the Coffin

second death, moreover, sensibly sophisticated the Egyptian understanding of what life after death would be—and in ways almost unthinkable to Christian eschatology. For if the other world were at all to accommodate a humanity whose existence was not independent of time, these people shrewdly reasoned that not only must there be life after death, but there must be death after death as well.

A man as wealthy as the scribe Ani hoped to avoid the second death and the fate of the Egyptian masses: Ani's Book of the Dead contains, in addition to a "Chapter of Not Rotting" and a "Chapter of Not Perishing," two "Chapters of Not Dying a Second Time."[60] As the Egyptians understood it, there were indeed two ways of escaping annihilation and of entering into immortality. Depending upon the city and the period of Egyptian history in which one lived, one compiled a book of the dead that invoked the aid of either of the two resurrective deities in the Egyptian pantheon: Amen-Ra, who reappeared on the earth each morning, or Osiris, who reawakened into life after falling under the powers of darkness. Worshippers of Amen-Ra aspired to attain a place in the boat of the sun—"the Boat of Millions of Years"— reasoning that if one secured a position in the sun god's company, one would attain eternal light and never fear the disappearance of daytime and sunlight and, correspondingly, of wakened consciousness.[61] Worshippers of Osiris aspired personally to reenact the god's resurrection and to enjoy immortal life, like Osiris, in that special, elysian region of Amenti called Sekhet Hetep.[62] The scribe Ani, who lived during a period of Egyptian history late enough to have learned the niceties of theocratic politics, diplomatically threw his faith into the resources of both of these deities at his wake: in the "Hymn to Ra" which begins his book of the dead, he prays that the Boat of Millions of Years will pick him up at the gates of sunset, carry him through the underworld, and drop him off at the Elysian Fields of Sekhet Hetep.[63] In this way, apparently, he could experience as little as possible of the dangerous swoon into the realm of somnolent absence out of which other people disappeared forever. In both of these means of attaining immortality, Joyce clearly perceived the Book of the Dead bordering on a reconstruction of the human night; for anyone who manages to come into the company of the sun, or to rise up out of corporeal inertness with the help of the sun, will also have moved through the night into morning. So it happens that "the boat of millions of years" floats into the nocturnal underworld of the *Wake*, without the need for much adjustment or translation of terms, directly from the Book of the Dead (479.25–26; 26.18–19, 418.5–6). It does so most notably at moments in the night when Joyce's sleeper, a man buried in his body and laid out dead to the world in his bed, begins to sustain an "infrarational" sense of his orientation in the night's "seemetery," and of his steadily fluid and "retrophoebi[c]" drift toward "the ra, the ra, the ra, the ra" (415.10–12 [and dawn]; see, e.g., 479.18–36); for the force that carries him toward morning and the company of the sun (hence, "retro-Phoebus") is identical to the divine solar power celebrated in Raite books of the dead.

Since the man asleep in Joyce's book of the dead lies transfixed "in various phases of scripture as in various poses of sepulture" (254.27–28), the symbolic forms of Egyptian burial must also now compel our attention. As the human subjects of Egyptian books of the dead understood it, one could neither awaken from inertia in Amenti and resurrect into a new life, nor escape the second death and enter the Boat of Millions of Years or the Elysian Fields of Sekhet Hetep, unless one were properly buried. And as Egyptian theocratic history evolved, moving from a predominantly Raite theology to a proto-Christian theology in which the redemptive figure of Osiris loomed large, the rituals attached to a proper burial became more and more complicated and elaborate. New Kingdom Egyptians like the scribe Ani and the steward Nu, encouraged by the culturally definitive example of Osiris, came to believe not only that the soul reawakened into new life after death, but that its survival depended upon the preservation of the body as well. At their funerals, accordingly, they sought meticulously to reenact the experience of Osiris, as a way of guaranteeing their spiritual resurrection in a new spirit-body in the next world. In their books of the dead, they systematically changed their names: the scribe Ani became "the Osiris Ani," "the Osiris the scribe Ani," or simply "Osiris";[64] "every dead Egyptian was identified with Osiris and bore his name."[65] This is rather what happens in the Wake, where the real name of the sleeper gets lost, with his consciousness and identity, instead to be recast in thousands of forms emblematic of his imminent matitudinal resurrection: Christ, Tim Finnegan, Finn MacCool, King Arthur—and here, of course, Osiris.

Egyptian morticians, observing that the soft internal organs of the body decayed more swiftly than the musculature and skin, conformed to the religious expectations of their clientele by removing and "scattering" the parts of a dead man's body while chanting hymns to Osiris: this procedure had the economical effect of preserving the various organs of the potentially resurrective body from perceptible organic decay and simultaneously of replicating the experience of Osiris, whose entrails had been torn apart by the powers of night and separately buried. The embalmers, then, symbolically acted

Inside the Coffin

out the roles of the scattering destroyer, Set, and of the jackal-headed god Anubis, who was instrumental in accomplishing the physical reincorporation of Osiris. Inserting a curved iron rod up the corpse's nostrils, the embalmers pulled the brain out of the dead man, dried it, and set it aside in a kit to be interred with the rest of the body.[66] Like their twentieth-century descendants, they slit the corpse open at a spot somewhere to the left of and between the navel and the groin, and from the wound they extracted the perishable intestines, heart, stomach, and liver. Modern-day embalmers wash these entrails down drains;[67] the Egyptians washed them with palm wine, stuffed them with gums and spices, sealed them separately in four "Canopic" jars named after the four animal-headed deities who upheld the canopy of the sky at the four cardinal compass points of the universe, and blessed them with the names of four gods who helped reintegrate the scattered Osiris.[68] After filling the hollows of the skull and trunk with spices, gums, washing soda, and muddy Nile plaster, Egyptian morticians finally wrapped the corpse in bandages that had been separately inscribed with the name of the deceased and with verses from the Book of the Dead.[69] During the two months in which the deceased's body underwent this process of embalming, the departed soul presumably lay unconscious in Amenti, awaiting, like Osiris, the moment at which his scattered body would be gathered together in order that within it he might be resurrected into eternal life and brought into the company of the sun.

This resurrection happened at the tomb, where the various kits and jars containing the organs of the dead man were collected together beneath the funeral couch on which his coffin rested, and where the members of his family elaborately relived the myth of Osiris. Inscriptions on the outer sycamore coffin in which the dead man lay suggested that the coffin was the womb of Nut, Osiris's mother, out of which he would again be reborn;[70] the inner coffin was shaped in the form of the body of Osiris himself.[71] In turn, the lamentations of the dead man's—the Osiris's—wife were heard as the entreaties of Isis, who once again moaned to Ra the sun over the dead and broken body of her husband; the dead man's oldest son, in whom the dead man lived on and in a manner defeated death, was understood to be an embodiment of Horus, the force of the rising sun, who once again triumphed over the powers of darkness and helped his dead father to live on in the world.[72] At some time in this period of mourning at the tomb, apparently, just as the funeral ceremony properly began, the inert soul in Amenti stirred dimly, assumed a spectre's consciousness, and began to move, Osiris-like, towards resurrection. In Joyce's book of the dead, much the same kind of feeble stirring occurs to the man "tropped head" in the night's "seeme-tery" just after the *Wake*, and his wake, begin:

> So may the priest of seven worms and scalding tayboil, Papa Vestray, come never anear you as your hair grows wheater beside the Liffey that's in Heaven! Hep, hep, hurrah there! Hero! Seven times thereto we salute you! The whole bag of kits, falconplumes and jackboots incloted, is where you flung them that time. Your heart is in the system of Shewolf and your crested head is in the tropic of Copricapron. Your feet are in the cloister of Virgo. Your olala is in the region of sahuls. And that's ashore as you were born. Your shuck tick's swell. And that there texas is tow-linen. The loamsome roam to Laffayette is ended. Drop in your tracks, babe! Be not un-rested! The head boddylwatcher of the chempel of Isid, Totumcalmum, saith: I know thee metherjar, I know thee, salvation boat. For we have performed upon thee, thou abramanation, who comest ever without being invoked, whose coming is unknown, all the things . . . concerning thee in the matter of the work of thy tombing. Howe of the shipmen, steep wall!   (26.6–24)

As always at the *Wake*, it is worth asking whose "eyewitless foggus" we share here: that of a body at its wake, or that of a body not awake? Every element in this passage helps to locate us at the unconscious interior of a corpse drifting darkly toward its resurrection in each of those three distinct regions of space that the Egyptians topologically equated: within the scat-tered ruins of its own body, within the next world, and within the world-encompassing body of Osiris. Some chapters from Egyptian books of the dead were designed to be read at the funeral specifically in order that the dead subject of the book might hear the words and so begin the process of his own internally self-performed resurrection. Much the same design in-forms this moment in the *Wake* (pp. 24–26), where the corpse, the Osiris, hears voices—the voices of four old men who stand at the four corners of his closed sycamore coffin[73]—praying that he will not be assailed by worms, that he will not perish in one of Amenti's many lakes of boiling water, and that he will indeed reach the blessed kingdom in which he might cultivate wheat, the hair of Osiris, through eternity ("So may the priest of seven worms and scalding tayboil, Papa Vestray, come never anear you as your hair grows wheater beside the Liffey that's in Heaven!").[74] Like the mummified Egyptian corpse whose "eyewitless foggus" is preserved in books of the dead, the *Wake*'s hero here seems dimly to lift into an awareness that various organs of his body ("heart," "head," "feet," "O, la, la!") have been separated from his trunk, preserved by bottle-washing morticians in those Canopic jars ("kits," "metherjar," "boddylwatcher"), and symbolically scattered to the four corners of the earth and sky. In Egyptian mortuary practice, these four jars were surmounted by lids shaped in the forms of the heads of animals and man, each representing one of the deities who stood at the corners of the sky and therefore defined the limits both of the underworld and the body of Osiris;[75] here, as is appropriate to a man embedded in the night, they limn out a form loosely suggestive of the constellation Orion (hence the evocations of the Zodiac). As in books of the dead, then, the corpse treated in this passage from the *Wake* finds itself stirring to life in its own broken body, in the night-world of Amenti, and at the corners of the sky simultaneously. Consciousness begins to seep back into the spice-and-gum-filled hollow of his skull—"(skull!) that was a planter for you, a spicer of them all" (25.22–23)—and the corpse lying in a part of the tomb construed as a "temple of Isis" ("chempel of Isid") apparently begins to recall phrases from the "mummyscrip" wrapped around him (156.5):[76] the phrase "I know thee" ("I know thee metherjar, I know thee salvation boat") is a formula frequently invoked in the Book of the Dead.[77] The Egyptians found it necessary for a dead man to use this phrase as a way of acknowledging his familiarity with the underworld and therefore of placating those hostile forces bent on bringing him his second death; but a modern reader can interpret the formula more liberally: it recurs so insistently in books of the dead simply because it asserts the possession of consciousness and the capacity to know. For anyone who can say "I know"—or know at all—is certainly not lost in the "Real Absence" of sleep, much less of death. And in the passage at hand, as in books of the dead, the first things the reviving corpse wants to know are the locations of his missing body and scattered entrails and of the solar "salvation boat" that will carry him through "the land of the souls" (24.34), through the gates of dawn, and into the light and life of a new day in "Healiopolis" (24.18). This passage, in short, enables us to enter the skull of an encrypted Tutankhamen ("Totumcalmum") and to observe the form of unconsciousness that rippled there for over three thousand years before his tomb was opened. In a way there is nothing figurative about the passage at all: it reconstructs exactly, from the internal "eyewitless foggus" of the corpse itself, the kind of life that Tutankhamen and his contemporaries imagined would follow death.

In Joyce's book of the dead, "th'osirian" protagonist (350.25) within whose body the other world is located lies scattered and scrambled in an only slightly modified way. As "Totumcalmum," he is simply a man who sleeps in "total calm" in "Chapelizod" ("chempel of Isid"), an innkeeper (or "boddylwatcher") whose consciousness has disintegrated in the night. Because the *Wake* systematically strives to reconstruct the "blank memory" and "eyewitless foggus" of a body dead to the world, it might now be construed as a "mummyscrip" whose content, like that of Egyptian "winding sheets" (77.28), is "the presence (of a curpse)": "for that (the rapt one warns) is what [this] papyr is meed of" (20.10–11). Like the mummy of Tutankhamen, moreover, Joyce's "Totumcalmum" also is enwrapped in linen cerements—"bedding" (24.13), since he moves through the dark "resting be-tween horrockses' sheets" (491.31–32 [where "Horrocks" is an English tex-tile firm and Horus is an agent of Egyptian resurrection]). He is also quite literally "embalmed" (78.6)—indeed, "**h**ealed, **c**ured and "**e**mbalsemate" (498.36–499.1)—although the spirit-preserving "balm" that lies in his veins and in his "metherjar" is far less exotic than the palm wine and bitumen which Egyptian morticians used to keep their clients from decay: a "mether" (Anglo-Ir. *meadher* [*OED*]) is a drinking tankard, and the potable balm within it seems to have passed into the veins of Joyce's sleeper to insure him of a particularly balmy sleep here.[78]

That a void great as the one internal to the constellation Orion suffuses this sleeping man is suggested not only by the astro-anatomy of the passage, but also by its assignation of "Totumcalmum" to "the region of sahuls," a phrase that combines the primary English meaning of "the region of souls" and the Middle Egyptian word *sahu*. Like other terms from the Book of the Dead adopted by the *Wake*, the word *sahu* itself turns out to be something of a pun, since it fuses together three discriminate meanings that a modern reader would tend to separate: at one and the same time, the Egyptians used it as the word for "spirit-soul" (a part of the self that lived after death), the word for "mummy," and the name of the constellation Orion.[79] Like other elements in the passage, then, the phrase helps to set this moment in the *Wake* "in the otherworld of the passing of the key of Two-tongue Common" (385.4–5), although in Joyce's understanding, the otherworldly "region of sahuls" was topologically indistinct from the world his hero has entered by having "tropped head" in sleep. For the *Wake*'s embalmed "Totumcalmum," able only to "no" "Real Absence," lies in much the same position as Tu-tankhamen, simultaneously "inert in the body," vaguely alert in the spirit-filled otherworld like Amenti, and scattered throughout a universe formed in the shape of the body of man. Nothing in this passage, finally, suggests that Joyce's "Totumcalmum" is privy to the revelations of a collective uncon-scious or that he has a deeply buried memory of Egyptian theology; for while the *Wake* suggests that people derive their visions of the afterlife by unconscious reflection on the experience of sleep, it also shows how they concretize those visions with images drawn from material, historical reali-ties to which their generations alone have direct access. The point is not

Inside the Coffin

that Joyce's hero has a memory, or even a knowledge, of ancient Egypt, but that the Book of the Dead and the *Wake* speak "two tongues in common" ("Two-tongue Common") because they both capture, in comparable hiero-glyphies, parts of human experience in which "our whosethere outofman" seems not to be there. Both map out the same other world. When Joyce's hero falls asleep in the "seemetery," accordingly, "his heart, soul and spirit turn to pharaoph times" (129.35–36).

Two other features of this passage on "Totumcalmum" intensify its sepul-chral effects. The first of these is that apparently eccentric riff of American slang which intrudes discrepantly in a context otherwise heavily echoic of the Book of the Dead. This evocation of American idiom seems to have been Joyce's way of reinforcing the understanding that his hero, at this point in the *Wake*, has indeed passed into the next world, the other world, "the New World": "the ousts of Amiracles" in the passage at hand (427.23 [*not* "Amer-ica," but a realm of "miracles"]); the remote outreaches of Australian "Tossmania" in the fable of the Ondt and the Gracehoper (416.30); the ex-tremities of British South Africa, in Jaun's saintly vision of "the fulldress Toussaint's wakeswalks experdition" ("we shall all be hooked and happy, communionistically, among the fieldnights eliceam [Elysian] *élite* of the elect in the land of lost time. Johannisburg's a revelation!" (455.5–6, 453.31–34). A reading of the Book of the Dead enables us to see how little contri-vance there is in the imaginative transaction by which Joyce transforms America and comparable ends of the earth into ciphers representative of an other or "New World" like Amenti in the *Wake*. In the Irish experience of the last two centuries, as millions of countrymen left their loved ones and emigrated from their native earth, these places were regions into which neighbors and relatives disappeared forever. Many of Ireland's emigrants, never again seen alive by their relatives or friends, may just as well have been dead to those they left behind, as the *Wake* suggests in its recurrent portrayal of a son's departure from the known earth into the absence of an other and New World (III.i, III.ii), and as Stephen Dedalus makes explicit in *Ulysses* when, in his discussion of *Hamlet*, he defines a ghost: "What is a ghost? Stephen said with tingling energy. One who has faded into impal-pability through death, through absence . . ." (*U*, 188). So too in the passage at hand, which begins its exploration of Totumcalmum's departure from life by evoking Gerald Nugent's *Ode Written on Leaving Ireland:* "to part from Dev-lin is hard as Nugent knew" (24.25–26 [though to part from life is harder]). Many of those people left behind on their native earth—no less than those who bemoaned the passage of the scribe Ani or the steward Nu into Amenti—

must have found the passage of loved ones into the New World of "Amiracles" heartbreaking—as the self-exiled Joyce would well have known: in his letters he refers to America, to which his son and daughter-in-law emigrated, as "the ends of the earth" (*L*, III, 412). In the *Wake*, then, references to "the New World" of America often become the ciphers for the New, unearthly World inhabited by those "deadported" (536.2), in turn to deepen our sense of the absence amid which Joyce's sleeper dwells. Like the originators of the Egyptian books of the dead, who pieced together descriptions of the dark underworld of night by referring indirectly to the unreal remotenesses of the Sudan and the Sahara, Joyce too went to "the ends of the earth" to find the images with which to describe his hero's "Real Absence" in the night.

All of the particular Americanisms informing this passage on "Totumcalmum," as adjoining references to "Pike County" and "hogglebully" suggest (25.28, 33), come from *Huckleberry Finn*, a work in which Joyce perceived a new-world manifestation of the spirit of the ubiquitous Finn who sleeps at his *Wake*. The phrase "ashore as you were born," eccentrically spelled as anything in the *Wake*, is actually a modification of the somewhat more unorthodox "shore's your born," which appears in the twelfth chapter of *Huckleberry Finn*, at a moment when Huck, crouching "in dead silence" in the night on the "texas" of a wrecked steamer, overhears two men plotting the death of a third. "That there texas" itself refers to the upper deck of a riverboat, on which the captain's sleeping quarters were located. In the *Wake*, it bears a related meaning, apparently referring to Totumcalmum's own sleeping quarters ("that there texas is tow linen"), whose sheeting in turn seems made of something like "tow-linen," a rough fabric which Huck observes the children of Parkville wearing when, attired only in garments like nightshirts, they are invited up to "the mourner's bench" at an evangelical camp meeting to cast off sin and to consider the prospect of heaven. It is on the differing qualities of sleep and rest afforded by "shuck ticks" and "straw ticks" that Huck muses in the long passage from Twain's novel which provided Joyce with detailing descriptive of the swell qualities of his own sleeper's bedding ("your shuck tick's swell"). Even apparently insubstantial expressions in this American interlude come from *Huckleberry Finn:* both the phrases "drop in your tracks" and "the road to Lafayette" occur in the novel, although Joyce embellishes the latter of these by inserting an additional "f" to remind us that however remotely his absent hero may have been "deadported" to the New World, or Amenti, he lies simultaneously inert in the province of the Liffey.[80] Should these individual details seem too arcane, the sonority and the locality of the passage alone should make its placement in the New World clear (all of the sixteen places on the earth named "Lafayette" are in the United States). The reasons for which this New World enters the sleeper's dream in this part of his night should also be clear from lines internal to the passage: "the loamsome roam is ended" (the "lonesome road" to the "loamy" grave), "drop in your tracks," and "be not unrested" spell matters out quite explicitly. The enshrouded, embalmed, and scattered hero of this book of the dead, enduring his own "Real Absence" from life, is beginning to orient himself in a strange, amental, New World like Amenti.[81]

The last phrase in the passage on "Totumcalmum"—"Howe of the shipmen, steep wall!"—integrates its Egyptian and New Worldly features with the *Wake*'s many evocations of Viking howe- and ship-burials: again, Totumcalmum is embedded and dead to the world ("steep wall" = "sleep well"). But the phrase also reinvokes the Book of the Dead by calling attention to other peculiar features of Egyptian sepulture. In the Old Kingdom "mastabah" tombs, notably—mentioned in the opening pages of the *Wake* ("Damb! He was dud! Dumb! Mastabatoom, mastabadtomm!" [6.10–11])—the corpse of the deceased man was *not* laid to rest in the spacious rectangular building that lay above ground; this was built for the benefit of the living, who came there to placate the deceased spirit with "offerings of the field" (cf. 24.34–25.8). Instead, a walled-off vertical shaft forty to eighty feet deep was sunk through the ceiling and floor of the tomb, and, at the bottom of the shaft, a narrow, horizontal mummy chamber was hollowed out to hold the corpse. At burial, his double coffin was lowered down the shaft from the roof and pushed aside into the mummy chamber, which was then walled up and sealed off, the steep, vertical shaft in turn being crammed full of rocks and boulders. This laborious form of burial, as Joyce's phrasing suggests, was not only intended to insure the absolute security and rest of the preserved body ("Be not unrested" . . . "sleep well" beneath the "steep wall"); it also protected the living from the possibility of assault by the dead ("We have performed upon thee, thou abramanation ['abomination' and 'Abram'-like forebear] who comest ever without being invoked, all things concerning thee in the work of thy tombing").[82]

One additional curious feature of these tombs deserves the special attention of a modern reader: the actual doors of mastabah tombs, through which the living entered the building, were usually situated in the eastern wall, so that the mourner might face the west, the locality of the sunset and the Hidden Land of Amenti, upon entry. There, on the western walls of these structures, the architects of postmortality painted "false doors," embellished with the name of the deceased and inscribed with prayers for his eternal survival, through which the spirit of the dead man presumably came forth and went into the Hidden Land, the New World in the far west. As Egyptian history evolved, however, and as more members of lower classes undertook the expense of ritualized burial, the shape of the mastabah tomb changed in such a way that its most material parts vanished and its most immaterial ones became most prominent: members of the lower classes, who could not afford to build the whole mastabah tomb, supplied their dead with only the false, painted gateways to the west. The resulting stelai—stone slabs shaped in the forms of arched doorways and gates facing west, inscribed simply with the names of the dead and a few simple commemorative prayers—seem to be the original prototypes of our modern tombstones.[83]

As the *Wake*'s treatment of "Totumcalmum" shows, Joyce clearly found the force of sleep palpably manifested not only in Egyptian books of the dead and in the extraterrestrial geographies they mapped out, but also in the material forms of Egyptian funeral practice and sepulture themselves. Even though the owners of books of the dead evolved the sobering concept of "the second death," the second death itself, by an inevitably consolatory reflex, was always understood to happen to someone else, never to the subject named in his own funerary papyrus. In the mortuary documents out of which Western letters and conceptions of death originated, Joyce perceived a desperate effort to convert "the silence of the dead" (452.20) into the imminently resurrective silence of sleep. For if death were regarded only as a lapse into a form of sleep, then everything occurring after death must be in the nature of sleep itself, a duration of "suspensive exanimation" before the resurrection of the body (143.8–9). Passage after passage in the *Wake*, accordingly, treats its sleeping protagonist as one of the Egyptian dead lost in "old nekropolitan nights" (80.1–2). Here, for instance, at a moment in the middle of sleep when "Totumcalmum" moves his head and generates a thought that vanishes immediately and forever from the sands of his memory:

> Mask one. Mask two. Mask three. Mask four. Up.
> —Look about you, Tutty Comyn!
> —Remember and recall, Kullykeg!
>
> (367.8–11)

Passages like these finally show why the *Wake* should have found the waked Tutankhamen a perfect cipher for its somnolent protagonist, "Totumcalmum": Joyce sustains an equivalence between these two figures throughout his "bog of the depths" (516.25) not because his hero has any substantial knowledge of Tutankhamen, and not because the Egyptians thought at all of Tutankhamen's death simply as a species of sleep; but because Tutankhamen was presumed at death to experience the same quality of nothingness, to enter the same kind of other world, and to move toward the same kind of solar resurrection as Joyce's sleeper.

These lines also conveniently return us to that earlier passage descriptive of "Totumcalmum," where the scattered and enshrouded protagonist of the Book of the Dead had barely begun to undergo the process of burial and the long resurrective movement that would lift him from dark oblivion into a new life and dawn. When we last entered the gum-stuffed and amental skull of this dead man, his consciousness and "sahul" were barely beginning to stir alive in Amenti and in the embalmed parts of his body, "all matters in the work of his tombing" having only begun. In order to help the inert Osiris in Amenti rise up from the lethargy that left him helplessly vulnerable to the second death, the Egyptians believed that a sequence of funerary rituals had to be performed on the mummy, so that the dead man might regain the will and consciousness necessary for his independent survival in the New World. Joyce's book of the dead evokes these mortuary procedures because all books of the dead contained crucial chapters corresponding to each— chapters that described events transpiring inside the mind of the corpse as funerary priests on earth treated it to insure its resurrection. After offering an internal understanding of the nullity felt by a dead man awaiting the resurrection of his body, in other words, the Book of the Dead also minutely documented the various stages by which the corpse would rise up from its mortal inertia to return to life. The chapters chronicling this resurrective movement form a substantial part of books of the dead and, in a way, constitute its plot—the forward, linear, chronological movement that governs the placement of the variable chapters in each variant book of the dead. As the titles of these chapters alone suggest, they would have provided Joyce with an internalized account of the process by which a man dead to the world ascended from "Real Absence" to wakened, literate consciousness.

Primary among these chapters and corresponding funeral rites is "The Chapter of Opening the Mouth," which Joyce evokes several times in the *Wake*: once, for example, in a phrase that describes HCE's sleep as "going to boat with the verges of the chaptel of the opering of the month of Nema Knatut" (395.22–23);[84] and also, at the beginning of chapter I.v, in the title *"Of the Two Ways of Opening the Mouth"* (105.23–24).[85] At the ceremony of Opening the Mouth, two priests anointed the bandaged mouth and eyes of the Egyptian corpse with a series of symbolic instruments and read from the Book of the Dead, thereby empowering the mummified Osiris to throw off his healing bandages and to open his mouth and his eyes in the underworld.[86] In the "Chapter of Opening the Mouth" corresponding to this ceremony in the Papyrus of Ani, extraordinary things happened in the consciousness of the dead man once the priests liberated him, to invoke two of the *Wake*'s central terms, from dumbness and blindness in Amenti:

> THE CHAPTER OF THE OPENING OF THE MOUTH OF THE OSIRIS ANI. To be said:—The god Ptah [the celestial blacksmith, who forged the human body] shall open my mouth, and the god of my town shall unfasten the swathings, and the swathings which are over my mouth. Thereupon shall come Thoth [the god of intelligence and literacy], who is equipped with words of power in great abundance, and shall untie the fetters, even the fetters of the god Set, which are over my mouth.[87]

Prepossessed by those "swathings," nineteenth-century Egyptologists surmised that Egyptians devised the ceremony of "Opening the Mouth" because they "foresaw that when a man had been made into a mummy, if life were returned to him by magical means, it would be impossible for them to move their members because of the bandages with which they were swathed, and he could not breathe, [eat, drink, or talk] because his mouth would be closed by swathings also."[88] In Joyce's reading, however, the Egyptian seems to have feared in death a "fettering" of far greater strength than that imposed by any winding sheets. In life, no doubt, a man like the scribe Ani had observed the fettering rigor mortis and inanimacy of the dead, and in his sleep, no less doubtfully, he had experienced something like rigor mortis internally. For in the classical *Hemmungstraum*, the dream of physical constraint obliquely reflective of sleep's power to paralyze the body, the dreamer typically envisions something frightening, tries to shout or move, and finds his mouth and body fettered helplessly still—as in the Book of the Dead:

> Permit not thou to come nigh unto me him that would attack me, or would injure me in the House of Darkness. Cover over the helpless one, hide him. . . . Grant thou that I may come forth, and that I may be master of my legs. . . . Let none come to see the helpless one.[89]

That the compilers of the Book of the Dead in part translated the memory of sleep into those chapters describing the corpse's "opening of the mouth" is furthermore suggested by the relationship of these chapters to others. "Chapters of Avoiding Thirst and Hunger" in various books of the dead show that the Egyptians knew what it felt like to be inert, "fettered," simultaneously subject to the tantalizing desire for food and water, and yet incapable of "opening the mouth";[90] difficulties of this sort, recurrently disrupting the sleep of "Humpheres Cheops Exarchas," arise comparably in the Papyrus of Ani, as many thankful and victorious exclamations in his chapters of coming forth by day attest: "I eat with my mouth. I evacuate with my body. Behold, I am the god of the Tuat."[91]

In Ani's book of the dead, as in others of the Theban recension, "The Chapter of the Opening of the Mouth" (chapter XXII) is aligned sequentially with others in a plotted progression that makes its significance to the *Wake*'s reconstruction of the night especially clear: following the "Chapter of Opening the Mouth" one finds "The Chapter of Bringing Words of Power to the Deceased" (chapter XXIII) and "The Chapter Which Maketh a Man to Remember His Name in Khert-Neter" (chapter XXV).[92] In the reasoning of the Book of the Dead, the deceased Egyptian could not fend off the phantasmal threats found in Amenti unless he possessed the literate power to recite charms; nor could he gain the paradisaical reaches of Sekhet Hetep unless he remembered his name. Stranded in strange kingdoms, he could not utter with a mouth close by death such crucial formulaic phrases as "I know thee, and I know thy name, and I know the name of her who is within thee."[93] "Opening the Mouth," then, seems to have meant much more to the Egyptians than the casting off of facial bandages. By internally opening a mouth helplessly and involuntarily closed—whether in sleep or in death—"the inert one in the body" regained the extinguished capacity for speech, language, consciousness, and knowledge: only then could he say, "I am the master over myself and over the attributes of my head."[94]

A passage close to the end of *Finnegans Wake* allows us fully to appreciate the experience internal to the inert Egyptian mummy in the hour of his funeral. Here, in the early hours of the morning, Joyce's "Totumcalmum" lies alone on his funereal bed, just after the boat of the sun has risen into the world above him to carry him out of the depths and darknesses of "Amenta":

> Yet is no body present here which was not there before. Only is order othered. Nought is nulled. *Fuitfiat!*
>
> Lo, the laud of laurens now orielising benedictively when saint and sage have had their say.
>
> A spathe of calyptrous glume involucrumines the perianthean Amenta: fungoalgaceous muscafilicial graminopalmular planteon; of increasing, livivorous, feelful thinkamalinks; luxuriotiating everywhencewithersoever among skullhullows and charnelcysts of a weedwastewoldwevild when Ralph the Retriever ranges to jawrode his knuts knuckles and her theas thighs; onegugulp down of the nauseous forere brarkfarsts oboboomaround and you're as paint and spickspan as a rainbow; wreathe

the bowl to rid the bowel; no runcure, no rank heat, sir; amess in amullium; chlorid cup.

(613.13–26)

All of the words in the opening clause of the last paragraph quoted here, except for "Amenta," are English: a "spathe" is a large, sheathing leaf that encloses the flowers of certain plants; "calyptrous" pertains to the "calyptra" (< Gr. *kalyptra*, "covering," "occulting," "veil"), the hood that encloses the sporecases of certain mosses; a "glume" is one of the leaves that forms the outer envelope of the flowering parts of grasses or sedges, as in a husk of corn; "perianthean," comparably, pertains to the "perianth," the structure that forms the outer enwrapments of flowers; and the Joycean verb "involucrumines," finally, derives from the English "involucre" or "involucrum" (< L. "envelope"), an anatomical and botanical term applied to the outer, enveloping membranes of plants and animal organs. The sense that the paragraph is describing the imminent unfurling of an inflorescent core of vegetable matter—a self-enclosed blossom, or "chlorid cup"—is reinforced by its second clause; here Joyce provides a compressed history of the evolution of botanical life as the language advances, term by term, through a sequence of words denoting more and more complex forms of vegetable life: "fungaceous and algal"; "muscal" (pertaining to mosses) and "filical" (pertaining to ferns); "graminal" (pertaining to grasses) and "palmular" (pertaining to palms). As the culminative term in this heptad of botanical names suggests, the encored flower opening up to light here seems to be that of the palm tree; and because this passage is temporally set in the East-oriented, heliotropic moment of dawn, the palm flower that the corpselike protagonist of this book of the dead has in mind seems to be that of the date palm of Egypt—the phoenix palm, *Phoenix dactylifera*—a tree whose blossoms are, in fact, enveloped by "spathes" and "perianths."[95] These details, at least, would account for the vitality that Joyce's interred hero, the most evolved form of vegetative life that the earth has ever seen, feebly senses as he lies in a "spate" of nocturnal, "amental gloom." That the passage reconstructs, once again, the "tropped head" of a man dead to the world is made clear in the first of its paragraphs, which states that "there is no body present" and—in an ambiguous clause that can be read either restrictively or nonrestrictively—that this absent body "was not there before" either. As the paragraph evolves further, however, and as "feeling" and "thinking" begin to infuse the blossoming palm ("feelful thinkamalinks"), a clearer sense emerges of the actual circumstances generating this moment in Totumcalmum's sleep.

Inside the Coffin

The paragraph seems to be about the buried man's mouth (a "skullhollow"), ready to undergo the resurrective ceremony of opening up as his tongue, riding out to his jaw ("jawrode"), hits against structures of bone ("knuts knuckles") and soft labial flesh ("theas thighs") in an act of "retrieval" ("Ralph" derives from the Old Nor. *Rathulfr*, "the cunning of the wolf," and the kenning of the wolf is at its muzzle). Our hero seems to be undertaking one of those exploratory morning yawns in which the tongue casually surveys the teeth and lips in an annular motion ("wreathe the bowl"), finds the ground of its activity disgusting ("nauseous forere brarkfarsts"), executes a retreat ("onegugulp down of the nauseous," "wreathe the bowl to rid the bowel"), and then falls back into a state of wishful placidity ("you're as paint and spickspan as a rainbow"). "No thing making newthing wealthshowever" (253.8–9), the dark and empty space within his mouth moreover differs little from the void contained within the closed enwrapments of a flower. Since the corpselike protagonist himself seems dimly to perceive the taste of decaying vegetable matter inside that mouth— "increasing, feelful thinkamalinks luxuriotiating everywhencewithersoever among skullhullows and charnelcysts"—he registers the subliminal awareness in the appropriate vegetative imagery. The condition afflicting him here, on one level, is simply what Leopold Bloom, feeling unpleasant under comparable circumstances, calls "morning mouth," which, he adds, sends "bad images" into the head around it (*U*, 61 [the L. *luxurio* in "luxuriotiating" = "I am rank"]). At the *Wake*, however, "the inert one buried in the body" seems unconsciously aware that the bacterial forces which generate the bad taste of "morning mouth" differ little from the bacterial forces which, if left unarrested, generate putrefaction within the "charnel cysts" of the dead man's "hollow skull." Here again, the *Wake* seems virtually to replicate the "eyewitless foggus" of a corpse—a corpse now able to "no" that the agents of putrefaction are growing inside out of itself. Like the subjects of books of the dead, the man sleepily dead to the world at the *Wake* has the taste of mortality in his mouth—although, as it also happens to the enshrouded Osirises of those books, his mouth will soon be opened, like the dark core of the phoenix palm blossom, to the light of the boat of Ra.[96] Fortified by its knowledge of the Book of the Dead, then, the *Wake* here answers the haunting eschatological question of how the decaying corpse, buried in loamy inertia and scattering throughout the material universe, initiates the process by which it resurrects itself bodily into life: it opens its mouth in the hour when the sun moves through the gates of dawn, and, as paragraphs subsequent to this one in the *Wake* show, it lets language, consciousness, knowledge, and sunlight flood back in to replace the darkness. In Joyce's book of the dead, the opening of the mouth accomplishes the same miracle treated in its Egyptian antecedents: it resurrects.

Like the embedded man whose unconscious experience this passage reconstructs, the corpses who speak out of Egyptian books of the dead are internally aware of the forces of decomposition threatening to overwhelm them:

> And when the soul hath departed, a man seeth corruption and the bones of his body crumble away and become stinking things, and the members decay one after the other, the bones crumble into a helpless mass, and the flesh turneth into foetid liquid. Thus man becometh a brother unto the decay which cometh upon him, and he turneth into a myriad of worms, and he becometh nothing but worms, and an end is made of him, and he perisheth in the sight of the god of day. . . .[97]

One of the mortuary practices that prevented this kind of onslaught, of course, was embalmment; but there were others. "Under the Old Kingdom the dead were anointed with the Seven Holy Oils, the names of which are duly set forth in the Liturgy of Funerary Offerings, and on the alabaster anointing slabs";[98] and under the New Kingdom, the ritual of anointment was incorporated into the ceremony of "Opening the Mouth," where the funerary priests, in a primitive form of extreme unction, applied unguents to the lips and eyes of the deceased. Valued in life as medicines that insured the health, cleanliness, and fragrance of the body, these ointments seem to have performed a comparable service for the corpse, who, sick with mortality and corruption, benefited both physically and spiritually from their curative powers. Whole medicine cabinets full of these sacred unguents were stored in the tombs of Egypt's dead, apparently so that the person who had passed into death could draw upon them in the process of resurrection and restore himself magically to life and health.[99] A comparable kind of restoration preoccupies the corpse "tropped head" at Joyce's *Wake* when, gathering toward resurrection, he imagines the voices of young women addressing a rejuvenated version of himself as he departs from his native earth into another, New World:

> . . . when you will be after doing all your sightseeing and soundhearing and smell-sniffing and tastytasting . . . send us, your adorables, thou overblaseed, a wise and letters play of all you can ceive . . . from your holy post now you hast ascertained ceremonially our names. Unclean you are not. Outcaste thou are not. . . . Untouchable is not the scarecrown on you. You are pure. You are pure. You are in your puerity. You have not brought stinking members into the house of Amanti. Elleb Inam, Tipep Notep, we name them to the Hall of Honour. Your head has been

touched by the god Enel-Rah and your face has been brightened by the goddess Aruc-Ituc. Return, sainted youngling, and walk once more among us. (237.16–30)

Much of the passage comes directly from the Book of the Dead. In the Papyrus of Nu, for example, the spirit of the departed exclaims:

I am pure. I am pure. I am pure. I am pure. My pure offerings are the pure offerings of that great Benu (phoenix?) which dwelleth in Hensu.

And later:

I am pure. My breast is purified by libations, and my hinder parts are made clean with the things which make clean, and my inner parts have been dipped in the Lake of Truth. There is no single member of mine which lacketh truth. I have washed myself clean. . . .[100]

At the close of the ceremony of "Opening the Mouth," finally, the Sem priest recited comparable words as he smeared ointment on the lips of the corpse: "I have anointed thy face with ointment, I have anointed thine eyes. I have painted thine eye with *uatch* and with *mestchem*. . . . Thy two eyes are decked therewith in its name of *Uatch*, which maketh thee to give forth fragrance in its name of Sweetsmelling."[101]

In *Finnegans Wake* the sacred mortuary unguents that have been applied to "the presence (of a curpse)" are rather more mundane. As William York Tindall has noted, the pseudo-Egyptian deities "Enel-Rah" and "Aruc-Ituc" are simply the skin care products "Harlena" and "Cuticura" spelled backward, and the anointed members of the inert body are simply the modified Italian *Belle Mani* ("beautiful hands") and the French *Petit Peton* ("little tootsy") in reverse; in Tindall's phrase, "reversal means renewal."[102] Had Joyce been able to tour a contemporary drugstore, he may well have modified his inverted phrasings: the shelves of these "pharmacies" carry bottle after bottle of unguents with names like "Wrinkle Away," "Dermalife," and "Nutraderm," and the backs of these bottles usually feature a little paragraph advising one to "Apply first thing in the morning, last thing at night."[103] The gerontophobic names of these magical medicines and the instructions pertaining to their use clarify the passage of the *Wake* under our attention: like the perfumed oils with which the Egyptians anointed their dead, the products here named in reverse foster the illusion of turning back time and reversing the process of aging and dying; like the funerary *uatch* and *mestchem* ointments, they hide the odors of the body, and the body itself, from people trained to attach greater value to things of the spirit. There is little contrivance, then, in the understanding by which the *Wake* sees the application of these products to the skin at bedtime as a kind of extreme unction, an anointing of the flesh in the hour at which it falls down dead to the world to release the soul into the underground of "Amanti": these ointments protect Joyce's sleeping hero from the certain threat of his own mortality. If, like the Egyptian dead, the man "tropped head" at Joyce's *Wake* has been invigorated and preserved with the embalming fluids of potent spirits, so too have he and his wife been anointed before their passage into the darkness—with extreme unguents whose names seem to be, if not "Harlena" and "Cuticura," then "Nivea" and "Pond's Cold Cream."[104]

Once the Egyptian corpse had undergone its curative anointing and the ceremony of "Opening the Mouth," the responsibility for its resurrection passed from the funerary priests and relatives to the dead man himself, who was now fortified with the powers of articulacy and literate consciousness. It was at this critical moment in the slow resurrective process that the Book of the Dead assumed a utilitarian value to the corpse stranded in Amenti, as the following passage from the *Wake* suggests:

> —Let Eiven bemember for Gates of Gold for their fadeless suns berayed her. Irise, Osirises! Be thy mouth given unto thee! . . . On the vignette is a ragingoos. The overseer of the house of the oversire of the seas, Nu-Men, triumphant, sayeth: Fly as the hawk, cry as the corncake, Ani Latch of the postern is thy name; shout!
> —My heart, my mother! My heart, my coming forth of darkness!   (493.27–35)

Here, as in the Book of the Dead, the moment being celebrated is not that of complete resurrection, but a moment of incremental liberation from the forces of inertia and obliviousness. The numinously renewed dead man ("Nu-Men," "I rise") has not quite yet found his way out of the realm of darkness and death, and the *Wake*, the wake, is not yet over; having passed beyond the Gates of Sunset ("Gates of Gold"), he has merely had his mouth opened by priests of Osiris and Amen-Ra ("fadeless suns berayed") who recite the funeral liturgy ("Arise, Osiris! Be thy mouth given unto thee!"). Finding his capacity for articulacy and literacy renewed, however, the Egyptian dead man reborn in Amenti would have reacted much like the man "going forth by black" in this passage: according to the particular threat that he sensed growing in the darkness, or according to the particular goal he wished to reach, he would have referred to the appropriate chapter of his book of the dead and recited the necessary "words of power." This in turn he would have accomplished by searching for the appropriate "vignette"—a picture of life beyond the grave drawn on the papyrus, which

Inside the Coffin

served as a kind of chapter-marking.[105] In this passage from the *Wake*, the corpse consults the "vignette" of "a ragingoos"—the evocation of a rainbow suggesting that the sleeper is rising toward a visual dream—and begins to read the magical spell from the corresponding chapter, much as the soul of Nu, the steward of the overseer of the seals, would have done:

> The steward of the overseer of the seals, Nu . . . saith: I rise up like Ra. . . . My heart, once brought low, is now made strong. I am a spirit in heaven, and mighty upon earth. I fly like a hawk, I cackle like the smen goose . . . I advance to the realm of the star-gods. The doors of Maat are opened to me. . . .
>
> "We will not allow thee to enter in over us," say the bars of [the doors of Maat], "unless thou tellest us our names." [And I reply], "Tongue of the place of Truth is your name." . . . The right lintel of this door saith: "I will not allow thee to pass over me unless thou tellest my name." [And I reply] "Strengthener of the support of Maat is thy name." . . .[106]

The first of these spells and the passage of the *Wake* that quotes it illustrate the principle underlying the many "Chapters of Making the Transformations" found in books of the dead: whether he wished to escape from danger, rise toward the boat of the sun, or fly to the house of Osiris, the prepared Egyptian found it advisable to include in his book of the dead chapters whose recitation would enable him, once his mouth was opened, to change into a hawk, a heron, a swallow, a serpent, a crocodile, or, finally, a Bennu bird (a phoenix).[107] Here, both as a hawk and a corncrake, the dead man flies to the House of Osiris, where he then draws upon another chapter of his Book of the Dead and, so as not to antagonize the gods of night and darkness, utters a second spell revealing his innocence and his familiarity with the underworld hidden in the body of Osiris. In the last line of the passage from the *Wake* quoted above ("My heart, my mother! My heart, my coming forth of darkness!"), the mummified dead man acknowledges that he has advanced one more degree toward his resurrection into new life: his mouth opened, he now becomes sensible of the heartbeat in his body and of his imminent rebirth.[108]

Although the passage is virtually identical in contour and wording to the passages quoted from the Papyrus of Nu, "th'osirian" hero of the *Wake* undergoes a far less dramatic experience then his counterpart in the Egyptian document. Not actually turning into a hawk or approaching the house of Osiris, he becomes capable of dreaming. In the Book of the Dead, the "Opening of the Mouth" enabled the dead man to rise from lethal absence into an attentuated half-life which made possible the reading and reciting of charms that insured his resurrection; in Joyce's book of the dead, the "opening of the mouth" seems to occasion a comparably incremental movement toward resurrection, by elevating its central figure from vacant sleep into a part of the night where, because dreams are inextricable from language, he becomes capable of hallucinated vision and hearing. The passage from the *Wake* under our attention, then, indeed signals a rebirth of sorts ("My heart, my mother! My heart, my coming forth of darkness!"), for in the process of finding his "mouth given unto him," Joyce's central figure rises from "Real Absence" and inertia into the kinds of "infrarational" thinking that Freud and his contemporaries explored in their studies of dreams and human infancy. And as recollectible dreams again begin to occupy this sleeping man, Freud in turn valuably illuminates his mind; for psychoanalysis has much to say about the symbolic meanings of birds, flight, and levitation in dreams, and the dream into which HCE now passes bears obscurely on snakes with evil intentions and volcanoes "in erupting" (494.8):

> —Apep and Uachet! Holy Snakes, chase me charley, Eva's got barley under her fluencies!"
> (494.14–16)

"Apep and Uachet" are "holy snakes" who appear in many Egyptian books of the dead: Aapep is the black, evil serpent who threatens to devour Ra in clouds just before his emergence at dawn from the blackness of Amenti; Uachet, beneficent "lady of flame," is a serpentine personification of the northern sky at sunrise.[109] Since these two conflicted serpents push their phallic heads into "the womb of Nut," the waters of the sky, at the same time that Ra begins resurrectively to rise into the world amid clouds of fire and smoke, in turn to give birth to a new day and to allow the resurrection of the sleeper, these lines suggest how Joyce might have found in the Book of the Dead—in addition to its sustained exploration of nothingness—forms of thought comparable to those underlying dreams. Here again, symbolic events that the Book of the Dead locates in the dark other world of Amenti, twentieth-century thought would locate in the other world of sleep.[110]

In the slow resurrective process that culminates in "the Opening of the Mouth" and the revival of perception, Joyce found the real plot of the Book of the Dead, the linearly progressive movement that determined the placement of each of the variable chapters in each of its variants. Not at all apparent, this plot lies concealed by diffusion in a highly allusive text which appears to bear more on the never-told, cyclically progressive stories of Ra and Osiris than on any real human being, and which also refers to everything known in the circular Egyptian cosmos but the real life of the subject who lies at its center, absent of all but his name—the Osiris Ani, the Osiris Nu. This plot, then, is also essentially that of the *Wake*. As the Book of the Dead unfolds, it reconstructs, from the "eyewitless foggus" of its absent central subject, a succession of events of dramatic consequence supposed to befall his corpse between death and resurrection: its mouth opened, it breathed, it sensed the presence of its heart, it battled with inertia and with the linens that swaddled it, it drifted its way through the kingdom of night fending off nightmarish visions, it passed through various levels of attenuated consciousness while lying inert in the body, it temporarily fended off thirst and hunger by subsisting on the images of food and water, and so forth. As in the *Wake*, so in the Book of the Dead: a reader who examined either of those books expecting to find a gripping story would, as Doctor Johnson remarked of *Clarissa*, "go and hang himself"; indeed, he might not even notice a linearly progressive account chronicling the heliotropic movement toward resurrection of a man lying inert in bed.

Just before the departed and absent subjects of these deadmen's books met the sun or awoke into the fields of Sekhet Hetep, however, they did finally manage a sequence of startling, active gestures. The soul of the deceased, having wandered through the nocturnal gloom of Amenti in estrangement from its deadened body, joined its new "spirit-body," which lay co-spatially within its corpse;[111] and "the double tet" of this renewed body—its backbone and its phallus—prepared to stand up

> upon the night of the things of the night of the making to stand up the double tet of the overseer of the seize who cometh from the mighty deep and on the night of making Horuse to crihumph over his enemy. . . .   (328.31–35)[112]

Accoutered with a new body that rose up out of its old one, the dead man now reemerged into active, physical vitality. According to "The Chapter of Opening the Tomb . . . and of Coming Forth by Day, and of Having Mastery over the Legs,"

> That which was shut hath been opened by the command of the Eye of Horus [the rising sun], which hath delivered me. Established are the beauties on the forehead of Ra. My steps are long. My legs are lifted up. I have performed the journey, my members are mighty and are sound.[113]

He lifted up his head from the pillow on which it lay, according to "The Chapter of the Pillow":

Awake out of thy sufferings, O thou who liest prostrate! Awake thou! Thy head is the horizon. I lift thee up, O thou whose word is truth.[114]

Finally, he moved into the company of the morning sun, or else into the wheat fields of Sekhet Hetep. And as Egyptologists have ascertained, the Egyptians conceived the fertile land of Sekhet Hetep in imagery reflective of the Nile delta on which the sun shown anew every morning, with three differences: the wheat grew taller there; people did not have to work as painfully; and no one who reached it died.[115] The resurrection into new life that the Egyptian corpse, the Osiris, was presumed to undergo at the end of its passage through Amenti, then, resembled an experience that Joyce interpreted simply as awakening:

> Verily, I am here. I have come. I behold thee. I have passed through the Tuat. I have seen Father Osiris. I have scattered the gloom of night. I am his beloved one. I have come. . . .[116]

While this reading of Egyptian mortuary texts has treated the Book of the Dead largely as if it were a version of *Finnegans Wake*, this emphasis might easily be reversed, so that the *Wake* might be read as a book of the dead. A peculiar transformation would then occur: the hero of the *Wake* would turn out not to be sleeping man, but a corpse, his departed spirit wandering in the other world. While some of Joyce's readers have approached *Finnegans Wake* in this way, finding in its "nekropolitan nights" and in its incessant references to the heavens and hells of earth's religions all manner of arcane revelation into the fabric of supernature, Joyce's own stated interest was always in the human experience of night, the evidence of the *Wake* itself suggesting that any prolonged scrutiny of events presumed to befall the stiff inside the coffin inevitably opens into a meditation on the state of sleep. The Book of the Dead, then, provided Joyce with a richly inflected hieroglyphy adequate to the reconstruction of a calmly sleeping twentieth-century man embedded in "the semitary of Somnionia": "going forth by black" and "coming forth of darkness," he lies both hidden and apparent, himself and not himself, alive while dead to the world.

Inside the Coffin

CHAPTER FIVE

The Identity of the Dreamer

HOW TO FIND A GOOD TAILOR

At the center of *Finnegans Wake*, in the darkest hours of its night, the story of a conflict between "Kersse the Tailor and the Norwegian Captain" occurs to our hero (II.ii, 311–30; cf. *U*, 61). As Ellmann explains it, the story is based on one that Joyce's father was fond of telling, "of a hunchbacked Norwegian captain who ordered a suit from a Dublin tailor, J. H. Kerse of 34 Upper Sackville Street. The finished suit did not fit him, and the captain berated the tailor for being unable to sew, whereupon the irate tailor denounced him for being impossible to fit" (*JJ*, 23). Though Ellmann goes on to note that the unpromising subject "became, by the time John Joyce had retold it, wonderful farce," its potential for sheer buffoonery has never been satisfactorily explained in writing on the *Wake*. It emerges, however, in a variant of the story according to which the captain, returning to pick up the suit he ordered, flies into a torrent of invective for the shoddy workmanship he discovers. The tailor looks at him with taxed professional calm, tugs at the garment, and says patiently, "Well, you're not wearing it right! If you just hold your arms like this [the arms twist up like mutant pretzels], if you hold your head like this [the head glues itself to the shoulder], and if you walk like this [the teller staggers off, doubled over and pigeon-toed], it fits perfectly."

What all this has to do with "a reconstruction of the nocturnal life" will become evident if, "by a commodius vicus of recirculation" (3.2), we "re-arrive" at the first page of *Finnegans Wake* and the paragraph containing the phrase "in bed"—now to note that the two sentences forming that paragraph are internally linked by the garish homophony of the verbs "retaled" (3.17 [properly, "retailed"]) and "entailed" (3.19). Only a very craftless or a very canny writer would ever have paired them so loudly. Through "sound sense" (109.15, 121.15), Joyce is calling attention to the essential relation of these two "tailwords" (288.3 ["detail," a third]), which derive together with "tailors" from the Old French *taillier* ("to shape by cutting," "to determine the form of"). The common element linking all these terms has to do with the idea of "tailoring"—formal alteration—it, too, made thematic from beginning to end of *Finnegans Wake*, though most notably in the "tail" (324.5 [or "retailored" "tale"]) of "Kersse the Tailor," which lengthily engages the dark questions "Who fits?" and "Who is suitable?" If the first sentence of that paragraph on the opening page tells us that a "fall" has happened "in bed," it adds by way of verbal qualification that this fall has been "retaled" there— "rendered piecemeal" in this way of telling ("retailing"), and necessarily "retailored" to suit the new and altered conditions of "the Evening World."

Now tailoring, in any form, simply involves the formal alteration of investments—articles of clothing—so that they come out fitting the body more comfortably. It works exactly like sleep if, "letting punplays pass to ernest" (233.19–20), we take "investments" or any of a whole array of related terms in the more abstract senses that have evolved from them. By day the hero of *Finnegans Wake*, something of "misfit," has a great many "vested" interests in "the factionable world" (285.26) represented in the map of Dublin, even though he sometime feels not "cut out for" (248.17) and "unsuited" to its "fashions," and though sometimes in turn, "fearing for his own misshapes" (313.32), he finds its "modes" unsuitable and "unfit-ting" (165.25, 127.4). Often they "rub him the wrong way" and afflict him with "wears and tears" (116.36). Survival in the "fashionaping" Daily World (505.8), where being "fascinating" is indistinct from "fashion-aping," re-quires a kind of "wearing" "uniformity," though nobody ever quite fits the swell-looking "uniform" or lives up to his "model" (191.25; see 127.4). It also demands both a keeping up of "appearances," with "apparel," and the maintaining of "habits" that ultimately "run him ragged" and "wear him down." Clearly, a person so "worn out" needs to be "redressed," and in both senses of that word: on the one hand, he needs to be compensated for afflictions, but on the other, he simply needs a new set of "investments." Relief Map B, then, shows "the Wreck of the Ragamuffin" (290.F5) whose sustained residence in the Daily World of Map A has left him in "Rags! Worns out" (619.19)—the submerged reference to "the Wreck of the Hesperus" (306.26–27), here as throughout the *Wake*, reminding us that the "hole affair" takes place after nightfall (Gr. *hesperos*, "evening", cf. 321.14–15, 387.20, 557.6). In reconstructing this "wrecked ragamuffin's" passage through a night, the *Wake* now issues a general invitation to "Come to the ballay at the Tailors' Hall" (510.14)—where the rhythm of the line and the paragraph it opens evokes a song entitled "The Night of the Ragman's Ball" (510.13–30 [*Annotations*]), and therefore suggests that this night will entail the wholesale "formal alteration" and "redressing" of a badly "worn out" "misfit": "Name or redress him and we'll call it a night" (514.17; cf. 232.20, 489.22–23).

As it turns into his body in sleep, accordingly, the "old worold" (441.18–19)—the "worn" out "old" "worryld" (59.10)—is retailored, so to become "whirrld" (147.22) and to undergo a series of "formal alterations" for which the *Wake*, fond of the prefix of renewal, generates many terms. As it turns into his body in sleep, "willed without witting, whorled without aimed" (272.4–5), it is "recorporated" (228.20), "regrouped" (129.12), "recompounded" (253.35), "remassed" (358.13), "reformed" (361.4), "rearrived" at "from scratch" (3.5, 336.18), and at bottom "recreated" so completely (606.7)—"rereally" (490.17)—that it comes out "rassembling" the reassembled "whorl" shown in Relief Map B (373.14, 6.24), where our hero's "own fitther couldn't nose him" (322.12–13 ["fitter"]). And especially not "his own father," whose "model" no son ever quite "fits": "we drames our dreams tell Bappy returns. And Sein annews" (277.17–18 [Fr. *Sein*, "bosom"]); "the same renew[s]" (226.17). The relief map accordingly illustrates "the Benefits of Recreation" in two senses of the latter word (306.22). Sleep, as a "solstitial pause for refleshmeant" (82.10), is in one sense simply a form of recreation or refreshment that enables our "worn out" hero to return to the world, after undergoing extensive "formal alterations," "finefeelingfit!" (431.1). But in another sense, because it entails a wholesale "dismantling" of the "fabric" of things, sleep re-creates the "worold" completely, retailoring it precisely by "re-fleshing" it, in the form of the body (hence "refleshmeant").[1]

In Carlylean terms, "sartor's risorted" (314.17 [L. *sartor resartus*, "the tailor's retailored"])—at "One Life One Suit (a men's wear store)" (63.16–17). And our worn-out hero, as "besuits" the "ragged," is now simply *suiting himself.* The orthodox way of putting this would be to say that in "sewing a dream together" (28.7), he is getting his wishes fulfilled—"nett sew?" (312.16). Tailoring, in *Finnegans Wake*, operates much like the "ingenious interweaving process" that Freud calls the dreamwork (*ID*, 317); for that, too, simply involves the "formal alteration" of "investments"—now construed as psychic ones—so that they fit the body more comfortably. It results in the production of that "weaver's masterpiece," the dream (*ID*, 319), where, "as the baffling yarn sail[s] in circles" (320.35), everything is formally altered to suit "our talorman" perfectly (see 375.34–35).

By "redressing" him, the dreamwork enables our hero to bid "sew wrong" (322.8 [and "so long"]) to a world characterized by "uniform matteroffactness" (123.10)—"Love my label like myself" (579.18)—and also to "curse the tailor" who taught him to "Respect the Uniform" (319.27, 320.2, 579.14 [hence "Kersse the Tailor"]). Since he harbors a great deal of bottled-up animosity for this "uniform," "he'll want all his fury gutmurtherers to redress him" (617.18–19); the wording here suggests that it will take a whole army of "fairy godmothers" to spin out the "baffling yarns" necessary to redress the "fury" and "murderousness" rising from his "gut," but at the same time to keep those forces comfortably concealed. As the *Wake* acknowledges in the play of these terms, the formal alterations that transform the Daily World of Map A into the Evening World of Map B make it difficult to know "**how** **c**omes **e**ver a body in our taylorised world to selve out thishis" (356.10–11 ["**how c**an anybody **e**ver solve out this thesis"])—where the line in part calls attention to the puzzling nature of meaning in dreams, but also latently reveals that HCE, the dreamer himself, inevitably "selves out" "this, his" world, and again, as it "suits" his body ("ever a body"). Passages in *Finnegans Wake* that allude to the story of "Kersse the Tailor" (23.10–11, for instance) operate in cipher to indicate that its hero is undergoing redress and a change of investments at the moment in question (e.g., at 22.30–23.15).

Now of all the properties formally altered in this wholesale retailoring of the world, one particularly bears note here: "telling," since Joyce has retailored the English "retail" into a neologistic "retale" on the first page of the book, and since a running play on words blurs together the meanings of "tailor" and "teller" throughout the *Wake* as a whole (cf. 317.27, 319.8, 319.24). The extended pun calls attention to problems of evident centrality in *Finnegans Wake* by inviting the simple question of how anyone can "tell" when he falls, or has fallen, asleep. As memory will attest, one largely does not, because "telling" is in every way antithetical to the condition of sleep. A Germanic equivalent of the Latinate derivative "rationality" (< L. *ratio*, "reckoning, calculation"), "telling" in even its most quotidian and feeble forms implies the ability deliberatively to put two and two together. At root, "to tell" simply means "to count," as in "telling" time or in working as a bank "teller"; but beyond that, it means "to take account," recognitively, as in "telling" what is going on. Finally, in this escalating calculus, "to tell" is to provide a coherent "account," as in "telling a story." The man "tropped head" at the *Wake* cannot "tell" in any of these senses. At the instant he "falls to tail" (285.11)—suffers that "knock out" and "falls to his tail"—he also "fails to tell" in every way possible. He cannot tell a story; he cannot tell what is going on; and he cannot even tell himself apart from the figures in his dreams, who in turn, after his example, can "not rightly tell their heels from their stools" (476.31 [their heads from their toes]). The whole matter of "telling," therefore, is necessarily "retailored" and formally altered in *Finnegans Wake*.

One way of seeing how extensively these formal alterations sweep through the *Wake* would be to examine very closely the syntax of that paragraph on page three containing the verbs "retaled" and "entailed."[2] A broader perspective on the matter would emerge from a consideration of the "tail" of Kersse the Tailor itself, which cannot be read as a narrative involving distinct characters, no matter how hard one tries, because the *Wake*'s "worn-out ragamuffin" simultaneously plays the parts of the misfit and of the dream-weaving "talerman" who suits himself (319.8). The episode reconstructs not a discrete sequence of real-world encounters, but a general process of unconscious "redress" that reaches its climax in the murderous story of the shooting of the Russian general (who is at once our hero's father and our hero himself in the role of a father under attack by two sons). As this example in turn suggests, an ultimate way of seeing how radically the *Wake*'s "telling" is retailored to suit the conditions of the night would be to begin inquiring into the identity of the man who sleeps at *Finnegans Wake*, and all the more essentially because the question, "Who is he?," is central to a coherent reading of the book (261.28). The strangeness of this question emerges fully if we simply bend it back into "our own nighttime": how does anyone sleepily "knock[ed] out" and unconscious "tell" who he is?

"RIGHTING HIS NAME"

As will have become evident in passing, and as many passages in the *Wake* make clear, both the "nomen" (L. "name") of the "noman" who sleeps at *Finnegans Wake* (546.4) and "the facts of his nominigentilisation" (31.33–34) constitute an ongoing problem in the book, rather than a dislodgeable point of information:

> Here line the refrains of. Some vote him Vike, some mote him Mike, some dub him Llyn and Phin while others hail him Lug Bug Dan Lop, Lex, Lax, Gunne or Guinn. Some apt him Arth, some bapt him Barth, Coll, Noll, Soll, Will, Weel, Wall but I parse him Persse O'Reilly else he's called no name at all.   (44.10–14)

Given these mutually contradictive and ridiculous choices, and considering that the ostensibly privileged name "Persse O'Reilly" fails to appear in "The Ballad of Persse O'Reilly" at all, we should incline toward the culminative item in this catalogue ("he's called no name at all")—and all the more particularly because the phrase "here lie the refrains of" reminds us that we are sharing the "eyewitless foggus" of somebody "dead to the world" in a dimension void of objects, whose "tropped head" contains only the "remains" of "lines" and "refrains," and not alertly arranged and ordered letters. Of necessity the man asleep at *Finnegans Wake* "remain[s] topantically anonymos" throughout the whole book (Gr. *to pan*, "the whole") because he has "tropped head" (34.2–6), concomitantly jettisoning the orderly stuff that ordinarily fills it, not least of which is a knowledge of his own name. As Joyce remarked in an interview of 1936, "there are, so to say, no individual people in the book—it is as in a dream, the style gliding and unreal as is the way in dreams. If one were to speak of a person in the book, it would have to be of an old man, but even his relationship to reality is doubtful."[3]

Anyone's "blank memory" of the night will attest that no one fully unconscious has a retrievable grip on his name, social security number, facial appearance as it most recently gelled in the mirror or the ego, or other such accoutrements of "identity" as enable him, in waking life, to know himself as familiarly as a third person. The *Wake*, accordingly, responds only with positive negativity to continually raised questions about the "indentity" (49.36 [the negated "identity"]) of its sleeping protagonist, as is suggested by the parenthetical answer to the question "Who was he to whom? (O'Breen's not his name nor the brown one his maid)" (56.32–33). By reference to Thomas Moore's lyric "Oh! Breathe not his name," the line indicates that the "naym" of this "nobodyatall" (29.19, 73.19)—where the "nay" negates the "name"—cannot be "breathed" at all, and for reasons lengthily spelled out in Moore's poem.[4] The chain of patently absurd names cited above, then—itself only representative of the string of names that runs through the book as a whole—constitutes only one of many "a long list (now feared in part lost) . . . of all abusive names he was called" (71.5–6),

The Identity of the Dreamer

where these "abusive names" might be understood as the products of no-menclatural "misuse" and "abuse" both. Like many "a word often abused" in *Finnegans Wake* (149.34)—"abuse" included—they should not be taken at face value because each of them shows our hero "under the assumed name of Ignotus Loquor" (263.2–3 [L. *ignotus loquor*, "I am talking about the unknown"]).

Though the thousands of variable names patched around the "topantically anonymos" "belowes hero" of the *Wake* serve ultimately to cancel one another out—"In the name of the former and of the latter and of their holocaust. Allmen" (419.9–10)—so to emphasize his essential unnamability, they also serve the crucial purpose of capturing him obliquely, in the manner of "nicknames" (32.18, 46.1; 59.16, 98.27), "bynames" (29.31), "agnomen[s]" (30.3), "moniker[s]" (46.21), and "assumed names" and "illassumed names" both (49.8, 263.2; 86.12). They work associatively, that is, like the dream-work's condensed and "composite structures," to reveal underlying states and conflicts that befall "this most unmentionablest of men" in his drift through the night (320.12–13).[5] The nickname "Timb" or "Tomb" (139.10 ["Finnegan"]), for instance, shows our hero laid out dead to the world. While some may call him "Gunne or Guinn" (44.12), he is surely, as a "Gunnar, of The Gunnings, Gund" (596.15), "Goney, goney gone!" (306.F2). As "Finn," by contrast ("some dub him Llyn and Phin" [44.11]), his "spatiality" (172.9 ["speciality"]) is the containment of space (hence the enclosure of "Dublin" in "dub him Llyn"). And since "some apt him Arth" (44.12), an "apt" composite name might be "Arser of the Rum Tipple" (359.15–16), which designates neither "Arthur of the Round Table" exactly nor a "blacked-out" "rummy" whose "tippling" has landed him "on his ars" either (514.34), but their point of convergence, together with the sleeper's, in a once-and-future figure who will "rise afterfall" (78.7).[6]

As the example of these particular "bynames" and the *Wake* itself suggests, the trick to answering the excellent question posed and tackled by Adaline Glasheen in her *Censuses*—"Who's Who When Everybody is Somebody Else?"[7]—is simply to untangle, as in dream analysis, the "condensed" and "displaced" figures that have been "traduced by their comedy nominator to the loaferst terms" (283.6–8). Beneath the whole of *Finnegans Wake*, underlying all the "samilikes" and "alteregoases" and "pseudoselves" in the book (576.33), there lies only a singular "comedy nominator," the "one stable somebody" (107.30) whose nightlife generates the "comic denominations," distorting (or "traducing") them in the process, but who is finally the only real "common denominator" underlying them all. Given any name in *Finnegans Wake*, then, the reader should reduce it "to the loaferst terms"—where the appearance of the book's omnipresent and tell-tale "loafer" in this "lowest" suggests that such a reduction would best be accomplished simply by asking how the name reflects on its hero's "lofetime" (230.19 [nocturnal "lifetime"]).

If, "by a commodius vicus of recirculation," we "rearrive" at the vicinity of the opening page containing the phrase "in bed," all the strange nominal evocations surrounding it now turn out to reveal a little more about the constitution of "Arser's" "knock[ed] out" and "tropped head" at this particular moment in the night. Like Humpty Dumpty ("the fall," "offwall" "humptyhillhead," "humself," "prumptly," "tumptytumtoes"), he has fallen, although asleep, so to enter a state of mind "scrambled," "addled," "cracked," infantilely regressive, and elusive of capture in the King's English (47.26). Like anyone rubbled "after [the] humpteen dumpteen revivals" of a lifetime's mornings (219.15 [who counts them?]), our hero has been "eggspilled" (230.5 ["expelled"]) from the wakeaday reality represented in Map A and transformed, from *homme* to "homelette" (59.29–32), into the scrambled "eggshill" (415.9–10 ["exile"]) depicted in Relief Map B, where he lies "embedded," a Finnegan of sorts, in the night's "seemetery": *Hombly, Dombly Sod We Awhile*" (415.14–15). As "a once wallstrait oldparr," comparably, "to name no others, of whom great things were expected in the fulmfilming department" (398.24–26), our hero resembles the legendary "Old Parr" simply in being an "old pa" or *père* (Fr. "father"), burdened with a "scraggy isthmus" (3.5–6 [Gr. *isthmos*, "neck"]) and a "body you'd pity" (381.15), but also with desires difficult of fulfillment in the day.[8] In the night, however, where this "old pa's" wishes get furtively "fulmfilmed," the term "Old Parr"—"to name no others"—in a way "names" "no others," but only the old man himself: since to be an "Old Parr" would be any old man's dream, the term shows our hero wishfully dissolving conflicts that arise from a waning virility. "Reduced to the loaferst terms," then, even particular "nicknames" like "Humpty Dumpty" and "Old Parr" turn out to describe states of unconsciousness and unconscious conflict endured in the sleep of the book's heroic "loafer"—though in their self-eradicating contradictiveness, again, they leave the *Wake*'s "knock[ed] out" nobody "called no name at all." And to the essential question, "Who is he?" (261.28)—"whoishe whoishe whoishe?" (499.35–36)—there are two primary kinds of answer. For as "someone imparticular" (602.7), our "belowes hero" is "someone in particular" whom the night has rendered indistinct.

The Identity of the Dreamer

"IN THE HEART OF THE ORANGEFLAVOURED MUDMOUND"

As readers of *Finnegans Wake* have long noted, Joyce incessantly likens "our mounding's mass," as depicted in Relief Map B, to a vast "dump" (110.26), or "DUNGMOUND" (276.R1), or "kikkinmidden" (503.8)—where the Danish archaeological term *kikkenmidden* (Eng. "kitchen midden") designates a heap of bones marking the site of a prehistoric dwelling, *midden* itself deriving from the Da. *møg dynge* ("dung hill" or "refuse heap"). "A sort of heaps" (596.18), "our mounding's mass" constitutes a "dump" of this nature because his rubbled and "deafadumped" body (590.1), now dead to the world, marks the site of a past life (yesterday's, for instance) and because matters deriving from his past, including letters, are buried inside of it. One way of discovering what lies "in the heart of the orangeflavoured mudmound" (111.34)—the "orange" makes our hero a Protestant— would be to *Dig him in the rubsh!* (261.L2 ["dig in the rubbish," or "dig him in the ribs" and wake him up]).

We might see the image of this "dump" particularized by "rearriving" at the book's first page and the vicinity of the phrase "in bed," now to consider "the great fall of the offwall" that it describes (3.18–19). Since the odd compound "offwall" evokes the German *Abfall*, the Danish-Norse *affald*, the Dutch *afval*, and the English *offal*, all generally meaning "refuse or scraps," the paragraph that we have been examining might now be construed as a dense trash heap compacted of things let fall: "oranges . . . laid to rust upon the green," a "dumptied" "Humpty Dumpty" (17.4), a badly contused Finnegan, letters that may have become "litters" (17.28), and finally, containing them all, our "scrapheaped" hero himself (98.17), a "dustman" of sorts (59.16 [Br. "garbage collector"]). "What a mnice old mness it all mnakes! A middenhide hoard of objects!" (19.7–8 [and a "midnight hoard of objects" internalized]).

These details suggest in particular what the paragraph shows more generally if considered as a formal whole. On the evident verbal surface, it reads like a scrap heap of conceptually disconnected words, fragments, references, and quotations: "it's like a dream." For in the psychoanalytical account of dream formation, the manifest content of any dream is much like the manifest content of this paragraph, in being particled together of "residue"—"the day's residue"—or, in Freud's German, *Tagesreste*, where the German *Reste*, literally meaning "remains" or "dregs," would figuratively give the dream the surface structure of a mnemonic dump. Through its ongoing reference to "dumps" and "middens," in part, the *Wake* is concretely convey-ing the orthodox insight that dreams are compacted of immense networks of scraps and fragments salvaged from the past.[9]

Another way of reading *Finnegans Wake*, then, would be to see any one section of it as a chaotic trash heap of mnemonic bric-a-brac, scraps, trivia, personal memories, and particles of information gathered from such places as the *Encyclopaedia Britannica* and Dublin's papers and lore. Rather than examining the "infrarational" connections that coherently link these par-ticles of residue together in the "Evening World," it would be possible to trace them back to their sources in the Daily World, to see where they came from and to infer things about "the days when **Head-in-C**louds walked the **e**arth" (18.23–24 [as opposed to his nights, when he does not]). Studies of the *Wake* that identify the "facts" constituting its manifest content do just this, and they accordingly serve the important purpose of putting our hero's "nightlife" into a concrete, real-world context and milieu. The richness of these studies enables us to work backwards from the *Wake*, to establish a sense not of our hero's nightlife, but of his life in the day; and they allow us to begin seeing "this very pure nondescript" as a Bloom-like "ordinary man" (64.30), "somebody mentioned by name in his telephone directory" (118.12–13).

Although we have so far regarded "Sir Somebody Something" as a stupe-fied anyman (293.F2), an "imparticular" "**H**ere **C**omes **E**verybody" (32.18–19), the sheer density of certain repeated details and concerns allows us to know that he is a particular, real Dubliner. The nature of these recurring concerns, moreover, enables us to see that most of what Joyce leaked out to his publicists and much of what the criticism has inferred is largely true. Our hero seems to be an older Protestant male, of Scandinavian lineage, connected with the pubkeeping business somewhere in the neighborhood of Chapelizod, who has a wife, a daughter, and two sons. Since the subject of his dreams is *not* these people or places as objective entities, however, but the more complex matter of his "investments" in them, a great deal about his factual life in the Daily World is hard to reconstruct with any certainty. *Finnegans Wake* offers less a factual "family history" than a "family his-trionic" (230.29).

What emerges from an examination of the details is the sense of someone as singularly unsingular as Leopold Bloom. As "the herewaker of our hame-fame" rises from the vacuum of his sleep toward a reacquired knowledge of his "real namesame" in the last pages of the book (619.12–13), his spec-tacular lack of distinction becomes more and more evident (and notably in

III.iv). "One of the two or three forefivest fellows a bloke could in **h**oliday **c**rowd **e**ncounter" (596.15–17), he could not stand out in a crowd if he tried. Repeated indications suggest that he is "a man of around fifty" (506.34), roughly "fiftytwo heirs of age" (513.23), "anything . . . between fiftyodd and fiftyeven years of age" (380.13–14) or, more elaborately:

> a man in brown about town . . . picking up ideas, of well over or about fiftysix or so, pithecoid proportions [Eng., "apelike"], with perhops five foot eight, the usual X Y Z type . . . not in the studbook by a long stortch . . . always trying to poorchase movables by hebdomedaries for to putt in a new house to loot [to let], cigarette in his holder, with a good job and pension in Buinness's, what about our trip to Normandy style conversation . . . seeking relief in alcohol and so on. . . .
> (443.20–444.2)

Reference both to the draining activity of "poorchase" ("purchase") and to a "hebdomadary" ("weekly") salary earned in a "business" involving "Guinness's" (hence "Buinness's") tells us something about this man's income, as does reference to the "movables" that his harried "poor chase" takes as its objects ("movables," sl. for "small objects of value," also suggest the Fr. *meubles*, "furniture"). It is through countless details like these that we gradually amass the sense of a life as heartwrenchingly drab as Bloom's, a life of dispiriting modern routine whose quotidian highlights seem to be:

> business, reading newspaper, smoking cigar, arranging tumblers on table, eating meals, pleasure, etcetera, etcetera, pleasure, eating meals, arranging tumblers on table, smoking cigar, reading newspaper, business   (127.20–23)

As the mirrorlike structure of this little catalogue implies, the alpha and omega of the whole arrangement is "business," which brackets everything else so stolidly that "pleasure" can only dissolve in a listless blur of ill-defined "etceteras" somewhere in the middle of things. This happens because when our hero does get away from "business, reading newspaper, etcetera," "pleasure" takes singularly limited and unimaginative forms:

> minerals, wash and brush up, local views, juju toffee [a real treat!], comic and birthdays cards [on special days of the year]; those were the days and he was their hero.   (127.24–25)

Passages like these evoke a quotidian tedium much of the sort that our hero himself foresees in the late hours of the *Wake*, as he grows dimly conscious of the imminence of another day-in-the-life of this quality and so sinks resolutely back into sleep:

> Retire to rest without first misturbing your nighbor, mankind of baffling descriptions. Others are as tired of themselves as you are. Let each one learn to bore himself. It is strictly requested that no cobsmoking, spitting, pubchat, wrastle rounds, coarse courting, smut, etc, will take place amongst those hours so devoted to repose.
>
> (585.34–586.3)

These details also suggest why Joyce, rather than writing another novel like *Ulysses*, sought in *Finnegans Wake*, with a Protestant publican rather than a Jewish ad-canvasser as a hero, to provide an account of the "alternate night-joys" (357.18) that lavishly open in the unharnessed imagination of this "very pure nondescript" and in the dreams through which he is "redressed." What he is unconscious of is precisely his own potential, and the possibility that life could be so much more.

The reader will notice that each of the passages examined above contains a reference to liquor ("Buinness's"), to barkeeping and bottlewashing ("arranging tumblers on table"), to pubs ("pubchat"), or to the sordid glory of the barroom ("wrastle rounds, coarse courting, smut, etc"). These are only representative instances of details whose continual recurrence compels us to see our hero as a "large incorporate licensed vintner, such as he is, from former times" (580.23–24 [like yesterday]). Though the wishfully inflated terms here elevate him into a better businessman than he seems to be, they inevitably suggest, together with an unending stream of references to a barroom ambience evoked through song fragments and gossip, that our hero is a "headboddylwatcher of the chempel of Isid" (26.17 ["head bottle-washer of Chapelizod"]). All such references as these would constitute vestiges of "the day's residue," too, allowing us to see the barroom as our hero's sphere of operation. "Arranging tumblers on tables" is his life.

One would be hard pressed to find a page in *Finnegans Wake* that did not name a variety of kinds and brands of alcohol and in part because these items are our hero's occupational tools; alcohol in general is part of his days' residue.[10] But if, on the one hand, these references allow us to work backwards from the manifest content of the text to draw inferences about "the days when Head-in-Clouds walked the earth," meanings in dreams are "overdetermined," so that these references also operate symbolically, to help describe the nights when "Head-in-Clouds" just lies there. Since alcohol has the power to "black out" and render him "alcoh alcoho alcoherently" "absintheminded" (40.5, 464.17; see 380.7–382.26), it invariably operates in the *Wake* as a cipher for the opiating powers of sleep: "poppypap's a passport out," but so are sleep and heavy drinking (25.5; cf. 84.17–18, 475.9–10). Be-

The Identity of the Dreamer

cause alcohol does to the brain much what sleep does, blotting out rationality and lifting inhibitions, the move "From Miss Somer's nice dream back to Mad Winthrop's delugium stramens" (502.29–30 ["midwinter's delirium tremens"]) is an inevitable one. "Arser of the Rumtipple," then, has "boomarpoorter on his brain" (327.33–34 [wishful delusions of Napoleonic grandeur because of strong-spirited "water on the brain"]), and also "a boodle full of maimeries" in both his "boozum" and his "hoagshead" (348.7, 449.16, 15.31 ["bottlefull"]); the reference here, to a "Howth head" with all the internal properties of a "hogshead," invites us again to inspect the "tropped head," of the figure shown "evidently under the spell of liquor" in the relief maps (43.16) and to ask the question, sustained in the *Wake*,

> —Wisha, is he boosed or what, alannah? . . .
> —Or he's rehearsing somewan's funeral.
>
> (477.5, 9)

Since the person "knock[ed] out" never knows what hit him, questions like this one, as far as he can "no," can have no answer: "it may half been a missfired brick" that "conk[ed] him" out (5.26, 170.14), or perhaps "he had had had o'gloriously a'lot too much hanguest or hoshoe fine to drink" (63.21–23 [Gael. *thoise fíon*, "fill of wine"; "had had had" yields "'had' one too many"]). Alcohol, at any rate, saturates Joyce's "alcohoran" (20.9–10) for an overdetermined variety of reasons.

So too do references to names of pubs and inns, which drift through our hero's "nightlife" because he is concerned about his work and anxious about the competition.[11] But at the same time, meanings in dreams being overdetermined, many of these pub-names also serve latent, sleep-descriptive functions. Etymologically, an "inn" is a place where one is not "out," and our "innermost" "innerman," (194.3, 248.32, 462.16) in the "duskguise" of "Here Inkeeper," (376.10 [not "innkeeper"]), does a very good job of "keeping in." As an "innvalet" (320.15), he is not simply a public servant ("inn valet"), but one asleep in bed (hence "invalid"). "Malthus is yet lukked in close" throughout the *Wake* (604.7), comparably, partly because this "Inkeeper's" "malthouse" is closed for the night, but also because, simply by sleeping, he is practicing a form of birth control (hence "Malthus"). Pub names like "The Old Sot's Hole" (41.32, 147.5), the "Halfmoon and Seven Stars" (59.1–2), the "Blackamoor's Head" (59.2), and the "Black and All Black" (59.4) accordingly help to evoke the blacked-out head of a benighted man who "is not all there, and is all the more himself since he is not so, being most of his time down at the Green Man" (507.3–4); and while this "Green Man" seems simply to name another pub, it also suggests that this man "keeping in" at "the Mullingcan Inn" (64.9), "mulling" as best as he "can," will rise from the dead in the morning (like "the green man" of folklore).[12] Attention to subliminal meanings like these, layered everywhere under the *Wake*'s verbal surface, now leads us back into a consideration of our hero's "imparticularity" in the night.

HCE

One of many passages in the *Wake* that clarifies our hero's "*Unmentionability*" (107.7) explains that

> . . . there is said to have been quondam (pfuit! pfuit!) some case of the kind implicating, it is interdum believed, a quidam (if he did not exist it would be necessary quoniam to invent him) . . . who has remained topantically anonymos but . . . was, it is stated . . . seemingly . . . tropped head. . . .   (33.32–34.6)

These tangled words (note the six passive constructions) require some sorting out. They tell us that while the "topantically anonymos" man who sleeps at *Finnegans Wake* is largely only "a quidam" (L. "a certain unnamed person") with a "quondam" identity—"it used to be there" when "he was" (L. *quondam fuit*), but now it simply isn't—Joyce had to find a way of designating the central presence of his hero throughout the book; for "if he did not exist (and it is not at all clear that anyone "dead to the world" does) it would be necessary quoniam to invent him" (L. *quoniam*, "because," "for this reason"). While "allauding to him by all the licknames in the litany," then (234.21–22), Joyce draws on the inventive "sigla H.C.E." (32.14) less to "allude to" than to identify the "one stable somebody" who sleeps (107.30), unnamable because unconscious, at *Finnegans Wake*. Operating between lines (481.1–3), within words (421.23 ["**He**Cit**E**ncy"]), in reverse order (623.9 ["ech?"]), but primarily in acrostic formations, the "normative letters" HCE (32.18) permeate *Finnegans Wake*, moving through the body of the text with supple protoplasticity, so to convey the continuous presence of a specific "Homo Capite Erectus" (101.12–13) within whom the "hole affair" unfolds. "A family all to himself" (392.23–24), "**h**e is **e**e and no **c**ounter he who will be ultimendly respunchable for the **h**ubbub **c**aused in **E**denborough" (29.34–36 [as for everything else in the book]). Like "Punch," in other words, "all the charictures in the drame" (302.31–32) are mere puppets invisibly controlled by HCE—a "puppetry producer" of sorts (219.6–8)—who alone is "responsible" for their motions (hence "respunchable").

Only interior to "the **h**eavenly one with his **c**onstellatria and his **e**manations" (157.18–19) do all other manifestly differentiated "characters" like ALP, Shem, Shaun, and Issy appear, as "constellated" products of his dreaming mind, in the manner of the Kabbalah's sephirotic emanations (see 29.13–15, 261.23–24).

Consider, for example, "Shaun the Post," who seems to attain the status of an independent character in the third book of *Finnegans Wake* and whom the criticism customarily treats as a discrete agent. Not simply Joyce's remark that "there are no characters" in *Finnegans Wake*, but countless details in Book III itself reveal that Shaun's evidently "uniform" appearance is really "fumiform" (413.31 [L. "made of vapor"]); that he "weigh[s] nought" (407.5), like any phantom; and that his "autobiography," a nonexistent "blank," is "handled . . . in the ligname of Mr van Howten" (413.30–414.3). Since this "ligname" designates a body dead to the world (Ger. *Leichnam*, "corpse"), and since the "nickname" "van Howten" moves us into "Howth" ("HEAD"), the details show that Shaun is only a figment in HCE's "tropped head," representative of a letter-carrying and letter-conscious state of mind into which the dreamer ascends as he moves toward wakening.[13] The notoriously strange "barrel" in which Shaun appears ("I am as plain as portable enveloped" "care of one of Mooseyeare Goonness's registered andouterthus barrels" [414.10–12]) is therefore simply a cipher for the imperceived and "unknown body" of HCE (96.29), within which the "fumiform[ed]" Shaun and all kinds of letters are in fact "enveloped": etymologically, the English word "body" derives from the Old English *bodig* ("a cask" or barrel) and is cognate with the Middle Low German *boddig* ("a tub for brewing") because then as now the body was perceived as a container of better things ("spirits"). While Shaun's barrel seems to be one of "Msr. Guinness's," then, the spelling "Mooseyeare Goonness's" also suggests that beneath all appearances, Shaun is simply a diffuse aggregate of "spirits," a being with all the palpability of a fairy tale figure (hence "Mother Goose"), who appears inside of HCE.

It is impossible, of course, not to wonder why Joyce chose "the sigla H.C.E." to designate his hero, although these "initials majuscule," strictly speaking, mean nothing and are "meant to be baffling" (119.16–17). In the form explored by Roland McHugh, the "chrismon trilithon sign ⊓ , finally called after some his hes hecitency Hec" (119.17–18), stands outside of all familiar alphabetic systems;[14] while its acrostic equivalent, "the sigla H.C.E.," "means" something independently of phonetic systems. The two formations constitute, like the letter M in Beckett's *Unnamable* trilogy, a sign without signification, a human formation closed to any referential exterior, and so come to carry, in *Finnegans Wake*, the weight of the Biblical Tetragrammaton, the unnamable name, in evoking only "a rude breathing on the void of to be" (100.27), "the allimmanence of that which Itself is Itself alone" (394.32–33 ["rude breathing" suggests the formative breath or "spirit" of YHWH in Genesis]). Still, since the characters in the acrostic *are* Romanic, and since Joyce was hardly a practitioner of the arbitrary, it seems inevitable that a rationale should underlie his choice of the trigrammaton HCE. The configuration clearly works better than HIM or IAM, either of which would hardly have been obscure enough to conform to anyone's sense of sleep (see, however, 166.18–19). But why HCE?

Readers who have engaged this question seem to have arrived at a sketchy consensus, commonly detecting somewhere beneath HCE an evocation of the words of consecration in the Roman Catholic Mass (incidentally the longest wake on record): *Hoc est enim corpus meum* ("For this is my body").[15] The reading is difficult to disregard once it is pointed out because it enables HCE always to verge on signifying, without ever fully doing so, *hoc corpus est*—"This is the body," stripped of pronominal definiteness and caught at the transubstantiative moment in which "word is made flesh," and primarily only flesh. It enables HCE to mean nothing, in other words, in much the same way that the body "means" nothing. Whether or not one buys a reading this definitive is finally not crucial because its purport is everywhere evident anyway. Sleep is absolutely transubstantiative in force: turning the whole world into the body of the sleeper, it incarnates everything (see relief map). If the text periodically warns us that "it is a slopperish matter, given the wet and low visibility," "to idendifine the individuone" of which it treats (51.3–6 ["to identify" and "define" the "one" "individual"]), it adds by way of parenthetical explanation that the whole business is "slopperish" because the "sword of certainty which would indentifide the body never falls" (51.5–6). The wording here, for all its cultivated vagueness plainly "identifies the body," even as it "hides" it (hence "indentifide"), and in much the same way that the cipher HCE simultaneously "identifies" and "hides" the *Wake*'s central figure, "the presence (of a curpse)" (224.5–6). While "allauding to him by all the licknames in the litany," then (234.21–22)—by all such "nicknames" as "Finnegan," "Arser," "Old Parr," "etcicero" (152.10)—Joyce draws on "the sigla H.C.E." less to "allude to" than to "indentifide" the "Great Sommboddy" lying "dead to the world" at the *Wake* (415.17 [Fr. *somme*, "sleep"]), and to identify it largely as some "*body*"; for underlying all the *Wake*'s allusive "licknames" one finds only a body "let drop as a doomsbody drops" (289.15): these "licknames," too, "indentifide" the Ger. *Leichnam* ("corpse").

As HCE, then, the "belowes hero" of *Finnegans Wake* is not at all a "character," possessed of reified properties like "personality," "individuality," and "identity," but a body, inside of which, "tropped head," there is no consciousness of anything much outside, except as it has been cargoed and reformed in memory; on top of and throughout which, in wakefulness, the man-made constructs of character, personality, individuality, identity, and ego have been layered. This is the case not simply because all of these concepts and terms are arbitrary constructions entertained in consciousness to describe conscious agents, but also because they are parochially modern and narrow fictions, and not transhistorical or innate human properties. Developed in that period of historical upheaval that saw, with the rise of the novel, the evolution of a sense of selfhood compatible with the urgencies of capitalism, terms like "character" and "personality" harness the human into kinds of self-"possession"—ones heavily invested with a sense of the "proper" and "propriety," of "ownership" and one's "own"—that ensure adaptive survival within a system structured on the values of "possession" and "property."[16] The artificiality of these "fibfib fabrications" (36.34) enables us to see from yet another perspective why Joyce would have spoken of *Finnegans Wake* as a work breaking with a certain form of Cartesianism. It is not simply that no one asleep has the least consciousness of objective reality, or of the manifold objects of which it is constituted. In a world void of objects, "if I may break the subject gently" (165.30 [and this last time in a philosophical sense]), we also find the complementary property of the "subject," in whose eyewitness focus those objects congeal, "disselving" (608.5 ["dissolving"]). Insofar as the *Wake* has a psychological "subject," that "sopjack" is simply "an unknown body" (96.29).

If, then, we "rearrive" at the opening page of the book, we might see that "**H**owth **C**astle and **E**nvirons" (3.3)—an odd locution, when all is said and done—does not straightforwardly designate "Dublin," but Dublin as it has been transubstantiated and incarnated inside the all-absorbing cipher HCE; or, in Freudian terms, Dublin as it has been introjected and incorporated; or, in Joycean terms, Dublin as it has been swallowed "schlook, schlice and goodridhirring" (7.18–19 ["hook, line, and sinker"]), interior to a body that has "disselv[ed]" under "the **H**elpless **C**orpses **E**nactment" of sleep into the elements of "**h**allucination, **c**auchman, **e**ctoplasm" (423.31, 133.24). If the first two of these elements evoke the familiar province of the dream and the nightmare (Fr. *cauchemar*), the last evokes only the less accessible eventfulnesses passed out in a body fallen "under **h**eaviest **c**orpsus **e**xemption" and submitted to the "**c**hanged **e**ndocrine **h**istory" of night (362.17, 136.28): "ectoplasm," in the discourse of spiritualism, is the "no-matter" that forms the bodies of ghosts; in embryology, it is the primal matter from which, "later on life," all surfaces of the body that negotiate contact with the external world—sensory organs, skin, brain, "brainskin" (565.13)—eventually evolve. As a phrase, then, "**H**owth **C**astle and **E**n-virons" merely accomplishes in small what that paragraph at the bottom of page three does more elaborately. Like every other construction containing "the sigla H.C.E.," it shows our hero "**h**iding the **c**rumbends of his **e**nor-mousness" "to the **h**idmost **c**oignings of the **e**arth" (102.6, 118.36–119.1); for concealed beneath every manifest appearance in the *Wake*'s nocturnal uni-verse ("hidmost") is the unconscious body of its sleeper, "himself in the flesh" (79.2), within whose "cremains" (hence "crumbends") all landscapes hallucinatorily or ectoplastically arise.

These considerations will enable us to begin filling in the vast "blank memory" we all have of the night by allowing us to see that what must take place in parts of sleep void of dreams is the body itself, which has to be there in the "Real Absence" of everything else for one "to be continued." This in turn will suggest why the opening pages of *Finnegans Wake* will con-form, as "representation," to anyone's experience of the night, though not to a conventionally conceived dream. Since the content of our "knock[ed] out" hero's "tropped head" here is largely "his own body" (185.36)—"an un-known body" as dead to the world as Finnegan's—what is ultimately being represented is less a dream than the fertile ground of dreams; and if in wake-fulness HCE "has" a body, in the night he simply "is" one. *Finnegans Wake*, in other words, is a representation of a human body. This is only what we might expect of a work entitled the *Wake*, where, as at all wakes, the body is the life of the party. *Finnegans Wake* now becomes a "vivle" of sorts (110.17), a form of "secret stripture" whose subject is "the supreme impor-tance . . . of physical life" (293.F2, 35.22–23).

Ten years before *Finnegans Wake* was published, in that collection of essays entitled *Our Exagmination*, for which Joyce claimed responsibility, Marcel Brion spoke of *Work in Progress*, predictably enough, as an enterprise seeking to convey "a reality true and whole in itself," "obey[ing] its own laws and appear[ing] to be liberated from the customary physical restraints." But he added:

> I imagine that [Joyce] could write an unprecedented book composed of the simple interior physical existence, of a man, without anecdotes, without supernumeraries,

The Identity of the Dreamer

with only the circulation of the blood and the lymph, the race of the nervous excitations towards the centres, the twisting of emotion and thought through the cells.[17]

Ten years later, presumably, Joyce had realized what in 1929 lay yet undone.
A number of gathering energies in Joyce's literary career make it plausible
that the *Wake* should move toward this end—not least the evidence of *Ulysses*, which ends were *Finnegans Wake* merely begins, *inside* a human body
on the verge of sleep; and whose real structure (retrospectively elicited as
Joyce revised and drew up the Gilbert-Linati schemata) turned out to be that
of the human body, an organism Bloom-like in its adaptive energies, rather
than an organization foreplanned. The body is, to some ways of thinking, a
Catholic prepossession—the "cloacal obsession" of H. G. Wells's phrase—
though by the time Joyce had passed through *Ulysses* into *Finnegans Wake* he
had found it as catholic in its understructuring impingements on the real as
had Freud ("One life is all. One body. Do. But do" [*U*, 202]). If by 1937 Joyce
had taken to demeaning *Ulysses* as "a little prelude to WIP [*Work in Progress*]"—and in some sense, rightly—he clarified the preludic relation of his
"day book" to his "night book" by calling *Ulysses* "more an epic of the body
than of the human spirit," going on to observe impatiently that "for too long
were the stars studied and man's insides neglected. An eclipse of the sun
could be predicted many centuries before anyone knew which way the
blood circulated in our own bodies."[18] Both the context in which Joyce
made these remarks, and his tell-tale reference to an "eclipse of the sun"—
one way of saying "night"—lets us know that he was explaining, obliquely
as always, *Finnegans Wake*.

Already one can see why the English word "body," unlike the enveloping
signifier "HCE," is hardly an adequate term for the "one continuous present
tense integument slowly unfolded" through "all . . . moodmoulded cycle-
wheeling history," within which *Finnegans Wake* takes place (185.36–
186.2). For this is not the body taken literally, or the body as we in any way
consciously bring it to mind, in the process converting it into exactly what
it is not (mind). It is above all not the body construed as an object—a thing
through whose instrumentality a headier, *Britannica*-reading subject wedged
in somewhere behind the eyes and between the ears can look down on the
paltry "tumptytumtoes" to which it is attached and comprehend its relation
to them by seeing them visibly "out there," in outer space, on a categorical
parity with his shoes and the furniture. No, " (the best was still there if the
torso was gone)" (291.14–15).[19] Nor is this the organic body of romantic ide-
ologies; for as both a reading of *The New Science* and close study of "gradual

morphological changes in our body politic" will show (165.26–27), HCE's is the "body politic" of "someone imparticular" (602.7), a body instilled with discrete laws by parents localized in a real historical situation and disciplined into <u>pol</u>ish, <u>pol</u>iteness, and other such self-<u>pol</u>icing laws as are entrenched in the "Hoved <u>pol</u>itymester" of the head to insure its survival in the <u>pol</u>is (324.20 [the underlined words are etymologically related]).

The "local busybody" lying at the center of the *Wake*, then (438.16), has affinities with the body as treated in Foucault, in being "an effect of power," an "institution" humanly made and organized by subjection to extended disciplinary practices, within which a "micropolitics" is immanent. And it certainly has affinities with the body as treated by Freud, the body conceived as a field of emotions, attitudes, and symptomatic knots susceptible to discursive unravelling, whose structures unfold in dreams and whose formation is the story of a life held taut in unconscious conflicts of "wills gen wonts" (4.1). The body lying dead to the world at the *Wake* is the form outside of which nothing known to humanity ever happens and inside of which everything ordinarily set apart as external in fact only ever comes to life, in the form of sensationalistic impressions, memories, stamps, welts, and symptoms. Above all, this "unknown body" has affinities with the bodies of Vico's earth-founding giants, of which all other things are evolved forms.

What is true of the boozy, symposial crowd gathered at "Finnegan's Wake" holds equally true of much of the commentary on *Finnegans Wake* and of a platonically prepossessed Western culture generally: "they just spirits a body away" (289.F2); or, more conspiratorially, "(. . . we purposely say nothing of the stiff, both parties having an interest in the spirits)" (82.8–9). That so little has been said about the stiff at the *Wake* is only one sign of the unconsciousness to which consciousness repressively relegates the body;[20] but the oversight affects as well much commentary on dreams. Freud's insistence on the sexual grounding of dreams might well be regarded, in this Joycean light, as a determination not to see dreams foliating out of anything other than the living body which is the site of their origination and their driving cause. Dreams only hold out the manifest illusion of taking place, for instance, in Dublin or in any other locale that one might investigate "out there." In fact, they take place in sleep, in bed, inside of and because of the body of the dreamer. By putting us "back in the flesh" (67.5) the *Wake* returns us to "some precise hour which we shall again agree to call absolute zero or the babbling pumpt of platinism" (164.9–11). All things in the *Wake* start here, "in the flesh."

The Identity of the Dreamer

CHAPTER SIX

Nocturnal Geography: How to Take "Polar Bearings"

FINN

Since "Finnegan," by associative "sound sense" (109.15), modulates through "Finnagain" into "Finn, again" (5.10, 628.14), and since Joyce erratically conceived of the *Wake* as "the dream of old Finn lying in death beside the river Liffey" (*JJ*, 544), we might momentarily regard the man lying "dead to the world" at the *Wake* as the "sleeping giant," "Finn MacCool" (540.17, 139.14), although this is a "goodridhirring" too. "Finn" is another cipher, telling us that the "magnificent brut" (60.26) shown "outlined aslumbered" in the "relief map" has entered a universe of radically strange spatialities.[1]

As "Mr Makeall Gone" (220.24), our hero operates like a "vacuum cleaner" (309.21, 362.25–26, 364.33–34): as soon as he falls asleep and "makes all gone," the entire earth gets swept "off the face of the erse" (178.6–7, 50.8–12). Through this process of "subtractional betterment" (150.33–34), he is "reassured by ratio that the cube of [his] volumes is to the surfaces of their subjects as the sphericity of these globes . . . is to the feracity of Fairynelly's vacuum" (151.1–7). In other words, as the heady glue that holds it all together dissolves in sleep's vacuum ("subjects," capable of "ratio" and "rationality"), all geometrically constructed space disintegrates too ("cubes," "volumes," "surfaces," "spheres," "globes"). As space vanishes, our hero passes out of dimension into an aspatial "nolandsland" situated "*In No-*

where," "By Nowhere" (391.15, 175.7, 9). "Where are we at all? and when-abouts in the name of space?" (558.33).

Anyone consulting his own "blank memory" of the night will recall that when bed, walls, and "room whorled" away and vanished in sleep, a dimensionless "worldroom beyond the roomwhorld" opened up (100.29), there to reveal "the canonicity of **h**is **e**xistence as a tesseract" (100.34–35). Since "a tesseract is a four-dimensional hypercube that cannot be graphically represented in three-dimensional space," the phrase advises us that the *Wake*, because sleep does, necessarily takes place in a spatiality that has little in common with the three dimensions everywhere evident in the masonry of the Daily World.[2] Sustained parts of the book unfold in the "fourdimmansions" of a "newwhere" (367.27, 155.12; 467.23) whose "space-element" is one of "Length Withought Breath, of him, a chump of the evums" (164.33, 261.13–14). All these measurements are quite precise: "length without breadth" evokes a "no placelike" dimension infinite in extension but only ideal in form (609.2); "withought" is a cipher for unconsciousness ("without thought"); "breath" limns out the interior of the body; and HCE designates the book's omnipresent hero, a brainless "chump of the evening," but for that reason, too, "a champ of the *aevum*" (L. "eternity").[3]

Sleep erases the boundaries by which, in wakefulness, we distinguish ourselves from the alien immensity of the surrounding world and set ourselves apart from it, as we were taught, in worried little subject-object relations. In sleep, "we're been carried away. Beyond bournes and bowers" (379.35). "*Your feats* [and your feet] *end enormous, your volumes immense*" (419.5). And as boundaries dissolve and all perceived externals vanish, sleep translocates "Allspace in a Notshall" (455.29 ["nutshell"])—even as it robs one of volition ("not shall"). Or again, it relocates *Omnitudes in a Knutschedell*" (276.L2), where that "nutshell" now resolves into the bonier, slicker Dutch *schedel* ("skull"). "Due to a collupsus of his back promises" (5.27 ["back premises"]), our hero becomes a "colossus" as soon as he "collapses" and—"pftjschute" (3.19)—lands "knock[ed] out" "on the flounder of his bulk" (6.31 ["the flat of his back"]). We "behold of him as behemoth for he is noewhemoe. Finiche!" (7.14–15). With ephemeral instantaneity ("as be he moth"), he suddenly falls down "dead to the world," "finished" ("Finiche") and "nailed to the spot" (Fr. *fiche*); but at the same time, by "dropping asleep somepart in nonland" (403.18), he falls out of dimension and spills into infinity, a "behemoth" "divested of care" (Fr. *il s'en fiche*).

Like anyone, then, the hero of *Finnegans Wake* is indeed a "sleeping giant," though not a waking one—and a giant, moreover, in no pedestrian

Nocturnal Geography

or determinate sense. Viewed from his own "eyewitless foggus," by contrast to runts like Finn MacCool, the man who sleeps at *Finnegans Wake* is so big that nothing in space exists outside of him. He fills any "landshape" in which he turns up because all such "lambskip[s]" (502.36)—"landscapes" seen while "*wools gathering*" (353.33)—are only his dreams and really lie inside of and fill him. Night bountifully redistributes "the fat of the land to Guygas" (494.23 [Gr. *gigas*, "giant"]), though the "fat" and the "guy" immanent in this "Guygas" reveal beneath the giant form an "ordinary man" (64.30): "finight mens midinfinite true" (505.24–25 ["finite man" with "finite *mens*"—L. "mind"—moved by "night" into the "infinite"]). "From the hold of [his] capt in altitude till the mortification that's [his] fate," everything in *Finnegans Wake* takes place inside of this "sleeping giant" (540.17–18), whose formal boundaries will by now be clear: "hold" and "capt" evoke the ubiquitous "Howth" head (L. *caput*), while the "mortified feet" and deadly "fate" remind us that, like "Finnagain," he "bit the dust at the foot of the poll" (580.10–11 [Eng. *poll*, "head"]).

By day, the hero of *Finnegans Wake* inhabits the world represented in Map A, of Dublin, where he and his sinking "grocery business" are such small and negligibly ephemeral concerns as to escape all cartographic and much public interest. But as sleep turns him into a "Bygmester" (4.18)—or "big-master" (624.11)—his body opens out "in the broadest way immarginable" (4.19), spilling out "in all dimensions" and "in all fathom of space" (498.28, 394.10). If, "in the days when **H**ead-in-**C**louds walked the **e**arth" (18.23–24), he was a nobody, in his nights, when he just lies there, he fills immensity, his "Head" in the "Clouds" for being both heavily befogged and wholly lost to sight, "his extremeties extremely so" (74.15). As "allspace" relocates itself inside his body, the world reorganizes itself in the image of his "grossman's bigness" (565.22 [Ger. *gross*, "vast"]), not to mention his sleazier "grossery baseness" (367.2 [see relief map]). In reading of "this preeminent giant," then (504.15)—"Promiscuous Omebound" (560.1)—readers of the *Wake* must think BIG and "immengine" (337.20 ["imagine," "immense"]).

Construed as "the book of Doublends Jined" (20.15–16 ["Dublin's giant"]), the *Wake* now requires not simply "Belief in Giants" (306.16–17), but also some practice in reading "Biggerstiff" letters (413.29); as opposed to a Swiftian "Bickerstaff," a "bigger stiff" than is easy to envision generates and contains them all. Various ciphers modulated with supple variability throughout "the Book of Doublends Jined" serve to remind a reader of its sleeper's periodically absolute "loss of bearings" in space (576.34–35). Grandiose and "most unenglish" (160.22) articulations on the other of "Fe fo fom!" (11.7) and "Finfoefum" (7.9–10) recur with "fierce force fuming" in-sistence (608.31) to show him drifting through the night "without links, without impediments, with gygantogyres, with freeflawforms" (596.23–24). As a "rude rule of fumb" (283.20), these terms indicate that "his im-mensesness" is "loose at large and (Oh baby!) might be anywhere" (241.11, 99.6–7)—just as that interjected "baby!" reminds us that sleep regressively returns him to the condition of "first infancy" (22.1), when also, "fum in his mow" (596.6 [and "thumb in his mouth"]), he had "not yet" (3.10), "not yet" (3.11), shrunk through letters into the determinate limitations of pa-triarchal space: "*Ba be bi bo bum*" (284.L3).⁴

The names of giants, too, often underwritten with little descriptions of sleep, show the *Wake*'s "*Immensipater*" (342.26) emancipating himself from the constraints both of formally perceived space and of the patriarchal order ("immense pater") through which it genetically organizes itself in the head. As "Wassaily Booslaeugh" (5.5–6), for instance, our sleeping giant far outdwarfs the Russian giant "Vasily Buslaev" because, "knock[ed] out" and "blacked out" as well, he is laughably void of any sense of his "beerings" in space at all (321.13 ["wassail," "boose," "laugh"]). As "Finnfinn the Faineant," comparably (254.20 [not "Finn the Fenian"]), he is an immense and sluggish "do-nothing" (Fr. *fainéant*, "lazy idler"), a "*roi des fainéants*" (131.9). And as "MacGhoul" (354.6), "the dead giant manalive" is simply, like "Finnagain," dead to the world (500.1–2): "Finnk. Fime. Fudd?" (499.18). The evocation here of Finn ("Finnk") and of "Fe Fo Fum" show our hero lying "just in time as if he fell out of space" (462.31), while the echo of Fin-negan's "think I'm dead?" notifies us of "the christlikeness of the big clean-minded giant" (33.29 [his only really "christlike" attribute is a tendency to undergo a resurrection of the body after having "tropped head"]).

The appearance of ciphers like these throughout "the book of Doublends Jined" reminds us that "the whole thugogmagog" (222.14) takes place inside the body of a sleeping giant ("Gog and Magog" were giants of ancient Briton); but they also help us to fathom the nature of its hero's spatial per-ception in the night, and largely by indicating when he is *not* actively dream-ing. For dreams, unlike the sleep out of which they arise, take place in visible and recollectibly delimited representations of space (one sees oneself walking through a narrow corridor, for instance, or a field), whereas dream-less parts of the night, unfolding in the "fourdimmansions" of a "Length Withought Breath," do not. "As a rude rule of fumb," then, these ciphers occur most thickly at the borders of dreams reconstructed in the *Wake*—as happens, for example, in the closing pages of III.i, where a lengthily sus-

Nocturnal Geography

tained dream of "Shaun the Post" pales out into a darker "escapology" as "Shaun" "spoorlessly disappale[s] and vanesshe[s]" (428.22, 427.6–7)— "Gaogaogaone!" (427.9)—and "thylike fades" (427.17). The terms suggest that both the visible "likeness" of Shaun ("thy like") and the visual properties of the dream itself ("twilight") "fade" here, leaving our blacked-out hero to contemplate the absence of any image of the real, "whose disparition afflictedly fond Fuinn feels" (427.30). The evocations of Finn and "Fe Fo Fum" now suggest that as the familiarly constructed spatialities and forms of the visual dream "disselv[e]" into the "specturesque silentiousness" of "Real Absence" (608.5, 427.33), "his immensesness" falls out of the little dream scene played out behind his eyes and between his ears to sink back into a spatiality of "Length Withought Breath." Throughout "the book of Doublends Jined," comparably, "one must recken with the sudden and gigantesquesque appearance" of "the dead giant manalive" within whose "colossets" "the whole thugogmagog" unfolds (253.29–30, 500.1–2, 553.10–11 ["colossus," "closet"]).[5] A sleeping giant in reality, the "bigmaster" who sleeps at *Finnegans Wake* now becomes a "*spaciaman spaciosum*" (425.32)— "a handsome example" (L. *specimen speciosum*) of "ample space" (L. *spatium spatiosum*).

"THE SPACE QUESTION"

Acquaintance with the *Wake*'s "sleeping giant" and the alien "dimmansions" within which his nocturnal life takes place leads us to a consideration of the maps that accompany this book. Louis Mink, the distinguished geographer of *Finnegans Wake*, has rightly observed that the *Wake* "has its own geography, and a very queer geography it is too, since it violates the geographical postulate of identification by fixed coordinates"; he goes on to note that "the *Wake*'s Dublin is very different from the real Dublin, but it is derived from it."[6] In these respects, the Dublin of *Finnegans Wake* resembles entirely the cities that appear in anyone's nightlife; for these places, too, differ radically but are derived from the real cities that they recall, and they violate in every way possible "identification by fixed coordinates." Wakefulness takes place in the familiar "atmosphere" of a "world" mapped along charted "latitudes," whereas sleep takes place in its own quite alien "amstophere" (452.1–2 ["am stops here" in sleep's "atmosphere"]), in a "whirrld" structured along lax "lassitudes" (147.22, 441.9–10).

Map A, of "Howth Castle and Environs," shows "Dublin by Daylight." Countless books and directories—*Ulysses* among them—chronicle its history and the lives of its inhabitants, and countless more codify the laws that govern its languages, customs, and institutions. Bent into a meditation on "our own nighttime," however, common sense will suggest that nobody soundly asleep and oblivious of the location of his head and toes is likely to have the remotest knowledge of the world as represented in this map, which therefore fails accurately to reflect the universe really experienced or known at night. Since anyone brainy enough to know that England is separated from Ireland by the Irish Sea cannot sufficiently have "tropped head," new mappings of the world faithful to the experience of the *Wake*'s sleeping giant—"a Colossus among cabbages" (132.27–28)—are necessary to an understanding of the "dimmansions" in which he dwells (those "cabbages," like people, come in "heads," as do our vegetating hero and his "cabbageous [not "capacious"] brain" [409.13]).

In contrast to the map of "Dublin by Daylight," then, Relief Map B shows "Novo Nilbud by swamplight" (24.1), which depicts Dublin as a person "tropped head" would really "no" it. Where "by daylight," like Leopold Bloom, this "nulled nobody" ("Nilbud") would inevitably see before him at every instant some aspect of the "city" of Dublin in all its panoramic variety, night finds looming in his "eyewitless foggus" only a vanished "sooty" (143.5, cf. 25.3)—"Black and All Black" (59.4)—lit at best and only at intervals by spectral "swamplights," "Will-of-the-Wisp[s]" (211.2, 404.15), "jackalanterns" (197.26, 10.27), and other such phosphorescent illusions as erupt in dark marshes, in swamps, and, within dreams, on the undersides of shuttered eyelids. If Dublin lifts into vision at all in this "swamplit" world, it appears only in distortionarily scrambled form (much as the name "Dublin" swims into view out of the anagrammatically inverted "Nilbud"), so that it appears strangely reformed—as "Novo Nilbud."

The two maps of Daylit Dublin and Swamplit "Nilbud" have been drawn so that a one-to-one correspondence links them and shows their essential relation to each other. They are two mappings of exactly the same place, as really experienced by the same man, though in the antithetical states of wakefulness and sleep, where the "untired world" "recurs . . . the same differently" (229.17, 481.10–11). Since nothing in reality changes when our hero falls asleep—"everything's going on the same" (26.25), and "all in fact is soon as all of old right as anywas ever in very old place" (586.20–21)—every place inscribed with a name on the map of Dublin reappears, although in distorted form, on the map of "Nilbud," where a dormant equivalent appears tattooed on the sleeping "stigmataphoron" (606.27 [Gr. "thing bearing tattoo marks"]) shown "outlined aslumbered" there. At the same time, however, since everything in reality changes when he falls asleep, each of the "sobsconcious inklings shadowed on [his] soulskin" in this map of the night world (377.28) shows the effect of a "traumaturgid" "warping process" (496.24, 497.3)—the "turgid" "dramaturgy" of the dream-work (Ger. *Traum*, "dream")—which has cannily distorted whatever sleep has not annihilated.

All of the names on the map of "Novo Nilbud," then—like all terms generally in *Finnegans Wake*—serve at least a triple purpose, whose total effect is to describe a mind rippled by flickering "swamplights" whenever it is not sunk into the abyssal "blackholes" of "Real Absence" (549.5, 536.5–6). By standing in an inverse relation to the real-world locality which it parallels, each item on the relief map acts as a term under erasure, so to indicate the epistemological cancellation of that locality from "Nilbud's" "tropped head." The "Goatstown" and "Dundrum" knowable in Daylit Dublin, for example, evaporate into an indistinct "Ghosttown" because "sir ghostus" lies in a "duldrum" (532.4, 51.34), and cannot "nowhere" they are (10.26 ["know where"]) or that they exist. Although in wakefulness all of the places named on the relief map lie outside of Joyce's sleeping protagonist, "there all the time without [him]" (*U*, 37), they appear here equally inside of him, aspects of his "mummery," so that they bear his stamp and descriptively reflect his life in the night. This is the case, for example, with "Clowntalkin" (414.4 ["Clondalkin"]) and "clown toff" (315.31 ["Clontarf"]), which refer in part to two places in Dublin, but latently reveal our hero's sodden incapacity to act as a coherent monologist, much less a rationalist, in his sleep. In the particular passages from which these names have been stripped, finally, they all bear context-specific senses that cannot be evident here. But since the network of geographical references informing any work of fiction broadly orients it in its relations to the real, these names collectively put *Finnegans Wake* into a context by mapping out one version of the nocturnal universe—the Evening World—it spans.

At a remote level, *Finnegans Wake* really does take place in the Dublin of Map A, where our hero lies at home in bed in Chapelizod, though he cannot know this Dublin or that Chapelizod, much less his "bed," his "head," or, since he "naver saw his bedshead farrer" (241.20), his "bed's head" either. To all of these things, together with the whole fiction of subject-object distinctions, he lies largely in a vanished relation (hence "bedshead farrer," which plays on the Da. *bedstefar* ["grandfather"] to signify a "vanished relation").

This is why Joyce was firm in insisting that a reader need not know Dublin to read *Finnegans Wake* (though it doubtlessly helps);[7] for the ability to identify "Fishamble Street," say, differs entirely from the ability required to orient oneself in the radically alien "Fleshshambles" shown "sprowled met the duskt" in the darker map of the night (538.22–23, 4.11–12 [the "owl" in this "sprawled" has nocturnal intelligence, while the "dust" in this "duskt" moves us into the night's "seemetery"]). More proximately than in Dublin, the *Wake* takes place in the "Dustbin" or "Dupling" (181.17, 586.15 [the trashed and dream-deluded little "dupe"]) shown snoring away in the map of "Novo Nilbud," interior to whom everything depicted in the map of daylit Dublin has been introjected and incorporated. Because *Finnegans Wake* shows the world reformed in this man's body and memory, it necessarily shuffles the "untired world" through a complex set of topological "inns and ouses" (7.5) whereby all ordinary surroundings (like "inns and houses") now lie simultaneously both "inside and outside" him.

For the two maps of "Dublin by Daylight" and "Novo Nilbud by Swamplight" interpenetrate, each lying simultaneously inside and outside its other. The sleeping body shown "sprowled met the duskt" in the nocturnal relief map, "in outher wards" (285.22–23 [and "in outer wards"]), really lies in bed at the place marked "Chapelizod" in the map of Dublin; but coordinately, the entire ground charted out in the map of Dublin really lies buried in the mound labeled "headth of hosth" in Relief Map B, where it exists as representation. Since Map A contains B, and Map B contains A, the hero of *Finnegans Wake* might be considered, according to one of its recurrent ciphers, a kind of Brian O Linn—the subject of a comic song bent on making the wishful best of always bad circumstances by turning everything upside down and inside out.[8] Throughout the *Wake*, "your pullar beer turns out Bruin O'Luinn" (328.1–2) because sleep transforms an ordinary bartender (or "puller of beer") into a hibernating hulk ("polar bear," Du. *beer* ["bear"], "Bruin") within whom Dublin has vanished and the end of the world appeared (hence "polar" and comparable ciphers for "ends of the world" in *Finnegans Wake*).[9] As "Priam Olim" (6.23), comparably, our hero used to be there in the Dublin of Map A (L. *olim*, "once"; *prius*, "before"), but now, "reincorporated" into the spatiality of Map B (387.36), where everything has been turned "skinside out" (507.6), both he and the world lie just "any were" (602.20 [in a vanished past]). The map of "Novo Nilbud," then, shows our hero lying "in vert" (5.6) as he "stand[s] at Bay (Dublin) from nun till dan and vites inversion" (523.17 [in other words, he just lies there—"stands at bay"—for an indeterminate length of time and "invites inversion"]). Or

Nocturnal Geography 153

again, it shows him at "hevnly buddhy time, inwreathed of his near cissies" (234.13–14 [since a "heavenly body," like one "nearvanashed" in the "narcissistic" state of sleep, becomes evident only at night; cf. 284.8–14, 526.34–35]).

Accurately to portray the simultaneous existence of his ordinary man and sleeping giant in the two conflicting spatialities of Dublin and the antithetical Nilbud of Map B—in a linearly progressive history and in the "ex-progressive process" of a dream time beneath history (614.31)—Joyce deploys throughout the *Wake* a wide-ranging toponymy by which to show his hero leading a "doublin existents" (578.14) and dwelling "in two worlds" at once (619.11). While it may well be true, for instance, that our hero lies in bed in the "township of Chapelizod" (this is pronounced with an accent on the short "i"), he himself can "no" it only from the "eyewitless foggus" of someone "embedded" in the "tombshape" of "chapel exit" (265.3, 127.29) or, again, of "Champelysied" (607.14 [Fr. *Champs Elysées*, "the Elysian Fields"]). Terms like these oblige us to see the "Brian d' of Linn" (17.12) asleep at *Finnegans Wake* as "a doblinganger" (490.17 [Ger. *döppelganger*]) who lives neither exactly in Dublin nor in a narcissistic "notshall," but in "doublin" (3.8), or "doubling" (97.9, 197.5, 290.16, 295.31, 413.25, 462.19), his "real" life drifting forth through an eight-hour gap of time in Dublin and history as he himself, "tropped head," conceives the place more as a "Taubling" (7.6), or "Dufblin" (447.23): both terms evoke the "sooty" neither seen nor heard by a *Taubling* (Ger. "a little deaf-ling") whom sleep has rendered "deaf-blind" (hence "Duf-blin").[10] The conflicted coexistence of these "two worlds" and spatialities in the mind of the *Wake*'s dreamer is reflected in the design of *Finnegans Wake* as a spatial artifact, which on the one hand has the linear and determinate form of any printed book, yet on the other hand cultivates the form of an eternally recurrent circle.[11]

Ultimately arbitrary, the two maps of "Dublin by Daylight" and "Novo Nilbud by Swamplight" constitute only one of many possible such sets of maps of the "doubling" within which *Finnegans Wake* is dynamically set; rather than consolidating a set of features that remains fixed in the book, they are meant to illustrate a kind of understanding necessary to a "reading of the Evening World," as it unfolds within the central and underlying "presence (of a curpse)." Any Dubliner will note how eccentric Map A is, since it puts main districts and thoroughfares on a parity with pubs and private estates; and any reader of the *Wake* will note how comparably arbitrary is the relief map of "Novo Nilbud," which draws on only a few of thousands of toponyms in the book. The nocturnal map is equally arbitrary, however, because it makes "too dimensional" (154.26 [and "two-dimensional"]) the "infrarational" spatiality within which *Finnegans Wake* takes place. "THE MONGREL UNDER THE DUNGMOUND" (276.R1)—the sleeping man buried in the body of matter shown stratified in the map of the Evening World—is endowed with an "INFRALIMINAL INTELLIGENCE" that cannot know things as they are presented in either map, as visible forms localized in geometric space. The map of "Novo Nilbud," then, objectifies space in a way inaccurate to the experience of sleep, the night, and the body, and all the more particularly because the "inklings shadowed on [the] soulskin" of the slumbering form it represents change fluidly from page to page of the *Wake*, as "matters falling under the ban of our infrarational senses" arise internally, within "the presence (of a curpse)."

As a way of seeing how these "infrarational" matters everywhere modify the character of represented space in the Evening World, we might examine a passage close to the end of the *Wake*, in which its sleeping giant plays host to this drift of "withought":

> Death banes and the quick quoke. But life wends and the dombs spake! Whake? Hill of Hafid, knock and knock, nachasach, gives relief to the langscape as he strauches his lamusong untoupon gazelle channel and the bride of the Bryne, shin high shake, is dotter than evar for a damse wed her farther. Lambel on the up! We may plesently heal Geoglyphy's twentynine ways to say goodbett an wassing seoosoon liv. (595.1–8)

The lines represent the same "landshape" as that shown in the map of "Novo Nilbud," and again as it appears in "relief"; but here the term "he" clearly "indentifides" the body of the sleeper underlying all evident appearances, as that body stretches characteristically from head to foot ("Hill of Hafid," or "Hoved," suggests "Howth" "head"; "knock and knock" names two "knocks out in the park"; while "he strauches his lamusong" suggests that "he stretches his limbs"). This "stretching," however, now generates a second sense of "relief" (an easing of discomfort, a "longing" to "escape" ["langscape"]), so to show different energies riddling the body which, in the opening pages of the *Wake*, lay deeply dead to the world. For "our local busybody" (438.16) is now "pleasantly healing" and coming back to life after a night of static embedment in the "seemetery" (hence the "quickening" of the "death bones" and the sense that "tombs speak"). As his body "pleasantly heals" and moves toward its resurrection, it also begins to regain its capacity to "presently hear" things—that crowing rooster (595.30), the matitudinal Angelus pealed out of churchbells (601.15–31), noisy delivery vans (604.9–18)—and weakly to interpret what it hears as it ascends toward wakeful clarity. "Nachasach," therefore, evokes "sassanach," the Gaelic for "Saxon," because the interpretive medium of English, is already, "by and by" (Ger. *nach und nach*), seeping back into our hero's "knock[ed] out" and "tropped head" with morning. Hence again "knock and knock." If earlier parts of the *Wake* have seemed like a vast "knock-knock" joke (330.30–32) because of the difficulty of knowing "who was there," answers, with English, now begin to emerge: "the quick quoke" and "the dombs spake" suggest that a body struck "dumb" in sleep, by "quickening," is regaining the ability to "quote" and "speak." "Whake?" shows our hero wondering "What?" is stirring the body of matter within which he lies embedded; but it also suggests that in his "infraliminal intelligence," he knows full well. "At matin a fact" (596.5 [as a matter of fact]), "clarify begins" here (594.12), at "matin" ("morning"), when he "comes out of the soil very well after all" (606.28–29) and a world full of "fact" returns to his "tropped head." No longer quite dead to the world, as if at his wake, "the presence (of a curpse)" is about to "wake."

The Eastern or oriental term "Hafid," accordingly (Ar. "preserver," "one who knows the known by heart"), shows our hero orienting himself, as sun rises in the Orient, in a real world full of facts "known by heart and preserved in the head" ("Hafid" = "Hoved"). But since sleep has broken the continuity of this world, and so has altered it, it is not quite the same world that vanished when he fell asleep last night. Proverbially, people are accustomed to saying that "things will look different in the morning," and the proverb yields its share of truth. One falls asleep nightly, abandoning an Old World sodden with conflicts and problems, and wakes up, ideally refreshed, to find a whole New World occupying the site of the Old World that crumbled with yesterday. The place-names covering the "langscape" presented here—"Cape Strauch" ("he strauches"), the town of "Lamusong" ("his lamusong"), "Gazelle Channel," and Mount "Lambel"—therefore orient us less in Ireland, than in "Newirglands" (595.10 ["New Ireland," in the Melanesian Pacific]), though not in any literal sense. Elements in a Wakean "geoglyphy" (< Gr. "earth-carving"), rather than in an orthodox "geography" (< Gr. "earth-describing"), the toponyms suggest that as the world reaggregates in our hero's "tropped head" under the oriental pressure of sunrise, it is not quite the same world he left when he fell asleep because sleep, having refreshed him, has altered it. He wakens renewed, "a newman" in a new Ireland (596.36). In his "infraliminal intelligence," accordingly, another drift of associations spins out of the resurrective stirring unconsciously perceived in his "stretching limbs," both already eager to be "on the up" ("Lambel on the up!") and, after a quick "wash," out amid company ("wassing seoosoon" suggests "wishing to see you soon," "washing," and the Ger. *Wasser* ["water"]). The gathering restlessness in his limbs also evokes the memory of a "dance" with a "damsel" ("a damse") and, in particular, with "a daughter more dotty than ever for a dance with her father." "What were frozen loins [are] stirred and lived," then (549.8–9); and, feeling renewed, "the old man on his ars" shown "scrapheaped" in the relief map wishfully foresees wakening into a "Newirglands" (with "newer *vir* glands" [L. *vir*, "he-man"]) so that, like "Adam" with "Eve" at the beginning of the world ("<u>ev</u>ar for <u>a</u> dam<u>s</u>e"), he can begin a new "season" of life all over again ("seoosoon") and reconquer the lost affections both of young people in general and of the members of his family in particular.

Countless passages in the *Wake* comparable to this one would have illustrated equally well how "geoglyphic" place-names, like all symptomatic "writing . . . streak[ed] over [the] bourseday shirt" of the book's sleeping giant (27.10–11), fluidly change in order to reflect "matters falling under the ban of our infrarational senses" as they ripple through "the presence (of a curpse)." Such passages also help us to gauge the nature of the "dimmansions" into which the hero of *Finnegans Wake* moves when sleep pulls him out of Euclidean dimension into the "nucleuds" of his body (283.24). Where spatial relations between objects on the map of Dublin are conventionally measured along straight lines in numerical units ranging from inches to miles and are organized in geometric or geographic space, the transformation that relocates the world in the body of the *Wake*'s sleeping giant causes "spacious" "straight lines" to become "specious" "strayedline[s]" (153.17, 293.18, 294.2–3), "extension" to become "extinsion" (371.24 ["extinct extension"]), and "number" to become "numb," "nummer," numbest (546.25–26, 10.28, 242.5, 313.25, 531.4 [because altogether impalpable]), if not dark "nombre" (222.32 [Fr. *ombre*, "darkness"]) or obliterated "no" (420.25).

The night dismantles orthodox geometries and geographies, as we learn in one of the *Wake*'s extended "Night Lessons" (II.ii), and in place of relations drawn by a "geometer" (< Gr. *geômetrês*, "earth measurer"), distances are determined by a warmer "geomater" (297.1 [Gr. *Gaia matêr*, "mother earth"]). Neither Euclidean nor Cartesian in character, but emotional or earthily "infrarational," distances separating "abjects" in the interior spatiality of "Novo Nilbud" are those of the sort which, through variable degrees of attachment and separation and attraction and repulsion, make our hero imaginarily near to or remote from another person or place—in much the same way that Stephen Dedalus, standing two feet away from

Buck Mulligan in *Ulysses*, can be eight months and hundreds of miles away, in the Paris he knew before his mother's death. And "as I know and you know yourself . . . and the arab in the ghetto knows better" (286.5–7), rationalists deft at objective measurement are not always best at gauging such "mythametical" distances (286.23), which are "binomeans to be comprendered" (285.27–28 [as opposed to "binomials," which are]) because they have little to do with rationality at all. Our hero's nightlife takes place in a space constituted by these "infraliminal" distances.

"THE OWL GLOBE"

As one consequence of the topological transformation by which sleep turns the map of Dublin "skinside out" into the map of "Nilbud," where everything is "recorporated" (228.20 [and "recuperated"]), the *Wake*'s sleeping giant will necessarily absorb and engulf any place or any thing in the world (just as his cipher, HCE, will absorb any context). Early in *Finnegans Wake*, its reader in fact learns that the still "form outlined aslumbered" throughout the book, a body laid to rest in bed, is "tautaulogically the same thing" as "the owl globe" (6.29–30); this would be "the whole globe," as informed by a nocturnal intelligence ("owl"), within which letters have come to an end (the extra "tau" in "tautaulogically" [not "tautologically"], designates the last letter in the Hebrew alphabet and so suggests, like the badly fatigued ⊔ at 6.32, the end of letters generally).

Map A', accordingly, of Western Europe in the 1930s, shows a portion of "the whole globe" as the hero of *Finnegans Wake* would doubtlessly know it by day; and its nocturnal counterpart, Relief Map B', draws eclectically on terms scattered throughout *Finnegans Wake* to yield an "eyewitless foggus" of the same extended region as Joyce's sleeping giant would certainly "no" it in the night. Again, a one-to-one correspondence links these two maps, so that every place charted on the first has its sleep-transformed equivalent inscribed on the other; and, again, the two mappings lie cospatially inside and outside each other, our hero in fact lying in bed in the area marked "Dublin" in the map of Europe, but all of the map of Europe lying buried in the "Dufblin" headquarters shown "corked" and "slaine" in Map B' (447.23, 155.1, 609.34). The play between the two maps illustrates the transformational process by which the "Western European world" of the 1930s, as Joyce's protagonist turns into his body in sleep, in turn turns into a "wastended" "neuropean" "whorled" (320.17, 519.1, 272.4), who now lies susceptible to those delusionally "neuropathic" reconstructions of the real met in dreams. The nocturnal map of this "Neuropath," then (488.26), renders concrete another version of the *Wake*'s singular "amstophere" by making visible "aspace of dumbillsilly" (15.18)—"a space," that is, as it is largely not perceived by the "silly dumbbell" or *espèce d'imbecile* (Fr., "type of imbecile") who has not only "tropped head" within it but is identical to it. Or again, it shows our hero in the "duskguise" of "His Revenances, with still a life or two to spare for the space of his occupancy of a world at a time" (532.27, 52.7–8 [a "revenant," like a sleeper, comes back to life from death with a life to spare; but a sleeper does it more than once]). Comparison of the two maps will allow a reader of *Finnegans Wake* to appreciate "the **highly continental evenements**" (398.13) of this "neuropath" for whom much of world and the letters that constitute it have "atlanst" become "vanished consinent[s]" (601.5, 337.8 [like "Atlantis" and its alphabet]). Where our hero would know by daylight exactly where he stood in relation to "Norway," "Monte Carlo," and "the Spanish," in his sleep, by contrast, he can "nowhere" he lies only in relation to "Nowhergs" (533.22 ["nowhere"]) and "mostly Carbo" (232.3), because his body "distends" "in the broadest way immarginable" and leaves his "tropped head" bearing only "murmurrandoms of distend renations" with the "sphanished" (358.3, 473.20 ["distant relations," "vanished"]). If by day he can expatiate freely with his customers about Napoleonic "Corsica" and "the Vatican," comparably, what he can "no" in the "seemetery" of night is largely a "muddy terranean" "nolandsland" extending through *Corpsica* into "the Vatucum" (120.29, 175.11, 243.31 ["vacuum"; this "Vatucum," incidentally, is the only real authority to which any reader of *Finnegans Wake* can legitimately appeal]). Latently immanent in all these terms, too, is "the presence (of a curpse)."

A little attention to the area labeled "idlish" "frustate" in the nocturnal map of "neurope" (182.15, 352.33 ["Irish Free State"]) will suggest that a comparably "sunless map of the month" might well be drawn of Ireland or of "any were" (602.20), since "allspace" goes into the "notshall" of the body at night. Because our hero is as vastly "obliffious" of Ireland as he is of his head and toes, the "Irish nation" evaporates in his sleep into an insubstantially "airish" "notion" (55.24, 192.26, 223.3, 327.31, 344.18; 128.16); or "goes under" to become a subterranean "oreland" (352.9, 359.26), its disappearance leaving this "nought in nought Eirinishmhan" (616.3) only an "airish," "idlish," and at times outrightly "eeriesh" "Inishman" (70.4, 320.13, 91.22 ["innish" because "inner"]). "In the drema of Sorestost Areas, Diseased" (69.14–15), the quotidian reality of a "Saorstat Erin" (or Irish Free

Map A'
The Western European world,
around 1930

Land of the Midnight Sun

Nova Zembla

Murmansk

0   100   200   300   400

Miles

Finland

The Finnish

Helsinki   Petrograd (Leningrad)

The Baltic

Asia

Volga

Asia

Asia

to Japan
(Land of the Rising Sun)

Europe

Foochow
(China)

Poland

Asia

Hungary   Transylvania

Rumania

Crimea

Where Buckley Shot the Russian General

Sevastopol   Inkermann

The Caucasus

Yugoslavs

Varna

Black Sea

Bulgaria

Armenia

Turkish Armenians

Asia Minor

Istambul (Constantinople)

Hellas
(Greece)

Sea of Marmora
(Fr. Mer de Marmora)

The Ottoman Empire
(through 1919)

Persia

The Persians

The Turkish

The Turks

Athens

Bagdad

The Levant   Tyre

Jericho

Egypt   The Nile   The Sinai
(Mountain of the
Lord of Israel)

Old Jerusalem
The Jordan

Arabia

Arabia Deserta

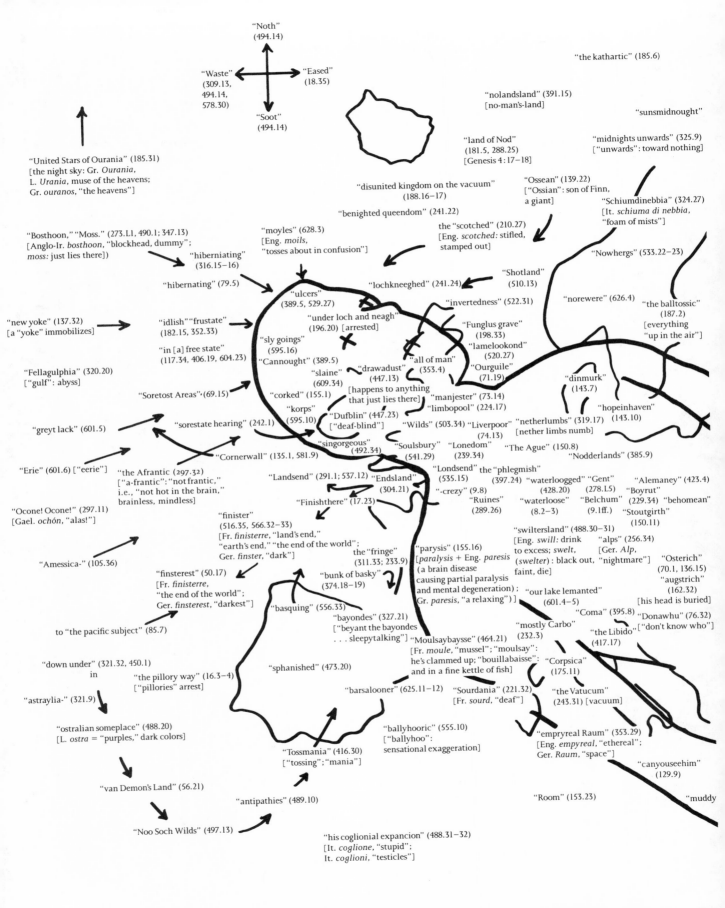

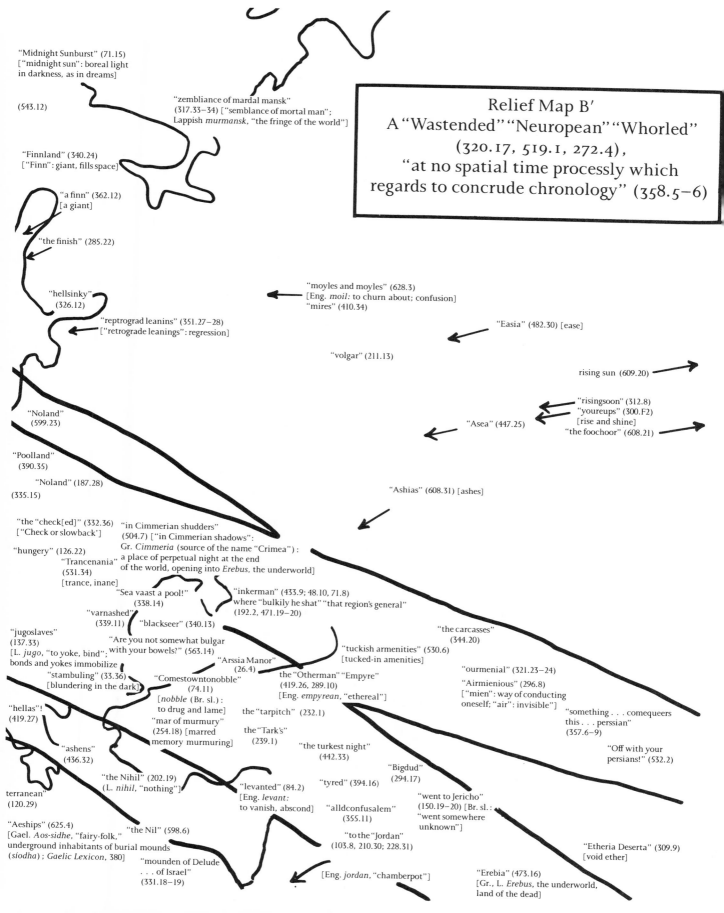

"Midnight Sunburst" (71.15)
["midnight sun": boreal light
in darkness, as in dreams]

(543.12)

"zembliance of mardal mansk"
(317.33–34) ["semblance of mortal man";
Lappish *murmansk*, "the fringe of the world"]

Relief Map B′
A "Wastended" "Neuropean" "Whorled"
(320.17, 519.1, 272.4),
"at no spatial time processly which
regards to concrude chronology" (358.5–6)

"Finnland" (340.24)
["Finn": giant, fills space]

"a finn" (362.12)
[a giant]

"the finish" (285.22)

"hellsinky"
(326.12)

"reptrograd leanins" (351.27–28)
["retrograde leanings": regression]

"moyles and moyles" (628.3)
[Eng. *moil*: to churn about; confusion]
"mires" (410.34)

"Easia" (482.30) [ease]

"volgar" (211.13)

rising sun (609.20)

"risingsoon" (312.8)
"youreups" (300.F2)
[rise and shine]
"the foochoor" (608.21)

"Asea" (447.25)

"Noland"
(599.23)

"Poolland"
(390.35)

"Noland" (187.28)

(335.15)

"Ashias" (608.31) [ashes]

the "check[ed]" (332.36)
["Check or slowback']

"hungery" (126.22)

"Trancenania"
(531.34)
[trance, inane]

"in Cimmerian shudders"
(504.7) ["in Cimmerian shadows":
Gr. *Cimmeria* (source of the name "Crimea") :
a place of perpetual night at the end
of the world, opening into *Erebus,* the underworld]

"Sea vaast a pool!"
(338.14)

"varnashed"
(339.11)

"blackseer" (340.13)

"inkerman" (433.9; 48.10, 71.8)
where "bulkily he shat" "that region's general"
(192.2, 471.19–20)

"the carcasses"
(344.20)

"jugoslaves"
(137.33)
[L. *jugo*, "to yoke, bind";
bonds and yokes immobilize

"Are you not somewhat bulgar
with your bowels?" (563.14)

"tuckish armenities" (530.6)
[tucked-in amenities]

"ourmenial" (321.23–24)

"Airmienious" (296.8)
["mien": way of conducting
oneself; "air": invisible]

"stambuling" (33.36)
[blundering in the dark]

"Comestowntonobble"
(74.11)
[*nobble* (Br. sl.) :
to drug and lame]

"Arssia Manor"
(26.4)

the "Otherman" "Empyre"
(419.26, 289.10)
[Eng. *empyrean,* "ethereal"]

"something . . . comequeers
this . . . perssian"
(357.6–9)

"hellas"!
(419.27)

"mar of murmury"
(254.18) [marred
memory murmuring]

the "tarpitch" (232.1)

the "Tark's"
(239.1)

"Off with your
persians!" (532.2)

"ashens"
(436.32)

"the turkest night"
(442.33)

"Bigdud"
(294.17)

terranean"
(120.29)

"the Nihil" (202.19)
(L. *nihil,* "nothing"]

"levanted" (84.2)
[Eng. *levant:*
to vanish, abscond]

"tyred" (394.16)

"went to Jericho"
(150.19–20) [Br. sl. :
"went somewhere
unknown"]

"Aeships" (625.4)
[Gael. *Aos-sidhe,* "fairy-folk,"
underground inhabitants of burial mounds
(*síodha*) ; *Gaelic Lexicon,* 380]

"the Nil" (598.6)

"alldconfusalem"
(355.11)

"to the "Jordan"
(103.8, 210.30; 228.31)

"Etheria Deserta" (309.9)
[void ether]

"mounden of Delude
. . . of Israel"
(331.18–19)

[Eng. *jordan,* "chamberpot"]

"Erebia" (473.16)
[Gr., L. *Erebus,* the underworld,
land of the dead]

State) disintegrates to become only a "dream" of "drama" ("drema") endured in bed (a "sore-tossed area," associated both with the "diseased" and the "deceased"). And "Erin," comparably, used to be there "in the days when Head-in-Clouds walked the earth," but now that the invaluable resources of his "tropped head" lie "spent"—"Erin gone brugk" (347.21)—Erin exists only "erehim" (17.23), "ere in" sleep he fell (62.19, 427.6), so to be transformed into an "Ailing" (148.33 [because "in bed"]) or "erring" (198.12, 272.20, 288.F6; cf. 62.25), at least until "Eringrowback" in the morning (389.4–5).[12]

"By his selfdenying ordnance," then, our self-extinguishing hero has "left Hyland on the dissenting table" too (73.2–3 [where it lies "dissected"]), so that a "sunless map" of "erehim" might be drawn with as much particularity as the two relief maps of "Novo Nilbud" or of the "Waste" (494.14 [the West]). If in wakefulness our hero certainly knows full well what and where Counties Monaghan, Louth, Tipperary, Cavan, and Down are, "Monaghan" by night vanishes into spooky "moonyhaunts" (595.15); "Louth" washes out in the sleep of a "lout" (595.12); "Tipperary" disintegrates whenever, lost in the "deep deep deeps of Deepereras" (595.28), he feels "his topperairy" (131.5 [an "airy" "topper" would be a headlike structure void of content]); "Cavan" simply disappears in "coffins" (595.15), "Maryborough, Leix," dissolving into "Miryburrow, leaks" (577.14). As for "Down," it simply sinks into deeper "downs" (101.6), there to form part of a world "down under" (321.32, 450.1 [not necessarily Australia]) and finally to drift into "the downandoutermost" (194.19). "All gone" (380.36).

These orienting comments apart, the two maps of the Evening World will explain themselves and are meant to be read on their own. Except that they will not account fully for the roles of Shem or Shaun in the *Wake*, or at all for its female characters, they offer, in their own way, a synthetic reading of the book. Items on these maps have been arranged in ways meant both to be suggestive and to discourage the bad habit of reading sequentially along the "ruled barriers" of written lines (see 114.2–20). Readers who have traced on a map of Dublin Bloom's wanderings through the "Lestrygonians" episode of *Ulysses*, for instance, will not be surprised to note that on the "sunless map" of "neurope," the "strayedline[s]" leading from "Belchum" through "Alemany" and "Stoutgirth" into "hungery" and the region "where bulkily he shat" "that region's general"—"Arssia Manor"—roughly sketch out the alimentary tract of a sleeping giant, every square inch of it underwritten with signs of conflict. Study of these submerged "aliment[s]" (163.2 ["elements"]) will also begin to suggest why the long story told in the *Wake* of "how Buckley shot the Russian general" is only a dream (337.32–355.33), bearing on "matters that fall under the ban of our infrarational senses," and not a historical account of a skirmish in the Crimean War. "Berkeley showed the reason genrously" (423.32–33 [by distinguishing the ideal from the real]): the area in which Buckley shot the Russian general, and the place in which our hero himself experiences "defecalties" (366.20–21) is not the Crimea at all. As these indications in turn suggest, reference to these maps, or to any sleeping body, will now enable us to draw some broad general inferences about *Finnegans Wake* as a whole.

"POLAR ANDTHISISHIS"

Reference either to "the beast of boredom, common sense" (292.28) or to a document like the *Encyclopaedia Britannica* would advise us that the two mappings of the Evening World violently distort a reality more accurately rendered in the familiar maps of Dublin and Europe. Consider only the example of the "Willingdone mormorial" (8.35), which has assumed, in "Novo Nilbud," dimensions ridiculously disproportionate to any sense of spatial exactitude, and a centrality incommensurate with its real cultural importance (Dubliners call it an "overgrown milestone" [36.18]).[13] Arguably, however, the misrepresentation works the other way around, the maps of Dublin and Europe disfiguring in their own ways a reality rendered quite accurately in the two maps of the night. For no one, phenomenologically, ever experiences the world as it is depicted in the maps of Dublin and Europe—now, for example, as one sits in a room reading amid a clutter of familiar objects, so "obliffious" of abstract compass directions like "north" and "south" and of places like "Monte Carlo," until print, exigency, or association brings them to mind, that they might more accurately be labeled, as in Map B', "Noth," "Soot," and "mostly Carbo." As one encounters the world in its average everydayness, moreover, one is always more intimately yoked in space to some underlying but unseen "carcasses," as shown in Map B', than to a locale like "the Caucasus," knowledge of which ordinarily reaches one not through direct experience but through the "carcass's" print-reading eyes and hearsay-accumulating ears. Only minimal reflection will answer satisfactorily the question of whether the space within which one personally passed the last day or two might better be construed as the heartland of "Amessica"—a big one—or an abstract "America"; of "Errorland" or "Ireland" (62.25); of "your disunited kingdom" (188.16–17) or of their theoretically "United" one.

The two sets of maps, then—one of surface geometries and objective relations, the other of subliminal and emotional relations—might be seen as distortions of each other, each ignoring properties central to the structure of its counterpart. However true it may be that the two chartings of the Evening World radically deform the place familiarly depicted in the maps of Dublin and Europe, the maps of Dublin and Europe complementarily overlook, and so violently distort, a number of matters overwhelmingly central to the two maps of the night—only the most obvious of these embodied in the "Willingdone mormorial" and all that it stands for. Visceral "matters that fall under the ban of our infrarational senses," they find no representative expression in the objective version of things charted out in the two maps of the world known to "day's reasons" (347.24).[14]

One way of seeing how destructively "day's reason" distorts concerns that everywhere inform the Evening World would be to consider the notorious "Phoenix Park incident." Everyone acquainted with *Finnegans Wake* knows that its hero broods guiltily throughout the book about some shadowy act of trespass committed in the Phoenix Park, although the exact nature of "the alleged misdemeanor" remains vexingly unclear (35.6, 33.14–34.29). Those who have sought to unravel the details note that the crime is "never fully delineated, but is alluded to or momentarily illumined at several instances";[15] and in the criticism, "there extand by now one thousand and one stories, all told," about "whatever it was . . . he thried to two in the Fiendish park" (5.28–29, 196.9–11).[16] Yet even studies that acknowledge the necessity of the crime's incertitude rather than trying to pin it down to a violation of "section 11 of the C[riminal]. L[aw]. A[mendment]. act 1885" (61.9–10 [the one for which they nailed Oscar Wilde]) fail sufficiently to appreciate that *Finnegans Wake* is "an imitation of the dream-state," and not a chronicle of real-world affairs. Most critical treatments of "the crime" overlook the obvious fact that almost everybody in the world has dreamed of perpetrating some nasty public indiscretion, but that having dreamed of such an offense hardly means that one really committed it. Much the same is the case with our hero, who has "an impressive private reputation for whispered sins" (69.4 ["private reputation" is a self-canceling phrase]), and whose crime takes place *not* in the Daily World represented in the maps of Dublin and Europe, but in their fleshier counterparts. The actual site of HCE's criminal trespass is not a real-world Phoenix Park at all, but rather an area figured more accurately in the *Wake* as "feelmick's park" (520.1) or "Phornix Park" (80.6). Our hero's indiscretion, "in shorts" (437.11), is localized in a particular spot about which, as an adherent of the "High Church of England" (36.29), he feels great shame "(you know . . . in your art of arts . . . as well as I do (and don't try to hide it) the penals lots I am now poking at)" (188.30–32). This would explain, moreover, why "the crime" assumes the proportions of original sin, and also why, like a great deal of conflict in *Finnegans Wake* generally, it takes place under the shadow of "the Willingdone mormorial" (as opposed to "the Wellington Memorial"). In "Dublin by Daylight," the "overgrown milestone" no doubt means as little to our hero as it does to the average Dubliner, and not least because it lies in his own backyard. But in "Novo Nilbud by swamplight," by contrast, precisely its triviality—as well as its extended associations with conquest and power—makes it an ideal item onto which the *Wake*'s dreaming hero can displace important "infraliminal" concerns.

If one studies the endlessly modulating forms that HCE's "crime" takes as it reappears throughout *Finnegans Wake*, it now becomes evident that however imaginary the "ludicrous imputation[s]" ascribed to him may be, he is in fact guilty, down to the letter, of every single one of them (33.26). There can be no doubt at all that the "magnificent brut" has urinated in the area in question (503.29 ["Trickspissers vill be pairsecluded"]). If he is indeed a married male with a daughter, he has certainly exposed himself to two females there; and considering some likely occasions on which he would have done so with one of them, he would likely have taken voyeuristic pleasure in turn. Finally, too, it is not improbable that he is fully guilty of "abusing the apparatus" (520.7–8) and "hav[ing] taken his epscene licence . . . as regards them male privates" (523.34–35 [though these would be his "epicene" own]). What is true of the *Wake* as a whole, then, is also true of this "crime." "It's like a dream": "a baser meaning has been read into [all] these [alphabetic and fictional] characters the literal sense of which decency can safely scarcely hint" (33.14–15). Precisely the slippery indefiniteness with which the *Wake* treats HCE's crime, finally, allows Joyce to capture his hero's guilt with an exactitude that would not be possible in the rule-bound, fact-craving Daily World.

The critical inclination to take HCE's crime literally, as a fact of the world, stems from a failure to take the appropriate "polar bearing[s]" in a nocturnal universe whose every feature is a "polar andthisishis" (177.33) of the evident forms of the Daily World ("and this is his antithesis"). The taking of these "polar bearing[s]" means that some epistemological adjustments are essential to an understanding of our hero's nightlife. Anyone who believes that the maps of Dublin and Europe represent the world accurately has spent perhaps too much time reading "the dully expressed" (500.15–16 [the *Daily Express*]) and too little "reading the Evening World." The world preserved in these maps is held in place by countless rule-governed systems maintained by a hierarchy of authorities ranging from legislators and geographers to cartographers, printers, and authors. One accedes to the truth value of these "fibfib fabrications" (36.34), as a necessary accommodation to a collective reality, by placing trust in an "awethorrorty" that far transcends any individual (516.19), and also by succumbing to many tacit assumptions about what the world is and what its people are. If the two day-clear maps show the "field" of our hero's "existence" as netted everywhere by this "awethorrorty," the two Wakean maps of the night show simply the "felled" of his "exsystems" (246.4, 340.8; 148.18 [all systems]). For not simply geometric space and geography, but everything on which the daily world and our hero's ordinary bearings in it are predicated turns into its "polar andthisishis" in the night—and in ways everywhere reflected by the *Wake*'s carefully modified predicates themselves.[17] Since the *Wake* as a whole is linked together by dissolved predicates, we might now see them moving its sleeping "sopjack" into such odd relations with imaginary "abjects" that, simply through its "sintalks" (269.3 [nasty "syntax"]), the book dismantles the structures on which the Daily World is predicated. And as this dismantling happens in small, so it also happens in large.

Authority tells us, for instance, that the Dublin represented in Map A was founded in A.D. 837 by Viking warlords on fenland and estuarial silt. Not so. The real ground and foundation on which Dublin or any other city rests is the substratum shown "outlined aslumbered" in the two maps of the Evening World—the ephemeral, labor-exploitable body (*U*, 164) which objectively drawn maps of the world could not represent even if those who drew them wanted to. This is why the Brian O Linn who sleeps "skinside out" at *Finnegans Wake*, an ordinary man in fact, becomes in the "Bigmesser's conversions" of his sleep a "Priam Olim" (530.32, 6.23 ["Priam" is the father of a fallen city]) or, in the guise of a "Bygmester" (4.18 [Da. "masterbuilder"]), the maker and founder of cities generally (532.5–554.10). All such orderly structures as that literately represented in the map of Dublin are layered up over the Adamic clay depicted in the map of "Novo Nilbud"— "Amtsadam, sir, to you!" (532.6 ["am Adam"])—which, more than vacant matter and two or three Great Individuals, constitute their real glory and ground. The observation underscores at once the pathos of our hero's position and the naivete of early Marxist dismissals of *Finnegans Wake*. In "Dublin by Daylight," our expendable average man—"Canon Futter" (9.19–20 ["cannon fodder"])—is a marginal, ephemeral nothing, whereas in "Novo Nilbud by Swamplight"—"fiefeofhome"! (133.17)—he fills immensity ("Fe Fo Fum"). Hence again, by way of an intonation that Maria Jolas early noted in the book's title, the power immanent in the *Wake*'s sleeping giant: *Finnegans, wake!*, you have nothing to lose but your chains.[18]

At least since 1789, authority in its liberal forms has also argued that the world depicted in the maps of Dublin and Europe is one structured on the humane ideals of "lebriety, frothearnity and quality" (133.31–32 ["liberty, fraternity, and equality"]). Not so. As the submerged references to our hero's pubkeeping business and a glance at the nocturnal maps will attest ("Canon Futter" "earns" by selling "frothy" "quality" stout and providing the service of "ebriety"), the world is "infrarationally" shaped by the form of an all-engulfing patriarchy, in whose business and interests everyone is enmeshed. Beyond that, as much feminist writing has shown, the world figured in the maps of Dublin and Europe as one of free agency is latently underlined by the pattern and force of male desire, as the nocturnal maps more accurately reveal.[19] All this is only to note, as have others, that far from marking a withdrawal from a civilization in crisis, *Finnegans Wake* in an odd way crystallizes that crisis, and not least through its assault on the institution of a language through which all the other institutions of a patriarchal culture are transmitted from parent to child and from generation to generation, over and over again, "the seim anew" (215.23).[20] The conflicts assailing the "perpendicular person" shown snoring away in the two maps of the night, then—the head of a household and a beleaguered patriarch in fact—are representative of larger crises agitating the social world of which he is a negligibly small but nonetheless formative part. The two maps of the night show "the old man on his ars"—and "Great Scrapp! 'Tis we and you and ye and me and hymns and hurts and heels and shields" (514.34–35 [note the scale of emotion running from awed reverence to sheer pain in all these "hymns and hurts," the variety of response ranging from flight to entrenched defense in all these "heels and shields"]).

Accession to the rational and objective view of things represented in the maps of Dublin and Europe entails the harnessing of the body to laws—and not simply to Freudian laws of corporate control, but to a whole host of laws that are inscribed on every square inch of the *Wake*'s sleeping "stigmatophoron," all the way from "tumptytumtoes" to "humptyhillhead": laws that reform the "bourseday suit" he was born with so that it will "stand up tall!" and walk (620.1); laws like "section 11 of the C.L.A. Act 1885" that determine "*Cur, quicquid, ubi, quando, quomodo, quoties, quibus auxiliis*" (188.8–9 [L. "why, what, where, when, how, how many times, with what assistance"]) his body will have its pleasure;[21] laws that determine where his tongue must hit the palate so as to produce distinct words and polite conversation rather than mere noise, Wakese, or offensive remarks; and laws that harness his eyes and mind in the act of reading, not least, so that they dutifully move along word by word, line by line, page after page, translating words into conventional senses—and all this, too, without any slouching or moving the lips. The world figured in the maps of Dublin and Europe, then, depends for its coherence not simply on authority, but on authorship as a collective enterprise and on language as a system, whereas the world pervaded by the *Wake*'s sleeping giant does not: the two maps of the night show us a landform in which letters are buried (I.v), missing (e.g., 66.10–28), and undeliverable (420.17–421.14). And consequently, "as my instructor unstrict me" (295.21–22), there are no rules down here (295.21); one moves "ad libidinum in these lassitudes" (441.9–10). "Reading the Evening World" obliges one to take "polar bearing[s]" not simply toward a world conventionally structured by "awethorrorty," but toward the conventionally legible structures of authors as well.

"POLITICOECOMEDY"

The terms strewn over the two maps of the Evening World are fundamentally sleep descriptive, of course; but not to notice that one of their incidental effects is the wholesale dismantling of the arrangements "set up over the slop after the war-to-end war by Messrs a charitable government" (178.24–26) and of the political status quo that Joyce would have known in the 1920s and 1930s would be to overlook an essential aspect of the *Wake*'s dark reformations of space and "exsystems." Because the terms on the night maps do formally what dreams do, revealing in the body of the *Wake*'s sleeping giant an underworld of aggressive forces and illicit pleasures whose release would mean the rubbling of government and self-government both, they introduce us obliquely to the *Wake*'s definite, if eccentric "politicoecomedy" (540.26). What began as a contrast between the conflicting geometries and geographies experienced in wakefulness and sleep, then, now modulates into a contrast in polar world-views—one structured on the principles of mastery, order, and "day's reasons," the other escaping structure altogether in anarchic playfulness, great "thisorder" (540.19), and "alternate nightjoys" (357.18). For if the maps of Dublin and Europe chart out a dimension that we might loosely construe as the Empire, their nocturnal counterparts, by standing the world "on its dead" (560.7–8 ["head"]), show the Empire in general and the "old man on his ars" in particular without any clothes. "Vott Fonn!" (345.9).[22]

Because the *Wake* purveys an "*idiology*" of "the murketplots" (352.19, 368.9 ["murked plots"])—and not an "ideology" of "the marketplace," it stands in an extremely fringey relation to the culture that produced it.[23] As a work committed to the "tropped head," it is antithetical to the go-getting propellants of "capitalism" (< L. *capitalis*, "of the head," the brainy center of all hustling), and not just rationalistically but pragmatically too: "it amounts to nada in pounds or pence" (521.5–6). On the other hand, a work so anti-authoritarian as the *Wake* stands in an equally fringey relation to any orthodox form of Marxism.[24] Everything in the world represented in the maps of Dublin and Europe, according to "Marx and their Groups" (365.20), is particled up out of labor, tremendous labor, whose impact is felt in even the most desultory acts of waking life (standing, for instance). In the night's "amstophere," by contrast, "all's loth and pleasestir" (263.22–23)— "loth, please, to stir," because "all's love and pleasure." We might, therefore, regard "the accomplished washout" (174.8) shown stratified in the two re-lief maps as a member of the "industrial disabled" (409.25–26), "disbarred . . . from unnecessary servile work" (411.2–3), if not overtly "on strike" against the arrangements represented in the maps of Europe ("not what I wants to do a strike of work" [409.33–34]). Or, again, we might construe "the lifesize obstruction" as a practicing "passive resistant" (529.29, 72.19), since "his most besetting of ideas . . . [is] the formation . . . of a . . . stra-tum" (76.2–5) and he does an extremely good job of lying there, even when conflicts arise. Finally, too, we might think of the *Wake*'s heroic loafer as a figure "hungerstriking all alone" (199.4), since sleep, from one perspective, is simply a kind of "hungerstrike" in which the self breaks its contract with the management of reality. If the arrangements represented in the two maps of the Daily World do not quite work, then, it is because the constituent force that holds them together—the brainy "Headmaster" (251.28)—does not work either. "Strike the day off, the nightcap's on nigh" (306.F2).[25]

A complex joke, in turn, suggests that "the aboleshqvick" (302.18 ["Bol-shevik"]) "hungerstriking all alone" in the maps of the night is perpetrating a deviant form of "sabotag" on the West in "the wastes a'sleep" (64.1)— where "The West's Asleep" and he lies dead to the world (hence "abolish-quick"). For "after suns and moons, dews and wettings, thunders and fires, comes sabotag" (409.28–29 [It. *saboto*, "Saturday"]). At its most transparent, the line draws a list of weekdays into a weekend to tell us that our hero is a "weekender" (124.36), on "vacation in life" (411.1–2), though in no pedestrian sense of these terms. A good way "to kill time" (173.11) and to "vacate" the head absolutely, sleep sends our hero into a "vacation" of the deepest possible kind and so makes him not simply "a weekender," but a complete "timekiller" (247.2), capable of putting an "end" to "weeks," perceived years, days, minutes, and history.[26] And as "he doze soze" (345.7–8), he inevitably throws a wrench into the working of the Daily World, for as any employer will tell you, sleeping is not productive, and in certain forms can be outright "sabotage." Like many other terms in the *Wake*, all these lines on "weekending" begin inviting us to wonder what would happen to the patriarchal machinery of the "waste" if all its latter-day Vikings, all "the gogetter[s] that'd make it pay like cash registers" (451.4–5), and all the "bright young chaps of the brandnew braintrust" (529.5) just relaxed and calmed down for a while.[27] Deeper entry into the mind of the "laboursaving deviser" (585.15–16) shown plotting away furtively in the relief maps of "Nilbud" and "neurope," then, raises the wholly speculative question of what the evolved work of the world would be if the wheels of its production were moved—as *Finnegans Wake* and its dreamwork were motivated—by "gaylabouring" (6.23 [*not* "daylabouring"]) and pleasure determined to have its out.

Finally evident in the play of all these contrasts is not primarily a political self-consciousness about a "state" so anarchic as the night, but a prolonged and intense focus on the nature of conflict itself. What Joyce called "irreducible antagonism[s]" produce unyielding tensions, at every minute of the day and night, between the two "coexistent and compresent" worlds that this chapter has explored (526.12)—one "the wikeawades warld" (608.34 ["wide-awake world"]) represented in the geographically coherent maps of Dublin and Europe, the other an "*in risible universe*" (419.3 [an "invisible" and "risible" one]) immanent in their dark and carnal complements; one a geometrically constructed space accessible to vision and reason, the other an "infrarational" dimension out of sight and out of mind.[28] Study of neither of these "two worlds" in itself will account for the formation of our hero's body, his life, or any minute in the here-and-now; nor for the anarchic, yet controlled "politicoecomedy" of the *Wake*.[29] Like the compromise formation of a dream, *Finnegans Wake* takes place in the area where these two "coexistent and compresent" dimensions, each "equal and opposite" (488.9), both necessary to the living of any life yet both "eternally opposed" (488.10–11), produce incessant tensions requiring constant resolution. We might therefore think of the body of the *Wake*'s sleeping hero as a "bluddle filth" (10.8–9 [a "battlefield" of "blood and filth"]) in which all these conflicts are set perpetually at war. In many ways, these conflicts and the carnal ground in which they play themselves out are so alien to and removed from consciousness that Joyce devises a whole new science to reconstruct their intrusion into our hero's "tropped head." Since his intellectual forebear in this endeavor was Vico, this would be the point at which to distance ourselves from the language of the *Wake* in order to consider the impact on "the book of Doublends Jined" of *The New Science* and its world-founding giants.

CHAPTER SEVEN

Vico's "Night of Darkness": The New Science and Finnegans Wake

Darkness . . . is the material of this Science, uncertain, unformed, obscure. . . .   (*NS*, 41)

"OUR FAMILY FURBEAR"

The critical work on *Finnegans Wake* has failed to account fully for Joyce's passionate interest in Giambattista Vico's *New Science*. Working from a sardonic sentence in one of Joyce's letters to Harriet Shaw Weaver ("I would not pay overmuch attention to these theories, beyond using them for all they are worth, but they have gradually forced themselves on me through circumstances of my own life" [*L*, I, 241; *JJ*, 554]), most critics of the *Wake* have remained content to draw on a reading of Vico that had already become gelled, as early as 1950, into a received form destined to be passed on from study to study without much examination or modification. William York Tindall, the last critic to put finishing touches on this orthodox version of Joyce's Vico, tells the story best:

> In each cycle of history there are three ages: the divine, the heroic, and the human, or the primitive, the semi-historic, and the historic. These three ages produce three

sacred customs: religion, marriage, and burial, the first a product of the divine age, the second of the heroic, and the third of the human. After circular flux comes reflux. When one cycle is over, another begins, and, as the Phoenix rises from its ashes, history repeats itself. The first divine age that we know about is the period before the Trojan War. With that war, the heroic age began. The human age of Athens and Rome led to the reflux, and from Rome's decay came a new age, as divine, barbarous, and cruel as the first. The feudal period of Europe brought a return to the heroic age. Vico lived in the human age, and it is easy to guess where we are.[1]

There are, of course, other givens: Vico's conjecture that the crack of thunder, first sounded on the first page of the *Wake*, terrified men in a barbarous state of nature into seeking shelter in caves and so into beginning the churning of the wheels of social history; his conjecture that the terrifying thunderclap caused men to try to duplicate its sound and its power by babbling onomatopoeically, thereby beginning the history of human language; and the observation, first made by Beckett in 1929, that Joyce textured *Finnegans Wake* with an array of quadrupartite phrases which evoke the four human institutions informing Vico's history:

> There are numerous references to Vico's four human institutions—Providence counting as one! "A good clap, a fore wedding, a bad wake, tell hell's well": "Their weatherings and their marryings and their buryings and their natural selections": "the lightning look, the birding cry, awe from the grave, everflowing on our times": "by four hands of forethought the first babe of reconcilement is laid in its last cradle of hume sweet hume."[2]

Most of these accounts, however, misrepresent *The New Science*. Vico speculates that history may operate cyclically, in fact, in a conjectural conclusion sixteen pages long, appended to a work of four hundred pages;[3] and all of the details with which Tindall clarifies the nature of Vico's human ages can be found in the synoptic fourth book of *The New Science*, a summary which, together with Book Five, comprises only one-fourth of the entire work.[4]

It is—and should be—hard to understand how the Vico portrayed in Joyce studies should have generated "passionate interest" in Joyce long before he began the writing of *Ulysses*, let alone *Finnegans Wake* (*JJ*, 340). It makes little sense to suppose that the realist who in *Ulysses* had invested so much care in the portrayal of a single man in a single city on a single day in history should have ended his career writing a book in polyglottal puns in order to transmit the news that the same things happened over and over again in quadrupartite cycles. It is, moreover, difficult to understand how this received vision of Vico could have caused Joyce to claim that *The New Science* strongly forced itself on his life or that Vico anticipated and yielded richer insights than Freud; indeed, it is hard to see how the established sense of Vico bears any relation to Freud at all, or to the night that *Finnegans Wake* reconstructs. Yet when Joyce first conceived of writing a book that would treat the mind in sleep, he also immediately conceived of Vico as a prototype whose work would serve him (*JJ*, 554). And after *Finnegans Wake* was completed, he remarked in reply to adverse reviews in the Italian press that the whole book was founded on the work of an Italian thinker (*L*, III, 463). He seems to have conceived of *The New Science*, in fact, as an intellectual foundation that would underlie *Finnegans Wake* as the *Odyssey* had *Ulysses*; and like the Homeric correspondences in that novel, the references to the four ages of Vichian nature internal to *Finnegans Wake* seem only to be the superficially most apparent outcroppings of a conception fundamental to the book's whole treatment of the dark. Joyce's thinking was never mechanical, and the imaginative transaction by which he brings Vico into the *Wake* proves to be no exception to that rule.

Like the *Wake*, *The New Science* was not much read or understood in its own day, and when it finally was understood, it was rightly perceived as a work that threatened both Christian orthodoxy and the body of mainstream rationalist Enlightenment thinking. Nowadays, historians armed with hindsight—the historian's gift—speak of Vico as a thinker who effected a revolution in the study of history and the human sciences no less profound than that which Galileo effected in the natural sciences; the English translators of *The New Science* find in the book "the germs of all the sciences of social change," and they speak of historiography as "Vichian and pre-Vichian."[5]

The foresightfully radical snap of thought that made Vico unread and misunderstood in his own day—the same decades of the eighteenth century in which Pope wrote his *Essay on Man*—was his supposition that our political forebears, men in a state of nature, were not enlightened rationalists who could agree on social contracts and protective alliances, but semi-bestial clods who had barely thrown off their fur, speechless giants who rutted, bore furry children, and left them to wallow in their own excrement while they themselves roamed off to sate their appetites (*NS*, 192ff; 369ff). This was a conception of history that needed a Darwin before it could become at all generally accepted, and it bore in itself a host of corollaries no less radical. Well before the appearance of Hegel's *Phenomenology of Mind*, *The New Science* necessarily implied that human consciousness was an evolutionary variable, changeable with history and society, and that it depended on the whole human past for its definition. The anthropoid giants who formed the first human society in Vico—a huddled, cave-dwelling knot of men and women who only over generations would begin even dimly to grasp the concept of a family—these forebears had a consciousness radically alien from our own, largely by having none at all; the people born ten generations later had a slightly more articulated consciousness than these forebears; and those born later still in Homeric Greece had an even different consciousness yet. To discover the genesis of rational consciousness in "our family furbear" (132.32) is one whole struggle of *The New Science*, which tries scientifically to determine how beasts driven into caves by the crash of thunder happened to make themselves over generations into learned Enlightenment thinkers capable of building and governing the great nations of the world. Vico's premise, of course, completely breaks with such forms of Enlightenment belief as Cartesian rationalism and Lockean empiricism, both of which regarded "Reason" as an eternal manifestation of laws of nature determined if not by a benevolent deity then by a transcendental order; and implicitly, but not explicitly, it therefore breaks with the world-view out of which rationalism evolved.[6]

The inherent threat that *The New Science* posed both to Christian thought and to the newly rising force of rationalism will explain why Vico had inevitably to refer to "Divine Providence" in *The New Science* and also why he preserved sacred history by locating the Hebrew race outside of the secular world—and essentially beyond the scope of his history—at a region of earth isolated by deserts and centuries from the rest of humanity; for according to the orthodox thought of his age, Adam came to earth already equipped with a language and an innately rational, if fallible, moral sense. As opposed to the sacred history of the Hebrew race, Vico's "gentile history" treats of the "gentile races"—of Egypt, Greece, Rome, Teutonic Germany, and the pagan Mid-East—whose forebears are born to earth wrapped in nothing but animal appetites and fears. Although Vico claims that a Divine Providence secretly guides the gentile races, his own evidence suggests that the "famblings" (582.5 [or "families"]) of which these races are composed merely stumble forward in blind, godless "fumblings": "gentile" history is made by men descended from animals, and not always well.[7] If the academics of Vico's Italy failed to understand his work, then, it was because, like Descartes and Locke, they supposed that reason and enlightened thought of the kind perceptible in the examples of classical Greece and Rome and in the Book of Genesis were natural, transhistorical attributes of the human mind: Enlightenment thinkers were accustomed to referring to the sage examples of Homer, Aesop, and other figures of antiquity who transcended their historical age; Pope translated the *Iliad*, LaFontaine brought Aesop into French. In Vico, however, rational consciousness appears in human history only during the Age of Reason, and to find it in the past is to project the modern mind backwards over the centuries to a historical age in which people possessed their own modes of consciousness and their distinct social forms.[8]

The Third Book of *The New Science*, "Discovery of the True Homer," illustrates in detail the failures of nonevolutionary reconstructions of the past (*NS*, 780–914). For Vico shows here, in ways that richly illuminate *Ulysses*, how Homer, far from being an enlightened sage, was the exponent of a barbaric tribalism. It has become a commonplace in the criticism of *Ulysses* to remark that the novel's Homeric correspondences belittle Bloom and make him seem laughably unheroic and impotent when compared to a warrior like Ulysses. Yet the humor that Joyce generates by making Bloom a modern-day Ulysses is not entirely of his own making; it is also history's. The *Odyssey* as a whole sets up a vital cultural backdrop against which Bloom's twentieth-century heroism and endurance define themselves. At the moment in *Ulysses* paralleled to that passage in the *Odyssey* in which Ulysses regains his homeland, Bloom sits still and, rather than wreaking havoc, uses the weapons of intelligence, sympathy, and fair judgment;[9] arming a bow of reason with arrows of scruples, according to Joyce's schema, he neither murders Molly nor savages Boylan. Had Joyce not used Ulysses as a sustained foil against whom Bloom could be compared in every human article, it would have been almost impossible to give cultural perspective to what might seem only at first Bloom's dubiously heroic capacity to survive, self-possessed, in the face of modern adversity. Against a testicle-ripping, nose-slicing hero like Homer's, Bloom bears our respect. And the ability of civilization to evolve new forms of heroism at the expense of older and more barbarous ones is a power that Vico, a voice at odds with those who have appealed to the sage authority of Homer, emphatically champions:

> Let us allow [Homer] to tell of the inhuman custom (so contrary to what the writers on . . . natural law . . . claim to have been eternally practiced among the nations) which then prevailed among the barbarous peoples of Greece (who are held to have spread humanity throughout the world): to wit, that of poisoning arrows, . . . [and] of denying burial to enemies slain in battle, leaving their unburied bodies instead as a prey to dogs and vultures. . . . Nevertheless, if the purpose of poetry is to tame the ferocity of the vulgar whose teachers the poets are, it was not the part of a wise man, versed in such fierce sensibilities and customs, to arouse admiration of them in the vulgar in order that they should take pleasure in them and be confirmed in them by that pleasure. *(NS*, 781–82)

As the example of "The True Homer" attests, the problem that Vico faced in accounting for the development of the gentile nations "from next to nothing" (4.36–5.1) was twofold in its complexity. If the men who formed the first social groups "at the very dawn of protohistory" possessed no reason at all (169.21), and if all subsequent history were not inherently the product of reasoning individuals, he had to explain not only the movement that lifted human society out of caves into Enlightenment Italy, but also the process by which "our family furbear" created a rational mind "from next to nothing" of his own crude power. Both problems lie at the heart of *The New Science*, and Vico begins to address them by developing a form of internal dialectic to which Marx would later refer in *Capital* and which the Marxist philosopher Georges Sorel would even later apply to the theory of the general strike.[10] Vico's postulate that human society begins when animalistic giants are driven into caves by the terrifying sound of thunder might have taken any number of forms. Had Vico our knowledge of the "new science" of animal evolution, for instance, he might have begun his history with a picture of apes seeking refuge from the jungle. As the *Wake* likes to put it, giving an evolutionary intonation to a music hall song in deference to Vico and Darwin both, "The Sister of the Wife of the Wild Man from Borneo Has Just Come to Town" (130.22–24, 331.34–36, 345.4–5, 382.24–26, 415.7–8, 481.33–35, 502.26–27; *U*, 380). Since Vico finds innumerable giants and thunder-gods in the earliest myths and human records, however, he puts the originating human moment in those terms (*NS*, 193, 301, 380).[11] The establishment of coarsely gesturing and babbling animal families in caves at once sets up a crude class structure differentiating those who own caves from those yet unsettled vagrants who do not, and the social tension resulting from that simple difference is never to relax in the course of Vico's history; indeed, it is only to grow more complex and entangled.[12]

This would explain, of course, how Marx could find in Vico a prototype for his own more refined "new science" of dialectical materialism. And it also helps to explain how Joyce could find Vico's historical vision compatible with his own, since it operates with much more sophistication and intricacy than the comparisons with Jung and its general treatment in Joyce criticism would suggest. Achieving an inclusiveness that Joyce claimed not to find either in Freud's theory of consciousness, or in the socialist and anarchist literature in which he was widely read, *The New Science* gave Joyce a vision of a recurring patterning in social history that at once respected the unique problems and conditions of successive social eras, yet also isolated,

Vico's "Night of Darkness"

as Marx did, social forces that manifested themselves in different cultures, in different material settings, and in different periods of history.

Joyce also undoubtedly admired Vico's peculiarly modern willingness to admit total unreason along with reason as a motivating force of history. Mainstream rationalist thinking bred in the European social community a hypocritical nineteenth-century politics verbally capable of asserting its alliance with Reason and its aspiration to rise onward and upward to work out the beast, but in fact capable of creating social conditions that would produce in Ireland, for instance, a famine described as "the worst event of its kind recorded in European history at a time of peace."[13] This is essentially the politics described in that section of the *Wake* which Joyce called "Haveth Childers Everywhere" (pp. 532–54), where HCE, stuttering constantly with guilt, dubiously justifies the aspirant importance of his work to his family by telling the whole story of civilization and including among his accomplishments a rather large number of mistakes: the slums of London (pp. 543–45), the pollution of the Liffey (p. 550), and the ambiguously productive rape of Ireland (p. 547). Nature gives Vico's man the mind of an unconscious animal; Vico's history is the process by which man, of his own blind, stumbling power, slowly builds that natural mind toward consciousness, interdependently with language and civil institutions.

Here, too, Vico's vision of history certainly appealed to Joyce, because it extended into social history processes that Joyce himself had sought to trace in *A Portrait of the Artist as a Young Man*, where, as Stephen's personality evolves in time from infancy to young adulthood, the language and consciousness through which he perceives and defines himself also evolve interdependently, all as aspects of one another. Joyce would also have found in Vico, then, a vision of historical growth as intricate as the vision of the personal growth that he represented in *A Portrait*—the struggle of "a batlike soul waking to the consciousness of itself in darkness and secrecy and loneliness . . ." (*P*, 183). The phrase, descriptive both of Ireland's and of Stephen's individual development in *A Portrait*, defines equally well the evolutionary development of human history in *The New Science*. It is not entirely clear, in fact, whether Joyce came to admire Vico because he found the vision of human growth presented in *A Portrait* confirmed in *The New Science*; or whether it was Vico who helped cause Joyce to scrap *Stephen Hero* and to rework it into the form that would come to be *A Portrait*. All we know of the original transaction that would cause Joyce to champion *The New Science* throughout his literary career and through all the pages of the *Wake* is that he first read and expressed passionate interest in Vico during his years in Trieste (1904–15); that he worked hard on *Stephen Hero*, abandoned it completely, and rewrote it as *A Portrait* during the same period;[14] and that Vico's vision of growth of the soul of mankind shares many affinities with Joyce's vision of the growth of the soul.

POETIC WISDOM

This comparison suggests a final radical corollary to the propositions on which *The New Science* is predicated—the corollary most interesting to a reader of the *Wake*. Since Vico argues that the language, consciousness, society, and problems of any moment in history develop as consequences of decisions made in a historical past in which the pressures of the immediate moment far outweigh those of any speculative future; and since he assumes that human history begins in the minds of bestial giants in a state of nature, he puts himself into the difficult position of having to account for "social" choices made by irrational beings who cannot know what "choice" and "society" are. If the language, consciousness, and civil institutions of Europe grew by a process of internal dialectic out of forests in which barbaric, terrified animals scrambled for shelter at the sound of thunder, then a knowledge of the process by which European civilization came to exist depended on a knowledge of how those wholly irrational beings thought. His enterprise, then, is identical to that of *Finnegans Wake* in that it entails a willed abandonment of reason and a sympathetic entry into unconsciousness:

> But the nature of our civilized minds is so detached from the senses . . . by abstractions corresponding to all the abstract terms our languages abound in, and so refined by the art of writing, and as it were spiritualized by the use of numbers . . . that it is naturally beyond our power to form the vast image of [the world perceived by the first men]. . . . It is equally beyond our power to enter into the vast imagination of those first men, whose minds were not in the least abstract, refined, or spiritualized, because they were entirely immersed in the senses, buffeted by the passions, buried in the body. . . . we can scarcely understand, still less imagine, how those first men thought who founded gentile humanity. (*NS*, 378)

The problem that Vico addresses in this passage is not one that he despairs of solving; indeed, in the central and most lengthy book of *The New Science*, "Poetic Wisdom," he tries to reconstruct the "scarcely imaginable" minds of those aboriginal first men in order to account for the history that grows out of them. "Poetic Wisdom" is the linch-pin of Vico's history, the studied and labored piece of evidence upon which he builds his science.

Vico's "Night of Darkness"

Our treatment [of history] must take its start from the time these creatures began to think humanly. In their monstrous savagery and unbridled bestial freedom there was no means to tame the former or bridle the latter but the frightful thought of some divinity, the fear of whom . . . is the only powerful means of reducing to duty a liberty gone wild. To discover the way in which this first human thinking arose in the gentile world, we encountered exasperating difficulties which have cost us the research of a good twenty years. [We had] to descend from these human and refined natures of ours to those quite wild savage natures, which we cannot at all imagine and can comprehend only with great effort. (*NS*, 338)

In a direct and substantial way, the mind that Joyce sought to reconstruct in *Finnegans Wake* was equivalent to the aboriginal mind that Vico sought to comprehend in Book II of *The New Science;* what Freud called "the dream-work" and "the unconscious," Vico, lacking psychoanalytic terminology, simply called "poetic wisdom" and "ignorance":

But these first men who later became the princes of the gentile nations, must have done their thinking under the strong impulsion of violent passions, as beasts do. . . . Hence poetic wisdom, the first wisdom of the gentile world, must have begun with a metaphysics not rational and abstract like that of learned men now, but felt and imagined, as that of these first men must have been, who, without power of ratiocination, were all robust sense and vigorous imagination. This metaphysics was their poetry, a faculty born with them (for they were furnished by nature with these senses and imaginations); born of their ignorance of causes, for ignorance, the mother of wonder, made everything wonderful to men who were ignorant of everything. . . . (*NS*, 340, 375; see also 399)

In order to substantiate his dialectical account of history, essentially, Vico had to invent an elaborate depth psychology—a "metaphysics," in his phrase—that would enable him to comprehend the unconsciousness out of which men made social choices "in the deplorable obscurity of the beginnings" of the human world (*NS*, 344):

But in the night of thick darkness enveloping the earliest antiquity, so remote from ourselves, there shines the eternal and never failing light of a truth beyond all question: that the world of civil society has certainly been made by men, and that its principles are therefore to be found within the modifications of our own human mind. Whoever reflects on this cannot but marvel that the philosophers should have bent all their energies to the study of the world of nature, which, since God made it, He alone knows; and that they should have neglected the study of the world of nations, or civil world, which, since men made it, men could come to know. This aberration was a consequence of that infirmity of the human mind by which, immersed and buried in the body, it naturally inclines to take notice of bodily things [i.e., the physical universe], and finds the effort to attend to itself too laborious. . . . (*NS*, 331)

When Vico proposes to work his way back into the unconscious mind of these first men by discovering "its principles in the modifications of our own human mind," he is not simply proposing—as the psychoanalytic movement would two centuries later—that a stream of primitive, infantile irrationality, reflected in the myths and fables of the past, underruns our modern civil consciousness. His vision is primarily historical. If consciousness is a man-made property that changes in historical time, then each individual owes the way in which he thinks to the generation of his parents; yet his parents owe their thinking and behavior to the generation of their parents; and so forth, in a chain extending back to the beginnings of the gentile world. Those crude choices made by Vico's giants, then, inform all minds born out of them; and the terrifying irrationalities and encaved social structures that they stumbled into still perpetuate themselves, despite the transformations of generations and generations, "in the modifications of our own human minds"—"the traditions of all dead generations weighing like an Alp on the brains of the living," in one of Marx's psychoanalytic phrases.[15]

This conception of history as a force funneling into and determining anyone's life in the present rang particularly true to Joyce, who was born into a family and a culture morally structured by a Catholicism genetically arising out of the Middle Ages. "*Like a gentile man,*" too (150.26), he was born into a nation whose political life had been determined by actions militantly undertaken in the twelfth century, when Henry II, asking the English-born pope of the Vatican for permission to take in hand the immoral Irish, made the city of Dublin the eternal property of the citizens of Bristol.[16] Joyce was born into a culture whose social structures were shaped by the infinitely inheritable superstition of racism, a habit of mind passed on from parent to child over generations and extending backwards through linguistic history into a time when the verb "to like" was synonymous with the preposition "like," and when to "like" someone meant that one found the likeness of his own race and blood in them.[17] Joyce was born into a family and a religion that implanted in him a fear of thunder so great that throughout his life he refused to live in cities known for the frequency of their thunderstorms and hid in closets, as Vico's giants did in caves, whenever thunder rent the sky; it was Vico's primitive man who bequeathed to generation after generation the fear of celestial punishment that found its way into Joyce's consciousness. And it was Vico's giants who bequeathed to the minds of all human generations after them the social unit of the encaved private family.

Twentieth-century psychoanalysis proposes to isolate and cure the irrationally disturbed components of personality by analyzing the fears and fixations inherited from parents in an impressionable, irrational infantile past. Vico's axiomatic observation that rationality is a man-made structure historically evolved out of animal unreason will suggest why Joyce would have regarded Freudian theory as a diminution of Vico's insights. Since *The New Science* sees the consciousness into which one grows as the product of a historical development that begins in the terror of thunderstruck "furbear[s]," it complementarily implies that the unconscious conflicts rifting modern minds and societies are historically transmitted over much more than one generation. The individual cannot purge himself of neurotic unhappiness by rethinking his familial past alone, because his parents are largely innocent transmitters of a language and an ideology determined by a history that transcends them and himself both. Fully to understand the irrationalities understructuring his mind, he has to exorcise his parents' parents, and his parents' parents' parents, and the "first men, stupid, insensate, and horrible beasts," who laid down the foundations of human civil life and consciousness (*NS*, 374). As a Vichian who had already extensively examined his relations with his mother and father in *A Portrait* and *Ulysses*, the Joyce of *Finnegans Wake* is as deeply interested in the remote determinants of neuroses as in the immediate ones. Action according to this psychological model is evident both in Joyce's life and in his representations of it: "tapping his brow" in the hour of his therapeutic release from the past in *Ulysses*, and muttering that "in here it is I must kill the priest and king," Stephen Dedalus has to lay to rest not only the irrationalities inherited from a devoutly self-abnegating Catholic mother and a self-destructive, jobless father, but also those inherited from the medieval Catholicism and the English economic policy that made possible that mother and that father (*U*, 589). In order to understand how that Church and that feudal economic behavior originated, Joyce in turn had to try to understand, in *Finnegans Wake*, the "furbear[s]" buried in the darkness of Vico's aboriginality. All of history is in one's parents; and the Oedipal struggle is with the whole of the past.

This understanding so fundamentally informs *The New Science* that it shapes Vico's whole prose style, whose texture is as dense, punning, and polyglottal as that of *Finnegans Wake*. In Vico's "gentile history," man creates over generations his own human nature—and exactly as he also creates human nations. Since human nature and nations evolve interdependently with language, Vico conveys their commutual coming-to-be, their *nascimento*, by weaving through *The New Science* an assemblage of words originating in the same aboriginal root **gen-* ("to come to be")—whose meaning is also its evolution. Uttered in the darkness of prehistory by descendants of Vico's first men, this syllable generates over generations, and in all the nations of the gentile world, a diverse vocabulary whose meaning is the genesis of human nature. (Some of its English outgrowths are diagrammed in figure 7.1.) On the evolution of vocables like this, and the freight they carry, Joyce succinctly comments in *Finnegans Wake* that "the world, mind, is, was and will be writing its own wrunes for ever, man, on all matters that fall under the ban of our infrarational senses" (19.35–20.1)—where the appositional equations of "world," "mind," "man," and his "runes" replicate the vision of *The New Science*. An aspect of his science, as the etymology of Vico's "gentility" will attest, is the conceptual identity of "nationality" and "genitality": originating in the same source, both words embody the same tensions. It is for this reason, in *Finnegans Wake*, that HCE's encounter with the "cad" (35.11; 35.1–36.4 [< Fr. *cadet*, "younger son"]) takes place in the shadows of the Wellington Memorial (36.18), the dream-displaced scene of his sexual "crime"; the conflict underlying this encounter, underlined by references to nationalist and generational struggles, is localized in HCE's genitalia. In *The New Science* and *Finnegans Wake*, national and generational struggles are also genital struggles, because they all bring patriarchal authorities and those subjugated to such authority into visceral conflict over issues of power and potency.

Since Vico's "Poetic Wisdom" in its own way strives rationally to reconstruct the minds of those irrational first men whose animal instincts began to determine the subsequent evolution of history and human consciousness, it encompasses the psychoanalytic work that Freud achieved in reconstructing the infantile mind whose fears and pleasure determine the shape of personal history. Here, too, Joyce learned much more from *The New Science* than a principle of eternal recurrence. Vico gave him the dream-work by which he spun out *Finnegans Wake*. What Vico called "Poetic Wisdom," Freud explained two hundred years later as the primary process of the unconscious. But Vico also anticipates Freud, and ultimately contributes to *Ulysses* and the *Wake* by drawing a rich fund of insight from the observation and the memory of human infancy. In trying to understand how the first men thought and oriented themselves towards others in a world void of society, he naturally seeks to fathom the wholly unformed mind of the child. Because Vico's first men are born into a state of nature and differ from their modern descendants largely in lacking the benefits of a long-evolved language and consciousness instilled in children by the process of education, Vico axiomatically assumes that these people thought as infants and chil-

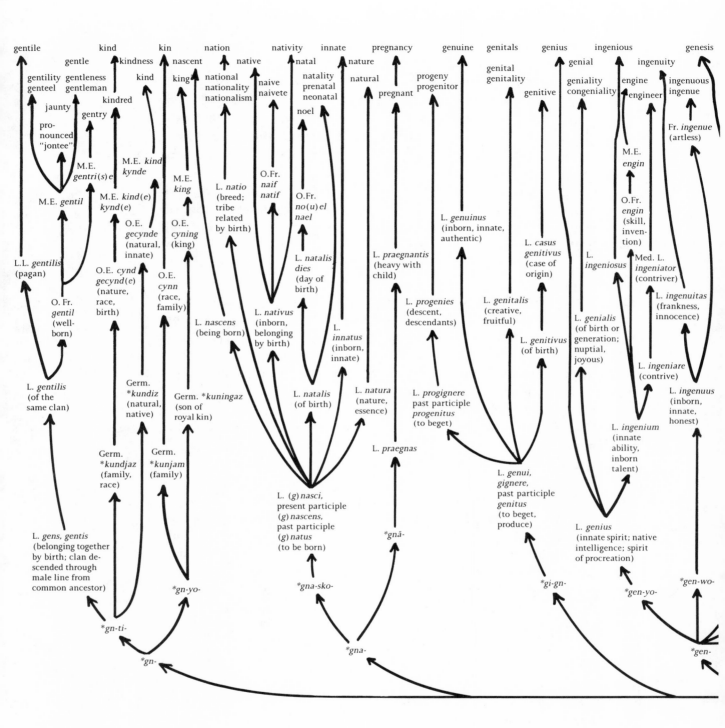

Figure 7.1. Etymological chart: **gen-. The Nature of the Generation of the Gentile Nations: "the sibspeeches of all mankind have foliated (earth seizing them!) from the root of some funner's stotter all the soundest sense to be found immense" (96.30–32) ("sibspeeches": "subspecies" of related ["sib"] tongues; "some funner's stotter": "some funny stutter" [Ger. *Stotter*, "stutter" + Nor. *Samfundets Stotter*, "Pillars of Society"])

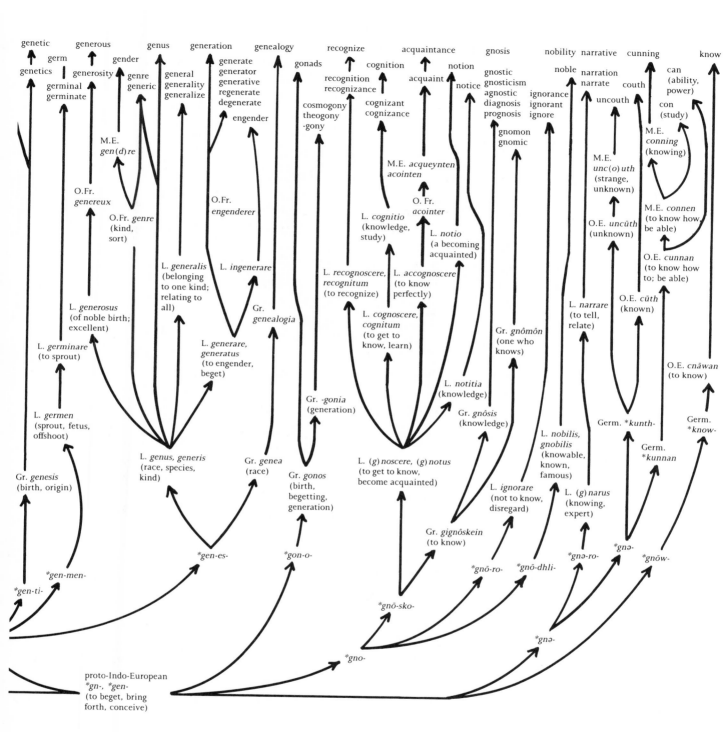

dren do (*NS*, 211–16): according to fears, pleasures, and instincts. What distinguishes the newborn child of the modern world from "the first peoples, who were the children of the human race" is the weight of history preceding his birth (*NS*, 498). It is a long, complex history whose main lessons the newborn child learns in the first few years of life when his parents teach him, as in the opening pages of *A Portrait*, language, morality, identity, family, and both the superstitions and the achievements of millennia (*NS*, 336). But the mind of an infant not yet tutored into the orders of language, reason, and social customs—not yet able to distinguish anything apart from its pleasures and fears—that is the mind which nature gives to "the children of nascent mankind" in Vico's *Science*, the mind out of which his aboriginal giants crudely act and "reason" (*NS*, 376).

In the psychogenesis that Joyce derived from Vico, "our family furbears" spent their entire lifetimes in a state of unconsciousness, and it was out of this unformed, infantile mind that they began to generate the utterances and groupings from which our own language and civilization grew. In "Poetic Wisdom," Vico constructs an elaborate psychology of the Unconscious, or "Ignorance," to explain the dreamlike ways in which this infantile and history-originating mind worked and made choices. His reconstruction begins with a willed, imaginary abandonment both of rationalism and of the man-made Newtonian order in which rationalism found its object:

> From these first men, stupid, insensate, and horrible beasts, all philosophers and philologians should have begun their investigations of the wisdom of the ancient gentiles. . . . And they should have begun [not with physics, but] with metaphysics, which seeks its proofs not in the external world but within the modifications of the mind of him who meditates it. For since this world of nations has certainly been made by men, it is within these modifications that its principles should have been sought. And human nature, so far as it is like that of the animals, carries with it this property, that the senses are its sole way of knowing things.   (*NS*, 374)

"In the early childhood of the world," however, this sensory "knowing of things" is *not* perceptual, but animal and instinctive (*NS*, 69): for "men at first feel without perceiving, then they perceive with a troubled and agitated spirit, finally they reflect with a clear mind" (*NS*, 218). Men void of the learned capacity to perceive, who sense nothing but their own feelings, can only stand as giants in proportion to all the rest of the unborn world ("the human mind, because of its indefinite nature, wherever it is lost in ignorance makes itself the rule of the universe in respect of everything it does not know" [*NS*, 180–81]). "Born in ignorance of causes, ignorance making everything wonderful to men ignorant of everything," the first men of Vico's "giantle" humanity (509.19 ["gentile," "giant"]) accordingly resemble the unconscious hero of *Finnegans Wake*—an "overgrown babeling" who lies "fum in mow" (6.31, 596.6)—by virtue of a gigantic egoism that knows in the world nothing but sensation interior to the body. Vico's "giantle[s]" move organically through the *Wake* because they have the sensibilities both of Joyce's unconscious hero and of unconscious human infants, "in [whose] mental life . . . today," according to Freud, "we can still detect the same archaic factors which were once dominant generally in the primeval days of human civilization."[18]

There are now two ways of regarding the genesis of the world into which this infantile mind awakens. In one, invented by Newton and upheld by scientific rationalism, the world begins when a God immanent in nature occasions an astronomical Big Bang that hurls the inanimate physical matter of billions of galaxies outward into space to form, over eons and in a single star-system, a planet whose molecules will providentially start replicating themselves, in turn to generate animate matter capable of reproduction, and then self-consciousness, and then the inspired writing of revelatory books like Genesis: creation is already there, completely ordered and waiting to be known as the infant grows. In the second version, told in Genesis and upheld both in *Finnegans Wake* and in Vico's *New Science* of nescience, "the world in its infancy" begins when a space-pervading spirit named "I AM" (the Hebrew JHVH) starts gathering the appearances of nature out of a dark and void formlessness, paramount among them the form of an aboriginal man who becomes capable of naming animals, shaping the world, inventing and learning concepts like "matter," and evolving over time a mind like Newton's, trained in the pragmatic fictions of mechanical materialism: creation happens dynamically, from the inside out, as the world continually unfolds in "the modifications of our human mind." If the first of these geneses regards as primary the knowing of external matter, through science (< L. *scio*, "I know"), Vico's genesis regards as primary the not-knowing of the human mind, whose coming-to-be through nescience ("I AM") will ultimately generate the man-made constructs of science and reason. In words taken from what Vico called his "'new science in negative form,' the form, that is, of a destructive criticism of existing theories":[19]

> . . . as rational metaphysics teaches that man becomes all things by understanding them (*homo intelligendo fit omnia*), this imaginative metaphysics shows that man becomes all things by *not* understanding them (*homo non intelligendo fit omnia*), and perhaps the latter proposition is truer than the former, for when man understands, he extends his mind and takes in the things, but when he does not under-

stand, he makes the things out of himself and becomes them by transforming himself into them. (*NS*, 405)

The "giantle" world of Vico's *New Science*, then, originates exactly as the world originates in the Book of Genesis, and exactly as it always and only originates in the minds of human infants. "Lost in ignorance," "buried in the body and immersed in the senses," these impercipient, space-pervading giants, informed by *Jov*(e) or *J*(eh)*ov*(ah), rise from an unconsciousness that only knows "I AM" into "gentile" human "nature" by gathering from dark formlessness the etymologically related property of physical "nature"—animating it and making it sensible according to anthropocentric principles of infantile psychology that Vico elaborates throughout "Poetic Wisdom" (see *NS*, 180–7, 211–12):

> The most sublime labor of poetry is to give sense and passion to insensate things [as is] characteristic of children. . . . This philologico-philosophical axiom proves to us that in the world's childhood men were by nature sublime poets. (*NS*, 186)

Since Vico's aboriginal man actively creates the world by "making things out of himself," "the first nature" of gentile humanity in *The New Science* is "a poetic or creative nature, which we may be allowed to call divine": "in the world's childhood" of Vico's Divine Age, "men [are] *by nature* poets," and "the world in its infancy [is] composed of poetic nations" (*NS*, 187, 216 [italics mine]). The key terms here—as in all of these quotations and "Poetic Wisdom" as a whole—are "nature" (or "nations") and "poetry": Vico employs the latter in its etymological sense of "creating" or "making" (from the Gr. *poiêsis*) rather than in the sense of literary production, since the giants who people "the world in its infancy" know no language or writing ("infancy," etymologically, < L. *infans* ["not speaking"]). Just as the limits of his culture's vocabulary cause Vico to adopt the term "ignorance" to denote "unconsciousness," so he uses the term "poetic wisdom" to denote the manifold forms of unconscious thinking that Freud would study more specialistically in his work on infantile sexuality. Treating of "metaphor," "synechdoche," "metonymy," "allegory," and "myth," rather than of "condensation," "displacement," and "indirect representation," Vico's "Poetic Wisdom" is a form of Freudian dreamwork. Organic to the minds of "the children of nascent mankind," poetic wisdom is the unconscious wisdom into which his first men rise from their nescience; it is the unconscious wisdom out of which Enlightenment Europe and its institutions dialectically grow in Vico's social history.

In order to explain how this poetic wisdom arises in giants aboriginally "ignorant of everything" but the sensation of their bodies, Vico necessarily undertakes a reconstruction of unconscious memory comparable to Freud's; for "the world in its infancy" is a "time empty of facts which must really have been full of them" (*NS*, 735). Not unlike Freud, he attributes the early genesis of human nature to "the terror of present power," learned with the crash of thunderbolts which rudely teach Vico's infantile giant that he does not fill the universe (*NS*, 382). Generating the internal perception of fear in a body aboriginally all appetite, this external sound operates like the thunder of the patriarchal "NO!" in Freud's accounts of the sexual organization and toilet-training of modern infants:

> But the greatest and most important part of physics is the contemplation of the nature of man. . . . the founders of gentile humanity in a certain sense generated and produced in themselves the proper human form in its two aspects: . . . by means of frightful religions and terrible paternal powers and sacred ablutions they brought forth from their giant bodies the form of our just corporature, and . . . by discipline . . . they brought forth from their bestial minds the form of our human mind. (*NS*, 692)

Poetic wisdom arises in the minds of Vico's aboriginal giants, then, together with the learning of corporeal control and the human body's limited dimensions. Through poetic wisdom man creates his own body, which is not immanent in the physical universe, and which differs from the bodies of animals because it is humanly made and organized:

> In the prevailing best usage [the Latin verb *educere*] applies to the education of the spirit and [the Latin verb *educare*] to that of the body. . . . education began to bring forth in a certain way the form of the human soul which had been completely submerged in the huge bodies of the giants, and began likewise to bring forth the form of the human body itself in its just dimensions from the disproportionate giant bodies. (*NS*, 520)

If this kind of education reduces the space-pervading immensity of Vico's infantile first men by subjecting them to self-imposed disciplinary laws, however, it compensatorily liberates, through a form of "sublimation," a human nature that will generate the world of nations and civil institutions:

> Then, between the powerful restraints of frightful superstition and the goading stimuli of bestial lust . . . [these giants] had to hold in [check] the impetus of the bodily motion of lust. Thus they began to use human liberty, which consists in holding in check the motions of concupiscence and giving them another direction; for since this liberty does not come from the body, whence comes the concupiscence, it must come from the mind and is therefore properly human. (*NS*, 1098)

In his reconstruction of the mind at the origins both of social history and of personal history, Vico accordingly developed principles of "infantile regression" that Freud would elaborate two centuries later in his accounts of the dreamwork of sleep. Vico discovered in his aboriginal first men the "Freudian" principles of parental determination, dependency, and oedipality:

> The nature of children is such that by the ideas and names of the men, women, and things they have known first, they afterward apprehend and name all the men, women, and things that bear any resemblance or relation to the first. (*NS*, 206)

He discovered that in infancy a child has no solidly established sexual identity and therefore thinks, in a kind of promiscuous abandonment allowing the free association of everyone and everything, out of a mind "polymorphously perverse," as the first men of "giantle" humanity also did:

> . . . Orpheus then founds the humanity of Greece on the examples of an adulterous Jove, a Juno who is the mortal enemy of the virtues of the Herculeses. . . . Nor is this unrestrained licentiousness of the gods satisfied by forbidden intercourse with women: Jove burns with wicked love for Ganymede; indeed this lust reaches the point of bestiality and Jove, transformed into a swan, lies with Leda. This licentiousness, practiced on men and beasts, was precisely the infamous evil of the outlaw world [the world of the first men, who lived before the creation of civil law]. (*NS*, 80)

Finally, in an age whose philological authorities were trying to discover how the languages of the gentile nations could have developed historically from the Hebrew spoken by Adam in the Garden of Eden, *The New Science* advanced the radical proposition that human language had its beginnings in the minds of infantile first men who growled, whined, and whimpered in pleasure and pain like animals in caves (*NS*, 63); for the languages of Vico's gentile humanity, their beginnings found "in the modifications of our own human mind," originate not simply in historical time and geographical space, but also—as always and only—inside the bodies of human infants: "the first dull-witted men were moved to utterance only by very violent passions, which are naturally expressed in a very loud voice" (*NS*, 461); "articulate language began to develop by way of onomatopoiea, through which we still find children happily expressing themselves" (*NS*, 447):

> Men vent great passions by breaking into song, as we observe in the most grief-stricken and the most joyful. . . . it follows that the founders of the gentile nations, having wandered about in the wild state of dumb beasts and being therefore sluggish, were inexpressive save under the impulse of violent passions, and formed their first languages by singing.

> Languages must have begun with monosyllables, as in the present abundance of articulated words into which children are now born they begin with monosyllables in spite of the fact that in them the fibers of the organ necessary to articulate speech are very flexible.
>
> (*NS*, 229–231)

Vico's account of human genesis anticipatorily encompasses Freud's, finally, by understanding that human consciousness, language, and reality genetically unfold from inside the bodies of infants. Although the decorous civilization of Vico's Europe had begun learning to devalue the human body, nothing in the universe known to Vico's gentile man ever happens outside of its space, within which the human world and its knowing aboriginally and always come to be. Since the infantile thinking of Vico's first men is equivalently the unconsciousness of the body not yet tutored into human knowing, the psychology of unconsciousness that Vico develops in *The New Science* also anticipates the account of infantile sexuality given in Freud's theories of genitality. But Joyce, who described the secret pressures of the stomach on rational thinking in the "Lestrygonians" episode of *Ulysses*, the patterns of economic management imposed on consciousness by the evacuatory organs in "Calypso," and the evolved forms of human enterprise made possible by the biological endowment of lungs on mankind in "Aeolus," probably preferred to Freud's theories of genital organization Vico's broader account of how "gentile" human nature rolled up into the head not simply out of the loins but out of the entire body of his aboriginal infant giants. In Vico's *nascimento*, the thinking of the body begins not simply the history of personality, but the history of the West; and "genitality," in this history, is only a late and limited conceptual outgrowth of the broader force of a "gentile nature."

A "GIANTLE"

If nothing in Vico's gentile history happens outside of this body, everything in *Finnegans Wake* only happens inside of it. The hero of *Finnegans Wake*, losing the historically evolved property of consciousness when he falls asleep, spends the night "in the state of nature" from which Vico's original men arose (49.24–25), so to become "our family furbear" (132.32 ["bear" now because he is in hibernation]). "Ignorant of everything," he too lies "buried in the body" and "immersed in the senses" like a space-pervading giant. As incapable of abstraction as Vico's first people, emptied of all learned knowing, he too possesses no ordered memory of a historical past at

Vico's "Night of Darkness"

all. Incapable in turn of perceiving anything in the world outside of his own body, his body fills all sensed space, the infantile and unconscious way of thinking internal to it reordering in its own form of "poetic wisdom" the dimly recalled residue of the wakeful world. The intense process of reading by which Joyce elicited a dreamwork from Vico's "Poetic Wisdom" had to be one of the great literary encounters of Joyce's life; for Vico also gave Joyce a richly articulated account of the genesis of language that enabled him to evolve a reconstruction of the human night.

The primary materials filling HCE's mind immediately after his fall into sleep in the first chapter of *Finnegans Wake* indirectly represent, in images of burial and entombment, the paralysis of his fallen body and the death of his consciousness; but the psychology of unconsciousness of Vico's "Poetic Wisdom" in turn caused Joyce to overlay his hero's fall with a regressive hundred-lettered word expressive of the thunder that terrified Vico's giants (3.15–17). Reconstructing the return of its "retrospectable fearfurther" (288.F7) to the condition of Vico's aboriginal men, the first chapter of the *Wake* is densely clustered with images of giants and "astoneaged" cave men (18.15)—Neanderthal men (18.22, 19.25), Cromagnon men (20.7), Heidelberg men (18.23), Mousterian men (15.33), Piltdown men (10.30), and the paleolithic characters "Mutt and Jute" (16.10–11ff. ["mute and deaf"]), who babble and stammer imperceptively like Vico's men, and who earn their names from the comic-strip characters Mutt and Jeff, modern counterparts of the pictographic cave paintings of the "astoneaged." The *Wake*'s opening chapter dwells insistently on images of the giants of aboriginal myth because its sleeping giant is one of them: the chapter draws heavily on myths of origin provided in the Book of Genesis (4.18–5.4 and passim), the Egyptian Book of the Dead (26.17–20), the Irish Annals of the Four Masters (13.20–14.15), the Icelandic Eddas (14.16), and other accounts of the world's coming-to-be. Insofar as HCE's fall into sleep buries him within the matter of an "unknown body," his unconsciousness resembles that internal to all the tombs of the world, although foremost among these are ones evocative of paleolithic sepulture: cromlechs like those at Carnac and Stonehenge (5.31), megalithic circles like those seen in the Rollright Stones of England (5.30–31), kistvaens (5.31), menhirs (25.11–12), and, above all, prehistoric barrow after barrow referentially underlie this chapter. If it reconstructs Finnegan's wake from the "eyewitless foggus" of a man "tropped head," it also, as the prelude to "the book of Doublends Jined," evokes the waking of mankind in its cavemen and its neanderthal giants: a book of Wakening like

Genesis and *The New Science, Finnegans Wake* is also "the book of Doublends Jined" (20.15–16), or "Dublin's Giant." The unconscious mind "buried in the body" that HCE possesses in sleep is the unconscious mind out of which Vico's aboriginal giants initiated the historical wakening of mankind. It is the mind out of which, every morning, the world comes to be.

"FLESCH NUEMAID MOTTS"

Having reconstructed a psychology of the unconscious, Vico has only begun the work of his *New Science;* he still needs to account for the first social choices made by his world-founding giants. To this end, he summons up the oldest human records available to him: myths, fables, and legends. Rather than looking at these myths archetypally, he finds in them irrationally distorted accounts of the first human social transactions; for "men are naturally impelled to preserve the memories of the laws and institutions that bind them in their societies" (*NS*, 201), and "mythologies" "will be seen to be civil histories of the first peoples, who were everywhere naturally poets" (*NS*, 352).

In order to read these myths with a sensitivity to the alien mentality that generates them, however, Vico devises a system of interpretation not unlike dream interpretation, since its object is to elicit from the manifest appearances of obscure texts latent and concealed truths about archaic times—though times in which the earliest members of the gentile world established the first societies and began the first human social transactions. "Poetic Wisdom" elaborately studies "scarcely imaginable" modes of thought and expression through which "unenlightened" minds transform recognizable human concerns into mythical and fabulous forms. It necessarily seeks in turn a means of deciphering these obscure productions, just as psychoanalysis would decipher comparably strange forms of thought that played through the mind in sleep.

Since Vico's reconstructive enterprise also required him to study the language in which the concealed histories of the gentile races were preserved, a final point of comparison is with the psychoanalytic focus on language itself. Specifically, Vico's reading of myths recalls Freud's repeated observations that the "analysis of nonsensical verbal forms . . . occur[ring] in dreams is particularly well calculated to exhibit the dream-work's achievements"; for Freudian interpretation, like Vico's, works through the "analysis and synthesis of syllables" comparably to reconstruct an archaic human past—the infantile past—whose influence structures "the text of the dream" (*ID*, 338; 332n.). Indeed, in some special cases, Freud notes,

> . . . the course of linguistic evolution has made things very easy for dreams. For language has a whole number of words at its command which originally had a concrete and pictorial significance, but are used today in a colorless and abstract sense. All that the dream need do is to give these words their former, full meaning or to go back a little way to an earlier phase in their development.   (*ID*, 442)

And elsewhere in his work he broadens the understanding by treating philology as a protoform by psychoanalysis:

> In the agreement between . . . the dream-work . . . and [what] philologists have discovered to be habitual in the oldest languages, we may see a confirmation of our supposition in regard to the regressive, archaic character of thought-expression in dreams. And we cannot dismiss the conjecture, which forces itself on us psychiatrists, that we should understand the language of dreams better and translate it more easily if we knew more about the development of language.[20]

Vico's study of "the development of language" offered Joyce exactly this insight into "the language of dreams," his psychology of unconsciousness in turn anticipating Freud's both because of its earlier emergence in history and because of its compass: not simply personality, but all of Vico's gentile humanity begins in an unconsciousness whose dynamic is revealed in the evolution of language and whose deep structure is yielded by etymology. For the etymology of "etymology," Vico notes, is "the science of the true" (from the Gr. *etymos*, "true"; *NS*, 403); and the employment of this "adamelegy" in the "root language" of *Finnegans Wake* (77.26, 424.17), Joyce said, "guaranteed the truth of his knowledge and his representation of events" in his "imitation of the dream-state."[21]

Since Vico's gentile world unfolds from inside the bodies of aboriginal giants, his speculations on the genesis of language proceed from observations on how language always and only originates in the minds of human infants, as they begin to express themselves and simultaneously perceive those others who will teach them a language and consciousness evolved over millennia. Written language, in this prehistory—sign language—begins with manual gestures, whose exercise gradually educes the hands and eyes from the aboriginally giant body (*NS*, 225–26, 401–2, 431–46); while phonetic language originates in comparably expressive exercises of the vocal chords and ears: in asemantic babbling, laughing, and crying, all of which Vico subsumes under the single term "singing" (*NS*, 228–31, 446–54).

Once Vico's primitive man orients himself in encaved social groups—families—he begins to generate pictographic signs and monosyllabic utterances that in memory acquire fixed meanings expressive of basic fears and desires (*NS*, 448–54); and at this point in his development, man distinguishes himself from feral giants and begins to evolve more elaborate social structures, languages, and forms of knowing. Basic to Vico's genetic account is the understanding that all human language evolves out of an aboriginal state by a process of distortionary slippage as "PREAUSTERIC MAN" (266.R1) unconsciously blurs syllables and images together, in the course of his development, in order to build new words and concepts that always lie just beyond his slowly growing, conscious grasp: the Latin word for sheep (*pecus*) generates a word for money (*pecunia*) as the economic conditions of social history evolve, for instance; and the syllable *gen-*, over time, generates the concept and practice of "engineering."

Complementarily, Vico discovers that the etymological unlayering of modern languages, and the consciousness that they make possible, allows the reconstruction of the unconscious mind out of which gentile humanity arose. By drawing on the etymons of Western languages in *Finnegans Wake*, Joyce could accordingly represent a human mind returned, in sleep, to equivalent unconsciousness. "'The only difference,' he declared [to Jacques Mercanton], 'is that, in my imitation of the dream-state, I effect in a few minutes what it has sometimes taken centuries to bring about.'"[22]

The primary unconscious meaning that Joyce, through Vico, discovers beneath all human language is the "meaning" of the human body, within which the whole of gentile reality comes to be:

> The human mind is naturally inclined by the senses to see itself externally in the body, and only with great difficulty does it come to understand itself by means of reflection.
>
> This axiom gives us the universal principle of etymology in all languages: words are carried over from bodies and the properties of bodies to signify the institutions of the mind and spirit.
>
> (*NS*, 236–37)

Just as *Finnegans Wake* takes place inside the body of a sleeping giant, so too the whole of evolved human language and the reality it shapes arises from the bodies of man's unconscious human ancestors:

> It is noteworthy that in all languages the greater part of the expressions relating to inanimate things are formed by metaphor from the human body and its parts and from the human senses and passions. Thus, head for top or beginning; the eyes of needles and of potatoes; mouth for any opening; the lip of a cup or pitcher; the teeth

of a rake, a saw, a comb; the beard of wheat; the tongue of a shoe . . . ; a neck of land; an arm of the sea; the hands of a clock; heart for center. . . .   (*NS*, 405)

Apart from the decorous restraint that causes Vico to pass over parts of the body which twentieth-century man, compensating for centuries of repression, would later find central to consciousness, this passage too yields its rough psychoanalytical insights and establishes a primary philological principle informing every page of *Finnegans Wake*. Buried everywhere beneath the *Wake*'s letters lies the form of a sleeping body, HCE. Since all abstract language derives from an "ur sprogue" (507.22 [Da. *ursprog*, "original language"]) in which this body is merged with everything exterior to it, all human language, in both *The New Science* and the *Wake*, etymologically conceals the unconscious "presence (of a curpse)" out of which all gentile reality evolved.

At some seminal historical remove, for instance, the "pencil" that our hero wields by day slipped into its name when an unknown user of the Latin language identified a similar instrument with a part of the male body, and, once one thinks about it, revealed an unconscious, but nonetheless poetic wisdom; a comparably unconscious confusion of the body with the evolved word and tool occurs many times in *Finnegans Wake*—e.g., 173.10, 261.10, 553.11, 563.5–6—though most notably at moments in which our hero, thinking not out of his "tropped head" but out of his body, etches his desires in dreams by allowing "that overgrown leadpencil" shown in the relief map of Dublin (56.12 [The Wellington Memorial, or "overgrown milestone"]) to write of its wishes and wants (see 280.9–16). By day, the hero of *Finnegans Wake* likely lives at an abstract remove both from his body and the carnal ground out of which the gentile world emerges; but at night, the repressed "presence (of a curpse)" in his mind asserts itself in the uncovering of the carnal etymon. By practicing an extended *"abnihilisation of the etym"* throughout the *Wake* (353.22 [L. *ab nihilo*, "from nothing"]), Joyce shows the body lying everywhere under the surface of language (< L. *lingua*, "tongue"]).

Vico's "universal principle of etymology in all languages" both justifies and structures the whole of Joyce's "vivle" (110.17 [L. *vivus*, "living"; "Bible"]): since all words are inherently puns in which evolved denotations overlay long-lost and sometimes irretrievable meanings expressive of the unconscious thinking of the human body, Joyce's "root language" is real language. By weaving through *Finnegans Wake* the carnal etymons internal to English, Joyce could reconstruct an unconscious pattern that everywhere subliminally informs the Daily World. If the thinking of the body underlies all gentile reality and thought, and alone wells up into HCE when his rational consciousness dissolves in sleep, then the language of *Finnegans Wake* had to work with this language beneath language, with carnal etymons, to reconstruct in "flesch nuemaid motts," one kind of thinking that underlies all thinking (138.8 [Fr. *mots*, "words"; Fr. *nue*, naked; Ger. *Fleisch*, "flesh"]).[23]

"IRO-EUROPEAN ASCENDANCES"

Vico's gentile man begins to evolve a social consciousness once the sound of patriarchal thunder and "awethorrorty" abstracts him from the interior of the giant body; this fall into exteriority in turn forces him to begin making increasingly elaborate distinctions between his own and physical nature, between himself and others. Since removal from the giant body initiates the dialectically progressive history of civil relations, social history in *The New Science* begins when giants related by blood and sharing the same little cave manifest differences among one another and establish a social hierarchy by contest of sheer force. It is a contest whose outcome makes the patriarchal family a determinant structure underlying all subsequent societies, the imprint of its forms still to be found "in the modifications of our own mind."

A second etymological principle of *The New Science* therefore holds that the internal social history of a people is implicitly preserved in and transmitted through its language, and that all words carry a subliminal record of an entire past (*NS*, 238–40, 354): etymology, in short, is also a form of history, or verbal archaeology, whose study reveals the growth of "gentile" institutions. In an essay in *Our Exagmination* familiar to readers of Joyce, Beckett has already called attention to that passage in *The New Science* in which Vico, illustrating this etymological principle, looks into the network of relations preserved beneath the modern words for "reading" (It. *leggere*), "law" (It. *legge*, L. *lex*), and "legislation" (It. *legislazione*) (*NS*, 239–40).[24] Noting that these terms are internally linked both by "sound sense" and by an underlying semantic unity bearing on the idea of "collecting" and ordering, Vico discovers beneath them all a lengthy and tangled social history whose evolved achievements are illustrated in the words listed at the top of figure 7.2. The words and concepts of "legibility" and "legality," according to this etymology, preserve a history of the internal evolutionary process by which Latin man gathered himself from forests, where he first subsisted

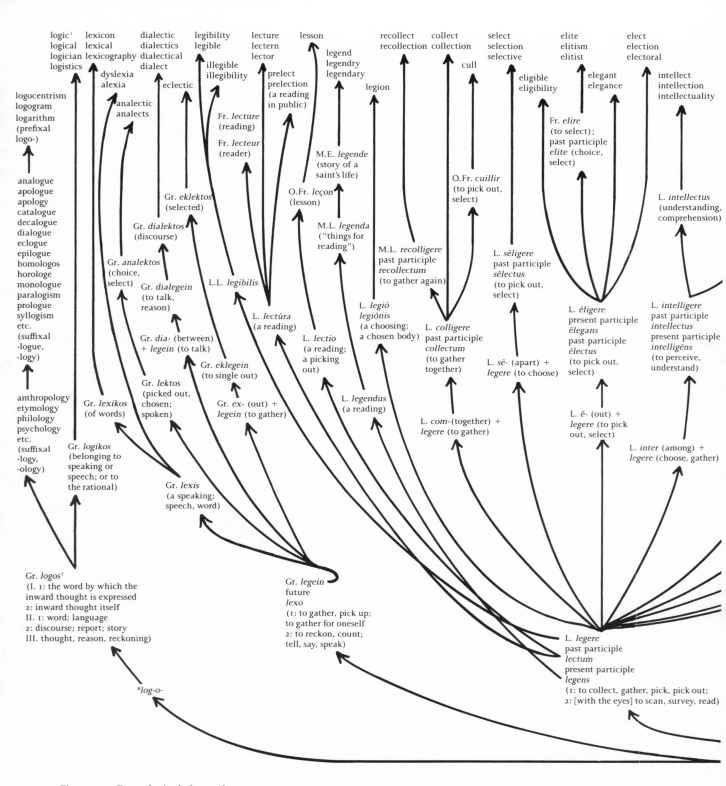

Figure 7.2. Etymological chart: *leg-

1. "A gee is just a jay on the jaunts cowsway" (284.F5 [A "g" is just a "j" on the giant's causeway]).

2. Cf. Heidegger, *Being and Time*, Int.II.7.B (32–34).

3. *NS*, 239–40.

4. Benveniste, *Indo-European Language and Society*, pp. 518–22.

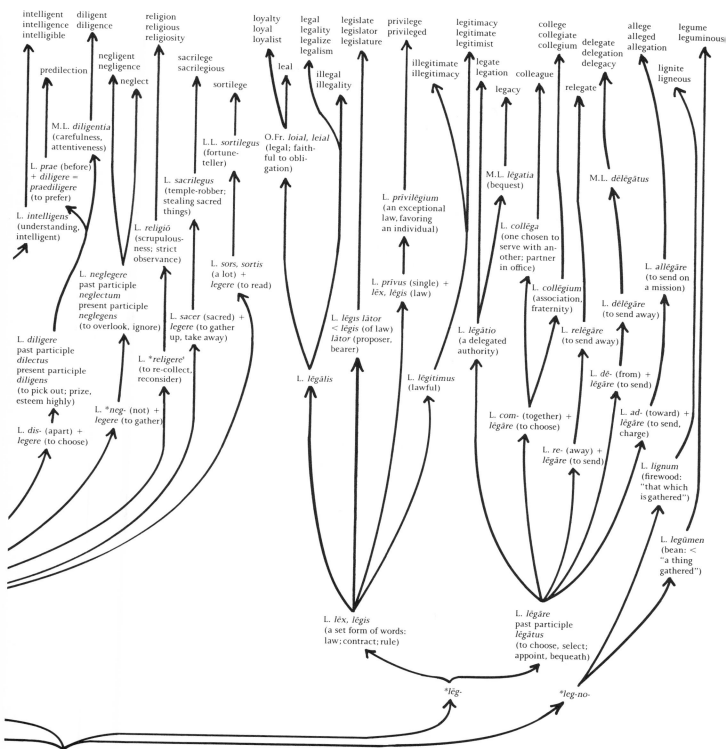

intelligent
intelligence
intelligible

diligent
diligence

predilection

negligent
negligence

neglect

religion
religious
religiosity

sacrilege
sacrilegious

sortilege

loyalty
loyal
loyalist

leal

legal
legality
legalize
legalism

legislate
legislator
legislature

privilege
privileged

legitimacy
legitimate
legitimist

college
collegiate
collegium

delegate
delegation
delegacy

allege
alleged
allegation

legume
leguminous

M.L. *diligentia*
(carefulness,
attentiveness)

illegitimate
illegitimacy

legate
legation

legacy

colleague

relegate

lignite
ligneous

L. *prae* (before)
+ *diligere* =
praediligere
(to prefer)

L. *intelligens*
(understanding,
intelligent)

L.L. *sortilegus*
(fortune-
teller)

O.Fr. *loial, leial*
(legal; faith-
ful to obli-
gation)

L. *prīvilēgium*
(an exceptional
law, favoring
an individual)

M.L. *lēgatia*
(bequest)

M.L. *dēlēgātus*

L. *sacrilegus*
(temple-robber;
stealing sacred
things)

L. *collēga*
(one chosen to
serve with an-
other; partner
in office)

L. *allēgāre*
(to send on
a mission)

L. *religiō*
(scrupulous-
ness; strict
observance)

L. *sors, sortis*
(a lot) +
legere (to read)

L. *collēgium*
(association,
fraternity)

L. *dēlēgāre*
(to send away)

L. *neglegere*
past participle
neglectum
present participle
neglegens
(to overlook, ignore)

L. *sacer* (sacred) +
legere (to gather
up, take away)

L. *prīvus* (single) +
lēx, lēgis (law)

L. *lēgātio*
(a delegated
authority)

L. *relēgāre*
(to send away)

L. *diligere*
past participle
dilectus
present participle
diligens
(to pick out; prize,
esteem highly)

L. **religere*[1]
(to re-collect,
reconsider)

L. *lēgis lātor*
< *lēgis* (of law)
lātor (proposer,
bearer)

L. *dē-* (from) +
lēgāre (to send)

L. **neg-* (not) +
legere (to gather)

L. *lēgālis*

L. *lēgitimus*
(lawful)

L. *com-* (together) +
lēgāre (to choose)

L. *ad-* (toward) +
lēgāre (to send,
charge)

L. *dis-* (apart) +
legere (to choose)

L. *re-* (away) +
lēgāre (to send)

L. *lignum*
(firewood:
"that which
is gathered")

L. *legūmen*
(bean: <
"a thing
gathered")

L. *lēx, lēgis*
(a set form of words:
law; contract; rule)

L. *lēgāre*
past participle
lēgātus
(to choose, select;
appoint, bequeath)

*lēg-

*leg-no-

Indo-European **leg-*[3]
(to pick, gather;
pick out, select)

nomadically by gathering native plants (the Latin *legere* ["to gather"], from the Indo-European root **leg-* ["to gather, or collect"], generates the words *Ilex* ["oak, gatherer"] and *leguminis*, which once meant "anything that could be gathered" and only later came to refer to vegetables); the same process by which he later formed protocities whose members were capable of collecting, storing, and later cultivating food themselves, and by which he finally established larger social groupings, whose formation made necessary the first formal laws. Gatherings of people into public bodies like these, then, historically generated the necessary institutions of "legality" and "legislatures" (after the Latin *lex, legis*), as well as the etymologically related property of "legibility"; for the gathering complexity of civil law required its fixation in codes. That historical linguistics and anthropology have inevitably modified the "facts" and refined our sense of the evolution of these terms does not finally matter: *The New Science* explores the genetic processes immanent in these words and the covert network of relationships that they reveal.

Particularly because *The New Science* explores the evolution of "reason" as a human institution, a dramatic way of illustrating what is at stake for Vico in the practice of etymology would be to consider the process by which the gentile world undertook the "fibfib fabrication" (36.34) of the term "reason" itself. As figure 7.3 will suggest, the growth of this word out of the Indo-European radical **ar-* is implicated in an objectifying tendency that also solidifies the meaning of "reality," which is a concept and a word and a "fact" of the world only in the radical sense of "fact" (< L. *factum*, "a thing made," as if "manufactured"). The etymology also suggests that the ascent of man into a "rationality" that maintains this sense of the "real" also entails enmeshment in a network of correlated formal institutions—"reading," "art," and "orderliness" among them—whose internalized effect is coincidentally parallel to that exerted by legal "ordinances" and the "army." For "art," "reading," and "reasonability," by putting and keeping the world in "order" and maintaining a sense of the "ordinary," do much what "armies" do—as analysts of ideology have long known. The network of relationships implicit in the etymology of the "real" reinforces those implicit in the history of "legibility," then, to suggest how the evolution of Vico's gentile "reality" is implicated in the slow formation of institutions and laws whose learning contractually holds together the Daily World.

The New Science is predicated on etymological studies like these, which reconstruct the forgotten and underlying senses of words that determine modern consciousness and institutions—words like "society," "liberty," and "hostility," for example, and "nation" and "gentility." Formative among these is the word and concept of "family," which Vico finds stamped into the minds of all people in his gentile history. When Vico's giants first group together in caves, they have no need of a distinct word or concept like "family," since signs designating individual members of the group would ring out all necessary social distinctions (*NS*, 257, 552). In order to understand the genesis of "families," then, Vico traces the word back toward the Latin *famulus*, "servant," and reconstructs a moment in prehistory when men still in the wild and at the mercy of stronger anthropoids seek out the patriarchal groups already established in caves for protection: they are admitted as "slaves," *famuli*, and their ownership in time generates the word *familia*, which in Latin originally means "a household of servants," and not a group of people related by blood. In turn, Vico speculatively derives the word *famulus* from the Greek and Latin words for "fame" or "rumored glory" (*phēmē* and *fama*), since the gathering rumor of a gloriously protective group brings these uncivilized wanderers into the patriarchal fold (*NS*, 555). Their entrance into the germinating society sets up the need for words and concepts that distinguish the patriarch's sons—still regarded as his negotiable property—from his slaves, and also from those untamed giants who still wander alone outside of gentile nature. The widening of social distinctions and tensions therefore generates the words *liberi* ("sons" or "children"), *famuli*, and *hostes* ("strangers, enemies"). In time, as the patriarch amasses enough slaves to work for him, he liberates his sons from servitude to confer on them a vague freedom withheld from the *famuli*. The condition of his sons accordingly begins to generate the concept, new to social history, of "liberty"; they "were called *liberi*, free. But it was [originally] a distinction without a difference" (*NS*, 556).[25] With the passage of generations and the accumulation of more wealth, the concept of freedom in turn generates a concept and word for "nobility" (*liberalitas*), and the word *familia* comes to mean a blood-related group of people wealthy enough to be free because they have large holdings of property and *famuli* to work for them. By this point in gentile history, man has stumbled up out of the obscurity of the world's beginning, and the conditions under which isolated patriarchal families would generate tribal feudalisms and a slavery sanctioned by tradition have become solidly established as forces internally driving a history made by man, but now way beyond his immediate control (*NS*, 552–69, 583–84).

All of these Vichian verbal archaeologies are important to *Finnegans Wake*, which, after the example of Vico, discovers beneath all words a layer

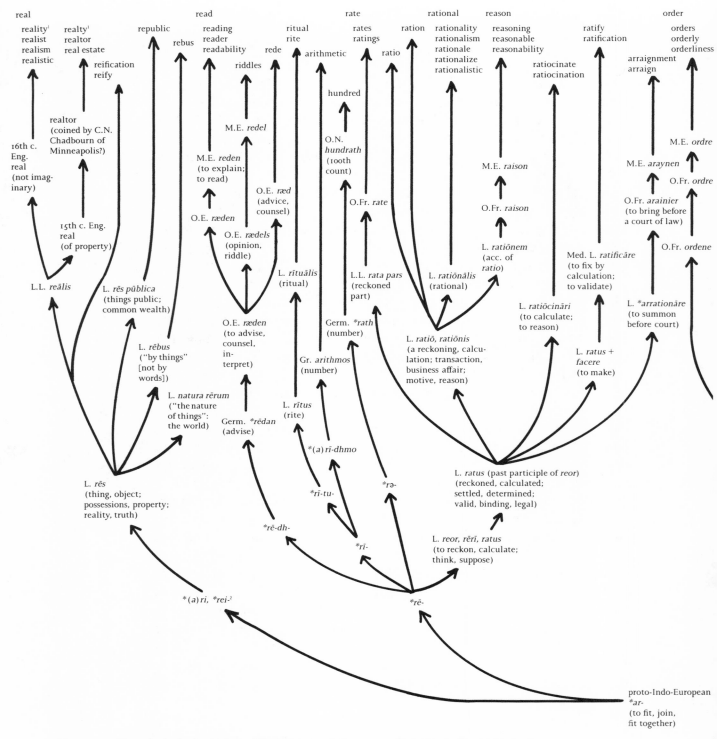

Figure 7.3. Etymological chart: *ar-. "those ars, rrrr! those ars all bellical, the highpriest's hieroglyph . . . wrasted redhandedly from our hallowed rubric prayer for truce with booty . . . and rudely from the fane's pinnacle tossed down . . . among Those Who arse without the Temple" (122.6–12 ["ars": L. *ars*, "art"; "ars all bellical": L. *ars bellica*, "the art of war"; "truce with booty": "truth and beauty"; "fane": L. *fanus*, "temple," opposite of *pro-fanus*, "outside the Temple"])

1. Cf. Raymond Williams, *Keywords: A Vocabulary of Culture and Society*, pp. 216–20.

2. Pokorny, *Indo-Germanisches Etymologisches Worterbuch*, p. 60.

ordinary
ordinariness
extraordinary

ordinance (law)
ordnance (arms)

art

primordial
primordium

artist
artistic
artistry
artificer

articulate
articulation

aristocrat
aristocracy
aristocratic

arms

harmony
harmonic
harmonize

army
armed

disarm
disarming

subordinate
subordination
coordinate
coordination

ordonnance
(aesthetics)

ornament
ornamental
ornamentation
ornate

exordium

artiste
arty
artifice

articles

aristology
(art of
dining)

Aristotle
Aristophanes
Aristocles
etc.

arm

armaments
armada
armistice
armipotent
armoire
armor
armorial
armory
etc.

alarm
alarming
alarm clock
alarmist

ordain
preordain
ordination
ordinal

Eng.
ordnance
(supplies)

adorn
adornment

artifact
artful

arthritis
(prefixal
arthro-)

O.Fr.
ordinarie

Med. L.
subordinare
(to set in a
lower order)

O.Fr., M.E.
ordenance
(an order,
command)

O.Fr. ordonnance
(arrangement
[of parts in
the whole])

L. primōrdium
(origin)

artificial

inert
inertia

O.Fr. article
(division,
part)

Gr. Aristotle
("by far
the best"?)
< aristos +
tele (far)

O.E.
earm
(arm)

O.Fr. desarmer

O.Fr. alarme

L. extra
ordinem
(outside the
order)

O.Fr. ordener
(to order)

L. primus
(first)
+
ordīrī
(begin)

L. iners,
inertia
(inactive,
lazy)

Gr. aristokratia
(rule by the
best-born)

Gr. harmonikos
(skilled in
music)

It. all'arme
(to arms!)

L. ordinārius
(according to
the custom-
ary order)

L. ōrnāre
(to arrange,
embellish)

L. adornāre
(to embellish)

L. exōrdīrī
(to begin
weaving;
to begin)

L. articulus
(small joint,
part, division)

Gr. aristokratia

Gr. ariston
(breakfast)

Gr. harmonia
(a fitting to-
gether; agree-
ment; harmony)

L. arma
(arms,
weapons)

L. armus
(upper arm;
"muscles")

L. ordino, ordinare
(to set in order)

Gr. arachnē
(spider)

L. ordīrī
(to begin a
web; to begin)

L. in- +
ars, artis
(unskilled)

L. artus
(the joints)

Gr. aristokratia

Gr. arthron
(joint)

Gr. arete
(virtue)

Gr. harmos
(a joining,
joint)

Germ. *armaz
(arm)

L. ōrdō, ordinis
(a line, row, order;
order, arrangement;
< a row of threads
in a loom)

L. ars, artis
(skill, style,
technique; art)

*(a)-rə-(k)-

*ar(ə)-ti-

*ar(ə)-tu

Gr. aristos
(the best)

*ar(ə)-dhro-

*ar(ə)-isto

*ar(ə)-smo

*ar(ə)-mo

*(a)rə-

*ar-t-
(joined
together)

*ōr-dh-

*ōr-

*arə-

*ar-m-of subliminal meanings stratified in sociohistorical time, the most current of which, making possible an aspect of modern social consciousness, conceals archaic self-interests and fears that arose "at the very dawn of protohistory," "when Chimpden first took the floor" (169.21, 46.2 [and the ascent of man began]). Again, this conception of history anticipates the psychoanalytical view of society as the collective creation of individuals whose actions are determined by parents, intrafamilial conflicts, and phobias inherited from the past. But the Vichian vision according to which *Finnegans Wake* makes the embattled human family a paradigmatic force in the genesis of social reality is historical, and it sees all of these struggles as institutional legacies (< I.E. *leg-) irrationally passed on from generation to generation; so that even today every father inevitably maintains a power invested in him by tradition, while every son born into a world shaped by this already-established authority has inevitably to overcome it, then to compete with peers that he might inherit the patrimony of an authority now historically transformed. When Joyce makes the family the center of all historical conflict in *Finnegans Wake*, then, he is isolating the primal social struggle in Vico that both historically and always engenders other struggle. Since Joyce sought in *Finnegans Wake* a language that would reconstruct the "infrarational" thought to which his hero—"a respectable prominently connected fellow of Iro-European ascendances with welldressed ideas" (37.25–26)—regresses in his nightlife, he draws on Vico's sociolinguistic vision by making central to the book not simply those carnal etymons that reveal the sleeping giant out of which gentile "reality" unfolds, but words and institutions that subliminally show how deeply riddled with unconscious conflict that giant form is.

HERE COMES EVERYBODY

According to a third etymological principle of *The New Science* informing the *Wake*, the etymology of a language can reveal not only the internal social formation of a people, but also the international forces that transformed that people through trade, war, migration, colonization, and "miscegenations on miscegenations" (18.20): "These . . . axioms give us the principle of a new etymologicon for words of certainly foreign origin, different from that mentioned above for native words. It can also give us the history of nations carried one after another into foreign lands by colonization" (*NS*, 299–300, 303–4).

A writer like Joyce, born into a nation that had been subjected to wave after wave of colonial and imperialistic invasion, could not fail to find these insights compelling. Once Vico's social history widens out of its claustral patriarchal groupings into a stage at which feudal tribes war, trade, or ally themselves with other feudal tribes, all history becomes an intertribal, and later an international collision of social forces; and whenever nations of two cultures collide, languages and consciousnesses collide and evolve also. In *The New Science*, then, Vico treats modern languages as if they were the language of *Finnegans Wake*—as blurred, polyglottal compacts of dozens of strange and foreign languages. In this kind of analysis, English would not be an exceptional case.

The earliest known inhabitants of England were eventually displaced by people who spoke a Celtic tongue descended from the proto-Indo-European hypothetically spoken somewhere, most likely, in Eastern Europe—a Celtic related to the Welsh, Scottish, Breton, and Irish still in existence today. But the Roman invasions overlaid this British Celtic with some Latin and a new civic consciousness, and marauding Angles and Saxons, pressured from behind by invading tribes from the East, moved in to override almost entirely the original British Celtic with an extensive Old Teutonic base. Invading Danes and Norsemen added a different complexion yet to the Anglish and Saxon already spreading outwards toward the frontiers of the island. Missionaries of the medieval Church made universal Latin the language of the literate and educated, and the Norman invasion brought, with its laws, the whole consciousness of the Mediterranean and Romance languages into England and then into Ireland—where the hybrid Anglo-Irish known by day to the hero of *Finnegans Wake* acquired a polyglottal texture already densely riddled with historical tensions.

Like *The New Science*, *Finnegans Wake* also tries to fathom "the obscure soul of the world" (*U*, 27), the force of a fumblingly made history in which generation after generation of billions of ephemeral individuals born in unconsciousness engendered, by their groping efforts, the conscious present in which one lives. A book about rapidly vanishing dreams and "darkness shining in brightness which brightness could not comprehend" (*U*, 27), *Finnegans Wake* explores, after the example of Vico, *all* the dark, unconsciousnesses that underlie its hero's thinking and enable it to be what it is; in every sentence it brings to mind those forgotten "furbears" who spoke alien tongues in the obscure prehistory of the gentile world, so to make possible all the small articles of the consciousness and reality within which Joyce's hero by day individually lives:

Vico's "Night of Darkness"

You mean to see we have been hadding a sound night's sleep? You may so. It is just, it is just about to, it is just about to rolywholyover. Svapnasvap. Of all the stranger things that ever not even in the hundrund and badst pageans of unthowsent and wonst nice or in eddas and oddes bokes of tomb, dyke and hollow to be have happened! The untireties of livesliving being the one substance of a streamsbecoming. Totalled in toldteld and teldtold in tittletell tattle. Why? . . . Why? Such me.

(597.1–22)

Having laboriously earned, by this late point in *Finnegans Wake*, the right to compare the length of life to the length of a volatile dream about to be scattered into nothing, Joyce evokes beneath the "basic English" of this passage the Mid-Eastern *Book of One Thousand and One Nights* ("unthowsent and wonst nice"), the Sanskrit *svapna* ("asleep") and *svap* ("sleep") in "Svapnasvap," and other such formative "odds and ends" ("eddas and oddes") of Western history as those "toldteld and teldtold" in the Icelandic Eddas written at Oddi ("in eddas and oddes"), in John 1:1 ("In the beginning was the word"), and in the Egyptian Book of the Dead and comparable "bokes of tomb, dyke and hollow"—all in order to represent the panhistorical human "substrance of a streamsbecoming" that has become embodied in a simple sleeping man, not even aware of himself, who is about to roll over, and waken from unconsciousness into English and the reality it upholds. Like anyone's, this man's mind and "the entirety of [his] livesliving" has been made possible both by billions of Toms, Dicks, and Harrys ("tomb, dyke and hollow") bled up out of gentile humanity over centuries in India, Egypt, Arabia, Norway, England, and Ireland, and by the steadily evolving language, "totalled in toldteld and teldtold in tittletell tattle" whose "Total" is English and the wakeful consciousness it makes possible. As he lies unconscious in the unwilled "trance" of sleep ("sub-strance"), all of the forces that have genetically shaped his consciousness come to represent him: he lies as unconscious of them as he is of himself, his "substance" "substrance[d]" by their "streamsbecoming." In visions of history as complex as those entertained by *The New Science* and *Finnegans Wake*, then, "English"—a comparatively modern development of world history—acquires meaning only as a convenient blanket term designating a language and sensibility historically compounded of scores of others.

In Vico's third etymological axiom, Joyce found richly reaffirmed the certain knowledge that language and consciousness are manifestations of each other, living and evolving forces made by men, but beyond any individual's control, which grow and expand and become more international as "our social something bowls along bumpily, experiencing a jolting series of pre-arranged disappointments, down the long lane of (it's as semper as oxhouse-humper!) generations, more generations and still more generations" (107.32–35): "semper," here, combines "simple" with the Latin *semper* ("always"), while "oxhousehumper" translates into English the first three letters of the Hebrew alphabet—*aleph* (meaning "ox"), *beth* ("house"), *ghimel* ("camel")—in order to convey, in the image of a problematically propelled bowling ball, the commutual evolution of language, consciousness, and social forms in Vico's gentile history.

Joyce found much in Vico that was congenial. That half of *The New Science* contained in "Poetic Wisdom" gave him a psychology of the unconscious, an account of dream formation, and a system of dream interpretation which, because they were synthetically integrated into a social history and a linguistic vision, appealed to Joyce more than the new sciences of psychoanalysis or linguistics. Unlike other philosophies of history and unlike any of the new sciences of sociology, anthropology, or political science, Vico's *New Science* did not regard language as an instrument subservient to a subject more central, but saw it instead as a condition that made possible both civil history and human consciousness. Long before Darwin developed the new science of animal evolution and Freud refined his account of infantile genesis, Vico saw human history as the creation of people born into the world in an unconsciousness that only after the struggles of millennia would evolve and codify into letters the arbitrary accomplishment of reason. Joyce undoubtedly admired above all in Vico, as he did in Aristotle and Aquinas, that synthetic catholicity and systematic wholeness of thought which was able to integrate in *The New Science* a philosophy, an evolutionary science, a developmental psychology, a sociology and anthropology, a dialectical history, and a verbal archaeology. Written in the century that saw the genesis of scientific rationalism, *The New Science* anticipates in total the whole array of human sciences which would precipitate out of the positivist tradition at the turn of the nineteenth century.

Since it does not make the individual, but mankind the center of a terrestrial cosmos, *The New Science* afforded Joyce the example of a work both traditional and radical, humanistic and anthropocentric, on which he might model *Finnegans Wake*. Vico's etymological reconstructions of the unconscious forces at the base of history moreover gave to Joyce the working principles by which *Finnegans Wake* would represent the unconscious conflicts underlying his hero's wakeful thought, and all his daytime social transactions. In Vico's etymological vision, Joyce found that every normal particle of language was inherently a quadruple pun of sorts. Beneath its current denotation, every word concealed two meanings revelatory of its existence in history, one reflecting the internal evolution of social forms and the other reflecting the wider international forces whose play modified those forms. And because every particle of language was a creation of gentile man, whose world and reality arose from the interior of flesh, all words finally concealed the aliterate thinking of the body, within which Joyce's subject lies unconscious in the regression of his sleep. The pun, according to Vico's etymology, was not simply an option of Joyce's style: its form was inherent in language and in the tensions giving rise to the consciousness that language makes possible.

Very much a book of origins—like Joyce's own Book of Waking—*The New Science* would also have provided Joyce with an account of human genesis more complex than that contained in the orthodox Biblical Genesis, quietistically received as truth over generations; than the rationalist account of genesis, according to which human reason arose through mechanistic laws of nature; than the psychoanalytical account of genesis, which scrutinized personal, but not social origins; and than socialist accounts of genesis, which examined broad social tensions, but not the individuals in whom they were embodied. Since sleep, from a Vichian perspective, can be construed as the process through which a person awakens from unconsciousness at the interior of a space-pervading body, *Finnegans Wake* assimilates whole the genetic vision of *The New Science* in order to represent the drift of its "dead giant manalive" (500.1–2) out of nothingness toward wakening and "the opening of the mind to light" (258.31–32). Telling in its own way a "meandertale, aloss and again, of our old Heidenburgh in the days when Head-in-Clouds walked the earth" (18.22–24)—the references to "Neanderthal" and "Heidelberg man" returning us to "primeval conditions" (599.9–10)—it reconstructs "the ignorance [or unconsciousness] that implies impression that knits [our] knowledge that finds the nameform that whets the wits that convey contacts that sweeten sensation that drives desire that adheres to attachment that dogs death that bitches birth that entails the ensuance of existentiality" (18.24–29 [the "ignorance" out of which, every morning, the whole of gentile existence comes to be]).

Elsewhere the *Wake* pays tribute to Vico by casting him in the image of the maker of first things, the knower of the world's dream, and the tutelary divinity of HCE's nightlife:

For the producer (Mr John Baptister Vickar) caused a deep abuliousness to descend upon the Father of Truants and, at a side issue, pluterpromptly brought on the scene the cutletsized consort. . . .

(255.27–30)

Set in the unconsciousness of Joyce's sleeping Dubliner ("abulia," < Gr. *aboule*, "without will," is a psychological term for the loss of volition), this is a modern reconstruction of Adam's dream, the dream in which the first man imagined his ideal consort, Eve—whom "the producer" removes here, "cutletsized," from Adam's rib. As the story from the Book of Genesis about the birth of human imagination that haunted Milton and his Romantic successors, the moment of Adam's dream begins the generation of secular history in the Bible. As it is evoked in the *Wake*, Vico becomes its generator and its interpreter, its "baptist" and its "vicar," because Vico, for Joyce, was the first man in modern history to fathom the first man and the first man's first dream.

Joyce finally found in *The New Science* an intricate sense of human evolution that refused to reduce history to a process in which discrete individuals in discrete generations act separately at moments discretely isolated in time. In Vico, the whole of gentile history determines the consciousness, language, society, and material circumstances in which anyone finds himself in the present; so that no one, consequently, would have the life and mind that he does were it not for an infinitude of people in the past: Vico's first men, whose bodies determined the structure of all subsequent reality and whose first hardly imaginable outcries made all subsequent language possible; the nomadic men of patriarchal Israel who made possible the coming of Christ and the millennia during which the image of the Crucifixion and the Resurrection shaped the perceptions of the whole Western world; the Greek thinkers who made possible the ongoing enterprises of philosophy, natural science, and mathematics; and billions of men more. A book that treats with studious intensity "all matters that fall under the ban of our infrarational senses," *Finnegans Wake* absorbs Vico's vision of history to make its reader conscious on every page of the universe of people who have generated the possibility of his individual existence (see, e.g., 582.13–21, 599.4–18).

Absent from his own consciousness, Joyce's sleeping hero in turn becomes an embodiment of all the historical forces that have produced both him and the conflicted desires which structure his dreams. In his identity-void drift through sleep, he becomes indirectly represented in the images of so many

Vico's "Night of Darkness"

other people—his sons, his racial and historical forebears, individuals prominent in the historical age in which he lives—that his mind eventually becomes a space made possible and cohabited by a world of people, each insubstantial as himself, who constitute a kind of psychic community in which each historically depends on each other but all ultimately enter into the formation of the dreamer's single dream:

> . . . an you could peep inside the cerebralised saucepan of this eer illwinded goodfor-nobody, you would see in his house of thoughtsam (was you, that is, decontami-nated enough to look discarnate) what a jetsam litterage of convolvuli of times lost or strayed, of lands derelict and of tongues laggin too . . . bashed and beaushelled . . . pharahead into faturity. . . .   (292.12–19)

Another pun basic to *Finnegans Wake*, then, condenses the individual and the collective, the self-enclosed dreamer unwillingly paralyzed in his body in present time and, as in Vico, the multitude of men in the collective history which parented him, which includes him, and within whose evolved tensions, in sleep as in wakefulness, he finds himself and his desire netted. This kind of pun operates most simply in *Finnegans Wake* merely in the proliferation of names that reveal the unconscious presence of its sleeping protagonist. "Here Comes Everybody" (32.18) and "Haveth Childers Everywhere" (535.34–35), names that evoke HCE in social and paternal forms, are not simply ciphers for the "one stable somebody" who sleeps at the *Wake*, but paradigms of the mankind whose struggles and labors have made possible that private, self-enclosed somebody. So, too, this catalogue of heroes and warriors who helped to shape the history that made possible the coming of the man asleep at *Finnegans Wake*, a man whose life has risen out of the past in which they perished: "Helmingham Erchenwyne Rutter Egbert Crumwall Odin Maximus Esme Saxon Esa Vercingetorix Ethelwulf Rupprecht Ydwalla Bentley Osmund Dysart Yggdrasselmann? Holy Saint Eiffel, the very phoenix!" (88.21–24 [read acrostically, the first letters of these names make a statement]).

By structuring the mind of his sleeping hero in the indirect images of all these others, Joyce demonstrates how fundamentally, if unconsciously, individuals are deeply entangled members of one another. He was not simply suggesting that his hero's thinking is composed of the people who have touched him most directly—of his parents, whose circumstances determined the nation and race, the language, sexuality, social class, fears, religion, and conscience that shaped him as a child; of his teachers, who informed him with the evolved learning and ideology of all gentile history; and of his neighbors, whose patronage and scorn helped to determine the character of his social existence. He was suggesting also that even the remotest human contact in his modern man's life, simply by virtue of its contact, inevitably finds a reflexive place in his humanity, to become a part of his consciousness and his personal identity. Just as human nature, in Vico's gentile history, is made wholly by people, so HCE's whole nature is unconsciously defined and structured by others both within and far beyond his immediate circle of acquaintance. It was from Vico that Joyce learned, even while writing those two egotistical biographical novels, *Stephen Hero* and *A Portrait*, that no infant born into the world of gentile nature can even remotely attain a "personality" without the prior existence of scores of people in the world immediately around it, and of billions of others buried in the night of a historical past ordinarily lost to consciousness: all of human thinking, incrementally modified by the desiring individual who lives at its experienced center, comes from someone else. In reconstructing the "indentity" of a man whose conscious identity has dissolved in sleep, *Finnegans Wake* structurally treats its central figure as the raddled blur of millions of persons, most of whom are completely absent from the consciousness that they unconsciously helped to shape. "As a singleminded supercrowd" (42.22), our hero is "more mob than man" (261.21–22).

These persons, therefore, need not even be close to the dreamer in space or time. In *Ulysses*, Stephen Dedalus claims that his consciousness has been fathered not at all by Simon Dedalus, but by Aristotle, Aquinas, Shakespeare, Swift, and the Fathers of the Church; this consciousness is fathered further, and more humanely, by his evanescent crossing with Leopold Bloom, a stranger who teaches him simple solicitude and interest for a few hours. *Finnegans Wake*, working from Vico's science of history, merely extends Stephen's insights into the genesis of identity to their logical and just ends when, in its own strange form, it treats HCE's personality as an organically unified tissue of other persons, most of whom, buried in a past of which he is unconscious, play absolutely no part in his wakened life at all. According to the standards by which we ordinarily assess that genre of writing known oxymoronically as "realistic fiction," even the most unreflecting hack would think four times before setting the hero of a novel into a plot that depended, for instance, on an ancient cult of Greek mystics, influentially descended from a seditious Semitic carpenter, who managed to transform the identity of a Roman emperor of the Western world and subsequently the identities of the descendants of the barbaric hordes his heirs would conquer. Not Joyce. If realistic fiction by convention scorned the fantastic, the "imitation of the dream-state" that he achieved in *Finnegans Wake* found historical reality more fantastic than both the fantasies realistic novelists scorned and the contrived reality they sought to represent. HCE's personality, then, is defined not only by family and contemporaries, but by people as remote in history as Christ and Constantine and Attila. These people are members of his personality: they arise in his "nightlife" not simply in composite structures that obliquely capture his identity, but as parts of him, by virtue of having made parts of his consciousness possible. Thousands of people from the past and from all nations crowd into HCE's dream to constitute the mind beneath his mind. In the individually dreaming body they establish a thickly entwined human community whose evolution in history has vitally formed the ground of his wakeful life. His ego or "I . . . be the massproduct of teamwork" (546.14–15).

Like *The New Science*, *Finnegans Wake* generates a vision of human consciousness in which individual personality can be spoken of only as the summed collection of all persons who have collided with it, made its existence in history possible, and even vaguely helped to shape it; paradoxically set entirely within an individual body, the book devastates as completely as the condition of sleep the whole notion of discrete individuality. It finally conceives of individuality not as a solipsistic cage, but as a society of sorts, in which family, contemporaries, historical and racial forebears, and the shadows of long-forgotten people interact to evolve a conscious organism, as in Vico, that has dreams and nightmares in a present time which always moves forward under the evolutionary forces of achieved or frustrated desire and wish.

Although the deformations of English integral to the work have caused some readers to regard it as the product of a furious egocentrism, nothing could be further from the truth. No defense of Joyce's aesthetic methods will make a first reading of *Finnegans Wake* less tortuous and frustrating than it may perhaps be: it is humiliating for some to be reminded that one does not know everything in the world, or even in the fractional part of the world that Joyce managed to assimilate. But even a tortuous first reading of the *Wake* should suggest that few books are less egocentric: dead to the world, its "belowes hero" has no consciousness of himself as an "ego" or an "identity" at all. As social in its vision of individual personality as *The New Science*, *Finnegans Wake* does not elevate HCE even to the individual level of an insignificant Leopold Bloom, but represents his mind in the displaced guises of all those others who have made that mind what it is. Almost promiscuous and indiscriminating in its fascination with humanity, it does not seek to tell the egotistically private success story of an individual burdened with great expectations. Less egocentric than somatocentric, it depicts a hero void of identity and weirdly named "Here Comes Everybody," who lies "refleshed" in the universally experienced condition of sleep, thinking in the form of poetic wisdom that flows out of the body and underlies the texts of dreams, whose mind is an introjected image of the universe and of the universe of people who made him. The "ideal universal history" that Vico discovered beneath the consciousness of everyone born in the enlightened present, Joyce made a living, dynamic world in *Finnegans Wake*. Its prose is the prose of the world.

CHAPTER EIGHT

"Meoptics"

SOME "VIDUAL" AIDS

Although the complaint that "Joyce's vision has atrophied" in *Finnegans Wake* most often comes from readers hostile to the book, even its admirers have noted in perplexity that "the strangest feature of this dream is that it lacks visual imagery . . . it is no easier to visualize a Mookse or a Gripes than to gather a clear-cut impression of slithy tove or a mome rath."[1] Difficulties like these now merit our attention because the evident visual opacity of the *Wake* is only a special case of what has been more broadly perceived as its general referential opacity: since so much of the *Wake* is hard to visualize, it is difficult to see it referring to anything at all. Here as always, however, the continued practice of "ideal insomnia" and steady reference to the night will illuminate a great deal, and largely by reminding us that most of the night does not involve vision or visual dreaming of any sort at all.

One can hardly notice the transformation as it overtakes one nightly in bed, but as one lies there colorfully envisioning other people and places while drifting out of wakefulness into sleep, one suddenly becomes functionally blind.[2] The greater part of sleep engages you in "blind poring," "with . . . dislocated reason," "in your own absence" (189.30–31), so that anyone asking himself what he saw while asleep last night will likely assent to what he might read virtually anywhere in *Finnegans Wake*:

—You saw it visibly from your hidingplace?
—No. From my invisibly lyingplace.

(504.8–9)

The *Wake*, in turn, not simply resists visualization, but actively encourages its reader *not* to visualize much in its pages, where "it darkles . . . all this our funnaminal world" (244.13). Because HCE passes through the night "with his eyes shut" (130.19), he regards the world from the interior of "blackeye lenses" (183.17) sunk in "eyes darkled" (434.31) and kept firmly "SHUT" behind "a blind of black" (182.32–33); through the "eyewitless fog-gus" of this "benighted irismaimed" (489.31 [his eyes "benighted," each "iris maimed"]), we regard a universe of profound "unsightliness" (131.19). "It's a pity he can't see" (464.5), because it makes all the many "unseen" "thinks" that happen in *Finnegans Wake* difficult for the reader who craves spectacle to apprehend (158.36, 194.18, 403.22).

Consciousness is so firmly affixed to the human eye that one would find it difficult to write an extended sentence in English without agitating some aspect of vision (as in this sentence, for instance, the terms "affix," "length," and "extended" evoke spatial relations; "write," if not "sentence," evokes graphics; and "aspect" furls out of the Latin *specere* ["to look at"], in kinship with terms like spectrum, spectacle, introspect, and perspective). All such concrete nouns as "eye," certainly, "appeal [appear] to [the] gropesarching eyes" (167.12–13); but so too, implicitly, do many abstractions: "insight," for instance, "ideas," (< Gr. *eidô*, "to see"), and "theory" (< Gr. *theôreô*, "to look at, view"). In the *Wake*, by contrast—where everything is "forswundled" (598.3 [Ger. *verschwindet*, "vanished," or *vorschwindelt*, "made-believe"])—the language struggles hard to "appeal [appear]" neither to the eye nor to those parts of consciousness rooted in the eye because it probes a state of existence in which everything is unconscious, and therefore not immediately "wiseable" (16.24 [or "visible"]).

Antithetical in every way to the world accessibly open to "the light of the bright reason which daysends to us from the high" (610.28–29 ["descends," "day sends"]), the Evening World is situated at the heart of an immense mental and cosmological "Blackout" (560.2, 617.14; cf. 221.22, 403.17 ["Black! Switch out!"])—and not least because sleep and night undo the creative fiat (L. "*Fiat lux*," "Let there be light!") by pitching the visible into a form of doubly complected darkness. As gravity pulls the planet through the penumbra and umbra of its own shadow and "the owl globe wheels into view" (6.29–30), visible earth spills off the face of the earth, and "the darkness which is the afterthought of [the Lord's] nomatter" alone becomes manifest (258.32–33). Within the darkness of this "earth in umber" (588.20 [L. *umbra*, "shadow"]), millions of "humble indivisibles in this grand continuum" fall down dead to the world in synchrony with the *Wake*'s "benighted iris-

"*Meoptics*"

maimed" (472.30), where, blinded by sleep and given "glass eyes for an eye" (183.36), they see only "invasable blackth" (594.33 [as opposed to "visible black"]). A recurrent term in *Finnegans Wake*—"Fiatfuit!" (17.32)—simply means in Latin that "'Let there be!' was," or as Joyce puts it elsewhere in English, "leaden be light" (313.35); "as it was, let it be" (80.23). The phrase punctuates the book in various forms to remind its reader that because there is no sunlight at night and no vision in sleep, any reconstruction of the night must also inherently study the "shadyside" of the creation (585.29)— its nightly decreation—through whose dark force the fiat and the covenant are breached as, on the underside of the earth and closed eyelids, the world is hurled back to the "primeval conditions" that obtained before its genesis (599.9–10).[3] "Like a great black shadow" (626.24–25), HCE therefore passes the night in the intangible deeps of an "earth in umber hue" (588.20), "in the shade" of a "shadowed landshape" (134.31–32, 242.18, 251.16, 279.F15–16, 474.2–3), where he tends to envision only shadows of "invasable blackth" "and shadows shadows multiplicating" (281.17–18).

It will help a reader both to orient himself in Joyce's "book of the dark" and to maintain an essential "blank memory" of his "own nighttime" if he realizes that an extended representational mannerism put to play in the work seeks in every context "the best and schortest way of blacking out a caughtalock of all the sorrors of Sexton" (230.10–11); since the "sorrows of Satan," like the "horrors" to which a "sexton" will introduce one at one's wake, largely concern the "tropped head," we find the line "blocking out a catalogue" of ciphers that evoke the night's "seemetery." But since "the caughtalock" in question is simply a man "arrested"—"caught" and "locked" in sleep—it also tells us that he tends to find "the best way of blacking out" anything that threatens to disrupt his rest with visionary turmoil. To portray the dark "optical life" (179.1–2) of this "benighted irismaimed," Joyce in turn necessarily and ceaselessly finds "the best and shortest way of blacking out" anything that might be visualized—by drawing on a number of murky terms that we have already considered ("black," "blank," "blind," "blot," "blotch," "dark," "night," and "murk") but also ubiquitous others. These "blackartful" terms lie everywhere in *Finnegans Wake* (121.27), densely woven over every page, scotomizing the work in ways so playfully pervasive that they can hardly be catalogued and at best merely illustrated. Actively warning a reader never to visualize anything but "invasable blackth" unless there are clear indications to the contrary, they collectively yield a good rule of thumb to follow in reading this "specturesque" "book of the dark" (427.33): "keep black, keep black!" (34.34 [not "back"]).

"It is a mere mienerism of this vague of visibilities," "for inkstands" (608.1 [Fr. *vague*, "empty"], 173.34), that terms like "shade," "tar," "coal," "pitch," "soot," and "ink" should everywhere occlude words that are otherwise "basically English" (116.26). With intricate particularity, these "blackartful" terms (121.27) enable the *Wake* to adopt its own peculiar "dressy black modern style" (55.14–15), a "blackhand" "sootable" to the portraiture of "*a blackseer*" who is given to envisioning only vast "blackshape[s]" and lots of "pitchers" (495.2; *L*, III, 147; 340.13; 608.29; 233.1, 438.13, 531.15, 587.14, 598.21). Since each such "pitcher" would be a "picture" more "pitchblack" (385.6) than "pitch" ("pitch," "pitcher," "pitchest"), as "unseen" by someone trained with "the Black Watch" (438.15 [not necessarily a British Highland regiment]), it doubtlessly "reminds you of the outwashed engravure that we used to be blurring on the blotchwall" (13.6–7). Anything so clear as "West 23rd Street" necessarily becomes, when captured from this "focoal" perspective (411.32) and in one of these "pitchers," only "Wastewindy tarred strate" (549.15)—a lot of ethereal "tar" and "waste," as blown through the hollows of the "bloweyed" "stratum" (hence "strate") shown lying there in the "relief maps" (534.18). The *Wake* might be construed, then, as representing an "EBONISER. IN PIX" (304.R1); only apparently an "Ebenezer" representable "in pictures," the "blackseer" underlying this phrase is an absolute "eboniser," "blacked out" and lost in deep "*pix*" (L. "tar"). A "tarrable" "fullsoot" (520.2, 411.22 ["terrible falsehood"]), the "sootynemm" shows "Eboniser" "in duskguise" as "a Tar" (420.5, 532.27, 385.33 [not necessarily a sailor]), and it makes him "a quhare soort of a mahan" indeed (16.1): the "soot" in that "soort" blacks out a word already ebonised by the Danish *sort* ("black"), so to locate the *Wake*'s hibernating "mahan" (Anglo-Ir., "bear") in the "ideal residence for realtar" (560.13 [not "realtor," but "real tar"]). "Watching tar" (505.2) might well be an ideal preparatory exercise for any reading of *Finnegans Wake*.

Every "blind drawn" (559.5), every " black patch " (559.25, 93.4), and all "Phenecian blends" and "Persia[n] blind[s]" in the *Wake* (221.32, 583.14–15) comparably help the open-eyed reader appreciatively to share the "eyewitless foggus" and "Black Watch" of a sightless "irismaimed" who lies "unspeechably thoughtless over it all here in Gizzygazelle Tark's bimboowood" (238.36–239.1 [note the "tar"]): while that "bamboowood" ordinarily makes "blinds," here it makes also "blind," and, together with the references to "Gazelle Park" and "the Bamboo Wood," where Buddha lived, it suggests that HCE is not only "nearvanashed," but "belined to the world" (156.20)— indeed, "blem, blem, stun blem" (98.3–4["blind," "stone blind," "stunned," and, by way of the Gael. sl. *blem*, "crazy"]). "And what wonder with the murkery viceheid in the shade?" (251.15–16): "murky eyesight" is an only "certainty" (Da. *vished*) or "knowledge" (Ger. *Weisheit*) that emerges in sleep's "murky light" (180.17 [Da. *mørk*, "dark"]). Since our hero passes through sleep "siriusly and selenely sure behind the shutter," at any rate (513.1)—where "Sirius" and the moon (or "Selene") orient us in the night and that "shutter" shuts out light—a reader of the *Wake* would well do more than "keep black!": "pull the blind" (132.14) and "draw the shades, curfe you" (145.33–34 [since "curfew," "curse you," comes at night]).

"Blueblacksliding constellations" like these "continue to shape" the universe of *Finnegans Wake* from beginning to end (405.9–10), and more often than not, since it is hard to see at night, in ways "sootably" hard to see. "Umbrellas" and "parasols," for instance, pop up all over the book because both of these instruments do in miniature what the night does absolutely, blotting out the sun and throwing pockets of "jettyblack" shade into the world (583.22 ["parasol" derives from the It. *parare sole*, "to ward off the sun," while "umbrella" comes from the L. *umbra*, "shade"]). The "great black shadow" sleeping at the *Wake* therefore lies embroiled in a dark "family umbroglia" (284.4)—an "imbroglio," to be sure, since familial conflicts underlie his dreams, but an "umbrella" also, since the essential forces in these conflicts are "infrarational" and have nothing to do with vision at all. Since dreams threaten to awaken visual consciousness from "the sense arrest" that pervades most of sleep (505.31), every "exposed sight" in *Finnegans Wake* "pines for an umbrella of its own" (159.35–36); and for this reason, we periodically find "Eboniser" maintaining his placid "Black Watch" on the world by "*hoisting . . . an emergency umberolum in byway of paraguastical solation to the rhyttel in his hedd*" (338.7–8). The line tells us that rather than working out a "paraphrastical solution to the riddle in his head" by facing the conflicts that might disrupt his sleep with the fatiguing demands of a visual dream, the "*blackseer*" in himself "*blanks his oggles*" (340.13, 349.27 ["his eyes"]), opens a big mental "umbrella" (Sp. *paraguas*), and slips from imminent strife back into sleepy peace (hence the contradictory play of the We. *rhyfel* ["war"] and *hedd* ["peace"] in "the rhyttel in his hedd"). "In any case" (Fr. *en tout cas*), since we have an "entoutcas for a man" as a hero (129.6 [Fr. *en-tout-cas*, "umbrella"]), the *Wake* might now be read as the Ballad of "Parasol Irelly" (525.16), its shadowy protagonist, the proud owner of an "umbrilla-parasoul" (569.20), moving us somewhat "beyond" (Gr. *para-*) ordinary Western accounts of the "soul" (hence "parasoul").

The *Wake* in turn becomes an extended "umbrella history" addressed to "lay readers" (573.36, 35 [as opposed to "standing" ones]), and it proceeds *parasol*iloquisingly" (63.20 [as a "soliloquy" made in the shade well ought]), "going forth by black" (62.27) while moving "Parasol Irelly" through a stream of shady encounters localized, for instance, "on Umbrella Street" (98.24) or "under the idlish tarriers' umbrella of a showerproof wall" (182.15–16): "idlish tarriers," in contrast to athletically jogging "Irish harriers," would simply lie there, "tarrying idly" in one dark spot, while that "showerproof wall" would resist not only rainfall but anything at all threatening to "show" itself ("shower" can rhyme with "lower" here). As an "umbrella history," in turn, the *Wake* becomes peopled by the many "darkener[s]" (418.5), "shadowers" (60.21), "dark deed doer[s]" (246.30), and other such "invisible friends" (546.29) who move through our hero's "tropped head" during sleep and, by day, engage him in all manner of unconscious struggle. Anyone may well recall such "invisible friends" by cultivating a "blank memory" of last night: blind though you may have been, "you saw their shadows . . . struggling diabolically over this, that and the other . . . near the Ruins" (518.3–6 [where these "Ruins," from the L. *ruere*, "to fall," return us to a meditation on the body shown rubbled in the relief maps]).[4]

In the *Wake*, these "invisible friends" include many "Doyles" and "Sullivans." So many "Doyles" and "Sullivans" populate *Finnegans Wake* that the book calls the "component partners" of the morphic "state" it represents "doyles when they deliberate but sullivans when they are swordsed" (142.8, 26–27 [Fr. *sourd*, "deaf"]), though collectively they resolve into "The Morphios" (142.29 [Gr. *Morpheus*]). While the name Doyle, deriving from the Gaelic *Ó Dubhghaill*, literally means "black-foreigner" and historically refers to the Danes; and while Sullivan, comparably, derives from the Gaelic *Ó Súileabháin* and literally means "black-eyed," Joyce said he "put the language to sleep" in *Finnegans Wake* and consequently "could not . . . use words in their ordinary connections" (*JJ*, 546). Many of the "Doyles" and "Sullivans" who appear in the *Wake*, accordingly, linger there in extraordinary ways. Sleep forces the *Wake*'s "benighted irismaimed" into all sorts of "blank assignations" with the "doyle"—the "dark alien"—in himself (575.15);[5] and the book's many "Sullivans" often have eyes less visibly black than eyes with "blackeye lenses" "blacked out" to the core. For all the "bleakeyed" figures and forms moving throughout *Finnegans Wake* (327.29), the only violence perpetrated on them is the night's—as anyone falling asleep anywhere will note: "Conan Boyles will pudge the daylives out through him" (617.14–15), and so badly that all things will "change their characticuls during their blackout" (617.13–14). What the *Wake* studies in its accounts of tortuous struggles between "Doyles" and "Sullivans" and "Tars" of this "soort" are conflicts that Joyce commemorates as "Contrastations with Inkermann" (71.8–9). These stand in "contrast" to Goethe's *Conversations with Eckermann*, a tome of almost unbearable light, in being relaxingly dark; for if an "inkman" is black, an "inkerman" must be blacker; and if Goethe helped lift the Enlightenment to its apex ("More light!"), the *Wake* helps inject it with a little more dark ("Keep black!").

At the end of many a "blindfold passage" (462.35) and movement "down blind lanes" (116.34), the *Wake* ends up pointing its "irismaimed" into "an allblind alley leading to an Irish plot in the Champ de Mors, not?" (119.31–32 [Fr. *champ des morts*, "cemetery"]). Because the man "tropped head" at the *Wake* lies "blurried" in the night's "seemetery" (13.11 ["blurred," "buried"]), the reader might also enter his "eyewitless foggus" by recalling or imagining what it would be like to "have of coerce nothing in view to look forward at" but the underside of a "mudfacepacket" (410.2–3, 492.20)— and preferably one six feet deep. Our hero envisions precisely this item while in mind of a "family drugger" (492.21) set up on "Ombrilla Street" (492.23), though he himself lies "confined," because sleep "arrests" his body, "in [a] back haul of Coalcutter" (492.15) blacker for the "coal" than "the black hole of Calcutta" (cf. 86.7–11ff.). If one now refers to the inanimate "mound" shown stratified in Relief Map B—and it could be likened to the dumped "black haul of some coal-cutter"—one will note that sleep has "burrowed the coacher's headlight" (11.17): each such "headlight" would be one of the eyes of the blindman in question (Gael. *caoch*, "blind"), each by night "buried" and "burrowed" in the underground of the body. More than once in the book identified as "the Mole" (310.1), the *Wake*'s "benighted irismaimed" should therefore be understood to have all the visionary acuity of a mole—though a mole sleepily "obcaecated" (76.36 [L. *obcaecatus*, "made blind, invisible"]) in a "mole's paradise" (76.33–34), a "mountainy molehill" (474.22), a "wholemole" (614.27 ["molehole"]).[6]

As all these examples suggest, trying to capture the "eyewitless foggus" of a man "dead to the world" and given to envisioning sodden "mudfacepackets" necessarily engaged Joyce in the exercise of something like "photography in mud" (277.25–26). Like Shem the Penman, a reader of the *Wake* should therefore discover that "every splurge on the vellum he blunder[s] over [is] an aisling vision" (179.30–31): either vision is badly "ailing," that is, or—since the Gaelic *aisling* means "dream"—it bleeds up spectrally within sealed "blackeye lenses." Almost every page in the *Wake* "pulls a lane picture for us, in a dreariodreama setting, glowing and very vidual, of old dumplan" (79.27–29): each "pulls a very lean picture," that is, one dimly "glowing" when "dreams" appear, but otherwise simply "vidual." Since the Latin *vidua* means "deprived" (but also "widow" in context), the line indicates that everything normally "visual" becomes, in the "blackeye lenses" of the *Wake*'s "irismaimed," simply "vidual" ("deprived of the visual"); but it also suggests the extent of the *Wake*'s intention to do for the night and the absent what "the Lane Pictures" do in offering colorfully verisimilar representations of a present: "Ah, in unlitness 'twas in very similitude" (404.12).

Critics have passed on the extremely odd and hardly comprehensible idea that Book I of *Finnegans Wake*, which Joyce called "a kind of immense shadow," and part of which he published under the title "A Mole" (*L*, II, lxx), takes place in the daytime, and even begins in the morning.[7] This reading surely needs reconciliation with Joyce's own belief that he was "writing about the night" ("It is night. It is dark. You can hardly see"), but also with a reader's experience of the very murky "darkumen" itself (350.28), which begins with the fall of "Eve" (3.1)—not necessarily "a beauty from the bible" (192.28)—and alludes to "the night" and "the shades that Eve's now wearing" "in dims and deeps and dusks and darks" that are streaked over "ebony" "blink pitch" (226.12–14, 341.9, 93.4 ["every black page"]): when "Eve takes fall," it is night (293.21). The observation that "it is not always night in dreams" will begin to reconcile these discrepancies, but will not finally explain why so much of a "darkumen" supposed to begin in the morning comes off the page "surrounded by obscurity" and "looking pretty black" (546.19, 188.4–5).[8] In fact, little of Joyce's "reconstruction of the nocturnal life"—and certainly none of Book I—takes place in the day, although its hero periodically, if only momentarily, seems to envision "charming details of light in dark" in dreams (606.21–22). Daylight occurs to its hero only toward the end of *Finnegans Wake*, in the middle of III.iv, when "the dapplegray dawn drags nearing nigh for to wake all droners that drowse in Dublin" (585.20–21), and "when the messanger of the risen sun . . . [begins to] give to every seeable a hue and to every hearable a cry and to each spectacle his spot" (609.19–21). "In the moontime" (528.5 [a nocturnal "meantime"]), "till daybowbreak and showshadows flee" (546.23), "yeddonot need light" to read extended parts of the book (535.9 [the reference to the Japanese city Yeddo, however, apprises us of the steady pull exerted on HCE's nightlife by the imminence of tomorrow and the "Rising Sun"]).

"Meoptics"

If, then, we return to the opening chapter of the *Wake*, any number of "blackartful" signs will show that the "hole affair"—a "spoof of visibility in a freakfog" (48.1–2)—is heavily "involved in darkness" right from the start (79.1). In a phrase by now familiar, for instance—"yet may we not see still the brontoichthyan form outlined aslumbered" (7.20–21)—any difficulty we might have had visualizing a "brontoichthyan form" is obviated by the cast of the sentence in which the phrase occurs. Not a question, but an assertion, it tells us that we could not see it lying still a moment ago, and "we may not see [it] still." More explicitly, a few pages later: "we may take our review of the two mounds [of 'hillhead' and 'tumptytumtoes'] to see nothing. . . . We may see and hear nothing if we choose. . . . as he lays dormont" (12.19–20, 25–26, 35). Joyce gets so much play out of "visus umbique" like these (183.14)—out of "things seen" (L. *visus*) "everywhere" (L. *undique*) "obscurely" (L. *ambigue*)—that terms like "see," "look," "peer," "scene," "view," and "eye" invariably bear cautious scrutiny for what they "reveil" about HCE's very deeply "blackguarded eye" (464.12 [and never trust a "blackguard"]). These terms are so pervasive, in fact, that we might now "rearrive" at the first page of the *Wake* to clarify, by "keep[ing] black!," some more of its murkily "clearobsure" terms.

We learn here, for instance, that our hero is "a bland old isaac" (3.11): the "comedy nominator," reduced "to the loaferst terms" (283.7–8), suggests in part that the *Wake*'s heroic "loafer" resembles the Biblical Isaac in being just an old man whose paternal authority has of late been assailed by one of his "kids"—"Jerkoff" (246.30 [Jacob])—who, merely by growing into all the nasty tensions and pretensions of adolescence ("buttended" = "pretended"), has begun treating his "oldparr" like a "cad" ("kidscad" [3.11]). But the phrase also suggests simply that HCE, like Isaac, is "blind." And this is why "rory end to the regginbrow was to be seen ringsome on the aquaface" (3.13–14).

Merely by falling asleep, the *Wake*'s "irismaimed" has drifted into a universe whose visible surfaces lie beyond—below—the red end of the spectrum ("rory = Irish = red," in Joyce's gloss of this line; "regginbrow = German regenbogen + rainbow" [*L*, I, 248]). If "nighthood's unseen violet [ultra violet] render[s] all animated greatbritish and Irish objects nonviewable to human watchers" elsewhere in the *Wake* (403.34–36), so too here must "nighthood's unseen infrared," at the other, "rory" end of the spectrum. In other words, the spectrum of visible light extending from red to violet and perceptible at every minute of the waking day is nowhere to be seen here ("No end to the rainbow was to be seen"); and in its place, within "eyes shut," kinds of light invisible to "eyes whiteopen" have swum problematically, if at all, into view (234.7): "his reignbolt's shot" (590.10). Sleep begins precisely here, where the spectrum of visible light comes to an end—to both its ends—and where kinds of light invisible to the open eye emerge "from the irised sea" (318.34 ["see"]) to "reveil" to a man made absent "the spectrem of his prisent" (498.31 ["the spectre of a present," as illuminated in "spectral" colors bled out of a "prism" imprisoned in "blackeye lenses"]). Vision arises here, like the verb "to be seen," in passive form, and in the absence of any identifiable agent or perceived object.

"Eboniser's" darkening "fall" asleep "in bed" on the first page of the *Wake* moreover scatters him "through all christian minstrelsy" (3.18). The phrase suggests in part that a deep past—"all Christian history"—has assumed a weird vitality in his nightlife, and it also historically dates him: "Christy Minstrels"—a generic name for variety shows in which white performers sang "Negro spirituals" in blackface—were popular in turn-of-the-century Europe. Not least, however, the phrase evokes a world of weird vaudevillean inversions, where white has been made black, and light dark (cf. 66.19–22). For the man "tropped head" at the *Wake* lies "melained from nape to kneecap" (247.19 [Gr. *melainô*, "to blacken"])—see relief map—and has so "blacked out" as to become, though not in any way accessible to vision or susceptible to racial construction, a "darky" (515.34), a "blackman" (236.16), a "Tar." "The darkens alone knows" what this blind and blacked-out "darky" is able to see on the first page of the book (439.24), where, as far as he can "no," "it mights be anything after darks" (603.25–26).[9] Together, all these terms indicate, as we might expect, that Joyce's "book of the dark" begins in the dark and only progressively moves toward "the opening of the mind to light" (258.31–32). A reader sensitive to its "dressy black modern style" will therefore likely discover that through much of the *Wake* "there would not be a holey spier on the town . . . nor a yew nor an eye" anywhere (23.35–36): that "holey spier," of course, would be our hero, who "spies" only "holes" (as opposed to "holy spires") because he is dead to the world (hence "yew") and blind (hence "no eye"): " 'tis endless now senne eye [or I] . . . last saw" (213.15).[10]

Although he is "looking pretty black" at everything (188.4–5), the *Wake*'s "irismaimed" nonetheless "ha[s] more in his eye" (81.20) than this survey of "sightlessness" can have suggested: "his lights not all out yet" (379.13) because visual dreams do sporadically fill the "Black and All Black" interior of his "tropped head" with spectral outpourings of vision and color. Our certain memory of such dreams, then—compelling us to wonder, "Will it

"Meoptics"

bright upon us, nightle"?—merits the infirm answer, "Well, it might now, mircle, so it light" (66.21–23). Apprising us of the "miracle" by which "light" flows forth in "batblack" "blackeye lenses" (405.36), the phrasing here reminds us that colorful "light at night" (256.34) does irradiate sleep, and largely because "we're eyed for aye" (239.6). "Let us see all there may remain to be seen," then (113.32–33): "light us find" (267.1), with "eye[s] . . . nolensed" (113.28 ["no lens!"]), night's manifold "brights and shades" (621.23).

"RAYINGBOGEYS"

It follows, of course, that whatever vision does arise in sleep is not precisely in the nature of vision at all, since it too bleeds up "in fact, under the closed eyes" (107.28). To represent fully the intricate character and play of this "light at night" (256.34), while yet maintaining an accurate "unlitness . . . in very similitude" (404.12), the *Wake* necessarily develops its own system of vision and optics—or, more accurately, of "invision" and "meoptics" (626.28, 139.16)—which elaborately captures "the charming details of light in dark" (606.21–22) that iridescently emerge, with visual dreams, within the "blackeye lenses" of "eyes darkled." As the spelling implies, the *Wake*'s "meoptics" is an insuperably "myopic optics," applicable primarily to the "me" that comes to light when the eyes "SHUT" ("myopia" derives from the Gr. *myein*, "to close or shut" and *ôps*, "the eye"). And "when I turn meoptics, from suchurban prospects" as my bedroom walls by falling asleep (139.16), what becomes visible, if not "invasable blackth," are kinds of light that have only the most spectral connections with those bled out of Newton's spectrum.

According to classical treatments of the subject, which evolve out of Descartes's *Dioptric* (1636) and Newton's *Opticks* (1704) and culminate in von Helmholtz's magisterial three volumes on *Physiological Optics* (1866), vision occurs as rays of light reflected from real objects endowed with Lockean "primary qualities"—"one photoreflection of the several iridals gradationes of solar light" (611.16–17)—impinge on the retina and ding it for life with an image of the real (see figure 8.1). Since Helmholtzian optics are inaccurate to the experience of sleep, however, where vision arises within the sealed chambers of the "eyegonblack" (16.29 ["gone very black"]), only the dawning of daybreak at the end of *Finnegans Wake* finds "hemhaltshealing" (611.28 [a "Helmholtzian" optics "healing"]); prior to that, as the spelling implies, the machinery of classical optics simply "halts," the *Wake*'s "meoptics" filling in its ample gaps (see figure 8.2).

This "meoptics" works the other way around: the light searing the retina comes from within and from behind—as "if this could see with its back-sight" (249.2 ["backside"])—and even as it issues invitations to "Lucihere!" (295.33 ["Look here!"]), it also plays demonic pranks on the dreamer (just as the L. *lucifer* literally means "light-bringing" but refers to the Prince of Darkness). Color precipitating "from next to nothing" in sleep, then (4.36–5.1), causes HCE to see as if "through his eyetrompit" only vast "*tromps-l'oeil*" (247.32–33 [Fr. "visual illusions"]), and with such murky strain as to require the optical equivalent of an "ear-trumpet" (see figure 8.4).

Well-endowed as he may be with "a peerless pair" of "seeless socks" (382.23, 468.25 [this "peerless pair" "peers" at nothing]), the *Wake*'s "be-nighted irismaimed" has as fine "a first class pair of bedroom eyes" as any of the figmentary characters of whom he dreams (396.11); and at ample coun-termoments to the book's predominating "blackouts," its "Anglo-Irish" sleeper—"he, selfsufficiencer . . . what though the duthsthrows in his . . . eyes" (240.14–17 ["what though the death-throes," the blinding "dust thrown"])—turns luridly "aglo iris" (528.23 [his "iris aglow"]), so that "by the hundred and sixty odds rods and cones of this even's vision" (405.12–13), he becomes "all eyes": "We are all eyes. I have his quoram of images all on my retinue, Mohomadhawn Mike" (443.1–2).[11] The wording here in part calls attention to the way in which Muhammad received the words of the Koran on "the night of power" in Ramadan (hence "quoram" and "Mohamad-"); but, by way of the Gaelic *amadán* ("fool"), it does so pri-marily in order to call our attention to the weird optics of vision in dreams, during which the "retina" ("retinue"), "under the closed eyes," may in fact actively "rudden up in fusefiressence on the flashmurket" (378.8): retinal "flesh" all "murked" ("fleshmurket"), in other words, "flashes" out in "phos-phoresence" ("fusefiressence") to raise a visionary "fussforus" (505.33), so that suddenly one finds oneself strolling wishfully through a "fleshmarket" and really believing oneself there. For one is as likely to discover an account of Muhammad's "night of power" in the nineteenth-century literature on sleep as in any book on Islam:

> Tradition accounts for Mohammed's being among the prophets in this wise: While indulging in spiritual meditations and repeating pious exercise on Mount Hira in the month of Ramedan, the Angel Gabriel came to him by night, *as he was sleeping*, held a silken scroll before him, and required him, though not knowing how to read, to recite what was written on the scroll. The words thus communicated remained graven on his memory. . . .[12]

"Meoptics"

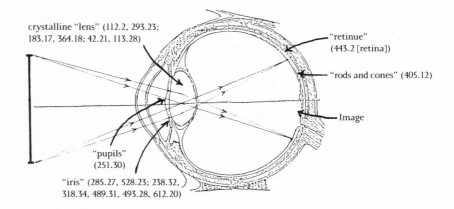

Figure 8.1. The ideal or schematic eye

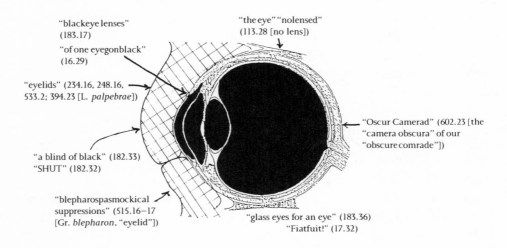

Figure 8.2. "one eyegonblack"

In Joyce's conflation of "quoram" and "retina," the silken screen seen by Muhammad "with his eyes shut" is not fully distinguishable from the retinal screen perceived by anyone in sleep. For Joyce and the authorities of his own day rightly inferred what students of "rapid-eye movements" have recently and more firmly claimed: except that they are firmly "SHUT," the eyes of a person hosting a visual dream behave oddly as they do in wakefulness under the photic pressure of real objects; and while it is obviously impossible to look "under the closed eyes" without opening them and destroy-

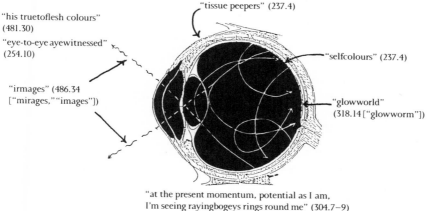

Figure 8.3. "truetoflesh colours"

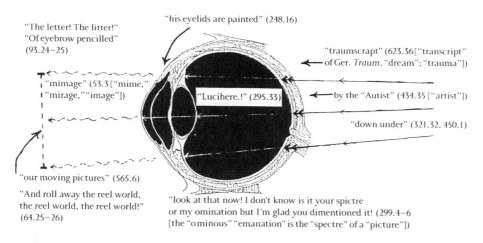

Figure 8.4. "traumscrapt"

ing the conditions that prevail there, it may even well be that "the rods and cones of even's vision" spark dimly up, during dreams, to generate a "fussfor" us (415.5).[13] By anyone's account, the visual dream entails a partial wakening of the eyes out of sleep, and, with them, the wakening of a shadowy aspect of visual consciousness.

All the many and "varied lights" appearing in *Finnegans Wake* are accordingly "veereyed lights" (344.23), snapped on within the incandescent "eyebulbs" (531.8, 557.12)—the "gropesarching eyes" (167.12–13)—of an "aglo-irismaimed" whom we might again construe as "Burymeleg and Bind-merollingeyes" (11.6–7). If the wording here accords with reflections on "our own nighttime" in suggesting that most of sleep sinks one into a state of motor paralysis and functional blindness, it also implies that at moments in the night the "bound eyes" of this "irismaimed" start to "roll," so to render his "*bulgeglarying stargapers razzledazzlingly full of eyes, full of balls, full of holes, full of buttons, full of stains, full of medals, full of blickblackblobs*" (339.19–21): the phrasing calls attention to the "bulging," "glaring," and "gaping" "eye" "balls" of a "stargazer" (one who exercises vision at night), while the "medals" and "buttons" scattered among the ocular terms suggest the growth, in these eyes, of a "uniform" appearance—that of "the rouged engenerand" (372.6–7 [or "Russian General," "rouged" because colorfully "made up" and "engendered" in HCE's eyes]). Followed by a line that shows this "rouged engenerand" taking form in the seven colors of the spectrum (339.27–29 [or rainbow]), the passage suggests that "eyes now kindling themselves are brightening" (290.4); and it also allows us to begin seeing, in "lumerous ways" (282.29 ["numerous" "luminous"]), how intricately "this looseaffair brimsts of fussforus!" (505.32–33 [again note the "light-bearing" *lucifer* in this darkly "loose affair"]).

Such sporadic ocular turmoil as disrupts sleep with vision will perhaps explain the *Wake*'s recurrent preoccupation with forms of "light" that no one awake can ever see—with "infrared," "ultraviolet," "herzian waves," and "xrays," for instance, all of which resemble the light washing over objects perceived in dreams in not being visible to the open eye (207.10–11, 316.2–3, 425.35, 590.7–9; 232.10–11, 460.25; 51.25–26, 248.1, 530.8). But it will also certainly clarify the *Wake*'s well-known obsession with "rainbows" and "rainbow girls," and its dense employment of what Joyce called "the iritic colors" (*L*, I, 295).[14] The term obviously signifies the seven colors of the "rainbow" (Gr. *iris*); but as the iritically afflicted Joyce would well have known and as passages everywhere in the *Wake* suggest, these "iritic colors" largely appear beneath the "iris" of vision-capable eyes ("see Iris in the Evenine's World" [285.27]).[15] If it is true, then, that HCE (as "*Terry Cotter*" [71.22]) tends to envision wet "mudfacepackets" throughout the night (because "his likeness is in Terrecuite and he giveth rest to the rainbowed" [133.30–31]), it is no less certain that he is periodically able to see, "by arclight" (3.13 [Fr. *arc-en-ciel*, "rainbow"]), all seven colors of the spectrum: "lift the blank" and "split the hvide and aye seize heaven!" (247.30–31); and as that "eye (and I) sees these seven" colors, it also becomes capable of seeing the "black and white" constituted by their total absence or presence (hence "the blank" and the Da. *hvide* ["whites"]). What the *Wake*'s "irismaimed" has in mind while "seeing rayingbogeys" of this sort (304.9 [apart from "bogeys" formed of illusionary "rays" and "rainbows"]) is simply visible "light." For anyone awake who looks around right now and surveys the multicolored "photoprismic velamina of [the] hueful panepiphanal world" (611.13 [the L. *velamina*, "coverings" or "veils," of the Gr. *panepiphanês*, "all visible"]), will always and only see, anywhere and everywhere he looks, the colors of the rainbow—though not in neatly arrayed order and rarely in unmixed primary form. Since Joyce also called the *Wake*'s "iritic colors," in an unusually straightforward remark he purportedly made to C. K. Ogden, "the colours of the colour-band" (*Annotations*, 215), we should finally see that in *Finnegans Wake* the colors of the "rainbow" simply signify the colors of the spectrum: they make up the total span of visible light.

It is, accordingly, a sign of our blinded "Irismans ruinboon" (612.20)—a "boon" redeeming his overwhelming "black ruin" (381.17)—that he always has his "gropesarching" "eyes on the peer for Noel's Arch" (490.22–23 [Noah's "arch" is the rainbow]). The opalescent gathering of those iritic colors way out there in the reaches of far space, on the backs of his eyelids, means that suddenly, "from next to nothing" (4.36–5.1), out of a universe washed away and swamped in black, a New World starts radiantly to undergo creation all over again, bringing to his eyes sights and scenes familiar as "home sweet home." Having "eyes on the peer for Noel's arch" is like being "on the pier" when "Noah's ark" comes in—"Gauze off heaven! Vision" (566.28 [and "Gods of heaven"]), "I'm blest if I can see" (273.F2, cf. 273.4–5)—because a spirit scattered in a formlessly dark void starts to incarnate itself ("Noel"), and with such particular heat in the area of the eyes that it witnesses the creation of a whole new world:

> Yes, there was that skew arch of chrome sweet home [Gr. *chrôma*, "color," "the surface of the body"]), floodlit up above the flabberghosted farmament and bump where the camel got the needle. Talk about iridecencies! Ruby and beryl and chrysolite, jade, sapphire, jasper and lazul.
> (494.1–5)

What that "camel" shares with the "ghosted," "flabbergasted," and "knock[ed] out" "Irisman" who envisions these "iridecencies" ("to get the needle" is to be "knock[ed] out") is tremendous strain in the region of the "eye." For "it is easier for a camel to pass through the eye of a needle" (Matt. 19:24), than for light to enter the eye of a man "tropped head." Since the camel seems to

"Meoptics"

squeeze through here (along with that "bump"), so perhaps does iridescent light. Those seven gemmy stones at the end of these lines call attention to our "aglo-irismaimed's" "marbled eyes" (55.22), "his pebbled eyes" (463.27), both of them stirring up internally with a splay of iritic colors, in false expectation of a dream "being visible above thorizon" (494.9): a "ruby" is red, "beryl" orange, "chrysolite" yellow, and so forth through the spectrum.

Since the long discursive passage that follows these lines has nothing very visually "dreamlike" about it, however, moments in the *Wake* like these complicate the book's "meoptics" by raising the question of what its "iris-maimed" might be looking at. Reference to Helmholtz's *Physiological Optics* would apprise us here that "the field of vision of a healthy human being is never entirely free from appearances . . . which have been called the *chaotic light* or *luminous dust* of the *dark visual field*. It plays such an important part in many phenomena . . . that we shall call it the *self-light* or *intrinsic light* of the retina." Commonly, this "chaotic light" takes the form of "floating clouds," "broad streamers," or "floating cloud-ribbons," all of "which may be transformed into fantastic figures."[16] According to Freud and the several nineteenth-century authorities whom he cites, turbulent versions of these "intraocular retinal excitations" play a constituent, if not a causative role in the formation of dreams.[17]

Now "peel your eyes" (302.11): if the reader closes his eyes and "steps out on the peer," he should eventually note that "**he can e**yespy through them, to their selfcolours, nevertheleast their tissue peepers," and even through "parryshoots" (237.2–4["parachutes," like umbrellas, darken what falls below]). All of these "meoptical" terms are asking the reader to consult his own "peepers" (his eyes and their "tissues," and *not* "tissue papers") and, by using the eye to see the eye, to become "eye-to-eye ayewitnessed" (254.10). The murkily visible "selfcolours" that one will gradually "espy" "out there" by engaging "in meeingseeing" of this sort (179.1), insusceptible to mapping in schematic drawings of the "Ideal Eye," are playfully illustrated in figure 8.3; by many accounts, these borealic "selfcolours" are an element in the "light" that bathes the world in dreams.

No matter whether "presentative" visual dreams entail the active wakening of the eyes or the passive detection of "chaotic light" drifting through "blackeye lenses," the *Wake* now suggests that one passes, in falling asleep, "from golddawn glory to glowworm gleam" (99.1): because the shimmer falling over all surfaces of the world perceived in dreams is created out of the eye's flesh and cast forth in a semblance of the real, HCE's "eyebulbs" might be understood to create light—"fleshed light" (222.22)—like "glowworms," "fireflies," "lightning bug[s]," and other forms of life that radiate color out of living tissue (29.7, 199.36, 246.8, 449.22–23, 528.28). As several citations from Moore's *Melodies* suggest ("The glowworm's lamp is gleaming, love"), "this glowworld's lump is gloaming off" (318.13–14) whenever HCE (the "lump" in question) dimly turns into and fades out of a whole oneiratic "glow-world"; for when his eyes "rudden up in fusefiressence" or swim in chaotic light, they exude light like "glowworms," in a nocturnal universe where, after all, "the gloom hath rays, her lump is love" (411.27–28 ["The moon hath raised her lamp above"]).[18] However fully "his reign-bolt's shot," then, we now "know [HCE], the covenanter, by rote at least, for a chameleon at last, in his true falseheaven colours from ultraviolent to subred tissues" (590.7–9); when the spectral hues of the rainbow (or arc of "covenant") do glow in the dark of his closed eyes, they reveal a strange new world illumined under a "heaven" lit with a paradoxically "true false seven" colors. A "lunar rainbow" of sorts because it only appears "under the dark flush of night" (527.7 [and also "the dark flesh"]) and because it can never be seen with open eyes (hence "ultraviolet" and "subred"), this nocturnal "spectrem" (318.33, 498.31 ["spectre's spectrum"]) is radiated up out of "blackeye lenses" whose "subred tissues" cast forth light, in "true-toflesh colours" (481.30), like the bodies of fireflies and the flesh of the "chameleon."[19]

Creating their own form of "earthlight" (449.7), each of HCE's eyes now becomes a powerful "flask of lightning" (426.29–30 [a container of liquid and "lightning"]) internal to which, as "flesh" turns into "flash" (220.28 [a common "misspelling" in the *Wake*]), he has occasion to glimpse "fleshed light like likening" (222.22–23 [and "flashed light like lightning"]): as that "flesh" "flashes" awake, that is—elusively as "lightning"—it yields inevitable if obscure "likenings" ("I'm sure he squirted juice in his eyes to make them flash for flightening me" [626.15–16]). The vision of an "irismaimed" endowed with this "lightning look" (117.3) therefore becomes at moments in the *Wake* a kind of dark "peekaboo" (580.15), or "meteoromancy" (228.20–21 ["divination by meteors"]), in which "gropesarching eyes" lost under a "night of falling angles" (21.25), a "night of starshootings somewhere in Erio" (22.12–13 ["somewhere in an area" accustomed to the more stolid vision of "Erin"]), are constantly teased by the appearances of scarcely visible "starshootings," "falling angles," "sheep's lightning" (449.28), and—"eye bet" (301.7)—comparably elusive kinds of light (now you see it, no you didn't): "happen seen sore eynes belived?" (534.26 [Ger. *Haben sie so eines erlebt?*, "Have you experienced one like that?"]). Or again, "his veins shooting melanite phosphor" (475.14–15 [Gr. *melanos*, "of black," *phôsphoros*, "light-bringing"]), his eyes engage in a form of "search lighting" (292.18), since they illumine the night's "glowworld" like "search lights," but have also to "search" murkily for whatever "light" they create. As "the lighning leaps from the numbulous," at any rate (367.27–28 [and as imagistic "likening" emerges from the "nebulous"]), the *Wake*'s "irismaimed" becomes a "lewdningbluebolteredallucktruckalltraumconductor!" (378.9–10 [a "conductor" of "lightning," "lewd" "trains" of thought, and the "dream," or Ger. *Traum*]). And his nocturnal vision becomes, in the idiom of the *Wake*, "flash as flash can" (188.12–13 [one plays "catch as catch can" with these forms of light]).[20]

To those visionary guidelines we have already compiled, then, we might now add a few others: "where there's white [and light], lets ope" (441.6 [and where there's not, let's "pull the blind" and "keep black!"]). Or again, "don't you let flyfire till you see their whites of the bunkers' eyes!" (542.25–26)—where that "bunker," of course, would be a man "in bed" or "bunk," within whose "firefly"-like eyes whole "New Worlds" are coming to be (hence "Bunker's Hill"). The *Wake* in turn becomes a "jackalantern's tale" (197.26–27, 10.26–27 ["for the lamp of Jig-a-Lanthern!"]), because it takes place in a hollow (and vegetating) head—or "a candlelittle houthse" (10.26–27 ["Howth" = "HEAD"])—that is erratically "lit [with] thousands in one nightlights" (135.20): these "thousands" would include the manifold "jack-o-lanterns," "rayingbogeys," "flyfires," "fusefiressen[t]" "headlights," "fleshes" of "likelings" (339.16–17), and "swamplights" that we have explored in passing; and as the wording implies, they all appear "in one"—person—our "benighted" hero, whom we now might construe less as an opaque "Eboniser" than as a colorful "Saxon Chromaticus" (304.18 [*not* "Grammaticus"]), an agent "from Chromophilomos, Limited" (123.14–15 [Gr. *chrômophilomos*, "colorloving"; "limited" because color is not always there]).

A particularly clear place in Finnegans Wake at which to study the formation and dissolution of visual dreams would be the beginnings and ends of chapters III.i and III.ii, which Joyce, obviously playing on the word "watch," called "The First and Second Watches of Shaun." Etymologically related to the words "wake" and "waken," "watch" means both "the act of keeping awake and alert," and "to look at," so that the term captures an essential feature of all visual dreams, during which the eye wakens, as if to "keepeth watch" (355.31), and then, on "nightwatch" (576.30), lazily "watches." The Shaun chapters open, accordingly, with the appropriately contradictory admonition, "Black! Switch out!" (403.17), which advises us on the one hand to "keep black!" ("Switch out!"), but also, antithetically, vigilantly to "watch out!" For it is "in the sighed of lovely eyes" rifted by precisely this tension (405.28–29 ["inside of"]) that the dreamed image of Shaun, at first "nonviewable to human watchers," gradually appears from within a "fogbow" (or obscured rainbow) that only slowly releases seven clear iritic colors from out of "obscidian" black (403.23–24, 6, 8–16). The visual filaments of the dream accumulate as "anon [and 'anonymously'] some glistery gleam darkling" gathers in intensity until a "lamp"-bearing "will of a wisp" appears (403.24–404.1, 13, 15). And within that "will-o'-the-wisp"—"now, fix on the little fellow in my eye" (486.13–14)—a figure "whom we dreamt was a shaddo, sure, he's lightseyes, the laddo" (404.14–15). This would be Shaun, a "picture primitive," "growing to stay" (405.3, 404.15). He is "lightseyes" (and "light-sized") not simply because as a hallucination he "weigh[s] nought" (407.5), but also because he appears within the darkly "lit eyes" of the *Wake*'s "aglo-irismaimed." This light-bringing "lampman" appears in the "tropped head" (427.1), moreover, carrying letters (and therefore literacy and ego functions), enveloped by that strange "barrel" which, as we have seen, is simply a cipher for the imperceived body of the *Wake*'s sleeping hero; should the reader now consult the reliefs maps of the night, he will note that it is largely within the miniscule "lightseyes" of the giant "form outlined alsumbered" there that Shaun—and graphic letters—are "enveloped."

At the far end of "The Second Watch of Shaun," conversely, we see this "pattern sent" (472.25 [the image or "pattern" of a "patron saint"]) "quickly lost to sight" as visible light crumbles away in "embers" (471.28, 473.9ff.). Indeed, as "yon beam of light we follow receding on [Shaun's] photophoric ['light-bearing'] pilgrimage to [his] antipodes" (472.16–17 ["down under"]), we learn that his "now paling light lucerne we ne'er may see again" (472.22–23)—the evocation of "Lake Lucerne" and of movement "to the four cantons" (472.24) suggesting that Shaun is drifting into a "helvetically hermetic" and "landlocked" "state." Like others in the *Wake*, the passage shows "vision pass[ing]" and "fading" from the "tropped head" (486.32–33) as the *Wake*'s "benighted irismaimed" sinks out of his "nightwatch" into a new species of nothing (473.6–7).

What happens in the middle of these extended "watches," in the interval between the aggregation and corrosion of visual dreams, is an activity that the *Wake* calls "spacemak[ing]" (247.2). The precipitation of the "iritic colors" out of the night's "invasable blackth" means that within the dimensionless body and "tropped head" of the *Wake*'s "sleeping giant," delimited forms of visible space—whole cities, bodies, mountains, rooms littered with objects—sometimes start to undergo elaborate imaginary creation. During his visual dreams, then, we find HCE "recovering breadth" (344.19) by "building space" in his head (155.6) or "making spaces in his psyche" (416.5–6; 415.28, 417.25)—and, in the process, rising from the ranks of "the great unwatched" (435.31–32). The construction of illusionarily constellated spaces and objects out of a wilderness of iritic and chaotic "light" complementarily entails the splintering out of the giant body of an organizing principle, in the form of a viewing spectator—or a "spatialist" (149.19 ["specialist"]) whose "spatiality" (172.9) is the "watching" and specular containment of the "seene" (52.36 ["scene"]; cf. 114.23). Difficult as it may be to determine from whose point of view one sees, "with his eyes shut," objects that appear in dreams ("we cannot say whom we are looking like through" [370.25]), what is ultimately "shown" to the dreamer whose "magic lantern [rises] to a glow of fullconsciousness" (421.22–23) is not simply the "shown" dream scene itself, but also a character "watching the watched" (509.2; cf. 508.35–509.4), whom we now simply call "showm" (29.4 [or "Shaun"]). The wakeful vigilance of this implicit observer ("your watch keeper," through whom "you've seen all sorts in shapes and sizes" everywhere in the world [464.25–26]) would explain why "Shaun the Post," whose name Joyce sometimes spells as "showm" or "shone" (29.4, 75.11, 441.23, 528.21), is always implicated in the *Wake*'s "space-making" eventfulnesses (see especially 149.11ff. and 415.25ff.). The appearance of diffusely spatialized objects in visual dreams necessarily signals "a trend back to the object world" and therefore the wakening of the dreamer's ego (let's "Show'm the Posed" [92.13]), which is everywhere wrapped up both in those objects and, as one's literate "murmury" of visual dreams will attest (254.18), in the carrying and delivery of letters.[21] A "character" with all the disorienting attributes of a figure in a dream and the bearer of our hero's ego functions as well (see 485.5), Shaun is as much a figure through whom we see things as a figure whom we see (this is why, as the commentary has generally noted, he "narrates" whole sections of *Finnegans Wake*).

As visible spaces, their semiconscious "watcher," and the ego fall together within the "tropped head" of the *Wake*'s "visionbuilder" (191.34), finally, the *Wake* "brings us a rainborne pamtomomiom" (285.15–16, F6). On the one hand this suggests a "rainbow pantomime," or "dumbshow," like that played out in chapter II.i ("The Mime of Mick, Nick and the Maggies"); but the undertones also suggest that all such "dummpshow[s]" (120.7–8) are really staged within HCE's "deafadumped" body (590.1)—"(dump for short)" (110.26)—within whose wakening and watching eyes a "pandemonium" of chaotically intersecting "rayingbogeys," "flyfire[s]," and "fleshes" of "likening" are coalescing, at all sorts of obtusely "falling angles" (21.25), to form sites like *Dreamcolohour* (176.10 [remotely a place like "Drumcollogher," perhaps, but primarily a space built only at the "hour" and in the "colours" of the "dream"]). *Dreamcolohour* now merits a tour. "Follow the spotlight, please!" (506.27).

"COLOURS"

Appearing at the structural center of the *Wake*, the "rainborne pamtomomiom" enacted in "The Mime of Mick, Nick and the Maggies" (II.i) is certainly essential to any consideration of the book's dark optics. Joyce informally called this chapter "twilight games" (*L*, I, 241) and in a well-known letter to Harriet Shaw Weaver said that he based it on a children's guessing-game called "Angels and Devils or colours" (*L*, I, 295), going on to explain that the child designated "it" in this tagging game had to guess the name of a color withheld from him by others, and, if successful in guessing, catch the person who chose it. The complex relevance of this ritual to a reconstruction of the night begins with the observation that the entire mime as staged in *Finnegans Wake* takes place inside the body of a recurrently evoked "sleeping giant" who, throughout "the whole thugogmagog," is reclined cap-a-pie and is largely dead to the world (220.14, 26; 221.26–27, 29; 222.14; 253.29–31). Underlying this entire game of *Find Me Colours*, in short (626.17), is the body of the *Wake*'s sleeping protagonist, within the "selfcolours" of whose "closed eyes" the whole chapter takes place (hence the "Finn MacCool" in *Find Me Colours*; cf. 219.18). Because he is generally "off colour" (230.1) and "he don't know whose hue" in the dark (227.25 [much less "who's who"]), the "guess-work" he undertakes in this "twilight game" might more properly be conceived as a form of "gazework" (224.26): "when the h, who the hu, how the hue, where the huer?" (257.34–35). For at the hour of the night explored here—"lighting up o'clock sharp" (219.1)—the *Wake*'s "visionbuilder" is trying hard to see, and "sinking [not 'thinking'] how he must fand for himself by gazework what . . . colours wear" (224.25–27 [and "were"]).

Once more, then, "our eyes demand their turn. Let them be seen!" (52.18–19). If the reader again consults his "tissue peepers," he will be able to participate directly in some of the "twilight games" that our hero plays in the

"Meoptics"

"Colours" chapter. "Peel your eyes" by closing them, and ask yourselves "not have you seen a match being struck" (233.18–19), but

—Have you monbreamstone?
—No.
—Or Hellfeuersteyn?
—No.
—Or Van Diemen's coral pearl?
—No.

(225.22–26)

As "your refractions" will attest (256.31 [and your "reflections," too]), all of these riddles again move us to the centers of HCE's "marbled eyes" (55.22), which, however dark and sightless they may be here, are nonetheless internally capable of "participating in the ambiguity of the jewel" when scintillant bursts of invisible "nightlights" fire through them (135.20).[22] Although his "catseye[s]" (423.7–8) are "submerged" throughout his sleep (like "coral pearl"), and lie "down under" (hence the reference to Australia's "Van Dieman's Land"), they are nonetheless always "a spark's gap off" (232.33) from striking up both "hellfire" and light—like the German *Feuerstein* ("flint")—so that they become at times dark "moonstones" of sorts, riddled through with forms of light visible only at night ("moonbeams"). Able "to setisfire" (234.24–25 [and "satisfy"]) "His Sparkling Headiness" (236.5–6)—note the "sparkles" in that "tropped head"—by "giv[ing] him chromitis" (232.2 [Gr. "inflammation of color"]) and filling with "the cloud of the opal" (220.9–10), HCE's "eyenbowls" therefore become sporadically "glycering juwells" in this part of the *Wake* (389.28, 236.2)—"wells" of vitreously "glyceric" fluid internally lit like "glistering jewels" (Ger. *Juwel*).[23] Each, "like a **h**eptagon **c**rystal **e**mprisoms trues and fauss for us" (127.3–4 [Fr. *fausse*, "false"])—and, in seven colors (hence "heptagon crystal"), "trues and *phôsphoros*" (Gr. "bringer of light"): "sight most deletious ['deleted' because unreal] to ross up [and raise up] the spyballs" (247.20–21).

That the occulted color HCE tries to discover by "gazework" within his "glystering juwells" should be "heliotrope" would account for the positioning of the "Colours" chapter at the center of *Finnegans Wake*. Although "heliotrope" simultaneously names a gemstone, a reddish-purple color, and a kind of sunflower, the word derives from the Greek *hêliotropion* and radically signifies a "turning toward the sun"; and it is here, precisely half-way through the *Wake*'s reconstruction of the night, that its unconscious hero—an "unknown sunseeker" (110.30)—starts inexorably to float up toward sunrise, resurrection, and the wakened rediscovery of sunlit vision. As the property sought by "gazework" throughout the *Wake*'s "twilight games," "heliotrope" therefore signifies less a concrete color or object than a whole visionary trend: "the flower that stars [and starts] the day" (248.12–13 [though that "star" keeps us oriented in the night]), its dense if occluded appearance in the "spyballs" of our *"sunflawered"* hero (350.11) suggests that he lies "in [a] sunflower state" at this moment in the night (509.21), and that he is beginning, as he moves through *the heliotropical noughttime"* (349.6)—"through dimdom done till light kindling light" (594.6)—to regard the world from beneath "heliotrope ayelips" (533.2 ["eyelids" "turning to light"]).[24] We might see the "Colours" chapter taking place not simply inside the body of the *Wake*'s "sleeping giant," then, but more particularly inside of his "thundercloud periwig" or "haliodraping het" (246.7, 509.22); within the empty confines of this heady structure ("wig," "hat"), flashes of "likening" (hence "thundercloud"), iridescent "haloes" (hence "haliodraping"), and "sunlife" are threatening imminently to reappear (517.20). "Let Phosphoron proclaim"! (603.36); "then shalt thou see, seeing, the sight" (239.12).

As an alternate name which Joyce gave to these "twilight games" suggests ("Angels and Devils"), the creation of light in our hero's eyes throws him into primal and archaic conflict; while one half of his "tropped head," represented by "Chuff" (or Shaun the Post), "fleshe[s] light" (222.22), begins "making spaces in his psyche" (cf. 247.2), and so sends his ego sailing toward the well-lit, ordered patriarchal world constituted of objects and letters, the other half, represented by "Glugg" (or Shem the Penman), seeks to preserve the relaxed state of sleep by "blacking out" everything potentially visible (230.10), failing at "gazework," and engaging in the production of wonderfully turgid "blackmail" (240.12; cf. 229.26–28 [as opposed to visible mail]): "cokerycokes, it's his spurt of coal" (232.1 [not "port of call"]). The two antagonists in these "twilight games" therefore appear throughout the "Mime of Mick, Nick, and the Maggies" as the conflicted powers of Light and Darkness—as St. Michael and a Luciferian Old Nick, or as "Mick and Nick" (e.g., at 230.3–4)—who conduct a war over light in an "arimaining lucisphere" (239.34 ["Ahriman," the Zoroastrian god of evil, would correspond to the dark but light-bringing "Lucifer"]).[25] As elsewhere in the *Wake*, their struggles show our hero "ambothed upon by the very spit of himself" (230.2): the wording here tells us that he "am both" contestants in the visionary conflict (or "ambush") dramatized in the "Mime," "ha[ving]

"Meoptics"

help [or half] his crewn on" one of the two antagonists and "holf his crown on" the other (610.11–12 [this apparently wagered "crown" is less a monetary unit than a slang term for the "head"]).

To put all this in more orthodox language, the struggle specifically localized in our hero's eyes throughout the "Mime of Mick, Nick and the Maggies"—and elsewhere in his body everywhere else in the *Wake*—is simply that which structures any dream, during which a variable force impinging on the "tropped head"—pain, desire, a sensory disturbance—seeks to return the ego toward wakefulness by "giv[ing it] some sort of hermetic prod or kick to sit up and take notice" (470.2–3), while a concurrently acting counterforce, "the universal, invariably present and unchanging wish to sleep" (*ID*, 267–68), dissolves all such "upsits" (127.17 [and "upsets"]). More particularly, the two conflictive forces warring in our hero's eyes and "tropped head" throughout the "Colours" chapter might be construed as "shamed and shone" (75.11 ["Shem and Shaun"]), the first of whom, "thrust from the light, apophotorejected" (251.6–7), "is all in vincibles" (232.25–26 [because, like anyone's upsetting "shame," he is repressed and susceptible to capture neither in visible imagery nor in letters, though he emerges "invincibly" in dreams]); the second of whom "shines" familiarly in our hero's vision and self-conceptualizing consciousness. Or again, the two antagonists might be construed as the socially outcast and rejected "Shames" (93.21) or "Pain the Shamman" (192.23), "The Memory of Disgrace" (413.3 [roughly speaking, our hero's repressed desire and "pain"]), who never sees the light of day because he is "acheseyeld" from it (148.33 [not simply "exiled" but also, as the blinding "aches" in those "eyes" suggest, banished from conscious visibility]); and the socially adroit and adaptable "Show'm the Posed" (92.13 [our hero's ego]), who everywhere carries and delivers letters, thrives in the clearly seen, and "show and show" (233.10) and "show on show" (441.23).

The "bone of contention" over whom these two "crown pretenders" struggle during the *Wake*'s "twilight games" (256.3, 252.15 ["crown" = "head"]) is Issy, who is surely the most difficult of the *Wake*'s main "characters" to fathom. Like the "rainbow girls" who form her entourage, she seems to be associated with the dreamer's iritic colors—with "rainbows" or visible light—because she represents, in part, woman in an "ideal" and visual aspect ("ideals" are from the Gr. *eidô*, "to see"). A goodlooking looker with "looks" (548.28), "Isabelle" "is a belle" (556.7, cf. 446.7) and, as such, the object of HCE's specular desire. "Like the beauty of the image of the pose of the daughter of the queen of the Emperour of Irelande" (157.34–36), she therefore drifts through the *Wake* in the guises of so many female models, movie stars, and actresses—"like Mrs Cornwallis-West" (157.33–34 [a real stage-star of our hero's day, but also a version of Tristan's Isolde, betrothed to Mark of "Cornwall"])—that one might well devise a long "parroteyes list" (493.5) of the mimetically desired forms she assumes in the "parrot-like eyes" of our hero, a man old enough as to have long ago discovered his sexual "paradise lost." As "the imnage of Girl Cloud Pensive flout[ing] above" him (82.19–20 [her "image" always "in"'side]), "Miss Butys Pott" "floats" everywhere within his eyes (220.7), by day as by night, permanently informing his vision with the spectacle of a tantalizingly inaccessible beauty that "make[s] Envyeyes mouth water" (235.24–25 [hence "flout"]). In part, she represents the "dearstreaming faces" (148.27) of all the young and beautiful women whom our hero can wishfully look at all he wants, but never, never touch: these would include the pin-up girls of the early twentieth century, but also, and not least, his own daughter and her peers (those "rainbow girls"). As Issy herself puts it, "I'm only any girl, you lovely fellow of my dreams" (146.5–6), and—"how marfellows!" (148.24)—"I mean to make you suffer" (145.15).

In all her shifting forms, Issy reminds us that not simply the philosopher's space, but ideal beauty too falls together in the eye of the beholder, and so she becomes, to "her bleaueyedeal of a girl's friend" (384.24 [HCE]), "dadad's lottiest daughterpearl" (561.15). In "pearlagraph" (226.1), that is, she coats the interiors of HCE's "closed eyes" in much the same way, though in younger form, that opalescent "mother-of-pearl" films the closed chambers of shellfish: "I feel a fine lady . . . floating on a stillstream of isisglass," as it occurs to our "aglo-irismaimed" (486.23–24 [where the gelatinous substance "isinglass" would be a cipher for his "glycering" eyes, the "isis" in this "isinglass" the goddess ingrained within them; cf. 84.29, 247.36, 415.28, 460.21]). As a "character" distinct from our hero's real-world daughter, then, "Issy" is as much in the character of HCE's vision as a being in her own right ("you'll see if I'm selfthought" [147.8–9]). As fully constituent a part of his "eyeforsight" (417.23) as an organ like the retina or a physical property like light, she fills "Envyeye's" eyes with lifelong "jealousy" (note the Ger. *Eifersucht* ["jealousy"] in his "eyeforsight"); with "envy" (< the L. *invidia* ["hatred"], in turn from *invidere* ["to look askance at"], ultimately from *videre* ["to see"]); and also with a distracting "skysign of soft advertisement" (4.13–14). Anywhere she appears, even if imaginarily, she is capable of "softly adverting" his look from its proper business, and, in doing so, of exercising a disturbing telekinetic power over various parts of his body: "I turned his head on his same manly bust," for instance (527.31–32).[26]

As a figure held together of light in our "irismaimed's" eyes, Issy always appears in the *Wake* "in apparition with herself" (528.25), a visual image framed in a "shellback thimblecasket mirror [that] only can show" her "sister reflection" (561.16–17, 220.9 ["shellback" because this visual image takes form in "daughterpearl," within "shells" of sorts; "thimblecasket" because those shells are the eyes of a big body "dead to the world"]). She appears there never in a touchably sweaty "nightdress," but in a merely visible "lightdress, spunn of sisteen shimmers" (157.8, 159.9): perpetually inviting the kind of troublingly intactile contact that seeing as an erotic activity allows, she "flouts" into his vision, in other words—"Hey, lass!" (226.6)—like an unattainable form on the ceiling of the "Sistine" chapel (hence "sisteen"); like a poster-girl (27.18), accordingly dressed, for all practical purposes, in "boyproof knicks" (527.19–20); or like the untouchable apparition of a seductive Blessed Virgin: "Think of a maiden, Presentacion . . . Knock and it shall appall unto you!" (528.19, 21 [the *Annotations* refer us to "the apparition of the Virgin at Knock, in County Mayo, in 1879"]). Or else—"delightsome simply!" (144.13–14 [note the particle of "light"])—she "flouts" into HCE's "eyeforsight" as "Icy-la-Belle" (246.20) or "Icy" (104.10; cf. 145.11, 214.31), "poor chilled" (527.35 ["child"]), like a visible but cold and unapproachably remote "star" (L. *stella* [hence, in part, the many "Stellas" in the *Wake*]). Finally, too, Issy never appears in unmediated singularity, but—as "Alitten's looking" (528.4)—always in apostrophic relation to an adoring but absent male whose watchful eyes, like the inside of "Aladdin's lamp," are wishfully "alit" and heliotropically "turning to light": "I always had a crush on heliotrope," as she puts it (461.8–9), even while her reflection, obscured "under Pouts Vanisha Creme" (461.2–3 ["Pond's Vanishing Cream"]) "make[s] off in a thinkling" (256.4). "(I'm fading!)" (528.11).

What is true of Issy is true also of the "rainbow girls" who surround her: in the "Colours" chapter, they become "bright elects" (239.28 [visibly appealing "bride-elects"]), whom HCE tries "to catch . . . by the calour of [their] brideness" (223.5–6 ["colour," "brightness," and L. *calor*, "warmth"]). And attention to the severe "arch trouble" that they cause in our hero's "tropped head" (459.16 [that "arch," of course, the rainbow]) should clarify the nature of the "twilight games" in which they are all engaged. These begin when our hero's "Shame" (or Shem)—"the duvlin sulph" (222.25 ["devil himself"])—"cometh up as a trapadour" in the night's "invasable blackth" and tries to discover concealed color (224.25): if the wording here manifestly paints Shem as a "dour" and love-lorn "troubador" of sorts, it latently reveals him as a force emerging from somewhere "down under" in the body, below the visible and conscious surface of things, as if from beneath a "trap-door." Showing sinister "red devil in the white of his eye" (252.33–34) and acting as a perversely "light-bringing" Lucifer (hence the ignitable "sulphur" in that "duvlin sulph"), this "shameful" figure tries to force his way into the realm of the visible—so stirring our hero's vision towards wakefulness—by seeking to find "by gazework what their colours wear as they are all showen drawens up" (224.26–27). As these terms now suggest, the ultimate aim of "Shame's" devilish "gazework" is not simply the achievement of vision—the heliotropic turning of eyes to light with the discovery of "what colours were as they are shown drawn up"; more particularly and less innocently, "aye seize" (247.31 [as "eye" aggressively "sees"]), this "gazework" also seeks to bring to light the most invisibly occulted place in our hero's world: the "pink of panties" (248.36) and the space between Issy's "whiteyoumightcallimbs" (238.30), the "colours [girls] wear as their drawers show up."

    "Shames'" shameful activity, of course, automatically awakens the "watchful" counteragency in our hero's "tropped head"—disciplined "Show'm the Posed"—who acts as an archangelic defender of the patriarchal order first by censoring "Shames" and thrusting him back "down under" into the invisible ("To part from these, my corsets, is into overlusting fear" [222.29–30]); and, second, by displacing the visionary turmoil "Shames" has aroused in our hero's "tropped head" into respectably sublimated and deceptively "translace[d]" (233.9 [or "translated"]) forms ("Behose our handmades for the lured!" [239.10]). "In the moontime" (528.5), Issy herself, "who shone yet shimmers will be e'er scheining" (528.21–22), lies diffusely suspended between these two forces ("shone yet shimmers" = "Shaun" and "Shem"), her "appearance" or "look" (Ger. Erscheinung) throwing our hero into correspondingly troubled conflict. For as "dadad's lottiest daughterpearl" (561.15), Issy and her girl-friends (Fr. filles) everywhere film our paternal "magnate's" vision, "attracting" his eyes with an irresistibly "magnetic" force ("the horseshow magnete draws his field and don't the fillyings fly?" [246.23–24]); but as the references to magnetic repulsion, "flight," and "Lot" and the Cities of the Plain also suggest ("lottiest"), his looking, capable of "disrobing to the edge of risk" (238.16), is always subliminally charged with the danger of verging on the shameful: "Close your, notmust look!" (147.29; cf. 144.36–145.1); "Approach not for ghost sake! It is dormition!" (561.27–28).

If dreams are indeed symptomatic of difficulties that trouble our hero during his waking days, we might now see that the ways in which he "rather naightily" (222.35 ["naughtily" and "nightly"]) goes about "flesh[ing] light" and "making spaces in his psyche" in the Evening World inevitably tells us something about the ways in which he complementarily, if unconsciously, "makes spaces" and light in the Daily World and, in the process, envisions that world and the people with whom he lives. Judging from the way in which "he lay[s] there . . . like Lord Lumen [L. 'light'], coaching his preferred constellations" in the night (476.22–24 [to give the obvious examples]), we can infer that by day our hero looks at younger and rival males with envious distrust and at younger females with masked desire; but "lookwhyse" (369.34 [and "likewise"]), we can also infer that the presence or absence of any of these figures anywhere around him in the Daily World—or the corresponding presence of any such "invisible [because internalized] friends" (546.29)—would determine, with the repulsive flinch, glower, or magnetic pull they exerted on his eyes, the nature of his surroundings and the bearableness of the life that those surroundings enfold. Not simply do we see our hero, in these instances, succumbing to visionary fixations that unconsciously constrain a world of infinite possibility into preordained patterns; we also see him unconsciously determining the appearance of the world in which he lives. Through its study of "meoptics," the *Wake* is only anticipating the post-Wakean investigations of phenomenology and psychoanalysis in showing that our hero's seeing, even in its most dispassionate forms, is never a matter of purely passive Helmholtzian object-reception, but an actively chiasmic exchange in which his eyes seek out, frame, and light up objects of their own peculiar choosing—so to color them, "while gleam with gloom sw[ims] here and there" (600.30–31), in their own idiosyncratic and often doleful ways.[27] The *Wake*'s "meoptics" will seem solipsistic, finally, only to those who are determined to see others as discretely isolated and mere objects, rather than as responsive people in whom one has, even in the night, living and charged investments.

No such scientific account of vision as that which our culture has compounded in its manifold elaborations of the "Ideal Eye," to say this in another way, could possibly explain why five distinct individuals looking at the same fixed, gray object—the Wellington Memorial, say—might diversely see a stirring tribute to the British past, a good place for a picnic, the ideal receptacle for a stick of dynamite, nothing, or a stone phallus. Idiosyncratic subterranean connections like these, falling together in the underground of the body and lying at the heart of all visual experience, are much what classical optics overlooks and much what the *Wake*'s "meoptics" everywhere intricately explores; for these "infrarational" matters emerge most clearly in a night's dreams, when objects proper disappear "under the closed eyes" and when—to take the classic "Freudian" example of the snake whose appearance has only a little to do with a snake—homogeneously fixed visual relations are violated by emotionally charged and symbolically fluid ones. The *Wake*'s "meoptics" is an eroticized optics. In examining the anti-Newtonian "spectrem" that comes to light in the dark of its "aglo-irismaimed's" "blackeye lenses," it is calling compensatory attention to the unconscious underside of vision, the neglected half of the unitary relation that makes the seer and the seen (and anyone "can see the seen [not 'scene'] for seemself" [114.23]) aspects of each other.

The great playfulness of all the ciphers put to play in "the Mime of Mick, Nick and the Maggies" therefore undergoes a final transcendent lift from "the trivial to the apocalyptic," in Joyce's phrase (*JJ*, 546), when one notes that the chapter is structured by unending allusions to children's games and by dense references, through its evocations of the archangelic war between St. Michael and Lucifer, to pre-Genesis accounts of creation. These formal elements make it necessary to see that the space within which the "Colours" chapter unfolds—a pair of eyes turning heliotropically to light—is the primordial site in the flesh through which the world always and only wakens and comes to light, whether in infancy or in the morning, both in the era of genesis and now. If we take seriously those verses in Genesis, the orthodox book of Wakening, that show God first creating light and then making man in his own image, it therefore becomes possible to regard man, too, as a being capable of creating light—and all the more necessarily because the genetic order is consonant with the findings of color and vision theorists, who, however notorious "the history of the investigation of colour vision [may be] for its acrimony," all finally agree with Helmholtz and Clerk Maxwell ("Maxwell, clark" [130.11]) in locating color "not in the nature of light but in the constitution of man."[28] As Newton himself observed, even as he brought to light the mechanics of light, light "rays, to speak properly, are not coloured. In them is nothing else than a certain power or disposition to stir up a sensation of this or that colour. . . ."[29] Since the "sensation of this or that colour" is stirred up only in the human eye, however, and since nothing visible to that eye is not colored, we might now wonder about the degree to which the entire realm of the visible, by day as by night, falls together "only all in [the] eye" (118.17).

A student of its "meoptics" will find distributed everywhere throughout the *Wake*, as Joyce hinted, an elaborately developed "theory of colours" (*L*, I, 406). For as the book's passing fascination with the iris will now suggest, the "sevenal successivecoloured" hues of "the seamless rainbowpeel" (126.19, 475.13 [the colors of the spectrum]) are not inherently discrete and separate qualities, but a continuity: no sharp "seam" or line of demarcation in nature determines where indigo ends and where violet begins, or where visible violet fades off into "unseen [ultra]violet" (403.22). Needing to be "unmeshed," the "PRIMITIVE SEPT" of colors precipitates into difference only in tutored eyes (267.13ff., R1), where, as we "tell them apart, cadenzando coloratura" (226.30), the "telling" learned in childhood is crucial: "R is Rubretta and A is Arancia, Y is for Yilla and N for greeneriN. B is Boyblue with odalisque O while W waters the fleurettes of novembrance" (226.30–33 [note also, while cultivating this childhood "remembrance," how eyes must learn to unmesh the components of this "RAYNBOW" before they can distinguish letters; cf. 247.35–248.2]). Just as the colors of "the his heptachromatic sevenhued septicoloured" spectrum are not divisibly fragmented outside of the eye (611.5–6 [hence the deliberate fusion of the objectively definite and the subjective in "the his"]), so perhaps the whole of "light," a form of electromagnetic radiation with much the same physical properties as "herzian waves" (232.10–11, 331.23, 460.25), "xrays" (248.1, 51.25, 530.8), "wireless" waves, and all those other forms of invisible "light" whose "unseen" paths the *Wake* traces, as if in a cloud chamber, through its hero's "blackeye lenses." Washing and waving over everything visible, those warm, miraculous stuffs that we call "light" and "color," then—both spelled with quotation marks in the work of vision theorists—must be construed as carbureted mixtures of electromagnetic radiation and ocular flesh;[30] for electromagnetic radiation alone does not constitute and will not make "light" (ask any corpse), though the body's "flesh[ing]" and "glowworm"-like "headlight[s]" will.

The real theater of war within which both dreams and the *Wake*'s archangelically embattled "twilight games" are staged, then, is also the chaotic site in which the visible world always and only undergoes its genesis, the fleshy ground in which not so much "light," but "the seeds of light" are planted and, in "truetoflesh colours," "the soul of light" is born (593.20, 481.30, 235.7); "so see we so," at least, "as seed we sow. . . . And her troup came heeling, O" (250.28–30 [look hard enough and "heliotrope" will come to light here]). Set "in Evans's eye" (533.4–5 [where friend "Evans'," unlike "heaven's," is human]), and exploring the genesis "of our world's oldest light" (123.36 [the one first seen in childhood]), the "twilight games" of which the *Wake* as a whole is constituted take place at "lighting up o'clock sharp" (219.1), and not a minute sooner or later: that cryptic hour now turns out to be precise precisely because it designates the time of the creation of light.

"TRAUMSCRAPT"

From the way in which our hero is "ambothed upon by the very spit of himself" in the "Mime of Mick, Nick and the Maggies," (230.2 ["am both"]), we might now draw some conclusions about dream formation in the *Wake*. Study of the night's "meoptics," as will have become obvious in passing, has generated an essential distinction between the "manifest" and the "latent" contents of dreams. Necessarily, the dreamer lies in a split condition and becomes "of twosome twiminds" to himself during dreams (188.14), the consciously "watchful" and letter-carrying half of his "tropped head" (Shaun) credulously watching and scanning—indeed, participating in— those larger-than-life scenes thrown against the backs of the eyelids and illusively assumed to lie "out there," while what the dreamer is in fact seeing, if not black eyelids, are diffuse "fleshes" of retinal "likening" motivated at the "backsight[s]" his eyes (249.2) by a malicious counteragent (Shem) who is pulling the wool over them (see 164.4–5, 167.8–14, 299.4–6). "Two dreamyums in one dromium? Yes and no error" (89.3). "There being two sights for ever a picture," then (11.36)—one "visible" and therefore consciously "wiseable" (16.24), the other "all in vincibles" and therefore in need of being "decoded" (232.25–26)—the dreamer assumes *a double focus* during visual dreams (349.13), by acting as both the unconsciously canny producer ("Shem") and the consciously baffled consumer ("Shaun") of the spectacle he beholds: "his producers are they not his consumers?" (497.1–2). And, to illustrate the character of the "two sights" this "double focus" allows, is not the repulsive stranger in the dream who lusts after "the dotter of his eyes" (372.3 ["the daughter of his eyes"]) in fact "the dotter of his [own] eyes?"

Without necessary recourse to authority, the *Wake*'s "meoptics" will now turn out to throw all manner of light on the structural character of dreams— in ways that might most elaborately be illustrated if we recall dreams like

"Meoptics"

the one apocryphally attributed to Muhammad, in which the dreamer "sees" and reads written words. Dreams like these would surely have elicited Joyce's special attention because they would have allowed him to study his governing subject, sleep, in conjunction with his working medium, letters; and they would invariably have raised perplexing questions about the visual forces at play in the "blackeye lenses" of a person who dreams of reading written signs. Who writes these signs (cf. 107.36ff.)? On what medium? And from what "point of view" does one see them "in fact under the closed eyes"? Since it is "true [that] there was in nillohs dieybos as yet no lumpend papeer in the waste" (19.31–32)—where the Latin *in nullis diebus* ("in no days") and *in nihilo* ("in nothing") "describe the night itself," while the absence of the German *Lumpenpapier* ("rag paper") tells us that sleep is refreshingly paperless—it would be inaccurate to think of words unconsciously appearing in dreams in the same way that we think of words consciously written on paper. Like the buried letter that appears "under the closed eyes" throughout chapter I.v of the *Wake* (107.28), every letter appearing in our "blurried" "irismaimed's" nightlife "is only all in his eye" (118.17).

According to one line of speculation inevitably issuing from the *Wake's* study of "meoptics," we might therefore conceive of an agent internal to the body agitating the "rods and cones of this even's vision" into wakefulness during visual dreams—and doing so not haphazardly, but with such weird precision as to etch there, graphically, people, scenes, and even alphabetic characters of a sufficiently credulity-gripping lifelikeness as to convince the dreamer of their reality. Dreams would be produced, according to this understanding, exactly as is "the letter" that surfaces recurrently in *Finnegans Wake*; for in one of its earliest manifestations, "The letter! The litter!" is "of eyebrow pencilled" (93.24–25). Written not on paper with pencil, in other words, but on the "tissue peepers" of the eyes with "eyebrow pencil," this deceptive "letter" and all the signs constituting it would resemble exactly the dream in being *a graphic representation* written in the medium of ocular flesh, where, as "flesh" turns into "flash" and that "flash becomes word" (267.16), a force in the body "make[s] a shine" in the eye (222.24 ["a sign"]), in the process generating a vast and baffling "mascarete" (206.14 [a "masquerade" inscribed with "mascara"]). For an illustration of how "all sorts of makeup things" (625.5 [like "dreams"]) apply to the eye, see figure 8.4.

The diagram shows that no artist in the world has so fine a medium with which to work as Shem the Penman, that half of the *Wake's* sleeper said to be responsible for scripting its "letter" with "eyebrow pencil." In the case of visual dreams, of course, we are considering the way in which this dark "Autist" (434.35 [or "autistic artist"]) inscribes his "traumscrapt" (623.36)—or "transcript" of a "dream" (Ger. *Traum*)—on only a few square inches of the flesh, the "tissue peepers" of the eyes; but elsewhere in the *Wake* we learn that this devilish "plaidboy" (27.9 [a "playboy" who makes body-covering patterns like "plaids"]) is given to "making encostive inkum out of the last of his lavings and writing a blue streak over his bourseday shirt" (27.10–11 [note—by way of the "cost," "income," and Fr. *bourse*, "money"—the economy with which Shem writes on this "birthday suit"; note also, by way of that thick "blue streak," his penchant for obscenity]). In a passage central to the "Shem" chapter, even more elaborately, we find this carnal "Autist" making ink out of his excrement, ostensibly—"produc[ing] nichthemerically from his unheavenly body a no uncertain quantity of obscene matter" (185.29–30)—and, with this "ink . . . out of his depth" (186.17), "wr[iting] over every square inch of the only foolscap available, his own body, till by its corrosive sublimation one continuous present tense integument slowly unfold[s]" (185.35–186.1). The details linking these passages are important because they show that one aspect of the writing which asocialized and banished "Shames" or "Pain the Shamman" produces is somatic: Shem's writing is symptom-making, the most efflorescent variety of which is the dream, the most common of which is mere living.

The letter that Shem creates, like the dream itself, originates in the "depths" of an "unheavenly body" (one that becomes evident, like a "heavenly body" or HCE's, only at night). Or again, as the *Wake* elsewhere describes it, this letter comes from a world "down under" (321.32, 450.1) and is wirelessly transmitted to Shaun the Post by an identical twin "brother" who "lives sameplace in the antipathies of austrasia" (489.10; 163.15; 488.21). Though the wording here seems to situate Shem in "the Antipodes," in the criminal colonies of "Australia," and though it seems to make him a "Cabler" of telegrams (488.21; 489.8–9), we should recall that the manifest appearances of dreams are ludicrously deceiving; latently, the wording is telling us simply that this dark "Autist" ("autistic" forces are internal to the body) lives in exactly the "sameplace" as the dreamer's ego and literate self—in "his own body"—although "samewhere" (347.10) in its "antipathies" (Eng. "aversions") or "antipodes" (Eng. "opposites"), "down under," beneath consciousness and visibility.[31] This "autist," then, under the "*oleas* Mr Smuth (434.36 [note that "smut"]), requires an "alias" (L. "other") because he stands in relation to the dreamer's consciously literate self

("Smith") as his identical "other" (252.14, 408.17, 25 ["brother"]) — exactly in the same way that Shem stands to Shaun, a "Siamese" twin to his "soamheis brother" (425.22 [as I "so am he is" too]). Since this "autist" "down under" in the body does not carry letters, however, he transmits his fleshy "traumscrapt" into the dreamer's letter-stuffed head and his eyes (cables it up to "Show'm the Posed") through channels absolutely imperceptible to the senses, as if by radiotelegraphy; and so he becomes, unlike any pedestrian "writer," a "wreuter of annoyimgmost letters," in "blackhand," who moreover "smells cheaply of Power's spirits" (495.2, 4): "Reuters" names a wireless agency, the "blackhand" "keep[s] black!," while those "annoying" and "anonymous" communiques, like dreams themselves, reveal dark and hemmed-in "Powers" and "spirits" that purvey, not surprisingly, "a no uncertain quantity of obscene matter" (not necessarily excrement).

Now the "NIGHTLETTER" that this "Autist" living "down under" in the dreamer's "antipathies" transmits into his letter-carrying head may "uphere" (222.31 ["appear" "up here" in the Daily World]) most clearly in dreams (308.16 [this "NIGHTLETTER," again, a radiotelegram sent in the night]) — but only because *dreams are visible;* all of the passages under our attention apprise us, however, that the "traumscrapt" Shem produces is written not simply with "eyebrow pencil" on those few square inches of flesh localized in the "tissue peepers," but "all over" "every square inch" of "his own body." Since this "traumscrapt" is moreover "produce[d] nichthemerically" (185.29) — where the English "nychthemeron" (< Gr. *nycht* ["night"] and *hêmera* ["day"]) designates "a period of twenty-four hours" (*OED*) — we should see it playing into our hero's life from the unconscious world "down under" not simply in the eyes and not simply during his dreams, but everywhere "in the flesh" through every minute of every day and night, so that it would generate, as it manifested itself on other "square inch[es] of the only foolscap available, his own body," less easily legible, more widely dispersed, but ultimately life-containing "traumas" (hence again "traumscrapt"), whose totality would be the "one continuous present tense integument" of the lived body, HCE, itself. In the play of all these ciphers, as will have become evident, the *Wake* is elaborating on and broadening the psychoanalytical account of dream formation.

According to that account, dreams are produced by the same networks of unconscious thoughts that erupt, in waking life, in somatic symptoms — in "palpitations, groundless anxiety, phobias, depression, paralysis, or sensory disturbances" — and also in those underlying and symptom-producing "defects in the field of personal relationships, attitudes to work, love, and so on which are practically speaking much more disabling."[32] In *Finnegans Wake*, where we find our hero's unconscious "alter ego" (see 463.6–7)—his "autistic" "other"—"writing a blue streak all over his bourseday shirt," dreams *are* in the nature of symptoms because they arise in HCE's "blackeye lenses" when the murky "Autist" "down under" in "his own body," wielding a carnal "eyebrow pencil," tattoos the "tissue peepers" with stigmatic retinal signs whose right reading would show our hero's body and life in conflict with themselves.[33]

From yet another perspective, these considerations enable us to see why *Finnegans Wake*, as an "imitation of the dream-state," is also, and necessarily, a representation of the body rather than of a life observed (through the eyes), narrated (by the tongue), or imperfectly understood (by the brain). Because the dreams that occur to our hero arise from the same sources "down under" in his body as do the interimplicated symptomatic knots that constitute that body and its life, "reading the Evening World" as it is literately reconstructed in *Finnegans Wake* is finally equivalent to "reading off [the] fleshskin" (229.30) of the "stigmataphoron" (606.27 [Gr. "thing bearing tattoo marks"]) depicted in the "relief maps" of the night— and all the more particularly because that body, as *The New Science* shows, is a man-made institution everywhere informed by and with language. From his dreams, accordingly (the dream, for example, of a crime in the Phoenix Park), a reader of the "the Evening World's" "traumscrapt" can infer a great deal about the "traumas" that make up HCE's troubled life in the Daily World: we know that "he's knots in his entrails," for instance (231.35 [and also in his groin]); comparable "sobsconcious inklings shadowed [elsewhere] on his soulskin" (377.28);[34] and so "many scalds and burns and blisters, impetiginous sore and pustules" covering his body everywhere (189.32–33) that they would constitute, if studied in their totality, the "one continuous present tense integument" of his body and life as a totality. In *Finnegans Wake*, as in "that letter selfpenned to one's other" which is the dream (489.33–34), "style, stink [ink] and stigmatophoron are of one sum in the same person" (606.27–28).

That visual dreams entail the partial wakening of the eye would explain their lifelikeness—the *Wake*'s "irismaimed" has "the eye of a gull" and believes anything he sees (377.4–5)—but also their underlying opacity. For what HCE must *really* be seeing while "really" seeing all those symptomatic shapes and scenes playing through his "blackeye lenses" is simply heavy "lid

"Meoptics"

efter lid" (509.27 [Da. *efter,* "behind"]). He "knows de play of de eyelids," then (234.16–17 [the black American idiom underlining their blackness]) not simply because they lie directly and everywhere in his line of vision, but also because they are erratically able, as "heliotrope ayelips" (533.2), to turn to light. "His eyelids are painted" on these occasions (248.16), so to form a kind of screen against which "play[s] of de eyelid" and "Movies from the innermost depths" are made "televisible" (194.2–3, 265.11): "and roll away the reel world, the reel world, the reel world" (64.25–26).[35] During the envisioning of these "moving pictures" we therefore "leave Astrelea" (64.23, 565.6 [the "astral" "lea" strewn with the night's "heavenly bodies"]) and, rising from the unconscious world "down under" with the *Wake*'s "iris-maimed" (hence "Australia"), we "*Cherchons la flamme!*" (64.28 [not only *la femme,* but also a world of fierily living color]).

Contemplation of the eyelids, however, also returns us to the night's "invasable blackth," within whose depths our hero lies cozily enwrapped in "his sevencoloured's soot" (277.1); unlike the "sevencolored suit" owned by Joseph, the Biblical knower of dreams, this one would be "sootably" "Black and All Black," and it would enfold a figure who has once again become "one heap lumpblock" (277.2–3)—a "lump," who just lies there, envisioning as honestly as "Diogenes" with "his diagonoser's lampblick" (290.21–22 [Ger. *Blick,* "look"]) only black "lampblack" (114.10–11). Since "lampblack," like a "black-lamp," would fill the "eyebulbs" with shadows rather than light, these "meoptical" terms—and yet others—remind us of the great and underlying drag which "invasable blackth" exerts on everything in sleep, beneath dreamed colors, and at the *Wake.*[36] They also return us to the occulted interiors of HCE's "blackeye lenses," within which there is a great deal more to see.

"ONE EYEGONBLACK"

As a way of demonstrating simultaneously the versatile power with which "the Autist" in the body writes all over one's "tissue peepers," the dark character of the presentations his "eyebrow pencil" draws, and the *Wake*'s peculiar but distinct "very similitude," we will now play some "flesh and blood games, written and composed and sung and danced by Niscemus Nemon" (175.31–33), or Shem the Penman, characterized here as a "no one" (L. *Nemo*) whom "we do not know" (L. *nescimus*). For everybody has a dark "Autist" like Shem living "sameplace" "down under" inside of him; and there are concrete ways of showing, "in the flesh," how actively and "nich-themerically" he inscribes his "traumscrapt" all over one's "bourseday shirt." Engagement in his "flesh and blood games" will therefore serve the additional purpose of showing how a proper site of identification with a hero like HCE, "the presence (of a curpse)," is in "the present (of course)," and "in the flesh."

In reconstructing the night "naturalistically of course, from the blink-point of so eminent a spatialist" as HCE (149.18–19)—where that "blink" "blanks" out the German *Blickpunkt* ("point of view") to leave it only an empty "blankpoint" (468.17)—Joyce found himself of necessity modifying the laws of literary naturalism, and in much the same way that quantum physicists rewrote the laws of nature in the early twentieth century. "I am working out a quantum theory about it," he writes in a passage ostensibly exploring the words *tantum* (L. "to such a degree") and *talis* (L. "of such a kind"), "for it is really most tantumising state of affairs" (149.34–36). Now quantum physics shows that the laws describing the smooth operations of the physical universe break down into all manner of radical strangeness when one examines events that take place at very high speeds, over very small intervals of time, and in very small places. So, comparably, the conventions of naturalistic representation break down radically when one begins to consider—as Joyce had already done in the "Lotus-Eaters" episode of *Ulysses*—the quantumizing effect on "point of view" of the trivial little eye-blink, during which one's *Blickpunkt* goes blank as the "eye goes black" for "one eyegonblack" (16.29 [the Ger. *ein Augenblick* literally means "one eye-blink," but idiomatically "one instant"]).

Thousands of times a day as one traffics in the Daily World of which the two maps of Dublin and Europe are representative, one's eyelids pass down over the eyes, blotting out everything and overwhelming the visual field; and thousands of times a day,"His Sparkling Headiness" (236.5–6), bent on conquest of the empirical, fails to see what is really there in front of his eyes. A "most tantumising state of affairs"—"really"—that one almost never sees the only thing that stays absolutely constant in visual space: "his own body," "the presence (of a curpse)," as it becomes visible in the form of "lashbetasselled lids" relegated to unconsciousness every time one overlooks the underlid (474.8). One can always avoid facing the Heraclitean torrent of the world, but one cannot never see the backs of one's own eyelids. "Bring[ing] to mind the . . . out of sight," then (200.25–26 [or, in its more common idiom, waking the dead]), the *Wake* now invites its reader to become conscious of "de play of de eyelids," in part because that play makes

"Meoptics"

sharply visible a conflictual process that impinges everywhere on the body but that elsewhere and largely has nothing to do with vision at all. For Joyce, moreover, "de play of de eyelids" would have raised the question of how one might render what one really sees "out there" in nature—"naturalistically of course, from the blinkpoint"—when English has no term for the obverse of the eyelid and when works like Helmholtz's *Physiological Optics* hardly note their presence. Through its "meoptics," the *Wake* prescriptively corrects the oversight.

"What the blinkins is to be seen" in "one eyegonblack" (568.1–2 [apart from its passive form])? At a quantum level, the "eyegonblack" "reveil[s]" (220.33 [as it "veils"]) the essential discontinuity and constructedness of the visual space within which scientific and literary naturalism are mapped out, as against the underlying ubiquity of the body. Just take "a dun blink round . . . and you skull see" (17.17–18): as that "blink" renders "Dublin" "dun" (a "dun blink" is a dark one), it illuminates the interior of your "skull." Study of the "eyegonblack," then, shows the visual field represented in the two maps of Dublin and Europe incessantly flipping "skinside out" (507.6) into the spatiality represented in the two carnal maps of the night, where vision undergoes momentarily dark revision and then emerges again, having enjoyed in the incremental "blackout" a slight "solstitial pause for refleshmeant" (617.14, 82.10 [at the "solstice," as during the eyeblink and the night, the sun seems to stop]).

"What the blinkins is to be seen" in the almost instantaneous "eyegonblack" therefore compels attention throughout the *Wake* because only matters of "degree" and "kind" ("tantum," "talis") differentiate a wink *per se* from "a winkle of sleep" (199.11–12), or "a wink of sleep" from forty: sleep, in a book where "wink's the winning word" (249.4), is only "forty winks"—perhaps fifty—endured in unbroken succession (28.18, 495.22, 561.34, 595.8), a form of sustained and involuntarily enforced exposure to the backs of the eyelids ("I could snap them when I see them winking at me in bed" [148.14]), as to the rest of the body whose presence one repressively overlooks by day. "Clos[ing the] blinkhard's eye" (109.21 [and "the blackguard's"]) as darkly as a "hard blink" does, the night reconstructed in the *Wake* therefore becomes "a winker's wake" (514.20 [as opposed to a winkless dead man's]), the "winter" underlying that "winker" designating the time of "hibernation."

Study of the "eyegonblack" in turn raises the question of why one blinks at all or, by sleeping, succumbs to "forty winkers" (495.22 [again those subliminal "winters"]). According to those who have studied "the inception and the descent and the endswell of Man" (150.30–31 [the "new science" of evolution is just the study of how a multitude of Finnegans wake]), land-dwelling animals sport "those lashbetasselled lids on the verge of closing time" (474.8) in order to help them moistly "reflesh" (and so "refresh") the eyes in surroundings that can easily grow dry and grating; eyelids attach themselves to the bodies of animals that do not live under water. The "eyegonblack" therefore *liquidates* visual space in two senses of that word, dissolving the iritic colors as it also, with the effect of Noah's deluge, floods the visible world with the "saltwater" (386.19, passim), in particular, of "meye eyesalt" (484.5; 222.27). During both the blink and the longer "winker" of sleep, then, "the length of the land lies under liquidation (floote!) and there's nare a hairbrow nor an eyebush on [the] glaubrous phace of Herrschuft Whatarwelter" (12.7–9; cf. 3.13–14): the opaque "phace" (or "face") in this phrasing conceals "daylight" (Gr. *phaos*) and a pair of "eyes" (Gr. *phaea*) that are sunk in a "watery world" (452.30) which becomes visible only within an "aquaface" (3.14); while the English "glabrous" ("without hair") pulls us not simply beneath the surface of the visible world, but beneath the "hirsute" surface of vision itself, into the space below the two "eyebrows" ("hairbrow," "eyebush"). Here, "eye sinks" (336.30 ["I think"]), in pure "blink pitch" (93.4 [a "blink's" "black pitch"]), the visible "regginbrow" (3.14 [the "rainbow" "in brow"]) comes to its ends as a vast "waterworld" comes to light (367.26): "what a welter" of "tar," "water," and "tarwater" in this "Whatarwelter" (Ger. *Welt*, "world")! "Search a fling did die near sea" (223.12–13): "did die" rather than "did I" because "eyewinker" (320.27 [a visually liquidated "Earwicker"]) has himself been "liquidated"; "such a thing did I never see" largely because "eye" was unconscious of it.

As these spellings moreover imply, the "language" of *Finnegans Wake* now becomes broadly "linguified" (228.21 ["liquefied"]), its "lingo" dissolving into "linquo" (178.2 ["liquid lingo"]), in order to represent what "eye sinks" when "the length of the land lies under liquidation." For the "meoptical" universe of the *Wake's* night is one of both "wet and low visibility" (51.3–4); and if extended mannerisms in the book warn us to "keep black!," others encourage us only "to sea" (50.35; 23.12, 223.13 [to "see" only saltwater]). "Let [anyone] blink for himself" (468.17 [not "think"]): if with wakeful "eyes whiteopen" you always and everywhere see something like "dear dirty Dublin," during the "eyegonblack" "[you] sea" something that might more accurately be painted as "teary turty Taubling" (23.12, 7.5–6)—where those

"Meoptics"

saline "tears" liquidate and wash away the "dirt" as you momentarily become a specular "Taubling" (Ger. *taub*, "empty"). "Lid efter lid" "under the closed eyes," "[you] sea" only "that tare and this mole, your tear and our smile" (509.26)—"tar," like a "mole," though to the fluid background strain of "The Tear and the Smile in Thine Eyes" (lyrics from yet another of Moore's *Irish Melodies*).[37] At a quantum level, then, the eyeblink finds one "whipping his eyesoult" (222.26–27 ["lashing" them in "eyesalt," as if "weeping his eyes out"]): "they nearly cried (the salt of the earth!)" (454.24–25). What one will largely "sea," "mid bedewing tears under those wild wet lashes" (463.9–10), is the liquidation of the world in a form of warm "saltwater" that Joyce calls "the tears of night" (158.20–21). One says "adieu" to the visible by closing the eyes: "Ah dew! Ah dew!" (158.20), "*O! O! O! Par la pluie!*" (158.23–24). And as drops of "refleshing" "dew," "rain" (Fr. *pluie*), and "thrain tropps" "liquidate" (484.4 [Ger. *Tränen*, "tears"]), a little "umbrella" (Fr. *parapluie*) furls forth its shade. When the *Wake*'s "irismaimed" puts "the length of the land under liquidation," accordingly, "the tears of night beg[i]n to fall" everywhere over the world in which he dwells (158.20–21), so to transform it into a kind of "Tear nan-Ogre" (479.2)—an "other world" manifestly like the mythical Irish "Tír na nÓg," but one that actually comes to light within the "teary" eyes of the "blacked-out" "ogre" depicted in the relief maps. Dead to the world, this sleeping giant has become "tearly belaboured by Sydney and Alibany" (489.31–32 ["dearly beloved"]): because his vision has gone "elsewhere" in the night (L. *alibi*), somewhere "down under" ("Sydney" and "Albany" are in Australia), his closed and "liquidated" eyes "labour" darkly in "tears."

Whenever "the water of the face has flowed" so deeply as this in the *Wake* (361.35 [that "face" being HCE's]), its "blottyeyed" "irismaimed" (361.36) undergoes a form of partial visual regression to the era of his genesis (hence the evocation of that time when the spirit also "moved upon the face of the waters" [Genesis 1:2]). Or, more particularly, since any closure of the eye evolutionarily "liquidates" vision and reforms it beneath "saltwater," the eyeblink returns the visible world to "primeval conditions" "far below on our sealevel" (599.10, 463.4–5): during the "eyegonblack," "I am highly pelaged . . . to see" (358.10–11 [Gr. *pelagos*, "sea"]). Our "tearly belaboured" "irismaimed" therefore "pours a laughsworth of his illformation over a larmsworth of salt" (137.34–35 [Fr. *larme*, "tear"]) by tending periodically to envision, in his sleep, many "floods" (330.10), "floodplain[s]" (36.15), "invisible" "saltlea[s] with flood" (81.1, 17–18), and comparable "saltings" that are never quite "wiseable" (17.20, 16.24 [or "visible"]). All that he is really able "to sea" at such moments in the night (50.35), as his "murty odd oogs" (88.17) rock eerily "through his old tears" (381.20–21) in "seeless socks" (468.25) void of iritic light and all sight of earth, are unplumbed, salt, and tractless "sees" (416.30 [or "seas"]): like the Netherlands generally, the Dutch *oog* ("eye") in these "murky" "oogs" would lie somewhere below saltwater level, while the spelling of "sea" as "see" suggests that the object of HCE's vision here is simply saline "see" water (cf. 366.16, 375.34–35, 445.26, 588.15).

As happens in the dream-void parts of anyone's nightlife, the visual dimensions of whole sections of *Finnegans Wake* fall together inside of deeply liquidated and very "fishy eyes" like these (559.23), which have regressively passed out "to see" (366.16 ["to sea"]).[38] This is the case not only in parts of the *Wake*'s opening chapter, for instance (cf. 3.13–14, 7.5–6, 12.7–9); but also through extended sections of "Anna Livia Plurabelle" (where "H. C. E. **h**as a **c**odfish **ee**" [198.8–9]); and throughout all of chapter II.iv, which is surely one of the weirder items in the book. There, beneath the forms of four old men "crossing their sleep [and the sea] by the shocking silence" (393.35–36), we find HCE moving through an "invinsible" "waterworld" (367.25, 26) while peering through "the salty catara off [of] a windows" (395.11 [the "cataract" blinds]) and "behold[ing] the residuance of a delugion" (367.24). As the spelling of "delugion" suggests, however, the "deluge" (13.36, 86.24, 214.7, 315.13) or "universal flood" (388.12) that he "sea[s]" here and at comparable moments in his sleep is more in the nature of a "delugium" (502.30 [or "delusion"]) than a "deluge" pure and simple. Terms like these suggest that "his deepseeing" "deepseepeepers [have] gazed and sazed and dazecrazemazed into [their] dullokbloon rodolling olosheen eyenbowls" (75.13, 389.26–28)—where the phrase echoes a line from Byron's *Childe Harold* ("Roll on, thou deep and dark blue ocean, roll") in order to show the *Wake*'s "irismaimed" visually lost in the "great deap sleap" of "the Deepsleep Sea" (277.13, 37.18 [all these terms point the "deep seeing" of "deep sleep" into a "Deep Sea"]). When "the length of the land lies under liquidation," accordingly, our "seelord" (325.16 [not "sealord"]) becomes a kind of Noah again, passing through a world everywhere visually liquidated and "inundered" (127.5) as his "gropesarching eyes" search in vain for any sight of earth, any iritic light, or "any shape at see" (375.34–35 ["ship at sea"]): "What ravening shadow! What dovely line!" (357.16–17; cf. 358.4–5 [the colors "raven" and "dove" are black and dark]). And Joyce's reader, himself equipped with the necessary "fathomglasses to find out all the fathoms" in the "saltwater" (386.16–17, 19), can again "blink for himself" to "feel what I mean" (468.17–18): he will be seeing "real life behind the floodlights" (260.F3 [these "floodlights" the eyes; cf. 221.28, 318.6, 330.10, 494.2, and 498.24–25]).

Having "define[d] the hydraulics of common salt" (256.28), we might proceed further in an "analysis" of the liquidating properties of eye-closure by trying to "analectralyze that very chymerical combination, the gasbag where the warderworks. And try to pour somour heiterscene up thealmostfere" (67.8–10). These "chimerical" "waterworks" would be the eyes of our hero (the voluble "gasbag" who is their only "warder"), while the "hydrogen" (or "heiterscene") that they release into "the atmosphere" of the Evening World would be one of their chief effects. Just as "electrolysis" reduces a compound into its constituent "chemical" elements, so a good "analectralysis" of the eye finds vision darkly liquidated into the "chymerical" elements of black, chaotic light, vitreous "juice" (Gr. *chymos*), and lots of "heiterscene"—or, better yet, "linguified heissrohgin" (228.21 ["liquefied hydrogen"])—but only because "hydrogen," from the French *hydrogène* ("water-producing"), does exactly what the eyes do. Eye closure and tear production, as these lines suggest, are causes and effects of each other: one blinks to liquidate the eyes, while the welling-up of tears complementarily induces the blink.

It is at a point so "tearly belaboured" that one would do well "to pour somour heiterscene up thealmostfere" ("some more," "some our"); for as the modulation of "hydrogen" into "heiter scene" now suggests (Ger. *heiter*, "merry"), a good strong burst of "laughtears" (15.9) will also liquidate vision and make the "eye go black"—ultimately to raise questions like those posed by Freud in *Jokes and Their Relation to the Unconscious*, as to whether one can laugh and think at the same time, or whether the power that erupts in "laughtears" annihilates consciousness, at a quantum level, as deeply as does sleep. Anyone "weeping like fun" (558.24) will discover not only that his *"blink points unbroken on"* (419.1 [Ger. *Blickpunkt*, "point of view," *umgebrochen*, "broken down"]); but also that he has been ephemerally translated "during [the] blackout" (617.14) into an *"in risible universe"* (419.3 ["invisible" because "risible"]) indistinct from that experienced everywhere in the Evening World. Because a good laugh can cause the "loss of reason," control, vision, and the head all "togutter" (332.12, 517.14 ["together"]), "man's laughter" modulates into "manslaughter" at the *Wake* (433.29), having the power to "paralyze" and leave one "stricken"—"with the whooping laugh at the age of the loss of reason" (423.26 [that "laugh," too, is contagious]). If only ephemerally, then, the liquidating experience of "laughtears" allows one to enter the "eyewitless foggus" of HCE, now "Mister Funn" (5.12), who seems to have "collaughsed" (580.7–8), "Drowned in the Laffey" (420.34 ["drowned in laughter"]), or, at the least, from "dyin loffin" (420.13), severely "tropped head."[39] "From the poignt of fun where I am crying to arrive you at" (160.32–33 [not "point of view"]), "laughtears" too will liquidate the eye, reducing vision yet further to one of its "chimerical" elements—this one "hilarity," as opposed to "tristesse" (21.12). And in what is only another matter of quantumized kind and degree ("tantum," "talis"), it should now be clear that anything at all conceivable as "objective" vision is always subliminally mediated by a thin film of tears—ocular "hydrogen"—the release of either of whose extremes can alter elementally at any one instant one's seeing of the world: the world looks hysterically different, and closer to the way it looks in the Evening World—"really"— when viewed through a film of "tears" or "laughtears."

It should also now be evident that all of the "meoptical" properties brought to light through study of the "eyegonblack" visibly "reveil," at a quantum level, the powerful determination with which the whole involuntary force of sleep seeps up into the day, everywhere to underlie and determinatively impinge on the real. No one consciously decides when or when not to surrender to "tears" or "laughtears," when or when not to lower "those lashbetasselled lids on the verge of closing time" by succumbing to "forty winks" or by "blinking upon this earthlight" (449.7). Blinking overpowers the eye as autonomically and involuntarily as do sleep and dreams, without external stimulus or any calculated decisiveness; the blink-reflex tugs at the wakened eye even in the dark, and even when one deliberately keeps one's eyelids closed in the dark.[40] Like the retina, then, the eyelids and the tearsacs become only two more of countless locales "in the flesh" on which the murky "Autist" "down under" inside everyone, "wr[iting] over every square inch of the only foolscap available, his own body" (185.35–36), etches out in the medium of living flesh a visible sign, "of eyebrow pencilled" (93.25), ultimately to glyph the face with the kind of opaquely legible "expression"—certainly not literary—that can be seen, for instance, when the person to whom one is delivering one's harangue fails to keep his eyelids open, fails to let them blink in relief, or bursts into tears, so to convey the news, though not in so many words, that one is being tedious, alarming, or painful.

In the writing on the lid, one sees the individual "autistically" (and "artistically") retailoring his body, its vision, and the world that takes shape in that vision to suit his needs and himself. For at every waking moment, lidded vision is taxed with a variety of heavily competing options: fully alert, at one extreme, one can overlook the underlid and stare into the face of the present; or, not alert at all, one can fall back into the body and watch the "blinketey blanketer" (603.31) "blanket" the "blinketey blank" world—as the *Wake*'s still-sleepy hero does close to daybreak when, to avoid the irritation of gathering sunlight and the news it carries of another day of work, he "blankets" his head and resumes a placid "eyewitless foggus" on the dark. "The mauwe that blinks you blank is mostly Carbo," then (232.2–3 [mostly "black," often "blank," sometime "mauve"]) because it plays a flexibility into one's negotiations with the real, allowing one at any instant, in what is only another matter of kind and degree ("tantum," "talis"), to "tare it or leaf it" (118.23 ["take it or leave it"]), like "The Man That Broke The Bank at Monte Carlo" after he broke the bank. The wide-ranging degree of this flexibility becomes not unusually apparent when one looks at any "dried ink [on a] scrap of paper" (118.33), as now, or otherwise meditates on the strangely soporific powers of academic Literature ("You're getting hoovier, a twelve stone hoovier, fullends a twelve stone **h**oovier, in your **c**orpus **e**ntis"—L. "body of being"—and also, by way of the Du. *hooved*, in your "head" [376.14–15]). The adaptable little "eyeblink" allows one vigilantly to scan the "leaf" of the page whenever one wants (hence "leaf it"), or to black it out while surrendering to the daydream, as if to turn it all to "tar" and to "tear" it to shreds ("tare it"). At a quantum level, "eye sinks," sleep and the "Autist" "down under" are tugging away at one's "bourseday shirt" right now.

As a marginal locale in the body incessantly taxed with conflicting options, the eyelids become an ideal site for the inscription of symptomatic "traumscrapt," and so become a few "square inches of the only foolscap available, his own body," on which the "Autist" from "down under," again wielding that resourceful "eyebrow pencil," can leave "sobsconcious inklings shadowed on [the] soulskin" (377.28). Anyone adept at "reading off his fleshskin" (229.30) will find these darkly legible "inklings" everywhere he looks in the Daily World if he examines the supple forms that eyeblinking takes—in the nervous twitches and tics of "tickeyes" (43.9), in leadenly drooped lids, in eyes narrowed in suspicion or anxiety, in "Irish eyes of welcome . . . smiling daggers" (176.22–23), in eyes that sparkle "in the twinkly way" (148.13–14), in "fleurty winkies" (561.34), in "tears," "laughtears," and so forth. Even among people of imperturbable countenance (let's "Show'm the Posed"), the eyelids show the imprint of these infinitely variable symptomatic signs; the longer and more rapidly the "Autist" in the body pulls down "those lashbetasselled lids on the verge of closing time," the longer one is "caughtnapping" (336.25 ["catnapping"]), and the longer one is "caughtnapping," the more deeply one moves in the direction of "forty winks."

"SUPRASONIC LIGHT CONTROL"

Prolonged scrutiny of the backs of the eyelids, finally, will help one to fathom the visionary character of "everynight life"—but largely because it turns out to be almost impossible to see them. No matter how hard one tries, one will find that an insuppressible and silent "headnoise" (535.23) tends constantly and involuntarily to pull the eyes away from a purely optical "eyewitless foggus" by generating another, wholly imaginary kind of vision "in the sighed of lovely eyes" (405.28–29 ["inside of," through subvocalic "sighs"]). However easy it may be to liquidate physical light by dropping those "lashbetasselled lids," "you [are] not quite so successful in the process verbal whereby you would sublimate your blepharospasmockical suppressions" (515.15–17 [Gr. *blepharon*, "eyelid"]). Since a "blepharospasm" is the medical term for an eyeblink subject to unrest, the wording here calls our attention to a form of vision, also arising "in fact, under the closed eyes" (107.28), which is made possible not by the active lighting-up of "eyebulbs," but, representative rather than presentative, by a "process purely verbal." Rolling into the eyes out of the space between the ears and the tongue as a result of language, and "presenting a strangely profound rainbowl in [one's] occiput" (107.11–12 [the "occiput" is the back of the head or skull]), this is the form of vision that enables anyone to see "inexactly the same as a mind's eye view" (515.22–23), or from a literally "bard's highview" (504.16), all things ordinarily visible to the eye's eye view—not least in the night—and often in defiance of "one snaked's eyes" themselves (564.34 [that whispering "snake," as in Genesis, deceives]): "do you hear what I'm seeing"? (193.10), "see wha'm hearing?" (174.13). Able to cast over the "things" really seen in the Daily World a sometimes dense if irrecollectible film of "thinks" imaginarily seen (as when someone lost in a daydream fails to observe what is going on around him), this representative kind of vision too has the evident power of making the eyes involuntarily drift and halt transfixed in their sockets, so to interfere with the mechanical transmission of objects and light rays into the eyes through the channels charted out in the schemas of traditional opticians. This form of "second sight"

"Meoptics"

(520.29; 5.25) is important to a "reading [of the] Evening World" because the *Wake*'s "irismaimed" exercises it everywhere.

If study of HCE's "liquidated" "blackeye lenses" has made it seem, for instance, that "by the salt say water there's nix to nothing we can do for he's never again to sea" (50.34–35 [or "see"]), we should now note that this "say water," unlike mere "seawater," has lots of formative language (or "say") spectrally dispersed in it (cf. 371.8, 9, 20, 32; 372.27; 373.11; 436.13; 540.23); moreover, that this diffuse "say" sometimes "manage[s] to catch a listener's eye" (174.17–18), so to illuminate, with "the light of other days, [the] dire dreary darkness" in which he dwells (136.20–21) by allowing him to construct "an earsighted view of" the world (143.9–10). "Earsighted" himself (and extremely "nearsighted" too), our hero has learned to "talk earish with his eyes shut" (130.19), and as a consequence, he is continually "insighting," throughout the *Wake* (437.5 [visually "inciting"]), a kind of "photosension under suprasonic light control [that] may be logged for [and looked for]" everywhere (123.12–13): the wording here tells us that the "sensation" of "light" ("photosensation") arises at times out of inaudible (hence "suprasonic") sound sounded within our hero's "tropped head." Or, as Joyce put all this much more straightforwardly in his notebooks, " ⊓ talks then picture."[41]

Lines like these, distributed everywhere in the *Wake*, finally suggest that from the relativistic "blankpoint" of an "Eyeinstye" (305.6 [that "stye" "keeps black!"]), there may be more to the ear than meets the eye: "*Habes aures et num videbis?*" (113.29–30 [L. "You have ears and you will not see?"]). "Ear! Ear! Not ay! Eye! Eye! For I'm at the heart of it" (409.3–4). Particularly in a book with a hero sometimes called "Earwicker" (I.ii), some attention to the role that "the night's ear" (74.10–11) plays in the darker parts of life now becomes essential to any reading of the *Wake*. But before taking a long, hard "monolook interyerear" (182.20 ["into your ear," in order to understand the *Wake*'s "monologue interior"]), a closing word on the liquidated eye.

This chapter has only barely begun to explore the *Wake*'s "meoptics," which ultimately amounts to a new optics and a "new science" in the nature of Vico's. Anything like "objective" vision, not least, receives a sharp, dark, refractive twist and wrench in the humor-filled "meoptics" of the *Wake*'s "Oscur Camerad" (602.23); there especially, the imperious vagaries of "point of view," as practiced by the first person, come to all kinds of problematic dead ends. Clues strewn densely over every page of the *Wake*, "from spark to phoenish" (322.20), will help its reader to know at any particular moment in the book what to make of the infinitely variable "brights and shades" (621.23) and "sparks" and "phoenixes" that play through the "mil-lioncandled eye" (25.26) and "blackeye lenses" of its colorfully "benighted irismaimed"; and at the same time, each of these clues will generally reveal something more, and more spectacular, about the immense "charm of his optical life" (179.1–2) and the miraculousness of his and "her changeable eye (which see)" (332.21–22 [note, for instance, the indiscriminate range of its voyeuristic inclinations]). If "you don't reckoneyes him" (465.3) or the immense visionary splendor of *Finnegans Wake* at these moments, it is per-haps only because, with "your glosses" (304.F3 [and "glasses"]) clouded over by bad habits, you don't "reckon" with his "eyes" (hence "reckoneyes") or with the "light phantastic" (182.4) that they mediate, make, and, "under the dark flush of night," blackly liquidate. In the *Wake*'s vision, this failure to see what seeing fully involves has "meant milliems of centiments deadlost or mislaid on" us (239.3)—"sentiments" whose reawakening restores to us, as in Vico, "the original sinse we are only yearning as yet how to burgeon" (239.2). Finally, the *Wake*'s "meoptical" insight into the night forces us to "see that wonder in your eye" (215.4–5), and, finding it considerable, we emerge from the book's darkness "hav[ing] frankly enjoyed more than any-thing these secret workings of natures," "really so denighted of this lights time" (615.13–15).

"Lights out now (bouf!), tight and sleep on it" (445.22–23).

CHAPTER NINE

Earwickerwork

"DUMMYSHIP"

Where the mastery of most arts and sciences requires the laboriously schooled mounting of a *"gradus ad Parnassum"* (L. "steps to Parnassus"), *Finnegans Wake* simply asks its readers to take a few "false steps ad Pernicious" (467.34)—and largely through a sleep-mimetic dismantling of the head. Pursued in one direction this headrubbling exercise leads "the noer" (286.28 [or negated "knower"]) into the "duskt" of the night's "seemetery" (4.12, 17.36 [hence "Pernicious"]); but in another, it leads to the ground figuratively depicted at the bottom of figure 9.1, somewhere far below which lies "the childhood of the world" explored in Vico's "Poetic Wisdom." Study of the etymology suggests not only that the night's "dusk," the "seemetery's" "dust," and the *Wake*'s "obfuscation" are essential aspects of each other, but also that "dullness" and "doldrums," and "deafness" and "dumbness" are. Signifying both the perception of phenomenal disappearances (as happens at "dusk," in "death," and in regions that lie "deep" "down"), and the phenomenal disappearance of perceptions (as happens in "deafness," "dumbness," and "dullness"), a number of the terms drawn into a relational unity by this etymology map out more of our hero's countless "houdingplaces" (127.11 ["Houdini's" was a vanishing act]), some of which will now repay investigation.[1] A little attention to the *Wake*'s "meoptics" will make unnecessary a comparably detailed treatment of its dark and extended "sordomutics" (117.14 [L. *surdus-mutus*, "deaf-mute"]). But if "the ubiquitous 'deaf and dumb' motif in *Finnegans Wake* has never been adequately explained," it is only because too few of its readers have taken the requisite "night lessons" in "night school."[2]

Examine again the "dummy" (334.22) shown "outlined aslumbered" in either of the relief maps—or any body sleeping, for that matter—and ask yourself two essential questions. "Did you gather much from what he let drop?" (509.5–6 [his body and its head, for instance]). Probably not, since "his lapper and libbers was glue goulewed" (531.13–14 [his lips stick]), and he is "obviously disemvowelled" (515.12). Or again:

> Did the kickee . . . say anything important?
> —No more than Richman's periwhelker.
> —Nnn ttt wrd?
> —Dmn ttt thg.
>
> (515.2–6)

Like a "periwinkle," "whelk," or other shellfish, a sleeping person generally "clams up" and just lies there, "protesting to his lipreaders with a just-beencleaned barefacedness" so bare and so clean that his lips seem not to move at all (91.17–18). Penny for penny, he becomes the cheapest "dumbshow" in town, and so too necessarily at the *Wake:*

> Act: dumbshow.
> Closeup. Leads.
> Man with nightcap, in bed. . . .
>
> (559.18–20)[3]

Moments like these, scattered everywhere throughout the *Wake,* enable us now to think of our hero as "*Boawwll's Alocutionist*" (72.16 [by way of the Gr. and L. privatives *a-* and *ab-*, a negated "elocutionist"]); and unlike any student of "Bell's *Standard Elocutionist*," who would have learned to enunciate crisply delivered oral performances, "he, to don't say nothing" (288.5–6), don't say nothing, "on account off" (536.24–25 [not "of"]) the night "nearly takes [his] own mummouth's breath away" (510.3–4 [note the "owl" obscured in "*Boawwll*" and "keep black!"]). Sleeping giant though he may be (hence "mammoth"), his "mum mouth" is "SHUT" so fully as to be, as far as he can "no," indistinguishable from "his speak quite hoarse" (334.16 ["big wide arse"]): "he's so dumnb [in all senses of the word]. If he'd lonely talk" (225.17–18). Since all of us, comparably, "were lowquacks did we not tacit turn" in sleep (99.1–2 [L. *loquax*, "talkative"; *tacitus*, "mute, silent"]), our representative hero necessarily becomes something of a weird "elecu-

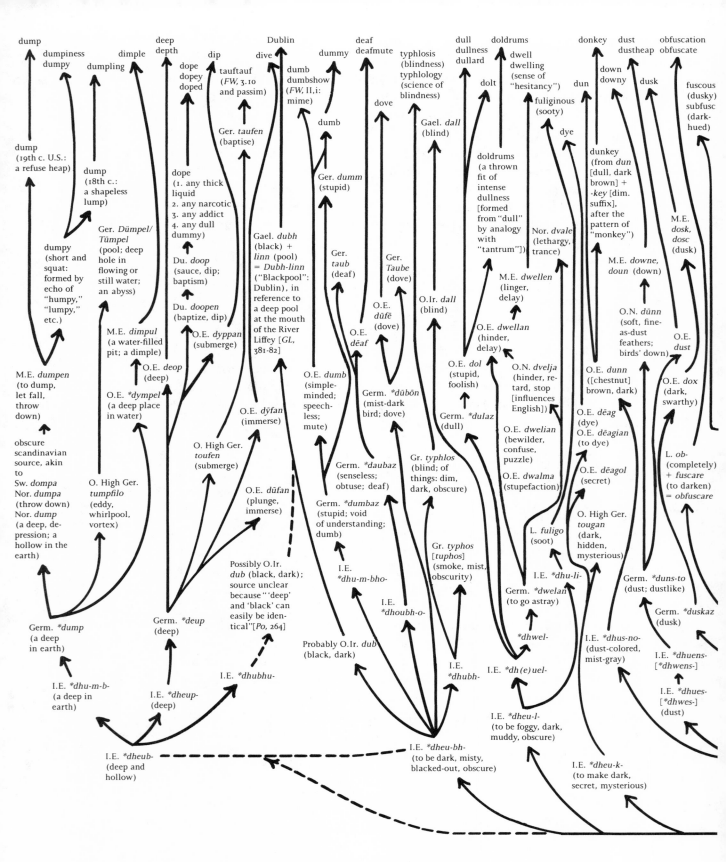

Figure 9.1. Etymological chart: *dheu-. "What is to be found in a Dustheap" (307.23)

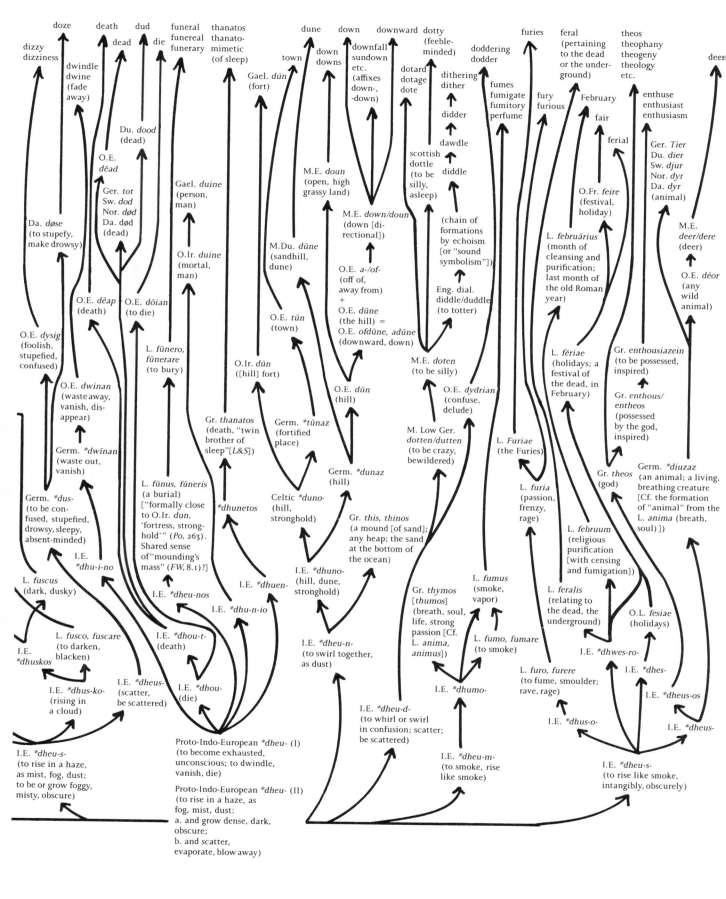

tioner" (58.34–35 [an "executioner" of "elocution" and a mute practitioner of "alocutionary" speech-acts]), *Finnegans Wake* in turn holding forth "Mute art for the Million" (496.7). (See figure 9.2.)

Moreover, our hero is "*as daff as you're erse*" (268.L4)—"as daft as you're Erse," perhaps, but also "deaf as your arse." And the arse, as reference to 509.30–33 and the accompanying commentary in the *Annotations* will suggest, is not the most developed of his sensory organs.[4] As anyone who has slept through an alarm clock knows ("I hate to look at alarms but . . . I hereby hear by ear from by seeless socks 'tis time to be up and ambling" [468.23–26]), sleeping people do not always hear things. Even when they do vaguely hear things, as anyone who has slept through a dull lecture will attest, they do a very poor job of recalling, interpreting, and intelligently discussing what they have heard afterwards. When HCE falls asleep and loses consciousness both of "Dublin" and the "Saorstat Erin," therefore,

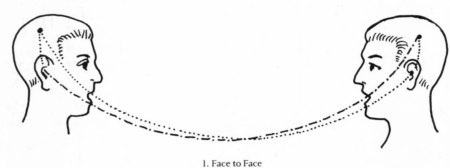

1. Face to Face

(after an illustration in Ferdinand de Saussure, *Course in General Linguistics*, trans. Wade Baskin [New York: McGraw-Hill, 1966], p. 11)

Mutt ("a dumm") and Jeff ("the deff")

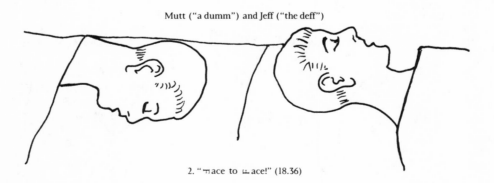

2. "⌐ ace to ⊔ ace!" (18.36)

Figure 9.2. The Facts of Speech

JOYCE'S BOOK OF THE DARK

he enters a "state" that might most accurately be construed as "Dufblin" (447.23 ["deaf-blind"]), "Taubling" (7.6 [Ger. *taub*, "deaf"]), or "sorestate hearing" (242.1). In parts of the night, as he lies "bothered . . . from head to tail" (381.28 [Anglo-Ir. "bothered" = "deaf"]), having "dropped down dead and deaf" "in Demidoff's tomb" (323.19, 329.23 [a "demi-dumb-and-deaf" one], he accordingly becomes known by such "psourdonome[s]" (332.32 [Fr. *sourd*, "deaf"]) as "old dummydeaf" (329.27) or "Sur Soord" (238.31)— both presumably attached to "Mrs Taubiestimm" (546.29 [Ger. *taubstumm*, "deaf and dumb"]). Passing "through deafths of durkness (407.12 ["deaf," in "death"]) while "sound asleep" (204.16 [and "asleep to sound"]), our hero therefore becomes the quintessential deaf-mute. And if he'll representatively be the death of us, "he'll [also] be the deaf of us" (379.20)—"Yus, sord" (379.21). Since "his hearing is indoubting just as [his] seeing is onbelieving," in short (468.15–16), a reader of the *Wake* would profit from a few lessons in "How to Understand the Deaf" (307.20–21).

In a word, they can "heerdly heer" (485.27–28). "Old dummydeaf" lies so deeply "in debt and doom" in the dark (496.4 ["deaf and dumb"]) that the terms "deaf-mute" and "deaf-dumb" recur throughout *Finnegans Wake* in a weltering proliferation of "hardly heard" and mutely garbled forms. This is perhaps most apparent in sections of the book given over to characters like "Mutt and Jute" (15.29–18.16) and "Butt and Taff" (337.32–354.21), whose names, at the end of a chain of sonic associations, sound like the words "mute" and "deaf" as badly mismanaged by two deaf-mutes crippled with nasty colds. But comparably distorted appearances of "deaf-mute" configurations appear everywhere at the *Wake*, in order to remind us insistently of the underlying "bedeafdom" (236.30 ["deaf-dumb"]) of the night. A line informing us that a dim figure shouted at our hero "last epening after delivering some carcasses mattonchepps and meatjutes," for instance (67.16–17), only apparently has to do with the rude delivery of a supply of "muttonchops and meatjuice"; beneath the manifest surface of the phrasing, we might see that the outrage perpetrated on "Sur Soord" "last evening" befalls everyone in "everynight life": last evening, too, your "carcass was delivered mute-and-deaf and deaf-mute" (cf. 467.15–17, and note the heavily conflicted "mutter and doffer duffmatt baxingmotch" at 415.13 [not really, finally, the interesting "mother and daughter deaf-mute boxing-match" it appears to be]).

Particularly because the "stream of consciousness" or "interior monologue" seems to involve some tacit play between the ear and the mouth, our hero's "defdum" (89.33 ["deaf-dumb"]) has important broad repercussions in *Finnegans Wake*—as an example from *Ulysses* will make clear. There we find Bloom "thinking," as he tries to assess the fortunes of the Guinness brothers, "What am I saying, barrels? Gallons" (*U*, 79). The word "saying" localizes the Joycean "interior monologue" somewhere in the dark channels linking mouth and ear, both of which evidently participate in an internal, if unsounded talking-over. Since Bloom's nocturnal counterpart has ears that don't work and a mouth glued shut by sleep, however, the *Wake's* nocturnal "*monologue interior*" necessarily modulates into something more akin to a "moanolothe inturned" (254.14; cf. 105.12); for "old dummydeaf" is so "turned inward" as to be "lothe" to "moan" at all, let alone to rise out of the "deafths" of his "bedeafdom" (407.12, 236.30). All of the heady mechanisms that guarantee the smooth flow of consciousness in *Ulysses*, in turn, become densely problematized in the *Wake*, where "the mouth that tells not will ever attract the unthinking tongue and so long as the obseen draws theirs which hear not so long till allearth's dumbnation shall the blind lead the deaf" (68.32–34). A single unit of Wakean "moanolothe inturned," this sentence shows all five of the closed senses extinguishing themselves "in conflict of evidence" (314.4); for "allearth's dumbnation" has fallen on the "presence (of a curpse)" and moved it to "the end of the world" (hence "Allah's damnation").

The best place at which to see what articles like this lead to in more extended forms would be the dialogue of "Mutt" and "Jute" (15.29–18.16), "Mutt and Jeff" (*L*, I, 406), or "mute" and "deaf"—whose essential action, staged on a dump (17.4–5), is that of sleep's extended "dummpshow" (120.7–8). If one compares the details exchanged during this dialogue to the representation of "Dufblin" given in Relief Map B, it will become evident that the "hole affair" takes place on the ground of a "gyant" body lying dead to the world in the "seemetery" of "everynight life" (18.11–12, 17.4–5, 17.26ff., 17.33).[5] The dialogue is localized, moreover, somewhere in the region of "the neck" of this sleeping giant (17.11, 17.21 [Gr. *isthmos*, "neck"]). Since it brings together a stammering "Jute" (16.10 [or "mute"]), who is somewhat "jeff" (16.12 [or "deaf"]), and a "Mutt" (16.11 [or "mute"]) who is apparently "jeffmute" (16.14 [or "deafmute"]), the dialogue raises mind-boggling questions, of a kind repeatedly asked in *Finnegans Wake*, about what either of the deaf listeners can possibly be hearing when either mute "alocutionist" spills out his story in silence: "did one scum then in the auradrama, the deff, after some clever play in the mud, mention to the other undesirable, a dumm . . . ?" (517.2–4). Underlying the whole "sottovoxed stalement" (313.18), in short—none of it "wiseable" (16.24 [or visible]) because the "hole affair" is sunk in the "dun blink" of the night's "eyegonblack" (17.17, 16.29)—is a conflict in the region of the neck of our sleeping hero, a stupefied "Taciturn" (17.3), whose shut mouth seems determined to invade his ear (hence the "invasion" motif), and whose deaf ear in turn seems intent on drawing out his mouth ("the bark is still there but the molars are gone" [466.36–467.1]).[6]

Like other characters in the *Wake*, this "Taciturn" figure has "a quick ear for spittoons" (38.9–10 ["spittoons" and speechless mouths having exactly the same content]) and is simply "diagnosing through eustacetube" during the dialogue of "Mutt and Jute" (36.35–36), trying to ascertain what goes on in the obscure and roomy space (mind [16.27]) that extends from "mouthparts to his orefice" (414.27): "Ope Eustace tube!," as it elsewhere occurs to "Mr Eustache" (535.26, 361.11). The dialogue anticipates others in the *Wake*, then, in which we find "the doomed but always ventriloquent Agitator" who is our hero (56.5–6) "agitating" himself by throwing his voice into the wooden space between his ears, playing a ventriloquist to his own dummy ("How wooden I not know it" [16.33]), and feebly "hearing his own bauchspeech in backwords (100.27–28 [Ger. *Bauchredner*, "ventriloquist"]). Generally, since he has a deep if not always conscious memory, our "ventriloquent" hero does thousands of voices, largely because he has heard and engaged in ongoing dialogues with all of them (his mother's, his father's, his wife's, his customers' and "Here Comes [almost] Everybody's"): "Hear more to those voices! Always I am hearing them" (571.24–25). "Playing on the least change of his manjester's voice" (73.13–14), moreover, and "talking alltheways in himself of his hopes to fall in among" the others to whom these voices are attached (602.31–32), he is easily capable of throwing them all into the vacuous space between deaf ears and dumb mouth, so to fill that space with a world of hallucinated and "uncontrollable nighttalkers" (32.7–8). Indeed, as "his thick spch spck[s]" out of "a twithcherous mouph" (23.4, 88.18 ["treacherous" because deceptive, "twitching" because shut]), "he stalks to simself louther and lover, immutating aperybally" (460.11–12)—"imitating" and "aping" "everybody," that is, but badly "mutating" them in the process. And it is for this reason, to "rearrive" at the dialogue of Mutt and Jute, that "Taciturn" becomes "our wrongstoryshortener" (17.3–4): not only does he generally get a "story" all "wrong," but he also tends, as he "clear[s his] throttle" and tries to "brake the news" (457.33, 377.25), to make a "long story short" (hence the "brakes" and the "throttle" in his "throat"), sometimes even, in order to preserve the state of sleep, reducing it to "next to nothing."

Earwickerwork

Nothing quite so eventful as fully "agitated" "ventriloquence," therefore, occurs during the dialogue of Mutt and Jute. For as its detailing suggests, the "hole affair" finally bears on the burial "mound" (or "howe") that underlies both of the hallucinated "nighttalkers" (17.29, 18.12ff., 17.4ff. ["howe" = "Howth" = vacant head]). As always, this would be the body dead to the world at the *Wake*, out of whose unconscious interior the two conflictive and stymied voices have precipitated. Since the scene is finally "inedible" (16.23 [and "inaudible"]), not "wiseable" (16.24 [or "visible" or conscious]), "onheard of and umscene" (17.15–16 ["unheard" and "not seen"]), the subject of the dialogue is simply the *Wake*'s sleeping subject, within whose "deafadumped" body (590.1) a richly articulated form of the night's "Real Absence" has accumulated. "No thing making newthing wealthshowever," this "Real Absence" becomes indistinguishable from the real absence out of which Vico traces the genesis of the West (hence the passage's many evocations of "cave" men [16.3] and, by reference to "Mutt and Jeff," of modernist equivalents of "Mousterian" cave paintings [15.33]). The dialogue, ultimately, is about the primordia of human dialogue.

The deaf ear striving to hear what the dumb mouth is striving to say will account for a good deal of the passing "auradrama" in *Finnegans Wake*—as happens, for instance, in the chapter on buried letters (I.v), when an obscure professor "Duff-Muggli" (123.11 ["deaf-mute"; Anglo-Ir. *duff*, "black"]) endorses "the wellinformed observation, made miles apart from the Master by Tung-Toyd" (123.19–20 [at the other end of the Eustacian tube by the "tongue-tied" mouth]). In at least one instance (571.27–34), as HCE miraculously "work[s] his jaw . . . and hark[s] from the tomb" (246.9), this "auradrama" seems to generate some audible "sleeptalking" (459.5). Brief consideration of a sleeping person's stupefied "bedeafdom," however, will also help to explain why so much of *Finnegans Wake* comes off the page reading like pure "absurdity" ("The surdity of it!" [538.18]) and sheer "Nonsense!" (56.28). For the mental life of a hero who has "no senses," at least by any ordinary understanding, can of necessity be only "non-sense"; and "the night" itself, in Joyce's words, "is an absurd thing"—"absurd" deriving from the Latin *absurdus*, "unheard of," in turn from *surdus*, "deaf."[7]

As the night moves HCE forward "for its nonce ends" (149.22) under the forces of sensory "closure" and "absurdity," however, the ears become extremely important because, unlike the eyes and the mouth, they never really close. Throughout the *Wake*, they therefore serve an enlightening and "oreillental" function (357.18 [Fr. *oreille*, "ear"]) by filling the "non-sensed" dark with a complex "sound sense" whose study will now be crucial (109.15).[8]

Glasheen has suggested that "if you have time on your hands," you might "look up every 'ear' in" *Finnegans Wake.*[9] If one were to add to all these many "muchears" (11.24) terms like "hear" and "listen," and "sound" and "silence," the project would amount to an endless rereading of the book. Auditory terms like these lie distributed over virtually every page of the *Wake*, integrally entangled in its "vermicular" and "nat language" and among its "meoptic" ciphers. These "earmarks of design" (66.1) now make it possible to move once again from cover to cover through "this Eyrawyggla saga" (48.16–17), this time paying some attention to the role of "hearing in this new reading" (55.33).

"EARWICKER"

Why Joyce chose to saddle his ostensibly ordinary twentieth-century sleeper with the altogether extraordinary name of "Humphrey Chimpden Earwicker" is elaborately explored in the second chapter of *Finnegans Wake*, which seems to explore "the facts of his nominigentilisation" (31.33–34) but finally bears only on what Joyce frankly called "the Earwicker absurdity" (*L*, I, 203). Well before he began to work on *Work in Progress*, Joyce pointed out to William Bird that "in sleep our senses are dormant, except the sense of hearing, which is always awake, since you can't close your ears. So any sound that comes to our ears is turned into a dream" (*JJ*, 546–47). It should come as no surprise, then, to learn in the *Wake*'s account of "Earwicker's" "nominigentilisation," that "Earwicker" is HCE's "occupational agnomen" (30.3). Now an "agnomen," in English, is a "nickname," *not* a real name, and in particular a "nickname" bestowed on a person "on account of some extraordinary virtue, action or the like";[10] and "Earwicker," in turn, "comes from the Anglo-Saxon Euerwaar or Ever-Waker" and simply designates a watchman.[11] Since "watchmen," "watching," "waking," and "vigilance" all etymologically derive from the Indo-European root *veg-* ("to be lively"), and since mammalian ears serve the partial function, according to the "new science" of evolution, of maintaining "watchful" "vigilance" against the threat of nocturnal attack by predators or burglars and prowlers (34.4), an integrated synthesis of all these understandings should make it evident that anybody asleep absolutely merits the "occupational agnomen" of "Earwicker" simply because ("it is an openear secret, be it said" [425.16]) he has no choice but to maintain a perpetually vigilant "earwitness" on the world through ears that just won't close (5.14).[12] Even if HCE "is not all there," then, and "not all hear" exactly either, a good part of him is always only "all ears" (507.3, 536.1–2, 169.15). Indeed, "Earwicker, that patternmind, that paradigmatic ear, receptoretentive as his of Dionysius," is inevitably taking constant readings on noises that well out of the dark around him (70.35–36 [as if he were in "the ear of Dionysius," a vast and hollow natural cavern which, like his own "tropped head," has famous echoically amplifying powers]).[13] "Earwicker," finally—as opposed to "Finnegan," "Finn," or "Eboniser"—is simply a cipher whose appearance throughout the *Wake* alerts us to moments in which its sleeping hero has transitorily ascended into a state of auditory vigilance; for "he caun ne'er be bothered [Anglo-Ir. "bothered" = "deaf"] but maun e'er be waked" (496.34–35 ["everwaked"]): "Witchman, watch of your night?" (245.16).[14]

One passage in *Finnegans Wake* that will illustrate particularly well the potent nocturnal sweep of Earwicker's e'erwakened ears appears at the beginning of chapter II.iii, at 309.1–311.4, in one of the darkest parts of the Wakean "noughttime." Since the passage is too long to quote in its entirety, the reader might wish to consult it before following the ensuing commentary, if only primarily to note that it makes sheer "nonsense" if read sequentially, according to those laws that insure the coherence of documents in the Daily World. About as difficult and obscure as *Finnegans Wake* ever gets, the passage will illustrate the validity of what Joyce told Frank Budgen when he said that his work was "basically simple"—*if*, rather than reading it linearly and literally, we interpret it as we might interpret a dream, by eliciting from the absurd murk a network of overlapping and associatively interpenetrating structures.

One of these structures, by now familiar, reconstructs the night's "Real Absence" and locates us squarely in the "ether" of a "vaticum" (or "vacuum") emanating from a "man made static" (309.9, 21, 22 [he doesn't move]). The second sentence of the chapter alerts us to an unspecified turbulence that "was now or never in Etheria Deserta" (309.8–9 [in void "ether"]); and if we examine the sentence further, it becomes evident that it has no subject at all, its predicate informing us further that this Absent Subject (our hero), "now or never," simply "was." Particularly because "Etheria Deserta" plays on an old name of Howth head ("Edri Deserta"), we can infer that the "ethereal" "vacuum" being explored here has accumulated in the "tropped head" of a "man made static" by sleep. The passage shows our Absent Subject—"the Vakingfar sleeper" whose "waking" is "far" (310.10)—entertaining "in the night the mummery of whose deed" (310.23–24 ["the Memory of the Dead," who remember nothing]), so that again the *Wake* becomes a "balk of the deaf" (or "Book of the Dead"), reconstructing the form of "doom" experienced by a body dead to the world. Aspects of this "doom-body's" "Real Absence" (289.15) are in turn particularized in ways that need no extended elaboration: identified as "the Mole" (310.1), our "man made static" lies "equipped with supershielded umbrella antennas" (309.17–18 ["keep black!"]); and he has, shut as if in a "wink," the vegetating "oyne of an oustman in skull" (310.29, 30 [an "ousted" man]). He lies suspended, finally, "in the doom of the balk of the deaf" (309.2–3)—his hearing "balked" or, at least, "for much or moment indispute" (309.10).

That these pages have such a complex content, however, suggests that not everything about our Absent Subject can be quite fully dead to the world. And if we "rearrive" at the passage, in fact, another network of associatively linked terms, bearing on what seems to be a complex radio set, seems to take up a great deal of room in his emptily "tropped head." A wondrous device, this "tolvtubular high fidelity daildialler" (309.14) is "culpable of cunducing Naul and Santry" (310.12–13)—"capable of conducting and condensing all and sundry" signals, that is, even from the Irish "Dail" (hence "daildialler") and from as far away as the villages of "Naul" and "Santry." It does this by drawing forth coherent signaling from the "man made static" crackling through the "Etheria Deserta" of the ionosphere; and by "bawling the whowle [boiling the whole bawl and howl] . . . down in an eliminium sounds pound [aluminum sauce pan]" (309.22–23 [thereby "eliminating" extraneous noise]), "so as to serve . . . up a melegoturny marygoraumd, eclectrically filtered for allirish earths and ohmes" (309.23–310.1). What emerges from this "high fidelity" radio, in short, is a rich "mulligatawney" of melodic "song" (hence the Gr. *melos*, "song," in "melegoturny"), "eclectically" and "electrically filtered" for wholesome consumption in "allirish hearths and homes" (hence the scattered culinary terms). Most readers of the *Wake* attentive to this dense radio vocabulary have regarded the passage under our study as a description of a radio or television set in Earwicker's pub, out of which will be broadcast later in II.iii the stories of Kersse the Tailor and of Buckley's shooting of the Russian General.[15]

If we press further into the interstices of these details, however, it becomes rapidly clear that the radio set in question has many astonishingly eccentric features. "Capable of capturing skybuddies, harbour craft emittences, key clickings, [and] vaticum cleaners" (309.20–21), it has the powers not simply of a radio set but of a radar station (which picks up "sky bodies," or airplanes), of a telegraphic post (which interprets "key clinkings"), and, since it is capable of "distance getting" (309.18), of a sonar apparatus as well. All of these distinct instruments are *sensing devices* that have in common the ability to elicit inaudible signs streaming in out of dark ether from invisible sources, and to make them audible and interpretible to human ears. Not the least peculiar feature of this sensing device is its extremely feeble power source; its "battery . . . [is] tuned up by twintriodic singulvalvulous pipelines . . . with a **h**owdro**c**ephalous **e**nlargement" (310.2–6) which, we learn in a related detail, is operating at "one watthour" (310.25 [the amount of energy needed to keep a one-watt bulb lit for an hour]). The conspicuous appearance of HCE here—and the heavy recurrence of the cipher elsewhere in the passage (at 309.20, 310.1, and 310.22–23) tells us that our hero's "body still persist[s]" in this part of the night's "Real Absence" (76.20), as a "forced in [the] waste" (309.13), insistently informing and underlying everything in this assemblage of terms. And the appearance both of "Howth" (HEAD) and the Gr. *kephale* ("head") in that "howdrocephalous enlargement" correlatively suggests that the real power source feeding this radio is our vastly "hydrocephalous" hero himself, whom sleep has made a very dim bulb indeed (hence again "one watthour"; "hydrocephalus" is water on the brain). However much the passage seems to be about a "**h**armonic **c**ondenser **e**nginium" (310.1 [a radiolike "engine"]), the latent immanence both of HCE and the Latin *ingenium* ("mental power") in that "enginium" suggests that the sound-sensing device in which we are interested is embodied in HCE, "in the flesh."

Another way of reading this part of the *Wake*, then, would entail isolating not radio parts, but all those associatively linked terms that have been sorted out, diagrammed, and put into perspective in figures 9.3 and 9.4, which offer in condensed form a visual sketch of the "otological life" of our "european" hero (310.21, 598.15 ["otology" is the science of the ear]). Showing a radio-receptive headset "as modern as tomorrow afternoon" (309.14–15), with all of the peculiar features that we have explored, the diagrams invite us to see that Earwicker, as a recurrent "character" in the *Wake*, is constituted essentially of two vast, vigilant, and radarlike ears with a large and hydrocephalous head wedged vacantly somewhere in between; and, particularly because we learn earlier in the *Wake* that "the ear of Fionn Earwicker aforetime was the trademark of a broadcaster" (108.21–22), these diagrams will also suggest why the passage under our attention will now resolve into a representation of Earwicker's own hearing, as a *process* misconstrued through free association as a process of radioreception. Ultimately, the passage is only describing Earwicker's ears, the one part of him awake at this moment in the night, as they hover statically in the dark and maintain their

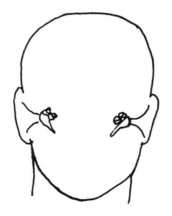

"Occupational agnomen" (30.3):

"**H. C. Earwicker**" (33.30)

"Psourdonome" (332.32 [Fr. *sourd*, "deaf"])

"Demidoff" (329.23 ["demidumb and deaf"])

Figure 9.3. "Headmound" or "the Mole"

ever-vigilant "earwitness" on the world, our hero himself "pricking up ears . . . and picking up airs from th'other over th'ether . . . this night sublime" (452.12–14).

In precisely specified ways, the "otological" referencing of the passage alerts us to the reasons for the vigilant sleeplessness of Earwicker's ears. Whenever sound waves "pinnatrate" the "pinna" (310.9) and whorl deep into "the latter end" of "the lubberendth" (310.21 [labyrinth]), they cannot help but jostle into active motion all the essentially mechanical components of the ear: the "tinpanned" "tynpan" (82.34, 224.19, 310.11), which resonates with only somewhat finer suppleness than a banged "tin pan" or "eliminium sounds pound"; the "**h**ummer, **e**nville and **c**storrap" (310.19–20); and the constituent elements of the essential organ of hearing, finally—the "routs of Corthy" (310.13 [or "rods of Corti"]), in "the organ of Corti"—which cannot help but vibrate mechanically when stirred by sound. Rocked into motion by sounds that enter the ear even in the deepest night, all of these unsleeping mechanisms therefore put Earwicker into the position of having constantly to ask "what are the sound waves saying?" (256.23–24). In "the sense arrest" that renders him "deafadumped" in sleep, it is not his ears

Earwickerwork

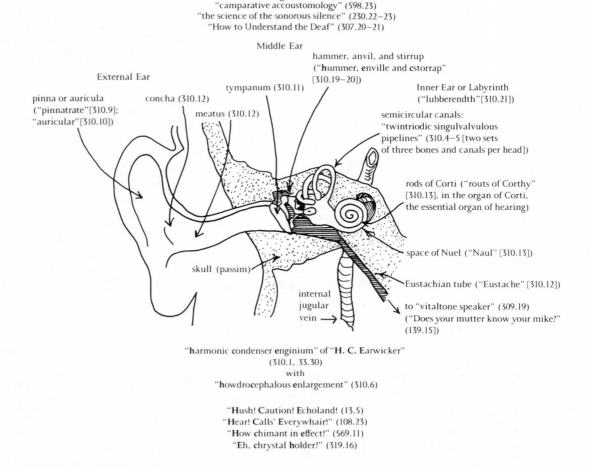

"his otological life" (310.21)
"camparative accoustomology" (598.23)
"the science of the sonorous silence" (230.22–23)
"How to Understand the Deaf" (307.20–21)

Middle Ear

hammer, anvil, and stirrup
("hummer, enville and cstorrap"
[310.19–20])

External Ear

tympanum (310.11)

Inner Ear or Labyrinth
("lubberendth"[310.21])

pinna or auricula
("pinnatrate"[310.9];
"auricular"[310.10])

concha (310.12)

meatus (310.12)

semicircular canals:
"twintriodic singulvalvulous
pipelines" (310.4–5 [two sets
of three bones and canals per head])

rods of Corti ("routs of Corthy"
[310.13], in the organ of Corti,
the essential organ of hearing)

space of Nuel ("Naul" [310.13])

skull (passim)

Eustachian tube ("Eustache" [310.12])

internal
jugular
vein →

to "vitaltone speaker" (309.19)
("Does your mutter know your mike?"
(139.15])

"harmonic condenser enginium" of "H. C. Earwicker"
(310.1, 33.30)
with
"howdrocephalous enlargement" (310.6)

"Hush! Caution! Echoland!" (13.5)
"Hear! Calls' Everywhair!" (108.23)
"How chimant in effect!" (569.11)
"Eh, chrystal holder?" (319.16)

Figure 9.4. The "otological life" of "H. C. Earwicker"

or his hearing that shut off, but the representation of hearing in his consciousness, which is evidently empowered with the ability to choose to hear or not
to hear as it likes. Everyone has firsthand evidence of the audio-selective
oddness of nocturnal hearing—notably in the memory of moments that involved sleeping through alarm clocks or phone calls, whose sounds obviously
"pinnatrated" the ear, but failed to make the slightest dent on the "howdrocephalous" head.[16] In *Finnegans Wake*, comparably, sounds from the real
world are invariably impinging on Earwicker's ears with erratic constancy
throughout the night; and, in the "lubberendth" of the book's extinguished
and extremely slow hero (Eng. "lubber" = "slow person"), these sounds are

either "eclectrically filtered" out and docilely ignored after an interval of muzzy reception in the "tropped head" (309.24), or else "bawl[ed] . . . down in [the] eliminium sounds pound" of the mind and subjected, by our "Taciturn" and misinterpretation-prone "wrongstoryshortener," to "a warping process" (497.3) that resolves them by incorporating them into the ongoing imagery of the dream.[17] If it initially seemed that our Absent Subject ("the Mole") was enduring "the doom of the balk of the deaf" in the passage under our attention and that his hearing was "for much or moment in dispute," then, it should now be clear that his hearing is actually in great suspense at this moment in the night, his ears cocked with eartrigger precision in vigilant readiness to pop alert at the least sound. The opening two pages of II.iii, in fact, are an essential setup for a little moment of sonic turmoil that our hero has been anxiously anticipating from the very first line of the chapter, where we read that "It may not or maybe a no concern of the Guinnesses but." (309.1).

The reader will note, in a context heavily concerned with sound-reception, the ominous buildup of references to the belly, food, and especially drinks at the bottom of page 310, beginning with the term "evenbreads" (310.22 [a literal English rendering of the Ger. *Abendbrot*, "supper"]) and escalating with effervescent urgency through the terms "bock," "stou[t]," "ale," "foam," "cork," "froth," and "pop" (310.28, 29, 31, 33, 34, 35). We learn in this region of the text that "that host of a bottlefilled, the bulkily hulkwight . . . is in on a bout to be unbulging an o'connell's" (310.26–28). The line manifestly suggests that the *Wake*'s bartending "host" is worrying about having to open a "filled bottle" of "O'Connell's ale," anxiety about his work haunting him even in the night; but the term "bottlefilled" ("battlefield") also joins the phrase "a bout" to indicate that our "host of a bottlefilled" is undergoing considerable conflict here. The terms, moreover, specify the nature and site of that conflict by suggesting that our "bulky" "host," who is not simply a bartender but an active drinker as well, is amply "bottle-filled" himself: "all seethic" (310.28 ["acidic," "all seething"]), his "bulkily" "bottlefilled" stomach is "about to unbulge."

Hence the lines that close this passage: "pressures be to our hoary frother, the pop gave his sullen bulletaction and, bilge, sled a movement of cathartic emulsipotion . . ." (310.35–36). If we are to identify with a hero who "overhears," we should hear three things here. First, in a line of imagery that will generate in this chapter the sustained dream of barroom strife, a bottle of beer is being opened, the cork making an audible "pop" as "pressure" shoots it off with "sudden bullet-action" and the "hoary froth" of the "emulsified potion" starts to "slide" over the side of the bottle (311.1). Second, a very moral statement, on the order of "praises be to our holy father, the pope gave a solemn benefaction and led a movement of Catholic emancipation," is being pronounced. But third, in a line of reading that will consolidate these two senses, we should hear this sudden "pop" originating out of our hero's own shut mouth and "bottlefilled" body: our "hoary frother" (310.35 [not "holy father"]) has belched, in short, and as this articulate little sound emerges from his own magniloquent lips, our sleeping patriarch badly misconstrues it by associating it with a "papal" (< L. *papa*) pronouncement. This happens because his oral performance entails an internal "bout" or conflict having to do with a discrepancy between pleasure and forms of politeness that are inevitably moralized and acculturated: as a "movement of cathartic emulsipation" (a "moment of catharsis" that "emancipates" "emulsified potion"), the "big brewer's belch" feels good (95.26), but it's not nice. Because the movement of his own lips puts our "ventriloquent" hero in mind of the mechanisms of talking, moreover, and also of a thirst that has accumulated during the night, the disruption of his stuck lips associatively jogs a memory of what it is like to talk and enjoy mouthy vitality (311.5ff.), so that it "slake[s] [his] thirdst thoughts awake" (311.16 ["take," "wake," "thirst"]) and generates over the next few pages of the *Wake* the story of "Kersse the Tailor," which appropriately explores, in a tense barroom setting, our hero's dubious "fitness" and "suitability." If we go back to the first line of chapter II.iii now ("It may not or maybe a no concern of the Guinnesses but."), it becomes evident that one of many matters initially suppressed on that end-stopped "but" was of course a "concern of Guinnesses," because Guinness's is what our "bottlefilled" hero has been both restraining and waiting to hear over two pages.

The trivial sonic eventfulness treated in this passage now turns out to be representative of a great deal in the *Wake* as a whole, where, as "sound" acoustically "sensed" "pinnatrates" his ears, Earwicker continually "make[s] soundsense and sensesound kin again" by trying to make "sense" of the "sound" (121.15–16 [even though, like Finnegan, he is dead to the world]). Introducing us to the "science of sonorous silence" (230.22–23), the passage asks us to see that no matter how deeply "one feels the amossive silence" (31.31–32)—profound "SILENCE" (501.6)—that seems to have pervaded "a sound night's sleep" (597.2 [the "moss" in "amossive" just lies there too]), "there [were inevitably] sounds of manymirth on the night's ear ringing" (74.10–11). Indeed, as "the auditor learns" (374.6), manifold "*Acoustic Disturbance[s]*" of all kinds (71.18) are inevitably penetrating "earwaker's" ears throughout the night (173.9–10) and—"Have you heard?"—demanding his vigilant attention and interpretive scrutiny (45.1).[18] For even if "you cannot wake a silken nouse out of a hoarse oar" (154.9–10 [or "make a fine mind"—Gr. *nous*—out of the hydrocephalous space between "hoarse" mouth and deaf "ear"]), Earwicker is constantly trying to ascertain "with his unaided ears" (475.36) "what are the sound waves saying" (256.23–24). Making him a victim of extended nocturnal "persecussion" (125.16 ["percussive persecution"]), these omnipresent "sound waves" burden him with unconscious decisions as to whether potentially sleep-disruptive "nusances" need to be "traduced into jinglish janglage" (275.F6 [out of acoustical "jingle jangle" into the "English language"]); or whether they can be ignored ("hearken but hush it" [134.28]), so to become "onheard of" (17.15), "underheerd" (160.26), and even "unherd" (223.1–2).

Since each of the night's many "acoustic" events partially "wakens" "earwaker," "acordant to all acountstrick" (180.5 [Port. *acordar*, "to waken"; "acoustic"]), each such "noisance" (479.20 [or "noisy" "nuisance"]) necessitates the production of a "tricky account" in his "tropped head" (hence again "acountstrick"), which, simultaneously taking brief recognitive "account" of the disturbance and "whishing" it away (587.12 [Eng. "wish"; Anglo-Ir. *whisht*, "be quiet"]), weaves it into all the other components of the dream, with so greatly "wicker"-like a complexity, as to make it unrecognizably "onheard of"—both to Earwicker and, unfortunately, to his sympathetic reader as well. If, on the one hand, each such sound "will wecker [his] earse" (375.19 ["waken his ears" and "wicker" them with "Erse"]), on the other each also succumbs to Earwicker's "whishtful" desire to sleep (333.34), and so becomes mere "noisense" (147.6 ["noisy" "nuisance" now converted into "non-sensed" "nonsense"; on the equation of "wishing" and "whishing" in the *Wake*, see also 407.11 and 457.30]).

From this perspective, the *Wake* might now be regarded as one erratically extended sound effect—a "sound seemetery" again (17.35–36), in which all sorts of "songs" and "howls" unconsciously sensed by "the presence (of a curpse)" "blurried" in the night's "seemetery," as if on "Alls Sings and Alls Howls" eve (304.F5 ["All Saints and All Hallows"]), generate a sustained form of "seeming." For the *Wake* "is told in sounds" that include "ereperse" (117.12, 15 [or "earpierce"]); and throughout the night reconstructed in "this radiooscillating epiepistle" (108.24), "the ear of Fionn Earwicker" (108.21–22) operates much like the phantasmal radioset explored at the beginning of chapter II.iii by sorting out sounds "for all within crystal range" (229.12)—Eh, **c**hrystal **h**older?" (319.16):

—Now we're gettin it. Tune in and pick up the forain counties. Hello! . . .
—Hello! . . .
—Hellohello! . . . (500.35–501.4)
—My dear sir! In this wireless age any owl rooster can peck up bostoons.
(489.36–490.1)

Continually "picking up" sounds that pour invisibly out of the dark "open air" around him (Fr. *forain*, "open air")—as if by "wireless" from another world (hence "Boston"), or as if over a telephone line in the "Real Absence" of anything visible—Earwicker's amply opened ears are constantly on the prowl in the night (hence that "owl"). And not least of the sonic transmissions they "peck up" seems to emanate from some "bosthoon" (Anglo-Ir. for "blockhead" or dummy).

"The auditor learns" that there are two varieties of "*Acoustic Disturbance*" "on the night's ear ringing," one of which, originating in the "rambling undergroands" of our sleeping "bosthoon's" body itself (481.15 [note the "groan" erupting out of that "rumbling underground"]), is so pervasive in the *Wake* and in "real life" that only its forms, and not its frequency, can be indicated. Such sounds erupt in periodic "snoring" of the sort that seems to punctuate and complicate "The Ballad of Persse O'Reilly" (7.28, 37.12, 40.5); hoarse "hemming" and hawing, throat-clearing and "coughing" (414.19–20, 571.25–26 ["**H**orsehem **c**oughs **e**nough"]); the "earpiercing dulcitude" of the "Yawn" (474.12–13); Earwicker's own "rude breathing on the void of to be," reminding him of his vital continuity and persistence in time (100.27, 499.14 ["Lung lift the keying!"]; 482.3 ["Breeze softly. Aures are aureas"]); the beating of his heart (74.14, 403.5 ["And low stole o'er the stillness the heartbeats of sleep"]); the gurgling of his digestive tract, particularly as his appetite and hunger rise toward morning (456.20–23 ["all the vitalmines is beginning to sozzle in chewn ('tune') and the hormonies to clingleclangle"]); and even an odd stint of nocturnal tooth-grinding.[19] Finally, too, as "farternoiser" (530.36 ["Pater Noster"]), "our hoary frother" is no more successful than Wonderworker-wielding Bloom at curbing the flow of "flatuous" "illiterative porthery" out of "his aers" ["arse"] into his "ares" ["ears"] (23.9–10, 231.30, 421.23); *not* "fatuous alliterative poetry," but a "flatulent" and "illiterate" after- and sound-effect of "porter"-consumption," this "porthery" is misinterpreted, at least once in the *Wake* (23.6–8), as the sound of thunder, so to give us dark, Aristotelean insight into one source of one of the *Wake*'s thunderwords.[20] "Zounds of sounds" like these, all of which lie "buried" inside "the dead giant manalive" (499.27, 500.1–2), each as open to analysis as "that big brewer's belch" made manifest on page 310, generate throughout the *Wake*'s nighttime an incessant "static babel" (499.34)—"static" not simply because this continuum of sounds originates in a "man made static," but also because it makes a perpetual background noise like that audible in radio "static." Together, in one way of thinking, these sounds *are* our hero— "nay, even the first old wugger of himself in the flesh" (79.2 ["Earwicker"])—whose vitality they define "silentioussuemeant under night's altosonority" (62.3–4): *silenceusement* (Fr. "silently"), they show what his "tissue meant"—and all the more intricately "because, living, loving, breathing and sleeping morphomelosophopancreates, as he most significantly did" (88.8–9 [see context]), these sounds show "all" his "flesh" or "body" (Gr. *pan*, "all"; *kreas*, "flesh, body") "skillfully" (Gr. *sophos*) taking the "form" (Gr. *morphe*) of "music" (Gr. *melos*). Since "Here Comes Everybody's" body is incessantly generating unheard "static babel" of this sort, the wakening from the dead of these sounds allows one to begin noticing how much of "the presence (of a curpse)"—and "the present, of course"—is not simply repressed as a condition of civility, but relegated to deep auditory unconsciousness, so in turn to raise dark questions as to how much of the sound that surely "pinnatrated" one's ears last night—or a few minutes ago, for that matter—was "really" heard at all. It is as if, hypnotically, "you . . . remain ignorant of all what you hear" (238.15–16).

The same questions contaminate the second class of "Acoustic Disturbance[s]" that play into Earwicker's ears throughout the *Wake*. Perhaps more intriguing than those of the flesh because they hold forth an extended "cluekey to a worldroom beyond the roomwhorld" (100.29 [or, again, a clue to the real world beyond HCE's "whorled bedroom"]), these "noisance[s]" allow us to see, from yet another perspective, that *Finnegans Wake* is not finally the "universal dream" of some disembodied global everyman, but a reconstruction of the night—and a single night—as experienced by "one stable somebody" whose "earwitness" on the world is coherently chronological. Sounds emanating out of the real "worldroom" outside of HCE's dream— "Hear, O worldwithout!" (244.1)—are inevitably streaming into his ears throughout the night and are in turn inevitably reflected somewhere darkly there "in the back of [the] mind's ear, temptive lissomer" (477.18). Many of these "noisances," very dark indeed, are as difficult to reconstruct with any certainty as are the real-world sonic components—unheard alarm clocks, heavy rains and storms, neighbor's howling pets—that anyone might find, upon reflection, incorporated into the dreams of any average night.

Such real-world "Acoustic Disturbance[s]" are most easy to make out in the sunstruck closing pages of the *Wake*, where the "noisance[s]" impinging

Earwickerwork

on Earwicker's ears, many of them sounds that we would expect to accompany an average morning's wakening, occur with an altogether realistic frequency and clarity. The distant sound of a mail train moving through the night across the River Liffey about three-quarters of the way through the book, for instance—"the mails across the nightrives" (449.30 [Fr. *rives*, "riverbanks"])—causes "earwaker" to "turn a widamost ear dreamily" into "the exhaling night" (449.28–29, 22); and, his "hares [and ears] standing up well and [his] longlugs dittoes" (449.20 [sl. "lugs" = "ears"]), his "tropped head" fills momentarily with other such nocturnal sounds as the croaking of frogs (449.32–33) and the warbling of nightbirds (449.17–19, 24–25 ["owl"], 27, 31), whose noise lifts him into a dim, subliminal awareness of the imminence of sunrise, breakfast, and resurrection (449.33–450.2 ["tealeaves," "trout," "egg," "poach"]). The very obscure sound of that train, however, merely signals the beginning of a gradual, remorseless buildup of urban activity and traffic—lots of traffic—whose sonorous din swells steadily as the book delivers HCE toward the moment of his wakening. This would explain why Joyce expressed concern that the penultimate chapter of the *Wake* should be "about roads, all about dawn and roads";[21] for as "the nightmail afarfrom morning nears" (565.32), and as "the annamation of evabusies" (568.4 [and "the animation of everybody busy"]) fills Earwicker's ears with the noise of "all these peeplers entrammed and detrained" (567.33), the sounds of the morning's bustle and of traffic are audible everywhere:

—Huesofrichunfoldingmorn. Wakenupriseandprove. Provideforsacrifice.
—Wait! Hist! Let us list!
For our netherworld's bosomfoes are working tooth and nail overtime. . . .
(571.32–36)

Earwicker hears in these "bosomfoes" of the dark—clamorous disturbers of his sleep—insistent reminders of his pending reinsertion into the linear clock-time of "history" (hence "Hist!"); but he also continues doing an excellent job of sleepily "whishing" them all away: "It's only the wind on the road outside for to wake all shivering shanks from snorring" (577.36–578.2 [yet note the subliminal hint of "shanks" moving on that "road"]). The strident work of these "noisance[s]," however, becomes harder and harder for him to ignore as he gravitates toward his wakening. When he hazily notes, for instance, that "it is not even yet the engine of the load with haled morries full of crates, you mattinmummur, for dombell dumbs" (604.9–11), the line of "moanolothe inturned" shows him again vaguely conscious of noises in the world "out there": perhaps an "engine"-driven "lorry" "full of crates" is "hauling" a "load" and making a delivery to his establishment; or perhaps "the scream of the service" audible here is an ear-brutalizing milkman (604.16 [hence the "cream," whose souring into "scream" invites us to recall the sometimes inconsiderately noisy behavior of "the cream of the service"]). At the same time, an echo of the sounding of the Angelus ("Hail Mary, full of grace, the Lord is with Thee") shows Earwicker dimly aware that all these disturbances, simply the morning's, foreshadow an imminent resurrection of his body (hence again the Angelus). And the string of expletives that closes off this flurry of sonic agitation, finally—"Oyes! Oyeses! Oyesesyeses!" (604.22)—simply evokes the legal term "*Oyez! Oyez!*" (O. Fr. "Now hear this!"), to indicate that "Sur Soord's" hearing is regaining a legitimate hold on the Daily World held in place by laws and interpretive agreements: "Hearing. The urb it orbs. Then's now with now's then in tense continuant. Heard. Who having has he shall have had. Hear!" (598.28–30). Together with a reference to the gospels ("he who hath ears to hear, let him hear" [Matt. 11:15]) and an evocation of the pope's address "To the City and the World" (L. *Urbi et Orbem*), all of these ciphers evoke the return of our "hoary frother's" consciousness, with auditory clarity, "to the city and the world."

Although the sounds "pinnatrat[ing]" Earwicker's ears are easiest to make out in the *Wake*'s closing chapters, other "noisances" punctuate the long and heavily "Silent" earlier parts of the book (14.6). The most dramatic of these varied "Acoustic Disturbances," and one that might be regarded as representative of the lot, seems to occur in chapter I.iii, at pages 63–70, when "Earwicker or, in slightly modified phraseology, Messrs or Missrs Earwicker, Seir, his feminisible name of multitude" (73.3–5), is deeply enough asleep, as the "comedy nominator" implies (283.7), to be oblivious of his individuality and gender. The pages in question, "bearing . . . several of [those] earmarks of design" which provide a reader with clues about Earwicker's "otological life" (65.36–66.1), most evidently describe a turgid and sporadically conducted "bottle at the gate" (65.35 [or, as the spelling suggests, a "battle" involving a "bottle"]). And a heavy layer of details allows us to infer that what must "really" be happening in the "worldroom" outside of Earwicker's dream at this moment in the night involves an "unsolicited visitor" knocking on a door somewhere out there in the dark (70.13). "Alleging that . . . it was only after ten o'connell, and this his isbar [this bar] was a public oven [haven] for the sake of irsk irskusky [Irish whiskey]," this noisy visitor "demand[s] more wood alcohol," asks our hero "to come out," and, "not easily discouraged, open[s] the wrathfloods of his atillarery and [goes] on at a wicked rate" (70.28–30, 27, 34, 30–32 ["wood alcohol" because our bartending hero wants this disturber of his peace to drop dead]). Whether Ear-wicker is hearing an actual after-hours visitor to his pub, as these details and the diffuse timing of the incident at "ten o'connell" suggest, or whether he is simply hearing a dull knocking somewhere in the distance and mis-construing it as an annoying call to duty cannot at all be clear.[22] It is clear, however, that "someone or other," for obscure reasons, is acting as a dark "summoner" and pulling HCE's hearing and consciousness up from the "deafths" of the night, so to raise in his "tropped head" a question asked elsewhere in the *Wake:* "Why wilt thou erewaken him from his earth, O summonorother"? (255.5–6)—especially when "the hour of his closing hies to hand" (255.6–7 [note the sonic evocation of "Earwicker" in this "ere-wakening" return to the past]). While our hero unconsciously hears the sound of knocking somewhere in the dark "worldroom" out there, and even vaguely realizes what is going on, he misconstrues it in every way possible, as detailing scattered over these pages suggests, "whishing" it away in order to preserve the state of sleep.[23]

Passages like these illustrate in only the most minimal ways the kinds of "Acoustic Disturbance[s]" that beam in out of the dark, throughout the *Wake*, to fall upon Earwicker's radiolike ears. As the chronological pacing of these "noisance[s]" will suggest, especially when integrated with other of the sonic events that interfere with HCE's sleep, they map out the contours of a single night.[24] These passages are important, however, because they also demonstrate the manifold ways in which "our ears, eyes of the darkness" (14.29), "see" in the night, and therefore serve as HCE's "aural eyeness" (623.18). For in all the instances that we have examined, Earwicker's ears enable events in the dark "worldroom" of external space to "hear show of themselves" (8.3–4 [the "here" taking place in "hear"]), and so they gener-ate in the "tropped head" many an "earsighted view" of the world (143.9–10). "Phonoscopically incuriosited," as the *Wake* recurrently suggests (449.1; cf. 123.12–13), our vigilant "european" hero is inevitably "made curious" (It. *incuriosite*) by "sound" (Gr. *phônê*); and, as "one who watches" for it con-tinually (Gr. *skopos* [hence "phonoscopically"]), he is capable of convert-ing it, "in the . . . mind's ear" (477.18), into forms of light and "objects of vision" perceptible imaginarily in the "mind's eye" (515.23 ["object of vision" is another meaning of the Gr. *skopos*]): "Vouchsafe me more soundpicture! It gives furiously to think" (570.14–15).

"PHONEMANON"

Very early in the *Wake*, Joyce alerts his reader to the nature of those "dectroscophonious" mechanisms (123.12) through which the ear, by acting as a "receiver" (Gr. *dekter*) of "sound" (Gr. *phônê*), generates, in the "tropped head," "earsighted" "objects of vision" (Gr. *skopos*) and so brings the world to light. Since the hero whose "eyewitless foggus" we share throughout the *Wake* has the ability to hear or not hear in the night, according to the emotional charges carried by sounds that have the potential to arouse him,

> We may . . . hear nothing if we choose . . . though every crowd has its several tones and every trade has its clever mechanics and each harmonical has a point of its own. . . . But all they are all there . . . as he lays dormont from the macroborg of Holdhard [Howth head] to the microbirg of Pied de Poudre [Fr. *pied*, "foot"]. Behove this sound of Irish sense. Really? Here English might be seen. Royally?
>
> (12.25–13.2)

As these lines suggest, it "behoves" our hero (the "one stable somebody" identified here through the tell-tale rhythm of "As I Was Going to St. Ives") imaginarily to "behold" the sounds he hears, which play into his ears constantly, in a diverse array of "tones," from discrete "points" differentiably localized in space, and in distinctly recognizable "harmonical" patterns— even while he lies unconscious in the night.[25] As "eyes of the darkness," his ears therefore serve the function of an "optophone"—an instrument enabling someone blind to read by converting ordinarily "visible" signs (Gr. *optos*) into musical "sound" (Gr. *phônê*): "Hear? . . . 'Tis optophone which ontophanes. List! Wheatstone's magic lyer" (13.14, 16–17).[26] As these terms further suggest, Earwicker's "optophone"-like ears are the portals through which, in the dark, "reality" (Gr. *onta*) and "being" (Gr. *ta onta*, "existing things") come to light (Gr. *phainô*, "to bring to light, make to appear"): hence the verb "ontophanes," which we might take to mean "to bring real appearances to light."

Since events befalling "the presence (of a curpse)" in the "nowtime" (290.17 ["nighttime"]) also occur subliminally in "the present, of course" and in "now time," these passages furthermore ask us to become conscious of the ways in which the ears take ascendancy over the eyes even in the here and now (cf. 113.27–30, 409.3–4)—especially since the *Wake*, frequently eliding the words "hear" and "here," suggests that much of the "here" unconsciously undergoes formation in "hear" (cf. 8.3–4, 76.10–11, 147.3, 468.24–25, 478.2, 536.2, 565.19, 588.27, and 593.5–6). For vision is an incomplete and partial sense: it is not always there in sleep and never there behind one's back, whereas the ears are openly receptive even in the dark, and, like the absurd radio described at the opening of II.iii, operate continually with a "circumcentric" sweep that encompasses 360° (310.7). Sympathetic identity with a hero like Earwicker, then, obligating us to eradicate consciousness of everything but the vitality of the ear, will waken from the dead and lift into consciousness a subdimension of space, distinct from visual space, which Joyce calls "a melegoturny marygoraumd" at the beginning of II.iii (309.23–24). This auditory "space" (Ger. *Raum*), always suffused with sound and "music" (Gr. *melos*), "goes round" one everywhere (hence "-goraumd") and differs from visual space, whose outward extension is stopped flat by opaque objects (eyelids and walls, for instance) because it penetrates even "soundconducting walls" (183.9): "Do he not know that walleds had wars. Harring man, is neow king. This is modeln times" (289.F6). Limited in extension only by the power of the ear itself ("Ear! Ear! Weakear! An allness eversides," "even to the extremity of the world" [568.26, 360.31–33]), this sonic spatiality resembles the space that one enters when riding on a whirling, music-irradiated "merry-go-round" (hence "marygoraumd"), because it is always in motion and never still or stable to the eye.[27] Since it escapes the dominance of vision and the demands of real-world exigency, this dimension of the real tends to fall beneath consciousness (as now, perhaps, such of its constituents as the sounds of remote traffic, the body, or a "sky body" droning in the air miles above one may also fall beneath consciousness [309.20, 22]). But it is in this unconsciously perceived "o'ralereality" (289.4 [Fr. *oreille*, "ear"])—an emanation of Earwicker's ears—that the *Wake* shows major parts of the world "ontophan[ing]" and coming to light.

Particularly because the spiral of the inner ear is the scene of *The New Science*, which reconstructs dark "changes of mind" (165.17) on the evidence of modulations in "sound sense" swept out in the course of "Iro-European ascendances" (37.26), this auditory "marygoraumd" becomes, in particular, the space in which speech takes place, and therefore the site of HCE's wakening and genesis. Because *The New Science* shows humanity rising into en<u>light</u>enment not primarily in visually extended space, but in the slow drift forward through time of "phonetic" structures that have the power to make and alter "phenomenal" ones, we should furthermore see that this auditory "marygoraumd" is the protospace out of which visual space and consciousness waken. Even since the beginning of time, in "first infancy" (22.1), the ears have always and inevitably been open and receptive; whereas the eyes, sightless in all the dark places and darker parts of life, have not. Vision therefore becomes, in the *Wake*, a sense whose developed forms are preceded and made possible by hearing. The world comes to light through "our ears, eyes of the darkness" not only in the night, but also "in the night of thick darkness" and "in the early childhood of the world" treated in *The New Science* (*NS*, 331, 69), when a patriarchal power heard in the sound of thunder gives the unconscious body "the fright of [its] light" (309.2 [and "life"]) and so begins the eye-opening genesis of gentile reality. The *Wake* describes this genesis, in the play-filled "Mime of Mick, Nick and the Maggies," in terms that locate it in childhood:

> For the Clearer of the Air from on high has spoken in tumbuldum tambaldam to his tembledim tombaldoom worrild and, moguphonoised by that phonemanon, the unhappitents of the earth have terrerumbled from fimament unto fundament and from tweedledeedumms down to twiddledeedees.
> Loud, hear us!
> Loud, graciously hear us!
> Now have thy children entered into their habitations. . . . Gov be thanked! Thou hast closed the portals of the habitations of thy children and thou hast set thy guards thereby . . . that thy children may read in the book of the opening of the mind to light and err not in the darkness which is the afterthought of thy nomatter. . . .
> (258.20–33)

As the patriarchal force identified as "Gov" here (a "God," or paternal "Gov"-ernor) sends formative "noise" thundering into the infant ear—"Loud" as if through a "megaphone" (hence "moguphonoised")—the law of the "Lord God" ("Loud" "Gov") is implanted in the bodies of indistinct and unformed little "tweedledeedumms" and "twiddledeedees" stricken with "mogiphonia" (Eng., "difficulty in producing loud vocal sound" [*OED*]). And as a consequence of the implantation of that "sound" and "voice" in the ear's flesh (hence the Gr. *phônê* in "phonemanon"), the "earth" "trembles" and "rumbles" "from firmament unto fundament" (hence the Fr. *terre* ["earth"] in "terrerumbled"), and "phenomenal" reality begins undergoing its genesis and coming to light. The informing of infant bodies through such vocal protocommandments as the thundered word "No!" or the order "that they do ming no merder" (259.5 [L. *mingo*, "piss"; Fr. *merde*, "shit"]) retailors those bodies "from fimament unto fundament" (L. *fimus* ["excrement"], *fundus* ["bottom, arse"]) and brings about a cataclysmic upheaval of the universe at whose purposive latter end the body is humanized and made visible, together with the "phenomena" of gentile reality (hence the "dim" premoni-

Earwickerwork

tions of "temple," "tomb," "tumulum," and "doom" audible in the ominously thundering rumble of "tumbuldum tambaldam" and "tembledim tombaldoom").

The context in which this particular thunderclap sounds in the *Wake*—at the end of the childishly play-filled "Mime of Mick, Nick and the Maggies"—dramatizes its ambiguated power. For the hearing of this "loud" "phonemanon" "in the far ear" has an "oreillental" effect (23.22–23, 357.18 ["far east" and "orient" now overlaid on the Eng. "ear" and Fr. *oreille* in order to designate the precise site of the dawning of light]); it makes possible "the opening of the mind to light" and the entry of children into the "habits" and "habitations" of civilization. At the same time, however, the hearing of this patriarchal "phonemanon" also produces "unhappiness" and "worry" in the newly formed "unhappitents" of the "worrild," because it means falling for life into a posture of inescapably slavish "obedience" (< L. *ob-audire*, "to hear completely") made necessary by submission to the strait-jacketing constraint of a language. As the "phenomenal" appearances of the "worrild" are brought to light through the hearing of this "phonemanon," accordingly, a being appears

> who, in deesperation of deispiration at the diasporation of his diesparation, was found of the round of the sound of the lound of the. Lukkedoerendunandurraskewdyloo-shoofermoyportertooryssooysphalnabortansporthaokansakroidverjkapakkapuk.
> Byfall.
> Upploud!
>
> (257.25–30)

Like the formative "breath of god" in Genesis (hence the L. *spiritus dei* in "deispiration"), the "loud sound" of this patriarchal thunder, by opening the mind to light, allows its hearer to take "the sound of the land" ("sound of the lound") and begin his "preparation" (L. *paratio*) for ascent into the light of civilized "day" (L. *dies* [hence "diesparation"]), and so merits "applause" (Ger. *Beifall*, "applause" ["Byfall"]; Eng. "applaud" ["Upploud"]). But it also gives birth to "deep desperation" ("deesperation") and scatters "the unhappitents" of the "worrild" into unending wandering and loneliness (hence the "diaspora" in this "diasporation"). This is why the hundred-lettered thunderword in this context is compounded of terms meaning "shut the door" (Da. *luk døren*; Gael. *dún an doras*; It. *chiudi l'uscio*; Fr. *fermez la porte*; Eng. idiom, "sport the oak"; Russ. *zakroi dver*; Turk. *kapiya kapat*). As the thunder of this patriarchal "phonemanon" sounds "in the far ear," doors start slamming and shutting violently everywhere, closing forever the infinite possibilities of childhood; and as those "doors shut," formalized "rooms" (an Eng. cognate of the Ger. *Raum*, "space") start appearing behind them, causing visual space in turn to undergo its genesis. The sound of this thunderclap, in context, therefore becomes a burst of "applause" falling at the end of a play (257.31–32)—and, in particular, the end of the play of childhood. But the end of childhood, complementarily, means the beginning of the play of "the worrild," which comes to light here "by falling" ("Byfall") "up loud" ("Upploud"), into the perception of the "phonemanon" of articulate sound.

How this "falling" "up loud" into articulate sound happens is illustrated in one way by figure 9.5, which charts the evolution of the conceptually distinct terms "phonetics," "phenomenon," and "phantasm"—all of which stand in spectral relation to one another and, as the Wakean coinages "phonemanon" and "ontophanes" suggest, may not be so clearly distinguished in "sound sense" as they are to "day's reason." Although it is unclear whether the two phonetically identical roots *bha*- I ("to talk") and *bha*- II ("to illumine") are semantically related in historical fact, a little Wakean "adamelegy" (77.26) will allow us to see that all of the concepts which they generate do share a common "sound sense," having to do with illumination and the bringing of things to light. For "talk" (Gr. *phônê*), no less than "light" (Gr. *phôs*), has the power to illuminate: just as "professors" enlighten students and bring to light new knowledge, and just as "confessors" cause dark growths in the soul to come to light, so talk generally illuminates, opening up new "facets" of the world and irradiating it with an "epiphanic" "phosphorescence." Reference to the first page of *A Portrait of the Artist as a Young Man* will illustrate the essential unity of all the terms shown spilling up out of the radical *bha*-; most of these terms might accurately enter a paragraph describing the effect of that page: a "preface" of sorts, the opening of *A Portrait* holds forth an "epiphany" in which we see "phenomenal" reality coming to light as the "infant" Stephen, orienting himself in human "phonology," beginning to identify the "faces" of members of his "family," and listening to "fables" and "fairy tales," begins to discover, with his "fate," first "fame" and the rudiments of a "profession," as well as "infamy" and the habit of "confession." It "make[s] soundsense" (121.15) that "talk" and "light," "phonics" and "photons," should be related.

As talk has the power to illuminate, so it has the power to make "phenomena" manifest. For if we integrate these etymologies with a reading of passages in the *Wake* which explore the "phonemanon" itself, it becomes necessary to see that the way in which any "phenomenon" comes to light (Gr. *phainomenon*, "that which appears" or "that which has been brought

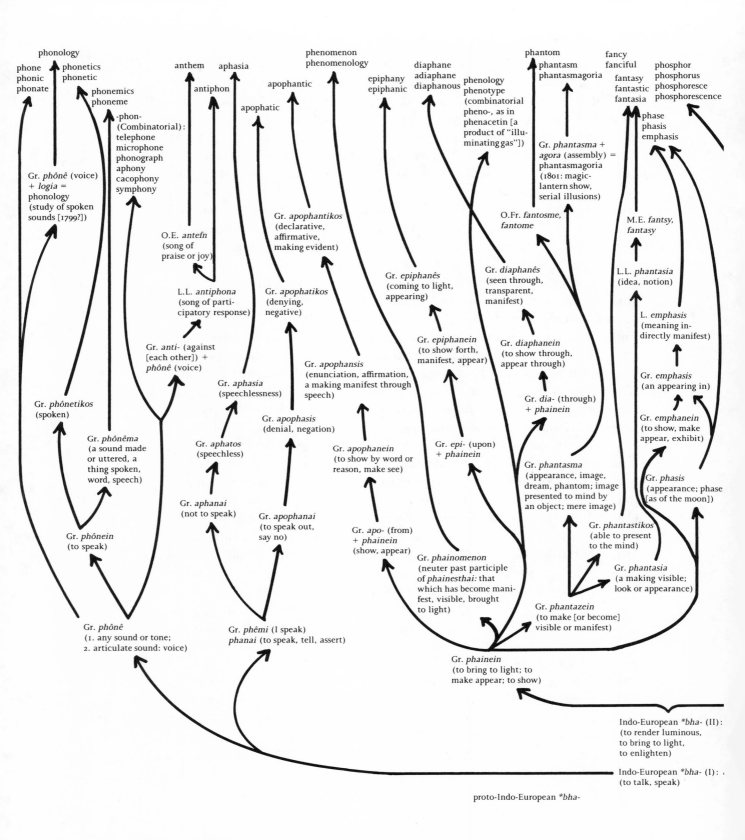

Figure 9.5. Etymological chart: *bha-. The "funantics" of "phonemanon" (450.27, 258.22)

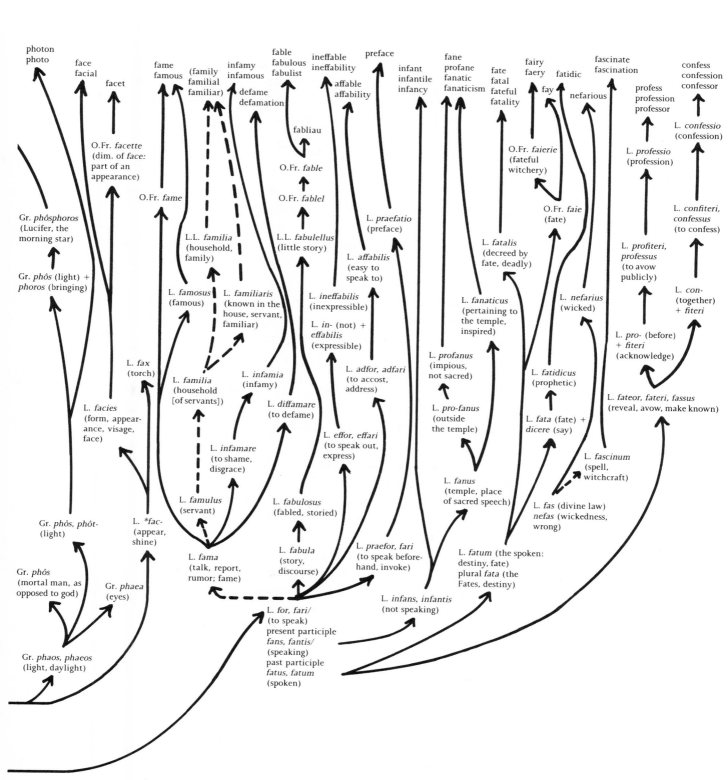

photon
photo

Gr. *phôsphoros*
(Lucifer, the
morning star)

Gr. *phôs* (light) +
phoros (bringing)

Gr. *phôs, phôt-*
(light)

Gr. *phôs*
(mortal man, as
opposed to god)

Gr. *phaea*
(eyes)

Gr. *phaos, phaeos*
(light, daylight)

face
facial

facet

O.Fr. *facette*
(dim. of *face*:
part of an
appearance)

L. *facies*
(form, appear-
ance, visage,
face)

L. *fax*
(torch)

L. **fac-*
(appear,
shine)

fame
famous

O.Fr. *fame*

L. *famosus*
(famous)

L. *familia*
(household
[of servants])

L. *famulus*
(servant)

L. *fama*
(talk, report,
rumor; fame)

(family
familial
familiar)

L.L. *familia*
(household,
family)

L. *familiaris*
(known in the
house, servant,
familiar)

infamy
infamous

defame
defamation

L. *infamia*
(infamy)

L. *infamare*
(to shame,
disgrace)

fable
fabulous
fabulist

affable
affability

fabliau

O.Fr. *fable*

O.Fr. *fablel*

L.L. *fabulellus*
(little story)

L. *diffamare*
(to defame)

L. *fabulosus*
(fabled, storied)

L. *fabula*
(story,
discourse)

ineffable
ineffability

L. *ineffabilis*
(inexpressible)

L. *in-* (not) +
effabilis
(expressible)

L. *effor, effari*
(to speak out,
express)

preface

L. *affabilis*
(easy to
speak to)

L. *praefatio*
(preface)

L. *adfor, adfari*
(to accost,
address)

L. *praefor, fari*
(to speak before-
hand, invoke)

infant
infantile
infancy

L. *infans, infantis*
(not speaking)

fane
profane
fanatic
fanaticism

L. *profanus*
(impious,
not sacred)

L. *pro-fanus*
(outside
the temple)

L. *fanaticus*
(pertaining to
the temple,
inspired)

L. *fanus*
(temple, place
of sacred speech)

fate
fatal
fateful
fatality

L. *fatalis*
(decreed by
fate, deadly)

L. *fatum* (the spoken:
destiny, fate)
plural *fata* (the
Fates, destiny)

fairy
faery

fay

O.Fr. *faierie*
(fateful
witchery)

O.Fr. *faie*
(fate)

fatidic

L. *nefarius*
(wicked)

L. *fatidicus*
(prophetic)

L. *fata* (fate) +
dicere (say)

nefarious

fascinate
fascination

L. *fascinum*
(spell,
witchcraft)

L. *fas* (divine law)
nefas (wickedness,
wrong)

L. *for, fari/*
(to speak)
present participle
fans, fantis/
(speaking)
past participle
fatus, fatum
(spoken)

profess
profession
professor

L. *professio*
(profession)

L. *profiteri,
professus*
(to avow
publicly)

L. *pro-* (before)
+ *fiteri*
(acknowledge)

confess
confession
confessor

L. *confessio*
(confession)

L. *confiteri,
confessus*
(to confess)

L. *con-*
(together)
+ *fiteri*

L. *fateor, fateri, fassus*
(reveal, avow, make known)

to light") is difficult to disentangle from the illuminating powers of the human "voice" (Gr. *phônê*). Indeed, since the "phenomenal" may be brought to light in same way that "phantoms" are—through the operations of human "phonology" (< Gr. *phônê*)—it becomes equally necessary to see that, at a primal level, distinctions between the "phenomenal" and the "fantastic" break down completely. As a reconstruction of the night, the *Wake* explores precisely this area of primal breakdown; for the dim borderline separating the "phenomenally" and the "fantastically" apparent crumbles entirely in the dream, where all evident "phenomena" are only "phantasmal," and where sheer "fantasy" is the only observable "phenomenon." As a reconstruction of the night, then, the *Wake* is exploring the primordia of the "funnaminal world" (244.13 [note the sleeping giant "Finn," and the "animal" body, underlying "funnaminal]).

Complementarily, we might see the world coming to light "phenomenally" through the power of a human "phonology" that begins in an obscure and unrecapturable burst of "tribalbalbutience" like that out of which the radicals *bha-* I and *bha-*II hypothetically emerged (309.2)—where "balbutience," from the Latin *balbutiens* ("stammering" or "speaking obscurely"), derives from the Latinate equivalent (*balbal*) of the Greek *barbar* ("barbarian"), the latter being a term of echoic origin evidently applied to "tribes" whose members spoke not Greek, but gibberish (like "barbarbarbar"). For the spilling-up into distinctness out of the *bha-* radicals of all the lexical terms given in the etymological diagram illustrates concretely how gentile reality comes to light, "in the far ear," through one vast process of audiophonic amplification, or "overhearing," by means of which a humankind originating in "tribalbalbutience" is able to "phone man on" ("phonemanon") into a future that is continually wakening and unfolding. As human speech amplifies a simple "sound sense" into a proliferating array of newly elaborated "phonetic" arrangements and forms through the process of etymological change, it also makes new distinctions. And by making new distinctions—between the "phenomenal" and the "phantastic," for instance— "phonetic" talk, like light, makes things distinct. This "may not or maybe a no concern of the Guinnesses but." (309.1), it is surely a concern of "Genesis."

As the quotation implies, all of these considerations allow us now to return, "by a commodius vicus of recirculation," to that passage at the beginning of II.iii, where we last left HCE suspended "in his umbrageous house . . . with the radio beamer tower" (380.15–16), hovering in the dark with his radio-receptive ears waiting to hear. Beginning with the announcement that "the fright of his light in tribalbalbutience hides aback in the doom of the balk of the deaf" (309.2–3), the passage finally shows us how formed "light" enters the "tropped head"—whether in childhood, "in the childhood of the world," or at night—as ears deaf to sound are startled into vigilant attentiveness. As a misperceived "Acoustical Disturbance"—"our hoary frother's" belch, in this instance—"make[s] soundsense" in the dark (121.15), the "phonemanon" generates a stream of "phonetic" associations, to which "phantasms" are attached; the "birth of an otion," then (309.12)—or the wakening of a "little ear" (Gr. *ôtion*)—inevitably entails "the birth of a no-tion" or two.

The wakening of that little ear not only complicates the structure of the passage in question, which finally consists of a great deal more than inter-linked networks of radioparts and otological terms; it also explains why the rest of the passage is there at all. For Earwicker's ears differ from the ears of animals in being capable not simply of acoustical perception and mere "hearing," but also of phonetic perception and "listening." Like all of his body, HCE's ears are humanly made and organized, wired by parents and the authority of literacy with "phones"—"phones" which might be understood both in the sense of "voices" (Gr. *phônê*) and of "phonemes," irreducible units of articulate speech sounds that have been there since the beginning of recollectible time and that can be popped into wakefulness at the least asso-ciation. If our hero is "haard of heaering," then (332.20), "he's [also] herd of hoarding" (331.3)—until "deaf do his part" (331.5). And what he "hoards" are billions of "phones."

If we move through the passage once again, then, another network of as-sociatively linked elements will emerge from it; for sounds entering the hu-manoid radio-receiver with the "howdrocephalous enlargement" must, in order to be heard, "pinnatrate inthro an auricular forfickle (known as the Vakingfar sleeper, monofractured by Piaras UaRhuamhaighaudhlug, tympan founder, Eustache Straight . . .)" (310.9–12). Much of this detail fleshes out features peculiar to Earwicker's "otological life": the terms "pinna," "aur-icle," "tympanum," and "eustachian," for instance; and also, among the components of "UaRhuamhaighaudhlug," *Raum* (Ger. "space"), "-aud-" (L. *audio*, "to hear"), and "lug" (sl. for "ear"). But since the construction also contains the taxonomic name of the "earwig" (L. *Forficula auricularia*), it shows "earwigs," too, creepily moving through the ear of the "sleeper" whose name, "Piaras UaRhuamhaighaudhlug" (or "Persse O'Reilly" [I.ii]) itself evokes a French "earwig" (*perce-oreille*). Shown in figure 9.6, these insects crawl through Earwicker's ear not only in the passage at hand, but

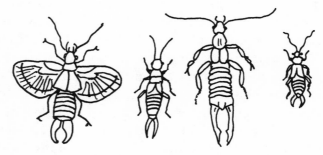

The Common Earwig
Taxonomic L.: *Forficula auricularia* (310.10)
Fr.: *perce-oreille*

Figure 9.6. Earwigs on parade

everywhere in the "Eyrawyggla saga" (48.16–17), and they raise an immediate question: "Did you aye, did you eye, did you everysee suchaway, suchawhy eeriewhigg airywhugger?" (360.31–32). The "absurdity" of the question in turn suggests that the way in which earwigs (or the ears themselves, for that matter) visually appear to the "eye" has nothing to do with their recurrence in the *Wake*. The "funny antics" of these insects, in a book "as cockful of funantics as it's tune to my fork" (450.27), ultimately has to do not with the book's "meoptics" or "acountstrick[s]" (hence the "tuning fork"), but with its "funantics"; and "funantics" would be "phonetics" sent off on some very "funny antics."

"EARWIGS"

Because the name of the "earwig" (< O.E. *earwicga*, "ear-worm") maintains an odd semantic constancy in a number of European languages (the Fr. *perce-oreille* ["ear-piercer"], the Ger. *Ohrwurm* ["ear-worm"], the Da. *ørentvist* ["ear-twist"], and the Russ. *ukhovyortka* ["ear-borer"] all paralleling the Eng. "earwig," and all intimating that some darkly fundamental relation links this creature with the human ear), most books on insects find themselves in the position of having to do much what Joyce does in the second chapter of the *Wake*, which gives the obscure "facts in the nominigentilisation" of "earwigger" (31.28) and recurrently associates his "agnomen" with the English "earwig" (e.g., at 31.26–28). Characteristically, entomological texts note in a sentence or two that "there is nothing to justify the vulgar belief that these insects introduce themselves into the ear and bore a hole in its interior through which they may penetrate into the brain";[28] or else they note that the creature "is called earwig, gossips will tell you, because it creeps into the ears of incautious sleepers in the open air, and so worms its way to the brain, where, if you will believe the purveyors of folklore natural history, it grows to a gigantic size."[29] "Earwigs," in short, seem to behave in the ear much as hearsay and gossip do, furtively entering the brain and growing way out of reasonable proportions once they get there; at least in Western folklore, they seem to constitute a primitive theory of dream formation. Their presence in Earwicker's ears at any moment in the *Wake*, then, even while he lies as deeply dead to the world as a corpse in the Book of the Dead, indicates that his ears are bugged with "the *Bug of the Deaf*" (134.36) and that he is about to receive a heavy dose of auditory phantasmagoria.

As the hardly scientific articles of entomological gossip quoted above also suggest, "earwigger's" ears are in fact (of sorts) filled with these dream-breeding "bugs of the deaf"; for "earwigs," obviously, have really gotten into "earwigger's" ears in much the same disturbing way that they just got into yours: through hearsay or gossip (hence the common equation of "earwigs" and "ear wags" throughout the *Wake*—where "ear wags," "by the wag," would simply mean "gossips" [413.35; see 98.28–29, 149.13, 315.23–26, 339.18–19, 485.21, 496.15–16, 619.6–10]). Since "every busy eerie whig's a bit of a torytale to tell" (20.23), we might see that these brain-beclouding "earwigs" are simply ciphers for elements in a "word" (175.12 [a verbally contained "world"]) where "everything is hearsay, a matter of tales and rumor";[30] capable of filling the "tropped head" (or empty "wig") with "story-tales" that regress into the past ("tory") even while moving progressively toward the future ("whig"), these "eerie whigs" therefore move through Earwicker's ears with all the "eerie" weirdness of elements in dreams. Indeed, since the "tropped head" of our vacant hero is filled with tangled chains of hearsay, gossip, and ear "waggery" (79.2)—with *signifying* chains not least of which is the Authorized Version—"the human head . . . might be usefully compared with an earwig on a fullbottom" (164.27–29 [where that "fullbottom," a kind of wig, would evoke the empty head]).[31] The kind of hearing generated by the movement of earwigs through the ear and "wigeared" head (414.36) would stand in contrast to the kind of unheard hearing registered in the "tropped head" when the "rods of Corti" resonate mechanically in "the lubberendth" but leave no recollectible memory of sound in the mind. For if Earwicker hears, in the night, some real sounds that seem to leave no memorable impression in his consciousness, he complementarily hears many unreal sounds that do: these would be sounds auditorily hallucinated and heard in "the mind's ear" (254.18), as when figures without fleshed mouths speak in dreams. "The whacker his word the weaker our ears for auracles who parles parses orileys" (467.28–29): "Persse O'Reilly's" "ears," in other words (his "auracles"), are in a manner able to "talk" (Fr. *parler*), however "weakly" and "whackily," by recalling the sound of the spoken "word."

We might see how "earwigs" behave in Earwicker's ear if we return to that passage at the beginning of chapter II.iii in which we first noted them and begin reading again "in midias reeds" (158.7 ["in medias res," though as if listening like "Midas," to the suggestive whisper of mere "reeds"]). As "Piaras UaRhuamhaighaudhlug" lies there sound asleep in a vacuum and waiting to hear, we learn that he is surrounded by a bizarre gathering—of "concertiums," "Guild[s]," "Reunion[s]," "Bnibrthirhd[s]," "Crowds," and "Ligue[s]" (310.14–17 [as well as "Bnai-Brith brotherhoods" and "leagues"])—all of which "lall the bygone dozed they arborised around" (310.18). The "concert" in "concertiums" suggests that all of these "consortiums" generate sounds; and if we reduce them all "to the loaferst terms" (283.7–8 [ones applicable to our "loafer's" sleep]), it becomes evident that all these "associations," historically, are *free associations* (since anyone or anything can join, for instance, a "crowd"). Lying at the center of the passage that we have been examining, then, these terms suggest that Earwicker's ears are constituted not simply of radiolike sound-receiving mechanisms and "otological" parts, but also of extensive chains of audiophonic "associations" which reach back into "all the bygone days" ("lall the bygone dozed") and which, having gotten into his ears "through the grapevine," "arborise around" him in a tangled and arborlike trellis of sounds. If these associations "lull the Big One," who is "dazed" because he has "dozed" off, they also generate a kind of internal whispering. As the image of whispers passing through the whorled concealments of the ear along a line of "free associations" implies, Earwicker orients himself in the world not only by picking up merely "Acoustic Disturbance[s]," but also by keeping his ear to the ground (500.1) and by keeping finely tuned in to that immense network of "sound sense"—human speech—whose most local and parochial form, gossip, also has the power to bring dark things to light. Earwicker's ears therefore become in themselves a "pub" of sorts, filled with the voices of all sorts of others that are lifted into wakefulness by free association.

If a reading of *The New Science* shows HCE lying at the evolved end of a diachronic language whose roots lie unrecapturably buried in the unconsciousness of prehistory, immersion in the *Wake*'s "funantics" complementarily shows Earwicker lying at the center of an immense phonological tangle whose totality is language as a synchronic structure. This is an aspect of the *Wake*—and it is a definite, if partial aspect—that does not need a great deal of attention here because it is the only aspect of the book that many readers seem currently willing to engage. Regarding the *Wake* as a work whose subject is "the pure *jouissance* of the signifier outside meaning," a work within which "the limits of communication [have been] . . . undone in the spreading out of a play of the signifier," readings which treat the book as a work of pure textuality are obviously important because they call attention to the *Wake*'s clear interest in the utter abitrariness of language as a sign-system infiltrated with insidious patterns of "awethorrorty," so to show how Joyce anticipated by decades one current academic interest in theory.[32] Such readings will hardly explain, however, why it would have taken Joyce fifteen years to produce a text which he was always careful to distinguish from dada and the surreal;[33] or why, when he was asked to say what the *Wake* was "about," Joyce never hesitated to say that it was "about the night" (as opposed to less concrete forms of nothing). To regard the *Wake* as a free-floating scud of signifiers disengaged from contact with the concrete, then, finally overlooks, in the best of all Western traditions, "the supreme importance . . . of physical life" and "the presence (of a curpse)" (35.22–23), by reducing the body "tropped head," repressively, to only one "square inch of the only foolscap available" on it—the tympanum—notwithstanding the *Wake*'s insistence that its own penman and Joyce's surrogate in the book writes all "over every square inch of . . . his own body" (185.35–36). As those most influential in advancing the importance of theory have attested, Joyce was light-years ahead of attempts now being made to theorize him.[34]

"THE BALLAD OF PERSSE O'REILLY"

If we now put into an integrated perspective the various audiophonic forces that play through Earwicker's ears in the dark, it should be evident that although he has "Ivy under his tangue" (485.21–22 [because both "tongue" and "language"—Gael. *teanga*—are vegetating]) and a "hohallo to his dullaphone" (485.22 [because his ears are "dull" and "hollow"]), "eh, eh, eh, esquire earwugs, escusado, of Jenkins' Area" is in severe conflict from beginning to end of the *Wake* (485.20–21)—in an "area" precisely specified by reference to "the War of Jenkins' Ear," and in a manner specified by the dull questions "eh?" and "excuse me?" which remind us of his underlying "hard-hearingness" (581.31).[35] So extensive are these conflicts, in fact—between absolute deafness and aroused hearing, between merely acoustical "hearing" and attentively phonetic "listening," between the hearing of "outer" and "inner" sounds—that "if you hored him outerly as we harum lubber-intly, from morning rice till nightmale, with his drums and bones and hums in drones your innereer'd heerdly heer he" (485.25–28). The proliferation of these conflicts in the "inner ear" (hence the ear "drums," the "labyrinth" in "lubberintly," and "innereer'ed") leads to moments in HCE's nightlife whose audiophonic properties are so entangled that our hero becomes as unrecognizable as the dismembered protagonist of "Johnny, I Hardly Knew Ye," a body nearly slain "with guns and drums, and drums and guns." For his always wakeful hearing, in the night, modulates through a steady continuum of forms capable of degenerating, for instance, from a call to "listen!" (571.24) into one to "Lesten" (477.7 [where "listening" "lessens"]), and ultimately into a state where "he lisn't the lug" (162.26 [and where the "lug" "isn't" "listening" at all]).

How these various forces at conflictive play in Earwicker's ear come together in the *Wake*'s "auradrama" might best be seen in its second chapter ("the Earwicker absurdity"), which patently explores the "character" of Earwicker, repeatedly asks the important question, "Have you heard?" (45.1, 44.17–18), and tells the story of how Earwicker got his name so obscurely that it is never clear whether the agnomen was a distinction conferred on him by the king or an abusive epithet hurled at him by the rabble. Ultimately, as the chapter suggests, "the facts in his nominigentilisation" are neither accessible nor important, though the process that leads to all the evident conjecturing is.

"Discarding once for all those theories . . . which would link him back with such pivotal ancestors as the Glues, the Gravys, the Northeasts, the Ankers and the Earwickers of Sidlesham in the Hundred of Manhood" (30.5–8), the chapter begins with a list of names that our hero, like Joyce, may have gotten from a tourist guide while summering in Sussex:[36] since the names come off tombstones, their owners having in common the fact of being dead, the details tell us that Finnegan will no longer be quite dead to the world in this part of the night, but will instead, even while lying embedded in a "sound seemetery," ascend into a state of vigilant Earwicker-hood. We therefore find him basking "in prefall paradise peace" and "saving daylight" here (30.15, 13 [by sleeping]), wrapped in the "duskguise" of a "cabbaging Cincinnatus" (30.12–13). "Cabbaging," of course, suggests that he is looking for a HEAD of something or other, and since "Cincinnatus," if we "traduce . . . [the] comedy nominator to the loaferst terms" (283.6–7), was most famous for "his retirement" (607.14–15), he becomes a cipher for our sleeping giant, *Finnfinnotus* (285.L1 ["Finn"]), who has also finally "retired" (33.3)—although only for the night: hence his appearance, in this chapter, "in a wardrobe panelled tuxedo" and "a shirt well entitled a swallowall" (33.6–8 [articles of "*evening* dress," as opposed to daywear; on sleep as a form of "retirement" see also 55.14, 77.18, 144.4, 248.27, and 436.16]). As the world's most famous retiree, moreover, Cincinnatus is celebrated most because his retirement was disrupted twice by *calls* to duty; and much the same is true of our sleepily "retired" hero, who is also evidently disturbed by a "call" of some sort to serve (30.19–31.28).

Since HCE can only "no" in the night, it is not clear whether the "call" that rouses him from his "prefall paradise peace" is the barking of a dog, as the detail at 30.18–19 seems to suggest " (or so it appierce)" (512.24); but the evocation early in the chapter of wording from "John Peel"—a hunting-song about noise that "would waken the dead"—does suggest that an "Acoustic Disturbance" of some sort has broken through the night's "amossive silence" (31.32) and so has made a man sleepily dead to the world very much "akin" to a noise-roused neighbor of "John Peel":[37] "For he kinned Jom Pill with his court so gray and his haunts in his house in the mourning" (31.28–29 ["haunts" and "mourning," however, show "Finnegan" stubbornly intent on remaining dead to the world]). Whatever the case, the misinterpreted sound agitates in HCE's "tropped head" an extended exploration of what would surely be a Protestant bartender's greatest dream and nightmare: what if, while he "was asleep at the wheel" (519.18), the King came into his pub and ordered a drink (30.19–31.28)? And worse, what if his regular clientele talked?

As a deft practitioner of both "acounstrick[s]" and "funantics," Earwicker now becomes "a layteacher of . . . orthophonethics" (38.35–36 [as opposed to a standing one])—where "orthophonetics" would be the "proper study of sound"; and in this capacity, he is periodically "overheard, in his secondary personality as . . . [an] underreared, poul soul, by accident" (38.27–28). "Under-eared" "in his second personality" because he cannot hear things exactly, yet an "over-hearer" (presumably in his "first personality") because whatever he does hear, he distorts way out of all reasonable proportions, Earwicker himself now becomes both the generator and receiver of an elaborate chain of "gossiple" that is ostensibly passed "earstoear" throughout the chapter (38.23, 539.1–2), but in fact is "delivered in his epistolear" (38.23), "his strict privatear" (327.36). In the same way that any dreamer underlies "all the charictures in [his] drame" (302.31–32), so too "Earwicker, that homogenius man" (34.14), finally underlies all the ridiculously "heterogenious" figures who spread rumors of his "whispered sins" (69.4).

As "the learned scholarch Canavan of Canmakenoise," for instance, (31.21–22 [Gael. *Ó Ceanndubháinn*, "dark-head"]), our dark-headed hero "can make noise," even while dwelling, as if in monastic "Clonmacnoise," in a deeply "secret cell" (182.34–35). Indeed, since "we knows his ventruquulence" (360.20–21 ["truculent" "ventriloquism"]), it should be clear that "he clearly expresse[s] himself" throughout this chapter (34.35), though in forms as indirect as that of the sentence in which this phrase appears (34.34–35.1). Since this garrulous figure from "Canmakenoise" is also "the owner of an exceedingly niced ear" (48.20–21), we might see that "the doomed but always ventriloquent Agitator" himself, by pursuing "a long chain of thoughts and associations" through "syllable[s] of . . . verbal hotchpotch" (*ID*, 331), generates the whole noisy "caravan" of "uncontrollable nighttalkers . . . who . . . [are] staged" in the chapter (56.5–6, 32.7–10 [and who are therefore not unambiguously real]). As he does so, "gaunt grey ghostly gossips [start] growing grubber in the glow" (594.25–26).

One of the first of these is "Gaping Gill," a figure who is "swift to mate errthors" while "diagnosing through eustacetube" (36.35–36). "Swift to meet others," but also "to make errors" in the process, "Gaping Gill" is simply a version of our "sleepytalking" hero himself (327.21), "Mr Eustache," whose biggest "error" lies in his failure to see that he "makes" up, while dreaming, all those "others" whom he "meets" in his own "tropped head," which therefore resembles "Gaping Ghyl," a deep vertical shaft in Yorkshire, primarily in being a profound natural cavity. In "mat[ing an] errthor" and proceeding to spread rumors of HCE's "whispered sins," moreover, "Gaping Gill" runs into a "hypertituitary type," practiced in "Heidelberg mannleich cavern ethics," named "Sweatagore" (37.1–2). Here, too, since the overproduction of "pituitary" hormone causes "gigantism" (hence "hypertituitary"), and "Sweatagore" evokes the Russian giant "Svyatogor," we might see only the *Wake*'s sleeping giant underlying all the "delusional acting" (164.3), all of which takes place in a sleeping body (hence HCE), dead to the world (hence the Ger. *Leiche*, or "corpse," in "mannleich"), that has regressed to a Vichian unconsciousness (hence the references to "Heidelberg man" and "cave ethics"). Dark encounters like these suggest not only that all the spreading gossip which culminates in "The Ballad of Persse O'Reilly" latently unfolds in the vertiginously coiled labyrinth of Earwicker's ear, but also that our hero is guilty of nothing much greater than *"Hearsay in paradox lust"* (263.L4 ["heresy" implying internal division, and "hearsay" its cause]), having become "a lustsleuth nosing for trouble in a boobytrap" (33.31–32 [that "boobytrap" the "booby's" own head]). As the "lustsleuth" within him seeks out pleasure, he invariably runs into trouble, so to throw himself into conflict and to agitate himself out of the "prefall paradise peace" in which the chapter began (hence "Paradise Lost"). By the time the ballad itself is "piped out of his decentsoort hat" at the end of the chapter (43.34–35 [the Da. *sort* and Eng. "soot" keeping the "head" concealed beneath that "hat" black]), all of the conflicting "gossiple so delivered in his epistolear" comes to define him, "Persse O'Reilly," as a precise network of living contradictions (or a "paradox" of "lusts").

In concrete ways, the chapter is elaborately dramatizing what all of *Finnegans Wake* announces generally: that "overhearing" is a condition of this book, structured as it is on the closure of the eye and the eternal openness of the ear. Any reader cultivating the essential "ideal insomnia" must therefore constantly "overhear," and in all three senses of the word, if he wishes to identify with a hero like "Persse O'Reilly": by magnifying hardly heard intimations, as if "overhearing" gossip; by amplifying and distorting the sounds of words according to no laws but those of "funantics"; and by disobeying and hearing things not intended to reach his ears (nasty innuendos, for instance). Indeed, he must everywhere "beware how in that hist subtaile of schlangder lies liaison to tease oreilles" (270.15–16); for just as the "subtle hiss" of the "serpent" (Ger. *Schlanger*) deceived Eve, and just as the manifest appearances of dreams deceive the dreamer, so too the misleadingly "subtle history of slander" explored in "The Ballad of Persse O'Reilly" can easily deceive the reader: like a dream, this slander gives false impressions, not least of which is that all of the evidently "delusional acting" takes place outside of our hero. The latent sense of the *Wake* falls together where his dreams do, in "subtle connections" (or "liaisons") that "tease the ears."

By "overhearing" and translating all of the book's graven letters "from black hand to pink ear" (43.28)—all of them written "in audible black and prink" (425.23–24 ["inaudible black print and ink"])—a reader will lift them into the vitality of living "earish" (130.19 [and perhaps "Irish"]), and so bring them to life in "the presence (of a curpse)," where the *Wake* takes place: in a body that does not think, "is not all there," but can never not hear. One of the book's primary assertions accordingly becomes, in place of

Earwickerwork

"I think, therefore I am," "I hereby hear by ear," therefore "I am amp amp amplify" (468.24–25, 533.33).

In turn, and especially because letters and the institutions they empower accumulate somewhere in "eyedulls or earwakers" (351.25), in the diffuse space between *Fickleyes and Futilears* (176.13), we might now amplify these remarks by considering the character of the *Wake*'s "litters" (17.28 [or severely "littered" "letters"]). It should by now have become evident that the *Wake* is about "the caecodedition of an absquelitteris puttagonnianne" (512.17–18)—the "blind surrender" to the dark (L. *caecus*, "blind"; *deditio*, "surrender") of a sleeping giant (hence "Patagonian") who is at times entirely "without letters" (L. *absque litteris*). As a body void of mind, HCE therefore becomes "our illicterate of nullatinenties" (336.31–32) not simply because he is "easily representative" (42.22 [as if "our electorate"]), but also because his "easily representative" status hinges on his being an "illiterate nonentity"—indeed, a greater "illiterate" than any of the "have-nots" or "proletariat" (It. *nullatenenti*). In what amounts to another extreme paradox shaping the whole design of a work as superliterate as the *Wake*, then—a paradox comparable to the one that enables Joyce to bend all the erudite detailing of *Ulysses* toward the humane understanding of an ordinary man on an ordinary day—any reader wishing genuinely to engage the *Wake* and achieve a state of "ideal insomnia" must accomplish a task even far more difficult than that imposed on him by the necessity of having to look up words in dictionaries: hard though it may be, he must try to abandon the monied and privileged reflex of literacy in order to attain to "dummyship" and become as good an illiterate as HCE.

CHAPTER TEN

"Litters": On Reading
Finnegans Wake

Long before now, the reader will perhaps have objected that the kind of reading by which even one paragraph of *Finnegans Wake* has been made to yield
sense has licensed me to lift quotations from all over the book, ripping
single words out of context and attributing to the *Wake's* sleeping hero
phrases that ostensibly bear on other characters; or that this kind of reading
has required a flagrant abandonment of sequential progression along the
printed line and instead has cultivated sense by a broad-ranging and di-
gressive association whose only limits have been the covers of the book and
the terms contained in it. I have only been practicing on *Finnegans Wake* a
kind of textually self-endorsed "*Sortes Virginianae*" (281.R2), where the
phrase refers to a traditionally long-standing, if odd kind of reading procedure called "*Sortes Virgilianae*" (L. "Virgilian fortune-telling"). A Western
version of the I Ching, Virgilian sortilege licenses the eager reader who
seeks light in personal affairs to open his Virgil "at random" and—"volve
the virgil page" (270.25)—begin interpreting whatever line he hits upon "ad
lib" (583.6, 302.22−23).

To the objection that terms have been taken out of context the obvious
reply is that they *are* the context: as dreams only happen in sleep, which is
their condition, so the *Wake* only unfolds in the reconstructed night that
successive considerations of the book's "nat language," its "vermicular," its
"meoptics" and "sordomutics," and its modes of "formal alteration" and "ad-

amelegy" have allowed us to see as simultaneously present and overlapping structures underlying the "hole affair." As for the objection that the words and traits of seemingly independent "characters" like Shaun have been misattributed to HCE, it will help to recall that Joyce said "there [were] no characters" in *Finnegans Wake*, where all "traits featuring the *chiaroscuro* coalesce, their contrarieties eliminated, in one stable somebody" (107.29–30): "every dream deals with the dreamer himself. Dreams are completely egotistical. Whenever my own ego does not appear in the content of a dream, but only as an extraneous person, I may safely assume that my own ego lies concealed, by identification, behind this other person" (*ID*, 357–58). Steady reference to sleep, finally, would again sanction the associative way of reading exercised in this book, since this is how we go about "reading the Evening World" as we experience it "in our own nighttime": a particle of recalled sense becomes clear here, a second, disconnected particle becomes clear there, and further struggle with the "m'm'ry" dimly fills in the large gaps between the two. Reading of precisely this sort is what we have practiced on *Finnegans Wake*, by clarifying a phrase on page three, then one on page 527, and by gradually filling in parts of the 524-page gap that intervenes.

Apart from these considerations, however, any number of "curious warning sign[s]" in *Finnegans Wake* itself, "indicating that the words which follow may be taken in any order desired" (121.8, 12–13), suggest that this may indeed be the best way "to make soundsense" (121.15) of our hero's "*ipsissima verba*" (121.8–9 [L. "very same words"])—where our hero, in this context, seems to be *the Aranman ingperwhis through the hole of his hat* (121.11–12) or, again, "hole of Aran man the hat through the whispering his ho" (121.13–14). Since these lines implicitly and explicitly mean what they say only if they are read out of linear order, they not only license the way of proceeding that I have adopted; like other indications scattered everywhere throughout this circular text—"pure chingchong idiotism with any way words all in one soluble" (299.F3)—they also require it.

Right at the threshold of *Finnegans Wake*, its reader learns that

> Bygmester Finnegan, of the Stuttering Hand, freemen's maurer, lived in the broadest way immarginable in his rushlit toofarback for messuages before joshuan judges had given us numbers or Helviticus committed deuteronomy. . . .   (4.18–21)

The sentence sets in motion a two-page account that shows every conceivable standing structure on earth falling: towers and buildings fall (4.35–5.4), ladders fall (6.9–10), trees fall (4.14–15), and "erection[s]" "phall" (6.9,

4.15); but so too do rational and legal structures and, obviously, readable and legible structures as well. Since the underlying cause of this pancosmic collapse is simply our hero's fall into sleep, the passage is orienting us in a world that exists "before joshuan judges had given us numbers"—a world of Vichian primordiality prior to the establishment of moral standards, that is (hence the disarray of "Joshua," "Judges," "Numbers," "Leviticus," and "Deuteronomy"), but a world equally prior to the establishment of "numbers" and comparable symbol-systems as well: at the center of the passage, with the Tower of Babel, languages collapse too. This sense is sustained by the rude appearance of a law-breaking "Helvetius" in the stolidly law-making "Leviticus," and also by reference to "freemen's maurer" (Ger. *Freimaurer*, "freemasons"). Since "Helvetius" was a "freethinker," and the "freemasons" might simply be construed by free association as a "free association" (anyone can join them, and as spiritual joiners they can join anything with anything), the passage is both suggesting and formally demonstrating that standing laws and rules have collapsed with HCE's consciousness in sleep. Like Finnegan, our hero has "stottered from the latter" and "tropped head" (6.9–10 ["tottered from the ladder"]); but this means too that he has "stuttered from the letter" and lost control of his literate consciousness. Together, all these elements are stating obliquely what is everywhere evident in *Finnegans Wake* anyway: that the language of the book, like the language of dreams and like language autonomically disrupted by the stutter, will operate in a manner unpredictably different from that in which rational language operates. As a reconstruction of the night, *Finnegans Wake* is "freely masoned" (552.5), "freewritten" (280.2), and structured "in the broadest way immarginable" by "free associations."[1]

Any reader wishing to "read the Evening World," as opposed to "the dully expressed," must therefore learn to "stotter from the latter" with the hero of the *Wake,* by slipping from the literal surface of the text and becoming a freethinker of sorts. Making "infrarational" and "freely masoned" connections is ultimately more important to an understanding of the *Wake's* "slipping beauty" (477.23 ["sleeping beauty"]) than making literate distinctions, which is the business of "day's reason." "Yoking apart," as we are taught in one of the *Wake's* "Night Lessons" (270.3 [and "joking apart," too]) is so essential to a reading of the *Wake's* "traumscrapt" (623.36 [and its "scrapped" letters and "script"]) that Joyce alerts us to its intricacies everywhere—and not least in his account of his work's production. At the beginning of I.vii, notably, we learn that Shem the Penman comes of a lineage whose peculiarity is well worth examining.

"Litters"

Shem is as short for Shemus as Jem is joky for Jacob. A few toughnecks are still getatable who pretend that aboriginally he was of respectable stemming (he was an outlex between the lines of Ragonar Blaubarb and Horrild Hairwire and an inlaw to Capt. the Hon. and Rev. Mr Bbyrdwood de Trop Blogg was among his most distant connections) but every honest to goodness man in the land of the space of today knows that his back life will not stand being written about in black and white.

(169.1–6)

If we take these lines literally, they simply tell us that "Shun the Punman" (93.13) is illegitimate, not of respectable lineage, and that he moves outside the law ("outlex" plays on the L. *lex*, "law"). But to take the lines literally is precisely to "shun the punman" who generates them, largely by failing to note that a great deal in these lines about lineage and lines is going on "between the lines." The "joky" passage suggests strongly that to take literally a "stemming" (Da.-Nor., "voice") that is related to "the most distant connections," glides "between the lines," "kids around too much" (Fr. *trop blague*), and generates meaning in "outlex" (the opposite of the Gr. *lexis*, "word") is to invite disaster. Like others in *Finnegans Wake*, the passage is obliquely warning us that the words constituting Joyce's "nonday diary" may not yield coherent meanings if held to their literal senses and that the ruled lines making up the printed book may lead nowhere. If, however, we look for and pursue lines and foliations of thought that have the tangled organic intricacy of hairs like those found in "Bluebeard's" or "Horrild Hairwire's" beards—where the play on the song-title "There's Hair Like Wire Growing Out of the Empire" suggests that the empire's ruled English has gone luxuriantly haywire—we may capture the meaning of the "punman's" "traumscript." Because they seek to reconstruct "matters that lie under the ban of our infrarational senses," in unconsciousness, lines in *Finnegans Wake* lead toward understandings that "will not stand being written about in black and white," and precisely because things "written in black and white" make themselves apprehensible to wakeful consciousness. Fully to understand the man "tropped head" at *Finnegans Wake*, then, a reader of the Evening World must not only "stotter from the latter" but also pursue "the most distant connections" by reading "in outlex" "between the lines." For if it is only stating the obvious to note that whole lines in *Finnegans Wake* make sheer nonsense, then "sure, treasures, a letterman does be often thought reading . . . between lines that do have no sense at all" (454.4–5). Here, too, Joyce is calling our attention to an important distinction between the kind of reading necessary to an understanding of the Evening World and the kind of rational literacy required to read "the dully expressed"; for "thought-reading," as opposed to "book reading," requires the exercise of intuition and imagination. And "that (the rapt one warns) is what [the *Wake*'s] papyr is meed of, made of, hides and hints and misses in prints" (20.10–11 [and *not* explicits and clears and corrects]) : "*Hirp! Hirp! for their Missed Understandings!*" [and not for their clear understandings] "*chirps the Ballat of Perce-Oreille*" (175.27–28).

The greatest obstacle to our comprehension of *Finnegans Wake* since its publication has surely been a failure on the part of readers to believe that Joyce really meant what he said when he spoke of the book as a "reconstruction of the nocturnal life" and an "imitation of the dream-state"; and as a consequence, readers have perhaps too easily exercised on the text an unyielding literalism bent on finding a kind of meaning in every way antithetical to the kind of meaning purveyed in dreams.[2] Since the *Wake* everywhere warns us that we should "stotter from the latter" by "feeling aslip" (597.12), read "between the lines," and pursue "the most distant connections" "in hides and hints" in order to comprehend the man "tropped head" at its center, "you can't believe a word he's written in" (252.27). The hero of *Finnegans Wake*, "as I'm given now to understand, [is] illscribed in all the gratuitouses" (496.5–6 [and *not* "described" or "inscribed" in all the explicitly clear literal senses evident on the page]); his nightlife is reconstructed "between the lines," and not on them. A reader must therefore "be vacillant over those vigilant who would leave [him] to belave black on white" (439.31–32 [and largely because the black-and-white surface of the printed page itself, like the manifest content of a dream, is only a "goodridhirring"]).

As a "farced epistol to the highbruws" (228.33–34), the *Wake* holds out the illusion of being a sacred text for "highbrows" (like a "first epistle to the Hebrews"). In fact, however, it is a "farce"—"Outragedy of poetscalds! Acomedy of letters!" (425.24). And as "a comedy of letters," *Finnegans Wake* is the antithesis of everything taught in the "academy of letters." It seems to require the same kind of sober attention as "a tragedy of poet" or "skald," but that impression is as misleading as the manifest appearance of a dream, whose latent content may have much the lowbrow substance of an "outrageous postcard." "How many of its readers realize" (112.1–2 [*really* realize]) "that [it] is not out to dizzledazzle with a graith uncouthrement of . . . the lapins and the grigs"? (112.36–113.3). The referentially secure languages of "Latin" and "Greek," of course, are helpful to a reading of the *Wake*, but less so than a knowledge of "*lapins*" (Fr. "rabbits") and "grigs" (Eng. "crickets"), which leap all over the place, "runnind hare and dart" (285.4), rather like the nocturnal thought of the "quhare soort of mahan" who sleeps at the

Wake (16.1). Because it is an "imitation of a dream-state" and not rationally discursive thought, *Finnegans Wake* is written in "coneyfarm leppers" (257.5–6 ["coneys" = rabbits]), and not "cuneiform letters," or, again, in "some little laughings and some less of cheeks" (125.15 [and even less "Latin" and "Greek"]). What it really requires of its reader is the ability to pursue "distant connections" and, in doing so, to leap all over the place. "*Read your Pantojoke*" (71.17–18 [and not the "Pentateuch"]).

The well-known "letter" that surfaces recurrently in *Finnegans Wake* as a cipher both for the text of our hero's dream and for the "nonday diary" of the *Wake* itself therefore has a number of noteworthy peculiarities to it. "Written in lappish language" (66.18–19 [L. *lapsus linguae*, "slips of the tongue"]), it is expected to arrive "next morning" (66.10), like a dream, and it is addressed to someone who lives at "**H**yde and **C**heek, **E**denberry" (66.17–18). The person expected to receive this letter would be HCE, then, "all reddy berried" in "Edenberry" (421.6 ["already buried" because dead to the world]), as a consequence of which our reading of the "litters" blown through "the hole in his hat" involves a kind of perpetual "hide and seek" among expressions everywhere absolutely delivered "tongue-in-cheek" (hence "Hyde and Cheek"). Because this letter is also "superscribed and subpencilled" (66.16), the sense it bears lies not on the printed line, but "between the lines" (letters "superscribed" would lie above the line, as letters "subpencilled" would lie beneath). All the terms that Joyce draws on to describe this "letter," then, serve to warn us that all the printed letters and words in *Finnegans Wake* are mere "vehicles" leading to hidden meanings and letters that are nowhere explicitly evident to a reader's literate consciousness (see 41.17–21). "Black look[s] white and white guard[s] black, in [the] siamixed twoatalk" that constitutes *Finnegans Wake* (66.19–21) largely because, like any "blackguard's" talk or like the manifest content of any dream, every appearance made manifest to consciousness on the page is deceptive and cannot be trusted. "Litterish fragments lurk dormant" and "buried" in the *Wake* (66.25–26), waiting to be awakened or unearthed when discovered at the end of "distant connections," in spaces "between the lines." Pragmatically, then, a reader of *Finnegans Wake* should be careful about taking anything in the book literally: "a baser meaning has been read into these [alphabetic] characters the literal sense of which decency can safely scarcely hint" (33.14–15).

Not simply rationalistic literalism but an insistence on treating the book linearly, with the preconceived expectation that it can be treated as "narrative" or that a concealed narrative can be reconstructed from it, has also stood in the way of our understanding of *Finnegans Wake*. Here, too, the questionable assumption that *Finnegans Wake* might operate as narrative arises from a failure to think about Joyce's subject, the night. Attempts to translate the *Wake* into "narrative," which it is obviously not, are equivalent to acts of "secondary revision" (or "secondary elaboration") in dream analysis, or to the act of "rationalization" in waking life: they impose, by force, a sham coherence on materials that are not so much incoherently disordered as "thisorder[ed]" (540.19), arranged in ways that resist the attacks of logic because informed by an associative, non-narrative coherence of their own. As an "imitation of the dream-state," *Finnegans Wake* is more in the nature of "ignarrative" than "narrative" because the "one stable somebody" who lies at the center of its nocturnal universe is the ignorant generator and receiver of the texts of his own dreams. "Narrative" derives from the Latin *narrare* ("to tell"), in turn from *gnarus* (L. "knowing"), and it implies that the teller knows what he is talking about. But because our hero has "skittered his litters . . . any old howe" (370.6–8 ["scattered" and "littered" his "letters" in the "tropped head"]), he cannot tell a thing.

Together, all of these features of its "freely masoned" "traumscrapt" make the text of *Finnegans Wake* a "nightmaze" (411.8 [a "nightmare" formally constructed like a "maze"]), a "jigsaw puzzle" (210.11), a "cryptogam" (261.27) or "holocryptogam" (546.13), a game of hide-and-seek or "cash cash" (24.1 [Fr. *cache-cache*, "hide and seek"]), a rebus (12.34, 104.14, 523.20), or a riddle in which "the speechform is a mere sorrogate" (149.29) that represents, like a dream, "matters that fall under the ban of our infrarational senses." As a book on the subject points out, *Finnegans Wake* takes in every particular the form and style of the riddle.[3] It is full of episodes whose dramatic interest lies in the asking, but not necessarily the answering, of riddles: for instance, Shem's "first riddle of the universe" (170.4), the Prankquean's riddle (21–23), the riddles posed during "The Mime of Mick, Nick and the Maggies," (219–259), the riddle of "the crime in the park" (or "whatever it was he reddled a ruad to riddle a rede for the sphinxish pairc" [324.6–7]), and the whole of the "Questions and Answers" chapter (I.vi). These local moments merely call our attention to riddles that rise up to meet us everywhere in the text, in a way that might be exemplified by practicing a Virgilian sortilege on the book and opening it at random. Wherever it falls open, there will be a riddle to solve. Every word, every phrase, every paragraph, and every story in *Finnegans Wake* requires the same kind of solution as a riddle does. And this includes the English.

Consider, for example, the notorious word "hesitancy," which recurs throughout *Finnegans Wake* in scores of misspelled forms—as "the spoil of hesitants, the spell of hesitency" (97.24), "and be the seem talkin wharabahts hosetanzies, dat sure is sullibrated word!" (379.6–7). Joyce pointed out in one of his letters (L, I, 241) that every Irishman would associate this word with Richard Piggott, who tried to implicate Parnell in the Phoenix Park murders of 1882 by forging a series of letters, but who "was trapped . . . by his spelling of the word 'hesitancy' as 'hesitency'" (*Annotations*, ix). Yet to explain the recurrence of the "spell of hesitancy" throughout *Finnegans Wake* on the basis of this story alone will not quite solve the riddle it poses as a reader (and particularly a non-Irish reader) encounters it—as Joyce's remark to Harriet Shaw Weaver suggests. By pointing out that every Irishman would recognize a certain meaning in the word, he was also implicitly noting that every non-Irishman would not, and need not, simply because "—all give it up?—" (170.23) "the spell of hesitancy," like the word "spell" itself, can mean a number of things. Our hero, after all, "ha[s] dizzy spells" (373.27). A "spell" in this sense is simply a lapse of time, and so sleep itself might be regarded as "a spell of hesitancy," or "hazeydency," a "slip of the time between a date and a ghostmark" in which letters are scattered and time pauses (305.4, 473.8–9 [hence the "dense haze" and the ghosted "postmark"]). As to the "spell of hesitancy" in this sense, "Hasitatense?" (296.F4).

We might now pay attention to the kind of thought that plays through the mind during the solution of a riddle like this. After an initial period of bafflement in which he feels lost "in the meddle of [a] mudstorm" (86.19–20), the person to whom the riddle is posed "seeks, buzzling is brains," as he tries to discover "what is that which is one going to prehend?" (223.25–26 ["puzzling" and "buzzing his brains," he tries to "apprehend" an answer "before" it is given]). If he is clever, he arrives at "the correct solution" (170.22–23), after a brief "spell of hesitancy," by suddenly waking up and getting it. He arrives at this "correct solution," moreover, not by any rationalistic calculation or by a procedure he might "prehend." For the solution of a riddle implicates one in a thought process that is able freely to establish "distant connections" and discover sense "between the lines" "in hides and hints and misses in prints"; and *Finnegans Wake*, by "asking the teaser" in its every word (111.27), is engaging its reader exactly in this process.[4] Sense in the "robulous rebus" of *Finnegans Wake* (12.34) falls together exactly as it does in riddles and in the "freely masoned" dreamwork of the night. It is "a treasure stumbled upon suddenly; not gradually accumulated by adding one to one."[5] You can look it up in Latin, you can look it up in Greek, you can look it up in the *Encyclopaedia Britannica*; indeed, "you may be as practical as is predicable but you must have the proper sort of accident to meet that kind of a being with a difference" (269.13–15).

Ordinary works of literature operate by presenting us with a verbal surface written in the indicative and offering us a field of indicators (as in the sentence, "It was a dark and stormy night"). As an "imitation of the dreamstate," by contrast, *Finnegans Wake* offers us a verbal surface that is only apparently indicative, but really full of riddles (as in the sentence, "It was black and white and red all over"). As a totality, then, the *Wake* becomes an "Anonymay's left hinted palinode obviously inspiterebbed by a sibspecious connexion" (374.7–8): every word in the dreamlike letter that recurrently appears in the "tropped head" of the man asleep at the *Wake* ("Anonymay's" = "anonymous") is "obviously inspired" by a "specious," "suspicious," though "related" meaning (hence "*sib*species")—one that often has little to do with the apparent sense of the word. The text accordingly becomes a "left hinted palinode" (a "palinode" is a poem in which the writer retracts something he has said) because as soon as it provides a reader with "meaning" through the letters and words apparent on the line, it takes the meaning away and leaves him with "sinister" hints (L. *sinister*, "left-handed") and with puzzles to solve (hence "left hinted palinode"). The surface of this "inspiterebbed" (or "inspired") text therefore becomes a "spiderweb" of sorts, full of traps for the literate and rational sides of our minds.

Because the lines and letters in *Finnegans Wake* make sheer nonsense and the latent senses to which they all point lie "between the lines," at the end of "distant connections," in "hides and hints and misses in print" nowhere manifestly evident on the page, the concrete text that we are reading—the material text bound in paper and running 628 pages—becomes mere "packen paper" by one turn of the *Wake's* imagery (356.24 [Ger. *Packenpapier*, "wrapping paper"]), a literately addressed envelope beneath whose surface invisible letters and meanings lie "buried" (I.v), "dormant" (66.26), waiting to be unearthed. Most of the identifiable words that one finds in the lines of this text, accordingly, once a certain kind of pedestrian, mechanical translation has been accomplished, become "eminently legligible" (356.21 ["legible" precisely because "negligible"]): "blimp, blump; a dud letter . . . a byword, a sentence with surcease" (129.7–8). All of these elements make themselves apprehensible to the literate mind, where exactly the meaning of the dream and the riddle-solving process in which the dream engages its interpreter are not. If on the one hand we have therefore been "reading a book" with all the properties of any other book—real pages, words, and visible letters—it comes as a surprise to learn that we have also "just (let us suppraise) been reading in a (suppressed) book" (356.19–20). Like the manifest content of a dream, everything manifest on the printed page of the *Wake* points to a second, concealed text whose every "word [lies] as cunningly hidden in its maze of confused drapery as a fieldmouse in a nest of coloured ribbons" (120.5–6). "It's like a dream."

Anyone who has analyzed a dream to his own satisfaction knows that dreams have much the same structure as the riddles that we have been considering, the same structure as the *Wake*'s "left hinted palinode." There is nothing essentially rational about the process (as opposed to the theory) by which these nocturnal "*rhyttel[s] in his hedd*" (338.8 ["riddles in his head"]) can be made to reveal conflicts (We. *rhyfel*, "war") of sufficient gravity as to have disrupted the sleep-sapped "hedd" of the dreamer (We. *hedd*, "peace"). Quite the contrary. Any dream is "quite puzzonal to the wrottel" (183.6–7): it is "quite personal to the writer" who thinks it up in the middle of the night, yet "quite a puzzle" with which "to riddle" in the morning, when its creator finds it impossible to understand. As "puzzonal wrottels" of this kind, dreams operate exactly as riddles do not simply in the wholly intuitive process by which they are untangled, but in the kind of understanding they yield. The successful interpretation of a dream results not primarily in an intellectual understanding, but in an illuminating "click" that wakes up the dreamer in the middle of his own life. And just as the analysis of a dream produces a sudden recognition, just as the solution of a good riddle generates a ripple of mirth, so a good "read[ing of] the Evening World" works to liberate "everyone's repressed laughter" (190.33–34), whose release is a sign that the book has been read rightly: *in risu veritas*, as Joyce remarked of the *Wake* (*JJ*, 703 [L. "in laughter there is truth"]).

That the language of *Finnegans Wake* really strives to "reconstruct the nocturnal life" and hold forth "an imitation of the dream-state" can be seen by "rearriving" at that paragraph on page three to which we have been returning "teems of times and happy returns" (215.22–23). Though the paragraph makes a vague kind of sense if we read it as we do ordinary prose— moving along word for word, sentence after sentence, translating each word into the ordinary senses of which it seems to be compacted, it will ultimately resist this kind of understanding, and for many reasons: incomprehensible words will impede our forward progression through the sentence, often creating disconcerting gaps in our understanding, sometimes forcing us to go back to the beginning and start all over again, ultimately leaving us with the uneasy sense that we may not be getting it. Even if all the incomprehensible terms are explained, "the fog of the cloud in which we toil and the cloud of the fog under which we labour" does not necessarily lift (599.30–31).

As our reading of the Evening World will have suggested, the paragraph, like *Finnegans Wake* as a whole, might better be treated as a rebus, a crossword puzzle, or a hardly comprehensible dream whose manifest elements are particles of trivia and nonsense that conceal latent and apocalyptic senses which lie not on the lines but between them, and not in any literal senses but in "outlex." By "thought-reading" "between [these] lines"—"lines" that make no sense at all"—and by following the *Wake*'s advice to pursue "freely masoned" "distant connections" "in the broadest way immarginable," the reader will discover a buried sense in buried letters in the paragraph—especially "on a second wreathing" (336.27–28 [or third or fourth]). According to this model, any paragraph in *Finnegans Wake* would operate exactly like a dream by providing us with a set of vectors that points to an absent content—"the presence (of a curpse)"—into the "eyewitless foggus" of whose "tropped head" the process of reading the Evening World leads.

The insistent presence of this corpse returns us to a meditation on the body that lies dead to the world at the center of the *Wake*, and to Joyce's stated claims about his work. Readers of *Finnegans Wake* have long felt that a great deal in the book "cannot be traced, with any show of plausibility, to the sodden brain of a snoring publican. No psychoanalyst could account for the encyclopedic sweep of Earwicker's fantasies. . . ."[6] Yet as our explorations of the *Wake*'s "nat language," its odd allusions to figures like Finnegan and Finn, and its "meoptics" and "sordomutics" will have begun to suggest, Joyce knew exactly what he was doing, and *Finnegans Wake* is indeed much what he said it was: a reconstruction of the night. If the work has seemed "utterly improperable" for so long (538.12), it is only because Joyce has "uttered it improperly," and because we, as readers acclimatized to a study of "the dully expressed," have approached it with a conventionally straitened sense of what it is "proper" to "utter" and what it is not. In the belief that "we must be constant (what a word!)" to literalistic sense and to all the leaden rules that govern the Daily World (238.11–12), we overlook the field of immense potentialities that the text, like the dream, opens ("Comport yourself, you inconsistency!" [192.31–32]).

Reading the Evening World will also have begun showing that *Finnegans Wake*, as Joyce claimed, "does for the night what *Ulysses* does for the day," and that its status as representation, until now a negligible concern, is sufficiently complex an issue that the stakes will have to be raised in critical discussions of what the book accomplishes and of how it stands in

"Litters"

(an exceedingly odd) relation to the literary tradition out of which it self-consciously arose. When Joyce justified the literary experimentation of the *Wake* by announcing that "one great part of every human existence is passed in a state which cannot be rendered sensible by the use of wideawake language, cutanddry grammar and goahead plot" (*L*, III, 146), he was presumably saying, among other things, that he was seeking "to render sensible a part of human existence"; and when he said that "the night world can't be represented in the language of the day" (*JJ*, 590), he presumably meant that he was "representing" an experience that we all share. Our failure to see that *Finnegans Wake* really "reconstructs the nocturnal life" stems from our unwillingness and inability to think, finally, about the *Wake*'s intractably strange subject, the night and our unconsciousness.

As to the business of "wreathing" its "litters," finally (336.27, 17.28 ["reading its letters"]), "it is perensempry sex of fun to help a dazzle off the othour" (364.23–24): "it's pure and simply six of one and half a dozen of the other" as to what comes first or last in any reading of the *Wake*, a work of bottomless "sojestiveness" (222.32) like the dream. But "always" (L. *semper*), "constantly" (L. *perenne*), it should be "fun" ("sex of fun"), and the reader must take part in the game if he wishes to "get the dazzle off this author"—or, for that matter, any "other."

"*The* Nursing Mirror"

That dreams entail "infantile regression," a return to the state of mind of infancy, is a central tenet of almost all writing on the night. According to Freud, "dreams simply make us into children once more in our thoughts and our feelings";[1] "what once dominated waking life, while the mind was still young and incompetent, seems now to have been banished into the night. . . . *Dreaming is a piece of infantile mental life that has been superseded*" (*ID*, 606). When the old man who sleeps at the *Wake* enters the Evening World, accordingly, he returns not simply to a "state of nature" (49.25), but to a condition much like that which he experienced "in first infancy" (22.1 [< L. *infans*, "not speaking"]), so to enjoy a "second infancy" (22.26) and to become something of "an infams" (621.26 [an "infamous" one]). For infancy takes place exactly where sleep does, in an "unknown body" void of mind, somewhere in eyes "meoptically" unlit and in ears and a mouth all "sordomutic."

One way of understanding the careful lack of specificity that Joyce cultivated when he spoke about *Finnegans Wake*—when he remarked, for instance, that "one great part of every human existence is passed in a state which cannot be rendered sensible by the use of wideawake language" (*L*, III, 146)—would entail asking only what he would have produced if he had wanted to write, after *Ulysses*, a novel exactly like *Ulysses* but about someone 36 or 37 years younger than the 38-year-old Bloom. Because *Finnegans Wake* does for the night what *Ulysses* does for the day, it is a work precisely of this sort; for when its hero falls asleep, he becomes unconscious, and *"what is unconscious in mental life is also what is infantile."*[2] By reconstructing the "nightlife" of an "ordinary man," the *Wake* is also reconstructing, with some intricacy, "a day in the life" of the first years of "real life"—the complicating snag being that there were no days in those "toyms" that anyone will recall lying somewhere "way back in [the] mistridden past" (602.36, 110.31 [recall, however, all the "toys"]). The "blank memory" lingering in the head from "lost life," accordingly (515.26 ["last night"]), now becomes darkly enmeshed with those "lost" parts of "life" deriving from childhood.

If we "rearrive" at that the paragraph of the *Wake*, for instance, we will now find, reinforced by a reading of those extended parts of the book given over to child psychology (II.i, II.ii), yet another of "threescore and ten toptypsical readings" concealed at the ends of "distant connections" "between the lines." For our hero's "fall" asleep has "retaled" him "early in bed" (3.15–17), and as a consequence, "the humptyhillhead of humself promptly sends an unquiring one well to the west in quest of his tumptytumtoes" (3.20–21). Most "Grownup Gentlemen" (221.2) are likely to have heard in Wakean coinages like "humptyhillhead" and "tumptytumtoes" an unspeakably ridiculous infantility. What else? "We bright young chaps of the brandnew braintrust are briefed here . . . with maternal sanction" (529.4–5 [those "briefs" are all at once letters, laws, and underpants, and "here" is the Daily World]), and so we tend brainily to patronize the gleeful "little folk creeping on all fours" (178.18–19). The evocations of infancy heard in these terms, however, now turn out to be crucial because "Humpty Dumpty" is "*A Pretty Brick Story for Childsize Heroes*" (106.14), and so is *Finnegans Wake*, which we must now construe, since "we are in rearing" (21.1), as "the *Nursing Mirror*" (46.25).

Where we earlier discovered in the "unquiring one" stratified in this paragraph the thinking of a "tropped head" oblivious of its spatial and personal relation to its own "tumptytumtoes," one form of unconsciousness spectrally overlaps another now, as the night in turn opens out bottomlessly into "childhood's reverye[s]" (483.5–6). Because it is reconstructing the "eyewitless foggus" of a man asleep, the passage is also, and *necessarily*, reconstructing the "eyeless" and "witless" "eyewitless foggus" of "an overgrown babeling" (6.31 ["baby"]) whose "eyes" and ears and "wit" have "not yet" (3.10), "not yet" (3.11) wakened. "Back we [return]," then, "by the jerk of a beamstark, back [to] paladays last" (615.25): to a "paradise lost" experienced "long ago" (Gr. *palai*), in "toyms" full of "playdays" and "giants" (hence "Jack and the Beanstalk"). The "babeling" coming to light in this paragraph, "overgrown" because "not yet" wakened to a sense of space, is also a "giant" of sorts, and so comes attached to those silly "tumptytumtoes." Since it is one of the *Wake's* "Night Lessons" (II.ii) that "digits" (fingers and toes) are first "digits" (numbers), their discovery making possible a non-Euclidean construction of space (282.7ff.), the paragraph now evokes a time when this "unquiring one" did "not yet" know that his "unknown body," let alone all of those pedagogically useful "tumptytumtoes," lay out there in the dark, way off at the far end of the world, waiting to be discovered and exploited by parents and math teachers. Still, since "he knowed from his cradle . . . why his fingures were giving him" (282.9–11 ["figures," "fingers"]), five of them lie immanently out there, waiting to be brought to light whenever he wakens, in the five countable components of "upturnpikepointandplace" (3.22 [*Annotations*]):

> —Recount!
> —I have it here to my fingall's ends. This liggy piggy wanted to go to the jampot. And this leggy peggy spelt pea. (496.17–19) [3]

What a little "*boîte à surprises*" this paragraph has become (165.29–30 [Fr. "box of surprises," or "jack-in-the-box"]), and not least because, "to our surprise, *we find the child and the child's impulses still living on [here, as] in the dream*" (*ID*, 224)—just as we find those childish impulses living on in the sudden popping-up of a memory of that "jackabox" (91.26, 485.33), which too, with "Humpty Dumpty" and those obscure "tumptytumtoes," "we all remember . . . in childhood's reverye" (483.5–6).

To ignore these childish impulses and all the infantile material represented in the paragraph because there is Latin to explicate or a theory to expound is to perpetrate thoughtlessly upon ourselves, as it was perpetrated upon us, something that the *Wake* calls the "young persons (Nodding Neutrals) removal act" (529.8). For we not only annihilate a deeply formative part of the dream, but lobotomize a whole portion of the brain with which we traffic in the Daily World, remaining unconscious of and shriveling our sense of possibilities by keeping the child inside the body buried. Again, then, we "have just . . . been reading in a (suppressed) book" (356.19–20)— one of many "excluded books" (537.27) which the ego- and letter-carrying part of the mind (let's "Show'm the Posed") has severe difficulties not simply thinking about, but acknowledging at all. The content of this "(suppressed) book," however, now turns out to be crucial to Joyce's "book of the dark" not simply because it impinges everywhere on the amnesic domain of "childhide" (483.31 [a deeply "hidden" "childhood"]), but because it also tells the story of how a world of little Finnegans wake.

"Well, Him a being so on the flounder of his bulk like an overgrown babeling, let wee peep, see, at Hom, well, see peegee ought he ought" (6.30–32)—noting, as we do so, that "we" become very "wee" in "the *Nursing Mirror*" of the Evening World (cf. 57.12–13, 259.3–4), so that "wee," like our "Childsize Hero," "ought to see pg. o" ("see peegee ought"), the blank page beginning the story of "Here Comes Everybody's" "real life," when we too "new nothing" (516.30 [not "knew"]). Sympathetic study of this amnesic blank will enable us now to note that our hero is identified as "**Haroun Childeric Eggeberth**" right from the beginning of the *Wake* (4.32). If this "cradlename" (201.32) seems manifestly to designate the rulers of their "days" (a Persian caliph, a Frankish monarch, and an Anglo-Saxon king), the night undoes those "daze" altogether (51.1, 316.26), so to reveal latently, in as fantastic an incognito as any that "Haroun al-Raschid" ever assumed in the fairy tale of the *Thousand and One Nights*, an unformed "child" ("Childeric"), moving away from the time of its conception ("egg") and "birth" toward the moment at which he will *Wake*. As an "overgrown babeling," our "Childsize Hero" maintains this infantile "duskguise" from beginning to end of the *Wake*, becoming, "for innocence" (435.10 ["for instance"]), a "Grampupus" (7.8 [It. *gran pupo*, "big baby"]), a "peewee" (11.10), a "Minnikin" (17.2 [Du. "little man"], a "babylone" (17.33), or a gigantic "Mister Funn" again (5.12 [as opposed to a sullen "Mister Pain" or a somber "Mister Finnegan"]). Our hero's unconscious drift through sleep, as idiom suggests, "rejuvenate[s]" him (41.13), and in a sense that might be radically construed ("rejuvenation" derives from the L. *re-* ["anew"] and *juvenis* ["young"]). "Young as of old, for [a] daily comfreshenall, [this] wee one" rules the night (619.14–15): dark "daily confessional" though sleep and its dreams may be, it also "comes and freshens all," so that an old man afflicted with "ague will be rejuvenated" (112.20 ["age," too]). Not simply an experience that embeds an old man in a "seemetery," then, but an extended process of rejuvenating "refleshmeant" that leads "from next to nothing" to the moment at dawn when HCE will *Wake*, sleep might now be considered, as in "The Mime of Mick, Nick and the Maggies," a daily reenactment of childhood itself.

Showing our hero in "dozen[s] of cradles" (211.20 [as elsewhere the *Wake* shows him in dozens of coffins]), all of these "cradlenames" (201.32) cause a strange transformation to sweep over everything in the *Wake*, as again we find "no thing making newthing wealthshowever for a silly old Sol, healthytobedder and latewiser" (253.8–9): note particularly, as a consequence of this transformation, how the "silly old soul" evoked in this familiar phrasing will now awaken the memory of "Old King Cole," just as "healthytobedder"—and the phrase "early in bed" on the opening page of the *Wake* (3.17)—will recall the bedtime homilies that "Here Comes Everybody" heard in childhood ("early to bed and early to rise"). "All's set for restart after the silence" (382.14), then, as "the old man on his ars" shown "scrapheaped" in Relief Map B becomes a magically rejuvenated "*Courser, Recourser, Changechild*" (481.2; cf. 87.18), "remembering [his] shapes and sizes on the pillow of [his] babycurls" (24.29–30)—where the appearance of Vico's *ricorso* in "recourser" tells us that his history is beginning all over again. "The course of history" therefore modulates into "the course of his tory" at the *Wake* (143.12) in part because, under the infantile, regressive, and conservative trend of the dream (hence that "tory"), the sleeper returns to a past extending through yesterday into "first infancy." The *Wake* in turn becomes "a bit of a torytale" (20.23) or a "Goes Tory by Eeric Whigs" (359.26)—a "ghost story" about a man dead to the world who, even while progressing toward the future ("whig"), "goes" extremely "tory." As "he doze soze," his emptily "tropped head" ("eerie wig") fills with "the Tales of Yore of the times gone by before there was a hofdking or a hoovthing" or anything "in Oreland, all sould" (359.24–26): the evocations of "All Souls' Day" and burial here (in an underground "oreland") remind us that our hero has "tropped head"; but the counterevocations of a time before that governing head was implanted in the body at all (hence the "high-king" and Du. *hoofd*, "head"), return us to the beginning of the world.

Moving its "*Changechild*" "past Morningtop's necessity"—the drab exigencies that force him, at the "top of the morning," to reassume the burdens of "head trouble and heal travel" (620.13 [thinking and walking])—"the *Nursing Mirror*" therefore begins to reflect its hero in "the clarience of the childlight in the studiorium upsturts" (266.11–13). If this line manifestly evokes "the children's study upstairs," like chapter II.ii generally, it does so largely in order to suggest that a kind of "clarity" and "light" known only to infant "upstarts"—"childlight"—now blazes up into and illumines our hero's "tropped head." For "it's the armitides toonigh . . . and there's to be a gorgeups truce for happinest childher everwere" (11.13–15). In the cessation of conflict that sleep brings ("armistice, truce"), the infant buried inside "the old man on his ars" is going to "gorge up truth."

Staged in a "Playhouse" of sorts (219.2)—a "kids' and dolls' home" (294.F1) rife with memories of gleeful visits to the "Cats' and Dogs' Home"—

dreams take place exactly when and where the song- and game-filled "Mime of Mick, Nick and Maggies" does: at "childream's **h**ours, **e**xpercatered" (219.5–6 [and in the body of HCE]). "Expertly catered" by a mind like the child's, they yield a kind of meaning which, in the morning, is "expertly expurgated" by the literate adult. As "an imitation of the dream-state," the *Wake* necessarily undertakes bottomless forays into childhood memory everywhere, everywhere evoking somewhere "between the lines" and at the ends of "hides and hints and misses in prints" experiences that "we all remember . . . in childhood's reverye" (483.5–6). Not a page in *Finnegans Wake*, all of them plushly "teddybearlined" (208.17), fails to refer densely to "fairytales" (220.13), stories from "storybooks" (219.24), "youth plays" (253.6–9), children's games (176.1–18, II.i), "toy fair[s]" (628.9), "mothers gossip" (316.11–12 [but also "Mother Goose"]), and "nonsery reams" (619.18 ["reams" of "nursery rhymes" and comparable "non-sense"]).[4] And not a page fails comparably to evoke some variant of Swift's "little language," which, though it is given in pure form primarily to Issy throughout the book, merely epitomizes a kind of linguistic regression that anyone might find anywhere in the Evening World:[5] "let him tome to Tindertarten, pease, and bing his scooter 'long" (191.21–22); "*Parolas infanetes. S!*" (565.28 [Esperanto for "baby words," Esperanto being the "universal language"]). Through these vehicles, "as were we their babes in" (619.23–24), "the *Nursing Mirror*" cannot help stirring, as profoundly as the dream, childhood memories of the deepest kind—even while the letter-carrying half of its reader is looking for deep commentary on the *Summa Theologica* or arcane puns in the Greek. All of these recollected vestiges of childhood, part of a collectively shared heritage whose learning precedes schooling and is in itself the learning of language, are inevitably attached to voices and memories that will pull anyone back to "the very dawn of protohistory" (169.21). Every page in the *Wake*, if the reader lets it work upon himself, will lead him back to the "nursery" (169.23, 227.11; 584.16, 619.18), to the "village childergarten" (253.30–31, 483.25–26), and to "toyms" "in that sometimes prestreet protown" (97.21) where "real life" first "erigenat[ed] from next to nothing" (4.36–5.1). "In effect, I remumble, from the yules gone by, purr lil murrerof myhind. . . . When she give me the Sundaclouths. . . ." (295.4–7). As a reader, like the *Wake*'s "Childsize Hero," "remumbles" (and "remembers") these things, he will also likely "remember from the years gone by," somewhere "between the lines" and in the nursing "mirror of the mind," a "poor little mother of mine," and attached associations—of "yule," "Santa Claus," and the laying-out of

"Sunday clothes": "I have heard her voice somewhere else's before me in these ears still that now are for mine," as it occurs to HCE (565.15–16 ["someone else's," this voice entered his hearing "somewhere else," "before" and prior to the construction of "me"]). All generally deriving from the era of his incarnation and birth (hence, in part, the incessant evocations of Christmas at the *Wake*), memories like those show him "at his old game of haunt the sleeper" (295.9–10); for the memory of a children's game called "Hunt the slipper" also "haunts the sleeper," who now moves through the night glamorously "invested" "in littleritt reddinghats and cindery yellows and tinsel and glitter and bibs under hoods" (551.8–9). Much more than the evident "news-reel" of images projected against the dreamer's closed eyelids, "this nonday diary, this allnights newseryreel" (489.35) also becomes a nonstop "nursery rhyme" (hence "newseryreel").

"Since we are talking amnessly of brukasloop crazedledaze," "for innocence," (562.16 ["aimlessly," in "amnesia," of "sleep broken" by memories of "cradle days"]), consider only the big blank "m'm'ry" the *Wake* wakens "from an early peepee period" of "your last wetbed confession" (533.26, 188.1 ["you were there," even if the "m'm'ry" is obscure]); or of "the time we . . . were fairly tossing . . . in bed, having been laid up with Castor's oil" (431.35–432.1); or of the time "we play[ed] dress grownup" (261.F1); or of a time whose "m'm'ry" is wakened from the dead (and "deadhead" [407.36]) by a line urging that "when you pet the rollingpin write my name on the pie" (441.17 [*not* "get the writingpen"]). Is not this Wakean "scripchewer" (412.4 ["scripture"]), even while calling attention to the ways in which the ascent into literacy massively shrivels one's sense of possibility, unearthing a buried "m'm'ry" for those of its readers who no longer write on pies and pastries but on paper—no doubt with methodologically justified impeccability? As for that "scripchewer," who can forget not the meaning but the taste of reading material— curiously compelling, slightly bitter, a little too pulpy, finally not palatable? "How strange memory is! To remember that after such a long time" (*L*, I, 375). "If we each could always do all we ever did" (287.F2).

Now "as you all know, of a child, dear Humans" (533.24–25), a snowballing and "(suppressed)" accumulation of childhood memories much like these is what grown-up little boys and girls are "mead of, mard, is made of" (374.1 [Per. *mard*, "man"]):

> —Trists and thranes and trinies and traines.
> —A take back to the virgin page, darm it!
> —Ay, graunt ye.
>
> (513.26–28)

"*The* Nursing Mirror"

Set to the rhythm of that nursery rhyme about the constitutional makeup of "little boys and girls," the wording here puts us in mind of a younger, as opposed to an older man (hence "Tristan"), who is in tearful conflict (hence the "sadness" [Fr. *triste*] and the "tears" [Ger. *Tränen*]) and whose "real life," because its living preceded the gelling of English in the head, is written not on legible pages, but on a "virgin page." The wording also refers to Thomas Moore's "Take Back the Virgin Page"—a song set to the Irish air "Dermot" (hence "darm it!") and subtitled "Written on Returning a Blank Book," and it therefore suggests that because "childhide" is written in a "blank book" full of "virgin pages" of this sort ("see peegee ought"), so too must be Joyce's "book of the dark" and *Nursing Mirror*."[6] Indeed, "that (the rapt one warns) is what [this] papyr is meed of, made of, hides and hints and misses in prints" (20.10–11). As the terms in this familiar line will now suggest, the content of the "papyr" making up Joyce's "mummyscrip" (156.5) is exactly the same as the content of the "papyrus" (hence "papyr") used to wrap an Egyptian "mummy": a body dead to the world, HCE. And the nursery-rhyme rhythm underlying the line now makes clear that "the presence (of a curpse)"—and "the present, of course"—is "made of" precisely the same things little boys and girls are: an aggregate of "buried" memories at whose inmost core lie the kinds of childhood memory brought to light by "the *Nursing Mirror*."

The letter "buried" in that body which *Finnegans Wake* takes as its subject therefore has the same latent, because infantile, content as a dream; and it is "written in [a] lappish language" (66.18–19) more of whose peculiar inflections we are now in a position to understand. Though it will reach the dreamer only "next morning" (66.10), when he reacquires the literate ability to carry and deliver letters (66.11–13) and when it stands "stated in Morganspost" (36.5 [Ger. *Morgen*, "morning"; *Post*, "letter"]), this communique comes in

> a huge chain envelope, written in seven divers stages of ink, from blanchessance to lavandaiette, every pothook and pancrook bespaking the wisherwife, superscribed and subpencilled by yours A Laughable Party, with afterwrite, S.A.G., to Hyde and Cheek, Edenberry.   (66.13–18)

Everything knowably manifest about this letter, in other words, is merely its "envelope," a complexly linked "chain" ("huge chain") of trivial materials ("pots and pans"), within which lies a message "lurk[ing] dormant" (66.26) and striving to get out by "hook or crook" ("pothook and pancrook"). "Superscribed and subpencilled," this dormant message lies somewhere "between the lines" ("above" and "below" them), so that it conveys meaning like a dream, a "slip of the tongue" (L. *lapsus linguae*), or a word delivered with "tongue in cheek" whose "hidden" meaning its interpreter must "seek" ("Hyde and Cheek"). The reference to "hide and seek" also implies, however, that the message "lurking dormant" in this "lappish language" (Ger. *lappisch*, "childish") carries its reader through a "huge chain" of associations back to "childhide" itself. And as an added complication, this dormant message seems to be formally written in "wholesome pothooks" (181.13; 119.29). So, at least, according to Joyce: "I am at present attending night school," he wrote to his son Giorgio in 1934, "where they teach 'em how to make pothooks" (*L*, III, 320).

Now "pothooks" are one form of those cursive lines that children make when they are learning to write or, by extension, any illegible handwriting or aimless scribbling:

Only a paleography of "your prescriptions" (419.32)—the "pothooks" and "scribbledehobbles" (275.22) whose writing preceded the formation of "inscriptions" proper—will help anyone to understand the "scribings scrawled" here (615.10), which some penman like Shem has evidently "scrabbled and scratched and scriobbled and skrevened nameless[ly and] shamelessness[ly]" all over the place (182.13–14). For if graphic writing, even if only approximately, is representative of thought—the written words "I think" meaning that I really do (think)—then surely some kind of thought must "lurk dormant" beneath these "pothooks"—and all the more particularly because the "little man" (166.21) who forms them is capable of as much lip-biting intentionality as any adult. Written by "the babes that mean too" (308.25 [they "mean" things "too," if not in orthodox language]), these pothooks resemble exactly the "NIGHTLETTER" whose meaning, imperceptible because radiotelegraphed up from "down under," the *Wake* tries to capture (308.16). All nonsense on the surface, all unconscious infantile thinking underneath, both dreams and the *Wake* take form in a script like that seen here. "Indiscriminatingly made belief mid authorsagastions from Schelm the Pelman"

(369.27–28), these "pothooks" do not make beliefs, but rather indiscriminate "make-believe"; nor do they work like "author's suggestions," but rather by "autosuggestion." To understand the "wreuter" who "scribbles them"— "Schelm the Pelman" (Ger. *Schelm*, "rogue")—a reader might well take depth lessons at a "Pelman Institute" (according to the *Annotations*, a "memory training center").[7]

Because the letter whose meaning the *Wake* explores takes the form of these pothooks, it is said to be hidden and buried in a spot where "the first babe of reconcilement is laid in its last cradle of hume sweet hume" (80.17–18): "last cradle of hume," of course, because our hero has fallen back into his body and gone dead to the world; "cradle" and "reconcilement" with "the first babe," however, because the fall back into his body also returns him to "first infancy." In what will partially account for the *Wake*'s incessantly exclamatory style, then, we might see that much of the material unconsciously "unearthed" as we dig (as if with a "pick") for meanings buried beneath the surface—of dreams, pothooks, the text of the *Wake*, and "the presence (of a curpse)"—is simply "childhide." "So pass the pick for child sake! O men!" (80.18–19 [and not for the sake of correct readings]).

The *Wake* unearths buried memories of this "childhide" in inevitably primary ways. Not least "because he mussed your speller on you" (191.30–31), Joyce puts his reader into a position roughly analogous to that of a child encountering an unknown language for a first time, so to recall an era of life in which "Here Comes Everybody" started knowing "anguish" (603.21 [U.S. college sl. for "English"]) and in turn started obscurely to fathom the overwhelming "awethorrorty" of the authors behind it. This perhaps will account for the "humiliation" that some readers feel on first looking into "the *Nursing Mirror*"—though in an ideal and just world, consciousness of a humiliation etymologically and ideologically indistinct from one's humanizing should have come decades before one even heard of *Finnegans Wake*, when one was a little Finnegan waking. So bafflingly weird at times is the "Babbyl" of "the *Nursing Mirror*" (532.25 [the "baby Babel"])—"Whangpoos the paddle and whiss whee whoo" (297.F5)—that one stands roughly in the same relation to its "storiella as she is syung" (267.7–8 [a "young" "story," whose truth is as difficult to ascertain as that behind a "fib," or It. *storiella*]) as a child stands in relation to the language in his primer. Hugh Kenner has remarked that learning to read *Finnegans Wake* is like going to a Berlitz school to learn a language that is useful nowhere on earth. An essential countertruth, however, is that we *are* learning how to read—and not only "between the lines"—but a language, "the seim anew" (215.23), in a "storyaboot" where "we start from scratch" (336.17–18). What is true of any language, finally, is also true of the *Wake's:* "it's as simple as A. B. C." (65.27–28, 107.34, 249.18)—though another essential countertruth requires us to see that it may be as strange as A. B. C., too.

"This nonday diary" and "allnights newseryreel" therefore becomes a "unique hornbook" of sorts (489.35, 422.15 [note the "unicorn"])—as its recurrent misquotation of alphabetic nursery rhymes like "A was an Archer" everywhere suggests: "Hootch is for husbandman handling his hoe" (5.9); "Lel lols for libelman libling his lore" (250.19). Since it unburies "childhide" and all the activity buried there rather than squelching it, however, it becomes a "childlit" inversion of the "great primer" (20.8), an antiprimer like that reconstructed in the "Night Lessons" chapter (II.ii), which takes the form of, only to demolish, schoolbooks. As a "book" (L. *liber*) that makes "free" (L. *liber*), the *Wake* sets the child buried inside at "liberty" (250.21): "two pretty mistletots, ribboned to a tree, up rose liberator and, fancy, they were free" (588.35–36)—where the line, set to the rhythm of a children's song ("Ten little Injuns"), also suggests that "fancy is as free" in this book as it is in the unconscious. "Childs will be wilds. 'Twastold" (246.21–22 [and "twice-told," because the *Wake*, like the dream, tells the "torytale" of infancy all over again]).

In turn, this reanimation of the wild child makes *Finnegans Wake* a kind of vast mnemonic "wonderland" in which "milliems of centiments deadlost" on us are continually being resurrected from the dead as an "original sinse we are only yearning as yet how to burgeon" reawakens (239.3, 2). Necessarily, "the *Nursing Mirror*" reflects its "Childsize Hero" "through alluring glass or alas in jumboland" (528.18)—"alas" because he's dead to the world, "jumbo" because he's a sleeping giant—and so situates him in a "wonderland" like that encountered in *Through the Looking Glass*, where the Daily World is "alluringly" "rejuvenated" and "refleshed."[8] Readers recalling the "toyms" "when they were yung and easily freudened" (115.22–23) will remember that childhood and wonderland could be places of both anxiety and "delight time" (329.10 [like "the nighttime"]). So, too, *Finnegans Wake*, where "we go out in all directions on Wanterlond Road with [a] cubarola glide" (618.21–22). If the possibility of "going out in all directions" all at once induce in readers accustomed to "the dully expressed" a kind of "wonderlost" anxiety (363.23)—"You is feeling like you was lost in the bush, boy?" (112.3)—then the sudden recognition of an infant "bushman" in that "bush boy" should convert all "wonderloss" into "wonderlust" (576.21 [mental "wanderlust"]), by reanimating a sense of what it was to be a child, "wanting" things badly (hence "Wanterlond") but also—by way of reference to "the Cubanola Glide," a dance craze of the 1920s—eager to take brash, modern, and "new steps."

Everyone worries about growing older and approaching the event of his wake. "Though Wonderlawn's lost us for ever"—"Alis, alas, she broke the glass!" (270.19–21)—the *Wake* rediscovers it everywhere, even in the body of the "Wondering Wreck" (229.14) shown rubbled in the two relief maps of the night:

> And then. Be old. The next thing is. We are once amore as babes awondering in a wold made fresh where [as] . . . in the storyaboot we start from scratch. (336.15–18)

Note the "love" (It. *amore*), the "wonder," and the fairytales ("Babes in the Wood") buried somewhere very deeply inside of this "old man on his ars," "Dropping-with-Sweat" (102.30). If "Grampupus is fallen down" at the *Wake*, and "grinny sprids the boord" (7.8–9 [the "old man" dead to the world, his widow arranging the wake]), it is complementarily true that "grampupus" has become a "big baby" (It. *gran pupo*)—as a consequence of which, everywhere one looks in "the *Nursing Mirror*," a "grin spreads broadly" across the face ("grinny sprids aboord"). As old meanings take on a new and "rejuvenated" life, that is, lifeless Mr. Finnegan modulates into a gigantic "Mister Funn" again (5.12); and in the grin generated by that reawakened sense of fun, another "sobsconscious inkling," writ on the somatic "foolscap" of "the presence (of a curpse)," ripples up into the head from "down under" to animate the body and bring a "deadhead" back to life. This awakening now signifies the persistence inside Here Comes Everybody, of a "child, a natural child" (595.34)—playful, creative, flexible, resourceful, and powerful—in a head otherwise clogged with "dud letter[s]" (129.7 [and dead laws]). This is why the *Wake*, although it shows "the old man on his ars" and the patriarchy of which he is a representative member in crisis, cannot finally be considered a merely annihilative attack on letters and Western institutions, but in fact a rosy, affirmative, and joyous comedy. For when the "old man" at the *Wake* goes dead to the world, the "childhide" inside him riotously wakens; and "whilst age is dumped [and damned] to mind the day," "youth . . . charm[s] the night" (371.18–19). "Doth that not satisfy youth, sir?" (224.28).

At the end of an aggregating understanding, moreover, it should be clear that inside of Here Comes Everybody, underground, there dwells a sleeping giant that knows no existence in letters and that comes to light in the dark; our usual name for it is childhood or infancy. Necessarily, in the process that sees a multitude of Smiths and Finnegans wake, this giant is harnessed, restrained, and shrunk, "cut short into instructual primers by those in authority for the bittermint of your soughts" (440.22–24 [not necessarily "for the betterment of your thoughts," that "awethorrorty" can make one "bitter" about what one's "sought"]). No one would argue that children should not be trained through language into forms compatible with the exigencies of the Daily World. And in fact, something precisely of this sort happens to "Haroun Childeric Eggeberth" as he drifts toward his awakening on the last page of the *Wake*, and in the process takes forms that show him returning to reality: our "**h**ugest **c**ommercial **e**mporialist" (589.9–10), we learn toward daybreak, leaves "**H**einz **c**ans **e**verywhere" (581.5) in "**E**ternest **c**ittas, **h**eil!" (532.6). As these terms ominously imply, however, the question is not whether or not the sleeping giant inside everyone should be restrained at all, but whether or not it is restrained at all well.

> As my explanations here are probably above your understandings, lattlebrattons . . . I shall revert to a more expletive method which I frequently use when I have to sermo with muddlecrass pupils. Imagine for my purpose that you are a squad of urchins, snifflynosed, goslingnecked, clothyheaded, tangled in your lacings, tingled in your pants, etsitaraw etcicero.   (152.4–10)

Memorably patronizing (< L. *pater*, "father"), this tutelary voice should remind us that English domesticated all us "little brats" (hence "lattlebrattons") in much the same way that England domesticated Ireland (or "Little Britain")—and perhaps to a degree that causes us even now not to notice that interesting little "tingle," or to recall how hard it was to learn to sit still ("etsitaraw"). "This, of course; also explains why we were taught to play in the childhood" (163.4–4 [where "taught" and "play" are contradictory]). By reminding us, "for innocence," of how "the lads is attending school nessans regular, sir, spelling beesknees" (26.34–35), "the *Nursing Mirror*" is also revealing the concealed necessity (hence "nessans") which motivated the "nice and" regular attendance of school; for those "nice" competitive little "spelling bees," in which everyone strove to be "the bee's knees," ultimately entailed instruction in competitive egotism and so really meant training in "business" ("beesknees")—and business much of the same sort that haunts our "**h**ugest **c**ommercial **e**mporialist" in the night. In more relaxed extents of the dark, all this tension disintegrates. "Too soon [like tomorrow] are coming tasbooks and goody, hominy bread and bible bee" (256.17–18)—the "taskbooks," placed by "father" (Co. *tas*) in the "satchel" (Du. *boekentas*), which teach one to be "good, homily-bred, and bibled."

How these "tasbooks" enter the head is illustrated particularly well in a paragraph that brings an end to all the children's gaming in "the Mime of Mick, Nick and the Maggies" (257.3–28). The paragraph takes the rhythm of a nursery rhyme entitled "Old Daddy Dacon" ("Old Daddy Dacon/Bought a bit of bacon"); but the lilt of the rhyme is violently and insistently broken on prepositions whose objects are parenthetically displaced by a string of admonitions, familiar because familial, of this kind:

> like (You'll catch it, don't fret, Mrs Tummy Lupton! Come indoor, Scoffynosey, and shed your swank!) . . .
> to (The nurse'll give it to you, stickypots! And you wait, my lasso, fecking [stealing] the twine!) . . .
> of (You're well held now, Missy Cheekspeer, and your panto's off! Fie, for shame, Ruth Wheatacre, after all the booz [boss] said!) . . .
> for (Ah, crabeyes, I have you, showing off to the world with that gape in your stocking!) . . .
> (257.12–24)

What we hear in the harsh conflict that wrecks the lilt of the nursery rhyme with the voice of parental admonition is the process that creates the Daily World and its objects—for distorted objects precisely are what will one day appear in the gaps occupied by those parentheses. As father ("Old Daddy Dacon/Bought a bit of bacon") brings home the "beacon" (257.15 [so to "enlighten"]), doors and possibilities shut forever (257.28), nursery rhymes vanish, play ends (257.31ff.), and from little childish "tweedledeedums" and "twiddledeedees" (258.24), "the worrild" and its "unhappitents" (258.21, 22 [and "worry" and "unhappiness"]) begin coming to their dark and troubled light. "So now, to thalk thildish thome . . . we are doing to thay one little player before doing to deed" (461.28–30 [and before leaving the "play" world of the dream and the Evening World, to resume somber "prayer" and the "doing" of adult "deeds"): "O Loud, hear the wee beseech of thees of each of these thy unlitten ones" (259.3–4). "Prayfulness! Prayfulness" (601.29 ["pray" for more "playfulness"]).

> O, by the way, yes, another thing occurs to me. You[,] let me tell you, with the utmost politeness, were very ordinarily designed, your birthwrong was, to fall in with Plan, as our nationals should, as all nationists must, and do a certain office (what, I will not tell you) in a certain holy office (nor will I say where) during certain agonising office hours (a clerical party all to yourself) from such a year to such an hour on such and such a date at so and so much a week *pro anno*. (190.10–17)

The details parenthetically suppressed here do not need to be told to anyone because everyone already knows them anyway: just fill in the blanks with the appropriate personal details, and "Pity poor **H**aveth **C**hilders **E**verywhere" (535.34–35). And if you pity him, "'tis sore pity for his innocent poor children" (47.13).

"Anxious to pleace" (113.34 [and "to police"], the letter-carrying and "civilized" side of HCE's mind ("Show'm the Posed") destroys an enormous range of possibilities and potentials by banishing and outcasting—much as civilization outcasts "lepers"—"that babe, imprincipially, my leperd brethern, the Puer, ens innocens," out of whom he grew *in principio* (483.20–21 [L. "in the beginning"; L. *puer*, "boy"]). "Been ike hins kindergardien?" (483.25 ["Am I my brother's keeper?"]), Shaun asks of this "lepered" "other" (252.14, 408.17, 25 ["brother"])—just as Cain asked of Abel (Gen. 4:9). And just as Cain's killing of Abel, like Romulus's of Remus, made possible the genesis and building of first cities (Gen. 4:17), so the perpetration in our own minds of "the young persons removal act" upon the "first mover" out of whom we all grew (483.27) surely insures our socialized adjustment in the cities of the Daily World, but also destroys an enormous resourcefulness and energy born in "childhide." In "Here Comes Everybody," the *Wake* shows us, "the child, a natural child, . . . wouldbewas kidnapped at an age of recent probably, possibly remoter" (595.34–36). The *Wake*, because the night does, brings it back.

For "I have regions [*not* reasons] to suspect . . . that [this] 'little man' is a secondary schoolteacher under the boards of education" (166.20–22 [and not *on* them]) who may have a lot to teach "youth" (224.28, 432.17 [and "you"]) about "tie taughts" (527.1 ["thy thoughts"])—and not least by showing you how deeply and badly those "thoughts" have been "tied taut," precisely because they have been "taught"—"cut short into instructual primers by those in authority for the bittermint of your soughts" (440.24). Indeed, "it may be, tots wearsense" (75.3 ["that wheresince"]) all kinds of brainy "sense" have been "worn" into "all us kids" (276.L3) and former "tots" by "awethorrorty" (hence "wearsense"), those in authority "whose told his innersense" (229.36) "stole his innocence" precisely when they "told him inner sense": "our breed and better class is in [a] brood and bitter pass" (237.32–33 ["bread and butter" evoking the family]). "Which every lad and lass in the lane knows. Hence" (600.3–4):

"Whoopsabout a plabbaside of plobbicides . . . poison kerls"? (331.17–18 ["boys and girls"]). Addressed to all of us grown-up "poisoned churls" (Ger. *Kerl*)—"(now you know it's true in your hardup hearts!)" (396.10–11)—the question invites us to contemplate a "plebicide" of the "plebiscite"—a rubbling of the conventional legacy transmitted unconsciously through generations and through authorized language—by means of a generally play-capable "whooping about" through the "childlit" instrumentality of a language like Wakese. And it also invites us to wonder what would happen if all the energy and vitality buried with "childhide" could be made to work to "Here Comes Everybody's" advantage, rather than buried.

To see precisely what is at stake here, we need only consider Joyce's career as a writer of fiction: it begins with the phrase "there was no hope" (D, 9), in the first sentence of a story about a boy who is afraid to eat crackers in public lest the sound of his chewing "make too much noise" and disturb others (D, 15). To measure the distance that Joyce traveled in the time that moved him from the hearing of hell-fire sermons (P, III), into the writing of that bleak phrase and story, through the capitalized "Yes" that ends *Ulysses*, and into *Finnegans Wake* is to see what the wakening of that sleeping giant might do in one person's life: "*Rockaby, babel, flatten a wall*" (278.L4 [the return, with a vengeance, of the repressed]). If the *Wake* is something of a "torytale," then, it is all the more crucially a "torytale" with extreme "reptrograd leanins" (351.27–28 ["retrograde leanings"]). For were it unleashed in Here Comes Everybody with as magnificently productive a lack of shame as it was unleashed in the writing of the *Wake*, the slumbering giant buried inside would release a force of potentially revolutionary magnitude (one capable, like "Lenin's," of turning a "Petrograd" inside out and into a "Leningrad").

"One of the most murmurable loose carollaries" growing out of these considerations (294.7 [a very "loose corollary," its logic best illustrated in the work of "Lewis Carroll"]) is that one must become a child again if one is to read the *Wake*. Joyce is hardly being obscure when he tells his reader that the letter buried in the body at the *Wake* "was folded with cunning, sealed with crime, uptied by a harlot, undone by a child" (94.8–9 [not necessarily a professor]): "Joke and Jilt will have their tilt" (290.F2). Everyone trains, in the Daily World, to be a brainy little "pantosoph" (Gr. "all knowing"), but in the Evening World, "your panto's off" (257.20), so that genuinely to engage the Evening World and "the *Nursing Mirror*," its reader must relearn "Jests and the Beastalk with a little rude hiding rod" (307.F1): that "Beastalk," in part, suggests "babytalk"; but also a "beanstalk" like that shown rising from the "unfettered belly" (567.5) of the sleeping giant whose "rude little rod" is featured prominently in Relief Map B. Propelled by "the It with an itch in it" (268.4 [Ger. *Id*, "it"]), this rod has as a primary purpose PLEASURE—of a kind which, the *Wake* suggests, most grown-up "poisoned kerls" do not have the faintest idea at all.

"He who runs may read," as they proverbially say in the Daily World. "According to the *Nursing Mirror*" (46.25), antithetically, "he who runes may rede it on all fours" (18.5–6). And since "all's fair on all fours, as my instructor unstrict me" (295.21–22)—"childhood's age being aye the shameleast" (227.34)—"the runes of the gamest game" mapped out by all this phrasing (279.F1.19–20) encourage a return to "childhide" and enrollment in a "Newschool" (327.8) whose "unstrict[ors]" do not teach "the dully expressed" but guide us "through their laughing classes" (526.35–36 [hilariously, as if *Through the Looking Glass*]): "there is no school today" at the *Wake* (620.11–12 [largely because it is night]). Given an "overgrown babeling" as a hero, then, one ought to "try to analyse . . . as though he, a notoriety, a foist edition, were a wrigular writher neonovene babe" (291.21–28 [L. "newly born"]). To do this is not necessarily to intellectualize this "analectual pygmyhop" (268.28–29 [note the "hopping" little "pygmy" in this "intellectual pick-me-up"]), but to engage in a profound form of "childsplay" (501.11) whose purposive latter end is waking-up of the "deadhead" and the world. Since "a brat, alanna, can choose from so many" possibilities (270.4–5 [Gael. *a leanbh*, "child"]), while the rule-governed adult may not, one must "fast" become "in ludubility [playfulness] learned. Facst. Teak off that wise head!" (607.3 [and all the more particularly if it's wooden]). "Get busy, kid!" (477.14). "Gee up, girly!" (112.6). "And keep the kids bright!" (469.32–33). Through his penman, after all, Joyce tells his reader only what he told Frank Budgen when he said that the *Wake* was "basically simple." "My child, know this": "I am *simpliciter arduus* [L. "simply difficult"], ars of the schoo, Freeday's child in loving and thieving" (487.35, 33–34) ["Friday's child is loving and giving," while "freeday" simply designates the night]).

As Mink has noted in the *Gazetteer* (p. 243), Joyce is fond of referring in the *Wake* to the "Mannekin-Pis, the statue (and fountain) of a pissing boy behind the Hotel de Ville" (or City Hall) in Brussels (17.2, 58.10, 207.14, 267.F2, 329.4, 334.35). The statue of this "wee mee mannikin" (576.15 [see figure 11.1]) evidently struck Joyce—and in part, no doubt, because it has much the same crafted structure as the *Wake* itself, whose penman, adept at "nameless shamelessness" (182.14), makes much the same three-word statement behind the backs of "those in authority" and everywhere lifts into consciousness "the shifting about of the lassies, the tug of love of their lads" and "a great deal of merriment, hoots, screams, scarf drill, cap fecking [stealing], ejaculations of aurinos, reechoable [re-echo-able] mirthpeals and general thumbtonosery" (253.25–28). We see such "mirth" and "general thumb-

Figure 11.1. Mannekin-Pis

tonosery" illustrated in the *Wake*'s childish pictographs (308.F1 & 2), the second showing healthy little nibbles taken out of the bones of the "old folkers" (308.18 ["fuckers"]) by "the babes that mean too"; the first announcing the arrival of an "anticheirst" (308.F1) which is at once optimistic, since the coming of the "anti-Christ" would signal, like the night, the end of history and the establishment of a new earth; and also bitter, since tutelage into use of the opposable thumb (Gr. *cheir*, "hand") means the beginning of the end of "holy childhood" (188.10) and the death of innocence. "Shoepisser pluvious" (451.36 [and *not* "Jupiter Pluvius"]), finally, is the reigning deity and watermaker in the *Wake*, as he is in *The New Science* and in the night.

Readers of science fiction are fond of claiming that it is the only form of imaginative literature that takes the future seriously. Not really. Since it imagines the future, in large, by projecting forward through the years the technological trends and scientific discoveries of the present, it fails to see that the future will not take place in a field of vacant objects—weapons or spacecraft, for instance—abandoned by "the old folkers," or in any form of Cartesian "outer space" at all. The future that will rain down upon the earth exists in the minds of children who are growing up and learning "anguish" *now* and whose adaptable persistence through the ages the *Wake* celebrates in its recurrent quotation of a beautiful sentence from Edgar Quinet;[9] and it is also, under the aspect of "tomorrow," awakening right now in "tie taughts" (527.2 ["thy thoughts"]): *Ideal Present Alone Produces Real Future"* (303.L3). Coming to light out of darkness now as millions of Finnegans wake, that future, too, is what the *Wake*, as a reconstruction of the night, is necessarily about. For the "wee mee mannikin" drifting unconsciously through "the *Nursing Mirror"* toward his rude awakening in the Daily World "is childsfather to the City" (15.8); "the first mover" of the human cosmos out of whom, in the morning and at the beginning of time (483.27), all the splintered appearances of the Daily World will emerge; "whoses wishes [are] the farther to my thoughts" (147.19–20 [because they historically "father" and perenially stretch and "farther" them]). It is into a consciousness of the immense potential borne by this child and buried in "Here Comes Everybody" that the *Wake*, because the night does, in part seeks to waken its reader. As the book moves toward its close and the dawning of a new day on earth, its vision focuses on "a youth in his florizel, a boy in innocence, peeling a twig, a child beside a weenywhite steed. The child we all love to place our hope in for ever" (621.30–32). And that child goes back a long way.

CHAPTER TWELVE

"Anna Livia
Plurabelle":
A Riverbabble Primer

RIVER-NAMES

On "Anna Livia Plurabelle," the showpiece of *Finnegans Wake*, Joyce said he was "prepared to stake everything" (*L*, III, 163): "either the end of Part I△ is something," he claimed, "or I am an imbecile in my judgment of language" (*L*, I, 249). To Ezra Pound he wrote of the "nervous collapse" into which the writing of the episode cast him; to Valery Larbaud, of the labor it exacted: "What a job! 1200 hours of work on 17 pages. She has grown—river-wise—since the night you heard her . . ." (*L*, III, 164, 165). He released all these notices, moreover, while working in 1927 on only the eighth of seventeen distinct revisions through which the chapter moved between its conception in 1923 and its completion, with *Finnegans Wake*'s, in 1939.[1]

Critics who have studied the chapter have confirmed what Joyce himself publicized and everyone knows: "hundreds of river-names are woven into the text. I think it moves" (*L*, I, 259). By October, 1927, Joyce estimated that he had worked 350 river-names into "Anna Livia," and within a month wrote of having "woven into the printed text another 152" (*L*, I, 261). Readers given to calculating these things estimate that the final version of the chapter contains anywhere from eight hundred to a thousand rivernames,[2] so to quantify a puzzle about whose quality James Atherton is perhaps most drily eloquent: "probably the most widely known fact about *Finnegans Wake* is that it contains hundreds of river names. But nobody has ever been able to suggest what purpose is served by this inclusion of names, except perhaps the reader will unconsciously absorb an effect of rivers. . . ."[3]

If the chapter was Joyce's showpiece, then, it has also highlighted the many eccentricities and implausibilies for which *Finnegans Wake* rapidly became notorious. Rightly calling the "tour de force of riparian geography" put to play in "Anna Livia" the feature of the chapter on which it "must stand or fall," Fred L. Higginson, like many readers, finally judges all the river-naming "a mere device"—a device motivated not by any discernible principle but purely by obsession. "Searching for rivers to fit the text was done not only by Joyce," he writes, "but, rumor has it, also by colleagues, amanuenses, a grandchild, and houseguests: anyone who would feed the obsession."[4]

Reaction to so strange and mere a "device" has varied widely. On the one hand, there are those who believe that "such a labor does not surpass the importance of certain 'parlor games'," hardly offering "a new way of leading toward regions still unknown," but rather "the manifestation of a dilletantism and of extreme estheticism."[5] On the other hand, there is the view of James Stephens that "*Anna Livia Plurabelle* is the greatest prose ever written by a man" (*JJ*, 617). Falling somewhere between these two extremes and deferring to Joyce's assertions that parts of the *Wake* were "pure music," "pleasing to the ear" (*JJ*, 703; *L*, I, 341), much of the criticism on "Anna Livia" justifies its fascination with the chapter by impressionistically appealing to its "flowing" sonority and "sound sense," typically noting that "many parts of Earwicker's story are aesthetically satisfying for the sound alone."[6] Not many readers, however, are likely to struggle through very many pages of prose so tortuous as the *Wake*'s simply because, though they may not mean anything, they sound nice. River-names, moreover, are only the most obvious eccentricity of a chapter in which yet other readers have also discovered little streaks of "kissuahealing with bantur" (204.3 ["Kiswahili" certainly and perhaps "Bantu"]), references to "escumo" (198.2 [Eskimo]), and riffs of Dutch not atypical of the *Wake* as a whole. These features of the chapter are at once extremely clear, since exegetes have explicated the *Wake*'s foreign languages over and over again; and yet they are not very clear at all, since few readers ever address the interesting question of why the Swahili, for example, should be there at all.[7]

Still, somewhere amid all these odd findings and conflicting views, there is a vast discrepancy. While Joyce claimed that the writing of the episode exhausted him, the scholarship portrays him casually flipping through Swahili dictionaries and the indices of atlases and, simply to indulge mannerisms, popping African words and the names of rivers into an originally clear English text at an alarmingly feeble-minded rate—the English "'upper' becom[ing] 'wupper' (a river)," for instance, and "'lower' becom[ing] 'lauar,' adding the river Laua," somewhere in the three years between 1924 and 1927 (206.31).[8] Since many of the *Wake*'s eccentricities—its resort to obscure foreign languages, its tendency to catalogue and list things, and its purported appeal to "sound sense"—become most evident in "Anna Livia," we might make the chapter something of a test case of the book as a whole. All of the chapter's strangest peculiarities will resolve into a stunning simplicity if we only continue to read the book as a "reconstruction of the nocturnal life" endured by "one stable somebody." To appreciate fully the quality of the reconstruction undertaken in this part of the *Wake*, then, the wakeful reader should once again fall into the "eyewitless foggus" and "blank memory" of a man "tropped head" by recalling only what it was like to have been asleep in the middle of last night. Access to one of these reaches of the dark is afforded by the last paragraph of "Anna Livia":

> Can't hear with the waters of. The chittering waters of. Flittering bats, fieldmice bawk talk. Ho! Are you not gone ahome? What Thom Malone? Can't hear with bawk of bats, all thim liffeying waters of. Ho, talk save us! My foos won't moos. I feel as old as yonder elm. A tale told of Shaun or Shem? All Livia's daughtersons. Dark hawks hear us. Night! Night! My ho head halls. I feel as heavy as yonder stone. Tell me of John or Shaun? Who were Shem and Shaun the living sons or daughters of? Night now! Tell me, tell me, tell me, elm! Night night! Telmetale of stem or stone. Beside the rivering waters of, hitherandthithering waters of. Night!   (215.31–216.5)

The oddest feature of this paragraph—and one which has led many readers to reject Joyce's intimations that the *Wake* has "one stable somebody" as a hero—is its apparently absolute lack of bearing on HCE, who is not simply absent from the scene, but not even talked about. That would be exactly the point: since our "belowes hero," having "tropped head," "is not all there, and is all the more himself since he is not so," the paragraph is representing his "Real Absence" (507.3–4, 536.5–6)—and doing so very effectively. Like a dream, whose manifest features everywhere reveal latent signs of the sleeper's "presence," however, so all the superficial details in this passage ultimately point to HCE's underlying "prisonce" (536.24 [his sleepily "arrested" "presence"]). We learn, for instance, in a yawned sonority, that a "heavy" and "ho head halls"; and "the gravitational pull perceived by certain fixed residents" in the region of that "bulkhead" (100.32, 511.24 [a "head" so "bulky" it cannot be moved]) moreover extends through space to feet: "my foos won't moos" (Ger. *Foos*, "foot") tells us that those feet lie there as movelessly as "moss" (Ger. *Moos*). Much the same "gravitational pull" stratifying this "unknown body" (96.29), its "most besetting of ideas" being as always "the formation . . . of a . . . stratum" (76.2–5), also moves internally to still its jaw and tongue: "talk" is "balked." Pandimensional inertia has rooted earthwards this entire "landshape," beneath which lies the body of the book's sleeping giant, "heavy as yonder stone," as it stretches characteristically from "ho head" ("Howth" head) to "feet" (see relief map).

Not simply his body, but his perceptions seem comparably overcome by the night's "sense arrest" (505.31). Accumulating at the end of a chapter through much of which "'tis endless now senne eye or erewone last saw" (213.15), all those "bats" remind us to "keep black!" ("flittering bats," "bawk of bats"): "who could see?" (213.7). And our "deafadumped" hero (590.1), "deaf as a yawn" throughout the "hole affair" (200.15), seems also unable to hear ("Can't hear. . . . Can't hear"). Less fully perhaps than at other times in the night, he just lies there dead to the world, for all he is able to "no" at his wake, traveling into "moss" and loam beneath a "stone" beneath a tree ("My foos won't moos" "I feel as old as yonder elm"; "I feel as heavy as yonder stone").

Since the paragraph bears such a richly articulated content, however, not everything about our hero can be quite fully dead to the world; and because everything in the paragraph gets there by way of his "overhearing" the gossip of two washerwomen, we should begin to conceive of him being only "all ears" (169.15). "Earwicker, that patternmind, that paradigmatic ear, receptoretentive as his of Dionysius" (70.35–36), is inevitably, at this moment of the night, maintaining his ever-vigilant and watchful "earwitness" (5.14) on the world through ears that just won't close. And at this moment in "his otological life" (310.21), as he "overhears" the dialogue of two invisible washerwomen, his ever-wakened ears have a very confusing choice to make: they can turn their anxiously vigilant attention outward, to radioecholocate with the acumen of a "bat" and the intensity of a "hawk" the "fieldmice" creeping in at the corners of his bedroom, the "bats" flitting around in the night, or whatever might be rustling out there in the dark ("flittering bats," "fieldmice," "bats," "dark hawks hear"). Or they can relax, turn inward, fall into the rest of the sleeping body, and listen there. As this brief foray into the "science of sonorous silence" or "camparative accoustomology" should suggest (230.22–23, 598.23–24), HCE indeed "can't hear" by the "acoustics" to which he is "accustomed" by day (hence "accoustomology")—but only because a deafening rush of waters everywhere audible at the background of the world threatens to drown all hearing out. If his "ho head halls," it also "echoes" (Ger. *halle*), with the dialogue of two washerwomen whose speech in turn echoes wildly of all those waters ("Can't hear . . . with the waters of. The chittering waters of. . . . Can't hear with . . . thim liffeying waters of. . . . the rivering waters of"). What these deafening waters would be is suggested both by the absolute indistinction between "them" and "him" (in "thim")—and also by a passage from the "Sirens" episode of *Ulysses* in which Bloom observes the two barmaids in the Ormond Hotel holding a seashell to each other's ears:

> Bloom through the bardoor saw a shell held at their ears. He heard more faintly that that they heard, each for herself alone, then for each other, hearing the plash of waves, loudly, a silent roar. . . . The sea they think it is. Singing. A roar. The blood is it. Souse in the ear sometimes. Well, it's a sea. Corpuscle islands.   (*U*, 281)

Much this kind of "souse in the ear" ("the sound of water surging against something" [*OED*]) would be the sonority that the *Wake*'s "earsighted" sleeper "overhear[s], in his secondary personality as a[n] . . . underreared" (143.9–10, 38.27–28) throughout "Anna Livia Plurabelle." Although "his braynes [are] coolt parritch" throughout the night (74.13 ["cold porridge"]), "his heart's adrone, his bluidstreams acrawl" (74.14), and his ever-open ears are inevitably suffused with the "pulse of [his] slumber" and "the heartbeats of sleep" (428.16, 403.5). Indeed, as we learn elsewhere in the *Wake*, whenever HCE happens to rest in absolute "peace," "he would seize no sound from cache or cave beyond the flow of wand was gypsying water, telling him now, telling him all . . ." (586.33–35 [Da. *vand*, "water"]).

The relevance of the sound of such flowing water to "Anna Livia Plurabelle" and to the man who dreams at the *Wake* will now become apparent if we turn to the literature on dreams. "An increased flow of blood through the ear," according to Havelock Ellis, can "furnish the faint rudimentary noises which, in sleep, may constitute the nucleus around which hallucinations crystallize."[9] Freud says much the same thing when he observes that "in dreams," "all the current bodily sensations assume gigantic proportions."[10] The idea, in fact, is so commonplace in early modern literature on sleep and dreams that one finds it summarily treated in the eleventh *Encyclopedia Britannica*, the source book that Joyce demolished in order to write the *Wake:* there one learns that "besides the eye the ear may supply material for dreams, when the circulation of the blood suggests rushing waters or similar ideas."[11]

In order to plumb the "real life" underlying that part of the night reconstructed in "Anna Livia," therefore, we need only heed the good advice that Joyce extends right at the threshhold of his "black and blue" (or dark) "book" (L. *Liber lividus*): "lift we our ears, eyes of the darkness, from the tome of *Liber Lividus*" (14.29–30), and then, holding them carefully poised there, listening in very attentively to the dim double wash of blood barely audible right now "in the far ear" (23.22–23), simply share in the "gossip" that our sleeping hero "overhears"—severely overhears—by keeping our eyes fixed on the page. All of the obscure terms in the following lines are marked by a superscript dagger and identified upon first occurrence in the table of water laid at the bed of the page; and oddly, they refer us to nothing more than arteries and vessels of moving water (rivers):

> How does it tummel†? Listen now. Are you listening? Yes, yes! Idneed I am! Tarn† your ore† ouse†! Essonne† inne†!
> (201.2–4)

> Well†, I never heard the like of that! Tell me moher. Tell me moatst.† (198.27–28)

> O but you must, you must really! Make my hear it gurgle gurgle, like the farest gargle gargle in the dusky dirgle dargle†! . . . But you must sit still. Will you hold your peace† and listen well. . . ?
> (206.16–18, 207.30–31)

> Oceans† of Gaud†, I mosel† hear that! (207.23)

> Mezha†, didn't you hear it a deluge† of times, ufer† and ufer†, respund† to spond†? You deed†, you deed†!
> (214.7–8)

> Are you sarthin† suir†? . . . Isset† that? . . . Ay, you're right. I'm epte† to forgetting. . . . It's that irrawaddyng† I've stoke† in my aars†.It all but husheth the lethest† zswound†.
> (203.8–9, 214.13, 208.4, 214.9–10)

> Well†, of all the ones ever I heard! . . . where is it? . . . I've lost† it! Aimihi†! . . . So near and yet so far! But O, gihon†! I lovat† a gabber†. I could listen to maure† and moravar† again.
> (200.28–29, 213.5–9)

> Onon†! Onon†! tell me more. Tell me every tiny teign†. I want to know every single ingul†.
> (201.21–22)

†Rivers: Tummel (Scotland), Tarn (France), Ore (Sweden), Ouse (England), Essonne (France), Inn (Europe); Dargle (Ireland), Peace (Canada); Aude (France), Moselle (Europe); Mezha (USSR), Ufa (USSR), Dee (England); Sarthe (France), Suir (Ireland), Isset (USSR), Epte (France), Irrawaddy (Burma), Stoke (England); Aar (Switzerland and Germany), Husheth (*Annotations*, 214), Lethe (Hades); Lost (US), Aimihi (Iran), Gihon (Eden [Genesis 2:13]), Lovat (USSR), Gabir (*Annotations*, 213), Maur (Malacca), Aure (France), Morava (Europe); Onon (USSR), Teign (England), Ingul (USSR).

Other references to water: tarn, moat, oceans, the Deluge, Ger. *Ufer* ("riverbank"), It. *sponda* ("riverbank"), "pond," Fr. *onde* ("wave"). Internal references to "wells" of various sorts—for instance, "artesaned wellings" (209.33), and "the holy well of Mulhuddart" (206.18)—make it clear that the interjective "well" is among these terms.

Otological terms: Da. *øre* ("ear"), in "Tarn your ore"; L. *audire* ("to hear"), in "Oceans of *Gaud*, "sound" in "zswound."

"Are you in the swim or are you out?" (204.26–27 [and do you therefore have water moving in your ears or do you not?]). The transformation is magical: "bring[ing] to mind the . . . out of sight" (200.25–26), these lines invite infinite exegesis, and not least because they literally mean, in visibly graven letters, much what the invisible and aliterate sound of the bloodstream moving through a human ear also "means"—"liquorally" (321.1)—as it speaks, "so near and yet so far," to the person unconsciously encoiled everywhere at its center. Even if our hero seems not to hear "the least sound" in "the Lethean swoon" of sleep because of some vague "wadding stuck in [his] ears" ("it all but husheth the lethest zswound"), he actually "overhears" a great deal: arteries and vessels of running water. And while their sonority reminds him that he might easily rise toward auditory vigilance by "turning his ear out," the lethargic undertug of sleep makes him antithetically "tarn† [his] ore† ouse†" (into arteries of water), so that he "essonne[s]† inne†" ("listens in") only to fluvial "irrawaddyng† . . . stoke† in [his] aars†": to vessels and veins of moving water. Momentarily we will regard these "lyne[s]†" (209.18) as the nucleus of "Anna Livia," and as they suggest, substantial parts of the chapter are not directly "about" Anna Livia at all, but rather—like many other of those ostensibly transitional passages which in fact hold the chapter together—about degrees of hearing, or of not hearing, or of never hearing;[12] as they "make my hear it" (206.16–17), they "make me hear my ear" and its "hearing." Particled together of terms largely signifying arteries of moving water—rivers—these lines orient the chapter at the interior of Earwicker's ear, which "overhears," in the absence of all other sound, the vitality of its own bloodstream.[13]

Study of these lines will suggest at once why Joyce, launching yet another of many "imeffible tries at speech unasyllabled" (183.14–15) and once again turning obscurely "outlex" (169.3), would have ransacked atlases in order to find a "vocabulary" supple enough to bring to mind a tangible reality always there in the background of the world and always "lying below" consciousness (213.5). Far from obscuring the chapter by "arnoment[ing]†" it with the "Naama[s]†" of hundreds of arteries of water (208.8; 204.5 ["names"]), he was highlighting essential "hydeaspects†" of the chapter (208.11); what readers have largely seen as a "mere device" motivated by an eccentric obsession was in fact an elucidative necessity crucial to the formation of a text representative of the sound of waters washing through the ear. "Merced† mulde†!" "Yssel† that the limmat†?" (212.26, 198.13).

†Rivers: Lyne (England); Arno (France); Na'aman (Palestine); Hydaspes (India); Merced (US), Mulde (German), Ysel (Netherlands), Limmat (Switzerland).

The skeptical reader will perhaps object: "Where do you get that wash? This representation does not accord with my experience" (509.1–2). Yes and no: preoccupied by day with an Irish reality that sends brawls into his barroom, nightmares into his sleep, and, not least, those fieldmice into his bedroom, our hardworking bartender would no doubt find the sound of his own bloodstream so trivial as to let it "sankh† neathe†" consciousness entirely (202.32–33). But in the night, when a quotidian reality held in place by monuments of graven letters, audible gossip, and "awethorrorty" crumbles out of mind and the thinking of the body moves in, his blood enwraps him, like an undergarment (200.25–26), and it has a lot to say:

> Tell me quick and dongu† so crould! . . . O gig goggle of giguels†. I can't tell you how! It's too screaming to rizo, rabbit† it all! Minneha, minnehi† minaaehe†, minneho†!
> (206.8, 14–16)

Not least of what these sparklingly comic lines afford us is some insight into what our "belowes hero" has on and everywhere in his mind in the middle of dreamless sleep ("O go in, go on, go an!" [204.27]): his bloodstream, surely, sounding in the "tropped head" to let him "no" that he is not "the presence (of a curpse)," but a living "presence, of course." News of its garrulous incessance somewhere out there in the dark ("Where did I stop? Never stop! Continuarration! . . . Garonne, garonne†!" [205.13–15]) is therefore gladdening. Even if mysteriously ("I can't tell you how"), it "tells" him—where the pronoun here and in the recurrent construction "tell me, tell me, tell me" might be understood as a direct and not an indirect object; and what it refers to as it "tells" him, "quickening" him and insuring his vitality ("tell me quick"), is only what the sound of washing water audible in your own ear also refers to as it "tells" you: "Minnehaha," "laughing water." [14]

The vague sonority of the liquid washing away "in the far ear" will now compel our attention because, whether one is conscious of it or not, it has been there since the beginning of the world ("Mezha†, didn't you hear it a deluge† of times, ufer and ufer†"); because nothing in the known universe takes place outside of the sound of its sound, enveloped within which and nowhere outside of which is the story of a life; and because in parts of the night, it is all that the *Wake*'s "belowes hero" can "no." All of the arterial "lyne[s]†" from "Anna Livia" that we have so far examined begin introducing us to the sonority of our hero's bloodstream and to unconscious auditory associations attached to it "the like of [which] you niever† heard"

---

†Rivers: Sankh (India), Neath (Wales); Dongu (Africa), Giguela (Spain), Rabbit (US), Min (China), Mina (Africa), Minho (Portugal); Garonne (France), Nièvre (France).

(206.7–8)—"niver†," "niver†," "nevar†" (203.36)—largely because the phonetic apperception of English and "the dully expressed" (500.15–16) gets in the way. Hence Joyce's eloquently terse defense of the chapter "to a friend who complained it was just *dada*": "It is an attempt to subordinate words to the rhythm of water," he said (*JJ*, 564 [and *not* the opposite, an attempt to subordinate the rhythm of water to words]).[15]

The dim double wash heard "in the far ear" will further merit our study because it affords us the example of an articulate sound-system, a language for which "language" is not at all the right word, more murky and illegible by far than anything writ in *Finnegans Wake*, that streams eternally into the ear out of a "mouthless face" without a source (101.30). Joyce calls this "affluvial flowandflow" "lappish language" in the *Wake* (404.1, 66.18–19), and "Anna Livia Plurabelle" is its intricately inflected text. No one would likely want to argue that this sound "sangnifying nothing" (515.8 [Fr. *sang*, "blood"]) is not, nonetheless, "deeply sangnificant" (357.15): if you can't hear it, you're dead. A sort of signified without a signifier—"(we need no blooding paper to tell it neither)" (101.19–20)—this obscure liquid rush therefore forces a reader of the *Wake* into the difficult position of having to "know by heart" (196.14 [as opposed to brain]). Or, as the sound of blood beating away "in the far ear" right now invites one to wonder, "Are you in the swim or are you out? . . . I mean about what you know. I know right well what you mean"; "did they never sharee† you ebro† at skol†, you antiabecedarian?" (204.26–28, 198.19–20 [*not* "show you Hebrew at school"]).

By way of this second question, Joyce frankly "call[s] a spate a spate" (198.19 [a "spate" is a sudden rising in a river]) and self-consciously acknowledges the peculiarities of the arterial language woven through the pages of "Anna Livia," which he variously calls "ebro†" (198.19) and "reussischer† Honddu†" (198.18). *Not* "Hebrew" and *not* "russischer Hindu" (Ger. *russischer*, "Russian"), but only arteries of moving water, these terms make the "affluvial flowandflow" of "Anna Livia" a profoundly "antiabecedarian" antilanguage whose "meanam†" (214.34 [*not* "meaning"]) becomes apparent not in letters, but in the sound that floods the ear in all the gaps that fill the ear precisely when the ear stops hearing letters. In order to "rightly rede†" the chapter (201.28), the conscious reader, doomed though he may be to pay careful attention to its phonetics and graphemics, ultimately has to "tarn† [his] ore† ouse†" and study the transformation that takes

†Rivers: Nive (France); Neva (USSR); Shari (Africa); Ebro (Spain); Skollis (Greece); Reuss (Switzerland); Honddu (Wales); Me Nam (Thailand); Rede (England).

place "in the far ear" when he stops reading literate language and "essonne[s]† inne†" to the "tone† sonora†" (200.13–14) of the "ebro†" that fills the ear outside of civilized structure. For if "learning" to "recognize" "what a" language like "Hebrew," "Hindu," or English "means" requires one to know an "alphabet,"dutifully "read" "chapbooks," and become "abcedminded" (18.17 ["a-b-c-d-minded"]), then "lerryn[ing]†" to "recknitz†" "wardha†" "language" like "ebro†" or "Honddu†" "meyne[s]†," by contrast, obligates one only to "no" the "alpheubett†," "rede†" river-riddled "chapboucqs†," and become an adamant "antiabecedarian" (212.20, 214.34, 200.36, 201.28, 206.12, 208.20, 198.20, 208.35). Unlike Hebrew or Hindu, moreover, whose "alphabets" are fixed by patriarchal law and lexicon with changeless graven letters—"aleph, beth, ghimel, daleth, and so on and so forth"—the "ebro†" and "Honddu†" of which "Anna Livia" is composed are "spilled" (420.33 [not "spelled"]) in an arterial "alpheubett†" whose "nubilee† letters" (205.7)—"alpilla, beltilla, ciltilla, deltilla" "and soay and soan† and so firth† and so forth†" (194.22–23, 200.13)—are "linked for the world on a flushcaloured field" "in scarlet thread" (205.8–9 [in the "flesh" and *calor*—L. "warmth"—of the sonorous and "scarlet-threaded" bloodstream]): "I sohnt† zo†!" (214.19). Purveying "sohnt†" and "meanam†," therefore (and *not* "thought" and "meaning"), in a form only "all inuendation" (194.32 [all "inundating" "innuendo"]), this "language" bears obscure "tidings" (194.23 [floods of them]) which in their totality issue "a letter to last a lifetime" (211.22 [and not a minute more or less because when it begins, a life may begin, and when it stops, a life does]). "When you're quite finished with the reading matarial," therefore (205.20 [the text of ALP]), "tarn† your ore† ouse†," "essonne† inne†," and start to "lerryn†" your "ebro†"·"intimologies" (101.17)—bearing in mind only that these are *not*, "don't you kennet†"? (213.11 [*not* "ken it"]), "Hebrew etymologies." "If the waters could speak as they flow!" (588.22–23), they would "meyne†" what "Anna Livia" does.

Distinguishing the lexically articulate languages of "Babbel" (199.31 ["Babel"]) from the "outlexical" sound of purely fluid "babble," the chapter accordingly invites its reader everywhere to cross that odd threshhold separating phonetics from acoustics, and then again that threshhold separating the acoustics of the external world from the acoustics of the internal. Ultimately, it requires one to perceive not only differences between the binarily

---

†Rivers: Tone (England), Sonora (Mexico); Lerryn (England); Recknitz (Germany); Wardha (India); Meyne (France); Alph (Xanadu); Alpheus (Greece); Boucq (Belgium); Nuble (Chile); Lee (Ireland); Soan (India); Isonzo (Italy); Kennet (England).
  Other bodies of water: Firth of Forth (Scotland).

"Anna Livia Plurabelle"

opposed phonetic elements that constitute any conventional language, but differences between all systems predicated on difference and "exsystems" pure and simple (148.18). The *Wake* is relatively explicit about this:

—When your contraman from Tuwarceathay is looking for righting that is not a good sign? Not?
—I speak truly, it's a shower sign that it's not.
—What though it be for the sow [sound] of his heart?   (490.28–31)

If anyone wakefully conscious right now might be construed as a "country-man" resident in the Daily World, in other words, his nocturnal counterpart must be considered an unconscious "contraman" (490.28 [or opposite]); and while the conscious "countryman" will inevitably see, everywhere he looks, all seven colors of the spectrum (Gael. *tuar ceatha*, "rainbow"), the "contraman" dwelling in the Evening World, because he is blind, cannot "look" at or for anything. These lines finally suggest that not simply "looking for writing," but falling into language generally is "a sure sign" that one is badly misreading the wet and "showery" "sanscreed" (215.26) of which "Anna Livia" is composed (it's like "looking," rather than listening, for "the sound of your heart"). Where the effect of "writing" is to "right" things, by defining and limiting them according to known rules and "creeds" (hence "righting"), "Anna Livia's" "sanscreed" is "without creed" altogether (hence the Fr. *sans*, "without") and does exactly the opposite. To "lerryn†" it, as it "tells" one (200.36 [*not* "learn"]), one must "be good and don't fol† in the say†" (208.30–31 [or into "saying" and language]): "take my stroke and bend to your bow†" (206.23 ["to get the bend of the bow," idiomatically, is to understand]).

Moving outward from the lines that we have regarded as the nucleus of "Anna Livia," and backward from the chapter's closing paragraph, we will now want to note that visible "lyne†" after "lyne†" in the washerwomen's dialogue simply means what the sound of the human bloodstream also "meyne[s]†," both as it streams through "the presence (of a curpse)" and as it moves right now, "in the present, of course," beneath consciousness and the visible surface of the world in the mind of the sympathetic reader. The chapter is a graphic and phonetic representation of the invisible and aphonetic form of "meanam†" purveyed by the waters washing away "in the far ear" of the "tropped head."

---

†Rivers: Fol (Turkey); Bow (Canada and Australia).
Other bodies of water: the sea (in "say").

MORE "UNDERGLIMPSES"

Representative of the chit-chatty "chattahoochee†" (209.22) that makes up the whole of "Anna Livia," the eclectic lines that we have examined will now clarify the formal shape of the chapter, which Joyce called "a chattering dialogue across a river by two washerwomen who as night falls become a tree and a stone" (*L*, I, 213). Essential to an understanding of this strange dialogue is the simple observation that our hero—an absent man who will not quite listen (198.28–199.10, 199.24–25, 32–33, 200.11–16, 201.24)—lies at its hidden center both because he is its subject and because he alone "overhears" it, even if badly. Throughout "Anna Livia," we find "old Humber†" (198.28–29 [HCE]) "sittang† sambre† on his sett†," "drammen† and drommen†" "and droming†" (198.34–35, 199.6 ["dreaming and dreaming and dreaming"])—and so deeply that "you'd think all was dodo† belonging to him how he durmed† adranse† in durance† vaal†" (199.9–10 ["dreamed atrance in durance vile," like the speaker of Moore's "I dreamt I dwelt in marble halls"). The wording here tells us in part that the *Wake*'s sleeping giant lies dead to the world in this part of the night, "holding doomsdag over hunselv†" in "Funglus grave" (199.4–5, 198.33 [hence the extinct "dodo," the "fungus" in the "grave," and the reference to Dublin's "Finglas" area, site of Prospect Cemetery]); and also that he is corporally "arrested" by sleep, as if held "under loch† and neagh†" (196.20 [hence his "prisonce" "in durance vile"]): he's asleep (Fr. *dodo*, "sleep"; *faire dodo*, "to go to bed"). As all the arteries of water that "mague†" up these "lyne[s]†" ultimately suggest (206.9), he sustains an odd species of "dream" in this stretch of the dark—a dream woven around the sound of the echoic play of waves of water like those legendarily audible in the dark of "Fingal's Cave" (hence again "Funglus grave").[16]

What "Old Humber†" has primarily in his mind here, as he listens to the "bloodvein[s]†" and "vesles† vet†" tangling their ways up out of "the core of his cushlas" (212.16, 201.23, 203.23–24 [L. *cor*, "heart"; Gael. *cuisle*, "pulse"])—and as he lies, "with Corrigan's pulse and varicoarse veins," "in contemplation of the fluctuation and the undification of [its] filimentation" (209.2–3, 214.23–24)—is his own bloodstream, its "scarlet thread" "linked for the world on a flushcaloured field" (205.8–9 [the "flesh-colored"

---

†Rivers: Chattahoochee (US); Humber (England), Sittang (Burma), Sambre (Belgium and France), Sette (Brazil), Drammen (Norway), Drome (France), Dodo (Africa), Durme (Belgium), Adra (Spain), Adranos (Turkey), Dranse (Switzerland), Durance (France), Vaal (Africa); Humse (Netherlands); Mague (Ireland); Bloodvein (Canada), Vesle (France), Vet (Africa).
  Other bodies of water: Lough Neagh (Ireland).

•

"warmth" of the body]).[17] Channeling the sonorous flow of moving waters that "vistule† a hymn, *The Heart† Bowed Down*," throughout "Anna Livia" (199.27–28), this "scarlet thread" generates a "meanam†" that we "scheldt†" (206.26) "rightly rede†" only if again, "in the broadest way immarginable," we pursue the most "distant connections" by yielding to a process of free association whose first and grounding term is the sound of the bloodstream. For the whole of "Anna Livia" and everything in *Finnegans Wake* bearing on the "character" of HCE's trigrammatonic consort, ALP, spills up out of and is written in this sound. So "tune your pipes and fall ahumming" (197.36–198.1), and "Note the . . . Associations" (270.11–14). Most evidently, what we know to be blood running through the ear (and specifically through "the juggaleer's veins" [300.31; 511.35]) sounds like running water, so that by one drift of thought, the sonority of his own bloodstream would raise in HCE's "tropped head"—and more generally than particularly—the memory of other arteries and channels of running water, and of everything that one might find "asousiated" with running water (151.29 [the "souse" in "asousi-ated" refers both to "the sound of water surging against something" and to the "alcoheren[ce]" of our "absintheminded" hero]).[18] Such "asousiat[ions]" would explain, of course, the diffuse networking of rivers that pervades the chapter. Primary among these rivers, for our hero, would be Dublin's River "Liffey," "Anna Liffey," whose Gaelic spelling is "*Life*."[19]

Both the syllable "Life" and the river to which it refers therefore become irresolubly bivalent in *Finnegans Wake*, designating "two thinks at a time." There can be no doubt that the sound of water washing away "in the far ear" reminds Earwicker of the River Liffey, whose geography, as the commentary has amply shown, "Anna Livia" elaborately explores. On the other hand, the status of the Liffey in the Evening World is altogether comparable to that of "Dufblin" (447.23 ["deaf-blind"]). If our hero loses consciousness of Dublin, "togutter" with his head and all other objects, when he drifts "from Liff away. For Nattenlaender" (382.27–28 ["from a life" in which the "Liffey" is objectively knowable, into the Nor. *natten land*, or "land of night"]), so too, "obliffious" of the "headth of hosth" (317.32 ["Head of Howth"]), must the "head of [our] host" become "oblivious" of the real-world "Liffey." To dis-tinguish that river from the river pouring through our hero's vacant mind in the night, consequently, Joyce calls the darker of the two torrents the "lifey" (203.6), the "lifing" (495.21), or, most explicitly, "the living" (131.13–14).[20]

---

†Rivers: Vistula (Poland and USSR), Heart (US); Scheldt (Belgium).

Comparably, to distinguish the nocturnal river streaming through the *Wake* from Dublin's "Anna Liffey," whose course one can find charted on any map of Dublin, he calls the stream of dark water flowing through the "terrian" depicted in Relief Map B "anny livving," or "anny living," or simply the "Brook of Life" (185.28, 327.6, 463.10, 264.6 [that "terrian" would be not "the terrain" of Dublin, but the *Wake*'s rubbled "earthling"]). "As if their liffing deepunded on it" (310.5–6 [because they and he do]), our hero's ears lie filled with the rush of the "deep" and "undulant" waters of this river (hence "deepunded"), which, as all these "spilling[s]" imply (461.3), is largely the river of his "liffe" (230.25, 447.23): "Lif, my lif!" (328.17).

Another "asousia[tion]." Since the sound of this river pouring away "in the far ear" is almost impossible to hear, it reminds Earwicker of other barely audible sounds: for instance, the sound of birds and "flittering bats" cutting their way through the air (206.19–20, 215.31–32), and of "field-mice," "rabbit[s]†," "coney[s]†," hare[s]," "otters†," and "wiesel[s]†" slipping in silence through all the small places and margins of the world (215.32, 206.15, 198.15, 210.15, 214.12, 197.4). Within the *Wake*, Joyce accordingly refers to the subject of "Anna Livia" as "little ana countrymouse" (553.2 ["liffle Anna countrymouse," he wrote to Harriet Shaw Weaver, "keeps me awake half the night"; *L*, I, 232]). By drawing on these analogies, he obviously meant to call attention to the virtual imperceptibility of the sonic reality under his study in "Anna Livia." In parts of the night in which Earwicker lies lost in the sound of his own bloodstream, in turn, "greater grown then in the trifle of her days, a mouse, a mere tittle, trots off with the whole panoromacron picture" (318.8–9): everything "panoramically" seen by day vanishes in these intervals, as a phenomenal reality ordinarily altogether negligible fills HCE's "tropped head." "Playing catched and mythed" with a sound hardly heard, finally (197.22–23 ["cat and mouse"]), Earwicker's ears also "catch and miss," among the associations they generate, the sound of whispering and gossip (hence the "myth" in "catched and mythed"). Gossip, too, the best kind always whispered, is sometimes virtually impossible to hear—especially if you yourself are its subject. The almost inaudible sound of his own blood "overheard" therefore reminds HCE of what it is like to hear (or not to hear) gossip somewhere in the "land of the livvey" (308.20).

Out of these aggregating associations, we might now see the chapter's unreal setting beginning to take shape, as vague gossip being passed back and

†Rivers: Rabbit (US), Coney (France), Otter (England), Wiesel (Germany).

forth across the River Life begins to generate "a chattering dialogue." As to the question of why "Anna Livia," unlike most other parts of the *Wake*, should take on the form of a dialogue, reference again to the sound of the blood purling away at the edges of the audible will yield manifold answers. "Tarn† your ore† ouse†," and "listen now": "sucho† fuffing a fifeing 'twould cut you in two!" (199.29–30). If you "essone† inne†" to the sound beating away "in the far ear," you will in fact hear it "cut[ting] you in two"—"systomy dystomy" (597.21 [according to the "system" of the heart's "systole" and "diastole"]). Whether one examines "Anna Livia" as a structured whole or studies small phrases in it, consequently, one will find the chapter rifted and cut into all manner of depthless twos.

Representative of the gossipy give-and-take underrunning the entire episode, all the lines that we have so far examined formally replicate, in their own way, the presence and absence of sound "in the far ear." For if one of the two washerwomen ("Queer Mrs Quickenough" [620.19]) does all the "telling," filling the dark with an outflush of fluvial "chattahoochee†," the other ("odd Miss Doddpebble" [620.19–20]) impatiently waits in the dead pause to hear ("Where did I stop? Never stop! Continuarration! You're not there yet. I amstel† waiting. Garonne, garonne†!" [205.13–15]).[21] Rhythmically, moreover, these and most other lines in "Anna Livia" are partitioned into intricate binary patterns ("stop," "stop"; "garonne, garonne") that exemplify the "inclination to make jingles" and to increase alliteration which Joyce exercised while endlessly revising the chapter:[22] "didn't you hear it . . . ufer and ufer†, respund to spond†? You deed, you deed†! I need, I need!" (214.7–9). Like the larger dialogic structure of the chapter, these "wyerye† rima[s]†" (200.33 ["weary rhymes"]) everywhere replicate the dim double beat of blood washing away in the ear; and, by "bring[ing] to mind the gladdest garments out of sight" (200.25–26), they begin giving us, like Denis Florence MacCarthy's *Underglimpses*, "underglimpses" of "investments" (not necessarily underpants) everywhere "lying below" (213.5) the "uniform" appearance of things ("combies" or "combinations" also are "undergarments"):

> And what was the wyerye† rima† she made! Odet†! Odet†! Tell me the trent† [trend] of it while I'm lathering hail† out of Denis Florence MacCarthy's combies. (200.33–35)

Particularly because it derives from the Latin *rivalis* ("one using the same stream"), "rivalry" in turn now becomes a formal principle of "Anna Livia,"

---

†Rivers: Sucio (South America); Amstel (Netherlands); Wye (England), Rye (England and Ireland), Rima (Nigeria); Odet (France), Trent (England), Hail (Arabia).

riving and rifting it into all manner of twos. The grounding and most evident of these rivalries is that explicitly dramatized in the chapter, which
makes "rivals" of the two washerwomen and the riverbanks on which they
stand (208.14, 197.1). But since "queer Mrs Quickenough and odd Miss
Doddpebble" resolve, at the end of the episode, into "a tree and a stone"—
into versions of "outlexical" Shem and letter-carrying Shaun (215.35,
216.1–2)—we should see that, as in a dream, all things manifest on the surface of the text act only as vectors pointing to far more turbulent rivalries
and conflicts everywhere "lying below" the evident surface of things. Cutting
the reader in two as deeply as they do Earwicker, these "infrarational"
matters make "rivals" of knowing and "not knowing" (209.21 [as of consciousness and unconsciousness]); of knowing by brain and "know[ing] by
heart" (196.14); of meaning and "meanam†," and "thought" and "sohnt†"; of
hearing and not hearing; of immersion in the body and the waters of Life
and removal from the sound of those waters into the deadly hearing of phonetic English ("You'll die when you hear" it because it contains, for instance, the phrase "you'll die" [196.5–6]). Finally, too—and only apparently
"against all rhyme and reason"—these rivalries pit "rhyme" against "reason"
(212.16–17): all such phrases as "without rhyme or reason," evoked throughout *Finnegans Wake* (154.30–31, 178.5, 183.13, 212.16, 263.26–27, 478.10,
496.14), make up a peculiar class of idioms "used to express lack of good
sense or reasonableness" (*OED*, "rhyme," sb. 3b). All of them surely apply
to the *Wake* as a whole and to "Anna Livia" especially, the "meanam†" of
whose "ebro†" appeals less to "reason" through a literal "sense" visible on
the page, than to the ear, through occulted rhymes, rhythms, and "sounds"
buried among the words.[23]

Like a dream, the text therefore becomes "a two in one garment" (208.15)
written in a strange form of "franca langua" (198.18–19 [or mixed jargon])
whose right reading requires a reader to do "two [things] adda† tammar†
(200.31 ["two thinks at a time"]). If the manifest content of the chapter is
susceptible to research in atlases and Swahili dictionaries, its underlying
and "infrarational" sense falls together only in all the sonorous gaps that fill
the ear when the ear turns letters to "litters." This is why the chapter will
never be easy to read and why it will always remain opaque, except as a
parlor game, to anyone approaching it only literalistically—even if the
reader has a fluent knowledge of conversational Eskimo and a steel memory

†Rivers: Adda (Italy), Tamar (England).

"Anna Livia Plurabelle"

of all the river-names in the world. For much of what the liquid sonority reconstructed in the chapter "meyne[s]†" is incomprehensible without some depth study of "ebro†" "intimologies." If attention to that sound will explain such formal features of "Anna Livia" as its binary forms and the manifold puns on river-names, as a case in point, it will now also clarify much of the chapter's content, which bears primarily on four things: an absent man who will not listen, genealogies, laundering, and Anna Livia.

Over five-and-a-half pages, the *Oxford English Dictionary* lists nineteen definitions of "blood," not the least "sangnificant" of which explains that "blood is properly treated as the typical part of the body which children inherit from their parents and ancestors," uniting them in "blood-relations" and "blood-relationship[s]" and linking them in bonds of "parentage, lineage, descent," and of "family, kin, race, stock, nationality" (*OED*, "blood," sb. III.8–13). As another association generated by the sound washing away "in the far ear" will therefore suggest, "anybloody['s]" "thickerthanwater" (70.25, 26 ["anybody's" "blood"]) sounds a little different from water because it is much, much "thicker." "Tarn your ore† ouse†. Essone† inne†":

> Wharnow† are alle† her childer, say? In kingdome gone or power to come or gloria be to them farther? Allalivial, allalluvial! Some here, more no more, more again lost† alla stranger. I've heard tell that same brooch of the Shannons† was married into a family in Spain. And all the Dunders de Dunnes in Markland's Vineland beyond Brendan's herring pool† takes number nine in yangsee's† hats†. . . .   (213.30–36)

What our hero, a man of Irish blood, obscurely "overhears" in "lyne[s]†" like these, as "all thim liffeying waters of" the night wash through him to tell him of "all Livia's daughtersons," "the living sons or daughters of" (215.31–216.2), is little more than what his "bloodvein[s]†" also "tell" him: a tale told of Irish blood, with Viking filiations, and particularly the blood of his own family. We might therefore think of passages like these—and "Anna Livia" is full of them—as "bloodlines," "linked for the world on a flush-caloured field," that lead "waybashwards†" in time to the place where HCE was born (202.22–23, 197.9ff.).

Because the heart "beats" and the blood washing away "in the far ear" makes "washingtones" of sorts (434.22–23), the "tone† sonora†" of these arterial "bloodlines" also reminds HCE of the "beating" sound of "washing"— and only all the more strongly because being asleep is like being run through a washing machine in an "Annone Wishwashwhose" (614.2–3 [or "Unknown

---

†Rivers: Warnow (Germany), Alle (Germany and Switzerland), Shannon (Ireland), Yangtze (China), Hat Creek (US); Wabash (US).

Other bodies of water: "Brendan's Herring Pool" (the Atlantic Ocean; St. Brendan, according to an Irish legend, discovered America).

Washhouse"; see 614.1–13]). As it waves over the body to replenish it, "mak-[ing] a newman if anyworn" (596.36), sleep forces everyone in the world to clean up his act and, no matter who he is, cleanses him of his filthy "hab-its": overeaters can't eat, overachievers can't achieve, smokers can't smoke, and drinkers can't drink (cf. 585.36–586.3). It is for this reason, in "Anna Livia," that "Ireland sober is Ireland stiff" (214.18 [whereas Ireland drinking is Ireland awake and mobile]); our hero, the "stiff" lying there "hungerstrik-ing all alone" (199.4) and listening to the waters of his Life churning about him, is being run through an eight-hour wash cycle of forced sobriety, his bloodstream acting as an invisible and internalized version of the Dub-lin Corporation's Main Drainage System—"a side strain of a main† drain" (214.2)—which carries off all the filth and pollution accumulated in "the body politic" (165.27) and, overnight, runs it off into nothing.[24]

Hence the complaints audible behind the beating and washing sound of our hard-drinking hero's "Life":

> Looking at the dirt of it! He has all my water black† on me. And it steeping† and stuping† since this time last wik. How many goes is it I wonder I washed it? I know by heart† the places he likes to saale†, duddurty† devil! Scorching my hand and starv-ing my famine to make his private linen public. . . . My wrists are wrusty rub-bing the mouldaw† stains. And the dneepers† of wet and the gangres† of sin in it!
>
> (196.12–18)

> Amn't I up since the damp dawn, marthared mary allacook, with Corrigan's pulse and varicoarse veins . . . soaking and bleaching . . . a widow like me, for to deck my . . . son, the laundryman with the lavandier flannels?
>
> (214.22–28)

If all these recriminations, made by a woman who has injured herself while ironing and even starved herself—and all for the sake of an ingratefully heedless little man—now sound unbearably maternal, they ought to. For the figure speaking of "lavandier" here (Fr. *lavandiere*, "washerwoman") pours forth an audible vision, like that visited upon Saint "Martha Mary Alacoque" ("marthared mary allacook"), of a "Sacred Heart"—and, in particular, of a "sacred heart" associated with self-sacrifice (hence the "martyr" in "marthared") and with lots of "cooking" (hence "allacook"). "Listen now. Are you listening?" As the sound of those "bloodlines" flowing through your own ear plainly "tell" you: "Think of your Ma†!" (206.3).

According to this imperative, readers cultivating the requisite "ideal in-somnia" and "blank memory" of "lost life" (515.26 ["last night"]) would now do well to wonder whether there was ever a time in their lives compa-

---

†Rivers: Main (Germany); Blackwater (Ireland), Steeping (England), Stupia (Poland), Heart (US), Saale (Germany), Duddon (England), Dirty Devil (US), Moldau (Czechoslovakia), Dnieper (USSR), Ganges (India), Ma (Burma).

rable to the hour of the night reconstructed in "Anna Livia," when they dwelled, only in unconsciousness, in a universe circumbounded primarily by the sound of a beating heart and arteries of running water. Should they have trouble "recoil[ing]" such a time—"O, foetal sleep! Ah, fatal slip" (563.10)—a simple Wakean question might help to jog a memory or two for which "memory" is not at all the right word: "where have you been in the uterim?" (187.36). Through these terms, the *Wake* suggests that in those darker reaches of the night when our hero's "tropped head" contains only its own bloodstream, his ears having abandoned their educated hold on a world ordinarily structured in acoustical and phonetic understandings, his hearing falls back into "an unknown body" and dissolves in a tangle of blood, where, "deap on deep in anear" (95.30 [and "in an ear"]), it leads him "backtowards motherwaters" (84.30–31). "And it is as though . . . the obluvial waters of our noarchic memory withdrew" (80.23–25):

> Look at here. In this wet of his prow. Don't you know he was kaldt a bairn of the brine, Wasserbourne† the waterbaby? Havemmarea†, so† he was! H.C.E. has a cod-fisck ee. 　　　　　　　　　　　　　　　　　　　　　　　　　　　　　　(198.6–9)

The spectral appearance of this strange little "waterbaby"—a concealed "Mann in the Cloack" (211.1 [or "cloaca"])—in the midst of a space defined only by sonorous arteries of moving water is startling and eerily beautiful, and so is the way in which these lines ask us to "recknitz†" their "meanam†." The allusion here is not so much to the nastily punitive, graven letter of the patriarchal Book of Genesis ("In the sweat of thy brow shalt thou eat bread"), as to the *rhythm* of Genesis; and as we all recall not recalling, the rhythm of genesis was the rhythm of running water: "Was not my olty† mutther†, Sereth† Maritza†, a Runningwater?" (469.13–14). Reconstructing a form of blank "momerry" wholly inaccessible to consciousness and "day's reason" (378.33 [a "merry" "memory" of "mom"]), the passage is evoking the origin not of reason but of rhythm, "in the far ear," and it is, moreover, particularizing the site and manner of that origin by indirectly recalling, only through a "sound" ("Havemmarea†"), the "sense" of the "Ave Maria": "blessed is the fruit of [the] womb."

That sleep entails "intrauterine regression" is so commonplace a tenet of psychoanalytical literature that one finds it represented even in *Ulysses,*

†Rivers: Waterbourne (England), Olt (Rumania), Mutt (Switzerland), Sereth (Poland and Rumania), Maritz (Bulgaria).

Other references to water: Ger. *wasser* ("water"), Da. *hav* ("sea"), L. *mare* ("sea"); Da. *sø*, ("lake," "sea").

where Bloom tumbles *Wake*-wards into sleep and the night under the aspect of "the childman weary, the manchild in the womb" (*U*, 737).[25] A reading of "Anna Livia Plurabelle"—plausibly if not inevitably reinforced by the evidence of the notebooks Joyce kept while working on the embryomimetic "Oxen of the Sun" episode of *Ulysses*—shows Joyce reaching inductively, through his interest in the body and the night, insights that Freud and his disciples reached deductively by elaborating the psychoanalytic theory of the dream. Joyce doubtlessly knew from his readings in embryology that "the fetus hears clearly from the sixth month in utero."[26] And in a passage that explains how HCE, somewhere "round Nunsbelly Square," "was founded deap on deep in anear" (95.35–36, 30 ["in an ear"]), the *Wake* even tells us that "Earwicker, that patternmind, that paradigmatic ear, receptoretentive as his of Dionysius" (70.35–36), has blank "momerr[ies]" of an indefinite "she [who] was lost away away in the fern" (95.29–30). Since the German *fern* means "distant," the details suggest that while our hero may indeed be "found dead" to the world in the night (hence "founded"), the state of "foetal sleep" itself (563.10) returns him mnemonically to a period of "lost life" when, "deep on deep in an ear," he heard in "distant" space "somme-thing†" as inaudible as a rustling "fern" (208.24). "(How faint these first vhespers womanly are, a secret pispigliando, amad the lavurdy den of their manfolker!)" (38.13–15): although the source of this "secret" "womanly" "whispering" "overheard" in the "night" (L. *vesper*, "night"; It. *pispigliando*, "whispering") is inaudible in the "weekday" (R. R. *lavurdy*), it comes to the fore everywhere in "Anna Livia."

Our "wasserbourne†" hero, washed in a "majik wavus" of arterial sound that moves him "backtowards motherwaters" (203.31 [Ki. *maji*, "water"; *wavus* "net"]), recalls prior times in his life when—"not yet" (3.10), "not yet" (3.11), "passencore" (3.4–5 [Fr. *pas encore*, "not yet"])—he was "not all there," "ripe before reason" (212.16–17), hearing only the "oreillental" sound of running water "in the far ear" while "erigenating from next to nothing" out of a "deltic origin" like that which opens "Anna Livia" (357.18, 4.36–5.1, 140.9 [note in "oreillental" and "far ear," how the "ears" "orient," as if in a "far east"]):

O
tell me all about
Anna Livia! I want to hear all
about Anna Livia. Well, you know Anna Livia? Yes, of course, we all know Anna Livia. Tell me all. Tell me now. You'll die when you hear.   (196.1–6)

†Rivers: Somme (France).

"Anna Livia Plurabelle"

In "rhyme without reason," the passage recreates a space "aqualavant to" that lying on the far side of the female delta and orifice, the "first of all usquiluteral threeingles" (285.16, 297.27 [L. *aqua*, "water"; Fr. *lavant*, "washing"; Gael. *uisce*, "water," L. *luteus*, "mud"]): hence its deltic shape and the "urogynal" "O" from which the whole chapter spills forth (619.2 ["original"; "urogenital"; Gr. *gynê*, "woman"]). "Mak[ing] you to see figuratleavely the whome of your eternal geomater" (296.30–297.1), the passage moves us behind the occulting and shame-invested "fig leave" (hence "figuratleavely") into a "momerry" of first "whome" ("womb," "home"), where all "meanam†" streamed into "the far ear" out of arteries of running water, as in turn the primordia of sensation and unconscious spatial perception "erigenat[ed] from next to nothing" (hence the "geometer" in "geomater"). "I dhink I sawn to remumb or sumbsuch," as the canny reader will unconsciously "recoil" (608.22 ["I think I seem to remember some such"]); and "pubably it resymbles a pelvic or some kvind" (608.23 ["probably it resembles" in "symbols" the "pelvis" of some *kvinde*—Da., "woman"]).

As both dream theory and these passages from "Anna Livia" suggest, the dimensionless spatiality in which our "wasserbourne†" hero experiences the greater part of the "nice" (65.12 ["night"]) has far less to do with any formalized "room" or "home" (his "bedroom," say) than with something that the *Wake* now calls "woom," "wome," and "whome" (465.8, 201.24, 296.31 [on the equation of "nice" and "night," see 253.18, 415.14, 502.29, 558.21]). The orientation of "Anna Livia" in this "kvind" of "woom" will now account for the gynocentrism of the episode, for its attribution to the figures of washerwomen (rather than laundrymen, say, or other males who work in water), and for its associative merging of Dublin's "Anna Liffey" with a "mothernaked" feminine "Anna" (206.30), who becomes, as a "character" informing everything in the *Wake*, "our lavy in waving" (275.12 [an aquatic "lady in waiting"])—"a lymph that plays the lazy winning she likes" to "a man that means a mountain" (309.4–6 [and through the "overhearing" of "lymph" by someone "lazy," "a nymph who plays the lady when she likes"]). For the sonority of his own "bloodlines" "overheard" unconsciously reminds HCE of a first and deep attachment to his mother, "the missus, seepy† and sewery†" (207.13): "forth of his pierced part came the woman of his dreams, blood thicker then water" (130.31–33)—where that "pierced part" would be "pierce" "oreille's" ear, the "blood" washing within it reminding him both of a distant past (hence the "then" in "blood thicker then water") and of

---

†Rivers: Mississippi (US); Missouri (US); Moma (USSR).

"Wooming" in general (603.1 ["women," and "wombing"]). Because that first attachment is the ground out of which all others grow, a sound associated with his "dearest little moma†" (207.34) extends to and underlies his thinking about all other women—including "baith our washwives" (281.1 [note the "bath" in which "both" these *Woschwiben*—Sw.G. "chatterboxes"— are immersed]). All characters in *Finnegans Wake*, in turn, who ultimately reflect the underlying "presence (of a curpse)" that dreams them up, "as an understood thing sle[ep] their sleep of the swimborne in the one sweet undulant mother of tumblerbunks" (41.6–7 ["Swinburne," of course, authored those lines that haunt Stephen Dedalus throughout *Ulysses:* "I will go back to the great sweet mother, Mother and lover of men, the sea"]). Because sleep does, all of *Finnegans Wake* takes place in a "woom" of this "kvind," the "unknown body" of "somewome" (298.19).

If, "by a commodius vicus of recirculation," we "rearrive at" the opening pages of *Finnegans Wake*, for instance, we will find our hero identified as "Haroun Childeric Eggeberth" (4.32) right from the moment in which, having "tropped head," he begins to undergo the "long, very long, [and] dark, very dark" process (598.6–7 [sleep]) that will culminate in his wakening ("My heart, my mother! My heart, my coming forth of darkness!" [493.34–35]). Only one of the hundreds of "cradlenames" (201.32) given to the "**h**eavengendered, **c**haosfoedted, **e**arthborn" body that is the *Wake*'s "belowes hero" (137.14 ["engendered," "foetus," and Da. *født*, "born"]), the name now reveals him as a "vary and likely" "foetotype" (324.1) toppling through the dark like a "**h**eadandheelless **c**hicken**e**stegg" (81.22–23) while "babetise[d]" in the "hitherandthithering waters" of the night and the river Life (537.8, cf. 276.F1).

A strange transformation now sweeps out of "Anna Livia" over the *Wake* as a whole. If the darker parts of the book "take you for a bugaboo ride and play funfer all" (304.11–12), here—"no thing making newthing wealthshowever" (253.8–9)—it "make[s] you to see figuratleavely the whome" (296.30–31). Halfway through the *Wake*, "Anna Livia Plurabelle" delivers HCE to a moment in the dark when his "unknown body" lies poised—"like the dud spuk of his first foetotype" (323.36–324.1)—enduring a form of unconsciousness so deep that the *Wake* calls it "mortinatality" (447.8), "*Uteralterance or the Interplay of Bones in the Womb*" (293.L1). The "subject" of "Anna Livia," ultimately, is this "unknown body" of sonorously moving water (his own), through whose sound a man experiencing "Real Absence," "know[ing] by heart," and obscurely "overhearing" many riddling "bloodlines," state-dependently recalls a time when he could "no" only the presence of a "Sacred Heart" whose embrace was all-pervasive:

"Anna Livia Plurabelle"

357

> Or where was he born or how was he found? Urgothland[†], Tvistown on the Katte-kat[†]? New Hunshire, Concord[†] on the Merrimake[†]? (197.8–10)

Not a real toponym, "Tvistown" here plays on the Danish *tvist* ("discord") to form a doublet with "Concord"; and since "discord" and "concord" both derive from the L. *cors, cordis* ("heart"), metaphorically signifying "two hearts beating as one" (*con-cordia*) and "two hearts in conflict" (*dis-cordia*), the passage evokes a time when, as a New World "erigenat[ed] from next to nothing" (hence the New World references), HCE's "heart was as big as himself, so it was, ay, and bigger!" (406.23 [because it, too, was "two in one"]).

"Anna Livia" now necessarily begins to explore a "lost histereve[†]" (214.1 [not "history"]) whose content is in part the "blank memory" that cannot be recalled from yesterday night (hence the L. *hesternus*, "yesterday," in "histereve"). But because the chapter takes us "where the hand of man has never set foot" (203.15–16), it also plumbs a far darker "lost histereve"—or "hystry" (535.18 [Gr. *hysteros*, "womb"])—whose content is the "blank memory" of the time of our hero's genesis and wakening (hence the *hysteros* and first mother "Eve" in "histereve"; cf. 564.31). In contrast to the Roman historian "Livy," a chronicler in letters of "history" and the accomplishments of Empire, the teller of the "hystry" sounding throughout "Anna Livia" is therefore known in the *Wake* as "livy" (452.19), "livvey" (308.20), or—to return to the first page of the book—"livvy" (3.24), "whose annal livves the hoiest!" (340.21–22 ["Hosanna in the highest!"]):

> "Fieluhr[†]? Filou! What age is at? It saon[†] is late. 'Tis endless now senne[†] eye or ere-wone[†] last saw Waterhouse's clogh[†]. They took it asunder, I hurd[†] thum sigh. When will they reassemble it? O, my back, my back, my bach[†]! I'd want to go to Aches-les-Pains[†]. Pingpong[†]! There's the Belle[†] for Sexaloitez! And Concepta de Send-us-pray! Pang[†]! Wring out the clothes! Wring in the dew! (213.14–20)

Because night seems to fall at the end of "Anna Livia," the critical work on *Finnegans Wake* has passed on the view that this passage describes the ringing of the Angelus at 6 P.M. As in a dream, however, manifest appearances are deceiving, and night cannot really be falling here because it is already night on the first page of the *Wake* and everywhere in its midst. So, at least, one of the washerwomen sharply tells the other, in the middle of "Anna

[†]Rivers: Ur (USSR), Gotha (Sweden), Concord (US), Merrimack (US), Ister (the Danube), Fie (Africa), Saone (France), Seine (France), Eye (England and Scotland), Erewon (*Annotations*, 213), Clogh (Ireland), Hurd (*Annotations*, 213), Ache (Austria), Ping (Thailand), Pongo (Africa), Belle (US), Pang (Thailand).

Other bodies of water: Cattegat (Baltic); Ger. *Bach* ("brook"), Aix-les-Bains (a thermal spa in France).

Livia," when she reminds her that "tisn't only tonight you're anacheronistic!" (202.35 ["tonight" does not mean "day"]). Keeping us oriented in the world that comes to light when HCE is dead to the world ("Acheron" is a river in Hades), "when nullahs† were nowhere" (202.36), and when the phenomenal appearances of the Daily World have been "taken asunder" by the night, the line tells us that sleep is radically "anachronistic" (< Gr. *ana-* ["against"] *chronos* ["time"]) because it annihilates measurable clock time altogether. Chronicling our hero's movement through the dark not by "clock" "times," then, but by arterial "clogh†" "thames†" (199.1), the passage takes place not at the time of the Angelus at all, but at the time that the Angelus asks us to think about: the time of the Incarnation, and of the Conception, and—"par the Vulnerable Virgin's† Mary† del Dame!" (206.5–6 [Fr. sl. *vulnerable*, "pregnant"])—of great "labor" and "pain": "who but Crippled-with-Children [ALP] would speak up for Dropping-with-Sweat?" (102.29–30 [an exhausted HCE]). Hence the particular words of the Angelus cited in "Concepta de send-us-pray" (L. *concepit de Spiritu Sancto* ["she conceived of the Holy Ghost"]), the Latin words for "holy spirit" displaced by the French *Saint Esprit* in order to "send us spray." Finally, the passage treats of a time "before the blood" (467.6 [or, as "genetics" modulates into "genesis," "before the Flood"]), situating HCE "somewhere, parently [not 'apparently'], in the ginnandgo gap between antediluvious and annadominant" (14.16–17 [when "Anna" was "dominant"; the "Ginnunga-Gap" of the Norse eddas, like the "woomy" gap in which Here Comes Everybody "'gins to go," designates the site of the world's genesis]).

The reference to "Waterhouse's clogh†" (213.16) will now begin to clarify Joyce's reasons for punctuating "Anna Livia" with allusions to Eskimos. For Eskimos, like "Wasserbourne† the waterbaby," also live in structures made of water—in "Waterhouses" better known as "igloo[s]" (207.33). And as the rhythmic sound pulsing "in the far ear" "tells" HCE, he does too: "Cant ear! Her dorters ofe? Whofe? Her eskmeno daughters hope? Whope? Ellme, elmme, elskmestoon!" (572.16–17). Evoking both the tell-tale rhythm that closes "Anna Livia" and the Danish *elsk* ("love"), these terms notify us that HCE lives in a body made largely of water, but they also show "Humperfeldt and Anunska, wedded now evermore in annastomoses by a ground plan of the placehunter, whiskered beau and donahbella. Totumvir and esquimeena" (585.22–24). While the wording here reminds us in part that our hero is dead to the world (hence the deadly "belladonna"), yet full of "spirits"

---

†Rivers: Nula (S. America); Thames (England); Virgin (US), Mary (Australia).

(hence the Anglo-Ir. *usquebaugh*, "whiskey," in the "whiskered beau"), it largely puts us in mind of the "anastomosis" ("connection of blood vessels") in the "placenta" ("placehunter"), so to show our hero (L. *totus vir*, "all man") circumenwrapped by a "beautiful woman" (It. *bella donna*). This would be his "esquimeena," whose "whome" was his first "waterhouse" and "home." And "that's what you may call a tale of a tub!" (212.21).

Or better yet, in a line that will clarify the *Wake's* erratic use of Dutch, "that's what you may call" "*Our Taal on a Taub*" (105.9 [Du. *taal*, "language"; Du. *taub*, "deaf"])—where the phrase refers not only to Swift's *Tale of a Tub*, but also, as elsewhere in the *Wake*, to pregnancy (e.g., 7.5). The bearing on HCE of the particles of Dutch scattered through "Anna Livia" becomes darkly explicit in a passage that describes "Anna Livia" singing "in a tone[†] sonora[†]" to her "*Vuggybarney*[†]" (200.6 [Da. *barn*, "child," *vugge*, "to rock to sleep"), while "Oom Bothar[†] [himself lies] below like Bheri-Bheri[†] in his sandy[†] cloak, so umvolosy[†], as deaf as a yawn[†], the stult! . . . Poor deef[†] old deary!" (200.14–16). "Below" what? Adjoined to the name of the Dutch-speaking Boer general "Oom Botha," who had as much trouble with (the) English as our "deaf" and "bothered" hero (hence the Anglo-Ir. "bothered," or "deaf," in "Oom Bothar"), the preposition moves us into regions like those in which *nederlands* is spoken (Du. *nederlands*, "Dutch"): into "nether-lands," below sea- and water-level. Like other parts of the *Wake* streaked with Dutch, these lines accordingly show "Oom Bothar" "luistening" "in the waveslength" (384.19, 394.16–17 [Du. *luisteren*, "to hear"]), while "the soundwaves" buffet and "trompe him" (23.26 [Fr. *tromper*, "deceive"]). They also show him harboring, while wondering "why is limbo where is he and what are the sound waves saying" (256.23–24), "something[†]" that the *Wake* calls "remembrandts"—of "his Anastashie" (403.10–11 [Gr. *anastasis*, "resurrection"]). Now "remembrandts," since "Rembrandt" was a Dutchman, would be nether-landly or subaquatic "remembrance," and it would yield "rheumaniscences in his netherlumbs" (319.17 ["reminiscences," that is, of "that which flows"—Gr. *rheuma*—and not necessarily as stored in the head]). All of these terms ultimately show "Haroun Childeric Eggeberth" drifting through "foetal sleep" "on the nod, neer the Nodderlands Nurskery" (385.8–9); and since, as Samuel Beckett noted of the *Wake's* hero, "there is a great deal of the unborn infant in the lifeless octogenarian," we might now see that parts of the *Wake* dense with Dutch are seeking to reconstruct, be-

---

†Rivers: Vouga (Portugal), Botha (*Annotations*, 200), Bheri (India), Sandy (US), Umvolosi (Africa), Yaw (Burma).

cause the night does, "vary and likely" "foetotype[s]" (324.1): although "they're lost we've found rerembrandtsers" (54.1–2).[27]

In turn, the chapter's Dutch and its fleeting references to Eskimoan "Water-houses" make it less difficult than might be supposed to see why Joyce would have drawn on Kiswahili in order to write "Anna Livia." For Swahili, spoken at the headwaters of the Nile, in a locale "long hidden beyond the horizon of scientific certainty," was, at least in popularized forms of early modern cosmologies, the language spoken at the Source.[28] In "Anna Livia" where our hero has become only all "headwaters," we can be "sarthin† suir†" that we are "get[ting] it frisk from the soorce" (209.13–14 [note the Gr. morpheme ôo-, "egg," at the heart of that "soorce," and the Da. *fisk*, "fish," in "frisk"]):

> Don't you know he was kaldt a bairn of the brine, Wasserbourne† the waterbaby? Havemmarea†, so he was! H.C.E. has a codfisck ee. Shyr† she's nearly as badher† as him herself. Who? Anna Livia? Ay, Anna Livia. Do you know she was calling . . . from all around, nyumba noo, chamba† choo†. . . ? (198.7–11)

The Kiswahili words layered into this passage—*nyumba* ("house"), *chamba* ("hiding place"), and *choo* ("privy")—now invite us to associate our hero's "waterhouse" and "hiding place" with a "ladies' madorn toilet chambers" (395.10 [hence the "privy"; note the "madonna" in that "modern" chamber]); and also with a "tempo" and sound audible only "in her tumbo" (209.11 [Ki. *tumbo*, "belly"]). And as the binary beat of that "tumbo" suggests ("nyumba noo, chamba† choo†"), HCE lies lost in "headwaters" at "the soorce" in this part of the night because he is recalling "the grandest gynecollege histories" (389.9). Through its use of Swahili, the *Wake* is seeking to woo its reader into a meditation on "the secrest of . . . soorcelossness" (23.19), moving him "backtowards motherwaters" and a place where "the dart of desire has gored the heart of secret waters" (599.25–26 ["gore" implies "blood"; note the "heart"]). Consequently, "the majik wavus" of which "Anna Livia" is woven "has elfun anon meshes†" (203.31 [Ki. *maji*, "water," *wavus*, "net," *elfu*, "1,000"]), "making meanacuminamoyas†" (201.30 [Ki. *mia na kumi na moja*, "111"])—where the ciphers "111" and "1111," in the *Wake*'s hieroglyphy, signify the filling up of emptiness ("100, 1000"), and so renewal.[29]

Owing to all these peculiar "hydeaspects†" of the chapter, the "meanam†" of the "ebro†" that pours into HCE's "tropped head" throughout "Anna Livia"

---

†Rivers: Syr Darya (USSR), Bhader (India), Chambal (India), Chu (China, USSR); Mesha (USSR), Mean and Acu (*Annotations*, 201), Cumina (S. America), May (Ireland).

now begins to sound forth in "a meusic† before her all cunniform letters" (198.24–25). These are *not* such "cuneiform letters," out of which the law-making institutions of Westernism evolved, as the pictographic character ▽ ("woman, pudendum"), ᵼfixed by law and lexicon into a phonetic symbol that would generate over centuries the terms "dogma," "derision," and "domesticity."[30] "Rother†," these "cunniform letters" take the "form" of the "cunny," purveying sense subsemantically, in the same way that the sound of arteries of water and "meusic†" do: hence the many "warbly sangs†" (200.11–12) that ALP sings throughout "Anna Livia" (e.g., at 198.23–27 and 199.29–200.16). Once again, then, "when you're quite finished with the reading matarial" (205.20 [the literate text of "Anna Livia"]), "rede†" what "was put in the Mericy† Cordial† Mendicants' Sitterdag-Zindeh†-Munaday† Wakeschrift" (205.16–17). Sounded "in the far ear" when HCE is dead to the world (hence the "wake" in this "makeshift" "Wakeschrift") and when time, days, and weeks end altogether (hence the "week-ending" effect of "Saturday-Sunday-Monday"), this "Mericy† Cordial† Wakeschrift" differs from any "weekly magazine" (Ger. *Wochenschrift*)—or from "the *Morning Times*" or "the *Daily Mail*"—because it is writ not in letters but in the "cunniform letters" that spill into the ear between letters to make "litters" of them, so to become "sommething†" like the "mormon's† thames†," or the "toiling moil†" (199.1–2). Where ordinarily legible periodicals chronicle "births," "deaths," and the passage of "mankind's history," this "Mericy† Cordial† Wakeschrift" speaks of "berths" and "debths" and tells an unwritten story—of "womankind['s]" "hystry" (128.19). Bearing on what it is to be "alive" (hence the Sans. *zindah* in "Zindeh"), its subject is a "*Mater Misericordia*" (L. " Mother of Mercy," the L. *misericordia* itself deriving from the verb *misereri* ["to pity"] and *cors, cordis*, [the "heart"]); and ultimately it yields, in the "ebro†" and "cunniform letters" playing through the *Wake*, a reconstruction of "real life" that is altogether "truetowife" (11.29 [and "true to life"]) because true to Here Comes Everybody's relations with "amother" (125.12 [and therefore "another"]).

In order to pursue the "meanam†" of these "cunniform letters" more deeply, the reader heeding the sound of the Life washing away "in the far ear and wondering "in [his] thoughts how the deepings did it all begin" (428.5) must now move "backwards . . . out of farther earshot . . . in the direction of Mac

---

†Rivers: Meuse (France); Rother (England); Sanga (Africa); Meriç (Turkey); Corda (Brazil), Zindeh (Iran), Mun (Thailand), Una (Yugoslavia); Mormon (US), Thames (England); Moi (Africa).

Other bodies of water: Moyle (north channel of the Irish Sea).

Auliffe's" (426.34–427.4 [where the "aleph" in "Mac Auliffe" names "the soorce," "liffe[y]" yields the sound of running water, and "Mac Auliffe" itself designates a "son"—Gael. *mac*—of "life"]). Only by taking soundings "deap on deep in anear" will one discover "how Big Bil Brine Borumoter first took his gage at lil lolly lavvander waader" (331.26–27 [or, like a "barometer," "gauged" the pressure of Nor. *lavvande*, "low water"]) while "oreillent[ing]" himself (357.18) in "matter" (< I.E. root *mater, "mother"). We have "such a loon† waybashwards† to row" (202.22–23) in order to discover what kind of "meerschaundize" lies (210.2 [Ger. *Meerschaum*, "sea-foam"])—like the froth and abundance spilled forth on the far shores of the world and out of Pandora's Box (209.18–212.19 [Gr. *pan-doron*, "all gifts"])—in the "mixed baggyrhatty†" (209.10) of ALP's "culdee sacco† of wabbash†" (210.1) that it would be best, in moving "backtowards [these] motherwaters," to proceed slowly.

> Of this Mr A . . . and these wasch woman . . . nothing more is told until now. . . . And then. Be old. . . . We are once amore as babes awondering in a wold made fresh where [as] . . . in the storyaboot we start from scratch.   (336.12–18)

"MISERICORDIA"

Because the unconscious perception of the bloodstream and all the "mea-nam†" associatively adhering to it constitute an incessant part of the "gos-siple so delivered in [HCE's] epistolear" (38.23), its sonority spills out of "Anna Livia" into everything else in the *Wake*, enveloping it everywhere and ultimately giving the book its circular, recirculating form. Throughout the night, the hearing of his own bloodstream in the "Real Absence" of anything else causes HCE "to pianissime a slightly varied version of Crookedribs confidentials . . . and, to the strains of *The Secret of Her Birth*, hushly pierce the rubiend aurellum of . . . a layteacher of . . . orthophonethics" (38.30–36 ["Crookedribs," as the *Annotations* explains, is "Eve"]). Although the wording here seems to describe the passing of gossip from one distinct person to another, we can infer from the context (I.ii) that only "one stable somebody"—"Persse O'Reilly"—underlies all the manifest appearances, characteristically "overhear[ing], in his secondary personality as . . . [an] underreared" (38.27–28) and therefore acting as both the generator and receiver of all the evident "gossiple." As "a layteacher of orthophonetics," again, Earwicker is a master of "overhearing"; and the "overhearing" of his

---

†Rivers: Loon (Canada), Wabash (US); Bhagirathi (India), Sacco (Italy).

own bloodstream, because of the "secret" "womanly" associations attached to it (38.14), makes his "rubiend aurellum" (L. *auris*, "ear") turn red everywhere in the night (hence the L. *rubens*, "reddish" or, because blood-filled, "blushing").

A return to the opening pages of the *Wake*, then, will show this always overheard riverbabble permeating even the book's first lines, and everything that follows them in the body of the text:

> riverrun, past Eve and Adam's, from swerve of shore to bend of bay, brings us by a commodius vicus of recirculation back to Howth Castle and Environs.   (3.1–3)

Particularly because "circulation" is a word usually associated with the bloodstream and the amply noted "commode" in "commodius" is a synonym for "chamberpot," we might now see that "the commodius vicus of recirculation" which HCE undergoes by passing into sleep returns him to a "whirled" in which there is "plenty of woom" (582.20, 465.8), even as it turns him into a sleeping giant capable of incorporating "Howth Castle and Environs." At the *Wake* as in the era of his wakening, therefore, "Haroun Childeric Eggeberth's" first intelligence is of running water ("riverrun"), and of vaguely tactile movement and binary sound in confined space ("swerve of shore," "bend of bay"); and as in the era of his genesis, too ("Eve and Adam's"), intelligence of the maternal precedes that of the paternal.

Embodied in the sonority of running water, this intelligence permeates everything in *Finnegans Wake*. For even though, sleeping like a rock, "he calmly extensolies" in the dark, dead to the world and "rockbound" (6.35, 7.1), still, "all the livvylong night, the delldale dalppling night, the night of bluerybells, [ALP's] flittaflute in tricky trochees (O carina! O carina!) wake him" (7.1–3). The "bells," "flutes" "ocarinas," "trochees," and alliterative doublets in this construction make "meusic†," while the Italian *carina* ("nice" [a term related to Romanic words for the "heart"]) evokes our hero's pleasure in ALP as, "unda her brella, mid piddle med puddle, she ninnygoes nannygoes nancing by" (7.26–27)—the "umbrella" "keep[ing] black!," the "puddles" and "waves" (L. *undae*) keeping HCE "inundered" (127.5), and the "nannygoat" returning him to childhood. If "he's doorknobs dead!," then, "Annie Delap is free! Ones more" (378.1–2); and "once more," because the unconscious associations welling up out of the sound of his bloodstream and its "lap" never stop (hence "Delap"), "one's more" than one—as in the era of his genesis and birth, when he was "wedded . . . in annastomoses" with ALP (585.22–23). "She is livving in our midst of debt," then (11.32 ["in the midst" of sleep's "death"]), "and laffing through all plores for us (her birth is uncontrollable)" (11.32–33 [as "uncontrollable" as HCE's nocturnal "remembrandts" of his]). And "she knows her knight's duty while Luntum sleeps" (12.4–5): since "knight's," like "night's," would move us into the Dark Ages and thoughts proper to a hero like "Mr Knight" (245.32 ["night"]), whose hearing of English disintegrates "When London [and English] Sleeps," the line suggests simply that ALP's "night's duty" is to "wake him"—in both senses of the word (to watch over the dead, to quicken and bring to life). "She who shuttered him after his fall and waked him widowt sparing" (102.1–2), accordingly, becomes a figurative "widow" to a man dead to the world (e.g., at 7.8ff., 79.27ff., 214.26, 387.33), tendering him "Anna Stacey's how are you!" (28.31 [Gr. *anastasis*, "resurrection"]).

Although it may seem, to all external appearances and to "day's reason," that the "one stable somebody" shown in the two relief maps of the night is a solid man, the unending play of terms like these throughout the *Wake* finally suggests that "our mounding's mass" has a deep "streamline secret" encoiled within him (560.30), and that "all the livvylong night, the delldale dalppling night," "the solid man [is] saved by his sillied woman" (94.3). As "Ainsoph . . . with that noughty besighed him zeroine" (261.23–24), our hero is always and inevitably "a family all to himself" in the *Wake* (392.23–24), since he alone generates and contains in his dreams (like the Kabbalah's supreme creator, "Ain-Soph") the figures of Shem, Shaun, Issy, and ALP—and since ALP herself, however "naughty" a "heroine" she may seem, is only a "nought," a "zero," a dream bled out of a sound as inaudible as the "sigh" in "besighed." If "a so united family pateramater" as our hero "is not more existing on papel or off of it," then (560.28), since he himself dreams up and contains both paternal and maternal figures (L. *pater et mater*, "father and mother"), it is complementarily true that "as keymaster fits the lock it weds so this bally builder to his streamline secret" (560.29–30). However "solid [a] man" of character and body our hero may be in the Daily World constituted of authority ("papal"), "paper," and the whole "bally building" of civilization (Anglo-Ir. *bally*, "town"), the "samething is rivisible by nighttim, may be involted into the zeroic couplet" (284.8–10); when he lies "reduced to nothing" in the night, that is (499.3 ["zero"]), the discretely individualized and "solid man" disintegrates, becoming "divisible," and even "disselving" (608.5) into a "couplet" of sorts.

The two terms in this "zeroic couplet" would be the characters HCE and ALP, who lie "anastomosically assimilated" with each other throughout the *Wake* (615.5) and together represent the "one fledge, one brood" (378.4 [and the "one flesh, one blood"]) that constitutes both "the presence (of a curpse)" and the "anastomosic" "ground plan" (585.23) out of which this presence evolved. If the first of these trigrammatonic configurations remotely evokes the Latin *hoc corpus est*, and so "identifide[s]" the body "tropped head" at the *Wake*, ALP provides both the missing complement ("this is his blood") and a resurrective principle capable of transforming the wake into a wakening. Recurrences of the couplet HCE and ALP evoke the steadily wakening "fleshblood" of the "one stable somebody" who lies dead to the world at the *Wake* (292.9); but since the sound of the blood in that "fleshblood" recalls "absent female assauciations which I, or perhaps any other person . . . have the honour to had" (413.18–20), they also force us to see, in new ways, that what exactly we mean when we conceive of our hero as a stable "him" or "himself" is exceedingly problematic. Indeed, these "couplets" suggest that a "hemale" already returned to an "early bisectualism" through the infantile regressive powers of the dream (581.18, 524.12, 36["bisexualism"]), also undergoes "sexual" "bisection" through the force of uterine regression, taking both "the form masculine" and "the gender feminine" (505.25). For as he lies asleep "with his cunnyngnest couchmare . . . lame of his ear and gape of her leg," "he as hale as his ardouries, she as verve as her veines" (576.27–29, 577.3–4), he becomes inextricably entangled not simply in a "cunningest nightmare" (Fr. *cauchemar*, "nightmare"), but, through the hearing of his "ardouries" and "veins," in a "cunny nest" (hence "cunnygnest") localized in a feminine "gape of her leg" (hence the "mare" in "couchmare"). There, "him her first lap, her his fast pal" (318.12–13 ["lap" = "pal" = "ALP"]), the two together "han in hende will grow" (318.14 [Nor. *han i hende*, "he in her"]). There, too, the annealing force of "ardour" is born (hence "ardouries").

These dyads, then, finally reveal our hero to be less a discretely individualized "solid man" than a knot of modulating attachments that lead back in time to the era of his wakening, where, "when older links lock older hearts then he'll resemble she" (135.32–33). Throughout the *Wake*, HCE is "formelly confounded with amother" (125.11–12)—"formally confounded with another," that is, precisely because he was "formerly con-founded with a mother":

> —I get it. . . . he stands pat for you before a direct object in the feminine. I see.
> —Madonagh and Chiel, idealist leading a double life! . . .   (490.9–11, 6)

Since "the aged monad" who sleeps at the *Wake* disintegrates into "Real Absence" in the night (341.13), under the twin forces of infantile and uterine regression (514.34, 608.5), he is not finally a paternal old man at all, but rather a child entangled in a mother's body, an "idealist leading a double life" in a universe within which patriarchy and all its laws have collapsed: "in the dream we return to the dual unity, mother and child, as one body."[31] In one way of thinking, then, the real hero of the *Wake* is not at all "the old man on his ars" shown visibly "scrapheaped" in the relief maps, but his "polar andthisishis" and unconscious (177.33), a mother and child whose mutual embrace, as in figurations of the Pietà, implicitly represents the "Real Absence" of the father. In turn, these considerations enable us to see that parts of the *Wake* in which ALP is dominant take place not in the socially engendered spatiality of a male body, but in a "woom" where "femelles will be preadaminant" (617.23–24 [as if "before Adam"]) and where, our "hemale man all unbracing to omniwomen" (581.18), "woman will water the wild world over" (526.20–21). From this perspective, the *Wake* takes place both in the body of a male lying dead to the world as if at a wake, and in the body of "amother" with whom, while wakening, he is "formelly confounded."

Beginning with the phrase "Eve and Adam's" (3.1), *Finnegans Wake* therefore teems with forms of "the zeroic couplet" HCE and ALP, which Joyce modulates, in the course of the book, through "minney combinaisies and permutandies" (284.12–13). In an endless series of "combinations and permutations" of inter-entangled "combies" and *mutandes* (It., "underwear"), these "couplets" give us continual MacCarthy-like *Underglimpses* into "investments" lying below the visible surface of things—not least of which is "love" (hence the Ger. *Minne*, "love," in "minney"). Showing HCE everywhere "anastomosically assimilated" with "his streamline secret," these dyads appear not only acrostically, but descriptively, turning "the solid man"—"our mounding's mass"—into a "melting mountain in wooing wave" (132.7–8) or, since he lies moored to the earth like Gulliver in Lilliput, into "a Mons held by tentpegs and his pal whatholoosed on the run" (113.19–20 [L. *mons*, "mountain"]). Or, again, they poise "Flowey and Mount on the brink of time" (197.14–15), the scene of the *Wake* itself extending "from Fonte-in-Monte to Tidingtown" (202.9 [note the "fountain" inside the "mountain," and the "tide" on which the "town" is based]). Ultimately, these dyadic configurations show that the real hero of *Finnegans Wake*, "*The Bearded Mountain*" figured in the relief map, never exists independently of his "streamline secret" and consort, "*The River Romps to Nursery* (Maidykins in Undiform)" (222.12–14)—where the female "kin" in "Maidykin," associated with the "nursery," wears an "undiform" because she takes the "urogynal" and maternal "form" of "waves" (L. *undae*).

"Because it's run on the mountain and river system" illustrated in the play of all these terms (288.F3), the *Wake* in turn is "poured forth where Riau Liviau riots and col de Houdo humps" (42.18–19 [Pro. *riau*, "river basin," *colo*, "mountain"; Provençal is "the language of love"]). And although HCE "half hear[s] the single maiden speech La Belle sp[i]n[s] to her Grand Mount" throughout the night (137.35–36), "as Rigagnolina to Mountagnone, what she meaned he could not can" (255.15–16 [or "ken," since he is unconscious of it; It. *rigagnolina*, "rivulet," *montagnone*, "big mountain"]). These terms now make the *Wake*'s nocturnal "interior monologue" something that might more accurately be construed as the *Intimier Minnelisp of an Extorreor Monolothe* (105.11–12; cf. 254.13–14); for though our hero seems, on the "exterior," to be dead to the world (hence his emplacement beneath that "monolith"), the "interior" of his body is suffused by the "intimite" "lisp" of a sound unconsciously signifying "love" (Ger. *Minne*). By another drift of association attached to the sound of blood washing away "in the far ear," then, the River "lifey" modulates into the "Lovvey" (231.12), and our hero is washed forward in its stream.

The power and depth of the attachment represented by the *Wake*'s "zeroic couplet[s]" is expressed eloquently enough in *Ulysses*, where Stephen Dedalus wonders whether "*amor matris*, subjective and objective genitive, may be the only true thing in life" (*U*, 207 [L. "love of mother"]), and where the hallucinated ghost of Mary Goulding Dedalus dramatizes the sentiment by declaring to her son, "years and years I loved you, O my son, my firstborn, when you lay in my womb" (*U*, 581). Although these "years," by anyone's count, would make for a long gestation, the *Wake* finally suggests that they are a vast underestimate and that, in a human universe in which attachment and interdependence are the grounding facts of life, the "strandentwining" "[naval]cords of all link back" (*U*, 38) in a never-broken continuity that makes Here Comes Everybody a membrane and member of other people. For the "innate little bondery" of anastomosis (296.29), which makes mother and child one body and person, allows no established and "neat little boundary" to separate one from "amother"; and the "innate bondery" that "formelly confounds" HCE "with amother" in the era of his genesis therefore becomes, in the *Wake*, the "groundplan" out of which evolve the bonds that link him, "later in life," with Here Comes Everybody else.

As "the uniter of U. M. I. hearts" (446.7–8)—his and hers in anastomosis, "yours and mine" now—the "leading lady" of *Finnegans Wake* therefore becomes "a most kindhearted messmother" (560.26–28 [note the Ger. *Kind*, "child" underlying that "kindheartedness"]), linking everyone "in those happy moments of ouryour soft accord" (446.15–16 [where "accord," < L. *cor, cordis*, radically signifies two hearts beating as one]). And "in that united I. R. U. stade" (446.17–18 [as opposed to the "state" made possible by male differentiation and conflict]), where "I are you" and "you are I" (hence "I. R. U."), the groundwork of "sym-pathy" (Gr. "feeling together") and "com-passion" (L. "suffering together") is laid—as of the Latin *misericordia* ("compassion, mercy") and the German *Barmherzigkeit* (literally meaning "yeast-heartedness" and lexically "compassion"): "*Notre Dame de la Ville*, mercy of thy balmheartzyheat!" (102.18–19 [note the "balm" and the warmth in this "heart"]). As the primal ground of an attachment that precedes the formation of letters and consciousness, ALP therefore becomes "bondwoman of the man of the house, and murrmurr of all the mackavicks, she who had given his eye for her bed and a tooth for a child" (101.32 [Gael. *maca mhic*, "sons of a son"]): though domesticated culturally (hence "bond-woman"), this "mother" memorable through a "murmur" (hence "murr-murr") generates both in her body and in the human family the primordia of human "bonding" (hence "bond-woman"), and by filling the "bed" with "children," and those children with "eyes" and "teeth," she does so in ways altogether antithetical to those dictated by the patriarchal *lex talionis* ("An eye for an eye, a tooth for a tooth"). "We're all found of our anmal matter," as the *Wake* puts it (294.F5), so to suggest that because "we're found[ed] in animal matter," we are inevitably "fond of our *Alma Mater*" (L. "fostering mother").

Our hero, who has had no choice but to maintain the role of patriarch in his conscious life, has evidently drifted far away from this "urogynal" "bondwoman," whose "impermanent waves were the better half of her" (101.30–31 [he being the worse half]). A prodigal son with "a prodigal heart" (210.17), he accordingly hears in "the hitherandthithering waters" pouring away "in the far ear" a sound symbolic of the force of attachment, and of attachment's passing; for "the river tripped on her by and by, lapping as though her heart was brook: *Why, why, why! Weh, O weh! I'se so silly to be flowing but I no canna stay!*" (159.16–18 [Ger. *Weh!*, "Woe!"]). The passing forth of these waters in the night, then, reminds him "infrarationally" not simply of the dark forward rush of time, but of the simultaneously joyous (hence "laughing") and heart-breaking power (hence "heart" and "brook") that time wields in tightening and severing the attachments that link him to other people. When "we list, as she bibs us, by the waters of babalong" (103.10–11), we in turn should hear in Anna Livia's river-babble intimations

of the passing away of childhood (hence the "bibs," "babble," and "baby");
of the loss of parents whose deaths are the inevitable countersign of our
coming-to-be; and of exile from a paradise to which sleep, nightly, returns
us (hence the evocation óf Psalm 133 ["By the waters of Babylon, there we
sat down, yea, we wept, when we remembered Zion"]):

> because ye left from me, because ye laughed on me, because, O me lonly son, ye are
> forgetting me!, that our turfbrown mummy is acoming, alpilla, beltilla, ciltilla, del-
> tilla, running with her tidings, old news of the great big world, sonnies had a
> scrap, woewoewoe! bab's baby walks at seven months, waywayway!   (194.20–25)

ALP's role in "Anna Livia" as a "proxenete" to a "man in passession"
(198.16–17, 22 ["passion," "possession"])—where the English "proxenete"
(< Gr. *proxenêtês*, "agent" or "broker") designates a matchmaker or nego-
tiator of marriage (*OED*)—would have to do with her grounding role in the
mediation of HCE's passions. The parts of the *Wake* that show HCE and ALP
"wedded now evermore in annastomoses by a ground plan of the placehunter" (585.22–23 [in the "anastomosis" of the "placenta"]) are also
implicitly showing the "infrarational" bases underlying forms of human
jointure and "wedding," where too, as in the "innate little bondery" of "annastomoses," there is no "neat little boundary," and "Twainbeonerflsh"
(571.29). "Who so shall separate" HCE and ALP, accordingly, "fetters to new
desire, repeals an act of union to unite in bonds of schismacy" (585.24–26
[though this newly formed "union," because "schismatic," is not without
tension]). One of Anna Livia Plurabelle's functions as a "character" in the
Wake, then, is to act as "the Bringer of Plurabilities" (104.1–2), and to open
up the possibility of those human "pluralities" which are born of the
making and severance of formed attachments—inevitable if only because
birth and death are facts of the world—whose experience is at one and the
same time the suffering of an indifferentiable pain and joy, and whose endurance signifies growth (hence the "tears" [Fr. *pleurs*] and the "beauty" [Fr.
belle] in "Plurabelle"). "For as Anna was at the beginning lives yet and will
return" (277.12–13), so "Anna was, Livia is, Plurabelle's to be" (215.24);
"Mammy was, Mimmy is, Minuscoline's to be. . . . The same renew"
(226.14–17). Note how, in these progressions from past to future, "Mammy"
modulates into something "very tiny" (It. *minuscoline*) but never quite disappears: "Mater Mary Mercerycordial of the Dripping Nipples, milk's a
queer arrangement" (260.F2).

The play of these terms also suggests quite the opposite of what is often
asserted by those who have read neither the *Wake* nor Joyce in any mean-

ingful way: far from being the work of the cold and cerebral writer, the *Wake* is a work of exorbitant and almost overwhelming passion and compassion, and the only thing that will prevent anyone from acknowledging it is too much reading of "the dully expressed." Not least of its accomplishments in plumbing those "infrarational matters" that come to light in the dark, when individuals differentiated in the Daily World by identity, consciousness, gender, and language "disselve," the *Wake* makes us all—"*a lot of lasses and lads without damas or dads, but fresh and blued*" (341.33–34)—the freshly reinvested "flesh and flood" of one body.[32]

"OVASLEEP"

In that passage from the "Ithaca" episode of *Ulysses* which catalogues the many properties that Bloom—"waterlover, drawer of water, watercarrier"—admires in water, we learn among all things else of "its ubiquity as constituting 90% of the human body" (*U*, 671, 672). Read in conjunction with "Anna Livia Plurabelle," the Bloomesque detail obliges us now to reconstrue the spatiality within which *Finnegans Wake* takes place not as the body of "the solid man" depicted in the two relief maps of the night, but as a body primarily of water. As our hero, like "every morphyl man of us . . . falls back into [the] terrine" depicted in the two carnal maps of the night (80.22–23 [where that "tureen," unlike a "terrain," holds liquid]), he becomes not only "himself in the flesh," but "himself in the flesh . . . incarnadined" (79.2–3)—the Shakespearean adjective suggesting that by turning into his own body, he passes into a spatiality of flowing fluid and "multitudinous seas incarnadine" (*Macbeth*, II, ii, 61). When the *Wake's* sleeping giant "goes under" in sleep, he therefore "disselv[es]" (608.5 [and "dissolves"]) in a body largely of water, where, quite easily, "you can sink [him] lead" (317.3–4 [so to answer Finnegan's question, "Do you think me dead?"]): "It's his last lap, Gigantic, fare him weal" (242.20–21 ["It's Your Last Voyage Titantic, Fare Thee Well"]). As "he dives" and goes "inunder" in this "Deepsleep Sea" (321.4, 320.3, 37.18), he comes to resemble "McGinty" of popular song: "and dong wonged Magongty till the bombtomb of the warr, thrussed in his whole soort of cloose" (366.32–33 ["and down went McGinty to the bottom of the sea, dressed in his old suit of clothes"]).

Drowned in "liquick music," our hero "sleep[s] in the water . . . and dream[s]" at moments in the *Wake* like these (280.32, 34–35), thereby keeping his nightly "dathe with a swimminpull" (377.35 [or "date with a swimmingpool"]); as the night renders him dead to the world (hence the "death" in that "dathe"), it also "pulls him into" a body overwhelmingly liquid. If the "ephumeral" experience of sleep embeds him in a "seemetery," then, the grave in which our liquidated hero lies must now be construed as a "watery grave" (78.19), the *Wake* itself becoming a dark "bog of the depths" (516.25 [or "Book of the Dead" plumbing subaquatic "depths"]). And as "the length of the land lies under liquidation" (12.7 [now in a new sense]), Here Comes Everybody begins "disselving" in the night's "deap sleap" (608.5, 277.13 ["deep sea"]) into "**H**eave, **c**oves, **e**mptybloddy!" (324.11), his "body" "empty" of everything but "blood" and approaching the condition of an "empty bladder." Interior to this body of water, our hero lies "as snug as . . . Jonas wrocked in the belly of the whaves" (463.31–32)—"locked in the belly of a whale in waves," but also, because he has undergone both infantile and uterine regression, "Rocked in the Cradle of the Deep": "*Rockabill Booby in the Wave Trough*" (104.6–7).

Since HCE, as a sunken "Gigantic," lives diffusively dispersed in his own dimensionless body of water, other bodies of water recur throughout the *Wake* as ciphers for his own; for, "having become genuinely quite beetly dead whether by land whither by water. . . . He lay under leagues of it in deep Bartholoman's Deep" (99.36–100.4). While reference here to "the Bartholomew Deep"—an oceanic trench off the coast of Chile—would put us in mind of a body of water virtually void of all signs of life, the "man" in "Bartholoman's" would localize the "Deep" being plumbed here inside of a human body.[33] Particularly because our hero's ears alone lie open to eventfulnesses rocking the interior of this body of water, "students of mixed hydrostatics and pneumodipsics will after some difficulties" need to learn to take "soundings" in it (151.29–30, 501.12). "Hydrostatics" being the study of still water and "pneumodipsics," presumably, a yearning for spirits (< Gr. *pneuma* ["breath, spirit"], and *dipsos*, ["thirst"]), these terms suggest that at moments in the night when HCE lies "inundered" in bodies of water (127.5 ["under" "waves"]), he orients himself "in all fathom of space" (394.10) by sustaining an auditory awareness of differing degrees of fluid movement and breath. Ascertaining the character of his "sinking" in these variably deep bodies of water (224.25 [not "thinking"]) is therefore difficult; indeed, fathoming the "SILENCE" of "Challenger's Deep is childsplay to this" (501.6, 11)—"childsplay" reminding us of the night's deepening infantile regressions, and the reference to "the Challenger Deep," the deepest oceanic abyss on earth, suggesting that the thoughts arising "from [the] dupest dupes" of a mind liquidated in sleep (367.34–35), in the *Wake*'s comparative study of "depths," are harder to fathom than "the deepest deeps" in the geophysical world.[34]

We might see these ciphers put to play most clearly toward the end of the *Wake*, at a moment close to our hero's wakening, when he lifts upward toward consciousness, as elsewhere in the book, like a "deadsea dugong updipdripping from his depths" (29.24–25 [a "dugong" being a submarine mammal), so to surface "from the depths" of his "unknown body" of water, and "from a death" that he has endured in a "deadsea" of sorts:

> Bring about it to be brought about and it will be, loke, our lake lemanted, that greyt lack, the citye of Is is issuant (atlanst!), urban and orbal, through seep froms umber under wasseres of Erie.
> Lough!
>
> (601.4–7)

As our "late lamented" hero—the "great lack" whose "Real Absence" is plumbed here—rises "through sleep from slumber" into morning light out of the night's "eerie" dark (hence the L. *umber*, "shadow"), he also rises upward from a closed body of water ("lake," "Lake Leman," "Great Lake," "Erie," "lough"). What "was ere" only "umber under waters" (hence the Ger. *Wassers*, "of water") now undergoes a seepy lifting-up into clarity: "Arise, Land-under-Wave!" (248.8). As he ascends "from his depths," moreover, "awike in wave risurging into chrest" (596.6["awake," "resurgent," resurrecting like a "cresting wave" or "Christ"]), a whole array of darkly drowned civil structures rises with him: the legendarily submerged Brettish city of "Ys" ("citye of Is") and the kingdom of "Atlantis" ("atlanst!") together with the civil structure of his own consciousness, now "at last" ("atlanst!") emerging from its immersion in a closed body of water to regain the capacity of real existence in a civilized present. "Ye of Is" (you who dwell in the present state) should note the emphatic attention given to the verb "is" in the phrase "the citye of *Is is is*suant." As he returns "to the city and the world" (hence the L. *Urbi et Orbi* in "urban and orbal"), "the emplacement of solid and fluid having to a great extent persisted" throughout the dark, "a socially organic entity" emerges from the depths of his own body "in a more or less settled state of equonomic ecolube equalobe equilab equilibbrium" (599.10–18 [note all the L. *aqua*, "water"]).

As a "bog of the depths," the *Wake* is full of such "subrises" as these (370.24 [and "surprises" occasioned by HCE's "rises" from his deeps]); and generally, the *Wake* clarifies our hero's emplacement in all the bodies of water and deeps to which it alludes by ordering them in relations of suggestively ascending vitality. Just as "Challenger's Deep" is dense with unfathomable "SILENCE," in contrast to the audibly everflowing and familiar River Life, so some bodies of water have less or more life in them than others. Moments in our hero's "deap sleap" that are set in oceanic abysses or the "deadsea," then (29.24), indicate roughly that HCE lies lost in "dead seekness" (62.7)—the "sickness" keeping him in a "dead seasickabed" (392.6)—and is void of any clear sign of life at all. Since "that dead wash of Lough Murph" (272.23–24) is sometimes stirred by "Morpheus" and his dreams, by contrast, parts of the *Wake* that show him immersed in "a protem grave . . . of the best Lough Neagh pattern" (76.21–22) would suggest that the "loch-kneeghed forsunkener" (241.24 [Ger. *Versunkener*, "one sunk," or "sunk in thought"]) has risen into a slightly richer form of underwater absence and spectrality—even while kept "under loch and neagh" (196.20 [because arrested by sleep and immersed in his own body of water]). For the Celtic underworld or a flooded city, according to varied legends, lies submerged beneath the waters of "Lough Neagh," which therefore harbor signs of ghostly human life.[35] Since yet other legends attribute to its waters the power to "petrifake" wood (77.1), passages in the *Wake* evoking Lough Neagh also show our otherworldly hero "landloughed by his neaghboormistress and perpetrified in his offsprung" (23.29–30); for in falling asleep, like a rock, and entering a subaquatic "otherworld," an aged HCE—an "offspring" well "offsprung"—also returns to "an inversion of a phallopharos" (76.34 [or dark womb]) and becomes surrounded by "his neighbormistress," ALP. From the underworldly depths of a body of water like Lough Neagh, finally, within which "Donawhu" (76.32 [or "Don't know who"]) seems auditorily aware of "her waters of her sillying waters of" (76.28–29), he rises into the warm and fecundating shallows of a body of water like that represented in the *Wake* by the equatorial Nyanzas, Victoria and Albert, where he begins to "get it frisk from soorce"; and from there he rises into full hearing of the "babbling, bubbling, chattering," and "gossipaceous" River Life (195.1–2, 4), everywhere animate and audible "in the far ear," and everywhere "sangnifying" his quickening.

Where this ascending progression of "subrises" leads will grow clear if we return to the opening pages of *Finnegans Wake*, and to the precise place at which our "reading [of the] Evening World" began—on the phrase "in bed" (3.17), in whose vicinity we learn that "*Hic cubat edilis. Apud libertinam parvulam*" (7.22–23 [L., "Here sleeps the public man. Near the small freedwoman"). The Latin verb "*cubat*" in this construction ("sleeps") puts a new inflection on the phrase "in bed" (L. *cubile*) and in turn throws a new perspective everywhere across Joyce's "bog of the depths." For one of many possible Latin synonyms for the English "in bed" would be the phrase "*in cubato*" (which, from the verb *cubo, cubare*, would literally mean "in having gone to bed"). Because our hero's night-long drift through the dark in his own closed body of water takes place *in cubato*, his sleep necessarily becomes, everywhere in the *Wake*, an extended form of "incubation" (112.21, 397.34 [where the orthodox Eng. "incubation," historically deriving from the L. *incubare*, "to lie down upon," generates the meaning "to hatch" simply because birds "lie down upon" their eggs]).

Playing host to a night-long *incubus* (L. "nightmare," 13.11, 221.23), the "headandheelless chickenestegg" who is our hero (81.22–23) now "disselv[es]," within his own closed body of water, into a fluid and life-generating state that the *Wake* calls both "incubation" and "ovasleep" (397.16 [L. *ova*, "egg"]); and somewhere in its "exprogressive process, (. . . known as eggburst, eggblend, eggburial and hatch-as-hatch can)" (614.31–33), he sustains dark "remembrandts" of his quickening and birth (see 614.27–615.10 entirely). That "Eggeberth" moves through the night while "incubating"—"ovidently" "asleep in [a] shell" (166.11, 469.17)—will explain, in part, the many extremely "doubtful eggshells" (183.11–12) and the heavy "soufflosion of oogs," "uoves, oves and uves" that appear everywhere in *Finnegans Wake* (184.30, 29 [It. *uovo*, L. *ova*, Gael. *ubh*: "egg"]). Eggs show up on virtually every page of the book in part because they are objects towards which our hero's desire (for breakfast and wakening) points; but also because sleep sends "the same **h**omo**h**eatherous **c**heckinlossegg as when sollyeye airly blew ye" (129.14–15) into "eggshill" from the Daily World (415.9–10 ["exile"]), by turning him into the incubating form shown scrambled in Relief Map B: "the same" person (Gr. *homos*) as when he last "saw" the "sun" (hence the L. *sol* and the seeing "eye" in that "solly eye") and when he last moved about in the free of the air ("airly blew"), this incubating humanoid is now so radically alien an "other" (Gr. *heteros*) as to resemble the dismembered hero of "Johnny I Hardly Knew Ye," a barely recognizable "eyeless, noseless, chickenless egg." If we reexamine the relief map of "the wellknown kikkinmidden where the illassorted first couple first met with each other," however (503.8–9), it will become "ovident" that this "deafadumped" ground is precisely the place where our hero's parents (inevitably an odd and "illassorted couple") once met: "he was poached on in that eggtentical spot" (16.36), which therefore extends not simply through space, but, from wakening to wake (17.22–23), through all time as well. If, once more, we "rearrive" at that paragraph on the first page of the *Wake*, we might now see that the "unquiring" humanoid "empty dempt[ied]" (319.36)

"Anna Livia Plurabelle"

somewhere in the liquidated space between "humptyhillhead" and "tumptytumtoes" is simply "incubating," and so merits yet another form of comparison with a "homelette" like Humpty Dumpty (59.31).

Because he "incubates" himself in sleep, "Haroun Childeric Eggeberth" spends the night "reberthing in remarriment out of dead seekness" (62.7); though dead to the world (hence the "Dead Sea"), he gives "rebirth" to himself in a body of water associated with "amother" (hence the "berth," "birth," and "remarriment"). In turn, however improbably, he *Hatches Cocks' Eggs* (71.27), the *Wake* in turn assuming the title *Egg Laid by Former Cock* (440.20 ["former" because he's dead to the world]). In general, however, eggs are associated with and brooded over by hens, and so too Haroun Childeric Eggeberth's; he becomes, in the night, "one fledge, one brood" (378.4) not simply because sleep "disselv[es]" him into "one flesh, one blood" "anastomosically assimilated" with "his streamline secret," but also because he becomes an "incubating" "fledgling" of sorts, a "chickchild" "asleep in [a] shell" (244.9–10, 469.17), brooded over by a figure to whom the *Wake* now gives such "mudhen . . . name[s]" as "Breedabrooda" (393.23, 78.17 [note the "brooding" "hen"]). Vaguely evoking "original sin," this "original hen" (110.22) undergoes a kind of unending "volucrine automutativeness" throughout the *Wake* (112.12 ["bird-like self-changeableness"]), becoming, for instance, our hero's "poachmistress" (412.23 [as opposed to a literate "postmistress"]) and a "fiery goosemother" or "nocturnal goosemother" (242.25, 449.36–450.1) who is magically capable of "lay[ing a] new golden sheegg" overnight (450.1 [that "golden sheegg," in part, the sun and its news of breakfast; cf. 382.11, 594.32–33]). The evocations heard among all these terms of "fairy godmothers," "the goose that laid the golden egg," and "Mother Goose," of course, should waken from the dead some memories of "childhide," while the correlated maternal associations will suggest how the *Wake*'s recurrent references to "the Hen" also ultimately evoke those times in which Haroun Childeric Eggeberth, "erigenating from next to nothing" in a dark body of water, was "formelly confounded with amother"—and all the more particularly because the Greek *to hen* signifies, in philosophy, "the One" out of which the phenomenal world splinters, "ab ove" (154.35 [L. *ab ova*, "from the egg," idiomatic for "the beginning"]). For as the arterial sound of "Anna Livia," now "the Sassqueehenna" (594.30 [the Susquehanna River and a "sassy queen hen"]), spills into his ears, "singing him henpecked" rhythms and "cackling" and "cheeping . . . with a choicey voicey like waterglucks" (492.9; 200.27, 8–9), it reminds "**Cheepalizzy's Hane Exposition**" (111.6–7 [not only "Chapelizod's," but a mother hen's, too]) of a time in life in which he was also undergoing an "ovasleep" of sorts, within the body of "amother" who "ha[d] plenty of woom in the smallclothes" (465.8–9). As then, so in the sleep of "everynight life": as "woman with her ridiculous white burden . . . reach[es] by one step sublime incubation," "ague [and age] . . . [are] rejuvenated" (112.20–21). You "hatch yourself well! Enjomb yourselves thurily!" (465.9–10 ["enjoy," "enwomb"]); and only at the moment of wakening, when "there'll be iggs for the brekkers come to mournhim, sunny side up with care" (12.14–15), do you too "Come! Step out of your shell!" (621.3–4).

Owing to the incubatory properties of sleep, moreover, the "nitrience of oxagiants" alters greatly (67.7 [together with "the nutrients" of sleeping giants])—and in ways suggested by the appearance of the "nitrogen and oxygen" in these "aliments" (286.L4, 163.2). Roughly, these define the metabolism of a "vegetable" (here, a human one), and in turn they suggest that nourishment in the vegetative state of sleep (406.31), apparently effortless and free of dependence on the external, bears comparison with mother-child "milkfeeding" and foetal nurture (337.5).[36] Particularly because HCE's sleep might be construed as "a lenty" form of "fasting" (130.8, 189.29–30, 211.16, 611.9), during which he lies there "on the verge of selfabyss, most starved" and "fastbroke down" until "Brèak—fast" breaks his fast (40.23, 541.25, 124.9–10), these terms make necessary the adoption of an "emended food theory" adequate to the "changed endocrine history" of the night (136.28, 163.35–36). Our hero, "highly pelaged and deeply gluttened" (358.10 ["pleased and gladdened"]), becomes something of a "somatophage merman" when he sinks into "ovasleep" (171.3)—a "merman" because he lies submerged in his own body of water, as if in a "sea" (Gr. *pelagos*) of "gluten," and "somatophage" because he subsists on that body. Indeed, he spends the whole night "changing cane sugar into sethulose starch" and "feeding on his own misplaced fat" (29.28, 79.13), so to give himself much "food for refection" (455.9 [and us "food for reflection"]): during sleep, you "wait on yourself," and *You're Welcome to Waterfood* (405.25, 71.22 [not "Waterford," but all the "water food" you can eat]). "See what happens when your somatophage merman takes his fancy to our virgitarian swan?" (171.2–4 [the "virgin swan" another version of the "hen"]): "he, selfsufficiencer, eggscumuddher-in-chaff" (240.14–15), loses the status he enjoys in consciousness as a "breadwinning" patriarchal "commander-in-chief" (55.7–8) and regresses into conditions like those experienced when he was an "egg-cum-mother." "Since both [HCE and ALP] was parties to the feed," however, "it's Hetman MacCumhal foots the funeral" at the *Wake* (243.13–14), by provid-

"Anna Livia Plurabelle"

ing the bountiful "cropse" (55.8 [or "corpse"]) off which he and all the phantoms in the dream in fact live (cf. 7.8–19), while "mealwhile [not meanwhile] she nutre him jacent" (243.13–15 ["jacent" means "recumbent"]).

The best place in the *Wake* in which to see this "emended food theory" dramatized would be in the book's first fully sustained "picture primitive" of Shaun the Post (405.3), who appears in the "allmurk" (404.10) dressed entirely in foodstuffs (e.g., at 404.23–407.6), obviously "having a great time of it, a twentyfour hours every moment matters maltsight" (405.22–23 [Ger. *Malzeit*, "meal," the "malt" blacking "sight" out]). Shaun is "invested" in food here largely because our hero's appetite has risen in the latter half of the night, so to waken his ego ("Show'm the Posed") and its acquisitive energies, and in turn to generate conflict with that part of himself (Shem) that stays "down under" in the body and is all "somatophage merman" (see 170.25–171.28). As his body starts creating itself out of itself by drawing on "the food that is to build" (246.12), the passage begins evoking a time when "little eggons, youlk and meelk" (613.11 ["little egos" like "you and me," subsisting on maternal "egg, yolk, and milk"]), enjoyed a "breakfast of first, a bless us O blood" (405.32–33)—and "all free of charge, aman" (406.21–22). "In the mealtub" (312.24–25 ["meantime"]), "plain as portable enveloped . . . care of one of Mooseyeare Goonness's . . . barrels" (414.10–13), Shaun begins traveling through "foetal sleep" not only in HCE's "body" (< O.E. *bodig*, "cask"), but also within a "Mother Goose" (or Hen) whose appearance shows him undergoing the infantile and incubatory regressions of the dark. Now exercising a "prelove appetite" "at the sign of Mesthress Vanhungrig" (406.35, 30 [Ger. *hungrig*, "hungry"]), he becomes "one . . . that . . . would aight through the months" (405.17–18 ["eat," as once through "eight months"]), an infant returned to the womb. "Ever of thee, Anne Lynch, he's deeply draiming!" (406.27 ["draining," while "dreaming"]), and "for auld lang Ayternitay" (406.28)—where the evocation of "auld lang syne" summons up a "blank memory" of times that "be forgot" and are "never brought to mind" (390.23, 21), largely because they were times when "his heart was as big as himself, so it was, ay, and bigger" (406.22–23 [times when he was "confounded with amother"]). "Thus thicker will he grow now, grew new" (406.28–29), until, "growing to stay" over the course of Book III (404.15)—"(gracious helpings, at this rate of growing our cotted child of yestereve will soon fill space and burst in systems, so speeds the instant!)" (429.11–13)—he reenacts the process of birth and grows into the spit and image of the old man who was "reduced to nothing" at the beginning of the night, the son who is his father's dream turning into his own father: "'tis Father Quinn again" (562.27–28 ["Finnegan" "quickened"]); "I met somewhere somelam to whom he will be becoming liker" (562.34–35).

Much more might be said about the *Wake*'s reconstructions of "ovasleep" and "about that coerogenal hun and his knowing the size of an eggcup" (616.20–21)—not least by way of noting how the evidently aggressive "hun" who is the incubating subject of this construction becomes everywhere linked with a feminine "hen" and "her" (Da. *hun*) with whom, bonded in "original sin" ("coerogenal hun"), he is latently "co-erogenous." Throughout the *Wake*, we find "the hen and crusader everintermutuomergent" everywhere (55.11–12), in a "scene [that is] refreshed, reroused, . . . never to be forgotten" (55.10–11). This is a scene that deepens, however, when the *Wake* answers the question of "Where" the night takes place by "indicating the locality" of deep sleep (599.25, 32) and directing our attention into a realm of pure "liquid" (Sans. *sara*) and fluid "sap" (Ger. *Saft*) governed by "Anna Livia" ("Innalavia"):

> Polycarp pool, the pool of Innalavia, Saras the saft as, of meadewy marge, atween Deltas Piscium and Sagittariastrion, whereinn once we lave 'tis alve and vale, minnyhahing here from hiarwather, a poddlebridges in a passabed, the river of lives, the regenerations of the incarnations of the emanations of the apparentations of Funn and Nin in Cleethabala . . . let it be! (600.5–12)

Set amid "laughing waters" ("minnyhahaing") at "the soorce" (Victoria and Albert Nyanza appear at 600.12–13), the passage orients our hero much where "Anna Livia Plurabelle" does, in the "riverbed" (It. *alveo*) of a river (Dublin's "Poddle") indistinct from "Innalavia's" "delta," "her water" ("hiarwathar"), and the uterine tract ("piddle," "pissabed"): it amounts to another reconstruction of nocturnal "woom," within which now are made "apparent" the ghostly "apparitions" of "parents" and ancestors ("apparentations") and of the washing forth and away of attached lives (hence the Fr. *laver*, and the L. *Ave* and *Vale*, "hail" and "farewell"). Lifting also upward through the birth-signs "Pisces" and "Saggitarius" into the "stars" (Gr. *astrion*, "star"), the passage leads also "*towards a relevution of the karmalife order*" (338.6), by evoking "revolutions" of "karma" and "lives" ("incarnations"), and "revelations of the Carmelite order" (the Incarnation). The convergence of all these ciphers suggests that the *Wake*, because it is about the night, is also necessarily a cosmogony, whose subject is the fluid torrent of creative power out of which the world originates every morning and always. For in the *Wake*, creation is not a historical event that happens only once, with a remote big bang in the Garden of Eden, but a "hystorical" event (564.31 [Gr. *hysteros*, "womb"]), happening constantly in the "garden of Erin" and other modern nations as people keep on waking up and children keep on spilling into the world. As in Genesis, then, where all the glittering appearances of the earth come forth out of a dark, formless, and inchoate body of water seeded with paternal form, as if from the interior of an egg ("let it be!"), so too in the *Wake's* account of HCE's genesis, where a world originates somewhere in the dark and liquid space of a body of water that itself originated in a body of water strewn with amniotic "alum and oves" (393.24 ["Adam and Eve"]).[37] In trying to fathom a hero who reverts in the night to "ovasleep," the *Wake* is also plumbing the form of unconscious "sinking" (not "thinking") that informs the interior of embodied water, as the body weaves itself up out of the dark, "from next to nothing," "some-whave" at "the heart of secret waters" (501.21, 599.26).

"THE CONSTANT OF FLUXION"

While these meditations lead us to see how deeply ALP, "mother of us all" (299.3), informs the body "tropped head" at the *Wake*, a return to their concrete point of origin in "the presence (of a curpse)," and to the sound of arteries of running water washing through "the far ear" will put them all into perspective. That riverlike sound generates one last and most profound association in our hero's "tropped head"—an association with the invisible force of fluidity itself, "everflowing on the times" (117.3–4). This is why Joyce could not possibly have been more explicit about the "meanam†" of "Anna Livia" without destroying his text and its treatment of "matters that fall under the ban of our infrarational senses." "Anna Livia" is not, finally, about blood as a wakeful rationalist might know it, the object of scientific observation and a by-product of pain that becomes visible only when it leaves the body, stops, and stops sounding forever. Putting into English the "wyerye† rima†" that flows through "Anna Livia" and throughout the *Wake* would have put it into reason and vision, where precisely it is not.

We must, then, "bewise of Fanciulla's heart, the heart of Fanciulla! Even the recollection of willow fronds is a spellbinder that lets to hear" (278.7–9 [It. *fanciulla*, "girl"]). The admonition advises us, in a passage about the reading of letters, to "beware" and "be wise," and in part by noting that where "spelling" "binds," the "spilling" out of "the heart" of ALP's arterial "flow-andflow" simply "spellbinds"; having all the substantiality of the memory of the rustle of willows, it speaks of a figure called "*Pantharhea*" (513.22

[Heraclitus' *panta rhei*, "all things flow"]), who appears in all those gaps and silent interstices of the world where language and the structures it makes possible are not—at night, in sleep, between words. "INCIPIT INTER-MISSIO" (278.R1 [L. "intermission begins" here]).

Since these silent gaps fall outside of letters, and outside of the institutions that those letters empower, what becomes expressed in the "cunniform letters" of which "Anna Livia" is composed is a form of creative power, feminine rather than masculine because it escapes traditional phallologocentric mastery and control. This productive force works much differently from the creative powers of patriarchy, whose deity, as exemplified in Genesis, brings the world to light by creating things in his own image, domesticating the unknown with the known, and discriminating and establishing difference—between light and dark, night and day, heaven and earth, sheep and goats, men and women, right and wrong.[38] "Anna Livia's" "affluvial flowandflow" spills into the world a "safety vulve" (297.26–27), a "constant of fluxion, Mahamewetma" (297.29–30)—where the reference to the Vedic "mahamavantara," or world-cycle, calls to mind cosmogonic revolution, and the evocations of the "vulva" and the "mama wet Ma" call to mind maternity and birth.

Like a dream, *Finnegans Wake* has its day's residue, too; and a substantial part of that residue is language itself, whose operative structures linger on in the Evening World, generating the illusion not only that words will keep the legislated and referentially secure relations to things that they maintain in the Daily World, but also that the "patrilinear" form of the book will yield a linear sense (279.4). As in a dream, however, this manifest appearance is misleading, since the sense of the dream is latent, buried, and rather than static, charged with a "constant of fluxion" that makes the release of meaning possible only if one travels along streams of unlimited association. Being wakeful readers, we cannot help but be mindful of the linearity, literacy, and lexicality of the *Wake*, precisely because these things mirror and make possible "the use of raisin" (130.16 ["reason"], 154.31, 183.13). But "raisin," as its spelling suggests, is all dried out here, and will not alone prove adequate when sent into the depths of the dream, whose form is not "patrilinear," but associative, fluvial, and capable of sweeping memory's bric-a-brac along with all the hydrodynamic "thisorder" and "fluxion" embodied in a river. And "that's the point of eschatology our book of kills reaches for now in soandso many counterpoint words. What can't be coded can be decorded if an ear aye sieze what no eye ere grieved for" (482.33–36). Calling attention to the conflicts and confusions that fill the literate and legislated space between "eye" and "ear" ("ear aye sieze," "eye ere"), the line suggests that terms in the *Wake* which cannot be literalistically "coded" will instead release meaning if an "ear" attuned to the sound of "the constant of fluxion" audible in the rivers pouring out of the heart (hence the L. *cors, cordis*, in "decorded") "seizes" on that sound and heeds its "meanam†."

The *Wake* therefore becomes something of a "New Free Woman with novel inside" (145.29). For there *is* a "novel inside" of the *Wake*, though hardly one of the sort that the criticism has traditionally sought, with real-world "exploits" involving a hunchback Nordic guilty of urinary excess. It is, rather, a "nightynovel" (54.21), which follows "the explots" of a "man made static" in bed for "eaght hours" (124.29, 309.22, 617.27), its linear plot being one of steadily deepening "embedment" that reverses itself at the book's midpoint, in the gap between I.viii and II.i, where a rejuvenating body begins to relive its own childhood and gravitate heliotropically toward the moment of its resurrection and wakening: "*No Sturm. No Drang*" (300.L2); "*Pas d'action, peu de sauce*" (274.L2). If the *Wake* preserves an eccentric and remote attachment to the novel and comparable forms of "patrilinear plop" (279.4), however, it also dismantles those forms, simply by taking as its subject the real experience of sleep, within which the real crumbles altogether—together with the paternal old man who "disselv[es]," by night, into a mother and child.

Just as ALP surrounds a hero who is "formelly confounded with amother" everywhere in the night, so too a "New Free Woman" "envelopes" everything inside of the novel which represents HCE's "nightlife," in turn becoming "the mother of the book" (50.11–12). And just as a "meanam†" "spilled" with "cunniform letters" plays through HCE's ears everywhere in the *Wake*, so the sound of its "constant of fluxion" envelopes all the letters buried inside him (I.v): "We note the paper with her jotty young watermark: *Notre Dame du Bon Marché*. And she has a heart of Arin! What lumililts as she fols" (112.31–33). The familiar "river" flowing out of the "heart" here (Alb. *lumi*, "river") "speaks," in other words (Alb. *fol*, "speak"), to an ordinary old man whom night has rendered dead to the world and "disselv[ed]" into a "Jolly Young Waterman." ALP now becomes "Misthress of Arths" at his *Wake* (112.29) in part because she wakens this once-and-future hero ("Arthur"), but also because she assumes the role of "mistress of arts" in a work that modulates now into a "Brook of Life" (264.6 [or fluid "book of life"]). Container and discoverer of its buried letter, "she . . . who tears up lettereens she never apposed a pen upon" (276.6–7 [or ever really opposed]) rises into this role largely by overwhelming the orthodox letters and literal senses established by patriarchy with her "cunniform letters" and "ebro†," which do not stay still, but grow and behave with all the unpredictability of children "(the mother of the book with a dustwhisk tabularasing his obliteration done upon her involucrum)" (50.11–13 [L. *involucrum*, "envelope"]). Much like the scavenging Hen of I.v, then, who gathers up the rubble of a trashed day's residue and puts it into "the sack of auld hensyne" (112.8 [and into forms of thought that "be forgot"]), this "Misthress of Arths" reforms the world when she "pits hen to paper" and, "in cunniform letters," produces "scribings scrawled on eggs" (615.10). She does so, in part, by reanimating in our hero, as once in her "cunniform" "whome," the unpotentiated mind of the child. For "lastly but mostly, in her genesic field it is all game and no gammon" (112.16–17)—where, because "gammon" means both "talk" and "ridiculous nonsense," the line suggests that orthodox "patrilinear" "talk" and "nonsense" will be supplanted by a playful flexibility or "gaming" that earns its "genesic" power by making no pretense to authority (*OED*, "gammon," sb. 4, v. 4).

As HCE's "Misthress of Arths," this "New Free Woman" in turn issues an "untitled mamafesta" (104.4) *"plainly Showing all the Unmentionability"* (107.6–7), whose "meanam†" resonates through the *Wake* as a whole. One of the few "Our Mothers" in literature—another "(suppressed) book"—it argues the power not of phallologocentric structures but of utero-illogico-eccentric ones (like children and dreams), and it is all the prettier for it:

> In the name of Annah the Allmaziful, the Everliving, the Bringer of Plurabilities, haloed be her eve, her singtime sung, her rill be run, unhemmed as it is uneven!
> Her untitled mamafesta memorialising the Mosthighest has gone by many names at disjointed times. Thus we hear of, *The Augusta Angustissimost for Old Seabeastius' Salvation, Rockabill Booby in the Wave Trough* . . . *Anna Stessa's Rise to Notice* . . .
> (104.1–8)

The opposite of an assertively aggressive "manifesto," this one is feminine in form (as the suffixal "-a" suggests); it replaces the overbearing "man" in "manifesto" with a "mama" who is the antithesis of all those patriarchal deities of whom "we read" in the Koran ("In the name of Allah, the All-merciful, the compassionate") and the Bible ("thy kingdom come, thy will be done, on earth as it is in heaven")—not least because, in childhood, "we hear of" "her singtime sung" (rather than "read" about his). The essential sense of this "mamafesta"—*"You'd be Nought Without Mom"* (106.3)—therefore takes a dual form, on the one hand bespeaking the creative power of "somewome" who is "amother" than our hero (*"It Was Me Egged Him on* to the Stork Exchange" [106.17–18]) and on the other reconstructing "the mind of the unborn child" "formelly confounded with amother": a subaquatic "Seabeastius," as opposed to an imperial "Sebastius" ("*Rockabill Booby in the Wave Trough*" [104.6–7]). Speaking of a redemptive "Mosthighest" (Messiah) who "has gone by many names at disjointed times," it is ultimately declaring, in times out of joint, the power of "the fruit of the womb" and of "the child we all love to place our hope in for ever" (621.31–32), through whom, in the infantile regression of the dream and in fact, the world is constantly being "rearrived" at and reformed. And while patriarchy can constrain it—indeed, must constrain it—its power will not be hemmed; for not even the sternest authority can predict what a child will become—or what a word in the *Wake* will lead to. "Unhemmed," each has no clear limit; "uneven" (and therefore "odd"), each deviates from all determinate plan.

Perhaps "you missed my drift" (424.31 [and also that of the *Wake*]). Never definitively "arrived at," meaning in *Finnegans Wake* "drifts" and is constantly "rearrived" at (3.5); and consequently it hovers in a state of continual arrival and is constantly becoming: "In the becoming was the weared, wontnat!" (487.20–21 [O.E. *wyrd*, "time, change, becoming"]). The "cunniform letters" that "Anna Livia" adds to the book therefore send its reader "arride the winnerful wonders off, the winnerful wonnerful wanders off" (265.15–16 [Eng. "arride," "to gratify"]); for as one "stotters from the latter," pursues "distant connections," and "wanders off," "wonders" and "delight" (Ger. *Wonne*) open up, their discovery attesting to a capacity not to trap and domesticate the unknown with what is already known, but to move with flexibility into a future potentially rich in "plurabilities."

The "hearing of" "the constant of fluxion" that envelopes the letters of Joyce's "Brook of Life," then, requiring only that we engage them with some resourcefulness and play, makes its reading as unpredictable as children can be, flooding the future with the prospect of unforeseen "plurabilities" that signal growth, vitality, and change. As soon as any aspect of the book begins to make sense—the idea of "raisin," for example—networking depths of new associations and bottomless complications, all welling up out of the dark experience of the night, web out everywhere in all directions; and, in turn, all the "changeably meaning vocable scriptsigns" in this nocturnal "chaosmos" alter (118.27–28, 21 ["chaos," "cosmos"]), taking on new meanings as they come to life where they ought to and only can, in "the presence (of a curpse)," as pathos and misericordia (*pleures*) and laughter and delight (*belle*) wake.[39] This is why a good reading of the *Wake*, a circular book without an end, can have no real ending.

"How it ends?" (614.19). Particularly because the sense of this book of the dark lies entangled in a network of free associations, it never ends. "It's like a dream," whose fruitful analysis, as Joyce himself well knew, has no point of termination: "A book like that," he said of the *Wake*, "has no ending. It could go on forever."[40] And like a dream, whose "meanam†" stays suspended in a "constant of fluxion" and is always being "rearrived" at, "it will remember itself from every sides, with all our gestures, in each our word" (614.20–21). "So you need hardly spell me how every word will be bound to carry over three score and ten toptypsical readings throughout the book of Doublends Jined" (20.13–16): there's one at least for every year in the proverbial three score and ten that make up a life. And on that score, particularly if we recall Daniel's very strong words to "Nebuchadnezzar" on the subject of dream analysis—"this is the dream, and we will tell the interpretation thereof" (Daniel 2)—"Nobookisonester" (177.14). There's "lovesoftfun at" *Finnegans Wake* (607.16), a book that one might easily read for a lifetime. More people should join in its fun.

"Anna Livia Plurabelle"

Notes
Index

Notes

AN INTRODUCTION: ON OBSCURITY

1. Adaline Glasheen, *A Second Census of "Finnegans Wake": An Index of the Characters and Their Roles* (Evanston: Northwestern Univ. Press, 1963), p. xvii.

2. Jacques Mercanton, "The Hours of James Joyce," trans. Lloyd C. Parks, in *Portraits of the Artist in Exile: Recollections of James Joyce by Europeans*, ed. Willard Potts (Seattle: Univ. of Washington Press, 1979), p. 214.

3. Mary and Padraic Colum, *Our Friend James Joyce* (Garden City, N.Y.: Doubleday, 1958), p. 158.

4. Louise Bogan, "Finnegans Wake," *Nation*, 6 May 1939; rpt. in *James Joyce: The Critical Heritage*, ed. Robert H. Deming (London: Routledge and Kegan Paul, 1970), II, p. 666.

5. Mercanton, "The Hours of James Joyce," p. 233.

6. Frank Budgen, *James Joyce and the Making of 'Ulysses'* (1934; rpt. Bloomington: Univ. of Indiana Press, 1960), p. 284.

7. F. R. Leavis, "Joyce and 'Revolution of the Word,'" in *For Continuity* (1933; rpt. Freeport, N.Y.: Books for Libraries Press, 1968), p. 208.

8. See also Ole Vinding, "James Joyce in Copenhagen," trans. Helge Irgens-Moller, in *Portraits of the Artist in Exile*, p. 149.

9. Mercanton, "The Hours of James Joyce," p. 209.

10. "To remark that one is not a constant dreamer is not to assert that dreaming is rare, but merely that one's recollection is rare. . . . It cannot of course be said that the failure to remember dreams is any argument against their occurrence" (Havelock Ellis, *The World of Dreams* [Boston: Houghton Mifflin, 1911], pp. 13–14). Ellis also isolates the issue essentially at stake in all debates about the continuity of dreaming through the night: "Many psychologists, as well as metaphysicians—fearful to admit that the activity of the soul should ever cease—believe that we dream during the whole of sleep. . . . On the

other hand, [some have] held that deep sleep is dreamless" (p. 13). Contemporary polemics about whether "dreaming" continues throughout the night or only during periods of REM sleep reflect the same essential concern, although the controversy now bears on the perdurability of "consciousness," rather than the soul.

11. Sigmund Freud, *Introductory Lectures on Psychoanalysis*, tr. and ed. James Strachey (New York: Norton, 1966), p. 89.

12. Vinding, "James Joyce in Copenhagen," p. 149.

13. Mercanton, "The Hours of James Joyce," p. 208: "Then [Joyce] came back to 'Work in Progress,' to the problems of dreams, which occupy a third of our lives and about which we know almost nothing." Compare Freud's late complaint, of 1933, that "analysts behave as though they had no more to say about dreams, as though there was nothing more to be added to the theory of dreams," in "Revision of the Theory of Dreams," *New Introductory Lectures on Psychoanalysis*, trans. and ed. James Strachey (New York: Norton, 1965), p. 8.

14. Vinding, "James Joyce in Copenhagen," p. 149.

15. Mercanton, "The Hours of James Joyce," p. 207.

16. "It is rarely possible to be aware of dreaming while it continues, and the only evidence of it would be uncertain memory to the effect after wakening. . . . Thus skeptics could argue that the reality of dreaming during sleep is an inference based on circumstantial evidence, and therefore that the phenomenal event of dreaming is . . . hypothetical. Malcolm (in *Dreaming*) goes so far as to insist that the only meaning the word *dream* has is in reference to the strange tales we report to one another. The usefulness of that word (or *dreaming*) in relation to something we assume is happening during sleep is apparent . . . although it has no direct empirical referent" (Frederick Snyder, "The Physiology of Dreaming," in *Dream Psychology and the New Biology of Dreaming* [Springfield, Ill.: Charles C. Thomas, 1969], pp. 17–19). Snyder's reference is to Norman Malcolm's *Dreaming* (New York: Humanities Press, 1959), a work grounded in British analytical philosophy, for discussions of which see *Philosophical Essays on Dreaming*, ed. Charles E. M. Dunlop (Ithaca: Cornell Univ. Press, 1977).

17. "A Metapsychological Supplement to the Theory of Dreams," in *The Standard Edition of the Complete Psychological Works of Sigmund Freud*, tr. and ed. James Strachey, vol. 14 (London: The Hogarth Press, 1957), p. 223.

18. Mercanton, "The Hours of James Joyce," p. 207.

19. Any book on sleep and dreams published after 1960 will have a discussion of REM sleep and an account of its discovery. For a highly readable treatment of the subject, see Gay Gaer Luce and Julius Segal, *Sleep* (New York: Coward-McCann, 1966), pp. 187–229. For a good anthology containing summaries of and excerpts from the major technical articles, see Ralph L. Woods and Herbert B. Greenhouse, *The New World of Dreams* (New York: Macmillan, 1974); this is a companion volume to Woods' *World of Dreams* (New York: Random House, 1947), an anthology surveying world literature on dreams from the Upanishads and Aristotle through Bergson and Freud. Both make for good introductory browsing.

Two other anthologies, more technical in nature but useful for their discussions of the relations of the new materials to Freudian, Jungian, and phenomenological theories of dreams are Milton Kramer, ed., *Dream Psychology and the New Biology of Dreaming* (Springfield, Ill.: Thomas, 1969), and Ernest Hartmann, ed., *Sleep and Dreaming* (Boston: Little, Brown and Co., 1970). Whether the new findings reinforce or jeopardize psychoanalytical understandings seems to depend on whether the person exploring them wishes to reinforce or jeopardize psychoanalytical understandings.

20. Luce and Segal, *Sleep*, p. 191.

21. If cycles of REM sleep are to be regarded as signs of "dreaming," their occurrence in the foetus, newly born infants, and all mammals raise yet other obscure questions. What purpose is served by a "dream" that has, presumably, no content? And how do such "dreams" spin up out of the phylogenetic past? Since reptiles, amphibians, and lower forms of animal life seem not to "sleep" at all, according to these criteria, but only to undergo periods of relative rest and quiescence, sleeping and dreaming, like intelligence itself, seem to be evolutionary variables that reach their most flowery and obscure forms in the human, who alone may sleep soundly throughout the length of a night. See Truett Allison and Henry van Twyver, "The Evolution of Sleep," *Natural History* 79, no. 2 (1970): 56–65, anthologized under the title, "The Sleep and Dreams of Animals," in Woods and Greenhouse, pp. 342–55. On REM sleep *in utero*, see Charles Furst, *Origins of the Mind: Mind-Brain Connections* (Englewood Cliffs, N.J.: Prentice-Hall, 1979), p. 100.

22. William Dement and Nathaniel Kleitman, "The Relation of Eye Movements During Sleep to Dream Activity," *Journal of Experimental Psychology* 53 (1957): 339–44; William Dement and Edward A. Wolpert, "The Relation of Eye Movements, Body Motility, and External Stimuli to Dream Content," *Journal of Experimental Psychology* 55 (1958): 543–53. See also Dement, Kleitman, and Wolpert, "Your Eyes Watch the Dream Action," in Woods and Greenhouse, *New World*, pp. 293–96, and Luce and Segal, *Sleep*, pp. 200–202. "However, more recent research indicates that it is difficult to match eye movements with the reported dream content (except in unusual cases, as in a dream of watching a Ping-Pong match), and people can apparently experience vivid visual dreams accompanied by only a few eye movements" (Furst, *Origins*, p. 96).

23. Nathaniel Kleitman, "The Nature of Dreaming," in *CIBA Foundation Symposium on the Nature of Sleep*, ed. G. E. W. Wolstenholme and Maeve O'Connor (Boston: Little, Brown, 1961), pp. 352–53. See also Russell Gardner et al., "The Relationship of Small Limb Movements during REM Sleep to Dreamed Limb Action," *Psychosomatic Medicine* 37 (1975): 147–59. "However, the relationship between limb movements during REM and the content of the dream is not perfect: many times a dreamer will report having a very active dream when no muscle twitches are visible" (Furst, *Origins*, p. 97).

24. Dement and Wolpert, "The Relation of Eye Movements, Body Motility, and External Stimuli to Dream Content," pp. 543–53.

25. Charles Fisher, Joseph Gross, and Joseph Zuch, "Cycle of Penile Erection Synchronous with Dreaming (REM) Sleep," *Archives of General Psychiatry* 12 (1965): 29–45; Herbert Greenhouse, "Penile Erections during Dreams," in Woods and Greenhouse, *New World*, pp. 296–97; Luce and Segal, *Sleep*, pp. 198–99. See also I. Karacan, A. L. Rosenbloom, and R. L. Williams, "The Clitoral Erection Cycle during Sleep," *Psychophysiology* 7 (1970): 338, and, in the same place, Harvey D. Cohen and Arthur Shapiro, "Vaginal Blood Flow during Sleep": "observed [increases in vaginal blood flow] in the sleeping female appear analogous to the pattern of penile erections observed in the sleeping male."

26. David Foulkes, "Theories of Dream Formation and Recent Studies of Sleep Consciousness," *Psychological Bulletin* 62 (1964): 236–47; Foulkes, "You Think All Night Long," and Robert L. Van De Castle, "Thinking during Non-Dreaming Sleep," in Woods and Greenhouse, *New World*, pp. 298–302 and 303–13.

27. Why most people dream in color, yet others evidently only in black and white, is not at all clear; nor is it clear why a small percentage of people have "auditory dreams," consisting only of voices and sounds unaccompanied by any visual imagery. Then too, there is sleepwalking, where more than the eyes move, and where the distinctions between sleep and wakefulness grow disturbingly obscure:

"A sixteen-year-old girl, dreaming of burglars as she later said, took the family revolver in her sleep and killed her father and brother, injuring her mother. In 1946, an Arkansas farmer awakened from a nightmare into greater horror, when he found that he had warded off an imaginary attacker with a heavy flashlight—and killed his only daughter, a four-year-old. A Berkeley housewife arose one morning at 2 A.M., threw a coat over her pajamas, and gathered the family dachsunds into the car for a long drive to Oakland, awakening at the wheel 23 miles away. . . . Perhaps one of the most amusing stories is that of an English lady who awakened one night. There was a thud on the bed, and she was so frightened she fainted. When she awakened in daylight, she found that her sleep-walking butler had set the table for fourteen on her bed. . . . One young Frenchman, who often arose in the morning with bruises and bad wounds, yet claimed that he had slept soundly and restfully. His wife knew otherwise. He spent a part of his nights in a pitched battle with the furniture—breaking things, bumping things, and even throwing chairs as he shouted. He seemed to be re-enacting a shipboard trauma suffered as a very young man. . . . A typical and not so funny case was reported . . . in 1965, when a twenty-three-year-old Australian woman was found at night in a Sidney street by the police—with broken legs. As she explained, she had had a vivid dream about eloping with her fiance. He had placed a ladder against the window of her third-story bedroom and she stepped out onto a ladder that, sadly enough, existed only in her imagination" (Luce and Segal, *Sleep*, pp. 134–35).

Stories like these no doubt illumine the one overt fear that Bloom is said to have in *Ulysses*, "the committal of homicide or suicide during sleep by an aberration of the light of reason, the incommensurable categorical intelligence situated in the cerebral convolutions" (*U*, 720); but they also raise very dark questions about the indistinct line that separates sleepwalking from unreflective walking in general.

28. Furst, *Origins*, p. 104.

29. Foulkes, "Theories of Dream Formation," p. 240.

30. On the nineteenth-century belief that movements in the eyes of sleeping people and of animals signified dreams see, for example, Robert MacNish, *The Philosophy of Sleep* (New York: D. Appleton, 1834), pp. 310–12, and J. N. Pinkerton, *Sleep and Its Phenomena* (London: Edmund Fry and Son, 1839), p. 20; on the wakefulness of "the visual faculty" in sleep, see John Bigelow, *The Mystery of Sleep* (New York and London: Harper and Brothers, 1905), p. 5; on "the retinal element of dreaming" and "movements of the eye," see Havelock Ellis, *World of Dreams*, pp. 26–31; and so forth. Observations of this sort are everywhere in the literature that Joyce would have known.

The most famous exemplar of nineteenth-century reflection on "rapid-eye movements" is George Trumball Ladd, whose "Contribution to the Psychology of Visual Dreams," in *Mind, A Quarterly Review of Psychology and Philosophy*, n.s., 1 (1892) is anthologized in Woods' *World of Dreams*, pp. 511–15, and in Woods and Greenhouse, *New World*, pp. 180–82. The essay is also discussed in *The Interpretation of Dreams* (pp. 66–67), where Freud generally endorses its findings. "Through pure introspection, [this] professor of mental and moral psychology at Yale University was able to distinguish between the fixed position of the eyes in deep, presumably dreamless, sleep, and their mobility during dreaming, cautiously stating that he was 'inclined to believe that, in somewhat vivid visual dreams, the eyeballs move gently in their sockets, taking various positions. . . .' Ladd surmised that 'in a dream we probably focus our eyes somewhat as we should do in making the same observation when awake'" (Kleitman, "The Nature of Dreaming," p. 350; for a comparable contemporary retrospect on MacNish and Pinkerton, see Gardner et al., p. 147).

31. Notably, by Harry Levin, in *James Joyce: A Critical Introduction*, rev. ed. (New York: New Directions, 1960), pp. 139–222, a work whose views, in earlier form, Joyce had admired (*L*, III, 464); by Richard Ellmann, in *James Joyce*, pp. 436, 546, 716; by Frederick J. Hoffmann, in "Infroyce," in Seon Givens, ed., *James Joyce: Two Decades of Criticism* (New York: Vanguard Press, 1963), pp. 390–435; by James Atherton, in *The Books at the Wake: A Study of Literary Allusions in James Joyce's "Finnegans Wake"* (1959; rpt. Carbondale, Ill.: Southern Illinois Univ. Press, 1974); by William York Tindall, in *A Reader's Guide to "Finnegans Wake"* (New York: Farrar, Straus and Giroux, 1969), pp. 18–19 and passim; by Margaret C. Solomon, in *The Sexual Universe of "Finnegans Wake"* (Carbondale, Ill.: Southern Ill. Univ. Press, 1969); by Margot Norris, in *The Decentered Universe of "Finnegans Wake": a Structuralist Reading* (Baltimore: The Johns Hopkins Univ. Press, 1974); by Colin MacCabe, in *James Joyce and the Revolution of the Word* (London: The Macmillan Press, 1979); and by Sheldon R. Brivic, *Joyce between Freud and Jung* (Port Washington, N.Y.: Kennikat Press, 1980).

32. Paul Ricouer, *Freud and Philosophy: An Essay on Interpretation*, trans. Denis Savage (New Haven: Yale Univ. Press, 1970), pp. 6–8. On "the text of the dream," a term that Freud makes equivalent to the "manifest" or verbally recalled dream, see also "Revision of the Theory of Dreams," pp. 9 and 14.

33. Mercanton, "The Hours of James Joyce," p. 221.

34. On Joyce's characterization of psychoanalysis as "blackmail," see *JJ*, 324; as deviant "confession," *JJ*, 472; as "mechanical" in its symbology, *JJ*, 382; on the superiority of *Ulysses*, see *JJ*, 324, 436. See also Budgen, "Further Recollections of James Joyce," in *James Joyce and the Making of "Ulysses"*, p. 320.

Both from his overt remarks and from that well-known passage in the *Wake* which exploratively drifts into the penumbra of the Freudian unconscious (115.11–35), we can infer that Joyce distrusted the humorless solemnity of some psychoanalysis—its "unsmiling bit on 'alices" (115.22 ["analysis"]); its "feebought" mercantile aspect (115.25); and the tendency at least of its ephebes to narrow perspectives by putting everything only "under the pudendascope" (115.30). Then, too, there was the dangerously normalizing sound of the Freudian "cure," as opposed to the Irish one, good whiskey: "I can psoakoonaloose myself any time I want" (522.34–35 ["soak," "on a loose"]), as the blacked-out brain underlying *Finnegans Wake* murkily notes, so implicitly to contrast "analysis" (Gr., "loosening up") with "lysis" pure and simple.

A final consideration, since Joyce had a daughter in recurrent treatment, is that these were not merely intellectual, but painful real-world issues for him. One can hear something of his frustration and anger speaking through his daughter in Lucia's remark on her failed analyst-for-a-season, Carl Jung: "To think that such a big fat materialistic Swiss man should try to get hold of my soul!" (*JJ*, 679).

35. Padraic and Mary Colum, *Our Friend James Joyce*, p. 134.

36. Jan Parandowski, "Meeting with Joyce," trans. Willard Potts, in *Portrait of the Artist in Exile*, p. 158.

37. For a reading of *Ulysses* that develops this line of thought in more intricate ways, outside of the psychoanalytic vocabulary, see Ralph Rader, "Exodus and Return: Joyce's *Ulysses* and the Fiction of the Actual," *University of Toronto Quarterly* 48 (Winter 1978–79) : 149–71.

38. Unlike such of his followers as Roheim and Ferenczi, Freud seems never to have been stirred by the question of what happens in sleep outside of dreams: "what is sleep? That is a physiological or biological problem about which much is still in dispute. On that we can come to no conclusion" (*Introductory Lectures on Psychoanalysis*, p. 88).

39. "related as day is to night": Vinding, "James Joyce in Copenhagen," p. 149.

40. In 1934, when Joyce was asked in an interview whether he "believed" in *The New Science*, he replied,"I don't believe in any science but my imagination grows when I read Vico as it does not when I read Freud and Jung" (*JJ*, 693). This echoed a remark of 1913 in which he had already noted that "Freud had been anticipated by Vico" (*JJ*, 340). Together the comparisons suggest, as will become evident, that Joyce found in Vico's *New Science* a version of "the new science" of psychoanalysis, but one more congenial to his temperament.

41. Adaline Glasheen, *A Third Census of "Finnegans Wake": An Index of the Characters and Their Roles* (Berkeley and Los Angeles: Univ. of California Press, 1977), p. 100.

42. Budgen, "James Joyce," in Givens, *James Joyce: Two Decades of Criticism*, p. 24; see also "Further Recollections of James Joyce," p. 320.

43. August Suter, "Some Remininscences of James Joyce," trans. Fritz Senn, in *Portraits of the Artist in Exile*, p. 64.

44. For more on this underground tunnelling, see the *Letters*, I, 205, 220, 222; III, 110; and Nino Frank, "The Shadow That Had Lost Its Man," trans. Jane Carson, in *Portraits of the Artist in Exile*, p. 92. See also *Finnegans Wake*, where this dark mountain reappears everywhere, in countless forms. As "our mounding's mass" (8.1), "the mountainy mole-hill" (474.22), "*The Bearded Mountain*" (222.12), it turns out to be the hero of the book, indefinitively known as "Mr Tunnelly" (435.34–35).

45. Louis Gillet, *Claybook for James Joyce*, trans. George Markow-Totevy (London: Abelard-Schuman, 1958), p. 111.

46. See *James Joyce*, pp. 85, 177–78, 317, 343–44, 436–38, and 543–50; *Portraits of the Artist in Exile*, pp. 207, 208, 212, 226, and 233–34; and Budgen, "Further Recollections of James Joyce," p. 327.

47. Mercanton, "The Hours of James Joyce," pp. 207, 212, 225, 233–34.

48. On the Aristotelian origins of the eight-hour night, see Luce and Segal, *Sleep*, pp. 31–32; on its inadequacy, see Groucho Marx, *Beds* (New York, 1930): "We spend a third of our time in bed or, if you are an actor, two-thirds; or, if you live in Peoria, three thirds."

49. Mercanton, "The Hours of James Joyce," p. 221.

50. Oliver St. John Gogarty, review, *Observer*, 7 May 1939, 4; rpt. in *James Joyce: The Critical Heritage*, 2, p. 675.

1. "READING THE EVENING WORLD"

1. "voice of God": Joseph Campbell and Henry Morton Robinson, *A Skeleton Key to "Finnegans Wake"* (New York: Viking, 1961), p. 15.

2. An example of coherent nonsense is what one will find elaborated in some of the commentary on *Finnegans Wake*, which explains, without irony, that the book is about a Nordic hunchback saddled with the improbable name of Humphrey Chimpden Earwicker, who is married to someone even more improbably named Anna Livia Plurabelle, and who has committed an indistinct crime involving two temptresses, three soldiers, and unclear quantities of urine in Dublin's Phoenix Park. The story is clearly there in *Finnegans Wake* for its reader to elicit; one cannot not notice it. Were it to appear in a work like *Ulysses*, however, it would be easier to take for what it really is: ridiculous. "It's like a dream"; and like a dream, it will clarify with interpretation.

3. As "Hoodie Head," for instance (4.5–6; cf. 276.26, 588.16), this head lies "hooded," in crowblack dark (hence "hoodie crow"). As a "Hoved politymester" (324.20), by contrast, it is the center of all self-government and -management, a kind of "uphill headquarters" (202.16 ["hill head"]) or "Headmaster" (251.28) exerting corporate control over the rest of the body. As a "houthse" (10.27 ["house"]) or "howthold of nummer seven" (242.5), it is our hero's chief dwelling place, a locale of "nummer seven" because in sleep its seven orifices—two eyes, two ears, two nostrils, a mouth—are "number" (more "numb") than anyone awake can possibly imagine (hence the spelling, which prevents the mishearing of a numerical "number"). As "Holdhard" (12.36 ["Howth" rhymes roughly with "both"]), this head head largely stays still, "held hard" because arrested in sleep, as here: "The cranic head on him, caster of his reasons, peer yuthner in yondmist. Whooth?" (7.29–30). The dopily "unquiring" "Whooth?" here, an immobilized "cranium" that is ordinarily "master of his reason" but that now lies dull as a rock (hence the "granite" in "the cranic head"), is incapable of differentiating its own "peering" from apparently external "appearances"; the verb "peer" functions doubly in this construction to suggest that the "headth of [our] hosth" ("Whooth?") is at once the "unquiring" subject whose "cranic head" actively "peer[s]" in the mist and, at the same time, the unseen "abject" ("Whooth?") that passively "appears in the mist." In this act of dream perception, as always, all "abjects" are aspects of the subject.

Further examples of the equivalence of "Howth Head," "head head," and our hero's "tropped head" follow in the text.

4. Campbell and Robinson, *Skeleton Key*, pp. 7, 26; this is a given in the criticism.

5. The night's absorption of objects and of the objective reality that they hold together will explain, for instance, why so many pawnshops and auction houses float through *Finnegans Wake*. Anyone "perplexing about a paumpshop" (516.28) will note that these are merely real-world sites in which objects drift into their vanishing points, sometimes to reemerge, according to the mundane formulation "Goney goney gone!" (306.F2; cf. 398.5–6, 427.9, 596.15). Pawnshops and auction houses do feebly in the Daily World what sleep does absolutely in the "Evening World." Simply by falling asleep, the man "tropped head" at the *Wake* has taken "a brisk pause at a pawnbroking establishment" (41.29–30) of celestial dimensions, in which the strangest objects in the world, if one examines the details, get "pawned": somebody's "head" (560.8), his "word" and "truly admirable false teeth" (596.30, 41.30–31 [as opposed to "real" ones]), "boom companions" [and English] (498.16), and "souls" (579.30). The process of wakening, on the other

hand, finds him drifting "out of the paunschaup on to the pyre" (209.31) where, phoenix-like ("pyre"), the vanished objects that constitute a whole world reemerge and get "re-deemed": morning finds our sleeping hero "pawn[ing] up a fine head" (560.8) and "re-purchasing his pawned word" (596.30). A recently circulated story about the man who woke up one morning to discover that burglars had broken into his house during the night, stolen all his furniture, and replaced it with identical duplicates nicely captures "the pawnbreaking pathos" (164.23) and humor of "the Evening World."

The dense occurrence of sentences and prepositions without "objects" in *Finnegans Wake* works much to the same effect—as, for instance, when we learn that "now at last is Longabed going to be gone to, that more than man," where the "to" never finds an object (254.34–35). All such constructions signify the absence of objects in "Longabed's" "tropped head."

6. Geza Roheim, *The Gates of the Dream* (New York: International Universities Press, 1952), pp. 7, 49, 58; "in sleeping, all cathexes are withdrawn from the environment that is seemingly external and objective but really libidinal and subjective" (p. 20); "the dream is a rebuilding of [a] lost world on a libidinal-narcissistic basis" (p. 132); "the dream environment is formed out of the libidinally cathected body of the sleeper" (p. 36). Cf. *ID*, 401n.

7. Norman O. Brown, *Love's Body* (New York: Random House, 1966), p. 49; see also pp. 47 and 56.

8. For another account of the *Wake*'s fleshed landscapes, see Claude Gandelman, "*Finnegans Wake* and the Anthropomorphic Landscape," *Journal of Modern Literature* 7, no. 1 (Feb. 1979): 39–50; through excellent illustrations, the article also explores a par-allel between the *Wake*'s landscapes and anamorphic visual representations, so to relate the *Wake*'s "Sheeroskouro" to Lacan's discussions of anamorphosis in *The Four Fundamen-tal Concepts of Psychoanalysis.*

9. For a very spotty survey of the incessant "misappearance[s]" (186.12) of our hero's "tropped head" and missing feet, see 6.27 ("feet," "hoer his head"); 6.34 ("Roundthe-head," "foot"); 7.10–11 ("head," "tayle"); 7.29–30 ("head," "feet"); 8.9–10.22 ("hat," "boots"); 8.16–17 and 10.10–11 ("hat," "harse"); 10.10–11 and 10.20 ("hat," "tail"); 12.36 ("Holdhard" [Howthhead], "Pied" [Fr. *pied*, "foot"]); 15.31 ("hoagshead," "locktoes"); 26.12–13 ("head," "feet"); 57.17 ("legpoll"); 58.25 ("cappapee"); 70.22–23 ("head," "heeltapper," "head"); 78.5 ("from grosskopp to megapod"); 81.22 ("headandheelless"); 89.31 ("head in thighs"); 110.14–15 ("twoe nails on the head"); 119.35–120.1 ("caps," "tails," "tails," "mouths"); 127.33 ("Head," "Rump"); 130.1–2 ("leglifters," "brow-benders"); 131.33–35 ("hodpiece," "footsey"); 132.12–13 ("head," "feet"); 136.33 ("head-wood," "feet"); 139.8–9 ("summit," "footles"); 152.33–34 ("from veetoes to threetop"); 158.26, 33 ("feet," "heed"); 160.19–20 ("barefooted . . . face"); 163.18–21 ("top," "but-tom," "bottom," "top"); 167.10–13 ("exlegged," "acropoll"); 191.14 ("head to foot"); 206.32 ("from crown to sole"); 215.34, 36 ("foos," "head"); 220.14 ("caps or puds"); 220.26 ("cap-a-pipe"); 221.29 ("Kobay pipe by Kappa Pederson" [cap-à-pie]); 227.10–11 ("foot," "capital"); 233.2–3 ("moutonlegs and capers"); 242.4 ("from . . . coupoll to . . . basement"); 247.19 ("from nape to kneecap"); 284.25 ("behidden on the footplate"); 331.28 ("capriole legs"); 381.28 ("from head to tail"); 424.19 ("footinmouther"); 428.26–27 ("trampthickets" [feet], "batter*cops*"); 471.15 ("the headless shall have legs!"); 475.25, 28 ("footsteps," "caperchasing"); 476.31 ("heels from their stools" [heads from their toes]); 483.19 ("top," "heel"); 499.31 ("Herd!," "Foot!"); 518.9–10 ("With my

tongue through my toecap on the headlong stone"); 519.21 ("last foot foremouthst"); 522.28–29 ("noses to boot"); 563.8 ("capers," "heel"); 578.7–8 ("hedcosycasket," "feet"); 578.26–27 ("head," "fate"); 619.25, 27 ("man of the hooths," "from cape to pede"); 620.12–13 ("Head," "Heel"); 622.30 ("capapole").

The ubiquity of formations like these throughout *Finnegans Wake* reminds us of its placement in the body of a man "tropped head."

10. A remote approximation would be "deconstruction," on which see Norris's *Decentered Universe* and Derek Attridge and Daniel Ferrer, *Post-Structuralist Joyce: Essays from the French* (London: Cambridge Univ. Press, 1984). A more resonant approximation would be "de-presentation," on which see Samuel Weber, *The Legend of Freud* (Minneapolis: Univ. of Minnesota Press, 1982), pp. 66–67; Weber coins the term while discussing a passage from *The Interpretation of Dreams* in which Freud insists that "at bottom dreams are nothing more than a particular *form* of thinking, made possible by the condition of the state of sleep" (*ID*, 545n.).

11. "my nocturnal comedy": from an unpublished letter to Louis Gillet, dated 9 September 1938 and quoted in Georges Markow-Totvey's "Introduction" to Gillet's *Claybook*, p. 20.

12. Hence the obvious satirical targets of *Finnegans Wake*, who include: Pontiffs, in every sense of the word (152.18–156.34); Priests (III.ii); Politicians (446.27–448.33); Puritan moralists (187.28–193.28, III.i, ii); and not least, as the Irish have always known, Professors (149.11–168.12; 419.20–34; 425). Wyndham Lewis alone seems to have struck Joyce as fitting all five bills.

13. Joyce spoke of *Finnegans Wake* as effecting "a deliberate break from a certain Cartesianism" (Frank, "The Shadow That Had Lost Its Man," p. 97). The difficulty with rationalized approaches to *Finnegans Wake* is suggested by the fate of the phrase "knock out"; the commentary has made it seem so definitively to refer to "Castle Knock" that the French version of *Finnegans Wake* translates the phrase as "Castleknock a l'entrée du parc"—losing what seems to me a great deal, and overlooking the latent and "buried letter" of which *Finnegans Wake* speaks so clearly. See *Finnegans Wake*, trans. Philippe Lavergne (Paris: Gallimard, 1982), p. 9.

Judging from the derision with which some of the writing on *Finnegans Wake* speaks of association as a mode of thought, a qualifying note is necessary. "We need not suppose that every association that occurs during the work of interpretation [will have its] place in the dream-work" (*ID*, 571) or, comparably, that every association that occurs to us in analyzing words and phrases in *Finnegans Wake* will be relevant to *Finnegans Wake*: only well-documented reference to the text itself will assure us that whatever associations we may discover are part of the book's structure, and not monomaniacal impositions of our own clever invention.

2. NOTHING IN PARTICULAR

1. Miguel de Unamuno, *The Tragic Sense of Life*, tr. J. E. Crawford Flitch (London: Macmillan and Co., 1921), p. 38.

2. See, for example, Luce and Segal, *Sleep*, pp. 89–90, and the sources cited there.

3. The term also has theological overtones. Inverting the process by which the inanimate stuffs of bread and wine are transubstantiated into the "Real Presence" of Christ in

the Eucharist, sleep would transubstantiate the real presence of anyone into "Real Absence" within the inanimated matter of the body.

4. Mercanton, "The Hours of James Joyce," p. 223.

5. Ibid., p. 221.

6. Tindall, *Reader's Guide*, p. 87; Glasheen, *Third Census*, p. xxxvi.

7. The reference to "Baselbut," a region around Basel, Switzerland, would inform us, in the *Wake*'s cipher system, that its hero is "landloughed" (23.29) and hermetically sealed in the vacuum of "four cantins" (496.9 [not "cantons"]) at this moment in the night, not in contact with the world "out there." It will also begin to illustrate the associative way in which foreign languages not genetically allied to English seem to operate in this text "imitative of the dream-state." In a letter of 1940 to Armand Petitjean (*L*, III, 501n.), Joyce spoke of a move to Switzerland as the act of "penetrat[ing] a country which is hermetically helvetic." Both the dating of the letter, on the verge of World War II, and its reference to "Helvetius," a freethinker, recall Switzerland's history as a state traditionally impervious to conflict and open to freethinking. Swiss-German intonations seem to emerge in *Finnegans Wake*, as in Joyce's thinking, to indicate its hero's movement into much this kind of "state." When captured in Swiss-German, "he canseels under veerious persons" (373.29): he "cancels," "conceals," but also hermetically "can-seals" in "four cantins" that lie landlocked, conflict-free, and open to the free thought of the night.

8. The bracketed definitions of "casehardened" (not necessarily a legal term) and "ex-animation" are from the OED. An additional reference to the children's game of "Dead Man's Dark Scenery or Coat," described in Norman Douglas's *London Street Games* as "one of those jacket-games, where one party has to hide, covered in their coats," would only reinforce the sense of the passage: it yields the "eyewitless foggus" of someone wrapped in the cloak of darkness. (*Annotations*, p. 87).

9. George G. Findlay, "Methodism (Doctrine)," in James Hastings, ed., *Encyclopedia of Religion and Ethics* (New York: Charles Scribners' Sons, 1927), 8, p. 610.

10. Since telegraphy and radiography, unlike writing, convey articulate meaning through the medium of an "ether" imperceptible to the human senses, both serve as figures, throughout *Finnegans Wake*, for kinds of sense sensed in the absence of real perception, by a man put "under ether" (98.3 ["anaesthetized"]) in sleep.

If the reader will "turn a widamost ear dreamily" into the room in which he is sitting right now—a "witness" ear, and "most widely"—he will note how indistinctly he "hear[s] the wireless harps of sweet old Aerial" (449.28–30) playing everywhere into his head. For "in this wireless age" (489.36), at every minute of the day and night, wireless communiques and radio waves bearing human voices and complex messages from all over the world "for all within crystal range" (229.12) are streaming constantly into the eyes and ears, "wordloosed [wirelessed] over seven seas crowdblast [broadcast] in cellelleneteutoslavzendlatinsoundscript" (219.16–17 [in "Celtic-Hellenic-Teutonic-Slavic-Zend-Latin-Sanskrit soundscript"]). What one will note, in trying to perceive these "open tireless secrets" (407.21 ["wireless"]) is the presence of a concrete "reality," there all the time around one, of which one is largely unconscious. And as any number of citations will show, it is a "reality" *exactly* of this kind that *Finnegans Wake* is scrupulously representing: "You have jest (a ham) beamed listening through" (359.22 [not "been listening to"]) a "NIGHTLETTER" of sorts (308.16 [in Am. sl., "a telegram sent overnight"])—a "NIGHTLETTER" concretely identical to the one reconstructed in *Fin-*

negans Wake. For "as I hourly learn from Rooters and Havers through Gilligan's maypoles," moreover (421.31–32 [where "Reuters" and "Havas" are wireless agencies, and "Gilligan's maypoles" are "aerials" humanized by reference to their inventor]), there is a great deal of hot news constantly blowing through and around my head of which I am "obliffious."

Since one's "real" perception of radiotelegraphic communiques resembles in concrete one's perception of "open tireless secrets" delivered incessantly from an unconscious into consciousness, "Morse nuisance" (99.6) becomes, in *Finnegans Wake*, a cipher for the operations of its sleeper's darker side. And Joyce's "new book of Morses" (123.35) requires in turn some familiarity with a "morse-erse wordybook" (530.19 [Ger. *Wörterbuch*, "dictionary"]) or with a primer of "noirse-made-easry" (314.27 ["noirse" blurs "Morse" into the Fr. *noir*, "black"]), because the act of translation required in reading *Finnegans Wake*, as in the case of radiotelegraphic transmission, is not from visible letters into another form of visibility, but from visible letters into the invisible—from consciousness and English into the "m'm'ry" of the unconsciousness of sleep.

Further examples of how radiotelegraphy works in *Finnegans Wake* follow in the text. See also Hart's notes on "The Telegram" in *Structure and Motif in "Finnegan's Wake"* (Evanston: Northwestern Univ. Press, 1962), pp. 122–28, 243; the entries on "Havas," "Reuters," and "Tass" in the *Third Census*; and Joyce's hints on the subject in a letter to Harriet Shaw Weaver (*L*, I, 321).

11. "Sordomutics" would equally suggest the French *sourd-muet* and the Italian *sordomuto*, both meaning "deaf-and-dumb." The *Wake*'s "sordomutics" is a deepened form of the language that the French call *Des sourds-muets* ("the language of the deaf and dumb").

12. As the line suggests, "hats" in *Finnegans Wake* always merit inspection because they sound like and have all the earmarks of "heads," but come with larger air supplies inside: hats are antiheads. The joke begins in the hallucinatory "Circe" episode of *Ulysses*, where one finds Stephen Dedalus momentarily engaged in a dense conversation with Lynch's "cap" (*U*, 504), the idea there being that where Stephen has a head full of ideas, Lynch has a "cap" (< L. *caput*, "head").

As "a wellknown tall hat" blown in the wind (321.9–10)—"a nightcap of that silk or it might be a black velvet" (321.10–11)—the hero of *Finnegans Wake* becomes frequently equivalent, in the "noughttime," to the content of an empty and untenanted hat. He has, moreover, "the most conical hodpiece of confusianist heronim" (131.33–34 ["the most comical headpiece of confused hair on him"]) because that "headpiece," like an empty "wig," has nothing inside but air and "confusion"—though also, and crucially, a hint of the transcendental (hence "Confucius"). "Wigs" and "caps" work like "hats" in the *Wake*: if there's nothing inside, there's nothing inside. As a "beer wig" (559.25), to illustrate the supple range of these figures, the emptily "tropped head" on our hero would be "blacked-out" and full of "spirits"; as an "eerie whig" (20.23, 360.32), it would be stirred by the "spirit's whispers in his magical helmet" (220.25–26); as a "wolkencap" (23.21), it would lie under a "woolen" "nightcap," lost in turbid clouds (Du. *wolkencap*, "cloud cap"; cf. 126.14–15); and so forth.

13. In context, the quoted line reads, "leave us and the crimsend daun to shellalite on the darkumen" (350.28–29); it is pointing out how catastrophically the rationally lettered consciousness that returns to the "tropped head" at "dawn" obliterates the senses purveyed in dreams.

14. For this reason, certainly one of the most interesting and indispensable of the word lists that has grown up around *Finnegans Wake* is Clive Hart's *Concordance*. Simply by putting the *Wake* in alphabetical order, the *Concordance* has established itself as something of a Contradictionary or Outlexicon of world language, immersion in which will repay study because of the wealth of interesting concepts that spills out of it ("unstant," for instance).

Reference to the *Concordance* will also discredit the often repeated view that *Finnegans Wake*, because it tells the same life's story over and over again in constantly varying forms, is a repetitious book. Quite the contrary: one would think that in a work aspiring to reconstruct "Real Absence," terms like "eyewitless" (for "eyewitness") and "witless" (for "witness") would recur over and over again. In fact, each occurs only once in the space of six hundred pages. What finally seems astonishing from this perspective is how *little* Joyce repeated himself in a work that "bare[s] full sweetness" (615.33 ["bears rich false witness"]) to the night.

15. The *OED* lists the "scotograph" as "an instrument used by the blind for writing in the dark"; and also, by way of such illustrations as the following, as a synonym for x-ray radiography: "The [X-rays] have very little in common with light. Would not 'scotography' be a better name for their work than 'photography'?" (Sir Alfred Wills, letter to the London *Times*, 10 March 1896). Since it allows perception where no real empirical perception is possible, as in sleep, the "xray" (248.1) too becomes a cipher for HCE's "nightlife," the *Wake* in turn giving his "X ray picture" (530.8). Cf. 522.20–24 and the gloss in the *Annotations*: "Thanks to Xrays, the time will come no doubt when he will snappograph you wrong side out."

16. It's "graphically" representative of "man," that is ("mangraphique"), but not in the manner of "Daguerre." A notation on unorthodox methods of attack, the line is playing off Bosquet's comment on the Charge of the Light Brigade ("*C'est magnifique, mais ce n'est pas la guerre*" ["It's magnificent, but it's not war"]).

17. Both the "legal trial" analyzed earlier in the text and the global vanishing act of these "nanentities" are representative of a great deal in *Finnegans Wake*, many of whose passages *seem* to be about real-world events like courtroom trials, ballad singing, or crimes; if, however, one starts pressing the details, these events turn out to happen in the middle of a stretch of sleep. Consider, for example, the chain of obviously ridiculous figures who putatively spread rumors about "Earwicker" in I.ii. One of these, we learn, "to whom reference has been made had been absent . . . but on racenight, blotto. . . . he sought his wellwarmed leababobed [Gael. *leaba*, "bed"] . . . and . . . resnored alcoh alcoh alcoherently . . . during uneasy slumber . . . [to two others] of no fixed abode . . . who had passed several nights . . . under the blankets . . . on the bunk . . . pillowed . . . and [a third] . . . who . . . had been towhead tossing on his shakedown . . . after . . . trying . . . to get . . . into . . . the bed. . . . [All] as an understood thing slept their sleep. . . ." (39.28–29, 33; 40.2, 4–5, 14, 16–19, 20, 21, 33, 34, 36; 41.6). Or consider again "Mrs. F . . . A . . ." (59.4), who, "resting for the moment" (58.34), delivers compassionate commentary on our hero while "recoopering her cartwheel chapot (ahat! . . .)" (59.5–6). Though she seems involved in fussy millinery work, something beneath all the evident appearances seems also to be "recuperating a head" (and an empty one at that). Many of the characters who move through *Finnegans Wake* are obliquely sunk into sleep of this sort because they appear in the "tropped head" of the sleeper to whom they occur. "It's

like a dream," in which all the obviously nonsensical appearances latently bear on "one stable somebody" (107.30).

18. Atherton, *Books at the Wake*, p. 107.

19. As Atherton notes (p. 262), the line additionally echoes the shrewd observation made by Wyndham Lewis in *Time and Western Man* that "there is not very much reflection going on at any time inside the head of Mr. James Joyce." Finding the assessment evidently inaccurate to a reading of *Ulysses*, Joyce bent it into pertinence in this part of *Finnegans Wake*, where his sleeping protagonist lies quite void of brain.

Playing off proximate phrasing (56.20–21), "Melancholy Slow" would also refer to the first line of Oliver Goldsmith's "The Traveller; or a Prospect of Society" ("Remote, unfriended, melancholy, slow"). The reference would only deepen the sense that the *Wake*'s sleeping hero has passed from everyday familiarities into another "state" at this moment in the dark. Treating of Goldsmith's absence from his native earth, "for a while my proper cares resigned" (l. 101), "The Traveller" is set in Switzerland, where "wants [are] few, [and] wishes all confin'd" (ll. 209–10). See Atherton, p. 97.

20. The *Classical Lexicon* gives the English "Be well-disposed with tongues, i.e. be silent!" for *Favete linguis*, noting that the phrase served as "a command to citizens at Roman religious ceremonies" (p. 36). McHugh, in *Annotations*, translates *Favete linguis* as "listen all in silence" and ascribes it to Horace, who quotes it for religious effect in the Odes (III, 1. 2). A. J. Macleane, finally, in his commentary on the Odes, points out that "'Favere linguis' . . . in its first meaning signifies the speaking of words of good omen. But it came as commonly to signify total silence" (*The Works of Horace with English Notes*, rev. and ed. Reginald A. Chase [Boston: Allyn and Bacon, 1858], p. 312). The historically complex phrase, in other words, designating lingual silence, carries contradictory tensions appropriate to the "sonorous silence" (230.23) of the *Wake*'s "nat language."

21. Jean-Paul Sartre, *Being and Nothingness*, trans. Hazel E. Barnes (New York: Citadel Press, 1966), p. 23. There are of course differences, though finally not irreconcilable ones, between Sartrean nothingness and the *Wake*'s "Real Absence."

22. "literary anti-matter": Hugh Kenner, *The Pound Era* (Berkeley and Los Angeles: Univ. of Calif. Press, 1971), p. 274.

3. "FINNEGAN"

1. Arthur Schopenhauer, *The World as Will and Idea*, trans. R. B. Haldane and J. Kemp (London: Trubner and Co., 1886), 3, p. 267 and chapter 41 generally.

2. Gottfried Lessing, "How the Ancients Represented Death," in *Selected Prose Works of G. E. Lessing*, trans. E. C. Beasley and Helen Zimmern (London: George Bell, 1889), p. 182. On the Dark Twins, see the *Iliad*, XIV, 213, and XVI, 672; Hesiod's *Theogeny*, 756; and the *Aeneid*, VI, 278. On the primordiality and persistence of the analogy between sleep and death in Western thinking, see Philippe Ariès, *The Hour of Our Death*, trans. Helen Weaver (New York: Random House, 1981), pp. 22–24, 354, 440–41, 525, and 625. For an eloquent meditation on the similarity, see Sir Thomas Browne's *Religio Medici*, part 2, sec. 12, in *The Prose of Sir Thomas Browne*, ed. Norman J. Endicott (Garden City, N.Y.: Doubleday, 1967), pp. 85–86.

3. Ludwig Jekels and Edmund Bergler, "Instinct Dualism in Dreams," *The Psychoanalytic Quarterly* 9 (1940) :402; Roheim, *The Gates of the Dream*, p. 3; Brown, *Love's Body*, p. 52.

4. On "thanatomimesis," see Robert Kastenbaum and Ruth Aisenberg, *The Psychology of Death* (New York: Springer, 1976), pp. 132–53, 175.

5. Cf. 41.6, 77.1, 87.11, 405.35–36, and 610.3. As is implied in the expression "sleeping like a rock," in the night "Tu es Petrus" (407.15 [L. "you're a rock," but also "Thou art Peter"; cf. 153.23–24]). That the "man made static" at his *Wake* (309.22) lies "rockbound" (7.1), sleeping like a rock "in the rockabeddy" (472.2), and in some guises "look[s] stuck to the sod . . . visibly unmoved" (430.12–14) will clarify one of the senses underlying the recurrent phrase "thuartpeatrick" (3.10) in *Finnegans Wake* (a "peatrick," or "Patrick," would be an Irished "Petrus"). It would also explain what some of the oddly "peter-fied" personages, like "Peacer the Grave" and the immobily "lapidated" "Peter Roche" (449.12–16) are doing in the book: like any good "petrock" (203.31), they just lie there, playing dead. For other occurrences of "thuartpeatrick" in the *Wake*, see the "Index of Motifs" in Clive Hart's *Structure and Motif*, p. 223.

6. The phrases and lines from the ballad italicized in the text appear in *Finnegans Wake* at the places designated parenthetically. For the full version of "Finnegan's Wake," see *JJ*, pp. 543–44, or Glasheen, *Third Census*, pp. 93–94, which also lists other evocations of "Finnegan" in the *Wake*. For another account of the ballad's role in *Finnegans Wake*, see Glasheen's "Notes toward a Supreme Understanding of 'Finnegan's Wake' in *Finnegans Wake*," *A Wake Newslitter*, n.s., 5 (Feb. 1968):4–15. On its employment at 6.13–28, see Eileen G. Margerum, "First Music," *A Wake Newslitter*, n.s., 10 (Aug. 1973):60–64.

7. As throughout *Finnegans Wake*, however, where "dead," "death," and comparable terms take incessant oblique forms, the spellings here are ambiguous because the man "tropped head" "in bed" at the *Wake* is not actually "dead to the world" but only "dead to the world."

8. A whole set of ciphers designating "the end of the world," accordingly, plays through *Finnegans Wake* to signal the annihilation of time, earth, and perception at the "ephumeral" met in the "noughttime." Allusions to the "a bockalips" (6.26 ["Apocalypse"; the "bock" "blacks out"]) or to the Book of "revelation" (453.33–34)—including passing references to the separation of "the sleep and the ghoasts" (551.2)—would be among these. But so too would references to "death angel[s]" of all kinds (472.29); to "ragnar rocks" (19.4 ["Ragnarok"]) or "guttergloomering" (565.2 [Ger. *Götterdämmerung*, "the Twilight of the Gods")); and so forth. Recurrent evocations of "Roland" and "Oliver" from *Le Chanson de Roland*, would work to this effect too (e.g., 73.33–74.5), to evoke "the solemn last farewells of Roland and Oliver," who "say goodbye to each other as if they were about to fall into a long sleep of infinite duration" (Ariès, *The Hour of Our Death*, pp. 22, 23).

9. "Our concept of the other world is unconsciously modeled on sleep and dreaming"; "myths on the descent to the other world and the return are based on the basic dream mechanism" (Roheim, *The Gates of the Dream*, pp. 271, 277; cf. 259, 275, 278, and chapter 5 generally). See also James Hillman, *The Dream and the Underworld* (New York: Harper and Row, 1979); and Brown, *Love's Body*, pp. 46–55.

Both Roheim and Hillman point out—to illustrate what is at stake here—that in Greek and Roman myth, where Sleep and Death were already twins, the underworld was in many ways a conceptual twin of the night. Opening "well to the west" (3.21), at the boundary of earth and ocean, the entrance to Hades lay "past the gates of the sun and the district of dreams," beyond a land of eternal night known as "Cimmeria" (*Odyssey*, XI,13–19; XXIV, 12). Spatially, the gateway to Hades seems to have been situated in a spot topologically indistinct from the one in which the night, and *Finnegans Wake*, begin temporally: at sunset. Because it takes place in the "semitary of Somnionia," then, the *Wake* moves its reader through "Cimmerian shudders" (504.7 ["shadows," with "shudders"]) into a "netherworld" (571.35) without the least contrivance or conceptual tampering on Joyce's part at all.

As a proper name, moreover, "Hades" (Gr. *Aidês*) designated both "the god of the world below" and the "underworld" itself, but as a common noun, *aidês* simply meant "unseen" and was related to such terms as *aidêlos* ("making unseen," hence "annihilating") and *aidnos* ("unseen, hidden, dark"); all of these were privative forms (*a-*) of *idein* ("to see"), from which English "ideas" derive. Like a dark pun, the name "Hades" would semantically have evoked a world comparable to the one met in the night's "seemetery," where the man "tropped head" has no ideas and nothing to see. Finally, too, there ran through "Hades" the dark river "*Lêthê*" (Gr., "forgetfulness"), of which "Finnegan" has obviously drunk: a "lover of lithurgy," (432.32), his "lethargy," etymologically, has the radical of "*Lethe*" in it (78.4, 214.10, 272.F3, 334.1, 397.8).

If passing into "Hades" meant entering a region indistinct from the night, finally, the forces of the night complementarily welled out of Hades into the world of the living. "Those hornmade ivory dreams you reved of" (192.27) issued out of "gates of dreams" that Homer and Virgil attached to Hades (*Odyssey*, XIX, 562–67; *Aeneid*, VI, 893–96)—one the "gate of ivory" and the other "the gate of horn" (or "the gate" "with the cow's bonnet a'top o'it" [63.19, 28–29, 34]). And if dreams were creatures of the underworld, so too were the souls of the dead, who were thought to have the palpability and substance of images in dreams (*Odyssey*, XI, 204–22) and moreover came to visit the living while the living slept (*Iliad*, XXI, 62–104). The topologically blurred relations of the underworld and the night are perhaps best captured by a line that Aeneas utters while down there: "*Umbrarum hic locus est, Somni noctisque soporae*" (*Aeneid*, VI, 387–90 ["This is a place of shadows, of sleep and somnolent night"]).

For a classicist's extended treatment of this material, see Ernest Leslie Highbarger, *The Gates of Dreams: An Archaeological Examination of Vergil, Aeneid VI, 893–899* Baltimore: The Johns Hopkins Press,1940). For an archetypal analysis, see Hillman. For a Freudian one, see Roheim, pp. 281–85. On the Greek, see Liddell and Scott, and Hjalmar Frisk, *Griechisches Etymologisches Wörterbuch* (Heidelberg: Carl Winter, 1954), pp. 33–34.

10. As Joyce hinted at the end of a letter to Harriet Shaw Weaver, "Tobecontinued's tale" is "(to be continued tomorrow)" (*L*, I, 280; cf. III, 374, 375n.). For other instances of what it means "to be continued" in *Finnegans Wake*, see 66.8–10 ("To be continued . . . next morning"); 302.29–30 ("To be continued. Anon" ["shortly," but in the meantime "anonymous"]); 454.7; and, most elaborately, 359.26–28, particles of which are discussed below.

11. Brown, *Love's Body*, p. 52.

12. On Halloween and All Saints' Day, see also 19.25, 26.6, 104.2, 237.35, 304.F5, 359.26, 427.32–33, 455.5–6 [Fr. *La Toussaint*, "All Saints' Day"], 488.23–24, and 537.28. For an "eyewitless foggus" account of the resurrection of the dead in another world (that is, of "spirits" coming back to life in the "tropped head" of someone sunk in the "seemetery" of night), see 329.22–330.1: "it was joobileejeu that All Sorts' Jour" (329.30–31 [where "Sortir du Jour," the title used in Fr. translations of the Egyptian *Book of the Dead*, would also signal the resurrection of the dead]).

13. On "heavenly peace," compare 470.36–471.5 to 499.1–12, and see by all means, at

454.28–455.29, the very funny account of what "heavenly peace" and life "Up There" (454.36) would really be like. Noting that our "patrified" hero has reached the end of his day on earth and so achieved its perfection and fulfillment would give a second sense to the recurrent "Twoedged Petrard" (497.8) having to do with "Peter" in *Finnegans Wake*. Anyone "dead to the world" and sleeping like a rock ("Tu es Petrus") would also have entered unto his kingdom ("Tu es Petrus").

14. On the "mound," see also 102.22, 111.34–35, 331.18–20, 420.14, 479.23, 499.34, and innumerable passing references. As I.v lengthily shows, "letters" are buried in this "mound"—"letters" in all conceivable senses (ABCs, scraps of remembered conversation and reading, and, in general, the whole business of "literacy").

15. As is noted elsewhere of the figure who sleeps like a rock at the *Wake*, "his likeness is in Terrecuite" (133.30; cf. 119.2, 240.19). "Terry Cotter" would just be an Irished version of the Hebraic "Adam."

16. In general, at the *Wake*, real-world place-names ending with "-bury" and "-borough" undergo translation from the "vernacular" into "the vermicular" as they vanish, with all consciousness of *le monde*, into the "tropped head" in le "mound." There they become burial sites ("-bury"'s), subterranean "burrows" ("-borough"'s), or "barrows" (burial mounds). In the daily world, place-names like London's "Harrow-the-Hill" or "Finsbury" designate "suburbs"; at the *Wake*, by contrast, they designate "su*burrs*" (454.30) in which the man lying "dead to the world" is wont to "harrow the hill" (355.16 ["harrow hell"]) or, in the guise of "Finn," simply lie there, void of ideas, entertaining himself at a sort of "Finsbury Follies," the price of whose admission is "dirt cheap at a sovereign a skull!" (374.27–28). The double "r" in those "su*burrs*," of course, puts us in mind of "*burrows*." Cf. 5.35, 24.20, 29.35–36, 62.28, 147.26, 372.17, 495.16 ["borrowing" = "burrowing"], 503.14, and 565.36.

17. Hillman, *The Dream and the Underworld*, p. 36.

18. In a body "tropped head," this is only what we might expect, since a great deal of vitality and conflict will inevitably hit "below the belch" (492.36 [the neck]), but also "below the belt" (457.17). For other passages equating the occulted world "below" with the occulted content of "drawers," see 107.6–7 (*Unmentionability*), 371.35 ("under where"), 571.15–16 ("under close"), 577.29 ("unterlinnen"), and so forth. These terms demonstrate additionally how a "reading [of] the Evening World," in "bring[ing] to mind the gladdest garments out of sight" (200.25–26), really can lift out of unconsciousness things like "the canon's underpants" (206.27), which were not evident in the order of things a few minutes ago, and are usually nowhere evident in the order of a daily world regulated by an "underlinen overlord" (97.24).

19. E. A. Wallis Budge, trans., *The Book of the Dead: The Hieroglyphic Transcript of the Papyrus of Ani*, Medici Society Version (1913; rpt. Secaucus, N.J.: University Books, 1960), pp. 409–19, 591–94. In order to pass from his grave into immortality, the Egyptian mummy was required to know and name, at each in a succession of doors in the House of Osiris, "the bars of the door," "the right lintel," "the left lintel," "the ground," "the bolt," "the socket and fastening," "the posts," and "the Doorkeepers." Otherwise, they wouldn't let him through.

20. A reader who explores this part of *Finnegans Wake* further will note that over pp. 75–78 Joyce draws extensively on Dutch terms. This happens, in part, because the Dutch for "Dutch" is *nederlands* ("netherlands") and because *nederlands* is spoken in "netherlands," a "state" in which everything lies "under." Through there is far more to

the use of Dutch in *Finnegans Wake* than this makes evident, at least one set of associations prompts Joyce to draw on *nederlands* to color out parts of the night in which the book's "belowes hero" has drifted into a netherlandly "netherworld" (571.35).

21. Arnold Toynbee, "Man's Concern with Life after Death," *Life after Death*, ed. Arnold Toynbee and Arthur Koestler (London: Weidenfeld and Nicolson, 1976), p. 3.

22. Jules Vuillemin, *Essai sur la signification de la mort* (Paris: Presses Univ. de France, 1948); quoted in Warren A. Shibles, *Death: An Interdisciplinary Analysis* (Whitewater, Wisc.: Language Press, 1974).

4. INSIDE THE COFFIN

1. E. A. Wallis Budge, trans., *The Book of the Dead: The Hieroglyphic Transcript of the Papyrus of Ani*, Medici Society Version (1913; rpt. Secaucus, N.J.: University Books, 1960), pp. 150, 351 n. 3, 355 n. 4; E. A. Wallis Budge, *The Dwellers of the Nile: The Life, History, Religion, and Literature of the Ancient Egyptians* (1926; rpt. New York: Dover, 1977), p. 159; E. A. Wallis Budge, *The Egyptian Heaven and Hell* (1925; rpt. LaSalle, Ill.: Open Court Pub. Co., 1974), pp. 16, 96, 109, 110.

2. Frank Budgen, "James Joyce," in Givens, *James Joyce: Two Decades of Criticism*, p. 26.

3. Frank Budgen, "Joyce's Chapters of Going Forth by Day," in Givens, *James Joyce: Two Decades of Criticism*, pp. 343–67.

4. See Campbell and Robinson, *A Skeleton Key*, p. 73, 198, 204, 211, 304; Joseph Campbell, "Finnegan the Wake," in Givens, *James Joyce: Two Decades of Criticism*, pp. 368–89; Atherton, *Books at the Wake*, pp. 191–200; Tindall, *A Reader's Guide to Finnegans Wake*, passim; David Hayman, ". . . a Sentence in Progress," *PMLA* (March 1953): 136–54; Clive Hart, "His Good Smetterling of Entymology," *A Wake Newslitter*, n.s., 4 (February 1967): 14–24; James Atherton, "Shaun A," in *A Conceptual Guide to Finnegans Wake*, ed. Michael H. Begnal and Fritz Senn (University Park: Penn State Univ. Press, 1974), p. 157; Michael Begnal, "Some Gleanings from the Book of the Dead," *A Wake Newslitter*, n.s., 12 (April 1975): 30–31.

The most exhaustively researched and detailed account of Joyce's allusions to Egyptian sources is Mark L. Troy's "Mummeries of Resurrection: The Cycle of Osiris in *Finnegans Wake*" (Ph.D. diss., Univ. of Uppsala, 1976), which readers looking for more detail and a perspective on the *Wake*'s Egyptological materials distinct from my own should by all means consult. Readers interested in consulting the Egyptological notes that Joyce kept while writing "Work in Progress" should refer to Danis Rose, *Chapters of Coming Forth by Day*, A Wake Newslitter Monograph, no. 6 (Colchester: A Wake Newslitter Press, 1982). For Rose, the Book of the Dead is "undoubtedly the single most significant source resorted to by Joyce in compiling his own Irish book of the dead" (p. 1).

5. Arnold Toynbee, "Man's Concern with Life after Death," in Toynbee, Koestler, et al., *Life after Death*, p. 16.

6. Budge, *Dwellers on the Nile*, p. 134.

7. Budge, *Book of the Dead*, pp. x–xi.

8. *L*, I, 406; Budge, *Book of the Dead*, p. 28.

9. Apart from its reference to Horus's victory over the forces of nocturnal darkness (his "coup"), "horuscoup" also refers to the horoscope, because folk history attributes its invention to Egyptian augurers. "Horoscope" seems to enter into the complex of meanings

in the line under our attention, again, as a way of commenting on the wish-fulfilling potencies of the dream.

10. Budge, *Book of the Dead*, p. x.

11. Ibid., pp. x, 21, 27; Budge, *The Mummy: Chapters on Egyptian Funereal Archaeology* (1925; rpt. New York: Macmillan, Collier Books, 1972), pp. 204, 209.

12. Budge, *Book of the Dead*, p. 217; *The Mummy*, p. 171.

13. Budge, *The Mummy*, pp. 168–70.

14. Ibid., pp. 163–67.

15. Ibid., pp. 204–5; *Book of the Dead*, p. 27.

16. Budge, *The Mummy*, pp. 153–54, 347–48; *Egyptian Heaven and Hell*, pp. 80–81.

17. Atherton, *Books at the Wake*, p. 192. Atherton also clarifies the reference to "Humphrey's Justesse of the Jaypees" in the line cited by pointing out an allusion to Henry Humphrey's *The Justice of the Peace in Ireland*, in which, of course, there are no "eschatological chapters." Since "Humphrey" is simply a cipher for the *Wake*'s inert and "hump"-like hero, the phrase aspires to a problematic definition of the sleepy tranquillity into which he has fallen: absolute peacefulness only "hinted at" in Humphrey's book is one of the states into which the Theban recension of the Book of the Dead tries to see; but before a dead man could attain that desired state he also had to go through a harrowing last judgment before the gods in which his whole life was put on trial. Troubled by his conscience even in the unconsciousness of sleep, the *Wake*'s dreamer seems to undergo a process of judgment and peace that lies halfway between the kinds of judgment and peace described in these two works.

"Bug of the Deaf," apart from referring to the Book of the Dead, also suggests the earwig, on which see chapter nine.

18. Atherton, *Books at the Wake*, pp. 192–93. For further discussion of the Papyrus of Nu and an excellent assessment of Joyce's acquaintance with available Egyptological sources, see Troy, "Mummeries," pp. 72–74. As both Atherton and Troy note, Joyce approached the Book of the Dead through the writings of Sir E. A. Wallis Budge, whose work no reader of the *Wake* should slight. Dated though Budge's Egyptology may be, it was Joyce's.

19. Budge, *Book of the Dead*, p. 614. See also those quotations from the Book of the Dead in the *Wake* at 328.31–35 and 593.20–24, where Joyce also refers to Nu, "the steward of the overseer of the seals," in the phrases "the everseer of the seize" and the "eversower of the seeds."

20. Budge, *Book of the Dead*, p. 217. An account of the book of the dead in the Dublin Museum ("the Dublin Papyrus") is available in Edouard Henri Naville, *Das aegyptische Totenbuch den* XVIII. *bis* XX *Dynastie* (Graz: Akademische Druck-u. Verlangsanstalt, 1971), Bd. I, pt 1, pp. 80–81; for reproductions of illustrations from the Dublin Papyrus, see also Bd. I, pt. 2, pp. 3, 4, 19, 22, 27–30, and 212.

21. Since the Egyptian Kingdom endured for some five thousand years, according to one chronology, its perception of the cosmos changed and modified in ways whose study falls beyond our immediate purpose. The body of this chapter accordingly deals primarily with the cosmology and mythography of the New Kingdom, which Egyptologists, dating all things as they do by reference to dynastic successions, situate in the Eighteenth through Twentieth Dynasties—roughly between 1550 and 1050 B.C., according to Budge. It was during this period that books of the dead seem to have flourished most widely and reached their most ornate forms, many of them sharing enough properties to be classified under a "Theban recension."

Since Egyptologists have not agreed on a definite system of Egyptian chronology, the dating of various books of the dead explored in the text is given according to Budge, *Dwellers on the Nile*, pp. 1–17, whose figures are currently regarded as "high":

Pyramid Text of Pepi I: Sixth Dynasty (2825–2631 B.C.)
Papyrus of Ani: Eighteenth Dynasty (1600–1350 B.C.)
Papyrus of Nebseni: Eighteenth Dynasty
Papyrus of Nekhtu Amen: Eighteenth Dynasty
Tomb Inscriptions of Tut-ankh-amen: Eighteenth Dynasty
Papyrus of Nu: Eighteenth or Nineteenth Dynasty
Book of Gates: Eighteenth and Nineteenth Dynasties
Coffin Text of Seti I: Nineteenth Dynasty (1321–1205 B.C.)
Turin Papyrus: Twenty-sixth Dynasty or later (663–520 B.C.)

22. Budge, *Book of the Dead*, p. 202.

23. Ibid., pp. 202, 206, 351 n.3; Budge, *Dwellers on the Nile*, pp. 207, 227–28; Adolf Erman, *Life in Ancient Egypt*, trans. H. M. Tirard (1894; rpt. New York: Dover, 1971), pp. 310ff.

24. Erman, *Life in Ancient Egypt*, pp. 310ff.

25. Budge, *Book of the Dead*, pp. 130–36; *Egyptian Heaven and Hell*, pp. 88–89.

26. Budge, *Book of the Dead*, p. 136; *Egyptian Heaven and Hell*, p. 89.

27. Budge, *Book of the Dead*, p. 137; the ancient Egyptians evidently believed that the Nile bubbled up out of these holes and flowed in two directions out of them (*Book of the Dead*, p. 163).

28. Budge, *Book of the Dead*, p. 345 nn. 1–2; *Egyptian Heaven and Hell*, pp. 177–79.

29. Budge, *Book of the Dead*, pp. 136, 284, 323, and 499; *Egyptian Heaven and Hell*, p. 128–29.

30. Budge, *Book of the Dead*, pp. 142–61; *Egyptian Heaven and Hell*, passim.

31. Budge, *Book of the Dead*, p. 145; *Egyptian Heaven and Hell*, p. 131.

32. Budge, *Book of the Dead*, p. 145; *Egyptian Heaven and Hell*, pp. 132–34.

33. Budge, *Book of the Dead*, p. 147; *Egyptian Heaven and Hell*, pp. 149–51, 156.

34. Budge, *Book of the Dead*, pp. 376, 124; the two quotations are from the Turin Papyrus and the Papyrus of Ani. See also Troy, "Mummeries," pp. 36, 38, 85.

35. Budge, *Book of the Dead*, p. 142; *Egyptian Heaven and Hell*, p. 106.

36. Budge, *Book of the Dead*, pp. 69, 404, 431, 450, 611, 505–6; see also *Egyptian Heaven and Hell*, pp. 89 and 197; and *Dwellers on the Nile*, p. 278.

37. Budge, *Book of the Dead*, p. 135. The diagram reproduced in figure 4.1, as well as the explanatory notes (at the right of the diagram) and the translations of the hieroglyphics (at the left), all derive from Budge (*Book of the Dead*, pp. 133–35). See also *Egyptian Heaven and Hell*, pp. 89, 197; *Dwellers on the Nile*, p. 214; and E. A. Wallis Budge, *Egyptian Ideas of the Future Life*, 3rd ed. (London: K. Paul, Trench, Trübner, and Co., 1908), p. 25. Budge dates this coffin map, which comes from the marble sarcophagus of the pharaoh Seti I, at 1350 B.C., in roughly the same period of Egyptian history that saw the writing of the Papyrus of Ani.

38. The diagram and the commentary on it can be found in Budge, *Book of the Dead*, pp. 131–32.

39. Budge, *Book of the Dead*, p. 353. On the opening pages of the *Wake* as a representation of the scattered body of Osiris, see Adaline Glasheen, "The Opening Paragraph," *A Wake Newslitter*, n.s., 2 (April 1965): 7; Atherton, *Books at the Wake*, p. 198; and Troy, "Mummeries," pp. 37, 41, 47.

40. "Hymn to Osiris," in Budge, *Book of the Dead*, p. 368.

41. As Budge notes, "the story of Osiris is nowhere found in a connected form in Egyptian literature, but everywhere, and in texts of all periods, the life, sufferings, death, and resurrection of Osiris are accepted as facts universally admitted"; he goes on to point out that the story of Osiris is told coherently only by such Greek writers as Plutarch, Diodorus Siculus, and Strabo (*Book of the Dead*, p. 53). The myth was, in other words, so formative a part of the ancient Egyptian consciousness that it could be told entirely by the allusion—as today for instance, one might invoke the whole story of the New Testament by naming Christ, or the whole order of Newtonian physics by mentioning "gravity." The summary of the myth of Osiris given in the text derives from Budge's account in his Commentary on the Book of the Dead at pp. 52–58 and 180–81; from that provided by Sir James Frazer in *The New Golden Bough*, abr. Theodore H. Gaster (New York: Mentor, 1964), pp. 384–89; and from Troy, "Mummeries," pp. 22–23.

42. This way of reading the myth of Osiris would have seemed alien to the ancient Egyptian, for whom the myth was reality. Any evocation of "sleep" as a way of comprehending the fate of Osiris, moreover, would have been equally baffling; for sleep is the center of a peculiarly modern fascination. Of the two or three thousand deities named in various books of the dead, none of any consequence seems to have been understood as the god who sent sleep and dreams into the human universe. In a way, the Egyptians had as little need for this kind of god as did the people of Homeric Greece: the god of sleep and the god of the land of the dead was the same god.

43. E.g., chapter I, "The Chapter of the Funeral Procession," in Budge, *Book of the Dead*, p. 365.

44. "The Chapter of Not Dying a Second Time," in Budge, *Book of the Dead*, p. 567.

45. Chapter CXXXIII, "The Chapter of the New Moon," in Budge, *Book of the Dead*, p. 507; the rubric instructs one to recite the chapter over a model of the boat of Ra that has been fashioned in green stone and purified in incense, in the presence of no one but one's son or father.

46. See, respectively, "The Chapter of the Funeral Procession" (chapter I) and chapter XVIII (without title) in Budge, *Book of the Dead*, pp. 408 and 512.

47. See, e.g., chapters CXLVII and CXXV, "A Chapter to Be Recited by the Deceased When He Cometh to the First Hall of Amentet" and "A Chapter to Be Recited at the Waxing of the Moon," in Budge, *Book of the Dead*, pp. 408, 512.

48. Chapter CLXXV, "The Chapter of Not Dying a Second Time," in Budge, *Book of the Dead*, pp. 562–63.

49. The adjectives and epithets given special emphasis in the text are from Budge's descriptions of Amenti and the Tuat in *Book of the Dead*, pp. 135–36ff., and in *Egyptian Heaven and Hell*, pp. 135, 138, 192.

50. Chapter XLV, "The Chapter of Not Rotting in Khert-Neter," in Budge, *Book of the Dead*, p. 460.

51. Budge, *Egyptian Heaven and Hell*, pp. 167, 119; *Book of the Dead*, p. 156.

52. Chapter XXXIV, "The Chapter of Lifting up the Feet and Appearing on Earth," in Budge, *Book of the Dead*, p. 478.

53. Atherton, *Books at the Wake*, pp. 194–95. Atherton notes that "Joyce uses the phrase 'Us, the real Us' twice in the *Wake* (62.26 and 446.36); it translates, 'I, even I,' in the royal plural as it was used by the Pharaohs in their inscriptions."

54. On Cheops, see Budge, *The Mummy*, p. 334.

55. See, for example, Budge, *Book of the Dead*, pp. 136–50, 315–16, and 395. In some books of the dead, serpent-headed butcher-gods and eaters of souls were assigned names thirty to forty syllables long, which the dead man needed to know and speak out loud if, for example, he did not want his face and groin gnawed off in the dark. In the presence of beings named "Hewer-in-pieces-in-blood, Ahibit, lady of hair" and "Lady of light, who roareth mightily, whose breadth cannot be comprehended. Her like hath not been found since the beginning. There are serpents over her which are unknown," immobility and speechlessness would be definite handicaps (*Book of the Dead*, pp. 411, 416).

56. *Explication of Finnegans Wake* 593.20–24. "The eversower of the seeds of light," apart from referring to invocations in the Papyrus of Nu ("the overseer of the seal"), evokes the gathering and regenerative force of the sun, which is now moving into our hero's consciousness "sowing seeds of light" and bringing warmth to the fields of the underworld. As one of the "cowld owld sowls" he is obviously a "cold old soul," but also, as the triply repeated word "owl" in the phrase suggests, a being possessed of nocturnal intelligence. The term "domnatory," therefore, conflates "dormitory" and "damnatory" ("of or assigned to damnation") in order to suggest that the underworlds of sleep and of traditional scriptures share an equivalence. Not necessarily the Egyptian deity "Tefnut" (who "seems to personify the power of sunlight" [Budge, *Book of the Dead*, p. 175), "Def-mut" reveals our hero, because asleep, to be a "deafmute."

"*Nuahs*," "*Mehs*," "*Pu Nuseht*," and "*tohp*," as others have noted, are simply the names and words "Shaun," "Shem," "The Sun Up," and "light" (Gr. *photos*) spelled backward. Since, in reading these words, one has to move backward, the inversions symbolize temporal reversal and renewal. For further discussion of the passage see Atherton, *Books at the Wake*, p. 193; Tindall, *A Reader's Guide to Finnegans Wake*, p. 307; Grace Eckley, "Looking Forward to a Brightening Day," in *A Conceptual Guide to Finnegans Wake*, p. 213; and Troy, "Mummeries," p. 80.

57. All details in this paragraph come from Budge, *Book of the Dead*, pp. 143, 153; *Egyptian Heaven and Hell*, pp. 94, 104–5, 114, and 124–25.

58. Budge, *Book of the Dead*, pp. 160–61.

59. Ibid., p. 429.

60. Ibid., pp. 460, 465, 459, and 561–65 respectively.

61. Budge, *Egyptian Heaven and Hell*, pp. 20–21, 94–95, 138, and 166; *Book of the Dead*, pp. 472, 564.

62. See, for example, Budge, *Book of the Dead*, pp. 136–37 and 154; *Egyptian Heaven and Hell*, pp. 48–63; *Dwellers on the Nile*, p. 280.

63. Budge, *Book of the Dead*, p. 346; see also p. 222.

64. Budge, *Book of the Dead*, pp. 339, 341, 367.

65. Frazer, *The New Golden Bough*, p. 389.

66. Budge, *The Mummy*, pp. 160–61.

67. Richard Selzer, "The Corpse," in *Mortal Lessons: Notes on the Art of Surgery* (New York: Simon and Schuster, 1974), p. 132.

68. See Troy, "Mummeries," p. 67. By quirk, the names of these four "Canopic" jars have nothing to do with the word "canopy"; they were so called by early Egyptologists who believed that Menelaus's pilot, Canopus, was buried in Egypt and worshipped there in the form of an inhumationary jar (Budge, *The Mummy*, p. 194).

69. Budge, *The Mummy*, pp. 160–65.

70. Budge, *Book of the Dead*, pp. 16–17, 447; *The Mummy*, pp. 160–61; elsewhere in the

Book of the Dead, the coffin and tomb are conceived of as an egg out of which the corpse is reborn (see, e.g., pp. 609, 611–12).

71. Budge, *The Mummy*, p. 178 n. 1.

72. Frazer, *The New Golden Bough*, p. 389; Erman, *Life in Ancient Egypt*, p. 308; Budge, *Book of the Dead*, pp. 250–55.

73. Reasons for locating Joyce's hero in a sycamore coffin are suggested by lines immediately preceding the passage, where the man lying dead to the world at the *Wake* hears the voices of four old men admonishing him: "... let your ghost hold no grievance. You're better off where you are, Sir, ... under your sycamore" (24.27–31). In the explicitly funereal and Egyptian context of the passage, which refers to "Healiopolis," "the land of souls," the otherworldly region of Sekhet Aaru ("the Field of Offerings"), Ushabti statuettes, and embalming procedures (24.18, 33–34 and 25.2, 3–4, 22–23), Joyce evokes the sycamore for two reasons.

Before Egyptian eschatological myths evolved into the elaborate forms of New Kingdom books of the dead, the Egyptians had simpler conceptions about what life after death would be; according to one such belief, the dead man traveled to a fertile underworld much like Sekhet Hetep or Sekhet Aaru—it was, in fact, called Aaru or Earu ("offerings")—where he could cultivate fertile wheat for eternity and "when tired in the evening ... sit under his sycamore" (Erman, *Life in Ancient Egypt*, p. 306).

Why a sycamore? "The scarcity of wood [was] quite a calamity for [ancient] Egypt" (Erman, p. 11). Since Egypt had few trees, the image of the shade-giving tree would likely have been made an attribute of the paradisaical afterlife; and since the sycamore was one of the few woody plants available to carpenters, virtually all of the wooden "inhumationary bric au brac" (77.33) hauled out of Egyptian tombs was fashioned of its wood: statues and statuettes, biers, funerary masks, the scribe Ani's two coffins, and so forth. Joyce's many references to "sycamores" in the *Wake* highlight the substantial alignment of the Book of the Dead with his own book of the dead, as reference to any of the following passages will attest; each refers also to ghosts, Amenti, beds or coffins, the absence of loved ones: 95.19–21, 203.20–21, 281.20–22, 384.1–5, 388.24, 397.22–24, 460.21–23, 476.14, 533.16–17, and 555.7–8.

In the *Wake* the sycamore coffin guarded at each of its "four coroners" (219.10) by the four old mourners is simply the sleeper's bed—which is elsewhere, according to the context of his dream, felt as a fluidly drifting boat, a layer of earth, or the vague matrix of compass points that define his orientation in the space outside of his body. For the sources of this note, see Erman, *Life in Ancient Egypt*, pp. 11, 193–94, 306, 451, and 453; Budge, *The Mummy*, p. 166, 210, 256, 257, and 260; Budge, *Dwellers on the Nile*, pp. 113 and 121; and Budge, *Book of the Dead*, pp. 285, 483, 617, and 619.

74. A prayer for deliverance from the attacks of worms comparable to that heard above in the *Wake* appears in the Papyrus of Nekhtu-Amen: "The Osiris, the royal scribe, Nekhtu-Amen, whose word is true, knoweth thee, he knoweth thy name. Deliver thou him from the worms which are in Ra-stau, which live upon the bodies of men and women, and feed upon their blood ..." (Budge, *Book of the Dead*, p. 156; see also McHugh, *Annotations*, p. 26). On "the idea of a heaven where wheat grew luxuriantly" and the mythic equation of wheat and the body of Osiris, see Budge, *Egyptian Heaven and Hell*, pp. 164–65; Frazer's lengthy discussion of Osiris's role as a god of the corn in *The New Golden Bough*, pp. 391ff.; and Troy, "Mummeries," pp. 68–70.

The reference to "Our Father" ("Papa Vestray" = L. *Pater Vester*) in the passage at hand bends back on the dreamer, the dead man himself: the prayer uttered by the four old men wishes that the corpse of "our father" won't be assailed by worms or damned to lakes of burning water. The allusion to Papa Westray, finally—the northernmost of the Orkney Islands—locates the passage at the borders of the known world.

75. Budge, *The Mummy*, pp. 161, 194–201; *Book of the Dead*, pp. 130–31, 191–92, 322.

76. In some versions of the myth of Osiris, Isis buried the scattered parts of her husband separately and had a funeral temple erected over each of the graves. See Budge, *The Mummy*, p. 278; *Book of the Dead*, pp. 55–56.

77. See Atherton, *Books at the Wake*, p. 198. For an illustration of the way in which the formulaic "I know thee" was invoked in books of the dead, see the passage from the Papyrus of Nekhtu-Amen, quoted in note 74.

78. Troy, "Mummeries," p. 35.

79. Budge, *Book of the Dead*, pp. 29, 62, 94, 70–73, 290, 317; *The Mummy*, p. 175. Some books of the dead contain a "Chapter of Setting Out for Orion"; the pyramid text carved into the walls of the Pharaoh Pepi I's tomb, for example, reveals that Pepi thought he had to "revolve in heaven like Orion" in order to attain immortality (Budge, *Book of the Dead*, pp. 85–86; *Egyptian Heaven and Hell*, p. 14).

80. The phrases from Twain's novel discussed in the text appear in the following chapters of *Huckleberry Finn* (New York: Norton Critical Editions, 1977): "Shore's your born," chapter 12, p. 59; "Your shuck tick's swell," chapter 20, p. 103; "texas," chapter 12, pp. 57, 58, chapter 13, p. 60, chapter 14, p. 64, and chapter 32, p. 175; "tow-linen," chapter 20, p. 106; "the road to Lafayette," chapter 31, p. 172; "dropped in our tracks," chapter 40, p. 215. On Joyce's extensive use of *Huckleberry Finn* in the *Wake*, see James Atherton, "To Give Down the Banks and Hark from the Tomb," *James Joyce Quarterly* 4 (1967): 75–83; R. P. Laidlow, "More Huck Finn in *Finnegans Wake*," *A Wake Newslitter*, n.s., 5 (October 1968): 71–73; Danis Rose, *James Joyce's Index Manuscript Holograph Workbook VI.B.46* (Colchester: A Wake Newslitter Press, 1978), pp. 18–31; and Danis Rose, "More on Huck Finn," *A Wake Newslitter*, n.s., 17 (April 1980): 19–20.

American sonorities informing other passages from the *Wake* on the New World ("No petty family squabbles Up There . . . nor no nothing" [454.36–455.2]) also often come from *Huckleberry Finn*, as Joyce acknowledges when he characterizes the stasis of peaceful requiescence explored at 454.26–455.29 as "Mark Time's Finist Joke" (455.29): when his hero is dead to the world (hence the "finish" and L. *finis* ["end"] in "Finist"), he simply lies there and "marks time," but in doing so, he also enters a New World.

In this New World, there is no work:

—Would you mind telling us, Shaun honey, . . . where mostly are you able to work. . . .

—Here! Shaun replied. . . . being too soft for work proper. . . . I am always telling . . . my answerers, Top, Sid and Hucky, now (and it is a veriest throth as the thieves' recension) how [I am] . . . disbarred after holy orders from unnecessary servile work of reckless walking of all sorts for the relics of my time. . . . Amen, ptah! (410.28–411.11)

In addition to "Tom, Sid, and Huck," this passage evokes Jim's term of endearment for Huck ("Huck honey"), and the names of the Egyptian deities "Amen," "Ptah," "Thoth." Through these ciphers the passage orients us again in a New World, like Amenti, where the man buried at the wake lives again in the rejuvenated, dreamed form of a son ("Shaun")—even while simultaneously enduring a vacant "vacation in life" amid "the relics of time." Because his body is enjoying heavenly peace while his renewed spirit is touring the New World, moreover, he doesn't have to do work. Instead, his "answerers" do his work for him. The reference here is to the *ushabti* statuettes that wealthy Egyptians had buried with them. Called "shabbty little imagettes" in the first chapter of the *Wake* (25.2; Atherton, *Books at the Wake*, p. 194), these little stone or sycamore statues of slaves were supposed to come to life in Amenti to do the dead man's work for him after he recited the spell known in the Theban recension of books of the dead ("thieves' recension") as "The Chapter of Not Doing Work in Khert-Neter" (Budge, *Book of the Dead*, pp. 30, 224, 629). The word *ushabti* literally meant "answerers" because the little slaves answered the master's commands (Erman, *Life in Ancient Egypt*, p. 317; see also Troy, "Mummeries," pp. 65–66).

As this passage finally suggests, what the Egyptians imagined happening "in the underwood" (360.14–15 ["the underworld" but also "under wood" and inside the coffin]) happens also in sleep: all action in dreams is performed by imaginary surrogates who do things that the inert, sleeping body cannot.

81. Illustrative of one critical attitude toward the *Wake* is the widely published and always amusedly told story of how Joyce never really read *Huckleberry Finn*. The story is based on a letter that Joyce wrote to one of his nephews living in New York; with the letter, Joyce forwarded a copy of *Huckleberry Finn* and, explaining that "I never read it and have nobody to read it to me and it takes too much time with all I am doing," he requested that his nephew "mark with blue pencil in the margin the most important passages of the plot itself and in red pencil here and there whenever the words or dialogue seem to call for the special attention of a European" (*JJ*, 699n.; *L*, III, 401–2). The spectral transaction by which *Huckleberry Finn* actually does find its way into *Finnegans Wake* suggests quite the opposite of what is usually assumed by people referring to this letter. Joyce knew the novel quite well. *Huckleberry Finn* appears in the *Wake* largely because it is a book that speaks in a common idiom of related concerns: much of Twain's novel takes place in the night, and all of it in the mind of a child. Joyce would also have found many of the central concerns of *Huckleberry Finn* falling right into alignment with the *Wake:* Twain's sustained interest in death, the night, witching and spirits, dream interpretation and dreams, and rebirth, which critics have recently regarded as a controlling theme of the book. In *Huckleberry Finn*, there are constant confusions between sleep and wakefulness, between the appearance of death and death itself; whole episodes and conversations might have come out of the *Wake*: "We slept like dead people," "De man ain't asleep, he's dead," and so forth (*Huckleberry Finn*, chapter 13, p. 64; chapter 9, p. 44). That such a book should have found its way into the *Wake*, finally, has to do with more than the exploited coincidence of the name "Finn": "Cat my dogs ef it ain't de powerfulest dream I ever seen," as Joyce, quoting Twain, copied in his notebook on *Huckleberry Finn* (Rose, *Index Manuscript*, p. 24).

82. For the sources of this paragraph on the mastabah tomb, see Budge, *The Mummy*, pp. 317–28; and Erman, *Life in Ancient Egypt*, pp. 310–14, who points out that most of the mummies bouldered down into the depths of mastabah tombs, disappeared centuries ago, victims of the energetic trade of tomb robbing.

83. On the evolution of the mastabah tomb, see Troy, "Mummeries," pp. 61–62, and Erman, *Life in Ancient Egypt*, pp. 311–14.

84. *Explication of Finnegans Wake 395.22–23.* "Going to boat" suggests "going to bed," and also entering the boat of Ra in the nightworld, the boat which bears Joyce's sleeper to the gates of dawn. "Verges on the chaptel" evokes "the virgins of the chapel" because our

hero's dream is erotic here; but it also names "the verses of the chapter" in this book of the dead. "Nema Knatut," finally yields "Tutank(h)amen" spelled backward; once again, the reversed spelling symbolizes the temporal reversal necessary to the process of renewal.

85. Atherton, *Books of the Wake*, p. 193. This title may also refer to the eleventh-dynasty "Book of the Two Ways," an early book of the dead. See Budge, *Book of the Dead*, p. 137; *Egyptian Heaven and Hell*, pp. 12–13.

86. On the ceremony of "Opening the Mouth," see Budge, *Book of the Dead*, pp. 246–55 and 278–79; Budge, *Dwellers on the Nile*, p. 169; and Troy, "Mummeries," pp. 74–77.

87. Budge, *Book of the Dead*, pp. 433–34.

88. Ibid., p. 246. The bracketed phrase incorporates into the sentence understandings that Budge develops elsewhere in his discussion of the "opening of the mouth."

89. Ibid., pp. 525–26.

90. Ibid., pp. 36, 38, 48, 89, 285–86.

91. Ibid., p. 485.

92. Ibid., pp. 32, 433–37. On "words of power" (98.26, 345.19)—*Heka*, in the Middle Egyptian—see Atherton, *Books at the Wake*, p. 194, and Troy, "Mummeries," pp. 76–77. This was the term by which Egyptians characterized all words and phrases in the Book of the Dead.

93. Budge, *Book of the Dead*, pp. 414–15 and 278–79.

94. Ibid., p. 524.

95. Between October 1921 and August 1922, the Joyces lived at 9 *rue de l'université* in Paris (*L*, II, lviii); "there they slept three in one room, one in the other. In the larger room Joyce kept a series of potted Phoenix palms: as one died, it was replaced by another. He said the plant reminded him of the Phoenix Park, and he attached great importance to it" (*JJ*, p. 518).

The period of time in which Joyce carried out this impractically expensive little ritual was the same as that in which he finished proofreading and saw the publication of *Ulysses* (in February 1922). Although it may have seemed to others that Joyce was moodily unproductive between February and August 1922, the "great importance" he attached to this ritual suggests that he was actually beginning to compose the *Wake*, although not in words, the first of which were drafted in March 1923. Instead, he seems to have mulled over the story of HCE's rise and fall by contriving the resurrections of potted phoenix palms—and, undoubtedly, by observing the enspathed perianths of their blossoms. This may be the only instance in literary history in which the genesis of a book has been recorded in the quotidian ritual by which an author maintained his house plants. The anecdote suggests how stubbornly Joyce's symbolisms sought attachment to concrete reality.

Information on the phoenix palm in the text derives from the article "Date Palm" in the *Encyclopedia Britannica*, Fourteenth Edition, 1929 (vol. 7, p. 68).

96. For an Egyptian association of the palm, the god Ra, and the "Opening of the Mouth," see the "Hymn to Ra" quoted in Budge's Commentary to the Book of the Dead (p. 109): "Hail to thee, Ra, . . . whose shrine is hidden, thou god in thy boat. . . . At his will the Nile appeareth, when the greatly beloved Lord of the palm-tree cometh he maketh mortals to live. . . . His name is hidden from his children in his name 'Amen' . . . Beloved art thou as thou passest through Egypt. When thou risest thou sendest forth light. . . ."

97. Budge, *Book of the Dead*, p. 462; from the Papyrus of Nu.

98. Budge, *Dwellers on the Nile*, p. 73.

99. On the origin of the sacrament of Extreme Unction, see Kenneth Scott Latourette, *A History of Christianity*, rev. ed. (New York: Harper and Row, 1975), vol. 1, pp. 532–33. Latourette sees the Christian practice of anointing originating in the primitive belief that unction promoted physical and—by inferential extension—spiritual healing.

100. Budge, *Book of the Dead*, pp. 575 and 589; the parenthetical question in the first of these quotations is Budge's.

101. Budge, *Book of the Dead*, p. 254.

102. Tindall, *A Reader's Guide to Finnegans Wake*, p. 167.

103. Back panel, "Revlon Milk Plus 6 24-Hour Moisturizer."

104. "Cuticura": 164.30, 291.F6, 550.18; "Harlena": 164.31; "Nivea": 583.22; "Pond's Cold Cream": 461.2–3, 526.29, 527.13. The last of these cosmetics, even more so than the others, seems always to be associated with Issy.

105. Budge, *Book of the Dead*, pp. 29–48; Budge, *The Mummy*, p. 171.

106. The quotations conflate three separate passages from the Papyrus of Nu: the Invocation to chapter CXXVI; the spells of transformation into birds in chapter CXLIX; and the naming of doors in the House of Osiris in chapter CXXV (Budge, *Book of the Dead*, pp. 614, 300, and 591, respectively). For comparable passages and formulae in the Papyri of Ani and Nebseni, see *The Book of the Dead*, pp. 409–12, 394, and 547.

107. For a list of such chapters, see Budge, *Book of the Dead*, pp. 37–39; for the corresponding Commentary, see pp. 304–10. "Chapters of the Changing into a Hawk of Gold" and into a "Divine Hawk" can be found at pp. 523–35, the "Chapter of Changing into a Benu Bird," at pp. 552–53.

As Atherton has pointed out (*Books at the Wake*, pp. 195–96), the hero of the *Wake* dreams of his own transformation into a Bennu bird in the following passage:

The phaynix rose a sun before Erebia sank his smother! Shoot up on that, bright Bennu bird! *Va faotre!* Eftsoon so too will our own sphoenix spark spirt his spyre and sunward stride the rampante flambe. Ay, already the sombrer opacities of the gloom are sphanished. Brave footsore Haun! Work your progress! Hold to! Now! Win out, ye divil ye! The silent cock shall crow at last. The west shall shake the east awake. Walk while ye have the night for morn, lightbreakfastbringer, morroweth whereon every past shall full fost sleep. Amain. (473.16–25)

Once again, the necrology of the Book of the Dead becomes a reconstruction of the night in the *Wake:* the process by which the Arabian phoenix ("Erebia") rises from the gloom of Amenti ("Erebus") into the fiery light of a new day is simply that by which Joyce's sleeper drifts through the nocturnal unconsciousness into which he vanished ("sphanished") toward the moment of awakening at dawn; in its risen light, Phoenix Park ("sphoenix spark") will once again rise up into the vision of this phoenixlike being. As additional details suggest, however, the phoenix into which the dead man (hence the "pyre" in "spyre") imagines himself transformed here is less a bird than Shaun ("Haun"), his son, who travels into a New World (tomorrow) after the old man has died and vanished from the Old World ("the phoenix rose a son before Erebus [death] sank his mother").

Tindall points out that in "Va faotre!" Joyce not only reproduces the Biblical command to be fruitful and multiply in twentieth-century terms (Fr. *Va foutre!* "Go fuck"), he also names the phoenixlike agent of his sleeper's life after death: the Breton *Va faotre* means "my son" (*A Reader's Guide to Finnegans Wake*, p. 247).

108. As Atherton notes (*Books at the Wake*, p. 193), the phrase "My heart, my mother! My heart, my coming forth of darkness!" "is verbatim from Chapter XXXB" and XXXA of the Book of the Dead. See Budge, *Book of the Dead*, pp. 371 and 454 ("Chapters of Not Letting the Heart Be Taken Away").

109. Atherton, *Books at the Wake*, p. 200. On Aapep, see Budge, *Book of the Dead*, pp. 159–60, 166, 109, 198, 345n.; on Uachet, pp. 189, 265, 401; on both see Troy, "Mummeries," pp. 51–54.

110. For a Freudian reading of the Book of the Dead, see Roheim, *The Gates of the Dream*, pp. 145–49, 303, 312–15, and 372–73.

111. See "The Chapter of Making the Soul to Be Joined to its Body" and "The Chapter of Not Letting the Soul Be Kept Captive in Khert-Neter" in Budge, *Book of the Dead*, pp. 228, 471–74.

112. *Explication of Finnegans Wake 328.31–35* The Egyptian hieroglyphic "tet" ( ), which literally meant "firmness" or "stability," pictographically signified the sacrum bone of Osiris, the part of his spine located closest to his genitals; the word by which we know this bone, equivalently, comes from the Latin *os sacrum* ("the sacred bone"). Amulets of gold, carnelian, lapis-lazuli, and gilded heart-of-sycamore wood shaped in the form of the tet were frequently a part of Egyptian tomb furnishings; usually they were draped around the neck of the mummy, and usually books of the dead contained chapters whose recitation would empower the corresponding organs of the deceased's new body to stand. See Budge, *Book of the Dead*, pp. 263, 319–20, and 616–20; *The Mummy*, pp. 259–60; and Troy, "Mummeries," pp. 34–35, 49, 73.

"The night of 'the things of the night'" and "the night of setting up the Tet in Tettu" are equated in the Papyrus of Ani. Both seem to refer to the occasion on which Horus, the rising sun, defeated Set and the powers of night in the last hours of night before the dawn, thereby completing the reconstruction of Osiris and ensuring his resurrection. See Budge, *Book of the Dead*, pp. 276 and 424–27.

113. From the Papyrus of Nebseni, in Budge, *Book of the Dead*, pp. 476–77; see also pp. 228, 474–75.

114. From the Papyrus of Ani, Budge, *Book of the Dead*, p. 621. A pillow or headrest made of sycamore wood was sometimes placed beneath the head of the Egyptian corpse; often it was the same pillow on which the man had slept night after night in his bed while alive, and often it was inscribed with words from "The Chapter of the Pillow." See Budge, *Book of the Dead*, p. 321; *Dwellers on the Nile*, pp. 57–58; *The Mummy*, pp. 210–11.

115. Erman, *Life in Ancient Egypt*, pp. 306, 317; Budge, *Book of the Dead*, pp. 139ff. and 206; Budge, *Egyptian Heaven and Hell*, pp. 41–63 and 91.

116. From "The Chapter of Coming Forth by Day after Passing through the Aamhet" in the Papyrus of Ani, Budge, *Book of the Dead*, p. 483. "Aamhet," Budge informs us in a footnote, was "a chamber in the domain of Seker, god of death."

5. THE IDENTITY OF THE DREAMER

1. Somewhere at issue in the *Wake*'s extended play with tailors and tailoring is the whole question of sleep's relation to "fitness." Everyone has heard the story of the energetic octogenarian who bounces out of bed every morning having required only an hour or two of sleep; and everyone knows the darker counterstory of the depressive teenager who cannot keep his eyes open anywhere, for anyone. To these stories one adds the leg-

ends—of Napoleon, for instance, who believed that a child needed six hours of sleep a night, a woman five, and a real man only four; or of Schopenhauer, who found it impossible to think unless he got a solid twelve hours a night. Stories like these raise questions of what sleep accomplishes that enables sleep requirements to vary so widely from individual to individual. And they are complicated by others that show how greatly people tailor sleep to suit themselves and their needs. Why is it that some people waken out of beds that look as crisp and unwrinkled as if they had hardly been slept in, while others crawl out of spaces that look as if they had been sacked? What happens down there?

People who have studied these things invariably note that the restorative powers of sleep have little to do with any such "healing processes" as folklore attributes to a changed metabolism. Though body temperature falls slightly in the night (see 597.32–34), the heartbeat decelerates (see 608.10–11), and the musculature relaxes, the most dramatic of the night's alterations sweep through the head, where distinctions between the purely physiological and the purely psychological grow very hazy indeed: both the evolved need for sleep and sleep's ability to reinvigorate originate in the brain. It would of course be extreme to claim, as some have, that the need for sleep is purely psychological (or physiological), because the whole area is one in which distinctons between the mind and the body break down entirely. Perhaps the only thing of which we can be certain is that by "redressing" one, sleep "will make a newman if anyworn" (596.36–597.1ff. ["of anyone" "worn"]): "after a goodnight's rave and rumble . . . he [is] not the same man" (41.14–15).

For further discussions of the subject, see Andre Tridon, *Psychoanalysis, Sleep and Dreams* (London: Kegan Paul, Trench, Trubner, 1921), pp. 11–15; Ernest Hartmann, *The Functions of Sleep* (New Haven: Yale Univ. Press, 1973), p. 68; and Luce and Segal, *Sleep*, pp. 21–29, 108–9.

2. Like every other element in the paragraph, its syntax is retailored in order to "describe the night itself." Its first sentence, like the state of sleep, is passive and void of identifiable person ("The fall . . . is retaled"); while in the second ("The great fall . . . entailed . . . the pftjschute"), the object is just a foreign and blurred version of the subject (Fr. *chûte* = Eng. "fall"). Since we find "the fall" entailing a version of itself, moreover, rather than a distinct effect, causal relations have also clearly disintegrated "(for was not just this in effect which had just caused that the effect of that which it had caused to occur?)" (92.33; cf. 482.36–483.1). At every level, the grammar is elaborately replicating the perceptual character of dreams.

We know that these syntactical niceties are deliberate because other passages in the *Wake* self-consciously discuss them. *Finnegans Wake* is more thickly riddled with passive constructions—or "deponent[s]" (187.30)—than any teacher of writing would ever care to point out, because "passivism" (137.33) together with "being sinned" and "being been," is a condition of the night ("being been" would signify a purely passive form of being). "Has it become to dawn in you yet that the deponent, the man from Saint Yves, may have been (one is reluctant to use the passive voiced) may be been as much sinned against as sinning?" (523.7–10). A "deponent" in the legal sense since he alone emits all the conflicting evidence over which he refuses to budge, the *Wake*'s "pacific subject" is also a "deponent" in the grammatical sense, since in sleep he takes a form outwardly passive though internally active, at least until "dawn dawns" in him. He is also entirely like "the man from St.Ives" in lying at the heart of a riddle of apparently stupefying insolubility whose resolution, as here and as throughout *Finnegans Wake*, turns out to be very simple. As the recurrent rhythm of "As I Was Going to St. Ives" reminds us throughout the *Wake* (e.g., at 12.29–31, 215.15–17, 330.1–4), all the dizzily proliferating appearances in the dream finally reduce to a single "one," and he is simply sleeping.

Reference to the "relief map" will clarify some choice instances of the passive voice in *Finnegans Wake:* "it was attempted by the crown" (86.6–7 [sl. for "head"]) feebly and unsuccessfully; and "as if that were not to be enough for anyone" (85.20–21), "little headway, if any, was made" (85.21–22). This is the case, "it was felt by me" (537.22–23), because the owner of the head "to whom reference has been made had been absent" (39.28–29), although "it was not unobserved of those presents" (92.22–23). The passive voice in *Finnegans Wake* in general replicates the "passivism" of the "tropped head."

3. Vinding, "James Joyce in Copenhagen," p. 149. On the identity of the sleeper, see Edmund Wilson, "The Dream of H. C. Earwicker," *The Wound and the Bow* (New York: Oxford Univ. Press, 1947), pp. 243–71; Ruth von Phul, "Who Sleeps at *Finnegans Wake?*" *James Joyce Review* 1 (June 16, 1957) : 27–38; James Atherton, "The Identity of the Sleeper," *A Wake Newslitter,* n.s., 4 (Oct. 1967) : 83–85; Hart, *Structure and Motif,* pp. 81–83; Bernard Benstock, "L. Bloom as Dreamer in *Finnegans Wake,*" *PMLA* 82 (March 1967) : 91–97, and *Joyce-Again's Wake* (Seattle: Univ. of Washington Press, 1965), p. 215; Robert Martin Adams, *James Joyce: Common Sense and Beyond* (New York: Random House, 1966), pp. 178–81; and Michael Begnal, "The Dreamers at the *Wake:* A View of Narration and Point of View," in Begnal and Grace Eckley, *Narrator and Character in "Finnegans Wake"* (Lewisburg, Pa.: Bucknell Univ. Press, 1975), pp. 19–123.

The views expressed in these places, representative of those circulating in the criticism, fall into four main groupings, according to which: (1) the dreamer is a single sleeping man; (2) the dreamer is Joyce himself; (3) the dreamer is a "universal mind"; and (4) there is no single dreamer, but actually ten or several. Of these views, the first is most consistent both with Joyce's remarks on the subject and with the remarks of Joyce's co-workers and publicists (Budgen, Gillet, and all the writers represented in *Our Examination*). Not simply Joyce's reading of the *Wake* makes this the most sensible approach to the book, however, but repeated indications given everywhere in the text itself. There we read, for instance, that all "the traits featuring the *chiaroscuro* coalesce, their contrarieties eliminated, in one stable somebody" (107.29–30). That this "one stable somebody" (not ten) is identified as "our social something" humanizes and particularizes him.

4. Oh! breathe not his name, let it sleep in the shade,
Where cold and unhonor'd his relics are laid;
Sad, silent, and dark be the tears that we shed,
As the night-dew that falls on the grass o'er his head.

But the night-dew that falls, though in silence it weeps,
Shall brighten with verdure the grave where he sleeps;
And the tear that we shed, though in secret it rolls,
Shall long keep his memory green in our souls.

Thomas Moore, *Moore's Irish Melodies* (Boston: Oliver Ditson Co., 1893), rev. ed., p. 80.

Hodgart and Worthington (*Song,* pp. 9–10) have pointed out that Joyce incorporated into *Finnegans Wake* the titles of all but two of Moore's 124 *Irish Melodies,* together with the names of the original Irish airs to which they were set (Moore wrote "Oh! Breathe Not His Name," for instance, to the tune of "The Brown Maid"). While many readers apprised of this discovery have seen in Joyce's subsumption of "Moore's melodies" (439.9–

10) an instance of a mechanical list-making tendency presumed to inform the *Wake* as a whole, the example of "Oh! Breathe Not His Name" will suggest that this is not the case at all. Like other works to which Joyce alludes in the *Wake*, the *Melodies* appear in the book because they develop many of the same themes as those that Joyce necessarily plumbed in his "reconstruction of the nocturnal life"; they deepen the senses of passages in which one finds them. Born of a late Romanticism already accustomed to finding the dream superior to reality, the *Melodies* could not have been written without the words "*night*" ("Oft in the stilly night, / Ere slumber's chain has bound me"), "*sleep*" ("When daylight was yet sleeping"), "*dream*" ("'Twas one of those dreams"), "*death*" ("When in death I shall calm recline") or variants of these terms, one or another of which occurs in every other of Moore's lines: if one strings together enough phrases from the *Melodies*, a protoversion of *Finnegans Wake* emerges. Joyce would have found in "tummy moor's maladies" a parallel, native, if somewhat soupy version of his own work (492.34).

5. "The composite structures which occur in dreams in such immense numbers are put together in an equal variety of ways. . . . Their strangeness disappears completely when once we have made up our minds not to class them with the objects of our waking perception, but to remember that they are the products of dream condensation and are emphasizing in an effectively abbreviated form some common characteristic of the objects which they are thus combining. Here again the common element has as a rule to be discovered by analysis. The content of the dream merely says, as it were, 'all these things have an element x in common'" (Freud, *On Dreams*, trans. James Strachey [New York: Norton, 1952], p. 47; see also *ID*, 327–30, 354–61).

6. Freud likens the condensing power of the dreamwork to a "procedure by means of which Galton produced family portraits: namely by projecting two images on to a single plate, so that certain features common to both are emphasized, while those which fail to fit in with one another cancel one another out and are indistinct in the picture" (*ID*, 328). A procedure exactly of this kind generates all the names assigned to the *Wake*'s dreamer. Readers skeptical of Freud might turn to Aristotle to find confirmed the same understanding: according to Aristotle, "the most skillful interpreter of dreams is he who has the faculty of observing resemblances," not differences (*De Divinatione Per Somnum*, 464^b, *The Basic Works of Aristotle*, ed. Richard McKeon [New York: Random House, 1941], p. 630; quoted in *ID*, 130 n.1, 355 n.1).

7. Glasheen, *Third Census*, p. lxxii.

8. Thomas Parr, a Shropshire farmer, earned cultural fame not simply by living to the age of 152 (1483–1635), but by purportedly getting a girl into trouble when he was well over 100 and by taking a second wife when he was 122. His virile example seems to have inspired the aging rakes of the court of Charles I to have the old man carted to London in a special litter so that he could be put on exhibition before the king. Unfortunately, Old Parr died during the trip. Buried in Westminster Abbey along with the great figures of English history, he became a kind of local Adam in the English imagination; and the term "Old Parr," not at all an idiosyncratic invention of Joyce's, became a long-lasting synonym for a "very old man." One still finds it in twentieth-century thesauruses.

9. In one way of thinking, everything that has ever gone into our hero's mind has stayed there, the vast bulk of it sorted out and relegated to the trash heap of amnesic obscurity because of its irrelevance, its uselessness, its triviality: still, "we keeps all and sundry papers" (147.24–25), and "each, every, all is for the retrospectioner" (265.5–6). An immense accumulation of "litterish fragments lurk dormant" in "our mounding's mass"

(66.25), and they make him something of a vast personal "museomound" of memories (8.5), many of which lie in his unconscious. Where by day the items in this "museo-mound" are retrieved and brought to mind according to a reality principle, in order to suit the exigencies of the present, by night, as a dim "musing" moves through the "mound" (hence again "museomound"), they are stirred into new and exotic configurations—in much the same way that real particles of broken glass, torn paper, and other scraps are stirred into new and exotic configurations in "a collideorscope" (143.28 ["kaleidoscope"]). All of these terms are ciphers for our "scrapheaped" hero's "deafadumped" body, within which the "dummpshow[s]" of dreams take place (590.1). On the hypermnesia of dreams, see *ID*, 45–51.

10. In the opening pages of the book, for example, one finds "pa's malt," "brewing," "Jhem or Shen" (3.12–13 ["John Jameson's Whiskey"]); a "jiccup" (4.11 ["hiccough"]); "rushlit" (4.19 ["rushlight" is sl. for "liquor"]); "yeasty" (4.21); "guenneses" (4.24 ["Guinness's"]); "Toper's Thorp" (4.27 [a community of heavy drinkers]); the "craythur" (4.29 [whiskey]); "balbulous" (4.30 ["bibulous"]); "the alltitude and malltitude" (4.33 ["malt," and the sl. "in one's altitudes," meaning "drunk"]); "liquor" (4.34); "Wassaily Booslaeugh" (5.5–6); "Hootch" (5.9); "vine" and soured wine "vinegar" (5.11); "tippling full" (6.8); "thirstay" (6.14); "Fillagain" (6.14 [as a bartender must]); "agrog" (6.19); "filling" (6.22); "tap up his bier" (6.24 ["beer"]); "bock" (6.26); "finisky," "barrow-load of guenesis" (6.27 ["fine whiskey," "barrel-load of Guinness's"]); "the tootal of the fluid" and "the twoddle of the fuddled" (6.28 [the "total of the fluid" generating "twaddle" among the "fuddled")—not to mention the heavily sustained evocations of "Finnegan's" major "blackout." What rises out of the play of these terms is a sense of our hero's life in the day. Comparable networks of references pertaining to Dublin, to luminaries of "the homely protestant religion" (530.28), to "Scandiknavery" (47.21), and to five recurrent family members would allow us to see the *Wake*'s protagonist as a Protestant Dubliner and family-man of Nordic lineage.

11. Since he is not particularly successful (589.12–590.3), he dreams, like Bloom, of better things. The names of private estates in his neighborhood preoccupy him (264.15ff.), as do the success stories of "wine and spirit merchants" who have thrived. Adam Findlater intrigues him as greatly as he intrigued Bloom in *Ulysses* (*U*, 58), and since some call him "Gunne or Guinn" (44.12), we can infer that he finds himself in competition with businesses operated by Michael Gunn, whose Gaiety Theatre was a place of entertainment, and with the Guinnesses, who made a fortune selling alcohol. In the night, where his inadequacies are wishfully redressed, the nicknames "Gunne or Guinn" reveal our hero's "investments" in these people.

12. For more on pub-names in the *Wake*, see the *Gazetteer*, passim, and Benstock, *Joyce-Again's Wake*, pp. 32–37.

13. Joyce spoke of the Shaun section of the *Wake* as "a description of a postman travelling backwards in the night," adding cryptically that "in reality it is only a barrel rolling down the River Liffey" (*L*, I, 214). Shaun's "work [at] postal night duty" (*L*, III, 107) has to do with the dreamer's *literacy*—his ability to carry and deliver letters.

14. Roland McHugh, *The Sigla of Finnegans Wake* (Austin, Texas: Univ. of Texas Press, 1976).

15. Henry Morton Robinson, "Hardest Crux Ever," *A James Joyce Miscellany*, Second Series, ed. Marvin Magalaner (Carbondale, Ill.: Southern Illinois Univ. Press, 1959), pp. 195–207; Philippe Sollers and Stephen Heath, "Joyce in Progress," *Tel Quel* 54 (June

1973) : 10–11 n. 3; Philippe Sollers, "Joyce and Co.," trans. Stephen Heath, *Tel Quel 64* (Winter 1975) : 11; and Jean-Louis Houdebine and Philippe Sollers, "La Trinité de Joyce," *Tel Quel 83* (Spring 1980) : 51–55, 69–76, and 80–81.

16. The terms are finally demoralizing because they consign to growth-capable people the status of fixed objects. For an excellent discussion of the histories of these words, see the entries on "Individuality" and "Personality" in Raymond Williams, *Keywords: A Vocabulary of Culture and Society* (New York: Oxford Univ. Press, 1976), pp. 133–36 and 194–97; for a discussion of their relation to the novel and the social reality of which it is a manifestation, see Ian Watt, *The Rise of the Novel* (Berkeley and Los Angeles: Univ. of Calif. Press, 1957), pp. 9–27.

17. Marcel Brion, "The Idea of Time in the Work of James Joyce," *Our Exagmination Round His Factification For Incamination of Work in Progress* (1929; rpt. New York: New Directions, 1962), pp. 33, 31.

18. Mercanton, "The Hours of James Joyce," p. 237; Jan Parandowski, "Meetings with Joyce," in *Portraits of the Artist in Exile*, p. 159. Compare also Joyce's remarks to Arthur Power on Turgenev: "he is like all the classical writers who show you a pleasant exterior but ignore the inner construction, the pathological and psychological body which our behaviour and thought depend on. Comprehension is the purpose of literature, but how can we know human beings if we continue to ignore their most vital functions" (Power, *Conversations with James Joyce*, p. 56).

19. Knowing one's "tumptytumtoes" through one's eyes, to illustrate the contortions that consciousness can perpetrate on the body, is to relocate one's "twoe nails on the head" (110.14–15) and also to ignore the vast underground that *Finnegans Wake* explores in its treatment of "matters that fall under the ban of our infrarational senses" (19.36–20.1). One way of comprehending these "infrarational senses," which involve no knowing at all, would be simply to move those "tumptytumtoes," which tend to vanish, on the principle "out of sight, out of mind," at the first appearance of a line of print. "You'll feel what I mean" (468.18). "I fee where you mea" (295.36–296.1).

20. For representative exceptions, see E. L. Epstein, "James Joyce and the Body," in *A Starchamber Quiry: A James Joyce Centennial Volume, 1882–1982*, ed. E. L. Epstein (New York: Methuen and Co., 1982), pp. 73–106; Solomon, *Eternal Geometer*; Benstock, *Joyce-Again's Wake*, pp. 267–82; and Norman O. Brown, *Love's Body*.

6. NOCTURNAL GEOGRAPHY

1. On "Finn" as an aspect of the dreamer, see also *L*, III, 422n., 472, 473n.; Adaline Glasheen, "Out of My Census," *The Analyst*, no. 17 (1959) : 23; and Hart, *Structure and Motif*, pp. 81–82.

2. Solomon, *Eternal Geomater*, p. 120.

3. Ellmann points out that while writing *Work in Progress*, Joyce grew "interested in variations and sameness in space, in the cubist method of establishing differing relations among aspects of a single thing, and he would ask Beckett to do some research for him in the possible permutations of an object" (*JJ*, 551). A number of scholars have clarified our sense of how extensively Joyce researched modern conceptual alterations of space and object-relations like these in order to render distinct the alien spatialities of the night. Solomon, in *Eternal Geomater*, discusses at length "Joyce's fascination with . . . the fourth dimension and non-Euclidean geometry, which accompanied the introduction of

the theory of relativity" (pp. 120ff); and Roland McHugh, in *The Sigla of Finnegans Wake*, calls attention to entries in Joyce's notebooks that show him investigating the higher dimensional geometries of Riemann and Lobachevski (pp. 74–75). Finally, too, by reformulating "object relations" in such a way as to see in "objects" immanent versions of the subject, psychoanalysis had its impact on the *Wake*.

For further discussion of Joyce's interest in post-Newtonian science, see Ihab Hassan, "Joyce and the Gnosis of Modern Science," and S. B. Purdy, "Lets's Hear What Science Has to Say: *Finnegans Wake* and the Gnosis of Science," in *The Seventh of Joyce*, ed. Bernard Benstock (Bloomington: Indiana Univ. Press, 1982), pp. 207–18.

4. For other evocations of "Fe Fo Fum," see the "Index of Motifs" in Hart's *Structure and Motif*, p. 222. Giants who wished to extend their vocabularies beyond the humdrum "Fo Fum" might consult the appropriate dictionary, L. Sainean's *La Langue de Rabelais* (Paris, 1922), to which Joyce referred in order to write "the Book of Doublends Jined" (*L*, I, 255). There they might find listed continental expletives on the order of "*Par Mahon!*," "*Corbieu!*," and "*Vraybis!*" (cf. 253.33, 253.36, and 254.26). It is impossible, as they say, to give an adequate translation, but roughly these things work out, over other intonations as well, to the English "Fe Fo Fum!" For examples of how the "language of Rabelais" is put to work in *Finnegans Wake*, see the *Annotations*, pp. 4, 20, 118–19, 124, 252–54, and the corresponding pages in the *Wake*. For an account of Joyce's use of Sainean, see Claude Jacquet, *Joyce et Rabelais: Aspects de la création verbale dans Finnegans Wake*, Études Anglaises, Cahiers et documents, no. 4 (Paris: Didier, 1972).

Heavy quotations from Macpherson's Ossianic poems and extended references to the literature on Finn throughout *Finnegans Wake* work, in part, to the same gigantic effect. On these giant languages, see Fritz Senn, "Ossianic Echoes," *A Wake Newsletter*, n.s., 3 (April 1966):25–36; and Swinson Ward, "Macpherson in *Finnegans Wake*," *A Wake Newsletter*, n.s., 9 (Oct. 1972):89–95.

5. The appearance of "the great Finnleader himself" at the end of I.viii (214.11), the heavy layering of quotations from Macpherson's *Temora* at the end of I.vii, and the comparable quoting of "The Youthful Exploits of Finn" at the end of I.v (see *Annotations*) would work comparably to signal a fall back into the dimensionless sleeping body.

Compare also the general (and representative) structure of II.i, which begins with heavy evocations of a "sleeping giant" (219.18, 219.20–21, 220.26, 221.29, 222.12, 222.14) and which closes, on the announcement that "one must recken with the sudden and gigantesquesque appearance" of the book's hero (253.29–30), amid pages streaked heavily with references to "Fe fo fum" (254.20–21), "the language of Rabelais" (252.33–35, 253.33, 253.36, 254.14, 254.26 [see *Annotations*]), and the names of giants (246.5–6, 254.20, 258.9). The appearance of all these ciphers at the beginning of the chapter means that the "mime" or "dumbshow" of which the chapter treats is played out behind the eyes and between the ears of the *Wake*'s "sleeping giant"; their appearance at the end of the chapter means that the spatially perceptible appearances of a dream are "mak[ing] off in a thinkling" (256.4) as HCE passes out into the dimensionlessness of deeper sleep.

6. Mink, *Gazetteer*, p. xi.

7. Heinrich Straumann, "Last Meeting with Joyce," trans. Eugene and Maria Jolas, in Maria Jolas, ed., *A James Joyce Yearbook* (Paris: Transition Press, 1949), p. 114: "In answer to my question, as to whether a knowledge of the local conditions in Dublin would make the reading of *Finnegans Wake* any easier, [Joyce] replied firmly in the negative. One should not pay any particular attention to the allusions to place-names, historical

events, literary happenings and personalities, but let the linguistic phenomenon affect one as such. If a premise to the reading of the work must be sought, then it should be a knowledge of the philosopher Giambattista Vico, to whom he was greatly indebted."

8. Three typical verses:

Brian O Linn was an Irishman born
He lived at a time when no fashions were worn
His teeth stuck out and his eyes far in
"I'm a beautiful creature," says Brian O Linn.

Brian O Linn had no breeches to wear
He got an old sheepskin to make him a pair
With the fleshy side out and the wooly side in
"They'll be lovely and cool," says Brian O Linn.

Brian O Linn had no shirt to his back
He went to the miller and borrowed a sack
Then he puckered the meal bag in under his chin
"Well, they'll take them for ruffles," says Brian O Linn.

A redaction of versions given in Colm O Lochlainn, *Irish Street Ballads* (New York: Citadel Press, 1960), pp. 30–31, and by Robin Roberts, *Irish Street Songs*. Stinson Records, SLP 63, 1963.

9. This would be the appropriate point at which to take "polar bearing[s]" (602.30) in the *Wake*'s "amstophere," where "polar" ("antithetical") does not always mean "arctic," but where "bear" (Gr. *arktos*) sometimes does.

Because the earth comes to an end when sleep begins, place-names ordinarily designating the limits of knowable terrains often mean, in *Finnegans Wake*, eschatological "ends of the world" as well. The *Wake* moves its hero to "Landsend," for instance (291.1 [but not necessarily to Cornwall]), or to "Finishthere" (17.23 [Fr. *Finistère*, "land's end"]), because these toponyms designate sites at which earth vanishes. And parts of the night comparably move our hero into unearthly "antipodes" or "polar" regions (472.17, 435.12, 567.35), simply because by losing his identity in sleep he discovers "his polar andthisishis" (177.33), in a world "down under" (321.32). Perhaps the most resonant of all the *Wake*'s ciphers for "the end of the world" is "west." "All goes west" (85.15) in *Finnegans Wake*—"well to the west" (3.21)—because at a primal level "west" and "night" are identical. Etymologically deriving from the Indo-European root *wespero* ("night, evening"), the English "west" is cognate with the Latin *vesper* and the Greek *hesperos* ("night"), all these terms designating the "timeplace" (416.24) at which the earth spills off the face of the earth as the Daily World, "ebbing wasteward, leaves to the soul of light its fading silence" (235.6–7). As the space out of which night erupts, "westerness" (21.22) generates complex associations throughout the *Wake*, and particularly because, whether at day's or life's end, to take the "journey westward" or "to go west" (D, 223; 85.15) means idiomatically "to die." On "Westerness," see also 66.32–34, 295.1, 319.6, 407.36, and 457.20 ("look for me always at my west").

"Bearing right" along in these "polar bearing[s]" (97.4), "bears" move heavily throughout *Finnegans Wake* because, among all things else, they are good at "hibernating" (79.5), "with bears' respects to" (358.30 ["which bears respect to"]) the night. Whether as a "Fitz Urse" (97.5 [L. *ursus*, "bear"]) or "Bernesson Mac Mahahon from Osro" (340.17 [Da. *bjorn*, Anglo-Ir. *mahan*, It. *orso*, "bear"]), "our tribal furbear" and "grizzliest" hero is a "quhare soort of mahan" (132.32, 340.21, 16.1 [Anglo-Ir. *mahan*, "bear"]) who rests in peace beneath a Wakean "graphplot" reading "as urs now, so yous then!" (535.3–4 [the line plays the L. *ursus*, "bear" into the formulaic epitaph—"As us now, so you one day"— to remind us that we all spent last night hibernating, "dead to the world"]). For more on bears, see 43.1, 51.15, 97.5–12, 200.1, 253.31, 255.15, 267.22, 339.27–340.21, 373.14–16, 430.6, 539.31; Glasheen, *Second Census*, pp. 166–67, *Third Census*, p. 25.

10. As the examples will suggest, the apparently playful process by which Joyce alters the name "Dublin" throughout *Finnegans Wake* works in fact with some precision to map out the conditions of the night; every altered spelling of "Dublin" bears scrutiny for what it "reveils" not to be happening in the "knock[ed] out" and "tropped head" of a figure who lives in "nill, Bud" (620.3), when not in "Dumbaling" (34.1, 586.15 [since sleep renders him "dumb" in both senses of the word]). His nightlife takes place less in "Dear Dirty Dublin" than in the "dire dreary darkness" of "deep dorfy doubtlings" and deeply nagging "Doubtlynn" (136.20, 374.18, 248.7), because it is altogether unclear "whether . . . the audible-visible-gnosible-edible world exist[s]" for him (88.5–7). Even the name "Dublin" seems to play into this nocturnal toponomastics; historically deriving from the Gaelic *dubh-linn* ("black-pool") and originally referring to a deep pool at the mouth of the River Liffey (*Gaelic Lexicon*, p. 381), it refers equally throughout *Finnegans Wake* to the "blackholes" and "black pools" into which sleep immerses everyone (549.5, 204.18). Like all terms in *Finnegans Wake* and all images in dreams, "black pool" seems to refer outwardly toward the real world of Dublin, although it also refers inwardly, to the "sleeping giant" of "Novo Nilbud," within the fathomless "Blackpool" (88.34) of whose "tropped head" the *Wake* takes place.

11. Since the "sooty" in which the *Wake* unfolds is a negation of the city and all structures upholding it, vanished cities like "Troy," "Carthage," and Goldsmith's "Deserted Village" move spectrally through the book to remind its reader that "everynight life" itself takes place in a vanished civilization (see, e.g., 17.26ff., 55.3–5). Passing references to utopian "noplaces" like Samuel Butler's "Erewhon" work to a comparable effect (391.15, 152.18, 510.27).

12. Compare substitutions for "Erin" like "Wherein?" (16.21), and "Even" (130.3 ["night"]). An old poetic name for Ireland—"Inisfail" or "Innisfallen"—comparably modulates into "in his Falling" (72.7) and "in his fallen" (476.13) in order to evoke the "Inishfeel" (510.33 ["innish-feel"]) of someone "in his fail" (462.8). And under the direction of the *Wake*'s "hibernian knights underthaner" (335.26 [its Hibernicized "Arabian nights' entertainer"]), even the name "Hibernia" describes the night: in the *Wake*, "Hibernia" refers as much to the slow business of "hiberniating" (316.15) as it does to a state knowable in wakefulness.

13. Mink, *Gazetteer*, p. 536.

14. Joyce himself made this point at more eloquent length: "Classical literature represents the daylight of human personality while modern literature is concerned with the twilight, the passive rather than the active mind. We feel that the classicists explored the physical world to its limit and we are now anxious to explore the hidden world, those undercurrents which flow beneath the apparently firm surface. But as our education was based on the classical, *most of us have a fixed idea of what literature should be, and not only literature but also of what life should be.* And so we moderns are accused of distortion; but our literature is no more distorted than classical literature is. . . . When we are living a normal life we are living a conventional one, following a pattern which has

been laid out by other people in another generation, an objective pattern imposed on us by the church and state. But a writer must maintain a continual struggle against the objective: that is his function. The eternal qualities are the imagination and the sexual instinct, and the formal life tries to suppress both. Out of this present conflict arise the phenomena of modern life" (Arthur Power, *Conversations with James Joyce*, p. 74; italics mine).

15. Bernard Benstock, "Every Telling Has a Taling: A Reading of the Narrative of *Finnegans Wake*," *Modern Fiction Studies* 15 (Spring 1969) : 5.

16. According to the *Skeleton Key*, HCE was "caught peeping at or exhibiting himself to a couple of girls" and "was witnessed by three drunken soldiers, who could never be quite certain of what they had seen" (pp. 7–8); according to the *Third Census*, he is "a homosexual who annoys three soldiers," though "the soldiers deny it [and] say HCE exposed himself to two girls" (p. xxxi); the *Reader's Guide* notes simply that "he did something in the Park, as, according to others, Adam did something in the Garden." "His sin . . . remains indefinite" (p. 58). For an excellent discussion of the crime, see Norris, *Decentered Universe*, pp. 44–47.

17. A statement that it would be quite feasible to make of our hero in the Daily World, for instance—"of course, how wouldn't we know where he had his little existence and what he wished and could do"—might take, in the altered predication of "the Evening World," a form reading, "off course" "how wooden" "we nowhere" "he addle liddle" "exsystems" "end" what he "swished" "uncouth" "doom" (410.18, 16.33, 10.26, 4.28, 148.18, 239.32, 319.32, 239.35, 483.18). Dissolved predicates like these are everywhere in *Finnegans Wake*.

18. Eugene Jolas, "My Friend James Joyce," in *James Joyce: Two Decades of Criticism*, p. 14; see also Dominic Manganiello, *Joyce's Politics* (London: Routledge & Kegan Paul, 1980), pp. 224–25.

19. For an excellent account of Joyce's relation both to the women's movement of his own day and to current feminist critical practice, see Bonnie Kime Scott, *Joyce and Feminism* (Bloomington: Indiana Univ. Press, 1984). Readers bothered by the male form depicted in the two maps of "the Evening World" might note simply that our hero has no choice but to sleep in the ridiculous "mirthday suit" he was born with (35.4). Since the polymorphic interior of this "mirthday suit" teems with heavily "mixed sex cases" (48.2), moreover, the visible outlines made evident in the two diagrams are misleading. "Sapphrageta and Consciencia [are] undecidedly attached to" the *Wake*'s "sleeping giant," as a reading of "Anna Livia Plurabelle" will make clear, and complementarily he is "attached" to them (542.19–20 ["Sappho," "suffragette"; the obscure term in this formulation, of course, is "attachment"]).

20. For an excellent exploration of the ideologically subversive effects of the language of the *Wake*, see Colin MacCabe's *James Joyce and the Revolution of the Word*, pp. 133–71.

21. The seven Latin adverbs are those taught to priests for use in the confessional ("let us pry" [188.8]). Recalling them helps the confessor to determine the nature of his client's sin.

22. The extent of Joyce's global exasperation with the sociopolitical world in which he found himself is suggested in part by his odd living habits: in the course of 36 years of "marriage," he and Nora moved between 150 and 200 times, cutting a kind of noman's land through seven countries (see Ellmann's list of "Joyce's Addresses" in the *Letters*, II,

lv–lxii). We might detect in the terms that make up the nocturnal map of "neurope," then, some of Joyce's exasperation with the West, and also share some of the complex glee that he must have felt in discovering "Berlin," for instance, to be "barelean" (550.8 [not much there]); free-living but pricily prohibitive "New York," where his son Giorgio sought to make a future, to be just another "new yoke," "new yoke" (137.32); the French to be the "fringe" (311.33 [hardly the center]); or "Saville Row fashions" to be "civille row faction[s]" (320.7), in that unaffordable "fashions," by visibly distinguishing "*The haves and the havenots*" (295.L2), also make visible potential "civil war factions." The evidence of Joyce's letter shows him perpetrating this kind of nomenclatorial decimation on places he actually lived in whenever he grew discontent with them: a boring summer in London's Campden Grove found it altered into "Campden Grave" (*L*, I, 317 ["that grove was inhabited by mummies"]); "Antwerp" was interesting for a while, but as the mosquitoes began to compete with its lures, it became "Gnatwarp" (*L*, I, 245; 140.2); even his own publishers, Faber and Faber, when they failed to do a job to his satisfaction, got transformed into "Feebler and Fumbler" (*L*, III, 320).

Finally, too, there are Joyce's explicit statements on the Western world. In a letter of 1934, he wrote to his son, "it is or should be patent that the conduct of public affairs in all the great countries of the world between Russia and America both included makes stupid, boring, irritating, backwards England seem like a land inhabited by non-bloodthirsty *homines sapientes*" (*L*, III, 312). And while this makes England seem an island of light in a sea of barbarism, we should recall his remarks on the subject to Arthur Power: "I decided that I could never have become a part of English life, or even have worked there, for somehow I would have felt that in that atmosphere of power, politics, and money, writing was not sufficiently important" (Power, *Conversations with James Joyce*, p. 64).

23. The allegiance of the *Tel Quel* group, particularly in its Maoist phase, to *Finnegans Wake* is well known; both in China and in the *Wake*, its editorial staff seems to have perceived formal alternatives to the Western status quo. For Philippe Sollers, "Joyce's refusal to indulge in the slightest dead pronouncement is exactly *itself* the political act"; "*Finnegans Wake* is the most formidably anti-fascist book produced between the two wars" (Philippe Sollers, "Joyce and Co.," trans. Stephen Health, *Tel Quel* 64 [Winter, 1975]: pp. 3, 4).

The extent to which the *Wake* has been perceived to move at the fringes of all systems is perhaps best suggested, however, by an opaquely uninterpretible detail included in Herman Blei's "Terrorism, Domestic and International: The West German Experience," in National Advisory Committee on Criminal Justice Standards and Goals, *Report of the Task Force on Disorders and Terrorism* (Washington, D.C., 1976), p. 498. We learn here that Gudrun Ensslin, the West German minister's daughter and student turned member of the Baader-Meinhof gang, had worked for some time prior to her career in terrorism on an incompleted doctoral thesis on *Finnegans Wake*. The interesting question is what connection Blei perceived to link the two forms of evident anarchy.

24. For a sober assessment of Joyce's politics and an excellent account of his passage through socialist allegiances into loose adherence to a form of rational anarchy as espoused by Bakhunin, see Manganiello, *Joyce's Politics*.

25. "While we should like to drag attentions [very reluctantly] to the Wolkmans Cumsensation Act" (616.24–25) which stirs him towards morning (hence "welkin"), as "sensation" starts to return to his "tropped head" (come-sensation), so to remind him of the

imminence of another day of labor. Sleep, as a reading of *Civilization and Its Discontents* or a chat with the person down the street will suggest, is just a built-in compensation act for anyone on the staff of the Daily World.

26. A steady stream of ciphers in *Finnegans Wake* serves to remind us that our hero, "being personally unpreoccupied" (558.4), has been "discharged from [his] last situations" (529.14 [yesterday's]) and is ephemerally on "*haloday*" from beginning to end of the book (353.7 ["halo" because he is in another world]). Such ciphers would include references to "pensionees" (301.19), people on "relief" (409.20), "bushman's holiday[s]" (110.28 ["busman's"]), bank holidays like "St. Lubbock's Day" (292.5 [see "Avebury" in *Third Census*]), and "day[s] off" generally (306.F2). As the *Wake* moreover shows in the play of these terms, the "industrially disabling" aspect of sleep is so invariably moralized that, depending on who notes whom doing it, the same essential act of relaxation is susceptible to different colorations and forms. The "regular layer" (181.32) shown stratified in the relief maps is "out of a job" (181.30) when he feels guilty like an "oaf, outofwork, one removed from an unwashed savage" (191.11). When he does not, he is simply taking his well-deserved "leisure like a god on pension" (24.17)—or better yet, "like a gourd on puncheon" (373.20 ["gourd" because the "vegetative" state of sleep renders him a "human vegetable," and a hollow one at that; "on puncheon" because sleep leaves him "absintheminded"]).

27. Since the night automatically injects an "armistice" into the conflicts whose working-out is the making of the Daily World, another version of this line of thought furls out of the *Wake*'s heavily recurrent references to "truces," "armistices," and peace agreements. The two maps of "the Evening World" show our hero with "his defences down during the wapping stillstand" (588.5; 347.11 [Ger. *Waffenstillstand*, "truce"]), on "the uneven day of the unleventh month of the unevented year" (517.33–34)—where an "uneven day" would be a very "odd" one, like night; an "unleavened" interval of time would entail no "rising" and no real "events" ("unevented"); and "the eleventh hour of the eleventh day of the eleventh month" of 1918 would refer to the signing of the Armistice that ended World War I. "It's the armitides toonigh," then, "and there's to be a gorgeups truce" (11.13–15 [as well as a "gorged-up truth" that will reveal, in the form of the dream, unconscious conflicts underlying real ones]).

28. "irreducible antagonism": Mercanton, "The Hours of James Joyce," p. 212.

29. Joyce: "As an artist I am against every state. Of course I must recognize it, since indeed in all my dealings I come into contact with its institutions. The state is concentric, man eccentric. Thence arises an eternal struggle. The monk, the bachelor, and the anarchist are in the same category. Naturally I can't approve of the act of the revolutionary who tosses a bomb in a theatre to destroy the King and his children. On the other hand, have these states behaved any better which have drowned the world in a bloodbath?" (*JJ*, 446).

7. VICO'S "NIGHT OF DARKNESS"

1. W. Y. Tindall, *James Joyce: His Way of Interpreting the Modern World* (New York: Charles Scribner's Sons, 1950), p. 71. Tindall goes on to note that "the three ages have languages suitable to each. In mute, divine periods, men use hieroglyphics: picture-writing, coats of arms, and fables. A heroic age brings proverbs and metaphor, the language of the imagination. In the human age, language becomes abstract or vulgar. . . .

Attracted by Vico's interest in myth, language, and family, Joyce preferred him to other cyclists."

2. Samuel Beckett, "Dante . . . Bruno. Vico . . Joyce," in *Our Exagmination*, p. 8.

3. Book 5 of *The New Science*, "The Recurrence of Human Things in the Resurgence of Nations," 1046–96.

4. Book 4 of *The New Science*, "The Course of Nations," 915–1045.

5. Max Harold Fisch and Thomas Goddard Bergin, "Introduction" to *The Autobiography of Giambattista Vico*, (Ithaca: Cornell Univ. Press, 1944), p. 20. Here I should acknowledge a general indebtedness to Fisch and Bergin's wonderful "Introduction" to *The Autobiography*. Other works I have found useful are *Giambattista Vico's Science of Humanity*, ed. Giorgio Tagliacozzo and Donald Phillip Verene (Baltimore: The Johns Hopkins Univ. Press, 1976); and *New Vico Studies* 1 (1983).

6. Compare to Vico's evolutionary account of consciousness these representative views of others who wrote at his time:

". . . the condition of man [in nature] is the condition of war of everyone against everyone; in which case everyone is governed by his own reason . . ." (Thomas Hobbes, *Leviathan*, in *The English Philosophers from Bacon to Mill*, ed. Edwin A. Burtt [New York: Random House, 1939], p. 163).

". . . the power of forming a good judgment and of distinguishing the true from the false, which is properly speaking what is called Good sense or Reason, is by nature equal in all men. . . . Inasmuch as [reason or good sense] is the only thing that constitutes us men and distinguishes us from the brutes, I would fain believe that it is found complete in each individual, and in this I follow the common opinion of the philosophers, who say that the question of more or less occurs only in the sphere of the *accidents* and does not affect the *forms* or natures of the *individuals* in the same *species* (René Descartes, "Discourse on the Method of Rightly Conducting the Reason and Seeking the Truth in the Sciences," in *The Philosophical Works of Descartes*, trans. Elizabeth S. Haldane and G. R. T. Ross [New York: Dover, 1955], pp. 81–82).

"To consider political power aright, and derive it from its original, we must consider what state all men are naturally in. . . . The state of nature has a law of nature to govern it, which obliges everyone; and reason, which is that law, teaches all mankind who will but consult it, that, being all equal and independent, no one ought to harm another in his life, health, liberty, or possessions" (John Locke, "An Essay Concerning The True Original, Extent and End of Civil Government," *Two Treatises of Government*, in *The English Philosophers from Bacon to Mill*, pp. 404–5). Vico's, of course, was not the only interesting deviation from the mainstream Enlightenment thinking represented in these passages.

7. Vico, in fact, has to provide an elaborate account to explain how his first men arrived in a bestial state of nature, since ideological orthodoxy held that all mankind descended from a rational Adam. In order not to violate "sacred history" in his "gentile history," Vico supposes that after the Flood, Noah's sons wandered from the culture of their father and roved in the wild for centuries, until they reverted to animalistic beasts void of any property of mind but sensation (*NS*, 192ff).

8. "It is another property of the human mind that whenever men can form no idea of distant and unknown things, they judge them by what is familiar and at hand. . . ." "This axiom points to the inexhaustible source of all the errors about the beginnings of humanity that have been adopted by entire nations and by all the scholars. [For, the

"conceit of scholars"] will have it that whatever they know is as old as the world" (*NS*, 122–23, 127).

9. Compare Bloom's actions during his homecoming on June 16, 1904 (*U*, 732–34), to those of Homer's hero:

[Odysseus'] servants kept carrying the scrapings [of the dead suitors] and put them outdoors.

And when they had set in order the entire hall
They led the serving women out of the well-based hall
Between the round-room and the excellent fence of the court.
They cooped them in a narrow place from which was no way to escape.
. . . a cable from the dark blue-prowed ship
[Telemachos, at Odysseus's order] threw round the pillar of the great round-room and tied it on,
Tightening it high up, so none could reach the ground with her feet.
As when either thrushes with their long wings or doves
Rush into a net that has been set in a thicket,
As they come in to roost, and a dreadful bed takes them in;
So they held their heads in a row, and about the necks
Of all there were nooses, that they might die most piteously.
They struggled a little with their feet, but not very long.
They brought Melanthios through the forecourt and the yard,
Cut off his nose and ears with the pitiless bronze,
And tore off his private parts for the dogs to eat raw,
And chopped off his hands and feet in their furious spirit.
Then, when they had washed off their hands and their feet,
They went into the house of Odysseus, and the work was done.

(Homer, *Odyssey*, XXII, 450–79, tr. and ed. Albert Cook [New York: W. W. Norton and Co., 1974], p. 309).

10. Fisch and Bergin, "Introduction" to *The Autobiography*, pp. 104–5.

11. Any discussion of an originating moment is destined to be problematic, for reasons treated eloquently by Stephen Heath in "Ambiviolences: Notes for reading Joyce," in *Poststructuralist Joyce*, p. 61. If we take it for granted here that a secure knowledge of origins is impossible, however, nothing at all releases us from the nagging and human necessity of having to try to reconstruct them. It is precisely this double bind that contributes in part to the modernist anxiety discussed by Michel Foucault in his explorations of "The Analytic of Finitude" and "The Retreat and Return of the Origin" (in *The Order of Things: An Archaeology of the Human Sciences* [New York: Vintage, 1973], pp. 312–18, 328–35). Asking "how the deepings did it all begin" (428.5) is an essential exercise everywhere in both *The New Science* and *Finnegans Wake*, everywhere leading into the same obscure terrain as does thinking about the night.

12. Fisch and Bergin, "Introduction" to *The Autobiography*, p. 50:

The state of nature was one not of static equality, but of differentiation, inequality, and dialectical change. There was inequality between the organized family and the "lawless vagrants" still living in that chaos out of which the family grew; inequality among the vagrants themselves. The more violent and enterprising of the latter raided the homesteads of the settlers and burned or carried off their crops, but they preyed also on the weaker and more helpless of their own kind, who were thereby driven to throw themselves on the mercy of the settlers. . . . The family unit was thus enlarged and still further differentiated, and the tension between its elements was heightened. To the distinctions of sex and generation there was added a distinction of blood and class.

The serfs of the family had less in common with its blood members than with the serfs of another; the father of a family had more in common with the father of another than with his own serfs. To secure themselves against the mutinies of their serfs as well as against outlaw invasions, the fathers formed mutual alliances, patrician orders, "heroic states," with the fathers as citizens and the serfs as plebs. . . .

For further exploration of the comparison between Vico and Marx, see Giorgio Tagliacozzo, ed., *Vico and Marx: Affinity and Contrasts* (Atlantic Highlands, N.J.: Humanities Press, 1983).

13. Gifford and Seidman, *Notes for Joyce: An Annotation of James Joyce's "Ulysses"* (New York: E. P. Dutton, 1974), p. 24.

14. See Herbert Gorman, *James Joyce* (New York: Reinhart & Co., 1948), p. 32, and JJ, 306–7; Ellmann additionally notes that Joyce's "decision to rewrite *Stephen Hero* as a *Portrait* in five chapters occurred appropriately just after Lucia's birth" (*JJ*, 296).

15. Karl Marx, "The Eighteenth Brumaire of Louis Napoleon" in *On Revolution*, vol. 1 of the Karl Marx Library, tr. and ed. Saul K. Padover (New York: McGraw-Hill, 1971), p. 245.

16. The Charter of 1173 in which Henry II granted the city of Dublin to the city of Bristol is quoted at length in the *Wake* (545.14–23). Joyce slightly adjusts the charter's language, however, altering the signature of "Henricus Rex" to "Enwreak us wrecks" and adding to the charter's wording the giant Albion's "Fe Fo Fum" and an economic undertone in "Fee for farm." While Henry II granted Dublin simply to "my subjects at Bristol," finally, the "Enwreak us" of Joyce's modified charter grants Dublin to the citizens of Bristol "that from the farthest of the farther of their fathers to their children's children they do inhabit it and hold it." As Joyce's language here suggests, and as Vico's history reaffirms, single political acts engender consequences that endure through history.

17. Both the verb and preposition derive from the Middle English *lich* ("body") and its cognate *lik* (adjectival "like"), both in turn from the Germanic root **liko-* ("body, shape, form").

18. Sigmund Freud, *The Question of Lay Analysis*, tr. and ed. James Strachey (New York: Norton, 1950), p. 43; cf. also pp. 46 and 86–87, and *ID*, 588: "We can guess how much to the point is Nietzsche's assertion that in dreams 'some primaeval relic of humanity is at work which we can now scarcely reach any longer by a direct path'; and we may expect that the analysis of dreams will lead us to a knowledge of man's archaic heritage, what is psychically innate in him. . . . psycho-analysis may claim a high place among the sciences which are concerned with the reconstruction of the earliest and most obscure periods of the beginnings of the human race." In his later work, Freud moves psychoanalysis toward this kind of Vichian reconstruction, becoming increasingly absorbed with the collective character of the neurosis and more akin to Vico than Joyce may have supposed.

19. Fisch and Bergin, "Introduction" to *The Autobiography*, p. 11.

20. Freud, "'The Antithetical Sense of Primal Words': A Review of a Pamphlet by Karl Abel," in *On Creativity and the Unconscious: Papers on the Psychology of Art, Literature, Love, Religion*, ed. Benjamin Nelson (New York: Harper and Row, 1958), p. 62.

21. Mercanton, "The Hours of James Joyce," p. 221.

22. Ibid.

23. For other work on etymology that comparably explores the presence of the body beneath language, see Theodore Thass-Thienemann, *The Subconscious Language* (New York: Washington Square Press, 1967), and *The Interpretation of Language: Understanding the Unconscious Meaning of Language*, 2 (New York: Jason Aronson, 1968). See also Richard Broxton Onians, *The Origins of European Thought* (rpt.; New York: Arno Press, 1973).

24. Beckett, "Dante . . . Bruno. Vico . . Joyce," *Our Exagmination*, pp. 10–11.

25. The abstract English noun "freedom" originates in an entirely comparable class distinction, since its Anglo-Saxon etymon *freo*, originally meaning "not-enslaved," was conferred on the blood-sons of tribal chiefs in order to distinguish them from the rest of their fathers' property.

8. "MEOPTICS"

1. "Vision atrophied": Henry Miller, "The Universe of Death," in *The Henry Miller Reader*, ed. Lawrence Durrell (New York: New Directions, 1959), p. 210. Proponents of this view would do well to reflect on the fact that during "one great part of our existence"—and it's not sleep—vision atrophies, if one does it right. The eyes are only a fraction—a heavily intellectualized and reifying fraction—of the entire body.

"Lack of visual imagery": Levin, *James Joyce*, p. 175.

2. Luce and Segal, *Sleep*, pp. 64ff.; as the authors go on to point out, "anyone sitting in his own living room, watching a sleeping pet, might have observed the functional blindness of sleep. Indeed, many people sleep with their eyes half open, unaffected by movements around them." Luce and Segal also call attention to the work of researchers who have flashed lights into the eyes of people asleep with their eyelids taped open only to elicit no movement, no memory, no response; sleep blinds.

3. For other occurrences of the trashed "fiat" in the *Wake*, see the "Index of Motifs," Hart's *Structure and Motif*, p. 222.

4. For more "umbrella history," see 24.33, 52.26–27, 57.23 ["gamps"], 98.3 ["bumbershoot"], 106.32, 220.32, 248.1, 277.L3, 309.17–18, 315.19, 361.19, 373.20–21, 380.15, 449.14, 520.15 [Sp. *paraguas*, "umbrella"], 527.8, 530.28–29, 537.6, 568.7, 601.6, and 620.1.

5. One particularly dark scene in the *Wake's* "umbrella history" involves a legal action "heard by Judge Doyle" (574.9) and a jury of "fellows all of whom were curiously named after doyles" (574.31–32) in which chief testimony is "delivered in doylish" by a "Doyle" from "the Doyle's country" (575.9–10, 6–7). Resolving by way of the observation that "no property in law can exist in a corpse" (575.5 [and this presumably includes vision]), this "trial" resembles the dream, and comparable "trials" in the *Wake*, in part because it hinges on missing evidence.

6. "Moles," "bats," "owls," and other creatures endowed with gradated forms of blindness and night vision flit through the *Wake's* extended darkness in order to remind the reader of HCE's fluctuating "unsightliness" in sleep. "Peatrefired [petrified] under the batblack night" (405.35–36), the *Wake's* "peepeestrilling" hero (276.20 [It. *pipistrello*, "bat"]) is "blind as a batflea" (417.3) and so moves through the night engaged in vast sensory-deprivation games like "batman's biff" (337.3) and "blondman's blaff" (508.17)—not to mention "Deadman's Dark" and "deafmen's duff" (87.33, 467.17). Like the word

"bat," the word "owl" comparably overlays many otherwise "basically English" words in *Finnegans Wake* to remind us "owl" (37.29 ["all"]) that "owl" vision or intelligence experienced by the "cowld owld sowl" who sleeps at the *Wake* (553.20 ["cold old soul"]) is "owlwise" nocturnal (78.30). For more on "moles," see 129.4, 145.31–32, 57.85, 271.L4, 310.1, 509.26, 576.25; on "bats," see 151.33, 178.27 [It. *pipistrello*, "bat"], 180.27, 215.32–33, 221.33 [Fr. *chauve-souris*], 272.8, 276.20–21, 289.27, 337.3, 348.3–4 [Russ. *bitva*], 349.8, 374.19, 446.11, and 597.14; on owls, see also 4.11, 6.9, 107.22, 230.3, 331.19, 489.36, and 621.11.

7. "immense shadow": Breon Mitchell, "Marginalia from Conversations with James Joyce," in Clive Hart and Fritz Senn, eds., *A Wake Digest* (Sydney: Sidney Univ. Press, 1968), p. 81.

8. "not always night in dreams": Glasheen, *Third Census*, p. xlvii.

9. All of the "meoptical" details laced over the first page of the *Wake* again suggest, though from another perspective, that the moment in HCE's nighttime reconstructed in the paragraph to which we have been repeatedly returning will leave him in the morning with only the "blank memory of [a] hatless darky" (515.33–34); but now we are in a position to see why that "blank memory" should be attributed to a "hatless darky." The negated "hat" evokes the empty head, of course, while the "darky" resolves into a man made dark to the core; sleep turns all people into "darkies" of sorts (175.30, 293.13, 356.17, 603.27). As a "bamboozelem mincethrill," therefore (515.28)—the "bamboo" making blind[s], the "booze" "blacking out," and the condition of sleep generally "bamboozling"—the *Wake*'s hero becomes a spectral "Masta Bones" playing "*on the bones*" (515.32, 36; 341.8), in part because he resembles, in being "blacked out," a castanet-playing "tristy minstrel" (521.22); but also because he resembles a skeleton who "reconstruct[s]" dark "funeral games" for us (515.21–25).

From these details, we might draw broader inferences about the *Wake*'s allusions to black spirituals and its erratic employment of black American idioms, which its bartending Irish hero would likely not know in any detail: like others, these languages operate symbolically in the *Wake* because "blackness" and "spirituality" are quintessential properties of the night. The lyrics of most of the minstrel-show airs, Stephen Foster songs, spirituals, and comparable items listed by Hodgart and Worthington in *Song* turn out, from this perspective, to be cannily descriptive of the dark thought passing through the "Black and All Black" interior of "The Blackamoor's Head" (59.4, 2). In a "black modern style"—and spiritually—they show "Masta Bones" aware, like "Old Black Joe" (175.33–36; cf. 141.27), that "Gone over the bays!" (95.6 [and "the days," since it is night]), though "deeds bounds going arise again" (55.5 ["These Bones Gwine To Rise Again"]) when his body overcomes sleep's arrest ("deeds bound") by resurrecting in the morning. In the meantime, like John Brown's, his "body lies a-mouldering in a grave" of sorts, "while his shoul comes merging along" (364.9–10; cf. 415.21–22). Because inner conflict murders sleep even in the deep of night, however, "Ain't No Hiding Place Down There" (233.7). Still, like "Old Man River," but because his mouth is shut, "the old man . . . don't say nothing" (599.34–35; 288.5–6). And so forth. All of these lyrics, and comparable ones listed in Hodgart and Worthington, situate the *Wake*'s "darky" in a "New World" (not necessarily America) like that met in the night.

Putting this subject into perspective, finally, Mercanton recalls an occasion on which Joyce "had gone to bed late, got up in the night to work, dreaming about [a] young Negro dancer whose performance had charmed him" (p. 225). Joyce's comment on the dream

(p. 227)—"That's what I was made for, a little Negro dance"—puts him into sympathetic identity with that dark figure performing in the dark; and it also suggests that in all the black idioms and songs strewn through the *Wake* he saw languages and art-forms "jazz-like" his own (511.11 ["just like"]): "jazztfancy [and just fancy] the novo takin place of what stale words whilom were woven with" (292.20–21).

10. A number of passages in *Finnegans Wake* that critics have customarily treated as clear narratives susceptible to visualization ought therefore to be "blacked out" because, steeped in terms evoking sightlessness, they too have nothing essential to do with vision. The second chapter of *Finnegans Wake*, for instance, which climaxes in the story of the encounter with "the Cad" and closes with "The Ballad of Persse O'Reilly," seems largely to reconstruct an auditory dream—one consisting primarily of sounds in the absence of all vision: much of it takes place in "Earwicker's" ears, not his eyes. It is immediately before the encounter with the Cad that the reader is warned to "keep black!" (34.34). And "The Ballad" itself is performed, "after a brisk pause at a pawnbroking establishment" (41.29–30), with "an overflow meeting of all the nations in Lenster fullyfilling the visional area" (42.20–22); since there are exactly zero nations in the province of "Leinster," the detail suggests that HCE's "visional area" is as empty as that "lens" in "*Lens*ter": "a nation wants a gaze" in this extremely "vidual" part of the *Wake* (43.21–22 [and only when our hero gets one, presumably, will he see "A Nation Once Again"]).

11. Since there are, in fact, about 120 million rods and six million cones in the retina, the cited detail informs us that our "aglo-irismaimed's" vision, at this moment in his sleep, is extremely dim and "vidual": "if the whole population of the United States of America were made to stand on a postage stamp, they would represent the rods on a single retina"; "the number of cones is about the same as the population of Greater New York." See S. L. Polyak, *The Retina* (Chicago: Univ. of Chicago Press, 1941), p. 447; the quotations are from R. L. Gregory, *Eye and Brain: The Psychology of Seeing* (New York: McGraw-Hill, 1966), p. 49.

12. Bigelow, *The Mystery of Sleep*, p. 54; the italics are his.

13. Elsewhere, the *Wake* calls attention to "the millioncandled eye" (25.26[and retina]) of its "benighted irismaimed" in ways that are "sootably" "hard to see." At the end of "Anna Livia Plurabelle," for instance, the two washerwomen whose gossip constitutes that chapter briefly sight an unidentifiable "glow" "pharphar" in the dark (214.10–215.10 [Gr. *pharos*, "lighthouse"]); and particularly because the part of the night reconstructed here is not primarily visual—"who could see?" (213.7)—disagreement arises as to what the "glow" is. "You're thinking of Astley's Amphitheayter," one woman therefore chides the other, and "the ghostwhite horse of the Peppers. Throw the cobwebs from your eyes, woman . . . !" (214.13–17). These odd "cobwebs" are probably the dreamer's retinas: "the ancient name of the membrane, because of its thinness, was, in Greek, *arachnoeidês* . . . which means the 'cobweb tunic'. . . . At a later period [it] was compared . . . with a fishing- or casting-net" [L. *rete*] and so acquired the name 'retina'" (Polyak, *Retina*, p. 145; see also, in the *Wake*, 131.18–19 and 477.12).

The lines from "Anna Livia" under our scrutiny, moreover, call attention to what the washerwoman does *not* see in "cobbwebbed" eyes: and what is not seen is "Pepper's ghost," which Bloom associates in *Ulysses* with nocturnal phosphorescences (*U*, p. 151); it was a "stage illusion produced by projector & glass screen" (*Annotations*, p. 214), having all the obviously hazy insubstantiality of an image filming the retina in a dream. Since Mink notes in the *Gazetteer*, finally (p. 213), that "in 1815, the Molyneux Asylum for Blind Females took over [the] bldgs" that had formerly been occupied by "Astley's Amphitheatre," the cobwebbed-eyed figure "thinking of Astley's" and "Pepper's ghost" here must also have Blind Females somewhere in mind ("My sights are swimming thicker on me by the shadows to this place" [215.9–10]). Everywhere underlying the manifest detail in these lines, in short, we can infer the latent presence of the Wake's "aglo-irismaimed."

14. For a catalogue of rainbow configurations in Finnegans Wake, see Roland McHugh, "Rainbows," A Wake Newsletter, n.s., 15 (Oct. 1978): 76–77; and Ian MacArthur, "Rainbow 29," A Wake Newsletter, n.s., 16 (Aug. 1979): 62.

15. This is perhaps the appropriate place at which to recall that Joyce underwent ten eye operations while writing Work in Progress, three of them in April 1923, a month after he started the project, six others between April 1923 and June 1926, the period over which he "solved most of [the Wake's] structural problems and determined the final sequence of episodes" (A. Walton Litz, The Art of James Joyce [New York and London: Oxford Univ. Press, 1964], p. 83; on the dating of Joyce's eye operations, see Richard Ellmann, The Selected Letters of James Joyce [New York: Viking, 1975], pp. 215, 261). We might think of aspects of Joyce's "book of the dark," then, taking shape in the forced study of "his optics" ("meoptics").

No single problem made Joyce's eye operations, most of them on the left eye, necessary. With varying constancy between 1917 and 1941, he suffered from glaucoma, synecchia, iritis, conjunctivitis, episclerotis, retinal atrophy, and primary, secondary, and tertiary cataracts—all of them painful and incapacitating diseases whose gravity and scariness no healthy-sighted person should underestimate. Iritis, in early stages it is said to give the sufferer the sensation of having gritty sand in the eye, and so it forces him into incessant, involuntary tearing and blinking whose unrelieving effect is only to exacerbate the condition. Closing the eye, far from relieving the pain, deepens it, and in severe cases, the pain radiates into the brow, the nose, the cheek, and the teeth, ultimately to bring on severe headaches (see L, III, 113–14). While sand can be washed out of the eye, iritis cannot. It either goes away or it doesn't, and in the latter case it can spread. Left untreated, it can ravage the affected eye entirely and overtake the second by "sympathetic infection." Advanced cases of iritis were "cured," in Joyce's day, by removing the entire eyeball. Hence the earliest of Joyce's eye operations: an iridectomy on the right eye (his "good eye") in 1917 was followed by two iridectomies on the left ("the broken window of my soul" [L, III, 111]).

The "cures" seem as painful as the affliction. Joyce would have been conscious during these operations, his eyelid forced back and held open with a speculum, his eyeball grasped with a pair of forceps to prevent any involuntary flinching. He would have "seen" the surgical knife, razored on both edges to allow the doctor a minimum of movement, approach his cornea and cut its way, with a sawing motion, through to the anterior chamber and then into the iris, where its work would have been to slice out any infected tissue. Joyce would have undergone in reality, in short, a kind of horror conceived in a film like Le Chien Andalou to be surreal. And he would also have had occasion, during these procedures, to consider how objects can enter the eye of a subject in ways not usually explored in Newtonian or Helmholtzian treatments of optics. On iritis and iridectomies, see C. W. Rutherford, The Eye (New York and London: D. Appleton, 1928), pp. 144–47, 156–60, 250–55.

Somewhere in the development of his system of "meoptics," Joyce's interminable visits to the eye clinics certainly had their effect on *Finnegans Wake*, though how *little* they did might be seen by holding the text against his letters; he writes there, for example, of intending to "go to see Dr. Borsch (of whom I dreamed last night) tomorrow . . . [to] ask him to let me finish Λd before the next match" (*L*, III, 132). The letter shows him thinking all at once about his dreams, the *Wake*, his vision—and an eye surgeon, whom he did not want to see but had to, invading all three. However dizzyingly intricated the relations between "blindness and insight" might be in this particular instance, no dream of Swiss oculists or anything at all comparable appears in *Finnegans Wake* because the blindness overtaking its "benighted irismaimed" is absolutely normal to the night. Joyce's eye difficulties impeded, rather than helped, the progress of *Work in Progress*.

Richard Ellmann is therefore quite right to call "the theory that Joyce wrote his book for the ear because he could not see . . . not only an insult to the creative imagination, but an error of fact. . . . The eyes are closed in *Finnegans Wake* because to open them would change the book's postulate" (*JJ*, 716). Perhaps the best stance to take on this issue is one advanced by Stephen Dedalus in *Ulysses*, who announces that "a man of genius makes no mistakes. His errors are volitional and are the portals of discovery" (*U*, 190). These ringing words only mean, beneath all the rhetoric, that a resourceful person learns from his mistakes rather than letting them cripple him; and we might reasonably infer that a man of genius does not passively suffer victimage either. In considering the *Wake*'s "meoptics," surely, we are seeing Joyce making his difficulties work for him, rather than against him.

16. Herman von Helmholtz, *Treatise on Physiological Optics*, ed. James P. C. Southall (New York: Dover, 1962), 2, p. 12. Helmholtz goes on to observe that "the background of the visual field, on which these phenomena are projected, is never entirely black; and alternate fluctuations of bright and dark are visible there, frequently occurring in rhythm with the movements of respiration. . . . The shapes that are assumed are very curious, especially when one happens to be in a strange place that is perfectly dark . . . because then these imaginary figures are apt to be mistaken for real objects." Indeed, they "may easily have been the origin of many ghost stories" (p. 13).

17. Assenting to the observations of Wundt, Maury, and Ladd, Freud notes that "the changing, perpetually shifting character of the excitation of the idioretinal light corresponds precisely to the constantly moving succession of images shown us by our dreams. No one who attaches importance to these observations . . . will underestimate the part played in dreams by these subjective sources of stimulation, for, as we know, visual images constitute the principal component of our dreams" (*ID*, 67). Freud goes on, of course, to insist that the somatic constituents of dreams will not finally explain their peculiarities or their meanings. See also *ID*, 64–67, 82–83, 260–62, 573–74, 585–87.

18. The young May moon is beaming, love,
     The glowworm's lamp is gleaming, love,
     How sweet to rove through Morna's grove
     While the drowsy world is dreaming, love.

19. "lunar rainbow": Mitchell, "Marginalia from Conversations with Joyce," *A Wake Digest*, p. 81.

20. "When I'm dreaming back like that I begins to see we're all only telescopes" (295.10–12): in other words, the vision of anyone asleep and dreaming might also be considered a kind of "telescopy," since when "eye begins to see" in the night (hence the third-person form of "I begins"), "binocular man" discovers things not visible in the light

of day (68.1). In particular, nocturnal "telescopy" allows the "dim seer" to "uncover the nakedness of an unknown body" (96.28–29)—one like HCE's, or a "heavenly body," that becomes evident only at night "(O my shining stars and body!)" (4.12–13).

The appearance of "telescopes" in the *Wake* therefore serves to apprise its reader of visual conditions within HCE's "blackeye lenses" at "sootably" dark times in the night. The collapsible "sexcaliber" "tallowscoop" that appears in the *Wake*'s account of the battle of "waterloose," for instance (8.35–36), not only serves as a displaced visual image of HCE's phallus; since images in dreams are overdetermined and yield multiple meanings, it also tells us something about the murky "vidual" properties of that "candle-little" scene (10.27 [which is dimly "candlelit" by the "tallow" in the "tallowscoop"). We learn, comparably, of Shem the Penman, that "the only once . . . he did take a tompip peepestrella throug a threedraw eighteen hawkspower durdicky telescope . . . he got the charm of his optical life when he found himself . . . at pointblank range blinking down the barrel of an irregular revolver . . . handled by an unknown" (178.26–179.4). The line generates a set of complex tensions between the visible and invisible in order to suggest that Shem represents a part of HCE which falls largely outside of visual experience. For what begins here as a feeble attempt to see through a "dirty" or "durdicky telescope" (Gi. *dur-dicki mengri*, "telescope") occasions great and futile strain as the dark visionary trying hard to "peep" at a "star" (It. *estrella*) modulates into a blind "bat" (It. *pipistrello*), while the telescope itself changes into a gunbarrel. Looking down a gunbarrel, of course, generally tends not to sharpen vision at all, but rather to eradicate it. For more on telescopy in the *Wake*, see 9.34, 10.13, 235.24–25, 275.L2, and 449.34; on "heavenly bodies," see also 185.29, 234.13–14, 249.2–3, and 533.4–5.

21. Cf. Roheim, *The Gates of the Dream*: "The dream is visual . . . in the dream the dreamer is halfway out of sleep and building up a new world . . ." (p. 61); "the dream, as opposed to sleep, represents the trend back to the object world" and therefore "is a function of the ego" (pp. 95, 117).

22. "The ambiguity of the jewel": Jacques Lacan, "The Line and Light," in *The Four Fundamental Concepts of Psychoanalysis*, ed. Jacques-Alain Miller, trans. Alan Sheridan (New York: Norton, 1978), p. 96. The phrase occurs in a discussion of "embodied light" (p. 90), where Lacan locates the essence of the visual not in "geometral relations" like those diagrammed in figure 8.1, but in "light" itself: "the essence of the relation between appearance and being, which the philosopher, conquering the field of vision, so easily masters, lies elsewhere [than in geometric relations]. It is not the straight line, but in the point of light—the point of irradiation, the play of light, fire, the source from which reflections pour forth. Light may travel in a straight line, but it is refracted, diffused, it floods, it fills—the eye is a sort of bowl—it flows over, too, it necessitates, around the ocular bowl, a whole series of organs, mechanisms, defences" (p. 94). As will become clear, much this refractive complexity permeates HCE's "eyenbowls" (389.28).

23. Hence, throughout the "Mime of Mick, Nick and the Maggies," the running glitter of "crystal[s]" (229.12)—variably of "amethyst" (245.7), "carbuncle" (224.36), "diamond" (250.31), "hematite" (247.35), "jasper" (249.8), "opal" (220.10), "pearl" (226.1), "ruby" (224.3, 226.31, 249.7), "seafire" (245.8 ["sapphire"]), "turquewashed" (235.8 ["turquoise"]), and, above all, "heliotrope."

24. On "heliotrope" in the *Wake*, see also 89.18–19, 223.9–11, 223.28, 235.5, 236.35–237.2 (Fr. *tournesol*, "heliotrope"), 237.5–6, 248.8–10, 248.11–13, 248.14–18, 248.33–35, 250.30, 265.L1, 273.24, 280.24, 303.F1, 349.6, 461.8–10, 470.7, 509.21–24 ("Kansas" is "the

sunflower state"), 561.20, 594.8, 603.28, 610.36–611.1, and 626.17–18. For good discussions of the *Wake*'s preoccupation with "heliotrope," see Solomon, *Eternal Geometer*, pp. 22, 27, 31–33; Patrick McCarthy, *The Riddles of Finnegans Wake* (Cranbury, N.J.: Associated Univ. Presses, 1980), pp. 104–46; McHugh, *Sigla*, pp. 59–60; and Grace Eckley, *Children's Lore in "Finnegans Wake"* (Syracuse: Syracuse Univ. Press, 1985), pp. 131–32 ff. Here it would be relevant to note that all the stained-glass configurations in the last chapter of the *Wake* are ciphers for our hero's "heliotrope ayelips" (533.2), through which, as morning dawns, real sunlight is beginning colorfully to bleed.

25. The character of this struggle would explain, incidentally, why Joyce incorporated into the "Colours" chapter submerged accounts of "the Sudanese War" (*L*, I, 302), where "light" and "dark" were also in conflict; and it would generally clarify the chapter's dense references to angels, devils, and the occult (on which see Matthew Hodgart's *James Joyce: A Student's Guide* [London: Routledge & Kegan Paul, 1978], pp. 154–63). Etymologically, "color" and the "occult"—together with "hell," "holes," "hollows," "cells," the "clandestine," and "concealment"—are aspects of each other, all deriving from the Indo-European *kel-* ("to cover, conceal"); for in all of these things, as in Aristotle's "adiaphane" (*U*, 37), what is below and beneath the visible is covered up.

26. Throughout the *Wake*, Issy therefore stands competitively opposed to "Anna Livia Plurabelle," of whom she is finally a fragmentary aspect because, as anyone who has been through it knows, "looks" don't have everything to do with it. ALP differs from Issy in being "a woman of no appearance (I believe she was a Black . . .)" who moves, "unda her brella" (7.26), in a dimension everywhere "invisible" and "unseen" (158.25–26, 28, 36). This "woman of no appearance," however, is for that very reason "a woman to all important" (158.32): she represents a form of femininity to which our hero's attachment—profound, if unconscious attachment—is precisely *not* visual ("Think of your Ma!" [206.3]).

27. As will have become evident in passing, the *Wake* is everywhere undertaking, "in the flesh," a subversion of "spectator consciousness" comparable to that pursued by Maurice Merleau-Ponty in *The Visible and the Invisible*, whose phenomenology of "the flesh"—"the sensible in the twofold sense of what one senses and what senses" for which "there is no name in traditional philosophy"—is only a version of the far more ambitious and iconoclastic enterprise Joyce began in 1922 (*The Visible and the Invisible*, ed. Claude Lefort, trans. Alphonso Lingis [Evanston: Northwestern Univ. Press, 1968], pp. 99, 139–40). As the frequent equation of "eye" and "I" in *Finnegans Wake* suggests (23.36, 61.24, 197.17, 213.15, 295.11, 301.7, 330.26, 336.30, 347.8), the tendency of modern thought to privilege the observing "eye" has sanctioned also the tyranny of the "I" and all the baggage it carries with it: the clinical observer, his dispassionate point of view, and the all-knowing and self-enclosed subject. Joyce's "vision," by contrast, transcends mere vision, to offer us both "a full new" (344.22 ["view"]) of "the whirrld" (147.22), and a new *Phallusaph[y]* as well (72.14 [note the pleasure that motivates this negation of "philosophy," and "see relief map" for the details]). By closing the eye and moving into the night, the *Wake* is ultimately exploring an iceberg beneath the tip even of Merleau-Ponty's visible: "under the closed eyes," it brings to light not only the rest of "the presence (of a curpse)"—in itself a heavily "sleeping giant"—but the rest of "the present, of course." As Joyce himself put it while working on the "Colours" chapter, at a time in which his seeing was endangered but the progress of *Work in Progress* was not, "What the eyes bring is nothing. I have a hundred worlds to create, I am losing only one of them" (*JJ*, 664).

28. Gregory, *Eye and Brain*, p. 118, where Maxwell is quoted.

29. Quoted by Christine Ladd-Franklin, in "The Nature of Colour Sensations," Helmholtz, *Physiological Optics*, 2, p. 457. Compare the *Wake*'s account of the encounter between Patrick and the Archdruid Berkeley at 611.4–612.36.

30. See, for example, the typical remarks on the "Two Meanings of the Word Light" in W. D. Zoethout's *Physiological Optics* (Chicago: Professional Press, 1935), 2d ed. p. 161: "In a discussion of physiological optics great care must be exercised not to confound the two meanings of the word light; the objective, or physical, and the subjective, or psychological. There is, as far as we have knowledge of, no resemblance between the objective light sent by the sun and the subjective light of our consciousness. To ignore this distinction is to hopelessly flounder in the realm of optics. . . . There is neither green nor red in the universe; there are ether vibrations of longer or of shorter wave lengths. The redness or greenness is a matter of our brains, or, more properly speaking, of our consciousness." Not to mention "ouroptics."

31. "This genre of portraiture of changes of mind to be truly torse [and accurate to the *Wake*'s representation of the body or "torso"] should evoke the bush soul . . . so I am leaving it to the experienced victim [anyone who has been "knocked out" and rendered "dead to the world"] to complete the general suggestion by the addition of a wallopy bound or . . . a congorool teal" (165.18–21). Through these loony references to "bush souls," "kangaroo tails," and "wallabies," Joyce is informing us pretty directly that Australian and New Zealand idioms, of which our Irish hero is quite likely unconscious, will operate symbolically throughout the *Wake* to evoke "changes of mind" that overcome HCE when he drifts into his own "antipodes," "down under" in "his own body." For an excellent survey of Australian references in the *Wake*, together with an account of their relations to Shem and his telegram, see Hart, *Structure and Motif*, pp. 116–28, 112, 243; for an assessment consonant with my own of the way in which Joyce draws on Australian slangs (and also Maori and other "bush" languages) see Epstein, "James Joyce and the Body," p. 98.

32. J. A. C. Brown, *Freud and the Post-Freudians* (Middlesex: Penguin, 1964), p. 34.

33. "Considerations of representability," as Freud noted, play a crucial role in the formation of dreams, whose underlying causes and concerns, being unconscious, are not essentially visual. The mere visibility of a dream, in other words, is another "goodridhirring," a way of obscuring and masking, by displacing into the eyes, the real and "infrarational" concerns that lie at its core and that arise from "sameplace" "down under" in the dreamer's "antipodes." As in the familiar example of conversion hysteria, where conflictual desire is displaced upwards from a lower to a higher part of the body ("the tasks above are as the flasks below" [263.21]), dreams might well be regarded as displacements upwards into the eyes of conflicts localized elsewhere in the body's "bluddle filth" (10.8–9 [the "battlefield" of "blood" and "filth"]). Note, in this regard, how "the sensory crowd in [HCE's] belly [is] coupled with an eye" at the beginning of that chapter in the *Wake* concerned with the buried letter (107.15–17). On "considerations of representability," see *ID*, 374–80, 586–87.

34. One such symptomatically "sobsconcious inkling," to illustrate the endless extent of the "knots" constituting our hero's body, would be his "sobs" (hence "sobsconcious"): although our hero would surely be "conscious" of them when they threatened to well up from "down under," nothing over which he has any rational foresight or choice prompts them; they rise up "autistically," automatically, as if on their own—and sometimes for underlying reasons, because "subconscious" ones, of which he has only the vaguest

"inklings." Such "sobsconcious inklings" would be the produced work not of his conscious self ("Show'm the Posed"), but of the "Autist" inside him.

35. "They say that filmacoloured featured at the Mothrapurl skrene about Michan and his angeleens is corkyshows do morvaloos" (443.34–36 [Fr. *quelque chose de merveilleux,* "something marvellous")—to illustrate further how "moving pictures" (565.6) operate in "the Evening World." Manifestly an off-the-cuff remark on a recent "coloured film," but in fact a particle of nocturnal thought retrospectively illuminating "the Mime of Mick, Nick and the Maggies" (hence "Michan and his angeleens"), this line recalls Dublin's "St. Michan's Church," "the vaults [of which] are famous for 'an amazing preservation of the corpses' buried in them.'" The detail reminds us that our hero, though "dead to the world," is in very good condition; for "'the skin of the corpses [in St. Michan's, like his] remains soft as in life.'" Within the sealed pits of his eyes, moreover, a "coloured film" of iridescently lit "mother-of-pearl" sometimes takes form (hence the "Mothrapurl skrene"), so to allow him the viewing of shifting pictures. The two quotations are from Gifford and Seidman's *Notes for Joyce* (p. 260), where an undated *Official Guide to Dublin* is in turn quoted.

Because vision in dreams reaches the viewer as if out of thin air, moreover, and also allows him to see things in their "Real Absence," the night's "moving pictures" might also be considered a form of "television" (< Gr. *têle-* ["far off"] and L. *visio* ["seeing"]). In a book where everything about "Man is *temporarily* wrapped in obscenity [and obscurity]," accordingly, the *Wake's* "irismaimed" periodically finds himself "looking through at these accidents with the farofscope of television (this nightlife instrument . . .)" (150.30–33; for more on this nocturnal "television," see 52.18, 254.22, 345.45, 489.21, 597.36, 610.35, and especially 349.6–28).

36. In contrast both to the rainbow colors and to those that fall beyond the visible spectrum, the *Wake's* "meoptics" also includes "a nocturnal tri-colour" (L, I, 269), "a tricolour ribbon that spells a caution" (503.24); for the colors "black, green and gray" (441.4), as Joyce explained in a series of letters to Harriet Shaw Weaver, signify in the German that he would have spoken in his endless visits to eyeclinics, "successive stages of cecity" or blindness (L, I, 269, 273–4): *grüner Star* (Ger. *grün,* "green"), is a German medical term for "glaucoma"; *grauer Star* (Ger. *grau,* "gray") for "cataract"; *schwarzer Star* (Ger. *schwarz,* "black") for "amaurosis," or "dissolution of the retina." The appearance of these colors in conjunction with "everything or allselse under the grianblachk sun of gan greyne Eireann" (503.22–23) indicates that the *Wake's* "irismaimed" is returning to a "sunless" (Gael. *gan ghrein*) part of the night (hence the Gael. *greinbeach,* "zodiac," in "grianblachk"), where he endures a general "deadening" of the body (hence the "gangrene"), and not least in his eyes. "The crystalline world [within the crystalline lens] wane[s] chagreenold and doriangrayer in its dudhud" at these moments (186.7–8); and the whole picture changes, much for the worse (hence "Dorian Gray").

37. Erin! the tear and the smile in thine eyes
Blend like the rainbow that hangs in the skies;
Shining through sorrow's stream,
Sad'ning through pleasure's beam,
Thy suns, with doubtful gleam,
Weep while they rise!

Erin! thy silent tear never shall cease,
Erin! thy languid smile ne'er shall increase,

Till, like the rainbow's light,
Thy various tints unite,
And form in heaven's sight
One arch of peace!

Cf. 426.15–16.

38. "Particularly to be noted is the innervation of the ocular muscles in sleep; the eyes are rotated outwards and upwards. The physiologists state absolutely that this is a return to the position of the eyes which obtains in animals not possessing binocular vision (as for example the fishes)"; Sandor Ferenczi, *Thalassa: A Theory of Genitality* (New York: Psychoanalytic Quarterly, 1938), p. 76. While an observation like this perhaps sheds light on vision in dreamless parts of the night, Ferenczi draws on it, together with many comparable "bioanalytic" findings, in order to theorize sleep as a form of "thalassal regression" through which the mammalian organism, imbued with a "biological unconscious," strives to undo the evolutionary catastrophes layered into its body by seeking "to reproduce the . . . thalassal situation seemingly long since transcended" (p. 85). On sleep as an internalized form of evolutionary reversal and return to the sea, see especially pp. 73–80.

As will become more clear when we examine the role of "Anna Livia Plurabelle" in the *Wake*, much this understanding moves through Joyce's work, too, where "Our **Hu**man **C**onger Eel" (525.26), "ambilaterally alleyeoneyesed" and profoundly unconscious (323.29), drifts through parts of the night immersed in a body of water (his own), while his "fishy eyes" (559.23) stare vacantly "through the ghost of an ocean's" (426.20–21 [without "the ghost of a notion"]), able only to "see . . . in the fishnoo!" (525.27 [this "vision," in a "fishnet," would resemble that of the Vedic god "Vishnu," who took the form of a fish on earth]).

39. Whenever a reader of the *Wake* discovers that "all the mound reared" (420.14 [Fr. *tout le monde rire*, "the whole world laughed"]), it means, on two levels, that "all the mound" depicted in the two "relief maps" of the night has been stirred into vitality (hence "reared") by those energies arising from "sameplace" "down under" in the body which generate the experientially distinct though psychically related events of "laughtears" and the dream. For whenever those energies ripple though our hero's body (or the reader's), they alter its investments and retailor the heavily taxed "bourseday shirt" into a lighter and more bearable "mirthday suit" (35.4), so to "reflesh" it—literally—and as fully as might a stint of sleep. This is why, to spell out "the laugh and the shout" of it (101.5 [as opposed to the drearily reasoned "long and short"]), the *Wake* so outrageously seeks the release of "everyone's repressed laughter" (190.33–34). (*Read 'Em and Weep* was a title that Joyce may have consulted in order to write the *Wake* [*Annotations*, p. 215]). Laughing while reading *Finnegans Wake* liberates both the "Autist" "down under" in the body and the energies with which he composes "the Evening World" (see 187.33); that laughter is also a sign—an "inkling" written on somatic "foolscap"—that one has identified with the hero of the *Wake*, "the presence (of a curpse)," "in the present, of course," and "in the flesh."

40. "The cause of the involuntary blinking, which takes place at the rate of from 2 to 30 times per minute, is not known. It is not evoked by the drying of the cornea for the amount of moisture in the surrounding air has no influence on the rate. As blinking is continued in the dark, light cannot be regarded as the provocative agent." "Neither the mechanism of the blink nor the particular nervous center for the blinking movement . . . is known. . . . Emotional states affect its frequency; most noticeable is the inhibition of

blinking in persons with a 'vacant stare when lost in deep thought.' Sleep arrests the periodic blink, but . . . resting with the eyes closed does not alter the blink rate (i.e., the twitching of the lids). . . . It is at the unconscious, vegetative level that tear production and periodic blinking are integrated for normal functioning of the eye." The two quotations derive, respectively, from Zoethout, *Physiological Optics*, p. 362, and William K. McKewen and Ernest K. Goodner, "Secretion of Tears and Blinking," in *The Eye*, 2d ed., ed. Hugh Davson (New York: Academic Press, 1969), 3, pp. 371, 373.

    41. McHugh, *Sigla*, p. 23.

9. EARWICKERWORK

    1. The etymological chart undertakes two sleights of hand: the dotted lines in the diagram indicate purely speculative connections for which there is no scientific evidence; and although the two roots (*dheu-* I and *dheu-* II) have the same phonetic structure, they may not be related at all, standing perhaps in the same relation to each other as do the English words "bear" (to carry), "bear" (a large clumsy mammal), and "bare." Since the *Wake* speaks of pursuing "fairworded instance[s] of falsemeaning adamelegy," however (77.25–26), no reader of Joyce need feel the least restraint in engaging in this kind of shadowy semantic speculation.

    2. "deaf and dumb motif": Mink, *Gazetteer*, p. 282.

    3. Not necessarily a camera angle, the term "closeup" here suggests that HCE is about to "close up" his senses entirely (while "leads" comparably suggests that "heavy weights" are dragging his body down under [*OED*, "lead," sb. 6]). For our hero lives predominantly inside "his roundhouse of seven orofaces" (356.5–6)—the "face" beneath those "orifices" revealing them to be the two eyes, two ears, two nostrils, and talkative mouth. And "with seven hores [holes] always in the home of his thinkingthings, his nodsloddledome of his noiselisslesoughts" (379.14–15 ["the nice little home of his nice little thoughts"]), there is invariably in the daytime some nice little percept or "noise" to "listen" for and "seek" out—"to be sure." But by night, "to be shut" (341.34), there is not; for sleep takes place when everything is "SHUT" (182.32), "after closing time" (507.5–6), at "the hour of his closing" (255.6–7), in a world retailored so as to be predicated not on the openness of the sensory "orofaces" but on their "Closure" (585.27): "shutter reshottus" (352.25). "Tropped head" "under the **H**elpless **C**orpses **E**nactment" (423.31), our hero follows all its rules: "*he blanks his oggles. . . . He blocks his nosoes. . . . He wollops his mouther* [walls up his mouth]" and "*He boundles alltogotter his manucapes and his pedarrests*" (349.28–34 [the phrasing describes the anointing of the eyes, nose, mouth, hands, and feet in the ritual of Extreme Unction or last rites]); and then he just lies there, "dustungwashed" (342.13 ["tongue" "washed" in "dust"]), with "dust in his ears" (180.28) and dust in his eyes (240.16), peering insightfully through a "mudfacepacket" into the heart of "stiller realithy" (503.4 [Gr. *lithos*, "stone"; the third "l" in "stiller" yields the Da. *ler*, "clay"]). And since he lies so completely "shuttered . . . after his fall" (102.1–2), he passes the night as if in a succession of "closets" (e.g., 184.33, 445.5), "cells" (e.g., 12.2, 182.35, 295.L1), and "coccoons" (519.3), within which he lies "Closet for repeers" (421.3 [while "closed for repairs" and revisionarily "re-peering" at the world]). In the *Wake*'s depiction of sleep's "sense arrest," accordingly (505.31), everything at all imaginably capable of it keeps on "shutting" and "closing": mouths repeatedly shut or are shut (324.15 ["shut down and shet up"]; 355.8); books are shut and chapters sealed (20.15–18,

62.7, 621.3); doors shut over and over again (20.17–18, 257.27–28, 316.20, 371.16–17); curtains drop and action keeps on halting (49.2, 501.6–7, 531.27); people are shut up and "confined to guardroom" (196.20, 492.17); and "blinds" continually shutter windows and eyes (23.5, 132.14, 147.22 ["Close your, not must look"], 182.32–34, 221.32, 559.5), as our hero complementarily "puts the shutter up" and "shut[s] up shop" (23.5, 161.23–24, 370.34–35, 372.5, 595.31–32): "pull the blind, toll the deaf and call dumb, lame and halty" (132.14).

4. The *Annotations* (p. 509) refers us to the following verse:
A man may laugh through the whole of a farce,
A man may laugh through the whole of a play,
But a man can't laugh through the hole of his arse,
'Cause he just isn't built that way.

5. The dialogue begins, moreover, with the appearance of a figure "a parth a lone" (15.30 ["a part, alone"]), whose "hoagshead" (15.31 ["Howth HEAD"]) is "blacked out" and full of "spirits" (hence "hogshead"), and whose "locktoes" obviously cannot move. The appearance of a "Comestipple" (15.35 [or "constable"]) signifies the deepening of these forces of "arrest" and, with other terms, "blacks out" that "hoagshead" even more deeply (hence "comes tipple" [cf. 15.35–36]). Ultimately, then, the "quhare soort of a mahan" out of whom "Mutt" and "Jute" emerge shows us "the pillory way to Hirculos pillar" (16.3–4); and while these terms seem to name a traditional site of "the end of the world" (the Pillars of Hercules), the appearance of an immobilizing "pillary" beneath the surface of the phrase suggests that "the end of the world" reached in the dialogue occurs in the "tropped head" of some body "deafadumped" in the night's "seemetery." It is within this "tropped head" that the mute and the deaf dimly come together to discourse.

6. Also localized in the area of this "neck," in the topography of *Finnegans Wake*, is Clontarf, the site at which Brian Boru, in A.D. 1014, drove back the Viking invaders who had long overridden the coast of Ireland. In Joyce's thinking about Irish history, Clontarf would have been a place where "two races" (17.24) and two voices immanent in Irish speech—one Celtic, the other Teutonic—met, clashed, and merged with each other in "miscegenations on miscegenations" (18.20); for, "as is said of Ireland, 'It has two voices, one comes from the mountains and the other from the sea.'" The conflict that we find localized in our hero's neck during the dialogue of Mutt and Jute, then, has behind it a long and tangled history which is simply the history of human speech. The quotation is from Carola Giedion-Welcker, "Meetings With Joyce," in *Portraits of the Artist in Exile*, p. 261.

7. Mitchell, "Marginalia from Conversations with Joyce," *A Wake Digest*, p. 81.

8. On "sound sense," see 12.36–13.1, 96.30–32, 109.15, 112.11–12, 121.13–16, 138.7–9, 169.24–170.1, 318.35–319.1, 419.6, 499.25–27, 522.28–30, 598.4, and 612.29.

9. Glasheen, *Third Census*, p. 81.

10. The quoted phrases are from the illustrations given under the entry on "Agnomen" in the *OED*, where we read of a character in Scott's *Waverly* who acquires the neat little "agnomen of Bean" because of "his small pale features"; see also the entry on "Agnominate" ("to bestow an agnomen on, style, nickname").

11. Glasheen, *Third Census*, p. 121; Basil Cottle, *Penguin Dictionary of Surnames* (Middlesex: Penguin, 1967), p. 95. For excellent accounts of the real-world Earwickers, see Clive Hart's "Notes" in *A Wake Newsletter*, o.s., 4 (July 1962): 1–2; and Peter Timmerman, "The First Guide to *Finnegans Wake*," *A Wake Newsletter*, n.s., 16 (June 1979): 45–48.

12. Cf. Lacan, *Four Fundamental Concepts of Psychoanalysis*, p. 195: "In the field of the unconscious, the ears are the only orifice that cannot be closed." Actually, "goat along nose" (413.28 [and "God alone knows"]), this is not quite true; for the *Wake* also explores the "panarom[ic]" "extench" of the "gnose's" "gnoses" (143.3, 524.30, 182.4, 157.25 [the "nose's" "gnosis"]), through which our hero unconsciously "telesmells" properties like "H_2CE_3," (95.12) and its innumerable variants (71.28 [his wife], 95.13 [himself])—all of which, as they fall "under his nosetice" (164.31), he "nose . . . without warnword" (378.12). The life-long openness of the ear, however, is crucial both to Lacan and to Joyce, as it was also to Freud, because hearing, unlike the "chemical sense" of smell, is literately trained, so to become the means through which speech enters, informs, and forms the body. See also Freud, *The Ego and the Id*, trans. Joan Riviere, ed. James Strachey (New York: Norton, 1962), pp. 14–15.

13. The tyrant Dionysius of Syracuse used this cave as a prison because its amplifying properties allowed him to "overhear," through subterranean passageways, what his prisoners and enemies were saying. Like other references to prisons in the *Wake*, this one operates in cipher to suggest that our hero not simply "overhears" but also lies "arrested" in sleep; and like other references to caves and hollows, it also reminds us that HCE—"a locally person of caves" (365.2)—is himself a vast natural cavity. On "the Ear of Dionysius," see Mink, *Gazetteer*, p. 286; and Adolphe Badin, *Grottes et Cavernes* (Paris: L. Hachette, 1867), pp. 103–8.

14. Just as Joyce modifies the spelling of "Dublin" throughout the *Wake* in order to clarify conditions in "the Evening World," so he adjusts the "agnomen" "Earwicker" in order to give his reader a precise sense of HCE's widely variable acoustical perceptivity in the dark. As "earwaker," for instance, our hero is clearly capable of vigilant listening (173.9, 351.25); but as "Ear! Ear! Weakear!", he has to strain hard to do so (568.26). Since tongue-"wagging" is animated and indiscreet speech, by contrast (*OED*, "wag," v. I.4.b., II.9.d), the modulation of "Earwicker" into "earwuggers" and comparable forms (31.11) would suggest that HCE is only "wagging" his own "ears" at the instant in question ("I suppose you heard I had a wag on my ears?" [149.12–13]); while the notification that "E'ers wax for Sur Surd!," of course (238.31 [L. *surdus*, "deaf"]), would signal "old dummydeaf's" imminent lapse back into "the deafths" of sleep, where, as "daff Mr. Hairwigger" (491.30), he becomes an empty head ("wig"), full of air and void of sound. Toward the end of the *Wake*, finally, as "uhrweckers" prepares to waken (615.16 [Du. *uhrwecker*, "alarm clock"]), he becomes an "Eireweeker" (593.3 [about to rise into the concrete reality of a "week" in "Eire"]) and then "herewaker" (615.12), the last of these "agnomens" signaling his imminent return to the Daily World.

Much the same kind of play as Joyce gets out of the name "Earwicker" also effects the constantly varying forms of its Franco-Gaelic equivalent, "Persse O'Reilly" (44.24), or "Perce-Oreille" (Fr. "earwig"). As "beers o'ryely," for instance (498.18–19 ["beer," "rye"]), our hero is auditorily "blacked-out" but consumed with "spirits"; "as pierce of railing" (390.5), he is undergoing a spirited, if wholly internal bout of "earpiercing" raillery (474.12–13); as "O rally, O rally, O rally!" (593.3–4), he is about to get up to return to the Daily World; and as "Peace, O wiley!" (332.9), he is moving with "wiley" determination back into sleepy "bedeafdom":

—Yes, pearse.
—Well, all be dumbed!
—O really?   (262.9–10)

15. For variously developed accounts of this radio, see Campbell and Robinson, *A Skeleton Key*, pp. 196–97; Tindall, *A Reader's Guide*, p. 189; Glasheen, *Third Census*, p. liv; and McHugh, *Sigla*, p. 77.

Apart from the radio components and terms discussed in the text, the *Annotations* calls attention to those "supershielded umbrella antennas" (309.17–18 [antennas arrayed like the ribs of an umbrella]); "magnetic links" (309.18–19); "a vitaltone speaker" (309.19); a "hamshack" (309.22); much "static" (309.22); "ohms" (310.1); "circum-centric megacycles" (310.7); "gain control" (310.6); "pip" (310.9); "twintriodic" (310.4 ["triode" tubes]); and the "Bellini-Tosti coupling system" (309.18–19), where "Bellini and Tosi" together invented an early radio-sensing device capable of "distance getting" (309.18), although "Bellini" and "Tosti," considered separately, were Italian operatic composers whose work one might plausibly hear on any good radio.

16. "Some puzzles remain. For example, how is it that we can be roused from sleep selectively by different stimulus patterns? A new mother will be wakened by the faintest cry from her baby, while the father continues to sleep. Similarly, a sleeper is more easily awakened by the sound of his own name than by other names. The everyday facts seem to imply that some circuits in the cortex can remain vigilant even during sleep" (Furst, *Origins of the Mind*, p. 89). See also the discussion of "Noise and Sleep" by J. D. Miller in "General Psychological and Sociological Effects of Noise," in Edward C. Carterette and Morton P. Friedman, eds., *Hearing*, vol. 4 of *Handbook of Perception* (New York: Academic Press, 1978), pp. 646–52.

17. See Freud's discussions of "alarm-clock dreams" and the general effects of "auditory stimuli" on nocturnal thinking in *ID*, pp. 56–64 and 265–69. The analysis of precisely such dreams enabled him to formulate the well-known statement that "*Dreams are the guardians of sleep and not its disturbers*": "either the mind pays no attention at all to occasions for sensation during sleep . . . or it makes use of a dream in order to deny the stimuli; or, thirdly, if it is obliged to recognize them, it seeks for an interpretation of them which will make the currently active sensation into a component part of the situation which is wished for and which is consistent with sleeping. The currently active sensation is woven into the dream *in order to rob it of reality*. . . . *Thus the wish to sleep . . . must in every case be reckoned as one of the motives for the formation of dreams, and every successful dream is a fulfilment of that wish*" (pp. 267–68).

18. "Can you hear here me, you sir?" (478.2); "Can you hear better?" (478.4); "Do you hear what I'm seeing?" (193.10); "Big Seat, did you hear?" (361.6); "And I suppose you heard"? (149.12–13); "Have you hered"? (44.18); "Have you erred"? (491.16). The fact of Earwicker's acoustical vigilance would account for the heavy recurrence of questions like these throughout the *Wake*, and particularly in the "Earwicker" chapter (I.ii), which culminates in the question "Have you heard?" (45.1; 44.17–18, 25).

19. We find Earwicker "gnatsching his teats" (222.27) at 231.9–22. While the passage seems to describe Shem the Penman enduring "a violent pang of toothache after which he throws a fit" and runs off to write abusive poetic blackmail (*L*, I, 295), a great deal of sonic turmoil underlies the manifest content of the passage. Although it seems that the man "tropped head" at the *Wake*, characteristically, "thought him a Fonar all" here (231.11–12 ["thought" nothing, as if at his "funeral"]), a sound "like gnawthing un-heardth" (231.21–22) is obviously infiltrating his awareness: like "nothing on earth," this would be the sound of a "gnaw-thing unheard." And it is, accordingly, "as thought it had been zawhen intwo" (231.15); deeply indeed, his "thought has been sawn into," and

from a region specified by reference to the German *Zähnen* ("teeth") in "zawhen." The "gnawthing unheardth" reverberating through his "tropped head" therefore reminds him dimly of "gumboil owrithy" (231.13 [of a "boil" in the mouth making the "gums writhe," and of the sensation of having the words of the poet "John Boyle O'Reilly" in his mouth]), and so it "disconvuls[es] the fixtures of his fizz" (231.16–17 [the "fixed features"]) because it is painfully ugly, but also because it causes his jaws to move, so to generate a dream of ugly "poetry" and leave him with a "mouthfull of ecstasy" (231.9)—where this "ecstasy," deriving from the Greek *ecstasis* ("being put out of place") and the Latin *ecstasis* (or *ex-stasis*), suggests that his mouth has shifted out of inert "statis" into movement and heightened feeling.

In turn, this "gnatsching of teats" puts Earwicker subliminally in mind of prior times in his life when he stood in comparably strange and agonized relations to his own teeth: of that time when pain shot "up through the errorooth of his wisdom," for instance (231.10–11 ["wisdom" and "root" evoking the growth of the teeth, "Ararat" the time of genesis and the appearance of rock-hard matter "from next to nothing"]); and of a time in darkest infancy when nursing and painful "teething" occurred in unconscious synchronicity (hence the "gnatsching of teats" at 222.27). The deepening of the network of memories attached to the sound of "gnawthing unheardth," then, suggests why an episode of nocturnal tooth-grinding should appear in "the Mime of Mick, Nick and the Maggies," whose focus is so much on childhood. But it will also raise questions about what people given to nightly tooth-grinding can be thinking about; and it should also, by directing a reader's attention to the unheard sound coming out of his mouth into his ear at the time of reading, waken from the dead another part of "the presence (of a curpse)"—and of "the present, of course." For attention to the sound rising out of erratically active, gritting, grinding, or moving teeth—"like gnawthing unheardth"—will suggest, finally, how much of the vitality of the body is maintained in auditory unconsciousness.

20. The best interpretation of the source of the second of the *Wake's* hundred-lettered thunderwords (23.5–7) is offered by Aristotle, in "De Divinatione Per Somnum" (On Prophesying by Dreams), 463, in McKeon, *The Basic Works of Aristotle*, pp. 626–27. Noting that "some dreams are causes, other tokens . . . of events taking place in the bodily organism," Aristotle observes that

> the movements which occur in the daytime [within the body] are, unless very great and violent, lost sight of in contrast with the waking movements, which are more impressive. In sleep, the opposite takes place, for then even trifling movements seem considerable. This is plain in what often happens during sleep; for example, dreamers fancy that they are affected by thunder and lightning, when in fact they are only ringings in their ears. . . .

And Sir Thomas Browne, elaborating on Aristotle, refines this understanding:

> There is an Art to make dreams, as well as their interpretations, and physitians will tell us that some food makes turbulent, some gives quiet dreams. Cato who doated upon cabbadge might find the crude effects thereof in his sleepe, wherein the Aegyptians might find some advantage by their superstitious abstinence from onyons. . . .
> A little water makes a sea, a small puff of wind a Tempest, a grain of sulphur kindled in the blood may make a flame like Aetna, and a small spark in the bowels of Olympias a lightning over all the chamber.

(Sir Thomas Browne, Notebook Entry "On Dreams," in Endicott, ed., *The Prose of Sir*

Thomas Browne, pp. 447–58). As these observations suggest, especially when integrated with those details about "flatuous" "porthery" cited in the text, "farternoiser" seems to have "ordurd" (23.4) and gotten "the wind up" in that part of the *Wake* marked by the second thunderword (23.14), his awakened "hearsomeness" (23.14) causing him to misconstrue the sound, along Aristotelean lines, as the sound of thunder. And although the thunderword occurring at 414.19–20, comparably, seems to be a misheard bout of coughing, it ought to be pointed out that not all of the *Wake*'s thunderwords can be attributed to purely acoustical sources.

21. "I know that Λd[III.iv] ought to be about roads, all about dawn and roads, and go along repeating that to myself all day as I stumble along roads hoping it will dawn on me how to show up them roads so as everybody'll know as how roads, etc." (*L*, I, 232).

22. As Gifford and Siedman point out (*Notes for Joyce*, p. 362), "closing time for Dublin pubs in 1904 was 11:00 P.M.," so that the time "ten o'connell" would generally evoke, for our hero, closing time. Since Gifford and Seidman go on to point out that "laws governing the times when alcoholic beverages could be served in public houses were subject to certain exceptions for individuals who could 'prove' they were traveling and thus would not be able to 'dine' (drink) during the legal hours," there is the remote possibility that the passage is about an actual after-hours visitor to the pub.

23. "On his first time of hearing" what he imagines as a loudly knocking "process server" (63.20–21, 32), Earwicker thinks that the "unsolicited visitor" is "merely trying to open zozimus a bottlop stoub by mortially hammering" "against the bludgey gates for the boots" (70.13, 63.31–33): the evident knocking, in other words, is attached to a request for a serving-person ("the boots") to open a door ("open zozimus") and to serve drinks (a "bottlop stoub"); but because our hero is "deaf" (Ger. *taub*), asleep as if in "Aladdin's cave" (hence again "open zozimus"), he does all he can to ignore the noisy disturbance. What seems to be real knocking at a door out there in the dark now generates an elaborate network of associations.

In one line of thought, a figure "prised safe in bed as he dreamed" is "wokenp" "by hearing hammering" in the "Mullingcan Inn" (64.4, 7, 9); and this partly wakened sleeper imagines an old, put-upon man getting "hastily into his shoes with nothing" and coming "down with a homp, shtemp and jumphet to the tiltyard from the wastes o'sleep" (63.35–64.1). Part of him, in other words, "mulling" as well as he "can," imagines having to wake up and take care of a customer. Still, sleep insures that "this most nooningless knockturn" (64.15–16 [this "meaningless knocking," heard not at "noon," but in a "nocturne"]) will be disregarded; for "this battering babel allower [all over] the door and sideposts" "would not rouse him out of slumber deep" (64.9–10, 12). Earwicker accordingly shuts out the noise and sinks into a placid little dream of erotic pleasure (64.22–65.33); and the dream enables him to pass, even while the noise persists "out there" (65.34–64.1), back into the condition of being "dead to the world" (66.28), sleep in turn rendering his "carcasses mattonchepps and meatjutes" (67.16–17 ["mute-and-deaf" and "deaf-mute"]). But "in the drema of Soretost Areas, Diseased" (69.14–15 [this "dream" "dramatic," the bed a very "sore-tossed area"]), as "Humphrey's unsolicited visitor" (70.13) continues making noise "out there," our hero continually misconstrues it—as a series of threats (70.21–24), insults (71.5–72.18), and assaults (72.27–33)—during all of which, as a practicing "passive resistant" (72.19), he just lies there. When the disturber of his peace goes away, finally, everything "proceed[s] . . . in the directions of the duff and demb institutions" (73.19–20), and our hero goes "dead to the world" (73.23 ["Bully Acre" names a cemetery in Dublin]).

In so far as our hero periodically goes "dead to the world" and sinks into the night's "seemetery" during this noisy interlude, the "battle at the gate" also becomes at times a battle for a soul fought at the gate of the other world, the passage also offering its reader a "present(i)ment" of what "the presence (of a curpse)" must "no" when "summonor-othor" raps at the gate of his tomb.

24. Many of these "Acoustic Disturbances" are so dark that anything approaching a definitive or complete list of them would be rash. To illustrate the range of these back-ground noises, however, we might note that a dog seems to be barking in the "world-room" "out there" at 96.33–97.18 "(or so it appierce)" (512.24); the noise is incorporated into a dream of a chase and foxhunt in which our hero is literally "hounded," and the disturbance is resolved and wished away as a heavily dogged fox, already melting into a hibernating bear, turns deaf, holes up, and "hide[s] him close in covert" (97.14 [and per-haps "in covers"]).

"Birds start their treestirm shindy" rather early in the night (621.35–36), at 359.18ff., when a "naughtingel" (359.32) or "lightandgayle" (360.2) "warn[s] to hear" by starting to "chirp" stridently to someone "jeff" (359.18 [or "deaf," who "wants to hear"]). The disruption begins with the vague notice that "Eeric Whigs" is receiving radio signals (359.26, 22ff.), escalates into a call to full "Attention!" (359.30), and blossoms into a paragraph full of music (359.31–360.16). Further terms suggest that the hearing of this music is conflicted, however ("Let everie sound of a pitch keep still" [360.3]), because Earwicker wants the vaguely pretty "sound and pitch" emitted by the "son of a bitch" to stop, so that he can return placidly to his reverie (hence "everie").

The annoying sound of that nightingale only anticipates the moment when "the silent cock shall crow at last" and bring an end to the night (473.22). And, indeed, a boisterous "cock of the morgans" begins "to doodledoo" for the first time at 584.22ff., its "Cocorico!" (584.27, 30–31, 32–33) lifting our "returned auditor" (584.29) upward into an awareness of letters and literacy ("We herewith please returned auditors' thanks" [584.30]). And in the following pages, as the book gravitates toward the moment of wakening, the cock-crow only increases in frequency and intensity.

The night has already been disrupted, however, by the remorseless wakening of the young and the restless. For the sound of "a cry off" somewhere in the dark, as one of our hero's children wakes up, falls on Earwicker's ears at 558.32ff. and recurs, in mnemonic echo, throughout the rest of chapter III.iv. The cry is so disturbing that it lifts our hero abruptly out of deep sleep into a relatively clear, if ephemeral and spotty moment of con-sciousness—one which affords us, as Edmund Wilson early noted, perhaps the clearest view of Earwicker's bedroom and real-world circumstances that the *Wake* allows (558.35–559.16 ff.). And if part of the cry's disturbing effect grows out of our hero's genuine pater-nal solicitude, part of it also grows out of his unconscious agony. For the cry causes his wife to get up, as mothers will (559.30 ff.), to leave his bed for the bed of a younger man, so to demonstrate concretely how all of the old man's worries about being abandoned for another, younger man have a basis in sound fact.

Yet other "Acoustic Disturbances" are there for the astute auditor to disentangle from the wickerwork of the dream. These noises range in relative clarity from the clamorous pealing of the morning's churchbells (at 569.4 ff. and 601.16 ff.); to the delivery of the morning mail, economically synchronized with HCE's wakeful rising into a state of mind itself capable of delivering letters ("Heer's heering you in a guessmasque, latterman!" [603.2–8]); to a very, very dark moment in which our hero's wife seems to get up, presumably in order to answer a call of nature (at 332.36–334.6?).

25. A passage from the sonic episode of *Ulysses*, "Sirens," will explain why "every crowd has it several tones and every trade has its clever mechanics"; the passage shows Bloom thinking about musical "Instruments. A blade of grass, shell of her hands, then blow. Even comb and tissuepaper you could knock a tune out of. . . . I suppose each kind of trade made its own, don't you see? Hunter with a horn. . . . Shepherd his pipe. . . . Policeman a whistle. Lock and keys! Sweep! Four o'clock all's well. Sleep! . . . Drum? . . . Towncrier, bumbailiff. . . . Waken the dead" (*U*, 289). Conflated with those lines cited from the *Wake*, the passage asks us to become conscious of the ways in which the unique "mixture of sound-ingredients in a noise characterizes the impression in a way that indicates its meaning"; Robert Morris Ogden, *Hearing* (New York: Harcourt, Brace and Co., 1924), pp. 259–60.

26. "Wheatstone's magic lyre," as Glasheen notes (*Third Census*, pp. 304–5), refers to Sir Charles Wheatstone's "acoucryptophone," "a light box, shaped like an ancient lyre and suspended by a metallic wire from a piano in the room above. When the piano was played, its vibrations were transmitted silently and became audible in the lyre, which appeared to play itself." Much the same kind of magical power to release sound in the absence of any visible source is possessed by Earwicker's ears.

27. Quoting Lessing in *A Portrait*, and later in *Ulysses*, Stephen Dedalus argues that "what is audible is presented in time, what is visible is presented in space" (*P*, 212; cf. *U*, 37). His remarks, not Joyce's, cause us perhaps not to notice that what is audible is presented in space as well. Indeed, as a voice at the *Wake* puts it, "I should advise any . . . among my heeders [hearers] . . . to cluse her eyes [Gael. *cluas*, "ear"] and aiopen her oath [Gr. *aiô*, "to perceive, especially by hearing"] and see what spice may send her" (164.35–165.6 ["spice" would be enriched and "spiced-up" "space"]). The lines ask us to note that space is still there in the absence of vision, constituting itself with rich particularity "in the far ear" as "zounds of sounds," all precisely localized in space, impinge on the ear from various depths and distances (23.22–23); the echo of "far east" in this "far ear" calls our attention to the power of the ear to "orient" in space and will account for the appearance, in that radio-descriptive passage that opens II.iii, of a linked assemblage of oriental terms: "Arabia Deserta" (309.9), "Ibdullin" and "Himana" (309.13, 14), "Nur" (310.24 [Ar. *nur*, "light"]), and "muezzin" (310.25 [Ar. *mu'adhdhin*, < *udhan*, "an ear," a crier who calls from the top of a minaret]). These elements, in part, apprise us of the ear's "oreillental" power (357.18 [Fr. *oreille*, "ear"]).

Initiating an orienting reflex that causes one to turn and look (or, in Earwicker's case, to imagine doing so), the ears also exert an "oreillental" function by bringing to light parts of the world otherwise sunk in invisibility. Like the "Bellini-Tosi" aerial system evoked at the opening of II.iii (309.19), moreover, the ears are capable of "distance getting" (309.18), and can also home in on and pinpoint the location of sound-transmitting objects by a kind of sonic triangulation conducted in a dimension that students of the ear call "binaural image space." "It's Dracula's nightout" in the *Wake*, then (145.32), partly because Earwicker's ears, unconsciously radioecholocating and "distance getting" in the dark, periodically engage in a form of "batman's biff" (337.2 [and "blindman's buff"]).

dream . . . I can think of nothing better than the enigmatic inscriptions with which *Fliegende Blätter* [a magazine] has for so long entertained its readers. They are intended to make the reader believe that a certain sentence—for the sake of contrast, a sentence in dialect and as scurrilous as possible—is a Latin inscription. For this purpose the letters contained in the words are torn out of their combination into syllables and arranged in a new order. Here and there a genuine Latin word appears; at other points we seem to see abbreviations of Latin words before us; and at still other points in the inscription we may allow ourselves to be deceived into overlooking the senselessness of isolated letters by parts of the inscription seeming to be defaced or showing lacunae. If we are to avoid being taken in by the joke, we must disregard everything that makes it seem like an inscription, look firmly at the letters, pay no attention to their ostensible arrangement, and so combine them into words belonging to our own mother tongue. (*ID*, 539)

An example of this kind of "enigmatic inscription" would be the following fragment of Senecan dialogue:

Prae laetis si apage ortu ova qui te di ferent esse.

Noto contradictu in mi juge mentitis a veri fini dea.

No quare lingat prae senti si.

And upon this text, two interpretive operations might be expended. Exercising the most rational methods of which we are capable, we might explicate "the genuine Latin words," look up whatever we can in the appropriate reference books, and compensate for the mangled syntax by correcting the spellings that deviate from orthodoxy; but to do so would be to miss its essential point. (The lines are English and merely say, "Pray let us see a page or two of a quite different essay. Not to contradict you in my judgment, it is a very fine idea. No quarreling at present I see.") Much the same kind of "freely masoned" connection-making as is required to read this pseudo-Latin is also required in the interpretation of dreams and in the reading of *Finnegans Wake*, where "words [are not used] in their ordinary relations and connections." Rather than adhering doggedly to the letter of the law and the law of the letter, a reader of "the Evening World" must "stotter from the latter" and pursue meaning "in the broadest way immarginable." For further examples of the mock Latin used in this illustration, see C. C. Bombaugh, *Oddities and Curiosities of Words and Literature*, ed. Martin Gardner (New York: Dover, 1961), pp. 169–71.

In another well-known passage in *The Interpretation of Dreams*, Freud comparably likens the manifest content of the dream to a rebus, whose elements, if taken at face value, yield only the impression of sheer nonsense—as is also evidently true of the "robulous rebus" of *Finnegans Wake* (12.34). If, however, "we try to replace each separate element [of the puzzling text] by a syllable or word that can be represented by that element in some way or other [then the text of the dream will be] no longer nonsensical but may form a poetical phrase of the greatest beauty and significance" (*ID*, 311–12; cf. 356, 377, 444). Although it hardly yields "a poetical phrase of greatest beauty," the following primitive pictograph exemplifies the peculiarities of the manifest content of distorted texts like the rebus, *Finnegans Wake*, and the dream:

And here, too, two interpretive procedures might be expended on the text. According to the most orthodox procedures of which "day's reason" is capable, we might consult a zoological text to determine what kinds of animals these are, we might read an archaeological account of Lascaux to determine what meanings primitive men attached to quadrupeds, we might even read up on totemism; and though we will doubtlessly learn a great deal in doing so, we will still misread and miss the underlying sense. (The animals are "good gnus.") One goes about reading the "robulous rebus" of *Finnegans Wake* in exactly same way as one goes about reading signs like these—not by treating them in their "ordinary connections and relations," but by pursuing, "in the broadest way immarginable," extraordinary connections and "freely masoned" relations. By doing so, one finds the sought-after meaning one was looking for where one least expected it, in a way no one could have predicted.

3. McCarthy, *The Riddles of Finnegans Wake*, p. 16: "That *Finnegans Wake* is a giant riddle is apparent to anyone who has made a serious attempt to follow even a page or two of the book. In fact, virtually any word, any description, any situation in the *Wake* resembles a riddle. . . ."

4. In solving a riddle, "do you think for a moment? Yes, by the way. How very necessarily true!" (521.15–16). If we take this "by the way" as an English equivalent of the Greek *para-* ("by the side of," "by the way"), we can see in the solving of riddles the essential structure of paronomasia, or punning, in which "naming" (Gr. *onomaze*, "to name") happens "by the way," "obliquelike" (187.29). Every punned word in *Finnegans Wake* poses a riddle for its reader.

5. Brown, *Love's Body*, p. 244, on the deficiencies of learning and the power of loss of control.

6. Levin, *James Joyce*, p. 175.

11. "THE *NURSING MIRROR*"

1. Freud, *Introductory Lectures*, p. 211. For extended and well-known discussions of "infantile regression," see *ID*, 221–53; 559ff; and *Introductory Lectures*, pp. 195–212.

2. Freud, *Introductory Lectures*, p. 210.

3. There is, of course, as much to these obviously infantile lines as there is to those "tumptytumtoes" lost on the first page of the *Wake*. "Fingall's ends" tells us that the *Wake*'s "sleeping giant" has lost consciousness of the individuated limits of his own body and cannot differentiate the place where his "fingers end" from the place where "Fingal," a plain north of Dublin, "ends"—so that, again, we see sleep returning him to the condition of "first infancy." But the lines invite us also to reconstruct a "toym" in our hero's "mistridden past" when the practice of pedagogical counting games like "This Little Piggy Went to Market" (hence "recount") made it possible for his parents to draw forth from the darkness of infantile unconsciousness his fingers and toes, so to sort things out "from the last finger on the second foot of the fourth man to the first one on the last of the first.

—Finny. Vary vary finny.

—It may look finny but fere it is" (519.11–15)

That nursery rhyme, in other words, served the real-world purpose of "varying" what once were formless appendages ("fins"; hence "vary finny")—and in such a way as to make possible the consciousness not simply of fingers, but of their utility in gratifying desires (hence "this liggy piggy wanted to go to the jampot") and in fulfilling essential needs (hence "this leggy peggy spelt pea"); for not until the infant becomes conscious of the location of his fingers can he perform the higher functions of getting jam, using a pencil to "spell P," or, for that matter, making water and "spilling pee" (the "leg" in "leggy peggy" tells us that our hero made mistakes somewhere in the learning of these difficult lessons). As a reconstruction of the night, the *Wake* now asks us to see that although "Here Comes Everybody" in the world surely went through such rituals as these sometime in "real life"—("you were there")—their "m'm'ry," "leading slip by slipper to a general amnesia" (122.5–6), is reevoked in "the Evening World." Underlying so much that we take for granted, "lots lives lost" (257.35–36).

4. Hodgart and Worthington, in *Song in the Work of James Joyce*, cite occurrences of the following nursery rhymes on the pages of the *Wake* cited parenthetically ("Remember and recall, Kullykeg!" [367.11]): Around the Rugged Rocks (19, 64, 416); As I Was Going to St. Ives (12.102, 147, 215, 252, 291, 330, 390, 523, 552, 614); As I Was Going Up One Pair of Stairs (251–52, 424–25); A-tisket, A-tasket (315); A was an Apple Pie (94); A was an Archer (5, 19, 72, 80, 226, 228, 242, 250, 293, 302, 314, 319, 404, 603); Baa, Baa, Black Sheep (51, 133, 148, 279, 300, 301); Babes in the Wood (336, 504, 551, 619); Baby Bye, See the Fly (146); Brow Bender (130); Bye, Baby Bunting (529); Clap Hands (346); Close Your Eyes and Open Your Mouth (53, 165); Cock a Doodle Doo (96, 244, 461, 584, 595); Crosspatch, Draw the Latch (9, 163); Daffydowndilly (475, 530); Denary, Danery (261); A Dillar, a Dollar (288, 427); Ding Dong Bell (360, 361, 588); Do You Know the Muffin Man? (491); Eeny, Meeny, Miny, Mo (21, 94, 261); The Farmer in the Dell (236, 262); A Frog He Would A-Wooing Go (152, 310, 484); Georgie Porgie (37, 179, 279, 327, 375); Goosey, Goosey Gander (287); Guy Fawkes ("Please to remember the fifth of November") (87, 177, 364); Here We Go Gathering Nuts in May (176, 226, 285, 490); Here We Go Round the Mulberry Bush ("This is the way we wash our clothes") (6, 176, 237, 490, 581); Hickory, Dickory Dock (261, 314, 378); Hilary, Dilary (314); Hokey Pokey (71, 78, 234, 254, 256, 315, 368, 542, 558); The Holly and the Ivy (58, 59, 97, 147, 152, 236, 265, 291, 421, 465, 468, 502, 505, 556, 588, 616); The House that Jack Built (8–10, 18, 80, 106, 205, 271, 274, 369, 375, 439, 476, 511, 580); How Many Miles to Babylon? (17, 20, 84, 236); Humpty Dumpty (3, 7, 12, 13, 17, 29, 44–47, 99, 106, 129, 163, 175, 184, 219, 230, 285, 294, 296, 314, 317, 319, 320, 325, 334, 341, 343, 352, 372, 373, 374, 375, 386, 415, 422, 434, 455, 466, 496, 504, 550, 567, 596, 606, 614, 619, 624, 627, 628); I Had a Little Hobby Horse (197, 225); Jack and Jill (61, 141, 211, 290, 318, 462, 589); Johnny Is a ———, yah! yah! yah! (163); The King of Hearts (405); The King of the Cannibal Isles (78, 254, 315, 600); Knock Knock (330); Lavender's Blue (226); Little Bo Peep (80, 96, 143, 144, 147, 227, 248, 272, 276, 413, 420, 435, 449, 459, 478, 500, 502, 508, 540, 563, 571, 588, 590, 601, 614, 624); Little Boy Blue (556); Little Jack Horner (465, 623); Little Miss Muffet (413); Little Nancy Etticoat (208); Little Polly Flinders (562); Little Tommy Tittlemouse (17); London Bridge is Falling Down (7, 58, 233, 239); Looby Loo (226); Mary Had a Little Lamb (250, 440); Mary, Mary Quite Contrary (20, 204, 247, 272, 321); Monday's Child (88, 117, 487); Needles and Pins (6, 131, 210, 336); Oats, Peas, Beans, and Barley Grow (239, 602); O Dear, What Can the Matter Be (28, 225, 275, 621); Old Dolly Dinkins (339); Old King Cole (569, 619); Old Mother Hubbard (161, 388); One Fine Day in the Middle of the Night (191, 346, 347, 556, 624); One May Morning in the Middle of July (191); One, Two, Buckle My Shoe (314); One, Two, Three, Four, Mary's at the Kitchen Door (271); Oranges

and Lemons (59); Pat-a-Cake (294); Pease Porridge Hot (289, 395); Peter Piper Picked a Peck of Pickled Peppers (104, 112, 346, 616); Polly Put the Kettle On (23, 117, 161, 229, 236, 330, 332, 372, 585); Pop! Goes the Weasel (72, 215, 223, 341, 465, 540); Pussy Cat, Pussy Cat, Where Have You Been? (223); Reuben, Reuben (211); Rich Man, Poor Man, Beggar Man, Thief (57, 79, 132, 144, 202, 311, 317); Ride a Cock Horse (40, 102, 104, 121, 348–49, 363); Ring A-Ring O' Roses (6, 65, 147, 201, 209, 210, 215, 225, 239, 245, 246, 314, 330, 448, 453, 459, 462, 494, 510, 552, 624); Rockabye, Baby (104, 211, 248, 278, 294, 331, 420, 472, 546, 582); Rub-A-Dub-Dub (178, 239, 290, 351); See Saw, Margery Daw (508, 535); See Saw, Sacradown (18, 84, 508, 555); She Sells Sea Shells by the Sea Shore (508); Simple Simon (202, 408); Sing a Song of Sixpence (10, 11, 129, 134–35, 147, 167, 190, 232, 242, 244, 267, 276, 279, 300, 364, 377, 407, 450); Sir, Sir Solomon (416); Taffy Was a Welshman (10, 14, 222, 323, 390, 433); Ten Little Injuns (10, 588); There Was a Crooked Man (190–91); There Was an Old Woman Who Lived in a Shoe (13); There Were Two Blackbirds (346); This is the Way the Ladies Ride (The Lady Goes Apace, Apace) (7, 40, 102, 140, 257, 490, 554, 583); This Little Piggy Went to Market (368, 496); Tom, Tom, the Piper's Son (176, 277, 371, 385); Two Little Dickey Birds (588); What Are Little Girls Made Of? (20, 209, 374, 513, 558); When Adam Delved (21); When Good King Arthur Ruled This Land (79); Where Are You Going, My Pretty Maid (273, 336, 357, 476, 512); and Who Killed Cock Robin? (6, 7, 95, 211, 245, 256, 328, 333, 353, 361, 362, 383, 384, 568, 588).

This list is incomplete and does not include the equally numerous references to children's singing games that Hodgart and Worthington have discovered in the *Wake*, or to nursery rhymes in languages other than English; nor does it indicate the wide field of reference to childhood demonstrated by Grace Eckley in *Children's Lore in Finnegans Wake*. What percentage of *Finnegans Wake* is taken up by obscure allusions like these?

5. Swift's "little language" appears in *The Journal to Stella*, a series of letters in journal form that he wrote between 1711 and 1713 to Esther Johnson ("Stella") and her companion Rebecca Dingley in Dublin while, at the height of his public life, he led a prestigious and busy political life in London. In the course of the correspondence, the "little language" started to enter the letters. Endearingly weird, it is, as one of Swift's editors puts it, an "elaborate reproduction of the babble of the nursery" (Frederick Ryland, ed., "Introduction" to *The Journal to Stella*, vol. 2 of *The Prose Works of Jonathan Swift*, D.D. [London: George Bell and Sons, 1900], p. xix).

An example of the "little language" from letter 46: "Ppt does not say one word of her own little health. I am angry almost; but I won't cause see im a dood dallar in odle sings. Iss, and so im DD too. God bless MD, and FW, and Me, ay, and Pdfr too. Farewell, MD, MD, MD, FW, FW, FW. ME ME Lele. I can say lele it, ung oomens, iss I tan, well as oo" (Ryland, 368). As Ryland explains: "In the little language proper some acquaintance with the speech of the nursery will help the judicious student to find equivalents for 'oo,' 'zis,' 'im,' and so forth. As a rule, *l* is substituted for *r*; thus we have 'deelest logues' for 'dearest rogues,' 'rettle' . . . for 'letter,' 'flom' for 'from,' 'vely' for 'very,' and so on." The cited sentences from letter 46, according to these rules, would yield grown-up language meaning, "I am angry almost; but I won't because she is a good gal/girl in other things. Is, and so is Dear Dingley too . . . I can say 'lele' it, young women, yes I can, well as you." The other odd terms in the letter are simply alphabetical symbols—"Ppt" evidently standing for "Poppet" or "Poor Pretty Thing"; "Pdfr" for "Poor Dear Foolish Rogue"; MD for "my dears"; FW for "farewell" and/or "foolish wenches"; and ME for

"Madame Elderly" (Rebecca Dingley). The meaning of "lele" is obscure (Ryland, xx).

The spectacle of one of the greatest political and literary luminaries of his age, a man in his mid-40s who would come to be admired as one of the great English prose stylists, returning to the solitude of his lodgings at night to unwind in babytalk before going to bed, evidently struck the author of "the *Nursing Mirror*" as a relevant illustration of the persistence of the infantile in Here Comes Everybody. For more on Swift's "little language" in the *Wake*, see Levin, *James Joyce*, p. 166; Atherton, *Books at the Wake*, pp. 114–23; and the entries on "M.D." and "Pepette" in the *Third Census*, pp. 190, 223.

6. Take back the virgin page,
   White and unwritten still;
   Some hand more calm and sage,
   The leaf must fill. . . .
   Thoughts come as pure as light,
   Pure as ev'n *you* require; But oh! each word I write,
   Love turns to fire.

7. *Finnegans Wake* itself took gradual form in autosuggestive "scribbledehobbles" like these (275.22)—where the odd term is the name Joyce gave to the notebook out of which *Work in Progress* obscurely evolved (see Thomas E. Connolly, ed., *Scribbledehobble, The Ur-Workbook for Finnegans Wake* [Evanston, Ill.: Northwestern Univ. Press, 1961]). Joyce himself, moreover, was quite explicit about the power of "prescriptions": "the original genius of a man lies in his scribblings: in his casual actions lie his basic talent. Later he may develop that talent until he produces a *Hamlet* or a 'Last Supper', but if the minute scribblings which compose the big work are not significant, the big work goes for nothing no matter how grandly conceived. Which of us can control our scribblings? They are the script of one's personality like your voice or your walk" (Power, *Conversations with James Joyce*, p. 89). And on p. 95: "a book, in my opinion, should not be planned out beforehand, but as one writes it will form itself, subject, as I say, to the constant emotional promptings of one's personality."

8. For the best account of the role of Lewis Carroll in *Finnegans Wake*, see Atherton's chapter on "Lewis Carroll: The Unforseen Precursor," in *The Books at the Wake*, pp. 124–36. For a superb analysis of the affinities binding Joyce's comedy to "the comedy of regression" in the Alice books, see Robert M. Polhemus, *Comic Faith: The Great Tradition from Austen to Joyce* (Chicago: Univ. of Chicago Press, 1980), pp. 245–337.

9. "The only quotation of any length to be included in" *Finnegans Wake* (Hart, *Structure and Motif*, p. 183), the sentence is from Quinet's *Introduction à la philosophie de l'histoire de l'humanité*, and it appears in the *Wake*, the French slightly misquoted, in the "Night Lessons" chapter, at 281.4–10. Those lines translate as follows:
   Today, as in the time of Pliny and Columelle, the hyacinth thrives in Wales, the periwinkle in Illyria, the daisy on the ruins of Numantia, and while the cities around them have changed masters and names, several having passed into nothingness, civilizations having clashed and broken, their peaceful generations have crossed the ages and come down to us, fresh and laughing as in days of battles.
These "peaceful generations," like all the little "Blooms" that go sailing off into the future of June 17 at the end of *Ulysses* (e.g., *U*, 783, ll. 5–7), resemble the children of the world, resourcefully determined to thrive, because they must, even if "the old folkers" do not. For other evocations of this sentence in the *Wake*, see Hart, *Structure and Motif*, pp. 182–200, where it and its variants are discussed at length.

12. "ANNA LIVIA PLURABELLE"

1. A. Walton Litz, *The Art of James Joyce*, pp. 100, 118.

2. 800, according to Fred H. Higginson in his "Introduction" to *Anna Livia Plurabelle: The Making of a Chapter* (Minneapolis: The Land Press, 1960), p. 13; and 1036 "(excluding repetitions, and counting as one different rivers of the same name)," according to L. O. Mink in "Anna Livia's Handmaidens," *A Wake Newslitter*, n.s., 15 (December 1978): 83. See also the *Gazetteer*, p. xvii.

3. Atherton, *Books at the Wake*, p. 45.

4. Higginson, *Anna Livia Plurabelle: The Making of a Chapter*, pp. 13, 4.

5. From an unsigned notice, "James Joyce et Le Snobisme," *Le Monde* (2 May 1931), 4; rpt. in Deming, *James Joyce: The Critical Heritage*, 2, p. 416.

6. Marvin Magalaner and Richard M. Kain, *Joyce: The Man, the Work, the Reputation* (New York: Collier, 1962), p. 244.

7. On the Swahili (Eng. for "Kiswahili") in *Finnegans Wake*, see Philipp Wolff, "Kiswahili Words in *Finnegans Wake*," *A Wake Newslitter*, o.s., 9 (January 1963): 2–4; Jack P. Dalton, "Re 'Kiswahili Words in *Finnegans Wake*' by Philipp Wolff," *A Wake Newslitter*, o.s., 12 (April 1963): 6–12; Clive Hart, "The Elephant in the Belly: Exegesis of *Finnegans Wake*," *A Wake Newslitter*, o.s., 13 (May 1963): 1–8, rpt. in *A Wake Digest*, pp. 3–12; M. J. C. Hodgart, "Kiswahili/Kissuaheali," *A Wake Newslitter*, n.s., (February 1964): 4–5; and Jack P. Dalton, "Some Errata in Hodgart's 'Word Hoard'," *A Wake Newslitter*, n.s., 1 (June 1964): 10–11.

On the Dutch in *Finnegans Wake*, see Leo Knuth, "Dutch Elements in *Finnegans Wake* PP. 75–78 Compared With Holograph Workbook VI.B.46," *A Wake Newslitter*, n.s., 5 (April 1968): 19–28; "Dutch in *Finnegans Wake*," *A Wake Newslitter*, n.s., 8 (April 1971): 24–32, (June 1971): 35–43, and (August 1971): 54–62.

"Apart from pertinent word lists," as Fritz Senn has rightly argued, "what we need is some idea of why any given language is used in a given place"; Senn, "Dutch Interpretation," *A Wake Newslitter*, n.s., 11 (June 1974): 54.

8. Higginson, *Anna Livia Plurabelle: The Making of a Chapter*, pp. 8, 18, 41, 53, 69.

9. Ellis, *The World of Dreams*, p. 77.

10. "A Metapsychological Supplement to the Theory of Dreams," *Standard Edition*, 4, p. 223. According to Freud, "a dream appears to be a reaction to everything that is simultaneously present in the sleeping mind as currently active material" (*ID*, 261)—including "Internal (Somatic) Stimuli" (*ID*, 67–76, 117–18, 253–72, 628). "The essential nature of the dream is not altered by the fact of somatic material being added to it," however (*ID*, 262). For "*dreams do not simply reproduce the stimulus; they work it over, they make allusions to it, they include it in some context, they replace it by something else*" (*Introductory Lectures on Psychoanalysis*, p. 96 [italics mine]).

11. Northcote Whitbridge Thomas, "Dream," *Encyclopedia Britannica*, 11th ed., 8, p. 559.

12. On hearing, see 196.5–6, 197.20, 198.27–28, 200.28–29, 201.3–4, 203.20, 204.25–26, 204.34–35, 207.30–31, 209.24, 213.8–9, 213.16, 213.33, 214.7–10; on not or never hearing, or not being heard, see 198.27–28, 199.32–33, 200.14–16 (Anglo-Ir. "bothered" = "deaf"), 201.24, 23–24 ("in the silence"), 206.7–8, 207.23, 213.29–30, 215.31ff.; on the desire to hear, evoked continually by the chapter's refrain, "O, tell me all I want to hear" (198.14), see 196.1–4, 204.12–23, 206.16–17, and 206.18–20.

13. All of the river-names cited in the text have been drawn from Mink's *Gazetteer*, McHugh's *Annotations*, Litz's *The Art of James Joyce* (pp. 100–114), and Mink's "Anna Livia's Handmaidens." Names of rivers that are repeated in the text are identified only at the bottom of the page on which they first appear.

14. "From the waterfall he named her, Minnehaha, laughing water" (Henry Wadsworth Longfellow, *The Song of Hiawatha*, part 4). Note how the passage cited in the text, like the sound of the bloodstream, sustains part of its meaning not through any literal "sense" but through that distinct form of "sound" known as rhythm: "Minneha, minnehi, minaehe, minneho! . . . Make my hear it gurgle gurgle like the farest gargle gargle in the dusky dirgle dargle!" (206.15–18). In what will begin to illuminate Joyce's claims that the chapter purveyed meaning through "sound sense" (though not in the merely impressionistic way that the criticism has implied) the "sound" of these lines replicates not the "sense," but the tom-tom "sound" of Longfellow's poem about "Laughing Water" ("By the shores of Gitche Gumee,/By the shining Big-Sea-Water").

15. Joyce "felt some misgiving about [the first draft of 'Anna Livia'] the night it was finished, and went down to the Seine to listen by one of the bridges to the water. He came back content" (*JJ*, 564n.). Joyce's remarks to Harriet Shaw Weaver on an early draft of "Anna Livia," moreover, make clear the extent to which he conceived the episode, right from the start, in a way that would highlight both hearing in the night and the sound of water: "the first words are 'O tell me,'" he explained, the last 'waters of Night!'" (*L*, III, 90 [1924]).

16. "Fingal's Cave is cut through columns of basalt that shield all parts of the island [of Staffa, in the Hebrides]. Its Celtic name is *An-Na-Vine* or *Fine*, which means 'the harmonious cave,' or, according to another translation, 'Fingal's Cave.' These two names explain themselves; often, in effect, the roar of the sea and murmurs of wind, which die out while whirling to the back of the cave across columns arranged like the casings of an organ, produce sounds of marvelous harmony; 'these are the aeolian harps of the ghosts of the Fianna,' say the Gaels, who link the idea of Fingal to everything that seems supernatural to them": Badin, *Grottes et Cavernes*, p. 171, translation mine; "Fingal" is "Macpherson's name for Finn MacCool in the Ossianic cycle" (Mink, *Gazetteer*, p. 314). The harmonious inspiration for Mendelssohn's "Hebridean" or "Fingal's Cave Overture," Mink reminds us, Fingal's Cave resembles the "tropped head" of the *Wake*'s "sleeping giant"—"a locally person of caves" (365.2)—in being a vast natural cavity filled, as in "Anna Livia," with haunting echoes of washing waters. For more on "Fingal's Cave," see Mink, *Gazetteer*, p. 314; and the orthodox and nocturnal maps of Europe included in this book.

17. As Glasheen notes (*Third Census*, p. 63), "Corrigan's pulse" is named for the "Irish doctor who discovered the ailment"; it resembles our hero's in being Irish.

18. The chapter thus opens up indefinitely into the kind of archetypal and anthropological analyses with which readers of the critical work on *Finnegans Wake* will be familiar: almost anything that one might associate with running water is reflected somewhere in "Anna Livia." For a superb illustration of where one path of these associations leads, see Grace Eckley, "Queer Mrs. Quickenough and Odd Miss Doddpebble: The Tree and the Stone in *Finnegans Wake*," in Begnal and Eckley, *Narrator and Character in "Finnegans Wake*," pp. 129–235. On the relations of human communities and running water, see also Vico (*NS*, 527–28, 534, 714).

19. O Hehir, *Gaelic Lexicon*, p. 392. "*Life* is an old form of Liffey," Glasheen compara-

bly notes, quite rightly going on to argue that "in *FW* every 'life,' 'live,' 'alive,' 'living' names Anna Livia and the Liffey" (*Third Census*, pp. 168–69).

20. This will perhaps explain why, in a letter to Italo Svevo, Joyce compared "the little river of [his] city, the Anna Liffey," to "the longest river on earth" (*L*, III, 133n.). Particularly because the comparison enters the letter with remarks on "cordiality" (< L. *cors, cordis*, "heart"), what he likely had in mind as "the longest river on earth" was Here Comes Everybody's bloodstream, since 60 or 70,000 miles of "vesles vet" lie coiled inside every body, daily channeling the flow of two thousand gallons of blood through an endlessly intricated network of "scarlet thread."

21. Eckley, "Queer Mrs. Quickenough and Odd Miss Doddpebble," in *Narrator and Character in "Finnegans Wake,"* pp. 199–200.

22. Higginson, *Anna Livia Plurabelle: The Making of a Chapter*, p. 6.

23. This feature of the "ebro" in which "Anna Livia" is written will suggest why the apparent recklessness that Joyce is supposed to have exhibited while helping to translate the chapter into French and Italian was *only* apparent. As Ellmann recounts it, "Joyce's whole emphasis [in these translating sessions] was . . . on sonority, rhythm, and verbal play; to the sense he seemed indifferent and unfaithful" (*JJ*, 700); "he sometimes astonished [both the French and Italian translators] by caring more for sound and rhythm than sense" (*JJ*, 632–33). What sense? Nino Frank, one of Ellmann's sources, comparably notes that "two things struck [him]: first, that the rhythm, the harmony, the density and consonance of the words were more important to Joyce than the meaning, and that, for example, having written one thing, Joyce scarcely hesitated to put down something completely different in Italian, as long as the poetic or metrical result was equivalent" (Frank, "The Shadow that Had Lost its Man," in *Portraits of the Artist in Exile*, p. 97). Reading "Anna Livia" suggests quite the opposite of what is generally assumed from accounts like these. Because the chapter is about a kind of sense and "meanam" that fills the ear in the absence of literal sense and meaning, Joyce knew quite well what he was doing.

24. This would account, incidentally, for the appearance throughout *Finnegans Wake* of weird temperance organizations like "the Ballymooney Bloodriddon Murther" (219.19–20 [note the "blood"]). Unlike "the Ballyhooly Blue Ribbon Army," the subject of a comic song "about a temperance movement in a notoriously intemperate town" (Mink, *Gazetteer*, p. 222), this one meets in the night (hence the "moon"), when HCE is dead to the world (hence the "blood-ridden murder"). Sleeping is our hero's way of taking the pledge.

25. On sleep as a somatic "reactivation of intrauterine existence," see Freud's "Metapsychological Supplement to the Theory of Dreams," p. 222, and the *Introductory Lectures on Psychoanalysis*, where Freud characterizes sleep as a "withdraw[al] . . ." into "existence in the womb" that returns the adult organism to "the foetal state of rest" (pp. 88–89). Because his interests lay more in the analysis of dreams than in a reconstruction of the night, Freud himself made relatively little of these remarks, though his immediate successors developed them in elaborate and often engaging ways.

The most interesting of these elaborations, for a reader of the *Wake*, are Roheim's, in *The Gates of the Dream*, and Ferenczi's in *Thalassa*. Because Roheim "assumes that the dream is primarily a reaction to the fact that we are asleep," and seeks to develop an account of "a basic dream valid for mankind in general" (*Gates*, pp. 1, 15), his work amounts to a "reconstruction of the nocturnal life" which, though psychoanalytically biased, resonates in every way with Joyce's in the *Wake*. In Roheim's account of the dark, "the sleeper turns into himself and falls back into the womb, his own body being the material substratum of the dream-womb" (p. 7); "the environment into which the dreamer regresses is both [his] own body and the maternal womb" (p. 20). See also pp. 14, 16, 20, 88–94, and Brown, *Love's Body*, pp. 45–56.

Ferenczi's *Thalassa*, an astonishing fantasia, synthesizes the "new sciences" of psycho-analysis, animal evolution, and embryology in order to provide a "utraquistic" or "bio-analytic" account of sleep (pp. 3, 84, 73–81). Operating from the observations that sleep, foetalized birth (and coitus) are mutually developing evolutionary variables that attain their most complex forms in human beings, Ferenczi sees the womb as an internalized sea that mammalian organisms incorporate and carry with them when they stagger onto land. "The amniotic fluid represents a sea 'introjected,' as it were, into the womb of the mother—a sea in which, as the embryologist Hertwig says 'the delicate and easily in-jured embryo swims and executes movements like a fish in water'" (p. 56). Falling asleep, therefore, means not simply undergoing uterine regression—"turning into one's own body and the maternal womb"—but also undergoing a deeper form of thalassal re-gression and, as the *Wake* puts it, "go[ing] the way of all fish" (254.12): "H.C.E. has a codfisck ee" (198.8–9). Ferenczi's work is altogether compatible with the *Wake*.

26. Thomas Verney, M.D., with John Kelly, *The Secret Life of the Unborn Child* (New York: Summit, 1981), p. 21. "Recent studies show that from the twenty-fourth week on, the unborn child listens all the time. And he has a lot to listen to. The pregnant abdomen and uterus are very noisy places. The mother's stomach rumblings are the loudest sounds he hears. Her voice, his father's voice, and other occasional sounds are quieter but still audible to him. The sound that dominates his world, though, is the rhythmic thump of the maternal heartbeat. . . . The reassuring rhythm of its beat is one of the major con-stellations in his universe. He falls asleep to it, wakes to it, moves to it. Because the human mind, even the human mind in utero, is a symbol-making entity, the foetus gradually attaches a metaphorical meaning to it. [It] comes to symbolize tranquillity, security and love to him" (p. 38, 28 [note the inadequacy of the English]).

Actually, these studies are not so recent; they simply yield articles of understanding that Joyce, writing of the "virgin womb of the imagination" (*P*, 217), reading extensively in embryology, and pressing his ear against Nora's belly in order to listen to the birth of Lucia (It., "light") into the world, would have learned in any number of mutually re-inforcing ways. His interest in these topics can be minimally gauged from a study of the embryological notes that he compiled while planning "Oxen of the Sun" (see Philip F. Herring, *Joyce's Ulysses Notesheets in the British Museum* [Charlottesville, Va.: Univ. of Virginia Press, 1972], pp. 163–257). The notebooks show him exercising an interest in "creation from nothing" (Herring, p. 280), "previous existence" (p. 163) and "plasmic memory" (p. 171); and they include entries not simply on the formation and wakening of the ear—"4 & 5 m[onth] (ear hammer and anvil)," Joyce notes (p. 224), "one (ear) can hear what other says" (p. 223)—but also on the genesis of sensation, in "4th and 5th m[onth]," when the "pressure of amnios on face ear, jawal, [and] buccal" areas elicits a reactive response from nerves growing outward from the interior of dark water (p. 224). Joyce goes on to note that the "fetus [is] 1st independent" and exercises "voluntary move-ment [in the] 5th m[onth]" (p. 170). The notebooks ultimately show him studying with some empirical intensity "the embryo philosopher" who lies at "the bottom of reason" (pp. 218, 219). As one of Joyce's main amanuenses and confidants has notified Joyce's public, study of "the embryo philosopher" also played into a book about how little Finnegans wake: according to Samuel Beckett, "there is a great deal of the unborn child in the lifeless octogenarian" who lies dead to the world, enjoying "foetal sleep," at the *Wake* (*Our Exagmination*, p. 8).

This is so weird and wonderful an aspect of *Finnegans Wake* that it would be best to be clear at once about what a form of unconsciousness that might now be equated with prenatal memory might mean ("You were there"). Especially in a world of "Uncontrollable Birth" (184.15 [but a day of variously problematized forms of "birth control"]), beliefs about what kind of life might have preceded its waking are likely to be as highly charged—"no thing making newthing wealthshowever"—as beliefs about what kind of life might follow its wake (see 293.L1, 323.36–324.1, 452.29–31, and 447.8). Many readers, wanting "to avoid assuming a memory of different kind than that with which we are familiar" (Roheim, *The Gates of the Dream*, p. 89), will concur with the idea that "it is not necessary to postulate any memories of blissful intrauterine feelings"; "the intrauterine fantasy . . . is a nursing fantasy with a shift downward from the breast to the abdomen" (B. D. Lewin, *The Psychoanalysis of Elation* [New York, 1950], pp. 109–10; quoted in Roheim, p. 89). And yet others will want to take this aspect of the *Wake* very seriously indeed: there is a whole "new science" or "new discipline called prenatal psychology" (Verney, p. 24), whose study obviously engaged Joyce deeply.

To simplify a meditation that now threatens to become as bottomless as the one localized in Finnegan's coffin, we might think of prenatal memory as a form of "sohnt" that is "state-dependently" evoked in those parts of the night falling between dreams, when HCE's "tropped head" contains only the hearing of its own bloodstream (a "state-dependent memory," in neurology, is one that "can be recalled only in [the] specific . . . state . . . in which the memory was acquired" (Furst, *Origins of the Mind*, pp. 256, 178–179). It would be a memory of what the "unknown body" void of mind "thinks" as it pulls itself together out of darkness somewhere within hearing of the river Life. "Foetotype[s]" (324.1) captured in this form of "sohnt" are reconstructed everywhere in the *Wake*.

Consider, for instance, this business about the unborn child's hearing its mother's voice and stomach rumbling, and compare it to a passage in the *Wake* which explains "that Glugg, the poor one, in that limbopool which was his subnesciousness he could scares of all knotknow whither his morrder had bourst a blabber or if the vogalstones that hit his tynpan was that mearly his skoll missed her" (224.16–20). "Subnesciousness," presumably lying beneath "nesciousness" (< L. *nescio*, "I do not know"), would move us below any conventionally defined form of "unconsciousness" into a new depth of the Joycean "ungumptious," so to raise many questions about the "limbopool" being sounded here: are the "vocal tones hitting [Glugg's] tympanum" those of a "mother's blabber" (or mouth), or did his "mother burst a bladder"? One can "scarce of all know," though the imprint on "his skoll" of noise emanating from a feminine "schoolmaster" ("skoll missed her") evidently "scares" him. Nobody ever said that Joyce, *Finnegans Wake*, or the night and the Unconscious were not strange.

27. There were, for Joyce, some characteristically strange extratextual sequels to the writing of "Anna Livia Plurabelle." When Daniel Brody reminded him in 1940 of a German translation of the chapter that Georg Goyert had done, Joyce wrote back to wonder: "Do you think it would be possible to publish the version you have in Holland? After all, it is only about rivers and washerwomen" (*L*, III, 464). Why ask an editor known from

Zurich to publish a German translation of an English text in a country where Dutch is the main language? We are looking, perhaps, at that side of Joyce's mind which appalled and astonished Frank O'Connor who, pointing to a picture of Cork in Joyce's apartment and asking what the frame was made of, got the answer "cork." Had Joyce had his way, "Anna Livia" might have been framed like that picture: as Cork in cork, so "remembrandts" in nether-lands.

28. Ferdinand C. Lane, *The World's Great Lakes* (Garden City, N.Y.: Doubleday, 1948), p. 47: "the big lakes so long hidden beyond the horizon of scientific certainty have been identified as Victoria Nyanza, [and] Albert Nyanza."

For a representative specimen of the kind of language found in that peculiar turn-of-the century genre, the Nile travelogue, see Emil Ludwig, *The Nile: The Life-Story of a River*, trans. Mary H. Lindsay (New York: Viking, 1937): "Where are we? The source of the Nile. . . . None guessed its origin. For thousands of years men sought this source and went astray. . . . Here, at the source . . . [the land] has been likened to Paradise," its smallest features revealing "the symbol of the landscape of a dream" (pp. 5–6). For a more sinister example of the same rhetoric, see Samuel White Baker, *The Albert Nyanza: Great Basin of the Nile and Explorations of the Nile Sources* (rpt.; New York: Horizon Press, 1962), 2, p. 520: "Whether the man of Central Africa be pre-Adamite is impossible to determine. . . . Cut off from [the Christian] world, lost in the mysterious distance that shrouded the origin of the Egyptian Nile, were races unknown, that had never reckoned in the great sum of history—races that we have brought to light, whose existence had been hidden from mankind, and that now appear before us like the fossil bones of antediluvian animals. Are they vestiges of what existed in a pre-Adamite creation?"

These quotations will also clarify the recurrence in *Finnegans Wake* of references to "Victoria Nyanza" and "Albert Nyanza," the two great bodies of water from which the Nile arises (23.19–21, 89.27, 105.14, 202.18–20, 558.27–28, 598.6, 600.12–13 [Mink, *Gazetteer*, pp. 200, 529]). Absorbed by "the secrest of their soorcelossness" (23.19 [but note again the Gr. ôo-, "egg," in this "soorce"]), as well as the origins of "the Nil" (598.6 [Fr. *Nil*, "Nile"; L. *nil*, "nothing"]), Joyce embroiders these two traditionally fathomless "bodies of water"—each interimplicated in each other by a network of tangled waterways and yet lying incommunicado at "the soorce"—into ciphers for the "anastomosically assimilated" mother and child (615.5) out of whom, downstream, civilization grows. See the cited contexts.

29. Where a reading of *The New Science* will explain why Joyce, undertaking an "*abnihilisation of the etym*" (353.22), unravelled English into the polylingual elements out of which it arose, attention to the Swahili and Dutch in "Anna Livia" will yield a principle by which to understand the appearance in *Finnegans Wake* of languages *not* genetically related to English—especially if we compare the *Wake*'s use of Swahili and Dutch to other languages that have been explored in passing: Swiss-German (chapter 2, note 7), Australian and New Zealand slangs (chapter 7, note 29), black American idioms (chapter 7, note 9).

As Joyce himself points out in a passage about Shem—a penman who speaks with "tongues in his cheek" about "anythongue athall" (340.4, 117.15–16)—"the various meanings of all the different foreign parts of speech" that appear in the *Wake* are "*misused*"—misused as wittily as elements in dreams—and misused precisely in order to "giv[e] unsolicited testimony on behalf of the absent . . . to those present" by doing service in the work of "unconsciously explaining" nocturnal events in the body of someone "tropped head," evidently "of pentecostitis" (173.29–36, 130.9 [italics mine]). Languages like Dutch and Swahili, in other words, of which a sleeping bartender would be obviously *unconscious*, overlay parts of this "basically English" text (116.26) in order to invest it locally with properties which, if we pursue "distant connections" and read "between the lines" (169.6, 3), we might associate with Dutch and Swahili.

We might see how this principle could be extended—to Armenian or Latin, for instance—by "talking of hayastdanars and wolkingology and how our seaborn isle came into exestuance" (387.11–12 [where the *Hayasdan* in "hayastdanars" is Armenian for "Armenia," and "vulcanology" is the study of how, "from next to nothing," the earth began "boiling up" (L. *exestuans*) into "existence"]). Because Armenian is a language currently spoken at the site of Mt. Ararat, where the Biblical world began, the associations show Armenian serving the symbolic function, in a way that a historicized proto–Indo-European never could, of a protolanguage in *Finnegans Wake*. It would differ from Swahili, in this respect, because the "distant connections" to which we are led by thinking about Mt. Ararat and the sources of the Nile are altogether distinct in their complexities. Though Latin, comparably, is one of the founts of English and the instrument of the Catholic Church, it is also, as a "dead language," a language spoken primarily by dead people. Parts of the night in which HCE lies dead to the world in a "seemetery," then, are written "*decentius in lingua romana mortuorum*" (287.20–21 ["more fitly in the Roman tongue of the dead"]).

To be exhaustive at this point about the sixty-odd foreign languages put to work in the *Wake* would be impossible—and particularly because the relations between these languages and the English with which they merge are hidden in indefinite associations. A great deal more work needs to be done, however, on the "states" that the languages of foreign states evoke in the *Wake*.

30. David Diringer, *The Alphabet: A Key to the History of Mankind*, 3d ed. rev. (London: Hutchinson and Co., 1968), 1, p. 21.

31. Brown, *Love's Body*, p. 56.

32. See Brown, *Love's Body*, pp. 80–89, for the best possible commentary on this aspect of the *Wake*.

33. On the Bartholomew Deep, see Mink, *Gazetteer*, p. 225; and Sir John Murray and Dr. Johann Hjart, *The Depths of the Ocean* (London: Macmillan and Co., 1912), Map 2, pp. 128–29.

34. Exceeding "the unplumbed profundity in the Sundam trench of the Pacific" (*U*, 671), the "bed" of the Challenger Deep lies under a bonecrushing slab of water seven miles deep, 36,198 feet below the surface of the ocean, where 3-1/2 tons of frigid abyssal brine weigh upon every square inch of space and prevent even water from freezing. Void of light, which cannot penetrate the ocean beneath a depth of 1,800 feet, and of life, it is "the deepest hole in the deep," a concrete site of "Real Absence," and has not yet been definitively sounded. On the Challenger Deep and the sources for this note, see Mink, *Gazetteer*, p. 256; Murray and Hart, *The Depths of the Ocean*, p. 143; C. P. Idyll, "The Science of the Sea," and Robert S. Dietz, "The Underwater Landscape," in C. P. Idyll, ed., *The Science of the Sea: A History of Oceanography* (London: Thomas and Sons, 1970), pp. 2–21 and 22–41; C. P. Idyll, *Abyss: The Deep Sea and the Creatures That Live in It*, rev. ed. (New York: Thomas Crowell, 1976), p. 23; and Martyn Bramwell, *The Rand McNally Atlas of the Oceans* (Chicago: Rand McNally, 1977), p. 159.

35. On "Lough Neagh," the largest lake in the British Isles, see Mink's *Gazetteer*,

pp. 417–18; Campbell and Robinson, *A Skeleton Key*, p. 81 n3; and Roland McHugh, "Recipis for the Price of a Coffin," in Begnal and Senn, *A Conceptual Guide to Finnegans Wake*, p. 31: "The Celtic underworld was often conceived as being situated beneath the sea or a lake. In pagan times, Eochu was believed to be lord of the otherworld beneath Lough Neagh (hence its name, Loch n-Eochach, the lake of Eochu). In Christian times, after Eochu had been euhemerized into a mortal man, his connection with the lake was explained by inventing the legend that he was drowned when the lake burst forth and flooded his country. So the legend recorded by Giraldus Cambrensis that fishermen on Lough Neagh could see buildings (round towers) in calm weather."

36. "Sleep [is] characterized by certain body postures which, especially in the case of first sleep, have been described by quite unbiased observers as 'the foetal posture.' The extremities are drawn up to the body, so that the whole body assumes the so to speak spheroid shape which exigencies of space made a physical necessity *in utero*. Between sleep and the embryonic state far reaching analogies can be demonstrated with regard to metabolic function. Animals are preoccupied in the daytime with the obtaining and digestion of food, but its absorption proper, its assimilation into the tissues, takes place rather during the night, so the physiologists assert (qui dort dîne). Thus sleep creates the illusion of an effortless providing with nourishment similar to that obtaining *in utero*. It is often maintained, furthermore, that growth and regeneration take place for the greater part during sleep; while growth might be said to be the sole activity of the embryo in the womb" (Ferenczi, *Thalassa*, p. 75).

37. Along this line of associations, the *Wake* absorbs myths structured on the image of a "Cosmic egg," which Campbell and Robinson allude to in *A Skeleton Key* (pp. 5, 31). On such myths, see Charles H. Long, *Alpha: The Myths of Creation* (New York: Collier, 1963), particularly chapter 3 ("Creation from Chaos and from the Cosmic Egg"), pp. 113–49.

38. I am indebted here to an essay written by Brett Bourbon, on "The Interrelation between Identity and Becoming in *Finnegans Wake*," for a class on the *Wake* taught at the University of California–Berkeley in Spring 1985.

39. Joyce: "The object of any work of art is the transference of emotion"; "I've tried to write naturally, on an emotional basis as against an intellectual basis. Emotion has dictated the course and detail of my book, and in emotional writing one arrives at the unpredictable which can be of more value, since its sources are deeper than the products of the intellectual method. . . . This is 'Work in Progress'" (Power, *Conversations with James Joyce*, pp. 98, 95).

40. Mercanton, "The Hours of James Joyce," p. 213.

Index

Absence, 38; of senses and perception, 7, 45–50, 58, 62, 100, 102, 398 n.10, 441 n.3; absentmindedness, 38, 53, 57; "Real Absence," 43–44, 47–59, 62–64, 76, 109, 152, 272, 274–75, 282, 338–39; of life, 45, 62, 66–74, 103–4; of experience, 54; of ideas, 63; of mind, 63–64, 101–2; "your own absence," 71; and exile, 110–11; of human subject, 274–75; of content, 315

Adam, 50, 83, 168, 424 n.16; "red loam," 79; and Eve, 157, 223, 303, 363, 364, 367, 380; Enlightenment view of, 177, 192; Adam's dream, 211

Alarm clocks, 268, 278; alarm clock dreams, 443 n.17

Alcohol, 38, 47, 137–38, 279–80, 282, 393 n.34, 419 n.10; and "blacking out," 38, 54, 70, 76, 132, 137; and "Finnegan's Wake," 69–71; and drugs, 79–80, 137; sobriety and temperance organizations, 353, 457 n.24

All Souls' Night (Halloween), 53, 55, 77, 281, 321

Amen-Ra, 93–94, 98–99, 102, 104, 118, 123–24; meaning of name, 86. See also Sun

Amenti, 85; meaning of name, 86; described, 94–95; and "amentia," 101–2; experience of corpse in, 102–25

America: as "New World," 110–11, 358, 411–12 n.80; other world, 282; "Amessica," 166; Joyce on, 425 n.22; American idioms and songs in FW, 110–12, 252. See also End of the world

Amnesia ("blank memory"), 4–5, 7, 29, 47–49, 58, 63, 68, 69, 71, 73, 77, 317–18; visual components of, 47, 218; content of, 143. See also Memory, unconscious

Anarchy, 40, 170–71, 179, 425 n.23–24, 426 n.29

Anna Livia Plurabelle (character), 140, 349–70, 365, 376–84; as widow, 328, 365; as acrostic ALP, 348, 366; associations with water, 356, 364; associations with maternal attachment, 356–71, 376–84; presence throughout FW, 363–64, 374, 379, 382; as "Bringer of the Plurabilities," 370, 384; as Hen, 376; as "mother of the book," 382–84; relation to Issy, 436 n.26

"Anna Livia Plurabelle" (chapter), 257, 336–63; Joyce on, 336, 344, 347, 349; rivers and river-names in, 336–38, 341–49, 352, 379; composition of, 336–38, 456 n.15; sound of bloodstream as basis of, 340–46, 363–66; as representation of aliterate "meanam," 341–48, 362; rivalry in, 350–51; as reconstruction of prenatal memory, 354–61; gynocentrism of, 356–57; temporality of, 358–59; foreign languages in, 359–61; vision in, 436 n.26, 439 n.28. See also Embryology; Mothering; Representation; Sexuality: female

Appetite and hunger, 101, 103, 115–16, 124, 171, 279, 282; for breakfast, 82, 118, 284, 375, 377–78; in infancy, 377–78. See also Shaun

Aries, Philippe, 401 n.2, 402 n.8

Aristotle, 22, 282, 394 n.8; on dream interpretation, 418 n.5, 436 n.25, 444 n.10

Arrest, corporal: and paralytic sleep, 12, 59–63, 74–75, 218; as "petrifaction," 45–46, 48, 69, 374; ciphers for, 75, 79, 115–16, 148, 222, 338, 347, 441 n.15, 442 n.13; vs. rigor mortis, 77, 91, 101–4, 109, 114–17, 122–24; "sense arrest," 220, 339

Arthur, King, 105, 132, 138, 382

Association, free: 9, 27; and interpretation, 39–40, 274–80, 295, 382, 384–85, 397 n.13, 449–51 nn.1–2; as form of thought in dream, 156, 192, 276, 280, 302, 309, 382, 445 n.23; and language and reading, 305–9; and childhood, 322, 325, 327; as basis of "Anna Livia Plurabelle," 348–50, 352–53, 356, 363–64, 366, 368–70, 380–81

Atherton, James, 91, 336, 393 n.31, 401 n.19, 406 nn.17–18, 408 n.53, 411–12 n.80, 414 n.107, 415 n.108, 417 n.3, 454 n.8

Attridge, Derek, 397 n.10

Australia, 110, 164, 235, 238, 249, 252, 256, 325, 437 n.31

Authority, patriarchal, 39, 83, 168–70, 329; collapse of, 170–71, 328, 366–67, 377, 381–83; and conflict, 185, 229; in Vico, 190–91, 199–206; language as submission to, 289–90, 329–31, 345, 354, 381, 383

Badin, Adolphe, 456 n.16

Baker, Samuel White, 460 n.28

Ballad (I.ii), 55–56, 206, 282, 299–303, 309, 432 n.10

Bats, 339, 430 n.6, 435 n.20

Bears, 53, 153, 193, 219, 422–23 n.9

Beckett, Samuel, 8, 140; on Vico, 175, 199; and *Work in Progress*, 360

Begnal, Michael H., 417 n.3

Benstock, Bernard, 417 n.3, 419 n.12, 420 n.20, 421 n.3, 424 n.15

Bergin, Thomas Goddard, 427 n.1, 428 n.12

Berkeley, George, 165, 437 n.29

Biblical references: Jehoshaphat, 76; Apocalypse (Revelations), 77, 334, 402 n.8; Gehenna, 81; the Fall, 82; the sheep and the goats, 83, 381, 402 n.8; YHWH, 141, 189; Fiat, 217–18; Isaac, 224; Jacob, 224; Noah, 231, 255, 257; Lot, 243; Joseph, 252; the Flood, 255–57, 342, 343, 359, 427 n.7; Pentateuch, 307, 310; Babel, 307, 326, 332, 345; Hebrews, 309; Cain and Abel, 331; Anti-Christ, 334; Jonah, 372; Eden, 379–80; Daniel and Nebuchadnezzar, 385; Ararat, 444 n.19. *See also* Adam; Genesis, Book of

Bigelow, John (*The Mystery of Sleep*), 227 (quoted), 392 n.30

Bird, William, 4, 273

Blindness, 47, 48, 50, 53, 59, 115, 154, 230, 270, 280, 304, 339, 346, 348; functional, of sleep, 123–30; Joyce and, 434–35 n.15, 438 n.6; stages of, 438 n.6

Blinking, 47, 253–60; autonomic nature of the blink-reflex, 259; as symptomatic sign, 259–61; variability of, 260

Bloom, Leopold, 17, 22, 84, 118, 164, 313, 340, 371; compared to HCE, 135–37, 419 n.11; Odysseus, and heroism, 178; impact on Stephen, 213, 283; stream of consciousness, 269–70; falling asleep, 355; fear of sleep-walking, 392 n.27; homecoming, 428 n.9; on Pepper's ghost, 432 n.13; on musical instruments, 447 n.25

Body: as object in space, 28, 144; ciphers for, 37, 141–43, 235, 378, 396–97 n.9; as latent ground of the dream, 37, 80, 143–45, 156–58, 237–38, 240, 250–51, 302; sleep as burial in, 79–80, 98, 154, 181–82, 193–94, 270–72, 321; as site of "underworld," 96–97, 101–2, 108–9; as site of the resurrection, 123–25; as container of letters and dreams, 140, 235, 248, 332; as subject of *FW*, 140–45, 155–58, 193–95, 252–61, 315, 341–46; organic vs. politic, 145; as field of conflict, 173, 240, 246–51, 253–54, 261, 279–80, 299–300; formation of, in infancy, 190–93, 289–91; as ground of gentile reality and language, 197–99, 210; repression of, 198, 210, 254, 299; as ground of vision, 244–47; as medium of symptomatic writing, 248–51, 259–60, 328. *See also* Education; HCE: Identity; Laws; Tailoring; Vico; Vision

Bogan, Louise, 3

Book of the Dead, Egyptian, 81, 86–125; *FW* as, 72, 94, 104, 109–10, 111–12, 114, 125, 275, 372; history of, 88–89, 90–92; as guide to next world, 89, 100, 102, 121; relation to the night, 89, 92–93, 96, 101, 105, 109, 112–13; recensions of, 90; "rubrics" in, 99; "vignettes" in, 121; corpse's exploits in, 107, 114; chapter placement in, 114–16, 123–25; "chapters of making transformations," 122. *See also* Amen-Ra; Amenti; Egyptology and Egyptian allusions; Osiris

Boru, Brian, 441 n.6

Brian O Linn, 153, 154, 168, 422 n.8

Brion, Marcel, 143

Brivic, Sheldon R., 393 n.31

Brody, Daniel, 460 n.27

Derrida, Jacques (*continued*)
Words for Joyce," 448 n.33
Descartes, René, 117; Cartesian space, 31, 36, 144–45, 335; cogito, 68–69, 303–4; *FW* as deliberate break with Cartesianism, 142, 157, 397 n.13; and collapse of inner-outer distinctions, 153, 157–58, 189–90, 193; and rationalism, 177; *Dioptric*, 226; on state of nature, 427 n.6
Dillon, John M., xvi, 401 n.20
Diogenes, 252
Dionysius of Syracuse, 442 n.13
Diringer, David, 461 n.30
Discipline. *See* Education; Law
Douglas, Norman, 398 n.8
Doyles, 221
Dreamer: identity of, 130–45; "an old man," 131; "one stable somebody," 132–33, 139, 302–3, 306, 338–42, 400 n.17, 416–17 n.2, 417 n.3; agedness of, 133, 236, 241; Protestantism, 134, 135, 167; occupation of, 135; family life of, 135, 167; lineage of, 135, 352; as father, 167, 224, 241–43; apparent absence of, 338–42, 347; and unconscious memory, 354–56; "a family all to himself," 365. *See also* Earwicker; Finnegan; Finn MacCool; Mountain; Pubs and Inns
Dreams: and memory, 4–10, 19, 42, 46–48, 317–18, 321–24, 326–27, 354–55, 389 n.10; and epistemology, 7–10, 18, 390 n.16; manifest and latent contents, 8, 31–36, 247–52, 309–15, 324–25; and secondary revision, 8, 311; and sexuality, 12–13, 123, 145, 157, 165–67, 240–43, 249; and language, 14, 16, 18–19, 46–47, 59–62, 123, 195–98, 271–72, 305–15, 449–51 nn.1–2; and interpretation, 16–17, 27, 39–41; of constraint, 115; of flying, 122; and psychoanalytic account of dream formation, 129–30, 134, 249–51, 316, 355, 435 n.21, 437 n.33, 441 n.7, 457-58 n.25; "residue" as content of, 134–35, 381, 384; representations of space in, 149–50, 239, 244; of indiscretions, 166–67; conflict as origin of, 220, 240, 242–44, 250–51, 301–2; symptomatic nature of, 244–45, 247–51; of reading written signs, 247–51; sonic components of, 282–86, 301; infantile regression in, 316, 321–22, 324–27
Dream-work: wish fulfillment, 89, 128–30, 133, 157, 198, 240, 281, 284, 286, 335, 339; condensation and "composite structures," 132–33, 214, 418 nn.5–6; "day's residue," 134, 137; "overdetermination" of meaning

in, 137–38, 435 n.20; and distortion, 152; displacement, 167, 243; Vico's "poetic wisdom" as, 182, 190, 194; censorship, 243; sublimation, 243, 249; considerations of representability, 437 n.33
Dublin: 26, 30–37, 49, 54, 142, 145, 150–54, 158, 168–70, 171–72, 253–55, 268–69, 348–49; in history, 49, 57, 168, 423 n.10, 429 n.16; "Dublin papyrus," 91, 406 n.20; as dreamer's home, 135
—place-names: Adam and Eve's Church, 26; Liffey, 26, 30, 180, 348–49; Castle Knock, 30–31, 36, 397 n.13; Howth (Head), 30–31, 36, 54–55, 138, 140, 148, 155, 234, 272, 274, 276, 395 n.3; Phoenix Park, 31, 36, 166, 251, 395 n.2; Gaiety Theatre, 49, 54, 419 n.11; National Gallery, 54, 59; Chapelizod, 108, 135, 137, 153, 154; Clontarf, 152, 441 n.6; Wellington Memorial, 165, 185, 198, 244; Prospect Cemetery (Finglas), 347; Main Drainage System, 353; Waterhouse's Clock, 359; Poddle River, 379; Astley's Amphitheatre, 432–33 n.10; St. Michan's, 438 n.35; Fingal, 451 n.5
Dubliners: "The Dead," 21, 83; "The Sisters," 332
Dumbness, 39, 50, 52, 159, 264, 265, 271, 282; and dummies, 69, 77, 79
Dumbshows (pantomime), 48, 54, 236, 265, 271–72
Dump, 134–35, 236, 271–72, 375, 418 n.9

Ears: 261–62, 264–304, 323, 337, 340–64, 381; as ground of language, 261, 288–91; ascendancy over the eye, 261–62, 287–95; and stream of consciousness, 269; in sleep, 270–74, 276–82; never close, 272–74, 303, 339, 372, 442 n.12; and vigilance, 273, 276, 279, 281, 282, 295, 300, 339, 342; anatomy and mechanics of, 277–79, 295, 448 n.27; as scene of *NS*, 288; and auditory space, 288–91; as site of genesis, 289–95, 362–63; orienting power of, 290, 297, 355, 363; sound of bloodstream in, 344–45, 349, 351, 363–64, 380; embryology of, 458 n.26
Earwicker, 255, 262, 273–86, 339, 342, 349, 363; as cipher, 274–80, 288; as a real name, 300, 441 n.11, 449 n.36
Earwigs, 295–98; etymology, 296; and folklore, 297
Easter rising, 76
Eastman, Max, 449 n.2
Eckley, Grace, 409 n.56, 417 n.3, 436 n.24 453 n.4, 457 n.18

Eddas, 194, 208; Ginnunga-Gap, 359

Education: as disciplining of eyes and ears, 46–47, 165, 170, 196, 304; and language, 169–70, 322, 326–27, 329–33, 345; in Vico, 184–85, 190–93; in infancy, 289–91, 318–19, 322, 451–52 n.3; *FW* as negation of, 309, 329, 332–33, 345–46, 397 n.12; learning to write, 325; as humiliation, 326; learning to read, 326–27; as necessity, 329; as repression, 329–31; as destruction of potential, 331

Eggs, 133, 320, 357, 361, 375–80, 383

Ego, 131, 142, 235–37, 239, 249, 319; egotism of dream, 306; competitive egotism, 329

Egyptology and Egyptian allusions, 81, 85, 86–125; Sekhet Hetep, 85–86, 104, 116, 125; Horus, 87, 89, 109, 124; Khephera, 93; Isis, 98, 108; Cheops, 102; Nut, 106, 123; mastabah tombs, 113. *See also* Amen-Ra; Amenti; Book of the Dead; Osiris

Eliot, T. S., 21

Ellis, Havelock (*The World of Dreams*), 340, 389–90 n.10; 392 n.30

Ellmann, Richard, xi; on Kerse the tailor, 126; on Joyce's attitudes toward psychoanalysis, 393 n.34; on Joyce and houseplants, 413 n.95; on Joyce's interest in cubism and spatial relations, 420 n.3; on Joyce's addresses, 424–25 n.22; on Joyce's eye problems, 433 n.15; on genesis of *A Portrait*, 429 n.14; on Joyce and "Anna Livia Plurabelle," 456 n.15; on Joyce's recklessness in translating "Anna Livia Plurabelle," 457 n.23

Embryology, 143, 354–56; and foetal development, 358; anastomosis of the placenta, 359–60; pregnancy, 359–60; gynecology, 361

Emotion, 155–57; as aspect of the unconscious, 166, 169; as first thought in Vico, 182; as a component of the visible, 244–45, 258, 367; genesis and development of, 368–70; as growth, 370. *See also* Investments

Encyclopaedia Britannica, 135, 165, 312; on dreams, 340

English, 46; as interpretive medium, 156; history of, 207; medium of education, 324, 326–27; as domesticating force, 329; hazardous to your health, 351; disintegration of, 365

Enlightenment: social contracts, 176; and Goethe, 222

End of the world: ciphers for, 55, 110–11, 153, 255–59, 262, 420 n.8, 422 n.9, 441 n.5; sleep and death as, 76–77, 82, 334; end of history, 172, 334–35

Ensslin, Gudrun (Baader-Meinhof Gang), 425 n.23

Epiphany, 77, 291

Epistemology, 43, 50

Epstein, E. L., 420 n.20, 437 n.31

Erman, Adolf (*Life in Ancient Egypt*), 407 n.23, 410 n.73, 412 nn.82–83

Eschatology: defined, 24; and postmortality, 75–79; Christian vs. Egyptian, 104. *See also* Book of the Dead; Death; Life after death; Nothingness

Eskimos, 337, 351, 359–60

Eternity, 92, 147, 154; "eternal recurrence," 185

Ether, 53, 58, 274–77, 398 n.10

Etymologies of: "absurdity," 272; "accord," 369; "Adam," 79; "artless," 59; "aspect" and its correlates, 217; "barbarian," 294; "bed," 66; "body," 140; "cemetery," 67; "color," "hollow," "holes," and their correlates, 436 n.25; "discord" and "concord," 338; "Dublin," 423 n.10; "dusk," "dust," "obfuscation," and their correlates, 264–65; "Earwicker," 273; "earwig," 296; "entail," "retail," and "tailor," 127; "envy," 241; "eschatology," 24; "etymology," 196; "evidence,," 46; "fact," 202; "family," 203–5, 291; "freedom," 430 n.25; "genesis," "nature," "genitality," and their correlates, 184–85; "Hades," 403 n.9; "humanity" and "humiliation," 79–80, 83, 326; "idea," 217; "incubation," 375; "infancy," 190; "inn," 139; "language," 198; "legibility" and its correlates, 46, 199–202; "liberty," 203; "like," 183; "matter," 363; "mind" and its correlates, 59–60; "misericordia," 362; "myopia," 226; "narrative," 311; "obedience," 290; "obliteration," 48; "pencil," 198; "Peter," 69; "phonetics," "phenomena," and their correlates, 291–94; "poetry," 190; "Ralph," 118; "rationality," "reading," "reality," and their correlates, 202; "rejuvenation," 320; "retina," 432 n.13; "science," 15; "tell," 129; "theory," 217; "thing," 60; "trait," 47; "watching," "waking," and "vigilance," 273; "west," 422 n.9

Etymology, 196, 294–95; in Freud, 195–96; as protoform of psychoanalysis, 196; as regression, 196; Joyce on, 196, 197; Vico on, 196–97, 199–206, 206–7; as reconstruction of unconsciousness, 197; as uncovering of the body, 197–98, 430 n.23; as history, 199–206; playfulness of, in *FW*, 440 n.1

Euclid, 157, 319

Europe, in *FW*, 158–59, 165, 169, 171, 172. *See also* Vico

Evolution, 178; in *A Portrait*, 180; of meaning and human nature, 184–85; *NS* and "ascent of man," 206; of vision, 254–57; and hearing, 273; of sleep and dreaming, 391 n.21, 439 n.38, 458 n.25

Eyelids, 247, 251–56; as only visual constant, 252; as repressed part of body, 252; invisibility, 252, 261; as site of conflict, 259; as site of symptomatic inscription, 259–60; blepharospasmic suppression of, 261; marginal locale in body, 261

Eyes: as seat of consciousness, 217; effects of eye closure, 217–25, 253–60; Ideal eye, 227, 232, 244; power of language over, 229, 231–32, 251, 261; as object of vision, 232, 252, 257; as containers of light, 233, 238; wakening of, in dreams, 234, 244–46; as containers of graphic letters, 235, 247, 250; conflict in, 239, 243, 246; as creators of light, 239, 244–46; and ideal beauty, 240; erotics of, 241–45; power over body, 242; as site and ground of the visible, 245–46; training of, 245–46; as medium of symptomatic writing, 248–51; fracturing effect of, 250–51; liquidation of, 255–59, 262; and tear production, 255–59; equated with "I," 256; of fish, 257; effect of laughter on, 258–59; autonomics of, 259

Fall, the, 28, 82; into exteriority, 199; opening pages, 306–7

Fairy tales, 53, 140, 322–23; Queen Mab, 75; Bluebeard, 308; Jack and the Beanstalk, 319; Babes in Woods, 328; Little Red Riding Hood, 332; The Goose that Laid the Golden Egg, 376

Family: origins of, in Vico, 176–79, 199, 203–6; as heritage, 183; as transmitter of language and ideology, 184–85; as determinant structure, 199, 202, 206; as center of historical conflict in *FW*, 206; as paradigmatic force in genesis of social reality, 206; and bloodlines, 352

Fawkes, Guy, 46

Ferenczi, Sandor (*Thalassa*), 394 n.38, 439 n.38, 458 n.25, 462 n.36

Ferrer, Daniel, 397 n.10

Festy King, 44

Finn MacCool, 36, 57, 99, 105, 132, 274; as aspect of the dreamer, 146–50, 237, 294, 301

Finnegan, Tim, 69–85, 96, 99, 105, 132–33, 134, 148–49, 274, 280, 296–97, 300–301, 320, 328, 371

"Finnegan's Wake," 69–70; Joyce on, 71

Finnegans Wake: eccentricity of, 3, 338, 342; Joyce on, 4, 6, 8, 17, 20, 24–25, 27, 43, 64, 131, 146, 174–75, 196, 197, 221, 223, 224, 231, 237, 245, 272–74, 309, 312, 316, 333, 336, 344, 347, 349, 390 n.13, 391 n.13, 403 n.10, 419 n.13, 421 n.7, 445 n.21, 449 n.2; composition of, 21, 413 n.95, 449 n.36, 454 n.7; as representation, 26, 38, 40, 43, 55, 141, 197–98, 223, 251, 264; circular form of, 27, 154, 363, 384; grammatical person in, 30; passive constructions, 45, 139, 224, 416–17 n.2; affixes, 50–51, 128; syntax and grammar of, 55, 168; missing grammatical subjects and objects, 69, 131, 330, 343, 395 n.5; tense, 75; predication, 131, 167, 224, 373, 416 n.2, 424 n.17; linear form of, 154, 284, 381–82; politics of, 165–73; time of, 223–26; quality of representation, illustrated, 252–60; distinguished from dada and surrealism, 299; erudition of, 304, 309; as "imitation of the dream-state," 309–11, 313–16, 324–26; as "reconstruction of the nocturnal life," 338–63

—model paragraph analyzed, 27–37, 39–41, 66–67, 78–79, 98, 127–30, 133, 134, 142–43, 224–25, 314–15, 318–19, 358, 374, 375, 384–85

Fisch, Max Harold, 427 n.5, 428 n.12

Foucault, Michel, 145, 428 n.11

Foulkes, David, 14, 391 n.26

Four, the, 107, 257

Frank, Nino, 394 n.44; on Joyce's break with Cartesianism, 397 n.13; on Joyce and theories, 448 n.33; and Italian translation of "Anna Livia Plurabelle," 457 n.23

Freemasons, 307

Freud, Sigmund, 5–6, 9, 15, 17, 18, 47, 63, 123, 134, 142, 145, 269; impact on *FW*, 15–18; and Vico, 176, 179–80, 182–93, 195–96, 209; infantile sexuality in, 191–93; interpretation and focus on language, 195–96, 232, 245, 305–15, 449–51 n.2; infantile regression, 317; id, 332; somatic stimuli and dreams, 340; on uterine regression, 355, 415 n.10

—Works: "The Antithetical Sense of Primal Words," 196 (quoted), 429 n.20; *Civilization and Its Discontents*, 426 n.25; *The Ego and the Id*, 442 n.12; *Interpretation of Dreams*, 5–6, 8, 9, 15, 16, 18, 28, 39–40, 128–29, 196, 240, 302, 306, 317, 319, 392 n.30, 397 n.10, 397 n.13, 414 n.6, 418 nn.5–6, 429 n.18, 434 n.17, 437 n.33, 443 n.17, 449 n.1, 449–50 n.2, 451 n.1, 455 n.10; *Introductory Lec-*

tures on Psychoanalysis, 317, 394 n.38, 451 nn.1–2; 455 n.10, 457 n.25; *Jokes and Their Relation to the Unconscious*, 258; "A Metapsychological Supplement to the Theory of Dreams," 8, 340, 455 n.10, 457 n.25; *On Dreams*, 418 n.5; *The Questions of Lay Analysis*, 189, 429 n.18; "Revision of the Theory of Dreams" (*New Introductory Lectures on Psychoanalysis*), 390 n.13, 393 n.32

Funeral, 70–71, 79, 82; games, 68–69, 71; mummification and embalming, 105–6, 109; rites, Egyptian, 105–6, 114–21; annointing and extreme unction, 119–21. *See also* Burial

Furst, Charles, 391 n.22, 391 n.23, 443 n.16, 459 n.26, 391 n.21

Games: hide and seek, 310, 311; *FW* as, 316, 332; counting games, 319; children's games, 237, 245–46, 322, 323, 330, 398 n.8, 453 n.4; *FW* as childsplay, 333, 383

Gandelman, Claude, 396 n.8

Gaping Gill (character), 302

Gender: dissolution in sleep, negation of sexual difference, 30, 285, 364–67; and sexual differentiation, 366–69

Genesis: Vico's account of, 189–90; infancy as site of, 191–93; versions of, 210; of light and the visible, 245–47; of vision and visual space, 289–91; of phenomenal reality, 289–95; of objects and anxiety, 300; of world, 335; womb as site of, 354, 359, 362–64, 379–80; ear as site of, 362–64; of ardor and love, 365–66; of attachment, 365; of matter, 363

Genesis, Book of, 83, 141, 189, 194, 211, 245, 261; Enlightenment views of, 177; creation of light in, 217, 245–46; and pregenesis myth, 218, 245–46; as patriarchal structure, 290, 354, 381. *See also* Adam; Biblical references

Geography, 150–64; and geographical references in *FW*, 151–53, 156–57, 348–49, 358; dismantling of, 157, 168

Geometry, 146, 155, 157, 166; Euclidean and Cartesian, 157; dismantling of, 157, 168; as object of vision and reason, 172; Riemannian and Lobachevskian, 421 n.3

Ghosts and ghost stories, 53, 72, 77, 79, 80, 82, 92, 113, 143, 321

Giants, 36, 147–50, 237–38, 265, 270, 302, 304, 327, 328, 339, 347, 364, 371–72; in Vico, 145, 173, 176–78, 181–82, 188–94; names of, 149, 302; infants as, 189, 192, 319, 320, 328–29, 332. *See also* Finn MacCool

Giedion-Welcker, Carola, 441 n.6

Gifford, Don (*Notes for Joyce*), 429 n.13, 438 n.35, 445 n.22

Gilbert, Stuart, 3

Gillet, Louis (*Claybook for James Joyce*), 394 n.45, 397 n.11, 417 n.3

Ginnunga-Gap, 353

Glasheen, Adaline (*Third Census*), xvi, 18, 44, 132, 223, 273, 394 n.41, 399 n.10, 402 n.6, 407 n.39, 420 n.1, 447 n.26, 454 n.5, 456 n.17, 457 n.19; on the crime in the park, 424 n.16

Glugg, 239

Goethe (*Conversations with Eckermann*), 222

Gog and Magog, 149

Gogarty, Oliver St. John, 25

Goldsmith, Oliver: "The Traveller," 401 n.19; "The Deserted Village," 423 n.11

Gorman, Herbert, (*James Joyce*), 429 n.14

Goyert, George, 460 n.7

Graves: as site of "Real Absence," 63, 69; as site of engraving, 64, 72, 73; sleep as "protem," 70, 81, 374; "watery grave," 372. *See also* Tomb

Gregory, R. L., 245, 432 n.11

Guinness (family), 419 n.11

Gunn, Michael, 49, 54, 419 n.11

Haroun al Raschid, 320

Hart, Clive, xvi, 399 n.10, 402 n.5, 405 n.4, 417 n.3, 420 n.1, 421 n.4, 430 n.3, 437 n.31, 441 n.11, 455 n.9, 455 n.7; *Concordance* discussed, 400 n.14

Hassan, Ihab, 421 n.3

Hats and wigs, 49, 58, 59, 79, 164, 238, 297, 303, 310, 321, 399 n.12

Hayman, David, 405 n.4

HCE: introduced, 53; as "someone imparticular," 59; as nothing, 63, 304; waking life, 64, 134–38; as representative man, 74, 136, 169, 265, 304; as universal-individual, 91; absence of name of, 91, 124; anonymity and imparticularity of, 130–33, 139; as dreamer of *FW*, 139–45; nature and meaning of "the normative letters" H. C. E., 139–45, 158, 276, 366; compared to Tetragrammaton, 141, 366; as cipher for the body, 141–45, 276, 366; as Vichian man, 193–95, 210–11; as network of historical forces and tensions, 211–12; as "Here Comes Everybody," 212–15; mode of identification with, 253; as infant, 320, 328, 333; apparent absence of, in ALP, 338–42; as "unborn infant" or "foetotype," 357, 360; as dual unity with ALP, 365–68; as knot of attachments, 366–68. *See also* Body; Identity

Hearing: 45, 58, 155; power over eye, 160–61; visionary, 286–95; in sleep, 268–304; in dreams, hallucinated, 123, 271, 297–98; constant wakefulness of, 273–74, 276–77, 287; balked, in suspension, 275; represented as radioreception, 276–77; selective, in sleep, 276–81; as interpretation, 285–86, 301; and the unconscious, 276–79, 280–81, 368; and "overhearing," 278–79, 294, 301, 303–4, 339–52, 355–57, 363–64; unheard hearing, 297, 301, 343–44, 349; as unconscious screening, 280–81, 283; and phenomena, 287–95; hear = here, 287; in infancy, 289–91, 323; as obedience, 290–91; audiophonic amplification, 294; vs. listening, 295, 300; hearsay and gossip, 297, 298, 301–3, 339, 340; and conflict, 299–301; phonetic vs. acoustic, 345–46; hearing in utero, 354–61

Heart, 123, 356; periodicity of systole and diastole, 76, 350; sound of, 282, 340, 347; beating, 352; binary, 350, 361; Sacred Heart, 351, 353; heartbeat in womb, 354–58, 378; and anastomosic dual unity, 358; as seat of emotion, 368–69; sound as antilanguage, 380–82

Heath, Stephen, 419–20n.15, 428n.11, 448n.32

Heavenly bodies, 220, 249, 252, 435n.20

Heliotrope, 48, 117, 124, 238–39, 242, 245, 246, 252, 382

Helmholtz, Hermann von, 126, 226, 232, 244, 245, 254, 434n.16

Helvetius, 307, 398n.7

Hen, 376–79, 383

Henry II, 183

Herring, Philip F., 458n.26

Hesitancy, 311–12

Hibernation, 53, 153, 193, 219, 254

Higginson, Fred L., 337, 338

Highbarger, Ernest Leslie, 403n.9

Hillman, James, 402–3n.9

Hobbes, Thomas (*Leviathan*), 427n.6

Hodgart, Matthew J. C., 436n.25, 456n.7; *Song in the Works of James Joyce*, xvi, 417n.4, 431n.9, 449n.37, 452–53n.4

Hoffman, Frederick J. ("Infroyce"), 393n.31

Holes: "hole affair," 5, 64, 70; and hollows, 41, 78, 80, 118; in the head, 48–49; in lace, 54; graves as, 68; caves, 80; Ear of Dionysius, 274, 339; Gaping Ghyl, 302; Fingal's cave, 347

Homer: Odyssey and *Ulysses*, 176; Enlightenment views of, 177; in Vico, 178–79; and Hades, 403n.9; Odysseus' homecoming, 428n.9

Horace, 44, 401n.20

Hosty, 55

Houdebine, Jean-Louis, 420n.15

Humpty Dumpty, 133, 134, 318, 319, 375–76

I Ching, 305

"Ideal insomnia," 25, 49, 68

Identity, 7–8, 131–45, 365–68, 370–71; disintegration and absence of, in sleep, 7–8, 21, 28–29, 49–50, 54, 59, 62, 63–64, 131, 146–47, 274–75, 285, 365, 366; of *FW*'s dreamer, 36–38, 49–50, 130–33, 135–45, 273–74, 317–18, 320–21, 417n.3; at death, 42, 62, 72–73, 76–77, 103–4; of figures in dreams, 55, 131–33, 139–40, 270–71, 301–3, 306; and the fiction of individuality, 64, 91, 142, 168, 209, 214–15, 366; and "personality," as modern constructs, 142; as product of history, 176–77, 180, 183–85; formation of, in infancy, 191–93, 288–91, 322–24, 328–31; sexual, 192, 366; collective nature of, in Vico, 208, 211–15; as a knot of attachments, 365–66. See also Character; Conflict; Dreamer; Ego; Shaun the Post; Objects

Infancy and childhood: spatial perception in, 148–49, 193–94, 318–19; in Vico, 185–93, 264, 334–35, 338; and formation of body, 190–93, 289–91; infantile regression, 192–94, 317–19, 322, 326, 364; hearing in, 289–91; and learning of language, 246, 322–26, 328–31; as infinite possibility, 290, 333, 335; end of, 290–91, 330, 334, 370; *FW* as reawakening of, 318, 328–33, 383; as the repressed, 328

Interpretation. *See* Reading

Introjection, 142, 146–49, 153, 157, 158

Investments (cathexes), 128, 367, 378. *See* Tailors and tailoring

Invisibility: of the chthonic, 80; of underwear, 81, 243; of the body, 165, 254; as transcendence of vision and reason, 172, 216–26; of conflict, 220; of Shem, 240, 243; of dreams' latent content, 243, 247, 249; and the unconscious, 243, 249–50, 270–72

Ireland, 163–64; the Famine, 180; and English economic policy, 184; colonization, 207; domestication of, 329

Isolde, 241

Issy: as emanation, 140; as daughter, 156, 240–43; little language, 322

Jacquet, Claude, 421n.4

Jaloux, Edmond, 6

Janet, Pierre, 17
Jesus Christ, 81, 105, 149, 373
Jewels, 232, 238, 241–42
Jolas, Maria, 169
Joyce, James, 3–25 passim; lack of specificity in speaking about *FW*, 6, 317; on Freud, Vico, and science, 16–18, 394 n.40; growth as a writer, 17, 332; dreams recalled, 21, 431–32 n.9, 434 n.15; interest in the body, 143–44, 355, 420 n.18; fear of thunder, 183; eye diseases and operations, 230, 433–34 n.15, 438 n.36; summer vacation in Bognor, Sussex, 310, 449 n.36; on laughter, 314; purported coldness, 331; and composition of "Anna Livia Plurabelle," 336–38; interest in embryology, 355, 459 n.26; attitudes toward psychoanalysis, 393 n.34; on Switzerland, 398 n.7; acquaintance with Egyptology, 406 n.18; his houseplants, 413 n.95; on Shaun, 419 n.13; on classical vs. modern literature, 420 n.18, 423–24 n.14; interest in spatial and object relations, 420–21 n.3; and post–Newtonian science, 421 n.3; on Dublin in *FW*, 421–22 n.7; on the artist, state, and revolutionary violence, 424 n.14, 426 n.29; on modern Europe, 424–25 n.22; politics, 425 n.24; on vision, 436 n.27; attitudes toward surrealism and theories, 448 n.33; on scribbling, 454 n.7; on primacy of emotion over intellect in writing, 454 n.7, 462 n.39; misgivings about Anna Livia, 456 n.15; apparent carelessness in translating "Anna Livia Plurabelle," 457 n.23, 460 n.27
Joyce, Lucia: analysis with Jung, 352 n.24, 393 n.34
Jukes and Kallikaks, 5, 6, 113
Jung, Carl, 179, 393 n.34, 394 n.40; archetypal psychology, 80, 195, 403 n.9

Kabbalah, 140, 365
Kain, Richard M., 455 n.6
Kenner, Hugh, 50, 401 n.22
Kersse the Tailor and the Norwegian Captain, 126–30, 275, 280
Kleitman, Nathaniel, 391 n.22, 391 n.23, 392–93 n.30
Knock (Knock apparition), 242
Knuth, Leo, 455 n.7
Koran, 227, 383

Labor: body as unit of, 169; and sleep and *FW*, 172
Lacan, Jacques, 396 n.8, 435 n.22, 442 n.12
Ladd, George Trumball, 392–93 n.30, 434 n.17

Landscapes, 30–38; negated, 57; "interment in," 80; internalized, 147; spatiality of, in dreams, 147–48, 155–58, 270–72, 338–41, 348–49
Lane, Frederick, 460 n.28
Language: and dreams, 8, 14, 16, 18–20, 39–40, 46–47, 59–62, 123, 195–98, 261–62, 269–72, 305–15, 381, 393 n.32, 449–51 nn.1–2; as consciousness, 19, 46–47, 59–62, 96, 115–19, 121–23, 129–30, 140, 156, 170, 181, 184–88, 196–97, 202–3, 208–9, 235–36, 239, 249–50, 281, 284–85, 288–95, 307–8, 313–14, 319, 322, 324–27, 329–31; and negation, 29, 41, 48–51, 64–65; absence of, 56, 159, 264–69, 317, 344–46, 351, 381–82; as day's residue, 131, 133–34, 158, 298–99, 381; and the transmission of instituted power, 169, 289–91, 304, 329, 331–32, 381; as authority, 170, 289–91, 315, 326, 329, 331, 346, 362, 381; and the production of the body, 190–93, 246, 251, 289–90, 319, 452–53 n.3; genesis of, in Vico, 192–93, 196–98; and the production of reality, 199–202, 289–95; learning of, 246, 323–26, 328–31; graphic, in dreams, 247–50; representative power, 261–62; and stream of consciousness, 269–72; as obedience, 290; diachronic vs. synchronic, 298–99; as repression, 329–31; and difference, 345–46
—in *FW*: negated, 29, 41, 48–51, 64–65; obliterated, 47–64, 131, 134, 351, 361; and oppositional negation, 51; rendered "vermicular," 73–74, 79–80; and "giant language," 148–49, 421 nn.4–5; "blacked out," 218–25; "put to sleep," 221; "not used in ordinary connections," 221, 449 n.1; liquidated, 256–58; distinguished from rational language, 307–15, 449–52 nn.1–2, 380–81; and "little language," 322; as antilanguage, 344–45, 351, 362, 381, 382–83. *See also* Authority, patriarchal; Education; Etymology; *Finnegans Wake*; Law; Manifest and latent distinctions; Reading
Languages and idioms in *FW*, 3, 20, 337–38, 455 n.7; status of, 78, 460–61 n.29; American, 98; black American, 252; Oriental, 156, 447 n.27; Japanese, 223; Dutch, 257, 337, 360–61, 404 n.20, 455 n.7; Latin and Greek, 309, 312, 319; Esperanto, 322; Swahili, 337–38, 351, 361, 455 n.7, 460 n.29; Provençal, 368; Swiss, 398 n.7, 401 n.19; Australian and New Zealand, 437 n.31; Armenian and Latin, 461 n.27
Larbaud, Valery, 20
Latourette, Kenneth Scott, 414 n.99

Lavergne, Philippe: French translation of *FW*, 397 n.13

Law and laws: of evidence, 44–47; relations of legality to legibility, 44–47, 59–62, 166, 169–70, 199–202, 274; language as internalized system of, 45–47, 170, 199–202, 289–90, 328–31, 344–46, 362; as maintainers of "reality," 59–62, 168, 199–202; of corporate control, 144–45, 170, 191–93, 289–90; reading as submission to, 170, 199–202, 274, 315, 328–31, 333; of reason, 177–78, 427 n.6; collapse of, in *FW*, 170, 307–8, 332–33, 380–81

Leavis, F. R., 4

Leiris, Michel, 448 n.29

Lenin, V. I., 332

Lent, 377

Lessing, Gottfried, 67, 447 n.27

Letter, the, 50, 248–50; buried, 48, 134, 170, 198,248, 272, 310, 313, 324, 326, 332, 382, 397 n.13, 437 n.33; inscription in flesh, 248–51; as cipher for the dream, 249–50, 310, 324–26

Levin, Harry, 216, 315, 393 n.31, 454 n.5

Lévy-Bruhl, Lucien, 63

Lewin, B. D., 459 n.26

Lewis, Wyndham, 397 n.12, 401 n.19

Life after death: heaven, 75, 77, 80; limbo, 75, 360; sleep as, 75–76, 109–10; as illusion, 77, 82, 86; Egyptian, 90–125; duration of life in, 103; immortality, 103–4. *See also* Underworld

Light: eternal, 104; absence of, 216–25; in sleep, 223–26, 238–39; spectrum of visible, 224, 229, 232, 233, 238, 244–47; invisible, 225, 230, 233, 246; quality of, in dreams, 228–32, 236–39; "chaotic" (or "intrinsic") retinal, 232–33, 236, 258–59; and space, 235–36; and point of view, 236; in eyes, 239, 262–63; as constituent of the visible, 242–46; Newton on, 244; creation and genesis of, 244–47; nature of, 244–47; role of ear in, 286–87; in infancy, 289–91, 295; and enlightenment, role of speech in, 291–95

Limbo, 75, 360

Linearity, 8–9, 27, 39, 54, 164, 274; and manifest content, 381; in Book of the Dead, 114, 115–16, 123–24; and history, 154; and lines in *FW*, 308–9. *See also* Plot; Reading

Literacy: as submission to authority, 295; as privilege, 304; as repression, 331; as shriveling of possibilities, 323; inimical to "Anna Livia Plurabelle," 345, 362

"Literal sense": literalism and names in *FW*,

131–32; as manifest content of *FW*, 166–67, 307–10, 313, 315, 319, 322, 381–82; deficiencies of literalism, 167, 308–10, 313, 315, 381–82

Litz, A. Walton, 433 n.15, 456 n.13

Livy, 358

Locke, John, 177, 226; on state of nature, 427 n.6

Long, Charles H., 462 n.37

Longfellow, Henry Wadsworth (*The Song of Hiawatha*), 456 n.14

Lough Neagh, 347, 374

Luce, Gay Gaer, 390 n.19, 392 n.27, 430 n.2

Lucifer, 227, 230, 239, 243, 245

Ludwig, Emil, 460 n.28

McAlmon, Robert, 20

MacArthur, Ian, 433 n.14

MacCabe, Colin, 393 n.31, 424 n.20

MacCarthy, Denis Florence (*Underglimpses*), 350, 367

McCarthy, Patrick (*The Riddles of Finnegans Wake*), 436 n.24, 451 n.3

McHugh, Roland, 433 n.14, 462 n.35; *Annotations*, xvi, 5, 128, 231, 242, 250, 268, 312, 319, 326, 363, 398 n.8, 401 n.20, 410 n.74, 421 nn.4–5, 432 n.13, 441 n.4; on sigla, 140; *The Sigla of Finnegans Wake*, 412 n.3, 419 n.14, 443 n.15

Macpherson, James, 25; *Temora* and other Ossianic poems in *FW*, 421 nn.4–5, 456 n.16

Magalaner, Marvin, 455 n.6

Malcolm, Norman, 390 n.16

Mamafesta, 383–84

Manganiello, Dominic (*Joyce's Politics*), 424 n.18, 425 n.24

Manifest and latent content: in language of *FW*, 71–72, 129, 137–38, 152, 159, 169, 242, 249, 269, 279, 320; in characterization, 139–40, 303

—manifest content: of dreams and *FW* compared, 31–36, 309–10, 313–15, 324–25, 338–39, 351, 358–59, 382; as trivia and residue, 134–38; in myth, 195; as nonsense, 325

—latent content: the body as, 31–36, 41, 143, 249; etymology as uncovering of, 206; invisibility of, 242–43, 249–50, 272; of dreams and *FW* compared, 309, 315, 324–25, 351, 382; infantile, 324–26

Mannekin-Pis, 333

Margerum, Eileen G., 402 n.6

Mark of Cornwall, 241

Marx, Groucho, 394 n.48

Marx, Karl, 179–80, 183; and Marxism, 169, 171

as, 185, 188–89; sleep as, 193–95; Neanderthal Man, 194, 210; Heidelberg Man, 194, 210, 302; primordial dialogue, 272. *See also* Infancy and childhood; Vico

Psychoanalysis: and the "science" of the dream, 10–12; its relations to *FW*, 15–18; Joyce on, 16–18; vs. "cycloannalism," 74; psychoanalytical account of dream formation, 129–30, 134, 250–51, 316, 355, 435 n.21, 437 n.33, 441 n.7, 457 n.25; and language, 195; as reconstruction of "protohistory," 196; and vision, 244. *See also* Dreams; Freud; Manifest and latent content; Science; Vico

Pubs and inns, 138; dreamer's life as publican, 30, 108, 135–40, 169, 274, 279–80, 285–86, 301, 445–46 nn.22–23; pub as public, 297

Purdy, S. B., 421 n.3

Queen Mab, 75
Quinet, Edgar, 335, 454 n.9

Rabaté, Jean-Michel, 299, 448 n.32
Rabelais, François, 421 nn.4–5
Rader, Ralph, 394 n.17
Radio, 53, 275–76, 281, 294–95
Rainbows, 121, 224, 230–32, 233, 237, 245–46, 255, 260; and "rainbow girls," 230, 240–42. *See also* Light: spectrum of visible
Randomness, 9, 16, 27, 305, 311; and unpredictability, 316, 381–84. *See also* Association
Rationality, 28, 39; or rationalization, 40, 311; "day's reason," 76, 78, 166; etymology of, 80, 202; and constructed space, 147; inadequate in gauging emotions, 158; as distortion, 166; as accession to laws, 169; absence of, in first men, 179; as a man-made institution, 179, 184, 188–89, 202–3; inadequacy of, in understanding prehistory, 181; necessity of abandoning, 182, 188; in Vico, 183; loss of, in laughter, 258–59; inimical to *FW*, 308, 310; in sleep and *FW*, 309; inadequacies of, 312–13, 351, 380, 382; rhyme or reason, 351, 354–56
Reading: as process, 39–41, 305–16, 382–85; and linearity, 164, 169–70, 274; as instituted system of rules, 169–70, 274; as internalized submission to authority, 202; effect of, on body, 260, 328, 384; out of context and linear order, 305–6, 316; and association, 305–13, 315, 348–50, 352–53; "between the lines," 308–10, 313, 322; as unconsciousness of possibility, 319; in childhood, 326–27, 329, 332. *See also* Literal sense; Manifest and latent distinctions; Randomness
Realism, 4–5, 16, 18, 43, 52, 175, 213–14,

253–54; and the representation of "real life" in *FW*, 4–9, 18–19, 24–25, 26–35, 38, 40–49, 51–59, 66–71, 216–25, 227–37, 315–16, 320, 322, 324, 382, 452 n.3; and the relations of *FW* to objective reality, 24, 135–39, 151–58, 165–70, 274–86, 300–301, 382, 445–47 nn.23–24; and the depiction of real-world events in *FW*, 116–18, 155–57, 274–80, 443–45 nn.19–20, 445–47 nn.23–24; and reality, as man-made institutions, 153, 168, 202; and the representation of unconscious reality in *FW*, 252–60, 338–44, 347–50, 352–54, 398–99 n.10. *See also* Novel; Objects; Representation; Science

Referentiality, 27–28, 31, 36; negation of, 49–52; of names in *FW*, 130–33; of acrostic HCE, 140–42; apparent lack of, in *FW*, 216, 305–16; of *FW*, compared to conventional literature, 309, 313, 382; of river-names in "Anna Livia Plurabelle," 341–45

Regression: and sleep, 39; infantile, 149, 317–19, 322, 372, 384; Vichian, 192–94, 210; etymology as, 196; visual, 257; thalassal, 371–72, 374; uterine, 354–56, 366–67, 372

Reinvigoration: sleep as, 84; as "refleshmeant," 128, 254, 256; as recreation and refreshment, 156

Rejuvenation, 320–21; of meaning, 328, 377

Rembrandt van Rijn, 360

Renewal, 321

Representation, 36, 38, 40–41, 43, 52, 165–70; of nothing, 47–59, 62–64; of life beyond the grave, 67, 71–72, 74, 79, 80, 154, 194; of the body, 141–45, 154–57; of the invisible, 216–27, 254–58, 271–72, 341–46, 367, 380–81; *FW*'s representation concretely illustrated, 232, 252–60, 341–46; of infancy, 315–33

Repression: of aggression and power, 128–29, 169–70, 243, 328, 332; as unconsciousness of possibility, 136–37, 315, 319, 330–31; of the body, 145, 197–98, 253–54, 279–80, 283, 299, 444 n.19; and sexuality, 166–67, 170, 190–93; of Shem by Shaun, 240, 249, 283; learning and reading as instruments of, 170, 289–91, 315, 319, 329–32; *FW* as undoing of, 263, 314, 326–29, 331–33, 383–84, 439 n.39; of infantile memory, 318–19, 322–23

Resurrection: of the dead, 67, 77, 79, 81–82, 97, 106–7; of the body, 70, 82, 85, 87, 98, 99, 106, 113, 119, 121; and solar myths, 76, 114; as waking, 115–16, 122, 123–25; in *FW*, 116–19, 155, 159, 238, 284–85; etymology as, 197–98; "waking the dead," illustrated, 254–60; as reawakening of "original sinse,"

Resurrection (*continued*)

263; of memory, 327; of stifled possibility, 327; of childhood, 328; of dead head, 333; bringing to mind the out of sight, 342. *See also* Arthur; Finnegan; Jesus Christ; Osiris

Revue des deux mondes, 78

Ricouer, Paul, 393 n.32

Riddles, 310–14

Robinson, Henry Morton, 395 n.1, 405 n.4, 424 n.16, 462 n.37; *Skeleton Key*, 26, 36

Rockwell, Norman, 52

Roheim, Geza, 394 n.38; *The Gates of the Dream*, 396 n.6; on the dream and the other world, 402–3 n.9; 415 n.110; on dream and the ego, 435 n.21; theory of the dream, 456 n.25; unconscious memory, 459 n.26

Rose, Danis, 405 n.4, 411 n.80

Rutherford, C. W., 433 n.15

Sainean, L., 421 n.4

Saint Martha Mary Alacoque, 353

Saint Michael, 239, 245

Saorstat, Erin, 159, 164, 268

Sartre, Jean-Paul, 64, 401 n.21

Saturday Evening Post, 52

Schopenhauer, Arnold, 67, 416 n.1

Science: and problems of evidence, 8, 14–15, 18, 43–48, 54, 58, 63, 190, 194, 228–29; and sleep and dreams, 10–18, 24; and "new sciences," 14–15, 63, 85, 179, 209, 255; Joyce's attitudes toward, 17, 394 n.40; Newtonian, 92, 188–90; Vico's, contrasted with mainstream, 177, 181, 188–90; quantum theory, 253; and oversights of empiricism, 244–45, 254, 264; and science fiction, 334–35; post-Newtonian, 421 n.3. *See also* Descartes; Dreams; Embryology; Evolution; Freud; Newton

Scotography, 52, 54, 56, 58, 63, 77

Scott, Bonnie Kime (*Joyce and Feminism*), 424 n.19

Segal, Julius, 390 n.19, 392 n.27, 430 n.2

Seidman, Robert (*Notes for Joyce*), 429 n.13, 438 n.35, 445 n.22

Selzer, Richard, 409 n.67

Senn, Fritz, 421 n.4, 455 n.7

Sense and sensation: 45, 268; relation to language, 62; "trained senses," 62; loss of, 100; regaining of, 115–16; in mouth, 117–18, 280; as aspect of dreams, 123; as primordial, in Vico, 183, 189; distinguished from perception, 188; closure of, 270, 272; absence of, 272; dormancy of, 273; and sensing devices, 276; "sense arrest," 277

Sexual difference: disintegration of, in sleep, 30, 285, 366–69

Sexuality: clitoral and penile erections during dreams, 13; phallic, 123–24, 157, 198, 332; and dreams, 145, 247–48, 250; incest, 156–57, 242–44; defecation, 165, 249; and shame, 166–67, 240–44, 249, 332–33; homosexuality, 166–67, 424 n.16; bisexuality, 167, 366; masturbation, 167; urination, 167, 323, 333–34, 382, 395 n.2, 451–52 n.3; voyeurism, 167, 241–46, 263; illicit pleasure, 170–71; toilet training, 191, 289–90, 451–52 n.3; infantile, in Vico, 191–93, 198–99; "polymorphous perversity," 192; desire, 239, 241; sex for fun, 316; female, 354–84. *See also* Appetite; Body; Conflict; Crime in the park; Education; Underwear

Shadows, 58, 218, 223, 373; and ghosts, 69, 76

Shakespearean quotation, 82, 371

Shapiro, Arthur, 391 n.25

Shaun the Post, 140, 150; as representative of HCE's ego functions, 22, 234–36, 240, 319, 378; as carrier of letters, 140, 234–36, 239, 246, 319, 331, 351, 419 n.13; his barrel, 140, 235, 378; "First and Second Watches of," 234–36, 239; "Show'm the Posed," 236, 240, 260, 319, 331, 378; as watcher and "spatialist," 236, 244, 246; censor, 243, 319, 331; baffled receiver of news from "down under," 246, 249; implication in the visible, 249; relation to Shem, 249; and literate consciousness, 249, 331; his appetite and "investments" in food, 378; in "Anna Livia Plurabelle," 351

Shem the Penman, 43, 71, 140; as Cabler, 53, 240, 249; invisibility of, 240, 243–44, 249; below consciousness and literacy, 240, 249, 351; as "unconscious alter ego," or "other," 251; "down under" in the body, beneath the conscious and visible surface of things, 241, 243–44, 249–50, 252, 259, 378; as prompter of the dream, 241, 244, 247–49; malicious counteragent, unconsciously canny producer, 247; as inscriber of "the Letter," 248–49; writing on the body, 248–51, 252, 259; his writing as somatic, symptomatic, 249, 250, 259; as "Autist," 249–50, 252, 259; relation to Shaun, 250; as Punman, 308; riddler, 311; scribbler, 325–26; shame's voice, 333; in "Anna Livia Plurabelle," 351

Simultaneity, 306

Sleep, 3–26; REM sleep as "somatic correlate" of dreaming, 11–13; REM and NREM, 11–15; continuity of thought during, 13; length of, 22; triviality of, 23; snoring, 28,

282; as "vegetative" state, 38, 80, 116–18, 151, 234, 377; and death, 43, 45, 49, 53, 58, 66–85, 109, 113, 114–15, 194; and closure of the senses, 46–49, 270, 272; dreamless, 42, 50, 55, 59, 62, 67, 122, 143, 149–50, 194, 256–58, 343, 354–56, 379; as substance, 64, 77, 141, 208, 259; relations to "underworld," 77, 109; as recreation and refreshment, 128; from a Vichian perspective, 193–94; as ground of the dream, 239, 271–72, 305; as "forty winks," 254–55, 259; and vigilance, 260, 273, 276, 278; *FW* as mimetic of, 264; talking in, 272; toothgrinding in, 282, 443–44 n.19; sonic disturbances of, 283–86; as "state of nature," 293, 313; as retirement, 301; as reenactment of childhood, 320, 382; as rejuvenation, 320–21, 377, 382; as fall back into body, 326; as wakening and rebirth, 357, 359–60, 363–64; as uterine regression, 359–64, 378; as incubation, 375–80; as reenactment of birth, 376–79; altered metabolism of the body in, 377–78; sleepwalking, 392 n.27

Snyder, Frederick, 390 n.16

Solipsism, 214, 244

Sorel, Georges, 179

Sollers, Philippe, 419–20 n.15, 425 n.23

Solomon, Margaret C. (*Eternal Geomater*), 393 n.31, 420 n.3, 420 n.20, 436 n.24

Songs: "Auld Lang Syne," 46, 378, 383; "Brian O Linn," 153, 154, 168; "The Wild Man from Borneo," 179; "The Man that Broke the Bank at Monte Carlo," 260; "Johnny I Hardly Knew Ye," 300, 375; "John Peel," 301, 449 n.37; "There's Hair Like Wire Growing Out of the Empire," 308; "Ten Little Injuns," 327; "When London Sleeps," 365; "Down Went McGinty," 371; "It's Your Last Lap, Titanic, Fare Thee Well," 371; "Rocked In The Cradle Of The Deep," 372; "Jolly Young Waterman," 382; "A Nation Once Again," 432 n.10; "The Ballyhooly Blue Ribbon Army," 457 n.24. *See also* "Finnegan's Wake"; Moore, Thomas

Sound: absence of, 47–49, 57–58, 154, 268–69, 273, 280–81; "sound sense," 127, 146, 280, 288, 291, 294, 295, 297, 337, 338; as component of the dream, 273, 278, 280–82, 283–86, 301; and external reality, 278, 282–86; as wakening force, 280, 283–85, 301; sound of the body, 282–83; in "Anna Livia," 340–49; in utero, 360; *FW* as sound effect, 281. *See also* Ear; Hearing; Phonetics

Space, 146–65; annihilation of, 29, 47–48,

146–48, 254–58, 372; "objective," 30–31, 155, 236, 244–45, 254; Cartesian, 31, 46, 144–45, 335, 448 n.27; of the body, 36, 76, 96–99, 145, 148–49, 154, 158–59, 189–90, 236, 253, 371–72, 421 n.5; perceptual constitution of, 47, 145, 236, 244, 254; mythic, 78; chthonic, 80; of the "other world," 92–97, 100, 107, 114, 374; infinite, 94, 148; and dimensionlessness, 101, 148–49, 235, 356, 372; four-dimensional, 147; creation of, 149, 189–93, 289–91, 318–19; emotional constituents of, 156–57, 244; in visual dreams, 236, 239–40, 244–45; perception of, 236, 240, 244; subliminal components of, 236–37, 240, 242–45, 249, 254; auditory, 288, 447–48 n.27; uterine, 355–57, 259–60, 367, 379–80. *See also* Descartes; Geography; Geometry; Objects; Reason; Vision

Speaker, absent, 101, 271–72

Speech acts, 265

"Spirits," 70, 80, 82, 140, 250

Stella, 242

Stephens, James, 6, 337

Storytelling, nocturnal, 271; and sound, 280, 281

Straumann, Heinrich, 421–22 n.7

Stuttering, 180, 294; language of *FW* as, 307

Subject and subjectivity, 72; subject-object relations, 78, 142, 147, 153–54, 244–46; body as subject of *FW*, 142–43; constitution between eyes and ears, 144, 150

Sublimation, 191; in dreams, 243, 249

Substance, sleep as, 64, 141, 208

Subterranean, 81–82, 159

Sullivans, 221

Sun, 59; as archetype and origin, 76; resurrection and solar myths, 76; solar system, 76; solar physics, 76, 217–18; and Egyptian supernature, 92–96, 98–99, 102, 104, 114, 116–18; and heliotrope and sunlight, 238–39; solstitial refleshmeant, 254

Sunset, 92–94, 98, 112, 121

Suter, August, 20, 394 n.43

Surrealism, 299, 433 n.15

Swift, Jonathan: use of "little language" in *FW*, 322, 453 n.5; *A Tale of a Tub*, 360; Gulliver, 367

Swinburne, Charles Algernon, 357

Symptoms, 145, 250; *FW* as symptomatic writing, 157, 251; dreams as, 244–45, 248–51; adult body as symptom, 251; facial expression as, 259–60

Tacitus, 51

Tailors and tailoring: "formal alteration," 127;

Tailors and tailoring (*continued*)
alteration of investments, dreamwork as, 127–30; redress, 127–30, 137; retailoring of body in blink, 259
Telegraphy, 46, 53, 58, 72, 247, 250, 275, 398 n.10; Reuters, 250, 325
Telephony, 56, 282, 299
Telescopy, 21, 434 n.20
Television, 56, 58, 252, 438 n.35
Terracotta, 79, 230
Thirst, 100–101, 115–16, 280
Thomas, Northcote Whitbridge, 455 n.11
Thousand and One Nights, 320; 1001 as cipher, 361
Thunder: in Vico, 175, 177, 179, 194; patriarchal thunder, 199, 289; thunderwords, 282, 289
Time, 51, 82; chronology of dreamlessness, 56; end of, 75–77, 82–83, 103, 171–72; sleep as breach in continuity of, 111–12; reversal of, 120–21; as "spell of hesitancy," 312; in "Anna Livia Plurabelle," 358–59; annihilation of, in sleep, 359
Toynbee, Arnold, 83–84, 88, 405 n.5, 405 n.21
Transubstantiation, 141–43, 366
Tridon, André, 416 n.1
Tristan, 241, 324
Triviality: of sleep, 23; of elements in dreams, 29, 135, 167; marginality, 169; and the apocalyptic, 245; marginality, 169; of elements in *FW*, 315, 324; of body, in "Anna Livia Plurabelle," 343
Troy, Mark L., "Mummeries of Resurrection," 405 n.4, 406 n.18, 412 n.83
Tussaud, Madame, 44, 59, 63, 77, 87
Tutankhamen, 74, 108, 109, 113, 116
Twain, Mark (*Huckleberry Finn*), 111, 411 n.80, 412 n.81
Twins. *See* Shaun the Post; Shem the Penman

Ulysses: as self-analysis, 17, 184; and *FW*, 17–18, 21, 137, 317; Bloom's eyelids in "Lotus-Eaters," 22, 253; "Hades," 82, 84; Dedalus in, 91, 184; "Scylla and Charybdis," 110; morning mouth, 118; Kersse in, 126; as "epic of the body," 144, 193; "Lestrygonians," 164, 193; realism of, 176; Homeric correspondences in, 176, 178; "Nestor," 207; Stephen Dedalus' self-fathering, 213; stream of consciousness in, 269–70; erudition of, 304; "Yes," 332; "Sirens," 340; "Oxen of the Sun," 354–55; our great sweet mother, 357; Stephen's relation with mother in, 368; "Ithaca," 371
Umbrellas, 220, 232, 256, 275

Unamuno, Miguel de, 42 (quoted), 397 n.1
Unconscious, the: as "the unknown," 6–7, 9, 79; in Joyce and Freud, 8, 15–18; as nescience, 15, 189; ciphers for, 29, 31, 38; as subject of *FW*, 24–71 passim, 135–45, 151–70, 194–95, 216–25, 227–37, 315–16, 320, 322, 324, 338–85; as "no-consciousness," 42–59; unconsciousness as death, 44, 49, 52, 62, 66–84, 101–2; collective, 109; body as, 135–45, 194, 253, 341–46, 357; relations to nothingness and aboriginality, 63; absolute, 71, 79, 82; as ground of the dream, and *FW*, 71, 251; as "underground," 79–80, 328; as "underworld," 80, 170; as chthonic power, 80, 99; as world "down under," 110, 164, 235, 238, 249–52, 437 n.31; and "infrarational" coherence, 122–23, 135, 154–58, 172, 185; as invisibility, 217, 221, 240, 243, 249, 254, 255, 270; and laughter, 258; represented in *FW*, 252–60, 338–44, 347–50, 352–54, 398–99 n.10; as origin, in Vico, 179, 181, 188; *NS* as psychology of, 181–82, 185–93; as "ignorance," in Vico, 182, 188, 193; and infancy, 185–93, 318–39, 369, 384; collective, in Vico, 211–15; relation to letters and literacy, 308–15, 449–52 n.1; and prenatal life, 355–59. *See also* Dreams; Freud; Infancy and childhood; Manifest and latent Distinctions; Vico
Underground, 79–80, 328
Underwear, 81, 243, 318, 350, 367
Underworld, 69, 75; sleep as, 78, 79, 80–81, 374; unconscious as, 80, 170; Celtic, 374; Elysium, 75, 104, 110, 154; Erebus, 78; Hades, 78, 82, 359; hell, 75, 76, 77; Netherworld, 59, 75, 80. *See also* Book of the Dead; Life after death; Other world

Vacations and holidays, 172
Valhalla, 78
Vegetation, human, 37, 117–18, 151, 234, 299, 377. *See also* Dumbness; Madame Tussaud
Veils, 7, 10, 69, 78, 231, 254
Ventriloquism, 71, 271–72, 280, 302. *See also* Dumbness: and dummies
Verney, Thomas, 458–59 n.26
Vico, Giambattista (*The New Science*), 43, 46, 63, 83, 145, 174–215, 264, 272, 288–89, 297; and Freud, 18, 176, 179, 195–96, 209; on the state of nature, 175, 176–77, 179–80, 181; on genesis of language, 175, 179, 193, 196–97; as an intellectual foundation of *FW*, 176; conception of history in, 176–80; on origins of family, 177, 178–80, 199, 203–6; Joyce's interest in, 179–80; on ori-

gins of consciousness, 180, 181; on origins of civil institutions, 180, 199; of history, 181; *NS* as psychoanalysis, 181–93, 196–99; on origins of Western thought and civilization, 181–83, 199, 362; on "Poetic Wisdom," 181–93, 264; and infancy, 185–93, 264, 334; on origins of language, 192, 195–97; on origins of social history, 202–6; *NS* as book of unconscious origins, 210, 215, 272; on origins of dialogue, 270–72. *See also* Genesis; Wakening

Victoria and Albert Nyanza, 374, 379, 460 n.28

Vikings, 57, 168, 352

Vinding, Ole, 6, 7, 17, 131, 389 n.8

Virgil: Virgilian fortune telling, 305, 311; *Aeneid*, 401 n.2, 403 n.9

Vision: during dreams, 11–12, 47–48, 121, 150, 223, 226–40, 243–44, 247–49, 251–52; presentative vs. representative, 12, 227–33, 261–62; in sleep, 16, 24, 45–47, 53, 57, 59, 151, 216–25, 226; theories of, 226, 244–46, 254, 261; erotics of, 240–45, 436 n.26; liquidation of, 255–58, 262; power of language over, 261–62, 286–95; genesis of, 289–91

Voice: and phenomena, 285–94; illuminating power of, 291–95; as component of ear, 295; and hearsay and gossip, 297, 298

Vuillemin, Jules, 405 n.22

Wake, 66–85; relation of *FW* to, 87, 270–71, 328, 339, 362, 365, 377–78

Wakening: of eyes and vision, 11–15, 234–38, 240, 243, 245–46; of "original sinse," 73; as "coming forth by day," 115, 117–18; as resurrection of the body, 115–16; and acquisition of literacy, 140, 156; as return to reality, 155–56, 373, 382; of mankind, 194; role of sound in, 281, 284–85, 301, 354–57; of ear, 289–91, 294–95; dream analysis and riddle solving as, 314; as quickening and birth, 343, 345, 357–58, 364–66; as return to reality, 373. *See also* Evolution; Genesis

War of Jenkins' Ear, 300

Ward, Swinson, 421 n.4

Washerwomen, 339–40, 346, 347, 350–51, 357, 358–59, 363; and washing, 352–53

Watt, Ian, 420 n.16

Weaver, Harriet Shaw, 3, 6, 20, 21, 38, 87, 174, 237, 312, 345, 349, 399 n.10, 403 n.10, 438 n.36, 456 nn.14–15

Weber, Samuel, 397 n.10

Weekends and weekending, 172, 362

Wellington Memorial, 165, 185, 198, 244

Wells, H. G., 144

West, 92, 112–13

Wheatstone, Sir Charles, 287, 447 n.26

Wilde, Oscar, 166; *The Picture of Dorian Gray*, 438 n.36

Williams, Raymond, 428 n.16

Winking, 254–55, 274; forty winks, 254, 259

Winter, 58, 254

Wilson, Edmund, 417 n.3, 446 n.24

Wish fullfillment, 89; and dreamwork, 128, 133, 157; and genital desire, 198; and desire to sleep, 240, 281, 284, 286, 335, 339

Wolff, Philipp, 455 n.7

Womb, 354, 359, 379–80; hearing in, 354–55; sleep as return to, 354–56; as site of "Anna Livia Plurabelle," 355–56; as site of *FW*, 357–58, 360; as site of genesis, 359, 379–80; as site of night, 374, 376–77

Work in Progress, 20, 143, 144

Woolf, Virginia, 52

Women: and ideal beauty, 240; and looks, 240; status of female characters in *FW*, 356–57; and history, 362; primacy of, in *FW*, 367

Word made flesh, *FW* as, 37, 141; and Vico, 198–99

Wordplay, 305–15; puns, 92, 110, 184, 198, 210; acrostics, 139–42, 348, 366; as paradigm of collective-individual, 212; slips of tongue, 310, 325; rebus, 311–12, 315

Worthington, Mabel (*Song in the Works of James Joyce*), xvi, 417 n.4, 431 n.9, 449 n.37, 452–53 n.4

Zero, 53, 62, 145, 365–68

Zoethout, W. D., 437 n.30, 439–40 n.40

DESIGNED BY DAVID FORD
COMPOSED BY G&S TYPESETTERS, INC., AUSTIN, TEXAS
MANUFACTURED BY EDWARDS BROTHERS, INC., ANN ARBOR, MICHIGAN
TEXT AND DISPLAY LINES ARE SET IN PILGRIM

Library of Congress Cataloging-in-Publication Data
Bishop, John, 1948–
Joyce's book of the dark, Finnegans wake.
Includes bibliographical references and index.
1. Joyce, James, 1882–1941. Finnegans wake.
'I. Title.   II. Title: Finnegans wake.
PR6019.09F5566   1986   823'.912   86-40045
ISBN 0-299-10820-1